THE MEANING OF
PUCK

THE MEANING OF

PUCK

HOW HOCKEY EXPLAINS
MODERN CANADA

BRUCE

DOWBIGGIN

KEY PORTER BOOKS

Library and Archives Canada Cataloguing in Publication

Dowbiggin, Bruce
    The meaning of puck : how hockey explains modern Canada / Bruce Dowbiggin.

ISBN 978-1-55470-041-7

    1. Canada—Civilization—21st century. 2. Hockey—Social aspects—
Canada. 3. Canada—History—21st century. 4. Canada—Social conditions—
21st century. 5. Hockey—Canada. I. Title.

FC97.D69 2008   971.07   C2008-902277-7

ONTARIO ARTS COUNCIL
CONSEIL DES ARTS DE L'ONTARIO

The Canada Council | Le Conseil des Arts
for the arts | du Canada
since 1957 | depuis 1957

The publisher gratefully acknowledges the support of the Canada Council for the Arts and the Ontario Arts Council for its publishing program. We acknowledge the support of the Government of Ontario through the Ontario Media Development Corporation's Ontario Book Initiative.

We acknowledge the financial support of the Government of Canada through the Book Pub-lishing Industry Development Program (BPIDP) for our publishing activities.

Key Porter Books Limited
Six Adelaide Street East, Tenth Floor
Toronto, Ontario
Canada M5C 1H6

www.keyporter.com

Text design and electronic formatting: Alison Carr

Printed and bound in Canada

08 09 10 11 12 5 4 3 2 1

Contents

In memory of Bill, who liked a good argument

Acknowledgements

He swore he was never afraid of the puck
We believe him
If anyone asks,
the inscription should read
'My face was my mask.'

—"Elegy For Gump Worsley," The Weakerthans

Only in Canada could a roly-poly, whisky-drinking goalie be the subject of a pop song by an indie band. And only in Canada could a book use the sport of hockey to explain our nation's current state of mind.

So let me thank publisher Jordan Fenn and managing editor Jonathan "Just A Little Bit Outside" Schmidt of Key Porter for supporting and nurturing the idea the past two years. Thanks to Emma Cole, who guided the copy throughout the edit process. Thanks to Key Porter for also sending me reference materials and new books to spark the analytical process.

My agent Linda McKnight is the best mentor and friend an author could have. She steers me through the shoals of Canadian publishing and is a first-rate navigator.

I would like to acknowledge the support of the *Calgary Herald* where some of these essays first took root. And to the numerous hockey executives, players and agents who contributed their thoughts to the project. Special thanks to Steve Paikin and Catherine Ford for their constructive criticisms and encouragement on the book.

Finally, love to my extended family who provide the encouragement and inspiration to get an author through the writing ordeal. During the creative process we lost my father, who always thought I should be a salesman. I hope this book honours his memory, his love of reading and his conviction that Pierre Trudeau was vastly overrated.

September 2008

Imagine If You Will...

BOB: O baby...O Harry...I can't remember when we've seen anything like this. Game seven of the biggest hockey showdown ever. O golly, O baby...this makes the 1972 Soviet series look like a tea party. Team Canada and Team Quebec have come down to this: the third period, tied at two. On the line is nothing less than the future of the nation.

HARRY: But what a way to solve this for good, Bob. Winner take all...loser goes home and forgets the past 135 years of bickering...

BOB: Yessir, Harry, quite a showdown ... as the teams skate onto the ice here at the Saddledome in Calgary after opening the series at the Bell Centre in Montreal...let's go down to Ron MacLean who's standing by at ice level.

RON: That's right, Bob and Harry...you remember how hard Team Canada fought to have this game seven played in the heart of the West rather than in the traditional venue of Toronto's Air Canada Centre...and what a support it's been here ... the sea of red as Canadians get behind the club ... here and there I see a patch of blue or a fleur-de-lys, but I wouldn't want to be a Team Quebec supporter in here if Canada loses ... Wait, what's that ... a disturbance in the crowd ... I can't see ... there appears to be a group of Mounties ... surrounding someone just beside the ice ... it's ... why, it's Gilles Duceppe ... and Team Quebec is skating over, sticks raised against the Mounties ... yes, they're freeing Duceppe from the clutches of the police ... here comes Duceppe over the boards ... dishevelled, angry at something, we don't know what it is ... the Quebec players are assisting Duceppe, who ... yes, he's just flipped the bird at the prime minister's box ... Bob?

HARRY: Bob, Ron ... it looks like Mr. Duceppe is standing at the back of Team Quebec's bench singing "Gens du Pays," the anthem played for Quebec before each game ... speaking of unforgettable sights, who'd have thought we'd see Paul Henderson and Yvan Cournoyer, the two men in the most famous sports photo in Canadian history ... who'd have thought they'd have come to blows on the steps of the Hockey Hall of Fame during a photo shoot ...

RON: And may I say that Paul got in most of the good shots before Yvan pulled Henderson's Team Canada blazer over his head ...

BOB: Alright, they're about to face off at centre ice and once again the crowd has launched into its favourite song, "The Fleur-de-lys is not for me ..." Yes, it's former Alberta

Premier Ralph Klein with the baton, conducting the crowd ... Now what's happening, Ron?

RON: It appears, yes ... it now looks as if Duceppe has convinced Team Quebec coach Mario Tremblay to take his team off the ice ... they are moving toward the dressing room ... let me get close to hear what this is about ... M. Duceppe? M. Duceppe?

BOB: Harry, the Quebeckers are leaving ... they're going home! The Quebeckers are going home!

RON: Guys, it seems like Team Quebec is insisting that a tie goes to the visitor ... talk about your amending formulas ... all they have to do is keep this score and Quebec finally gets to leave Confederation ... and, oh no ... Don Cherry has shoved aside his walker and is now throttling Duceppe ... Peter Mansbridge is trying hold Cherry back ...

BOB: O golly, O baby, where's the notwithstanding clause when you need it, Harry?

CHAPTER ONE

The Warmup

"If you can't beat 'em in the alley, you can't beat 'em on the ice."
—Conn Smythe

"My boy's gonna play in the big leagues
My boy's gonna knock 'em dead."
—Tom Cochrane

Every nation begins with a transcendent myth and is sustained by moments that support that myth. Thus, the Americans have total recall of where they stood when they heard about Pearl Harbor or John F. Kennedy's assassination or, recently, 9/11—moments where the national will was galvanized and every citizen was called to the flag. Where the U.S. has a surfeit of such moments, Canadian history is less generous in such moments. The most iconic political moment—René Lévesque hushing exultant Quebec separatists in 1976—is hardly cause for celebration.

For people of a particular age in this country—anyone over the age of thirty-five—the "where were you?" moment probably came as Paul Henderson raised his arms in Moscow one September

afternoon in 1972—having delivered Canada a win over the
U.S.S.R. in game eight of the famous hockey showdown. Many feel
that moment was a unique triumph for a modern Canada, a brave
western warrior vanquishing the evil Soviet empire. Even as the
puck nestled behind a fallen Vladislav Tretiak, there was a sense of
new possibilities in the country. But now, thirty-six years later, the
moment is remarkable more as the culmination of the national
myth that existed since the Second World War rather than the start
of another. Even as Prime Minister Pierre Trudeau greeted the
beer-soaked heroes of Team Canada as their plane returned to
Canada in 1972, the deconstruction of the post-war Canada that
the hockey players defended so fanatically was well under way.
The dismantling of the military—perhaps the only symbol that
rivalled hockey on a national scale at the time—the bilingualism
policy, multiculturalism, economic nationalism, feminism, and,
most crucially, the Charter of Rights and Freedoms, would, in the
years ahead, radically transform the country that celebrated the
Cold War triumph of Henderson and his teammates. Just as
hockey changed in the days after the win over the Soviets—with
rampant expansion, million-dollar contracts and European players
heading to the NHL—the country that worships the sport was propelled on a new, uncharted course that left it unrecognizable to
many members of the older generation.

There remains a great sense of satisfaction when Canada's
men win gold on the international hockey stage today. But the
sense of national will that inspired Team Canada at Luzhniki
Arena in 1972 is gone for good in the diffuse foster home known
as twenty-first century Canada. Fifteen million Canadians watched
the country's best male players win the 2002 Olympic gold for the
first time in fifty-two years, but for symbolism in the modern age,
it paled next to the win by the amateur women's team. The women

epitomized the postmodern values of Canada better than did the
NHL stars who beat the U.S.A. 5–2. Who'd have ever thought that
as Foster Hewitt bawled out, "Henderson has scored for Canada"?

Recently, a Calgary colleague asked me why I had left the
security of my Toronto job and home for the unknowns of Alberta
back in 1998. (Said one of my CBC bosses: "But you're a city guy.
Toronto. Montreal. What do you want to go to Calgary for?")
Frankly, I hadn't thought about it much in the past few years as
my family and I integrated into the new West. Asked to recall
my rationale for abandoning a secure job and friends at the age of
forty-five, I temporarily drew a blank. I knew I wanted to write a
sports column for a major paper. Having seen local sports coverage killed across the nation by the CBC, I was—justifiably it turned
out—afraid of where the CBC was headed in relation to sports journalism. (And how long can you count on boyish looks in broadcasting?) I also felt it might be good for my kids to see something
different from Toronto's urban sprawl.

But it might have been something even more ephemeral.
Looking back, it was "a lonely impulse of delight" that drove me
west. I had been a judge for Magna Corporation's *So You Want to
be Prime Minister* competition in 1998. For three days, my fellow
judges and I heard an array of impressive young minds from across
the country expound on what made Canada work—or not work.
It was sobering, but it was also exhilarating to see the bright young
minds from across the nation challenging the status quo in post-
Meech Canada. While the arguments and presentations were all
impressive in their ways, it seemed clear to me that those contestants who had lived in more than one region of the country had
the fullest visions of the nation: the young woman from the West
who'd studied in Quebec, the Ontarian who'd worked summers in
B.C., the Nova Scotian who'd seen the Rockies. Hearing them, it

struck me that, as a journalist and a Canadian, it behooved me to do the same. Since returning with my family from Alberta in 1960, I'd been tucked into the secure cradle of the East with all its inherent convictions and assumptions about the country.

But to hear many of the scholarship contestants, there were different visions of the country to be found elsewhere in what novelist Yann Martel approvingly described as "a great hotel" full of competing cultures and values. Calgary, in particular, seemed to be simmering with a concoction of prosperity, rage and petroleum. The *Calgary Herald*'s managing editor was also on the judges' panel (along with Belinda Stronach—who knew?) and she asked me would I be interested in moving to Calgary to write a sports column. My immediate reaction was "Sure, and I'll grow a third eye, too." But the idea would not leave me alone. A visit to the city blew away my Stampede-soaked images of the place. My friend Allan Gregg said he thought Calgary had the best living conditions of any city in the country. There was no PST, lower taxes, lower housing costs, great skiing. So when the *Herald*'s editor Crosbie Cotton told me that no one would offer me the columnist's job that I desired after age forty-five, I was Alberta bound. Or bound to Alberta. From my new perch in the Foothills, I might better appreciate the country I'd known for almost half a century.

Covering sports can be a window into a nation's soul and having now lived and/or worked in five of the six Canadian NHL cities I believed I'd have a clear-eyed view of the torments and treasures of the country.

And so it has been. Looking back almost a decade now, I can't say I'm more optimistic about Canada for having lived in the West. Frankly, we've been struggling to reinvent ourselves after the Charlottetown and Meech debacles, and the results are inconclusive. The centralized, bilingual Liberal state envisioned after Expo

67 ("Trudeaupia" in Mark Steyn's immortal phrase) has more or less unravelled in the face of Quebec's indifference and the New West's economic clout. The traditional power corridor running from Toronto to Montreal via Ottawa is scrambling to remain relevant to forces such as the revived dollar that threaten its hegemony on the national debate. Multiculturalism and, most recently, the environment have redefined the old cultural and voting assumptions in vogue since Lester Pearson handed over power to Trudeau in 1967. After controlling the prime minister's job for all but eighteen months from 1968 to 2006, there is the potential for Quebec to lose its primacy over the highest political office in Canada. There is a sense that the old conceits are waiting to be blown away by a strong new wind. And just as strong a sense that those likely to be blown away will not do so without a fight.

But I do not say these things in despair. Any nation remains a work in progress, and the challenges that lie ahead can be seen as a defeat or an opportunity to recast ourselves in a new light. What are those challenges? (Pause for breath) Oh, you know ... regionalism, Quebec, the environment, Native issues, gender equality, America, economic sustainability. The things that send most of us screaming into the streets when brought up in polite company. Chatting with friends about this dread shopping list, I was struck by how these major themes facing Canada are also played out in that one constant of Canadian life: hockey. Through the national sports obsession, it's possible to better understand the dramas being played out in the nation's political and social drama. Reading Franklin Fehr's examination of globalization *How Soccer Explains the Modern World*—where he used soccer as a metaphor for the global economy—it became clear that hockey's lessons are Canada's lessons as well. And a book viewing contemporary Canada through hockey might provide a different way of looking at the country.

Like Canada struggling to make sense of rapidly morphing conditions, hockey in the modern nation is not a tidy spectacle, either. In fact, it's undergoing changes that shake it to its roots. Canadian teams that seemed doomed by a 62-cent dollar at the start of the decade are now robust powerhouses with the dollar near par. (So much so that Blackberry mogul—and Canadian hockey fan—Jim Balsillie wondered aloud why they weren't using their power to create more Canadian teams in the NHL.) The country may get one or possibly two more cities in the NHL (Balsillie hopes to put a second team in southern Ontario to challenge the Maple Leafs) as the dollar stabilizes and the American branch of the league withers under the indifferent management of commissioner Gary Bettman and the owners who prop him up. Changes in how the rules are called in the NHL have also meant that the smaller player—anyone under six feet tall—may have a future in the sport after all. The long held assumptions about fighting and violence in the sport, nurtured by Don Cherry on the otherwise pacifist CBC, are in danger of finally being debunked.

With their vast horizons and often passive nature, Canadians (English more so than French) are not necessarily a contemplative people and hockey is not a contemplative game. The Pulitzer Prize winner Richard Ford called it "an uninteresting sport played by Canadians." For many Americans—used to the pauses and ellipses of baseball or football—it is a busy, baffling spectacle. "Hockey on radio sounds like one long mistake," said former NBA coach Gene Shue. Like dental surgery, hockey is a business best gotten on with briskly and without too much contemplation. Even when the pauses arrive in the sport—be they intermissions or the contrived TV breaks—there is little self-examination involved in hockey. Players have just enough time to catch their breaths, spit multiple times and then go at it once more. Fans seize a beer, put the kids to bed and then resume their appointed rounds. That matter-of-fact approach appeals to Canadians, its brisk rhythms warming them against the snow.

In its quick, brutal fashion, hockey is a perfect wedge in the emerging urban/suburban-rural split in Canada—the so-called Tim Hortons versus Starbucks. Hockey lovers regard urban Canadian culture as some extended episode of *Queer Eye for the Straight Guy*, a fashion/design industry that keeps Canada out of wars and in designer jeans. If Canada were a TV program, it would be *The Odd Couple*. Hockey is Oscar, lounging in his underwear in a fraying Barcalounger. The rest of Canada is Felix, asking Oscar to pick up his pizza boxes, put on a clean shirt and take the empties back to the beer store. If Don Cherry is Oscar, then Jeffrey Simpson of *The Globe and Mail* is Felix. "These guys don't get it, because having grown up in the culture publicly glorified by Mr. Cherry, they buy into this notion that hockey violence is okay up to this imaginary line way out on the edge of acceptable behaviour," wrote Simpson in the wake of the Todd Bertuzzi incident in 2004.

As Fehr demonstrated in his book, soccer has become the Trojan Horse of a people's aspirations in many nations. In Canada, a country once sneeringly described as Belgium with an immigration culture, the vessel carrying its hopes is hockey (never, ever called ice hockey). It's a brave game played by young men and women seemingly impervious to pain and oblivious to the danger of skating on razor-sharp, razor-thin blades at thirty-five km an hour amid pucks that whizz by your ear at 130 km. And that, at least in our Afghanistan mission, is thought to be Canadians at their best. But as the petty factionalism over scheduling the Maple Leafs in western NHL cities showed, the sport is also a fault line that runs across the culture, separating regions and cities even as it unites them.

Increasingly, the game devised by Victorian swells as a gentleman's pursuit explains Canada in the twenty-first century. How, for instance, does the nation that has (until the recent Afghan mission) cherished its image as an international peacekeeper reconcile its pacifism with the brutal, pitiless heart of hockey, its national sport? How can it project the increasingly multicultural face of Canada (where the percentage of immigrants is growing at four times the rate of the Canadian-born population) on a largely white culture personified by Don Cherry, the pied piper on the national broadcaster? If nations are known by the idols they worship, what do we make of Wayne Gretzky as a symbol of how Canadians flatter themselves? Why do we behave so atrociously toward America, our best neighbour and trading partner? And what do Garth Drabinsky, Brian Mulroney, and convicted felon Alan Eagleson all have in common?

The short and long answer is hockey. Scratch a Canadian and you will get a hockey story. It may be the first atom game played on a subzero winter night or a hat trick in a beer league contest of forty-year-olds. Or a fight. I got into my first and only hockey fight at the age of sixteen. It was a park league in the Montreal suburb of Pointe Claire and we were entering the playoffs . . . or had they already started? It's not important anymore.

The stakes?

Who remembers? Other than it seemed like an all-encompassing experience at the time, my own version of the Stanley Cup rendered on a smaller canvas. I clearly recall the warm-up, skating in large, loose circles around our end of the rink with parents and spectators watching through the Plexiglas from above. It felt like there was iron in my hands and arms. My legs were bursting with pent-up power. I was a poster child for teenaged testosterone.

I knew the boy I fought that day—we'd played against each

other in a range of sports over the years. I can't recall what pretext I used to start the fight—did we bump into each other or exchange provocative comments about our mothers?—but at a stressful moment in the third period, when our team needed a spark, a fight seemed a great way to inspire my team and win the game. Why did I feel that? Because I'd seen what happened when John Ferguson or Eddie Shack or Reggie Fleming fought for their teams on TV. It looked dangerous and grown-up. So when the moment came, the gloves came off and were sent flying towards the picture of Queen Elizabeth that—like a Christian cross—hangs upon the wall of every hockey rink in the land.

I must have connected solidly with one of the first punches because he disappeared so quickly that I briefly lost sight of him. I found him lying at my feet and instinctively I jumped on top of him to continue the pummelling. (Hey, that's how Fergy did it.) Mercifully, the referee grabbed me before I could do more damage. As I moved away from the scrum I could see that the boy was bleeding near his nose and cheek.

And he was crying.

As I stood up, tugged my sweater back in place, picked up my helmet and skated to the penalty box, I could plainly hear him above the sound of the arena's generators. Where was the cheering, the adulation that showered down upon Fergy and Shack when their epic battles had ended? The faces behind the Plexiglas windows at the end of the rink—where the parents often stood to watch games in warmth and comfort—looked away or at their shoes. It was so deathly still I can remember clearly the sound of the latch on the penalty gate opening to accept me, showered in the blood and sweat and a sixteen-year-old's tears.

As I sat down, a few of my friends leaned in the penalty box to congratulate me. Over the thumping of my heart in my chest I could hear them, their teenaged voices filled with awe and excitement. "Way to go!" "Hey Killer!" and "Man, you were awesome." But I could only look down at my hands, pink and raw from the fight. My first thoughts were not of victory. "Why did he have to cry?" Why did I fight? Because I could, I suppose. But after that, I never fought again.

I tell this greying story, because (with apologies to Robert Frost) I too have been acquainted with the night. In the Luddite world of Canadian hockey, it is considered essential that you played the game, felt the rush of adrenaline when you hit full stride, the flash of anger when high-sticked, the sense of communion when your team won. Without it, no one in the traditional community will take you seriously. Pedigree comes from a thousand nights in musty dressing rooms, the stink of old sweat and socks in the nostrils. Men who bonded in the maelstrom of hostile arenas, challenged by opponents and fans alike, become members of a cult, oblivious to the outsiders.

No doubt, some will say that my fight in a minor-hockey game thirty-five years ago is no great thing, carries no authority. I beg to differ. The first brushes with the Canadian pastime are the most long-lasting, the most authentic. And leave the deepest marks. Matthew Barnaby may be the poster boy for the Canadian hockey personality. "For me it was the NHL or cleaning floors," says Barnaby (who had 2,257 lifetime PIMs when post-concussion syndrome ended his career in 2006).

> I had no backup plan. My Mom mortgaged our house twice to keep me in hockey. I have many friends who did not make it. It's tough. I approach every game like it's my first. I also try to remember that there are fans that may only see one game this year and they are in the stands tonight. Tickets aren't cheap. I want them

to say 'That Barnaby tried his best every shift.' I want the blue-collar guy to relate to me ... if they could skate, hopefully they would play like me.

Not that all hockey encounters are quite so dramatic or blood-tinged. Mark Starowicz, the renowned documentary filmmaker who went on to make the CBC's *People's History of Hockey* in 2006, was a recent immigrant from Argentina in the 1950s, with little or no English, when hockey built a bridge. Scared and not a little intimidated in the playground of his new Montreal school, Starowicz produced hockey cards. "My mother knew that back in Argentina we used to have player cards for the big footballers," Starowicz recalled. "So she bought me five packs of hockey cards. When I got to school I showed them to the kids. And even though I had just a little English, I had a Rocket Richard card and that was enough for them." Starowicz saved himself the schoolyard initiations with those cards and went on to tell Canadians about themselves for decades.

Polish immigrant Greg Przygocki had a similar experience when he decided to get citizenship for himself, his wife Iwonna and son Antek.

So we applied, passed the test, were moved during the citizenship ceremony. And then ... we thought we were Canadians. About a year later I was coming back home after work. It was late and I wanted to get home for the hockey game. Traffic was, as usual, bad in Toronto. Finally I got to the little streets of my neighbourhood. Unfortunately, I was running all stop signs—The Leafs were ready to play, for goodness sake! I was really rushing. Then, I turned one corner and just down the road, I saw a bunch of kids playing street hockey. I slowed down, smiled ... the guys saw me, stopped playing, moved the nets. I slowly drove through, waved to them, they waved to me, put the nets back and started playing again. I didn't think it was any delay, any wasted time. I was happy. I was Canadian!

There are the more conventional Canadian hockey stories from Roch Carrier's iconic *The Hockey Sweater* to the Rankin Island roots of NHL star Jonathan Cheechoo. Forests have been felled to chronicle the careers of players from garden spots such as Floral, Saskatchewan (Gordie Howe), Parry Sound, Ontario (Bobby Orr), or Victoriaville, Quebec (Jean Beliveau). Recently, the success of Canada's women's teams has added to the "in the bone" connection to the game by incorporating the other half of the nation into the game's mythmaking.

And while soccer has had its own wars—Paraguay and Uruguay answered the call to arms over a disputed World Cup qualifier—hockey has been said to have, in part, fostered a quiet revolution in Quebec with the 1955 Rocket Richard riot. The aftershocks of that night when francophones rioted in the streets of Montréal over the suspension of hero Richard by the NHL can still be felt passionately in the soul of modern Quebec where hockey is code for culture. Just ask Saku Koivu, the star-crossed captain of the current Montreal Canadiens.

Few hockey players have given so much of themselves as has Koivu. Over ten years in the tricolour of the Habs, Koivu battled abdominal cancer in 2001–02, torn ligaments in his knee, and a series of other setbacks and injuries. On a team decidedly short of elite talent since the departure of celebrated goalie Patrick Roy in 1995, Koivu laboured mightily to keep up the lofty standards of the Canadiens, the most successful team in NHL history. And he did it all at an undersized five foot ten, 184 pounds in a game filled with men forty or fifty pounds heavier and a half-foot taller.

The 2005–06 season, his tenth with the team and seventh as captain, was typical of Koivu's commitment to the Habs. The modestly talented Canadiens flirted with respectability at various points in the season, scrambling into the postseason in seventh in the East. In the playoffs, they grabbed a 2–0 lead on the Carolina Hurricanes in the next round, winning both games on the road in Raleigh. Then, leading Carolina 1–0 back in Montreal, disaster struck Koivu. Justin Williams' stick inadvertently caught Koivu in the right eye beneath his mask. The Finnish product grabbed his eye as blood flowed through his fingers. Koivu was immediately taken to a Montreal hospital. It was soon apparent that his season— perhaps his career—was over. Without their captain, the disheartened Habs lost four straight games, falling to the future Stanley Cup–champion Hurricanes in six games. Even then, Koivu's ordeal was not over. A Montreal newspaper cameraman snuck past security into his darkened hospital room, snapping a flash photo of a bandaged Koivu, infuriating doctors who said the bright light might permanently damage his eye.

Weeks later, Koivu sat before the assembled Montreal media in a conference room at the Bell Centre, the enormous building that replaced the famed Forum in 1996. An amorphous body that follows the Canadiens the way phytoplankton follows the Gulf Stream, the Habs bilingual press corps often churns out 2,000 words a day whether events merit it or not. No morsel of Habs trivia is too arcane or too pointless to escape the scrutiny of the men and few women who chronicle the club with the most Stanley Cups in NHL history. Hence the competitive mania to snap a photo of the distressed Koivu in his hospital room.

On this day Koivu could expect many questions on the state of his eye (still blurred) and the sudden collapse of the Canadiens without him. Perhaps there would be some questions about the direction of the club over the summer. As is his wont, Koivu handled the urgent rabble with calm and poise. With the press conference winding down, a new voice popped up from the back of the room. It was veteran reporter Charles Fairbault of TVA, the largest private television network in the province, asking his first and only question of the presser—in French. Koivu said "I'll have to have that in English." Fairbault then asked why, after ten years, was it that the captain of Quebec's team still could not speak French?

In almost any other press conference this question would be considered cheek of the highest order. Professional discourtesy. Never mind that Koivu had left significant pools of his blood on the ice in defence of the hockey honour of Montreal. Or that, gaunt and wan from chemotherapy, a bald Koivu had been feted by Canadiens' faithful with wave after wave of cheers on his return to the Bell Centre after starting treatment. Or that the Saku Koivu Foundation had raised enough money to buy a new PET/CT scanner for the Montreal General Hospital. Or that he was a polite visitor in a foreign land.

This is Quebec and the language kill shot is always in season in the political culture. And, while the Canadiens are a sporting enterprise, they are also very much a part of the political culture of the province. And so Koivu found himself in the crosshairs of a tribal fight that had burned for generations in the province where he worked. It was pointed out that while Koivu could not speak the *lingua franca*, his wife was able to speak the language. Montreal's general manager Bob Gainey was similarly fluent in both languages. Koivu apologized for his deficiency as if explaining away a weak backhand or inadequate skating style. In an "ideal situation," he conceded, the captain of the Canadiens should speak the first language of the province. "Should I or could I make an effort to learn? I think, yeah. I guess when you're not forced to do something, you become lazy. And the [hockey] schedule is very demanding."

Koivu, who does speak Finnish, Swedish, and English, then tried to plead for understanding. "I've gone through a lot here in Montreal, with this community and all the history that I have," Koivu said. "I've showed by giving back to the community that I love this place." But Koivu also said the language issue is not a very important one to the players and that team pride is the most important factor in selecting a captain. "I don't think it's a problem for the people I deal with every day that I don't speak French." Koivu's bilingual general manager Gainey—who had played for Montreal during the rise of the Parti Québecois—tried to deflect the heat from Koivu, joking that his captain would have learned more French if he'd hung out more with his wife Hanna. But the blood was in the water. By the weekend, the debate was transferred to the newspapers. In the English-language *Gazette*, American-born Jack Todd labelled Fairbault's performance "an ambush, pure and simple." In the French-language *Le Journal de Montréal*, Patrick Legace's column was entitled "Saku Koivu Speaks White," a reference to how francophones had once been told to speak "white," (English). Todd then accused Legace of stirring up the old hates and resentments against Anglos that were thankfully dying down in the twenty-first century. Legace riposted by saying that his great-grandmother was Scottish, and that Todd should learn to speak the language of Quebec himself before he opined on the subject.

That brought one of the great Canadiens legends into the fray. Henri Richard, the Rocket's brother who won the most Stanley Cups of any player in NHL history (eleven), came to the defence of Koivu. "Koivu hasn't done much this week, right? He's only committed to raising $750,000 for the Montreal General Hospital," Richard said to the *Gazette*.

"I mean, how much can this guy do? I'm lucky to speak two languages, but he's supposed to learn a third, on top of all he's been through and does for his team, and does for the city he loves that some people are trying to make him hate."

The issue simmered for much of the next season as Koivu struggled to learn some French and the media pounced on other stories, such as the loss of Gainey's daughter Laura at sea.

Hockey as a template for modern Canada?

Play on.

CHAPTER TWO

Hors Jeux

Montreal (CP)—A prominent Quebec publisher is calling on the government to force the Montreal Canadiens to spin more French-language tunes for the Bell Centre crowd. Michel Brulé says he was shocked the team's DJ played only one French song during Game Seven of the Habs first-round series against the Boston Bruins in 2008.

Brulé stood on a Montreal street corner and circulated a petition demanding the Quebec and Canadian governments set a quota for how much francophone music is played in the arena. The petition calls on politicians to create content rules similar to CRTC regulations and demands French-language songs make up at least 65 per cent of the tunes that echo through the Bell Centre.

Brule says the Canadiens organization has "no respect" for francophones in Montreal, the second-largest French-speaking city in the world. (April 2008)

If you believe in the power of human communication in the age of talk-show guru Don Imus and the iPod, then Bob Nicholson, president of Hockey Canada, should have been able to clear up any controversy swirling around Team Canada's captain Shane Doan when Nicholson visited Parliament Hill on a May afternoon in 2007. The same Shane Doan who was, at that moment, half a world away, putting his summer on hold while he represented Canada at the World Championships.

Forget for a moment that, in a time of war, healthcare meltdown, and environmental challenge, the elected assembly of Canada had nothing better to do than play politics with the reputation of an NHL player who was representing the nation for free. If one wants to know how hockey reflects modern Canada, the Doan Debate on Parliament Hill is an object lesson. An exemplary athlete was being asked to explain why he had been exonerated over a year earlier of a charge that he used an ethnic slur in an NHL game against a French Canadian linesman.

That's right. Seventeen months after the alleged incident, Doan was still guilty by not being guilty in Quebec's nationalist press. And, by that curious Canadian extension, rendered highly suspicious in the eyes of many, many Parliamentarians. "I don't understand how people can attack somebody when I was cleared by the NHL," a bewildered Doan said to reporters in Moscow covering the 2007 World Championships. "Anybody that does any type of investigation into it would realize I never said it. And yet, they can just throw it out in the House of Commons? Those are our leaders. Those are the people that we're supposed to look to."

Here's how Doan fell prey to the people we're supposed to look to for leadership: In a game in December 2005 between Doan's Phoenix Coyotes and the Montreal Canadiens, NHL linesman Michel Cormier said he heard Doan use an ethnic slur against francophones while skating by him. Doan said he was trying to calm down goalie Curtis Joseph during a skirmish and wasn't even talking to any of the four officials—who were all French Canadian. Doan vehemently denied using any ethnic slurs.

A subsequent NHL investigation verified Doan's version of events, but Cormier was apparently not appeased. He swore out a report that, in effect, contradicted his bosses' findings. (While saying they supported their own findings the NHL deputy commissioner Bill Daly was not inclined to muzzle Cormier. "The fact that both individuals can have different accounts of what transpired on the ice doesn't mean that either one is lying and we don't suspect that either one is." Heck of a vote of support there.)

Nor were the arbiters of Quebec indignation satisfied. Back in Cormier's home province, Liberal Denis Coderre, a former Minister of Sport who's never met a camera he didn't love (the most dangerous place on the Hill? Between Coderre and a microphone) picked up Cormier's cause, demanding that—due process be damned—Doan not be allowed to represent the country at the 2006 Torino Olympics. That unleashed the usual rhetoric from the chattering classes who benefit from such prattle. Jean-François Bégin of La Presse suggested there is a simple lesson to be learned from the NHL's handling of the issue: "The National Hockey League truly has no respect for its francophone players, referees and fans." Despite the complaints, Hockey Canada rejected Coderre's demand, and Doan played in Torino for Canada alongside five Quebec-born players and one Quebec-born coach—none of whom ever complained about Doan's presence.

Back from the Olympics, Doan subsequently sued Coderre $250,000 for libel for calling him, among other things, "unfit" to represent the nation. A defiant Coderre, declaring the NHL's findings of no value, countersued. And there the case went off into the legal underbrush to be resolved. But with Cormier still shopping his hurt self to receptive ears in Quebec's media (and the NHL inexplicably letting him do so) Coderre and the press in Montreal sniffed another chance to grind their axe when Doan was named captain of the 2007 version of Team Canada.

Columns were written about the lack of francophones on Team Canada (ignoring that seven or eight prominent French Canadians turned down General Manager Steve Yzerman's request to play) and stating that Doan's ascension to team captain was a clear provocation to those in Quebec who cling to resentment the way René Lévesque clung to his comb-over. An emboldened Coderre, supported by Liberal leader Stéphane Dion, NDP leader Jack Layton, and Bloc Quebecois leader Gilles Duceppe, demanded that Hockey Canada—a non-profit body receiving federal funds—be summoned to testify before a parliamentary committee about Doan's suitability as captain. While Canada does not vet its Supreme Court justices, it apparently decided that approving hockey captains is in its purview.

The governing Conservatives, stumbling badly on the environment and Afghanistan files, acquiesced to the powers of organized outrage rather than upset their precarious inroads into Quebec. Labour minister Jean-Pierre Blackburn offered a lame, "If we hadn't done it, how would we look as francophones?" excuse. (Gee, hard to say, Jean-Pierre, but it can't be worse than you look to the rest of the country now.) In less sympathetic circles, Doan was labelled a bigot, a racist, a disgrace, etc. over the mistaken accusation of an NHL linesman that the Phoenix captain called him a "f***ing Frenchman." All of this drive-by venom tossed by people who don't know Shane Doan from Melanie Doan.

Hastily summoned by the people's elected representatives to explain why Quebec's political elites were barking up the wrong tree, Nicholson described Doan as an exemplary choice as captain of the Nation's hockey team at the world championships in Moscow. "You should get to know Shane Doan," said Nicholson. "You can talk to all of his teammates that have played with him. He says 'fudge' a lot if he gets upset. He's a Christian and a person that I am proud to know." (A point many French-speaking players in the NHL later endorsed.)

Nicholson tried to enlighten them about the man Parliament was duly dissecting instead of working on more pertinent business. "We're taking Shane Doan, his wife, his mom and dad, his four kids through an allegation that could have been dictated by someone else," Nicholson said. "This is not right." Nicholson explained that while someone on the ice may have uttered an ethnic slur against an all-French refereeing squad at the Bell Centre in December of 2005, it wasn't the man whose reputation has been impinged on since that day.

"There is no question those words were said on the ice," said Nicholson. "The National Hockey League's investigation clearly shows that that was stated, but it also clearly shows that they felt that it wasn't Shane Doan . . . That is why we are here today—to protect Shane Doan." (Ironically, it was a European, Ladislav Nagy, not an Anglo-Canadian, who uttered the curse. But there are no votes in the optics for pitting defenceless Quebec up against citizens of the European Union.)

This should, in civil societies, have produced an apology to Doan from the politicos who stood aside while the usual suspects tried to create another Riel trial from these meager morsels. It's the least they could do while he played for free in Moscow with the maple leaf on his chest. But Bloc Quebecois Leader Gilles Duceppe was unappeased, saying the verdict on Doan's guilt could not be declared until the libel suit was resolved. "When someone robs a bank he's presumed innocent until proven guilty—but I don't know many people who'd name them bank manager while the trial's still on," Duceppe said. "They want to name him captain even before the verdict comes in. It makes no sense. It's an insult to Quebeckers." Ah, the Pains of Abraham strike again.

Then there was the corrosive prose from influential columnist (and committed separatist) Réjean Tremblay in *La Presse*: "Named by Steve Yzerman and by his coach Andy Murray and approved, it goes without saying, by the bosses at Hockey Canada, [Doan's captaincy is] proof that racism is tolerated in this country when the victims are francophones." Tremblay, for the uninitiated, is a master of *souveraintiste* agitprop and the sentence is riddled with code words. "Bosses" echoes the dreaded *patrons anglais* from the Duplessis days. The list of Anglos (Yzerman, Murray, Hockey Canada) hammers home oppression of the francophone linesman, Michel Cormier, who fingered the wrong guy.

And then of course, that hallowed buzzword "racism" that harkens back to Pierre Vallières' '60s separatist tome *The White Niggers of America*. Forget that Quebec may be a "nation" but it is not a racial entity. The redolent term implies Quebecois had been hanged by the hundreds as were the African Americans in the U.S.—a suggestion at odds with the facts, of course. All in all, it was standard rhetoric from one of the oracles of Quebec's grievance industry. It could have been Shane Doan, it could have been Ryan Smyth. Quebec's Bonfire of the Vanities required another log.

But at least Tremblay knows who he is. He's part of the 88 per cent of francophones who identified themselves in 2005 as something other than Canadian first (up from 68 per cent in 1970). He's one of the 80 per cent who want to separate or only remain in Canada for economic reasons. He's among the clever folk who understand that the present state of shaken-but-not-separated is the best of all possible worlds for Quebec's elites. You can't blame them, of course; in the finest traditions of Al Sharpton, the tactic of smearing the innocent has worked splendidly to assure the accusers a pulpit and a pension on the public purse. In both languages. When one unfairly attacks Doan or three white Duke University lacrosse players (as Sharpton did) in the name of a long-standing grievance, no apology is required.

But Tremblay and others are a known quantity pitching a well-worn message. What puzzled many Canadians is why those representatives of the rest of Canada—such as NDP leader Layton—allowed Doan to be roasted unfairly on the spit, had no idea who they were, or what people stood for outside Quebec's borders. It would have taken maybe one or two phone calls to learn they were targeting the wrong guy. Doan's values are those of millions who think that Canada is a swell place to call home.

So feeble seemed the grasp of what Doan represented in the rest of Canada, so petrified were the NDP leader and others from outside Quebec of the linguistic schism, that they held the coat of BQ leader Duceppe while he and his supporters put the boots into Doan. There was no third-man-in penalty required to keep the Laytons from defending an innocent man. There was no demand, for instance, to discover why Coderre and Duceppe, elected members of the federal assembly, had marched in a parade during the 2005 Lebanon war in Montreal that featured the flags and supporters of Hezbollah—a terrorist organization banned in Canada.

There was only the tin ear of Canada's elected representatives. Prime Minister Harper—who professes himself a big hockey fan—dithered in the earliest days of the story, finally reading the public mood three days after the volatile hearing stirred up so much passion in the Conservatives' home base. After saying Canada's government had no place in the hockey world, Harper called Doan in Moscow to offer support. But by then the damage had been done.

With the Doan file added to his other challenges, Harper soon saw his hopes for a spring election and a majority government disappear in the polls. An Ipsos Reid poll done May 8–10, 2007 (just after the Doan hearings), for CanWest News Service and Global National showed that the ruling Conservative Party's numbers had taken a precipitous dip the previous two weeks in Alberta and British Columbia. Specifically, the Conservatives saw their support drop by 13 percentage points in Alberta and 19 percentage points in British Columbia in the national poll. Nationally, Harper's Tories suddenly dropped behind the struggling Liberal leader Stéphane Dion with the Grits at 32 per cent, followed by the Conservatives at 31 per cent, the NDP at 17 per cent, and the Green Party at 9 per cent. (The poll surveyed 1,000 Canadians and is considered accurate within 3.1 percentage points, 19 times out of 20.)

Ipsos Reid principally attributed the collapsing Conservative vote to the environment, claiming the Tories' climate-change strategy was a dud, and that many Canadians wanted nothing to do with Harper as a result. That may be so. But the Tories had been playing hot potato with climate change for months, with varying degrees of impact on the polling numbers. Ditto Afghanistan prisoner exchange and federal/provincial wrangling over funding. One word explained what produced the sudden crack in the Tories' façade—particularly in the West: Doan.

The Conservatives' inept performance on the Doan file just prior to the polling resonated with many voters who couldn't find Kabul on a map or explain equalization policy. But they know hockey—and hockey players—and when the politicians tried to manipulate that agenda it accelerated a Tory slide building for months in the ROC (Rest of Canada). Allowing the usual parliamentary suspects to march Doan and Hockey Canada before a committee on trumped-up ethnic charges played very poorly in the Tories' heartland. When honourable members allowed Doan's reputation to be sullied on the floor of the House of Commons, it came as a shock to many core voters who saw the Tories as their bulwark against the constitutional circus produced by decades of answering every slight to Quebec's pride. Looking at the polling numbers through hockey eyes, the Doan file demonstrated to the ROC that, in their newfound thirst for votes in Quebec, Harper's Tories has seemingly forgotten about the core issues that Doan represents. Loyalty. National pride. Hard work. Fair play. That while the parties have changed in government, the agenda on appeasing Quebec's political elite evidently remains the same.

Doan could at least console himself that he was hardly the first outsider caught in the vortex of Quebec's language wars. While the furor of the '70s and '80s has calmed with the acceptance of French as the dominant language of Quebec, there remain the constant reminders of the primacy of French—and the vigilant watchdogs who keep it that way. When front-runner Bob Rae waited four minutes to speak French in his speech to the 2006 Liberal leadership convention the delay was considered big news to the chattering classes of Quebec who monitor such things. Rae's leadership bid eventually failed. Then there are the people who count the number of French songs played during Habs games at the Bell Centre. Or the size of letters on public signs across the province.

Doan, who'd grown up on the opposite side of the country, received a crash course in how Quebec politics work in the twenty-first century. As Saku Koivu also discovered when he was outed for his lack of French, nothing stirs linguistic passions in Quebec quite like hockey. And in Quebec hockey inevitably means *les Canadiens*. If all this cultural vitriol seems a little odd about a sports team, it's useful to note that the Canadiens serve as more than a sports franchise to the city and the province. They are a combination hockey club/soap opera/morality play all breathlessly covered by a prolific media that compete for even the most mundane story.

The sense of community provided by rooting for the Habs has made it—along with the Caisse Populaire, Cirque du Soleil, or the provincial government—a symbol of the modern Quebec "nation" declared by Stephen Harper. The Canadiens' success is Quebec's success; the sense of pride engendered by the *bleu-blanc-rouge* is a cultural touchstone for a province that so often sees itself as besieged. The Habs' failures are not considered Quebec's failures, however; those are often explained away by the cultural prejudices of a hostile world. In this sports fanaticism, however, it seems no different from the communities described by the fans of the Maple Leafs or Flames or Canucks. The thrill of the chase for a playoff position or the winning of a Stanley Cup—something not done by a Canadian team since 1993—provides a rallying point in cities that are increasingly transient and multicultural. Like a barn raising, a long playoff run galvanizes a community like no other experience in contemporary Canadian life.

What makes the Canadiens' place in the culture so unique is its metaphorical position in the interminable language/sovereignty war. The painful dichotomy of Hugh MacLennan's celebrated *Two Solitudes* was sewn into the Canadiens just as surely as the famed CH logo. The product of rivalries between warring Montreal businessmen in the second decade of the twentieth century, the Canadiens were the fevered brainchild of Montreal Wanderers owner Jimmy Gardner. The boisterous Irishman had just been shut out of the new Canadian Hockey Association when he turned to Ambrose O'Brien, son of Senator Michael O'Brien, and said something like, "Ambrose, why don't you and I form a league . . . and I think if a team of all Frenchmen was formed in Montreal it would be a real draw." Thus were the Canadiens formed not by French Canadians but by a sharp English-speaking cookie who was looking to exploit the burgeoning francophone community of Montreal—then 54 per cent of the residents of the city.

However they were concocted, the Club de Hockey Canadien soon became keystones of the National Hockey Association in 1908 and the home to Quebec stars such as Didier Pitre, Newsy Lalonde, Jack Laviolette, and "Skinner" Poulin. (In 1917, the Canadiens became a founding member of the newly minted National Hockey League.) While the province was full of players, there was a natural disinclination from the Anglo elite to value these Quebecois as highly as the gentlemen sportsmen or products of Ontario or the West. Instead it was the Irish—the other "untouchables" in Montreal society—who championed the French players and gave them a chance as the NHA morphed into the National Hockey League during World War One. The rivalry between the Habitants and the darlings of English Montreal fashion such as the Wanderers (and later the Maroons) was based on a real fissure line in the community. There was no need to fake emotion. For a culture humbled by Montreal's Anglo–Scots business crowd and subdued by their own Catholic hierarchy, the Canadiens were a chance for French Canadians to celebrate vicariously. The difference in Montreal's two realities was exploited by the flamboyant Leo Dandurand, Leo Letourneau, and Joe Cattarinich ("The Three Musketeers") who bought the Canadiens in the 1920s and gave their team pride of place in Montreal's French community. They lured Aurel Joliat, Billy Boucher, and that most un-French creature Howie Morenz from Stratford, Ontario, to play for the "Flying Frenchmen" through the Jazz Age. The Canadiens won the Stanley Cup in 1924, '30 and '31 and while not successful every season, became synonymous with the French fact in the city. Joliat, Morenz, and the Habs were known around North America and cheered in a famous doggerel of the day:

Wen I am tired of travail-trop
I put on coat of coon
And go to see Canadiens
Mak' meence-meat of Maroon.
When Joliat skate out I yell
Unteel I have a pain.
I trow my 'at up in de hair
And shout, "Harrah," again.
"Shut up, Pea Soup," an Henglishman
Sarcastic say to me;
So I turn round to heem and yell,
"Shut up, you Cup of Tea."

Not that the success of a French hockey institution did much to reform Quebec society or the power structure of the province in the years between the wars. The succession of an entrenched Liberal party in Quebec by the populist Union Nationale of Maurice Duplessis guaranteed the status quo in the province. So did the church's censorship of liberal notions of art and science that kept Quebec both intellectually and socially isolated even from the modernism of France. Marcel Trudel summarized the unique cultural climate of the first half of the twentieth century:

French-speaking Canadians were inculcated with exalting theses that placed them above the other nations. You have been chosen, they were told repeatedly, to propagate the civilization of Christ; unlike your neighbours, you are inspired by spirituality rather than the passion for material riches; you constitute a human entity without foreign elements, you are a white population, with you the family is the most beautiful in the world; as a highly moral society, you have respected the rights of others and you have accomplished extraordinary feats. In a word: if one goes looking for perfection in a human collectivity, it will be found in your midst, French of America, and it will be found there because you are of the French race.

While still financially powerful, Montreal remained a divided city. The Canadiens shared Montreal with the Maroons and were very much parvenus in the corridors of hockey power as the '20s roared. The real power in the NHL resided in Conn Smythe's Toronto Maple Leafs, the Boston Bruins of Art Ross, and the growing hockey empire of Montreal-born, Chicago-based industrialist James Norris. Matters only became worse in the Depression after Dandurand sold his interest in the Habs to concentrate on his horse racing enterprises. Even as the financially strapped Maroons disappeared from the NHL, the Canadiens could not exploit the opportunity in a city ravaged by the financial collapse afflicting much of the world. After their Stanley Cup in 1931, the Habs' prospects were perhaps best summed up by the Howie Morenz tragedy. Traded from the Habs in 1934, an aging Morenz later attempted to come back with Montreal in 1937. Robbed of his blinding speed, Morenz was checked into the boards by Earl Siebert of Chicago. Crashing into the boards he broke his left leg. Six weeks later, he died mysteriously in a Montreal hospital—of a broken heart, some said. Morenz' body lay in state at centre ice at the Forum, and his funeral attracted hundreds of thousands to the Forum and the procession route.

By the time the Second World War broke out in 1939, the Canadiens were a sorry franchise, existing on loans and charity from other NHL clubs. Their financial and hockey resources were at low ebb and it seemed their every move went wrong. When the Canadiens tried to hire Babe Siebert as their head coach in 1939, the former star player drowned before ever getting behind the bench. A concerned Conn Smythe loaned his head coach Dick Irvin to Montreal to help them survive on and off the ice. The fiery Irvin eventually got results on the ice, especially from an equally volatile player, Maurice "The Rocket" Richard. A distillation of Gallic fever and an unquenchable desire to score, Richard teamed with linemates Toe Blake and Elmer Lach to turn the Canadiens into a scoring machine during the war years. Richard smashed the existing records for goals in a season and, for the first time in thirteen seasons, the Habs won the Cup again in 1944—losing only five games in the regular season.

Once more, however, events outside the rink thrust the Canadiens into the national spotlight. While English Canada overwhelmingly supported the Second World War conscription in a 1942 plebiscite, much of "official" French Canada remained bitterly opposed. As such, the issue of Quebec's contributions to the war threatened to tear apart the nation. Suspicious as ever of British imperialism and seeing the Canadian army as an English-language institution, French Canadians represented a small percentage of fighting troops. Units such as the Royal 22e Régiment, Les Fusiliers Mont-Royal, the Régiment de la Chaudière, and the Régiment de Maisonneuve all served with distinction and bravery during the War (future Governor General Georges Vanier lost a leg in the service). But critics said that if these units had been allowed to serve together under French-speaking officers (as now exists in the Canadian Armed Forces), it might have encouraged more Quebeckers to serve and support the war effort.

In the pain of the sacrifices being made elsewhere in Canada, this argument drew little sympathy. And so bitterness grew between the two founding nations of Canada. As the need for fresh soldiers, sailors, and airmen for Europe grew more urgent in 1943–44,

Prime Minister Mackenzie King did an elaborate dance to placate both his power bases ("conscription if necessary, but not necessarily conscription" was his ambiguous rallying cry), creating home service as an option for Quebec while simultaneously jailing Montreal's mayor Camillien Houde for urging his citizens to avoid military service. In the end, King was forced to order overseas some of the Home Reservists (derisively called Zombies), but the war ended in 1945 before fewer than 3,000 saw frontline service.

Into this seething debate landed Toronto's irascible owner Smythe—who had left the Maple Leafs to form his own Sportsmen's artillery battery and was subsequently seriously wounded in France in 1944. While convalescing from wounds that would nag him the rest of his life, Smythe created a national controversy by stating that untrained young Canadians were dying in the fields of France, Belgium, and Holland while the well-trained Zombies sat safely back at home, protected by the Liberal government. He then accused the Canadiens of winning tainted titles because they kept their stars—such as Richard—from active service. Smythe pointed out how he and many of his own Maple Leafs had enlisted while the Canadiens seemed able to defer service for their best players. Richard had been medically rejected three times for service because of injuries to his legs and held a wartime job as a machinist. Still, thundered Smythe, how could Richard be healthy enough to score fifty goals in fifty games but not fight for his country? Smythe was notoriously anti-French (he once addressed a Montreal gathering as "Gentlemen, ladies and Frenchmen . . .") and so his critiques of Richard were seen as thinly veiled indictments of the Rocket's courage and character—and those of his fellow French Canadians. The old antagonism between loyal Protestant Ontario and contrary Catholic Quebec came to a quick boil in King's cabinet and Parliament at large. Once more, war concluded before the status of Montreal's hockey heroes became a bigger issue, but the comments of Toronto's crusty British imperialist found their way along the fault lines of Quebec culture, assuring the resentments would survive the Second World War.

The fault lines were in clear view in 1955, and once again the Rocket was the flashpoint. This time, however, Richard would be seen as a symbol of his Quebec's frustrating battle for respect in an English world, and the outcome would not be so easily forgotten. Richard vied with Gordie Howe as the NHL's top player in the postwar years until the spring of' '55. Howe led Detroit to seven straight first-place finishes and three Stanley Cups. Richard's Habs won three Stanley Cups between 1944 and 1955. Both rewrote the scoring books. Howe was a quiet, menacing force, amassing records and carving out space with his elbows and quick fists. Richard, by contrast, was a wild force of nature, continually exploding in highly public displays of anger and violence. It was all but certain that he would erupt whenever he was held, hooked, or slashed by those who tried to check him. In a 1947 playoff series against Toronto, Richard used his stick to knock Vic Lynn and then Bill Ezinicki cold when he felt their attentions too closely. In 1948, an irate Rocket broke his stick over Milt Schmidt's arm in Boston, then needed a police escort to get him to the dressing room after he was given a match misconduct for leaving the penalty box to harangue referee Bill Chadwick. In one Toronto game in 1954, Richard was tossed from the game for hitting a linesman with his glove during a brawl with Bob Bailey.

Conn Smythe was a firsthand witness to Richard's fury one night at Maple Leaf Gardens when the Rocket was sent to the Habs' dressing room. "The door flew open, and he charged out again, his eyes blazing the way he sometimes got, in what somebody once called the Rocket's red glare, so mad he wasn't seeing anything. I stepped in front of him and said, 'Rocket! Where are you going? Won't do any good...Get back.' He seemed to come to. He stared at me. Then, without a word, he turned and stomped back into the dressing room."

The high-strung Rocket, goaded by his coach Dick Irvin, acted from anger at the men checking him, not a desire to intimidate opponents. As always, his excesses—and those of others—were met with the tacit approval of the men who ran the NHL. "I admired that man tremendously," said Smythe of Richard in his memoirs, adding that he "would have given anything to have him play for me." But while the NHL saw Richard as the ultimate gamer, French Canada saw him as a bound Prometheus, a talent so large he could only be contained by the English through harassment, intimidation, and, ultimately, suspension. Played out against the first nationalist struggles after the war to break free of Duplessis' iron grip and the smothering Catholic church, Richard resonated with a younger generation of Quebeckers, one less afraid than its parents and grandparents to rebel. His iconic status was later poignantly summed up by Roch Carrier in *The Hockey Sweater*, a boy's veneration of the Number 9 jersey worn by Richard.

No film exists of the March 1955 incident in which Richard, prodded by the Boston Bruins, went wild, breaking sticks and finally slugging a linesman. Descriptions of Richard's blow-up range from him harmlessly tapping the official after a melee with Bruins defenceman Hal Laycoe to Richard breaking three sticks over various Laycoe body parts before punching linesman Cliff Thompson senseless. Whatever the truth, NHL president Clarence Campbell, a Rhodes scholar and Nuremburg war trials lawyer who ran the NHL from an office in Montreal's Sun Life building, decided to make an example of Richard. Citing the many previous incidents of undisciplined behaviour, Campbell suspended Richard for the remainder of the regular season and the entire playoffs. Losing their emotional leader till the next season, the Canadiens were effectively doomed in 1955. To the rabid fans of Montreal, it was nothing less than an assault on the pride of French Canada by a *maudit Anglais* lawyer doing the bidding of Conn Smythe and the English managers such as Detroit GM Jack Adams, who said that Richard needed to be "put in his place." In a precursor to the nationalist-inspired violence of the 1960s and '70s, the Richard suspension resulted in a smoke-bombed riot that caused Montreal to forfeit their final regular season game to Detroit and caused $500,000 in damage to the neighbourhood and the Forum itself. A mix of hooligans and disenchanted hockey fans looted hundreds of stores within a fifteen-block radius of the Forum. Twelve policemen and twenty-five civilians were injured while police arrested hundreds of people. The riot eventually petered out at 3 a.m., but Saint Catherine Street was a smoking shambles.

Detroit's Adams—never at a loss for words—was quick to place blame after the game with the French media. "I blame [the media] for what's happened. You've turned Richard into an idol, a man whose suspension can turn hockey fans into shrieking idiots." Richard himself had to take to the radio the next day to appeal for calm and say he was accepting his punishment. While Richard himself curbed his temper in his final seasons with Montreal before retiring in 1960, leading the Habs to an unprecedented five straight Stanley Cups, Quebec society never completely settled down from the dramatics of the Richard riot and the bitter, violent strikes in the asbestos industry in the postwar years. Spurred by separatist sentiment, the overturned cars and burned storefronts became FLQ bombs in the 1960s and, eventually, the killing of Quebec cabinet minister Pierre Laporte as the '70s dawned. The separatist movement went from fringe political movement to the governing party in the province, even as Pierre Elliot Trudeau became the putative federalist champion and provocateur supreme in the body politic—on one hand espousing bills of individual rights while also declaring the War Measures Act that called the army into the streets of Montreal.

Yet while the slogan of "*maître chez nous*" swept aside many of the lynchpins of Quebec society—the church, the Union Nationale, the Anglo ascendancy—the Canadiens remained outwardly secure, the very model of a bicultural success story for the next forty years in the tumultuous province, winning seventeen more Cups with a series of stars such as Jean Beliveau, Guy Lafleur, and Patrick Roy succeeding Richard as the icons of French Canada. Even as the language of Quebec was forcefully wrenched from English to a French/English blend and then to exclusively French under Bill 101, the Canadiens did business internally in English and celebrated their wins in French. They knew how to adapt to the new reality. For Anglos, optimistic that a little compromise would achieve an idyllic blend of the two cultures, one strengthening the other, the Habs were a wonderful petrie dish experiment that gave hope for a brighter day when everyone just "calmed down a little bit." For francophones, the Canadiens represented the strength and potential of an independent, strong Quebec that could stand shoulder-to-shoulder with its neighbours.

For those listening carefully, however, the reality of Quebec's change made itself loud and clear in episodes on and off the ice. Perhaps the most prominent eruption came in 1975 when an aging Henri Richard, the diminutive brother of the Rocket, got into a feud with head coach Al McNeil over his ice time during the playoffs.

Richard, whose record of eleven Stanley Cups will likely never be broken, called out McNeil for benching his captain after game five of the final series against Chicago. Richard called McNeil "*incompetent*," which in other NHL cities might have meant that McNeil was poor at line matching or strategy. But in the charged atmosphere of Quebec in the early '70s as the Parti Quebecois closed in on respectability and the establishment fought rearguard actions against the coming language flood, Richard was saying that McNeil, a Maritimer, had disrespected a French Canadian in his own home city. The French—especially a revered figure such as the Pocket Rocket—were not going to be pushed around any longer in their milieu by an *Anglais*. The Canadiens understand the optics. Despite winning a Cup in his rookie campaign as coach, McNeil was dispatched to the minor leagues the next season, leaving Richard vindicated in the public eye as he went into a satisfied retirement.

The Canadiens knew enough to bend to language politics in the new Quebec, although they rarely let it get in the way of winning before the 1990s. For every Rocket Richard there was a counterbalance of Doug Harvey. For Jean Beliveau there was Dickie Moore. For Guy Lafleur, Larry Robinson. For Patrick Roy, Bob Gainey. The tension between the two camps was converted from a handicap to an asset, a sharpening of the minds and senses within the dressing room on a daily basis. Teammates Peter Mahovlich and Mario Tremblay engaged in a bloody fight one night in the mid-seventies. While the drunken tussle between an anglophone and a francophone was seized upon by the province's chattering classes as ammo for their incessant language battles, the club quickly glossed over it on its way to four straight Cups between 1975 and 1979. For Ken Dryden, the Ivy League-trained goalie on that 1971 Canadiens championship team, the balancing act performed by the hockey team was a drama played out every day via French and English. "Language is the principal source of tension and rivalry," he wrote in his 1980 masterpiece *The Game.*

> It has to do with status—majority status and minority status— and the correlation between numbers, influence and language that has never been quite direct . . . For if the team is no longer truly of the society of which it is part, it remains its most visible symbol. It has been, and will continue to be, used by both sides as they play out the tension.

In the end, the *égal à égal* of the Canadiens' dressing room could not work in a Quebec daily becoming more bold and confident of its leverage within Canada. The rivalry, the tension that Dryden, an Ontario native, felt as Quebec approached its first referendum, suffused the Montreal hockey scene for a little over a decade and two more Cups in 1986 and 1993—both products of the magnificent Roy in net. But by 1996, when Roy left Montreal for Colorado in a snit over his coach Mario Tremblay, the rivalry between cultures that spurred the great teams of the '60s and '70s had largely dissipated on the team and in the province, a victim of the crushing victory of the French faction in the years that followed the glory days of Dryden's Habs in the '70s.

The signs of capitulation by the remaining English were summed up when former Péquiste Premier Jacques Parizeau famously sniffed that the narrow 1995 referendum loss was caused by "money and ethnics." Parizeau's ill-tempered analysis (while likely correct) was a bracing whiff of entitlement, the bitterness of a man denied the drumstick in his own house by the annoying downstairs staff. And a far cry from René Lévesque's underdog charm on the night of November 15, 1976, when he called for calm and compassion.

There is no real talk of a return to power sharing between the two old rival camps in Montreal; after the diasporas of the seventies and eighties, the remaining English are a curiosity, a museum artifact swallowed in a sea of unilingual French culture and the wave of allophones who replaced the fleeing English geese. Former MLA Reed Scowen summed up the mood of even the most accommodating, bilingual Anglos in his 2006 book, *Time to Say Goodbye*:

> Quebec today is not a community that a significant number of English-speaking people would choose to live, work or raise a family. This will not change, because it's the way the French-speaking majority want things to be. They have a language and a culture to preserve, and their project leaves too little room—too little state-sanctioned room—for a viable English presence. Quebec is French, and will remain so.

Perhaps it's a coincidence, but since the removal of the old antagonisms and passions between the Two Solitudes, the Canadiens have withered too. While expansion has naturally made winning the Cup more difficult, the Canadiens had never gone more than seven years without a Stanley Cup since the Second World War. At this writing, it has been fifteen years since the Habs last raised the Cup that bears their name twenty-four times. The balancing act of the famous Habs dressing rooms has disappeared, leaving only petty language attacks on Finnish and Russian hockey players as a reminder of the great social dramas once played out in the name of the Canadiens. The Canadiens have become—dare we say it?—just another hockey team loaded with polyglot millionaires from North America and Europe. The only compelling game left in Quebec is that of playing off dreams of independence against the fears of quaking federalist politicians in Ottawa for the financial and emotional profit of the province. As author Alan Cairns has written of the constitutional sport, "Quebec has consistently played both games simultaneously, with a division of labour between the two main (federal) parties."

By the 2007 provincial election, the landscape and loyalty of Quebec was clear, according to Jeffrey Simpson of *The Globe and Mail.* "The Liberals," he noted, "attracted less than a third of the francophone vote, while capturing the lion's share of the non-francophones. Most francophones, then, voted for parties with no interest in Canada (the PQ) or almost no interest (the ADQ), except as a matter of convenience." For the first time since the early twentieth century, Quebec had a minority government.

Former Ontario premier Bob Rae, defeated for the Liberal Party leadership in 2006, best summed up the current state of a unilingual, contented Quebec:

> For generations people outside Quebec have persisted in asking the typical media question: "What does Quebec want?" I think Quebec is now entitled to say, "Well, we have a pretty good idea of what we want . . . we've given you some sense of the direction we want to go." Now Quebec is entitled to ask English Canada, "What do you want?"

Even in this climate of ambiguous loyalties, however, the Canadiens provide a metaphor for the changes. The desertion of Patrick Roy, the darling of the Quebec hockey nation, on December 2, 1995, provides a vivid tableau illustrating the profound changes in Quebec society since fans rioted to protest how Richard, the francophone hero, was treated by the English establishment of the day. Having surrendered nine goals on twenty-six shots against the Detroit Red Wings—and hearing boos from the crowd at the Forum—Roy mockingly raised his arms when he stopped a soft shot. Finally relieved of his torture in net by Coach Mario Tremblay, a humiliated Roy stormed past his coach and confronted team president Ronald Corey. "It's my last game in Montreal," he said in French. A few days later Roy was traded to Colorado; a few months later the Avalanche were hoisting the Stanley Cup. But there was no English coach to call *"incompétent"* this time, no English owner to blame for cultural insensitivity. This was a native son of Quebec blowing off the French-Canadian coach and the French-Canadian president before a TV audience of French-speaking fans. And then taking his act to the United States. Nothing could better illustrate the state of modern Quebec than the evolution from Richard's riot in 1955—the perceived product of bias against a French Canadian—to the sight of Roy turning his back on the greatest institution of Quebecois pride for the riches of the Americans.

Put simply, the Canadiens are a very close approximation of how Quebec institutions will survive after independence. The Habs are Quebec without a parachute, a bold traveller in the global world. They carry the pride of the new Quebec formed since 1976 with them on their journeys across the National Hockey League. But it's not simply in the patriotic fervour that the Habs model independent Quebec. They also demonstrate the considerable compromises that Quebec will need to make if it wishes to pursue a continued French domination of the province's businesses, politics, and media. The Canadiens, for instance, are now owned by American George Gillett, who purchased them when the hallowed link to the Anglo establishment symbolized by the Molson family and its breweries was severed. Although some Quebec figures— notably Céline Dion—discussed purchasing the Habs, there was not enough money or commitment from within the province. (Lack of Quebec money also doomed baseball's Expos in 2002.) So to keep the team in Montreal before its rabid fans, the Denver businessman Gillett bought the club. Despite Quebec's punishing taxes, Gillett has done very well financially by Quebec's most hallowed symbol, and it's hard to imagine where the local money might come to save the team in Montreal should he sell the franchise. By most financial accounts on both sides of the sovereignty debate, Quebec is living well beyond its means within Canada (Quebec spends almost double the amount per person on social programs than do other provinces) and dangerously past its own purse if it wishes to be a sovereign state.

Even Quebec's most revered nationalists have voiced concerns that the now-content Quebecois must adapt to global forces and spend less time obsessing about old grievances with Anglo Canada. Former Premier Lucien Bouchard painted a bleak future for Quebec in a 2005 report outlining the province's economic future. "They work less than other North Americans; they retire earlier; they benefit from more generous social programs; both individually and collectively, their credit cards are maxed out. In a few short years, our dreams—or rather our children's—will be brutally interrupted by a knock on the door when the bailiffs come calling."

For a number of Quebec institutions the Canadiens' mix of American money and European skill will be the likely formula if the province wants to perpetuate the symbols of French cultural domination in the province. Likewise, the makeup of the hallowed lineup for the Flying Frenchmen will look much as it does today. Gone is the celebrated legacy of French stars that began with Rocket Richard and progressed through Jean Beliveau to Guy Lafleur and Patrick Roy. If a player is French on the twenty-first-century Habs it is strictly a coincidence of drafting or trading. The heroes of the Canadiens today are men such as the Finn Koivu or the Russian Alexei Kovalev or the American Mike Komisavek. The lustre of putting on the Habs' famous jersey has long ago dimmed, as Habs fans realized when free agent Daniel Briere—a Quebecois superstar—passed up the *bleu-blanc-rouge* for the Philadelphia Flyers' black and orange (and $52 million) in 2007. There is no hometown magic to draw players to Quebec any longer. The price of survival for the symbols of Quebec will mean accepting the position of outsiders (implacable separatist Jacques Parizeau might call them "ethnics") to produce a world-class product.

That's a point that Henri Richard, he of the subtle cultural diss of Al McNeil in 1971, now understands better than most. A concerned Richard voiced his concerns to the *Gazette* when Montreal sports media had seized on quotes given by the Canadiens Russian star Kovalev to a newspaper back home about the shortcomings of Coach Guy Carbonneau. Said Kovalev, "If you (media) are going to keep embarrassing me here, there's no reason for me to stay, because I don't want to ruin my reputation and ruin my career. Sometimes you wonder why anyone would want to be a good player when things like that happen." Richard worries that the corrosive media coverage was keeping star players from coming to play for the Habs. In particular, Richard says the obsession for a developing Quebecois player to be the next great French Habs star—a position unoccupied since Roy fled to Colorado and two Stanley Cups with the Avs—is putting too much stress on young francophone players. So when Don Cherry suggested Daniel Briere might come from Buffalo to his home province, Richard snapped.

"That's a lousy thing to say . . . I'm French, but I'm also a Canadian. A guy's language makes no difference."

Richard's teammate Yvan Cournoyer, a participant in the quintessential Canadian hockey goal in the 1972 series against the U.S.S.R., echoed Richard's qualms about Quebec's voracious media culture harming the province's ability to attract talent. In an interview with Dave Tubbs of the *Gazette*, Cournoyer cited the example of a big name who avoided Montreal for the New York Rangers:

> We ask why players like Brendan Shanahan don't want to come here. A lot of guys don't say it, but they don't want to come here because it's not as simple as coming to just play hockey.
>
> If I'm playing now, I'd be worried about coming to Montreal, knowing I'd be crucified if I said something even a little wrong. The mentality when a player considers the Canadiens now is: "Oh (expletive), do I want to go to Montreal?" And that's a shame, because this is a great hockey town and fans here are crazy about the game.

Going forward, the question will be: Does Quebec want to pay the price for institutions such as the Montreal Canadiens that stem from these concerns? How much will be enough? Don't expect Saku Koivu to supply the answers.

CHAPTER THREE

The Greatest One

"My husband was up early to listen to the radio so he could hear the score," she said.

"Oh," I smiled. I had misjudged her. Forever I would be sorry for it. "Yes," I said, "did he find out?"

"Yes—he's heartbroken."

"No," I said, "Not heartbroken—we won—Canada won 3–2."

She looked at me, as if I really was such a country bumpkin. And I suppose when considering it, I have been looked at like this almost all my life over something or other.

"But we were going for the Russians," she said.

"No," I said. I had the same tone as a man might who had just learned that the *Titanic* had sunk or Passchendaele had cost us thousands of men for fifty yards of mud.

Hearing my tone, the tone of a person bleeding, maybe she felt as if she had won a moral victory. "Well, we both hate Gretzky, you see." Her accent now turned slightly British.

"Why?"

"Oh, he's just such a Canadian." She smiled.

—*Hockey Dreams* by David Adams Richards

By the winter of 2006, it would be fair to say that Wayne Gretzky had never faced a press conference that didn't like him. Even at his most emotional—dabbing tears in front of Edmonton's press corps as he departed for Los Angeles in 1988—the former hockey star always had the empathy of the media crowd and the people they represented. Whether celebrating one of his myriad records or acknowledging another honour from the sport or the nation of Canada, Gretzky had always played to friendly audiences among the most cynical of crowds—a media horde. As befits the most brilliant scoring machine who ever played the national pastime and one who, in 2002, led Canada to its first gold medal in Olympic men's hockey in fifty years, Gretzky is held in something higher than high esteem.

But this February day in 2006 is an altogether different assembly of the fourth estate. Gretzky is here in his role as the general manager of the men's hockey version of Team Canada headed to the Winter Olympics in Turin. In a typical conference, he would reliably expect gentle probing about player selection as Canada seeks to repeat its gold medal from 2002. Such as the inclusion of the infamous Todd Bertuzzi, fresh off an eighteen-month suspension for breaking the neck of Colorado opponent Steve Moore. Or the exclusion of wunderkinds Sidney Crosby and Jason Spezza. And there would be the usual fatuous questions about comparisons to previous Team Canadas. It simply goes with the territory.

But as the media converge on a small conference room in Mississauga, Ontario, it's clear that a grim-faced Gretzky will not be playing softball with the press this day. His lean face tight in a rictus smile behind the dais, he can see, mixed among the familiar faces of hockey reporters, many people he does not recognize. They are news reporters with cameras, recorders, and pens, eager to jump on a story that threatens to tear apart Gretzky's family image and soil his spotless public image as Canadian national hero and (now) coach/co-owner of the Phoenix Coyotes of the NHL. The previous week New Jersey state authorities had announced charges against Phoenix assistant coach Rick Tocchet, a New Jersey state trooper, and another New Jersey man for running a sports gambling operation. State police said that the wagers—primarily on professional football—exceeded $1.7 million in the five weeks leading to the 2006 Super Bowl. Among the alleged bettors: Gretzky's own wife, the former actress Janet Jones, and his close friend and (then) Phoenix GM Mike Barnett. The sensational story was front-page news this winter day, even in American newspapers that otherwise ignore hockey 24/7. The betting rumours surrounding the blonde Jones—who has remained in Los Angeles while her celebrated husband moved to Phoenix—have become comic fodder for the likes of Jay Leno and David Letterman (top Dick Cheney excuse for shooting Harry Whittington: made a bet with Gretzky's wife). In Canada, it taints the man who was voted among the Top Ten Canadians of all time by a CBC poll.

As he surveyed the jostling reporters and camera operators, Gretzky could have few illusions about what was going to happen. Questions about hockey will be few. Since the gambling story had broken a week earlier, what he knew of his wife's betting is the only topic anyone wants to discuss. Tocchet, the linchpin in a betting scheme with alleged ties to the Mafia, is now an afterthought while the world's sporting press trains its sights on a man who chooses to remain in the spotlight but not feel the heat of the glare it brings this day.

Gretzky had already insinuated that it was unfair to link him to the story and that the media is hounding him unfairly. The hockey legend insisted from the first news leak that this story was not about him, but about Tocchet and his wife Janet. "You'll have to ask them," he protested when first confronted about the police probe. In his clinical attempt to distance the Gretzky name from the spreading stain, some thought it ungallant how Gretzky quickly threw his wife to the media when asked about the case. But Janet Gretzky, too, moved briskly to distance her husband and his pristine image from the growing scandal. She issued a terse press release saying that while she might have put down a dollar or two on a football game, her husband was blameless. So far as Janet Gretzky was concerned, her husband knew nothing of her gambling activities, nor had he ever bet on any sports event.

Not that the earnest attempts to protect the Gretzky franchise from reproach placated anyone in the press. The facts placed Gretzky squarely at the heart of the story—if not making him liable or guilty of any charges. 1) His friend and chosen employee Rick Tocchet was about to be arraigned for bookmaking and related charges conducted while employed by a team Gretzky partly owns and coaches. 2) Janet Gretzky had admitted that while she did not bet on hockey or on behalf of her husband, she had bet with Tocchet—perhaps as much as $100,000, said some stories. 3) Coyotes GM Mike Barnett admitted to placing a Super Bowl bet with his employee, Tocchet. 4) Tocchet's fondness for betting was an open secret in the hockey circles that included Gretzky. 5) New Jersey police had served Tocchet with legal papers and were trying to serve Janet Gretzky at her husband's home when he was there. 6) Police allegedly had a wiretap recording of Gretzky discussing the case just as it hit the news.

From these facts, media assembled for the Hockey Canada presser might justifiably ask what Wayne knew and when he knew it. Why he alone was ignorant of the betting when all around him seemed to know? And finally, was any hockey information passed along by Tocchet that organized crime was able to take advantage of it? ("It's not a hockey-related issue, it's a football thing. And at this time I can't comment any further," Tocchet told reporters at the time.)

In short, as the media noose tightened on this Monday afternoon shortly before Team Canada set off for Europe, professing no involvement wasn't washing with Gretzky's skeptics in the media. They had come to Mississauga to demand an accounting before the Olympics. And if Gretzky stonewalled or dissembled, some believed he should not be allowed to accompany the Olympic team to Europe where he might create a huge distraction at the Olympics.

But the Team Canada GM had long ago decided to tough out the media frenzy that stretched beyond Canada to the U.S. and Europe. In his adamant refusal to either tell all or issue a "no comment on a legal matter" he is fully supported by Hockey Canada, the NHL, some media (one Toronto writer called it "a crucifixation") and many loyal fans. He will not give his critics satisfaction as the inquisition begins. In less than five minutes of questioning, he only says "There's no story about me, that's what I keep trying to tell you. I'm not involved." He refuses any discussion of the propriety of him going to Turin. His answers are clipped, and he affects a nervous laugh as a Hockey Canada official attempts to keep order in the room. At one point under questioning, his shoulders sag in resignation, as if the weight of the country's hockey hopes has been loaded upon him. Asked about the integrity of the sport in light of the betting story, he says, "That's not for me to talk about." And with that, the conference is abruptly ended by Hockey Canada.

Gretzky's unequivocal denial of a role in the scandal is about preserving the franchise. The carefully cultivated persona he adopted when still a boy in Brantford, the lovable prodigy from small town Canada who is both above and with the people at the same time. He has paid a real personal price to maintain this perch, and he will not give it up easily. And so he grimly separates his hero's mantle from even his loved ones. Still, he has no escape route from the Olympics, even if he did want to go hide from public scrutiny. His unassailable image as the aw-shucks Canadian hero demands that he fulfill his obligation to Hockey Canada at the Olympics. And while he is thought to be well off financially, he still has advertising contracts with Roots and Ford that are contingent upon him going to the Olympics.

Even if Gretzky is found blameless, the family's private life—the one thing that hockey stars and celebrities try to protect above all else—is being turned upside down in the international spotlight of the NHL and the Olympics. There's an intruder in the home, going through the cupboards and looking under the bed. Secrets are spilling out. Why do he and Janet live in separate cities? Where did the mother of five get the money to bet? For Gretzky, the questions of credibility and culpability are bad enough. But the worst scenario for him is to see his marriage laid bare before the world, his wife reportedly betting large sums on sports events and racking up considerable debt while he stood by. (Apparently, the wiretaps record a man pleading with Tocchet to rescue his wife from a bad situation.)

In the contemporary world—where women often make more money and wield more influence than their husbands or partners—Gretzky's dilemma would be simply a cautionary tale. In the twenty-first century, women can stand on their own and suffer the consequences of their actions without a male filter. Unfortunately for Gretzky, hockey is still living in a social climate comparable to the 1950s. In the NHL's macho code, guys are supposed to control their significant others. Women are supporting actors, men the leads. Now the hockey world—as catty a place as Wisteria Lane on *Desperate Housewives*—will be clucking about Wayne's dilemma with Janet. By the time the last curious reporter or blogger has grown bored with Wagergate, it will take a lot of healing to get over the hurt produced by this maximum exposure. It is hard to see the Great One in a more uncomfortable or unflattering bind.

Coming on the heels of the loss of his mother and grand-mother in the previous year, this added stress seems like piling on to his supporters. For a man whose greatest sin seems to be the unreliable friends he chooses—hello Bruce McNall, *ciao* Rick Tocchet—you can see a normal human being cracking under that strain. But Gretzky—the public man—is no ordinary character, and any tears he might have shed were far from the public spotlight.

It did not immediately get better in Turin. The media waiting there again raised the betting scandal in their limited exposures to the team's GM. Once more, he stonewalled, affecting a bemused attitude at times, with his wife off shopping elsewhere in Italy. In time, the focus did shift, as he'd hoped, to the hockey club. Ironi-cally, the betting scandal only faded when his hand-picked squad never found its scoring touch at the Olympics. Shut out in three of the six games it played, Team Canada was ignominiously elimi-nated in the quarterfinals of the tournament, falling 2–0 to Rus-sia. A dearth of scoring and a lack of discipline among the NHL stars in Italy doomed the defending champions and left Canada with one gold medal in men's hockey in fifty-six years.

In a delicious irony, Bertuzzi—the man whom Gretzky and the Canadian staff had insisted be part of the club instead of Sid-ney Crosby—was in the penalty box when the Russians scored the decisive goal against Canada. The men wearing the maple leaf wound up a humbling seventh overall. Allowed to address a hockey issue, Gretzky was defiant. "People are going to question who was on the ice and who was on the team and that's OK," Gretzky told CBC Sports. "I'm a pretty big boy. I can stand up [to any criticism]. [But] obviously we have to do something different for 2010 . . . I'll take all the responsibility for not winning . . . This country will regroup and this team will be ready for 2010."

It would be difficult to imagine a lower estate than the one to which Gretzky had fallen in early 2006. Personally and professionally he'd been repudiated by events and touched by personal tragedy. His two hockey ventures—Team Canada and the Phoenix Coyotes—were remarkably unsuccessful. The media had dredged up his personal life, showing apparent cracks in the facade of his marriage. Comedians mocked his family and disparaged his efforts to bring hockey to the Arizona desert.

Yet, his iconic status in Canada remained unassailable. Public support was unflagging even when he seemingly placed himself ahead of Team Canada and casually offered his wife up for public scrutiny. Marketers still scrambled to attach the Great One's name to their products. In every sense, Gretzky remained Canada's Teflon man, protected by his amazing hockey feats and the accumulated weight of his myth.

In a country famous for humbling its chosen sons and daughters (Malcolm Lowry once wrote of his native land: "Success is like some horrible disaster. Worse than your house burning . . .") this balancing act was remarkable. Gretzky still managed to strive without any seeming ambitions. He was successful without appearing self-satisfied. He was patriotic without even living in his native land. He was unrelenting without appearing threatening. Most of all, he was about Wayne Gretzky while also being seen as the ultimate team player. In a nation that has traditionally cut down its tallest wheat (Jim Carrey still smoulders at his treatment in his own country before finding American fame) the young legend from Brantford managed the tricky proposition of rising high above Canadians' heads while still keeping his head down.

But there must be more to it than simply Gretzky's overarching fame and accomplishment? If it were simply hockey stardom, then Bobby Orr, not Gretzky, would lead Team Canada to Olympic gold in the current decade. It's often said that Orr could have played centre like Gretzky, but number 99 could never have played defence the way Orr did in his brief decade as hockey's pre-eminent star. But for all his brilliance, Orr never let the public get close to his real self in the way that Gretzky has done. Orr functioned somewhere above the rabble, untouchable and unassailable. His marriage was a closely guarded secret, not a public spectacle. He let few media people into the inner sanctum and ostracized those who violated his privacy. By the time his career ended prematurely because of knee problems, Orr was more of Boston than of Canada, a legend in New England and an enigma back in Canada.

The same might be said for Mario Lemieux, Gretzky's contemporary and every bit his equal as a scoring genius in the '80s an '90s. But Lemieux was French Canadian, stuck in Pittsburgh, and aloof to the blandishments of the average Canadian. Besides, Lemieux's health issues also disrupted his career and made him more a figure of sympathy than awe. Of the other hockey stars, Phil Esposito was considered too brash and goofy, Eric Lindros too calculating and self-obsessed, Guy Lafleur too much of Quebec, Mark Messier too primal and threatening.

If it were simply national sporting glory, then Donovan Bailey, not Gretzky, would still be celebrated from sea to sea for his double gold-medal performance at the 1996 Summer Olympics, when he kicked the ass of American sprinting and demanded they come back for a second helping. But Bailey is treated with suspicion by the Canadian public for his in-your-face confidence and scorned by a media that (unfairly) saw him as a quitter for not returning completely from a torn Achilles tendon suffered before the 2000 Sydney Olympics. Bailey's fierce black pride also seemed a little too real for conservative Canada coming to grips with the multicultural reality of its present day. By different criteria, Ken Dryden, the cerebral Montreal Canadiens goalie-turned-activist-turned-politician, should be a model for the modern Canada. Articulate, sensitive, sports hero, bilingual—a hero in both of Canada's solitudes where Gretzky was an Anglo phenomenon—his resume seems natural for myth. But where Gretzky artfully avoided being tied to any position or issue until becoming a coach himself in his 40s, Dryden continually allied himself to controversy and partisan political or cultural positions. As generations of politicians have discovered, to adopt a stance is usually fatal in Canada.

So why does Wayne Gretzky remain the quintessential Canadian hero in the earliest years of the twenty-first century? He didn't win a war, build a railroad, or repatriate a constitution. He speaks only one of the two national languages and now lives in the Sun Belt of the USA. Yet he endures a decade after retiring from the NHL. He makes Canadians feel like winners—without the problem of prisoner exchange.

Gretzky's place in the Canadian pantheon has been considered by many. The renowned writer/broadcaster Peter Gzowski, who watched Gretzky and his Oiler teammates obliterate the goon era in the '80s with their creativity, summed it up best for his generation of Canadians who came out of the Second World War experience. "To those of us who had grown up on the outdoor rinks, Wayne's accomplishments were especially pleasing," he wrote in 1982. "He was a throwback. He played the game of our lives. We cheered his rise to stardom."

Perhaps a look at the members of CBC's Top Ten (voted on by English-speaking viewers in 2004) reveals a few clues about the country that worships him but that he has not called home since 1988. Here they are:

1   Tommy Douglas
2   Terry Fox
3   Pierre Elliott Trudeau
4   Sir Frederick Banting
5   David Suzuki
6   Lester B. Pearson
7   Don Cherry
8   Sir John A. Macdonald
9   Alexander Graham Bell
10   Wayne Gretzky

What conclusions would an alien draw about twenty-first century Canada from that list? What themes run beneath the people's choices (besides the fact that they're all male)? There are two hockey personalities, four figures connected with health and science, two prime ministers who sought a peacekeeping role for the nation, the founding father of the country, and the inventor of the cell phone ... alright, its ancestor. Allowing for the vagaries of an unscientific poll, there are still no generals on the Top Ten List, no decorated soldiers or sailors (unthinkable before Trudeau became prime minister in 1968). Outside of Fox, the wounded martyr to cancer, there are no "ordinary" people. There are no explorers or voyagers, no Native Canadians, no teachers or trailblazing women. No great novelists or poets or filmmakers or actors or philosophers or artists or singers. Two scientists but no engineers, no architects, no chemists, no accountants, no bankers. And while Tommy Douglas was a preacher by calling, his legacy is predicated on his secular notion of universal health care. (And—in a curious Canadian way—the concept of something as valuable as health care for nothing.) There isn't a hint of organized religion on the list—at a time when religion still consumes the daily agenda in the U.S. and many other nations.

So, the Top Ten list is a concise catalogue of Canada's most cherished values at the start of the twenty-first century. The secular icons of health care, hockey, anti-Americanism, peacekeeping, and communications are not a bad platform upon which to run for office in a nation that projects itself (in the words of former Foreign Affairs minister Lloyd Axworthy) as a "soft" power, an honest peacekeeper of the world. Even though it had fewer than 60 of its 68,000 troops dedicated to peacekeeping in 2006—and a considerable combat role in Afghanistan—modern Canada now prefers to storm the beaches of reason, not the beaches of Normandy. So while the defence of modern feminism has become a sacred trust of Canada's Left, that does not extend that right so far as to defending it by force of arms in Afghanistan. With a few very prominent exceptions, Canada has graduated from the Ten Commandments to the commanding heights of moral relativism— especially in comparison to the United States, whom we so closely resemble. "Each country has certain values," writes Robert Fulford, "and Canadians appear to have decided that ours are superior."

No wonder historian Jack Granatstein describes Canada's twenty-first century foreign policy as the triumph of values— compassion, multiculturalism, environmentalism—over its interests—nations such as the U.S. or Britain that constitute its closest partners and, hopefully, defenders. Better to feel good than to feel guilt in an age where the new catechisms are the environment or racial harmony or personal self-awareness.

Having jettisoned large parts of its collective memory as too scary or too offensive for the new rapprochement, with Quebec and immigrant communities, the Rest of Canada (ROC) is now a place largely without a narrative—outside of hockey, of course. The men who perished at the Somme or Cortona or Korea must now be seen as earnest—but gullible—victims of the military-industrial complex. The civilizing effects of British law and custom are now trappings of an imperialist past. Moral equivalence is everything. The result, Mark Steyn writes, is that "In the space of two generations, a bunch of tough *hombres* were transformed into a thoroughly feminized culture that prioritizes the secondary impulses of society—rights and entitlement from cradle to grave—over all the primary ones." Symbolic of this tortured history has been the Official Languages Policy, which the government has employed for over thirty-five years to make services available in both official languages across the nation—in the hope of fostering bilingualism and a professional class of French speakers within the government and business. French-dominant language laws now underpin Quebec's society and the program is seen as a success in *La Belle Province*. But outside Quebec, the OLP is a patchwork quilt, cost-ineffective and loathed by many in English Canada.

So, where a linguistically confident Quebec has set one great movie after another, one great novel after another, against a canvas of mutual assumptions about purpose, the ROC has largely had no compelling backdrop since Paul Henderson's goal against which to frame its identity or art. Despite the injection of hundreds of millions into the cultural industry, just a small fraction of English Canadians (under 5 per cent) ever see their own movies, theatre, or art (significantly, pop music, which operates in a freer market, has successfully penetrated the market). Predominantly, English-speaking Canadian authors and directors either reflect the immigrant experience (Mordecai Richler, Michael Ondaatje, Austin Clarke) or are *auteurs* serving an international market (David Cronenberg, Atom Egoyan.). What emanates from the most celebrated native writers such as Alice Munro, Margaret Laurence, or Alistair McLeod is more the internal personal dialogue, divorced from mainstream culture. Their Canadian experience is framed less by the broader ROC than by an isolated sense of self or landscape. (Joseph Boyden's *Three Day Road* is a remarkable exception.) How can there be a great Canadian novel without a great Canadian narrative to support it? And how can there be a narrative without a set of mutual agreements about who we are or why we exist apart from the United States?

Despite this basic tenet of nationhood, the airbrushing of Canada's British past—with echoes of head taxes and immigrant quotas—has been fostered to lessen the culture shock for its 6.2 million foreign-born citizens (making Canada the only post-modern culture where the settlers adapt to the newcomers). Pollster Michael Adams believes the lack of identity is not a weakness but a strength that frees us of prejudices and makes us more universal. "We do suspect, deep down, that we're superior to other countries," writes Adams in *Unlikely Utopia: The Surprising Triumph of Canadian Pluralism*, "precisely because we don't think we're superior." But Patrick Luciani sees the inherent flaws in the "myth that Canadians live in this 'inclusive, genteel, ethnically diverse Nirvana.'" Writes Luciani, the product of immigrant Italian parents: "Some even cheer the hyphen in the hyphenated Canadian as 'a bridge, not a minus sign.' But in the end, such gestures signify reluctance among immigrants, a lack of commitment, and sense of waiting to see how things turn out ..."

The lack of success in making many newcomers feel more welcome in their country has done nothing to stop the re-ordering of Canada's past. "What do the entrants know about Bobby Orr or Lester Pearson or Gordon Lightfoot?" asked Lawrence Martin in *The Globe and Mail.* "The image blurs. If we had trouble defining 'Canadian' before, what do we do now—and what do we do as the trend accelerates, as it is bound to do, and as we witness the unseemly impacts of the immigration waves across Europe."

No surprise, then, that the cbc Top Ten list reflects the traditional suspicion of authority figures in Canada's new age, the wariness of commitment. The idea of waiting to see how things turn out before "buying in" is a perfect reflection of a culture reluctant to impose its narrative on fellow citizens or recalcitrant members of the world community. In the words of Michael Adams, in the last generation Canadians have become "more skeptical of authority and more confident about their personal decisions and informal arrangements."

And so the inclusion on the cbc list of Nobel prize winner Lester Pearson, who could never win a majority in Parliament (something Trudeau immediately accomplished in 1968). Pearson's humanity and peacekeeping appeal to our current value set, and his political humbling keeps him accessible. Or the iconoclast Douglas, the passionate Saskatchewan advocate of health care who was never to grab the top rung in Canadian political life— leaving him remarkably unsullied by the heavy lifting of leaders such as Brian Mulroney or Jean Chretien. The tragic one-legged runner Terry Fox is benign and unfailingly polite, while the putative strong man (Cherry) is in fact a harmless blowhard. The environmentalist Suzuki represents the Canadian suspicion of multinational corporations nurtured for half a century by populist politics and the left wing. MacDonald led only a peacetime Canada where railways, not wars, were the preoccupation.

Perhaps the presence in the number three position of the enigmatic Trudeau—the civil libertarian who called out the army in 1970s Quebec Crisis—speaks best to the polymorphous nature of the Canadian character in the twenty-first century. Trudeau, the man who motorcycled around Montreal during the Second World War wearing a German helmet as neighbours and friends were being killed by the Wehrmacht. Trudeau, the unflinching conscience who defeated Meech Lake and Charlottetown with the singular power of his intellect. Trudeau, who dated Streisand, married a woman who ran off with the Rolling Stones, fathered a child in his seventies. Trudeau, who marks the end of English Canada as we know it and the beginning of the French Canada we know today—despite his strenuous objections. Trudeau, the anti-authoritarian authoritarian who called out the troops. But ultimately it's Trudeau's impact as the pop figure more than as repatriator of the Constitution or father of the Bill of Rights that most resonates with Canada's MuchMusic generation. In this squishy pop sensibility, the CBC list seems built to avoid conflict rather than forge consensus. (In a delicious bit of Canadiana, CBC later had voters choose the Seven Wonders of the Canadian World in 2007, then allowed a select panel to override those decisions to guarantee that every region was represented.)

This straw poll also betrays the reflexive anti-Americanism that has existed since the Revolutionary War—and fed by the estimated 70,000 draft dodgers who rejected their country for Canada during the Vietnam War. Comedian Rick Mercer is just the latest to mine the deep vein of Canadian amusement at American vanity with his "Talking to Americans" spoofs. This is the

same superiority that lets Canadians label American vice president Dick Cheney as a puppet of the giant Haliburton Corporation (when he in fact owns no shares) while sitting Canadian
cabinet ministers take direct contributions from the very industries they legislate—as happened in the Chretien Liberal government. Who can forget how Canadians thrilled as Trudeau's famous
flirtation with Castro vexed the Americans? Or Paul Martin's refusal to participate in a anti-ballistic defence system for North
America in 2005? Gretzky sensed that willingness to blame America on the part of Canadians at the Salt Lake City Olympics in
2002, when, as Team Canada's executive director, he bitterly observed, "Americans love our poor start. Nobody wants us to win
but our players and our loyal fans." Lacking the ability to trump
America, Canada has adopted intellectual guerilla war, nipping
here and there at the exposed U.S. flank.

In short, the CBC's heroes are comfort figures who accept the
national reluctance to embrace heroic figures and tolerate diminished expectations. Where select individuals buck this trend, the
national consensus loves conformity the way Mackenzie King
loved a chat with Mother. Hugh MacLennan thought it was the
Scottish forebears who created the type. "The Irish," he wrote,
"only brought the cholera with them, but so far no antibiotic has
been able to eradicate from the national bloodstream what the
Scotch brought. It makes us allergic to great expectations. These
are for other people, not us."

Whatever the origins of Canada's self-abasement, Peter
Gzowski understood the syndrome in his 1982 book *The Game of
Our Lives*. "We are not good with our heroes, we Canadians.
Starved for figures of national interest, we, or our media, seek out
anyone who shows a flicker of promise and shove them on the
nearest available pedestal. We leave them there for a while, and

then we start to throw things at them." In his book *Canadians*, Roy MacGregor saw humility as a germ passed along through the hockey culture. "The greatest player in the game should not only be Canadian," he wrote, "but suitably humble, as the country demands of its heroes. Richard's reserve and Howe's shyness are in fact the real torch that is passed down to Beliveau, to Orr, to Lafleur, to Gretzky, to Lemieux, to Crosby." So much so that when Steve Santos was selected first overall in the 2008 NHL draft, his humility was cited along with his hockey skills.

And so we are left with Gretzky and his remarkable leg lock on Canada's conscience. It could be said that of the figures on the CBC list, Gretzky's story perhaps best embodies the hopes, the pride, the fears, the prejudices of the modern Canadian prototype. Product of the immigrant experience—a Belorussian grandfather who moved to small-town Ontario—Gretzky is simultaneously a member of the essential North American cohort known as the baby boom. Yet he retains strong influences from both experiences. Diffident to a fault in a traditional old-country persona, the product of central Canada also achieved fame in Alberta and then succeeded beyond his wildest dreams in Hollywood. He helped to save the national sport from its darkest days as a thug spectacle in the 1980s, married a movie star, and returned home to help Canada win its first Olympic gold medal in fifty-two years. And he did it all in an unthreatening fashion that seemed—on the surface—selfless and without ego. While Gretzky has ranged far and wide to collect his just due, most Canadians still think they have him exactly where they want him—back in Brantford with father Walter and the little backyard rink of his youth.

The real Gretzky—a serious, self-critical fellow—is an abstraction he has buried within the confines of his family and friends while he cultivates his public image. Few see the private man lying beneath the widely held image sold via commercials and the hockey business.

To understand why he's pursued this balancing act, it's necessary to review the legend of Gretzky, a story so well-known by now that almost any young Canadian boy or girl can recite it by rote. Gretzky grew up at the tail end of the Baby Boom in small-town Brantford, Ontario. His father Walter was a hyperkinetic phone company employee whose ideas on how to train hockey players were years ahead of his peers—and ahead of the professionals in many cases. His mother was that staple of the boomer years, the stay-at-home mom. Scrawny and unassuming, Wayne was moulded at a young age by Walter on the backyard rink into the greatest scoring machine ever seen. In one season alone he scored an astounding 378 goals. Walter Gretzky knew what he had. "You're a special person," he told his young son. "Wherever you go, probably all your life, people are going to make a fuss over you. You've got to remember that, and you've got to behave right. Remember that. You're very special, and you're on display." (Gretzky later reflected his acceptance of his special status when son Ty began playing hockey at the advanced age of seventeen. "He's not the best player in the world. As I tell him, he's not Wayne Gretzky. He understands that.")

While his accomplishments spoke loudly about his talent, Gretzky followed Walter's advice and was polite to a fault. (Even in his late forties, Gretzky still publicly refers to people of substance as "Mister," as in "Mr. Burke" for Anaheim GM Brian Burke, a man just four years his senior.) And here begins the connection with Roy MacGregor's Canadian myth, as Gretzky the prospect embodied all the humble, self-effacing Canadian qualities culled from the sacrifice of two world wars and the unending struggle for identity against brash Americans. With no wars for Canada's boomer generation to fight, that ethic transferred itself to the national game. And so emerged the stock character who dominates the hockey media to this day. Amiable, respectful, slightly befuddled by the attention, the public Gretzky largely speaks in clichés so shopworn it's a wonder they don't smell of mothballs. ("One of the biggest challenges the NHL has is that there isn't one player that we all know is going to be quotable, and the media is going to run with and pay too much attention to," understated NBA owner Mark Cuban of the Dallas Mavericks in his blog.)

Gretzky took to the proscribed hockey character like he took to winning Hart Trophies later in life. In a classic 1972 photo, an awkward young Gretzky posed with his hero, Gordie Howe, hockey's quintessential hard man of few words. Howe playfully considers Gretzky by hooking him in with a mini hockey stick while the towheaded boy looks straight into the camera in awe and wonderment. The transfer of power takes place here with one god, Howe, muscles bulging beneath the suit, transferring the secret to a younger god, Gretzky, in his ill-fitting, store-bought suit. Judging from the "aw-shucks" quality of both men in the black-and-white photo, there is a tendency to see the two hockey stars as cut from the same Canadian cloth. After all, Gretzky has hewn closely to Howe's folksy image since that memorable day. But Howe was a product of the Depression and the Prairies, rough and exceptionally violent when the occasion called for it. (He broke the jaw of the hapless J.C. Tremblay of Montreal only moments after receiving a standing ovation from the Forum crowd for his 600th career goal.) That was Howe's generation—unapologetic and dutiful at the office. Away from the rink, however, Howe remained a western gentleman, almost boyish. Some compared Howe to Gary Cooper, the iconic cowboy actor. Howe struck the symbolic Canadian male figure in the postwar years: virile, non-flamboyant, a man of action and nobility. But the violent, venengeful Howe who once lifted an opponent off the ice by his nostrils could never have fit in a modern Canada where politicians achieve the trick of opposing military action while still "supporting" the same troops in those actions they oppose. Like sucking and blowing at the same time.

Despite their hockey tie, Howe and Gretzky represent very different national myths. As a product of an urban, more sophisticated Canada in the '60s and '70s, Gretzky never suffered the privations visited on Howe as a boy in the Depression. He is a product of the space age, a time of experimentation and questioning. As opposed to Howe, he was a puppy, not a pit bull. His long blond hair flowed beneath his patented Jofa helmet, causing young girls to swoon. Inflation, not recession, was the economic ill of Gretzky's youth. As such, his numbers defy earthbound comprehension. He did not simply erase Howe's records, he obliterated them—many almost immediately in his career. And in contrast with Gordie, Gretzky very rarely fought, getting just 577 PIMs in his nineteen seasons. (Howe accumulated 2418 in his thirty-two seasons and inspired the Gordie Howe hat trick: a goal, an assist, and a fight in the same game). In short, Gretzky is as much a man of his time as Howe was of his.

It's deceptive to see the innocent Gretzky in the Howe photo and assume that the wide-eyed boy represents the man. The hostility of some in his hometown forged an iron will in the young man, a refusal to let criticism bend him from his goal—the single-minded determination on display years later as he faced down the media before the 2006 Olympics. At fourteen, he took the unusual (and hotly contested) step of leaving Brantford for Toronto to continue his training at a higher level, away from the petty jealousies that dogged his progress in the smaller city. While Brantford now touts him as the perfect hometown boy, there were many who had trouble abiding his success. His father told reporters, "He was cheered, booed and criticized by other players and parents. Some said he was ruining the leagues, because he scored so many goals. It upset his life, and his schoolwork suffered. He's a quiet sort of kid who keeps things bottled up inside. At one time, we thought he was going to explode." Walter remembered hearing fellow parents after the Brantford team lost 5–4 saying that "Sure [Wayne] got four but he cost us five." Getting out of Brantford and the hands pulling him back probably saved Gretzky from the disillusionment that destroyed many other players who peaked young and burned out.

While he still displayed the fawn-like innocence that would become his accepted public image, he felt both his power and his responsibility to the myth he was creating—the money and the fame and the worship of the hockey culture. And yet he still managed to preserve his image as the boy next door even though he was the greatest hockey scorer to emerge in a century. Soon the world was taking notice, as in a 1978 article by Frank Orr in *The Sporting News*:

> The name is Gretzky, Wayne G-R-E-T-Z-K-Y. All hockey fans should make a note of it, because they're going to hear the name often in the next few years. Unless, of course, most knowledgeable hockey scouts are wrong. In that case, many strong men will weep.

Strong men stayed dry-cheeked as Gretzky tore through every test offered, even when pitted against men five or six years older than him. And though he continued to act in his own best interests, he was rarely held to account for it—as would others later on. When it came to the Ontario Hockey League draft, Gretzky and his parents warned everyone not to draft him unless the team was within close proximity to the family home in Brantford. He couldn't miss education and overnight bus trips to the far-flung regions of Ontario, his father insisted. And when Sault Ste. Marie ignored the warnings and selected the skinny kid in the 1977 draft, the Gretzkys initially refused to go to the steel city six hours away from Brantford. There was indignation and outrage that a player might actually try to dictate his destiny in defiance of traditions that said a boy should go unquestioning to the city that drafted him. Eventually a compromise was reached to allow Gretzky to play in the Sault and live with family friends. No one much remembers the controversy today, but when the next Ontario phenom, Eric Lindros, likewise warned a number of teams off drafting him into the OHL, people did not forget or forgive his impertinence.

It would not be the last time that the fair-haired boy was held to a different standard. When Gretzky began smashing the records set by Howe a generation earlier—often with Howe in attendance—his hero was on another quest to have the pension money of retired NHL players restored to the plan after being misappropriated by the league. Howe, Carl Brewer, and others went to court to have surpluses returned to the plan. Gretzky initially promised to help any way he could to get Howe's paltry $13,000 annual pension increased to a proper level. But when Howe and Brewer asked Gretzky to challenge NHL Players Association director Alan Eagleson about the contributions from his Canada Cup promotions, Gretzky demurred. (Eagleson later went to jail, in part because of his handling of benefits from those tournaments that were promised to players but diverted to him and his family instead.) Howe was wounded by the failed promise and for a time refused to participate in the Gretzky record caravan (they later reconciled). But only a few dared whisper of the problem at the time, and the public saw only the Old Man and the Young Star as inseparable friends in hockey.

Satisfying the gruelling public demands with his own ambitions is a dance that has worked well for Gretzky. But the price was—and remains—strict adherence to a public persona that reassures Canadians that while Gretzky has a $25 million home in Bel Air, he's still just like you and me (a performance that Lindros, large, muscular, and aloof, refused to give to support his own image). Having set a standard by letting the public in on his 1988 wedding to Janet Jones, he's been forced to keep aspects of his life an open book for the public to probe via TV and other media. They, in turn, have been largely respectful outside the Tocchet affair. In selling the still-the-same-kid-from-Brantford image, it has helped that Gretzky remains boyish looking to this day, washed by the warm glow of California sun and his movie-star family. His lean unmuscular frame makes him the antithesis of the steroid-choked figures in other sports. His work in TV commercials and programs remains hopelessly hokey, but always endearing and slightly self-deprecating. In short, the public Gretzky is the kind of guy your grandmother loves.

For those who cannot quite buy into that homespun hockey package, Gretzky has also endeared himself to his fellow Canadians in another manner. Like Jim Carrey, Rick Moranis, Mike Myers, Steve Nash, and others—Number 99 has lived the real unspoken Canadian dream: making it big in the United States. Anti-Americanism may be a virulent strain that runs through Canadian politics, but succeeding in the lucrative U.S. market has never been included in that bias—quite the opposite. While those who choose to remain in Canada are usually brought down by the backdraft of jealousy, moving south to cash in on America's riches is still the litmus test of success for most of the boomer generation.

And Gretzky made it very big in Canadian eyes.

It's difficult to say whether the Gretzky of legend was a construct of his own or he had it thrust upon him by the market and the nation, but there's little doubt that he embraced the part completely at the public level. And the public reciprocated. So there is ample forgiveness in Gretzky's bank of favours with Canadians. In May of 2007, he managed to survive the Tocchet legal scandal. His buddy pleaded guilty in a New Jersey court to charges of encouraging a betting operation, but the veteran Tocchet avoided the more serious charges of money laundering that might have brought him jail time. The sensational tales of the mafia and Vegas gambling trips disappeared with the plea bargain. In copping the plea, Tocchet spared Gretzky the ordeal of watching his wife and best friends potentially testifying in open court about their behaviour, stories that could only restart the nagging questions about his knowledge of the betting schemes. The NHL's own internal investigation was likewise gentle on Gretzky, absolving him of any responsibility in the ugly episode. The sports historian in Gretzky knows it could have been otherwise: baseball commissioner Kenesaw Mountain Landis had suspended eight Chicago White Sox players for life in 1921 despite the fact that they were never convicted of throwing games to help gangsters.

How he will emerge from his Phoenix coaching experience is anyone's guess. The Coyotes missed the playoffs in Gretzky's first two seasons behind the bench but now seem to have a core of good young players. The greatest athletes rarely make good coaches but Gretzky seems to be relishing his job working with the young Phoenix players. Whether the Coyotes blossom or wilt, it's unlikely to reflect on Gretzky; in exchange for playing the role of its hero, Canada has granted him blanket immunity within the confines of the rink. Besides, Gretzky would likely get out before it caused his legacy any damage. As the gambling episode demonstrated, he will not let anything—be it his wife or close friend Tocchet—tarnish his very positive image. It's hard to see Canada reeling Gretzky back in at any point, considering his accomplishments and the flattering reflection he paints for them. As long as Gretzky has prestige in the United States, Canada will never bring him low; that's the fate reserved for those who remain at home and disappoint. (Witness the grovelling it took to lure Shania Twain back to her hometown after becoming a huge international success.) Out of reach, yet lodged in the heart—that is Gretzky's position as Canada's iconic figure. And will remain so as long as it flatters Canadians.

CHAPTER FOUR

Silence on the Lam

"Look, kids, you should never, ever, do anything like this. Todd was wrong—he knows he was wrong. If you have a beef with somebody, and you want to do something, it's face to face. Face to face—you settle it that way. You don't sucker-punch, ever, from behind. Do it face to face. That's the Canadian way."
—Don Cherry on *Hockey Night in Canada*, March 2004

"There's no place for stuff like that in our game. It's disgusting."
—Todd Bertuzzi in 2000 after Marty McSorley hit Bertuzzi's teammate Donald Brashear on the head with a stick.

A t the heart of hockey's Code of Intimidation there has always been the silence.

What happens in hockey *stays* in hockey.

The shroud of silence blanketed those who got hurt and those did the hurting. It was insurance, a guarantee that the outside world would never disrupt the comfortable culture of intimidation within the sport. The silence meant outsiders could never make a case against on-ice violence.

The *omerta* embraced players, coaches, GMs, and presidents. So long as everybody bought into the silence and said, "Who, me?" justice would be settled by the guys in hockey uniforms, not business suits. Keeping the peace yourself meant allowing police, judges, and politicians to conveniently look the other way when someone got a little out of hand.

Todd Bertuzzi threatened to change all that in the spring of 2008 with his demand to include his former Vancouver coach, Marc Crawford, in the $38 million lawsuit launched by Steve Moore in Ontario court against him and Orca Bay, the former owners of the Canucks, over Bertuzzi's infamous 2004 attack on the Avalanche player. Breaking the sanctity of the dressing room where "what happens here stays here," Bertuzzi was alleging that Crawford "failed to exercise control over, and caution his players against, physical aggression toward Moore" during the game in which Bertuzzi broke Moore's neck during a vigilante attack on the Colorado forward.

In hockey parlance, Bertuzzi was claiming Crawford ordered him to "get" Moore for his heavy hit three weeks earlier on captain Markus Naslund of the Canucks. (The allegation has yet to be proved in court.) Under the NHL's code, a scrub like Moore wasn't allowed to touch a star like Naslund. He had to be made accountable, and Bertuzzi was saying he was variously manipulated into exacting that price by Crawford. Testimony in Moore's suit revealed that Crawford scribbled names—including Moore's—on a board and asked that they be made to "pay the price." Crawford denies this.

Bertuzzi drew his coach into the controversy mostly to cover his own vulnerable butt, not to destroy hockey's code and its conspiracy of silence. He was hardly a rebel; he simply needed to deflect the liability for the vicious attack on Moore. Implying that he was following Crawford's orders made him simply a pawn in a bigger game, not the key figure in a retribution scheme against Moore.

Had Moore simply played by the code, keeping quiet in exchange for a small favour or two, this all would have been moot. But the Harvard product had not done the "accepted" thing by NHL standards: accepting a payout, maybe getting some minor scouting job as recompense, and disappearing into the wallpaper. Having seen B.C. justice give his case the minimum diligence when Bertuzzi received a conditional discharge with no jail time after he pleaded guilty to assault, Moore wanted his day in court to answer questions about which levels of the Canucks' management might have supported or ordered Bertuzzi's attack on him. And a nominal financial handout or shabby NHL sinecure would not suffice.

By simply persisting in his quest for four long years, Moore had exposed the divisions between Bertuzzi and Crawford that lay beneath the surface. If successful, he might show how the code sanctions and excuses the use of lethal force as a means of intimidation in the sport from the NHL on down. (Interestingly, Bertuzzi did not implicate Brian Burke, who was the Canucks' very fiery GM in 2004.)

The lawyers and judges will be asked to sort through the conflicting evidence given by Bertuzzi and Crawford regarding the attack on Moore. (As of this writing, no trial date has been set.) But lifting the shroud from the NHL's brand of intimidation might be equalling as damning for the parties involved. No wonder NHL commissioner Gary Bettman has been scrambling to effect a settlement of Moore's lawsuit against Bertuzzi and Orca Bay Corporation.

As Bertuzzi stalked Moore on the ice of Vancouver's GM Place on March 8, 2004, the code still rested firmly on its principles as a harsh manhood ritual, a fast game, a game of risk and reward, a game of blood and bone. "Cowards Don't Play Hockey" sang the

Soviets back in 1972, and it was one of the few points of agreement between East and West in the Cold War. Even as Bertuzzi culminated three weeks of overt threats with his sickening slug on Moore, the NHL had every reason to believe its code of intimidation would still continue for the foreseeable future: a manageable degree of mayhem for folks with anger issues. NHL disciplinarians had long cited the belief that hockey's "volatile" nature demands an "outlet" for the frustrations of the game. That, as opposed to other sports, hockey is inherently wilder, more untamed.

"A flying elbow in the face may provoke instant retaliation with two players dropping their sticks and gloves and fighting," said NHL referee-in-chief Scotty Morrison in 1971. "I view this as entirely more acceptable than a player retaliating by slashing his stick. If there was a rule that automatically ejected a player for fighting there would be a definite increase in slashing, a dangerous practice and one which I personally detest." In short, you think fighting is bad ... wait till you see what we can do with our sticks if you'll let us.

Morrison's maxim had many supporters over the years and few critics. But the Bertuzzi episode exposed the rationale in the public mind. By the time the shock waves from the highly public spectacle had dissipated, the rules for how much violence was too much in the NHL would change for good. At six foot three, 245 pounds, Bertuzzi is an intriguing blend of malevolence and teenage angst. A skilled scorer when the mood strikes (he tallied forty-six times in 2002–03) and a fan favourite for his swarthy good looks, he's also something of a loose cannon on the ice, another thing that endeared him to Canucks supporters heading into the fateful game. He had missed 10 games in 2001–02 for leaving the bench to join a brawl. Since becoming a fixture with the

Canucks, he'd amassed 469 penalty minutes—122 thus far in the 2003-04 campaign.

A few weeks earlier, in a February 16 game in Denver, Bertuzzi's best friend Markus Naslund had been levelled by a shoulder check from Colorado's Moore, a borderline blow that left the Swedish star bruised and dazed. While Naslund himself would only say he was out of position and had left himself vulnerable, many in Vancouver—including Crawford and Burke—saw it differently. The Vancouver coach was demonstrably upset behind the Canucks' bench that night, exhorting his players to settle accounts, while GM Burke said later it was "a headhunting shot on a star player by a marginal player."

The Canucks' indignation and the furor whipped up by sports-talk-radio demanded a reckoning for Moore, a journeyman Harvard product who had the temerity to touch a star of Naslund's magnitude. Under hockey's crude code of retribution, he had to answer to the Canucks in kind. "There's definitely a bounty on his head," Vancouver's Brad May said matter-of-factly of Moore. "Clean hit or not, Nazzy is our best player, and you respond. It's going to be fun when we get him."

This revenge would be at a time and a place of the Canucks' choosing. Nothing happened when the clubs met next in Moore's hometown of Denver. But the following game on March 8 was on Naslund's home ice in Vancouver. Moore understood that the time had come. Even though he was from an Ivy League school, Moore also knew old-school hockey. So when challenged to a fight early in the game by Matt Cooke, the twenty-six-year-old readily agreed to the scrap—to the delight of Canuck fans who howled with glee when Cooke landed a few harmless haymakers on Moore. Evidently, Colorado coach Tony Granato thought the score has been evened between Moore and the Canucks when his player and

Cooke were separated, and so he left Moore on the ice in the third period of a lopsided 9–2 win for the Avalanche.

But the scrap with Moore did not even the score, at least not in the estimation of Bertuzzi and his coach Crawford. Moore may have fought, but with the game out of hand, the Canucks under-performing, Crawford taking heat in the media, and Bertuzzi having a poor season by his standards, further retribution might solve many issues plaguing the Canucks. Despite warnings from the officials, Crawford dispatched Bertuzzi to the ice late in the third period of the blowout. To anyone watching the game, it was apparent that Bertuzzi had more punishment in mind for Moore.

The referees made half-hearted appeals for calm, but they carried no real sting in the menacing atmosphere of GM Place as Bertuzzi stalked Moore, taunted him, and tugged at the back of his sweater as they skated up and down the ice. When this provocation failed to provoke a response, Bertuzzi pulled up behind the Avs forward and swung a gloved right hand into the right temple of Moore. The Colorado forward was stunned by the blow and fell forward, defenceless, onto his face. Bertuzzi, still grasping the scruff of Moore's sweater, fell on his opponent's back. He attempted to pull Moore's head up off the ice, but before he could land a second blow, he was restrained by Moore's teammates, who frantically blocked Bertuzzi from landing another punch on the vulnerable Avs player. A melee ensued, but when it was done, Moore remained pitched face forward on the ice, motionless.

Watch enough hockey before this night and the scene would not have been unfamiliar to those who accept the by-products of hockey's inexhaustible well of passion. In fact, the Bertuzzi attack came just a few nights after an open feud erupted between the Philadelphia Flyers and Ottawa Senators. Like the Bertuzzi incident, the Flyers–Senators brawl was about retribution. Asked why he started the fighting, Donald Brashear, then of the Flyers, said, "Why wouldn't I? Did you see the last game?" The Flyers were upset, because a week earlier Senators forward Martin Havlat had viciously slashed Mark Recchi in the face with his stick, an infraction that cost Havlat just a two-game penalty while Recchi lost teeth and blood in the attack. After the Havlat attack, Flyers' coach Ken Hitchcock publicly announced he'd like to see Havlat "eat his lunch" for slashing Recchi—an open threat of violence that went unpunished by the NHL's earnest justice minister Colin Campbell who claimed that Hitchcock's published words were not explicit orders to attack Ottawa players.

Emboldened by Campbell's ineffectual response, Flyers' general manager Bob Clarke ratcheted up the tension after the game: "They [Ottawa] come in here one more time. They won't be able to hide Alfredsson and Hossa and all the guys then." In other words, take out our skill player and we'll take out one of your skill players. Despite the blatant threats, Commissioner Gary Bettman, (whose league automatically fines any player, coach, or GM who dares question the referees) played the blind cop. Everyone should just calm down, Bettman said. "99.99 per cent of the time, nothing comes of those comments. They're idle threats in the heat of the moment. And when they do come, we have a mechanism for dealing with it."

The mechanism Bettman trusted so implicitly failed to prevent the rematch between the Flyers and Senators, which featured five fights and numerous expulsions. "My teammates didn't forget what happened," Recchi said. "There was a lot of emotion." And Bettman's mechanism broke down in spectacular fashion in the Bertuzzi incident as well. Before the league could perform its usual sweep-it-under-the-carpet routine, cutting Bertuzzi from the herd as lone wolf, mass media in North America picked up the video of Bertuzzi's attack. With numbing regularity, American TV outlets such as CNN and Fox News (that normally avoid hockey like the plague) repeated the incident from every possible angle. In slow motion, the savagery seemed magnified. Within days, few in possession of a TV in North America had not seen the incident. In much the same manner that they vilified Democratic presidential candidate Howard Dean for an ill-advised war whoop after his disastrous 2004 New Hampshire primary loss, the 24-hour news channels made Bertuzzi into a figure somewhere between Tony Soprano and Jack the Ripper. On shows as disconnected as *Regis and Kelly* and the CBS *Morning News*, the Vancouver player was vilified and the sport of hockey portrayed as some charnelhouse activity. For those who view the NHL as akin to wrestling on skates, the Bertuzzi tape confirmed their worst prejudices. For those who defend and promote the sport in America, it was their worst nightmare writ large.

So NHL officials and apologists first blamed the media messengers. Never let it be said that there isn't a situation that the NHL brass can't make worse with a little trying. Caught unprepared by the severity of Moore's injury, they howled, "How dare the U.S. and Canada press exploit Todd's weak moment?" The hurt tone was vintage NHL: "You can't understand what happened unless you've played."

Bertuzzi's teammate (and NHLPA president!) Trevor Linden was flabbergasted by public opinion in the days after the attack: "It's ridiculous. Players make mistakes on the ice ... by no means I'm saying he shouldn't be punished, but everything that's being said is way over the top." A blustering Brian Burke added that his player had been "crucified" by the electronic press. "You've taken this opportunity to kick the crap out of him, and I think it's been just shameful," Burke lectured the media at a press conference in which he tried to assign blame for the embarrassment anywhere but where it really lay.

At a hastily arranged press conference in Toronto, a grim-faced Campbell and NHL vice-president Bill Daly announced that the hulking Vancouver forward was suspended for the rest of the regular season and playoffs (he eventually served twenty games in total for ending Moore's career with a broken neck). Campbell even chided a reporter who asked if fighting wasn't the real problem—even though Bertuzzi was indeed trying to get Moore to fight.

But the NHL pulled its punches when it came to expanding the ring of culpability. Rather than point a finger at coach Marc Crawford or GM Brian Burke, the entire Vancouver organization was fined $250,000 for actions detrimental to the NHL (against which Burke predictably raged). Bertuzzi, the marked man, then conducted a tear-stained press conference a few days afterward at which he accepted his punishment and asked for the return of his good name. "Steve, I just want to apologize for what happened out there," he said between sobs. "I had no intention to hurt you. I feel awful for what transpired." Bertuzzi—who had averaged 120 PIMS a year since 1999-00—then claimed that he's not the player he'd just proven himself to be.

"I am truly sorry. I don't play the game that way. I am not a mean-spirited person." Choked with emotion, he disappeared from view, a tragic hero to the hockey community, a symbol of the NHL's denial to the rest of the world. (A symbol that persists. When Bertuzzi was signed by Calgary in 2008, Flames GM Darryl Sutter compared Bertuzzi's assault on Moore with a simple traffic infraction. "I guess I expected certain members of the media to bring that up," said Sutter.

Whatever Betuzzi's intentions when walloping Steve Moore

from behind, it's clear that he felt it worth the risk in the court of Canadian opinion. In the moments he skated behind Moore, trying to goad him into a face-to-face, Canadian-style confrontation, there was enough time for Bertuzzi to measure the possible outcomes of his plan. He saw the possibility of a minor or major penalty for his act—but with the game out of hand that was hardly a punishment. Heck, he'd be showered and gone before the media ever made it to the dressing room post-game. He saw the possibility that one of Moore's teammates might retaliate and fight him—but, at six foot three, he had little to fear from any Avs on the ice. He saw the outside possibility that he might cut or bruise Moore with his punch.

A broken neck? Please, be serious.

And legal action? The courts never bothered with hockey fights.

Against these outcomes were ranged an array of positive responses: the gratitude of his friend Markus Naslund and the rest of the Canuck dressing room. The huzzahs of Canuck Brad May, who'd declared the bounty on Moore following the Naslund hit and said how much fun they'd have collecting it. The approval of his coach Marc Crawford and GM Brian Burke, who'd both openly insinuated that Moore pay a price for decking Naslund. The making of a "contribution" when his scoring total was down. The roars of the Canucks fans, who would have one positive to take from an otherwise dismal Canuck performance. (Declared Canuck fan Sean Karl afterward: "They are making an example of Todd Bertuzzi to cover up the poor management of Gary Bettman and the cadre of owners in whose pocket Bettman resides.") And finally, the overwhelming approval of those such as Don Cherry in the Canadian hockey community who see these dramas as integral to the national pastime, indispensable to a winning side. Could there be any surprise that, faced with such options, Bertuzzi wound up and slugged Moore when the Avs forward obstinately refused to turn around?

If he needed more precedent, Bertuzzi could cite the legend of 1972's eight-game challenge series that pitted Canada against the Soviets, when conclusive proof of the superiority of Canadian hockey—which included fighting and intimidation—was at hand. But, as everyone who knows a Yakushev from a Kaleshnikov understands, the predictions of Soviet incompetence did not come to pass. In a stunning series of games on Canadian and Russian soil, the Soviets demonstrated skill, creativity, fanatical fitness, and yes, toughness, in taking the lead in the series three games to one (with one tied). Humiliation was nigh for the NHL's vaunted propaganda machine as speedy Soviets circled the Canadian stars as if they were pylons and reduced legendary Canadian goalies such as Ken Dryden and Tony Esposito to statues in net. Tony's brother Phil, the NHL's top scorer at the time, went on national TV to plead with his countrymen to stop booing them; they were doing the best they could against these Rooskies.

The most talented—and thus infuriating—Soviet was a short, stocky forward with the burst of a Soyuz rocket named Valeri Kharlamov. With a mocking smirk, the star Soviet was single-handedly reducing Canada's illusions of grandeur to a pipe dream, scoring three goals and six points in the first five games. He went around the Canadian defence, in the immortal words of Howie Meeker, like a hoop around a barrel. Canadian coach Harry Sinden was secretly awed by Kharlamov. "All of us were impressed," said Sinden after the series, "but none of us wanted to let on. I've seldom seen anyone come down on two NHL defencemen and beat them to the outside, go around them and then in on the net. It just isn't done."

Kharlamov could not be allowed to continue such magic if Canada was to escape the series with its product and dignity intact. How could the league's franchises sell North American ticket buyers on their brand of shinny if a bunch of guys with funny names were reducing their box-office stars to stumblebums—all without so much as a single fight? Thankfully for Canadian nationalists, with the home team down three games to two (with one tie), Philadelphia captain Bobby Clarke found a prescription in Game Six in Moscow. After a brief chat on the bench with Canadian assistant coach John Ferguson—the same man employed by the Canadiens to police the Montreal Forum from 1963 until 1971—Clarke was dispatched to the ice surface at Moscow's ancient Luzhniki Ice Palace to enforce the Code. With all-powerful Soviet premier Leonid Brezhnev looking on in heavy-browed concentration, Clarke stalked Kharlamov around the ice, much as Bertuzzi would follow Moore thirty-two years later. As attention was briefly diverted, Clarke applied a full two-handed slash to the ankle of Kharlamov as they skated into Canada's zone. After briefly confronting Clarke (Imagined conversation . . . K: "How many cord wood you chop, Bobby?" C: "Yabbadamarastfraga.") Kharlamov limped off the ice, tried to return, then disappeared. Though it was not revealed immediately, Kharlamov's ankle was broken by the slash. The man who'd brought Canada low in the Summit series was a factor no longer. "I am convinced that Bobby Clarke was given the job of taking me out of the game," recalled Kharlamov after the series. "Sometimes, I thought it was his only goal. I looked into his angry eyes, saw his stick which wielded like a sword, and didn't understand what he was doing. It had nothing to do with hockey."

With Kharlamov disabled and Paul Henderson leading the Canadian team with his great skating and timely scoring, Canada rallied to win the series four games to three with one tie. It was an inspirational win by players who showed incredible guts, and in the confrontational atmosphere of the Cold War, a grateful nation celebrated Clarke's ingenuity and resourcefulness with his so-called Flin Flon love tap as much as it did Henderson's heroics. All was fair in love, war, and hockey in those stressful weeks of 1972, and Clarke's enterprising use of lumber had rescued the good guys from the evil empire of hockey. Clarke's strategic chop was a reminder that with Canadian pride or a Stanley Cup on the line, anything is acceptable to Canadians. Questioned years later about his two-handed contribution to national well-being, a grinning Clarke said: "If I hadn't learned to lay on a two-hander once in a while, I'd never have left Flin Flon."

Thus, a myth was born that slashing in the defence of Canadian hockey culture was no vice. The end justified the means and, to the Don Cherrys, anyone who argued otherwise was a Commie or a kook. Clarke's fervent patriotism indirectly gave Bertuzzi a get-out-of-the-penalty-box-free excuse thirty-two years later. A player who crossed the line from passion to psycho, such as Rocket Richard or Dave Schultz, was considered "a competitor," a man who'd lay it all on the line by leaving an opponent lying on the ice. As Swedish NHL star Ulf Nilsson later observed. "We wanted very much to win. But the Canadians HAD to win. They'd literally kill you to win." Todd Bertuzzi came very close to doing exactly that— killing Steve Moore. And because he didn't—by the margins of millimetres in Moore's spine and brain—the myth of unbridled passion as Canada's secret weapon still kept its currency under the NHL's tent (if not in the outside world). By unleashing his sucker punch to Moore's head, Bertuzzi was simply following in Clarke's vaunted tradition.

Moore's pain didn't end with the broken neck and the end of

his career, either. The public outrage outside Vancouver had finally caused the Crown in B.C. to lay assault charges against the popular Canuck four months after the event. What was most interesting wasn't the assault charge itself—the same charge had been laid in the McSorley case in 2000—but who wasn't charged in the incident. The other players and management on the Canucks who provoked the incident were excluded from blame. The Crown clearly did not see the public threats by Brad May and the deliberate selection of players on the ice by Crawford as incitement to assault. In its desire to make the larger issue disappear, the Crown pretended that Bertuzzi was some isolated agent, not acting in concert with vengeful teammates and coaches. The trial was set for January 17, 2005.

Throughout his rehab, Moore contented himself with the thought that the Crown in British Columbia, which had reportedly spent ten months investigating the assault, would do its duty and discipline Bertuzzi for breaking his neck. And that he'd be able to make a victim-impact statement to tell Bertuzzi how he blighted Moore's life. To look him in the eye—a courtesy Bertuzzi hadn't allowed Moore before crushing his temple with his right hand.

Then Moore found out that the B.C. Crown had given Bertuzzi an expedient plea bargain that allowed him to escape a public trial or jail, a deal hastily assembled in the week before Christmas 2004 that allowed Moore just a single day to get from the east coast to make his victim-impact statement in court. Moore also discovered that the bargain negotiated between the Crown and Bertuzzi was less harsh than one the same Crown office made to Marty McSorley (an out-of-town player) after his stick attack on Canuck Donald Brashear in 2000, a plea bargain that actually had some teeth in it. This in spite of the premeditated nature of Bertuzzi's assault on Moore—something that hadn't occurred in the McSorley cheap shot. When Moore's lawyer Tim Danson demanded to know why Moore had been denied a reasonable chance to make his victim statement in person, B.C. Crown officials sniffed that they were under no obligation to hear Moore in person. Which not only cross-checked the rights of victims of crime but cemented the perception that Canadian courts still gave the NHL a very wide berth when it comes to violence.

Moore knew Bertuzzi was a popular guy in B.C.; he just didn't think he was so popular that the Crown would move up the court date to accommodate Bertuzzi's wish for reinstatement in the NHL. Why was the Crown so anxious to make the case go away that it denied Moore his opportunity to make a victim statement in person? And whose sensibilities were being considered— Moore's or the attacker's—in the rush to complete the plea bargain a month early? How could someone rob him of his health and livelihood but—after weeks of threats—escape with no criminal record, no jail time, no probation? And not even face his victim in person? So Moore stopped trusting the B.C. justice system and decided to hold Bertuzzi to a higher standard than does the Crown in British Columbia. He sued Bertuzzi—and the people who employed him in Vancouver. As a subset of the Code, coaches and GMs were never connected to incidents that happened on their watch. Instead players silently took their punishment, branded as lone wolves who acted in a vacuum. But Moore was making the connection between a player and coach when violence erupts on ice. If successful he'd throw a massive legal scare into the fraternity of coaches and GMs that has felt itself insulated from reality.

Whether Moore was the cause, that same connection was made in the 2008 suspension of NHL Hall-of-Famer Patrick Roy and his son Jonathan, now the head coach and backup goalie respectively with the Quebec Remparts of the QMJHL. League officials suspended the senior Roy for five games for encouraging a brawl that featured his son's rink-length dash to pummel the goalie of the opposition Chicoutimi Sagueneens. Videos of the game seemed to show Roy directing his son to turn 180 degrees on the ice and assault Bobby Nadeau after Quebec trailed a playoff game by 10–1.

By suggesting that the younger Roy and his teammates were goaded by their coach, the QMJHL is getting at the real causal relationship that produces hockey violence. It made the direct link between assault and conspiracy to commit assault from behind the bench. And it might shred the final, intimidating barrier to making the game safer and more sane for everyone:

Silence.

CHAPTER FIVE

Pleasure Fighters

"I've had a couple of fights with friends that I've played with on other teams. You look over in the penalty box, and the guy gives you a little wink because he knows you've done your job. . . . Any friend who's a real good friend would probably understand at the end of the game when you're out for a beer, or a pop."

—NHL defenceman Andy Sutton

Ballistic missile defence in North America has always been a hot-button topic for Canadians, going back to the October Crisis of 1962 when Prime Minister John Diefenbaker reneged on an agreement with the U.S. to bring our air force to readiness in the face of the Soviet threat in Cuba. The acceptance of American leadership and armed warheads on Canadian soil was seen as an issue of Canadian sovereignty first and national defence second. Thus the resistance when Ronald Reagan first promoted his Star Wars idea to defend the continent in the 1980s. And the refusal of Prime Minister Paul Martin to participate in a ballistic program in the years following 9/11. Despite the fact that Canada would not have to contribute either money or soil to the

American initiative, Martin rejected the overtures of President George W. Bush to give the program tacit political support. The Americans were flummoxed that Canada would not even want a seat at the table to participate in the project.

"I don't understand this," Bush told Martin. "Are you saying that if you got up and said this was necessary for the defence of Canada, it wouldn't be accepted?"

Martin, who knew the answer to that question was "yes" in many corners of the nation, did not reply. In its almost pathological need for independence from American hegemony, the Canada of Martin's Liberals preferred the label of peacekeeper to the world over the shared defence interests of the continent. While the Harper government's combat involvement in Afghanistan has tempered that pacifism somewhat, there is clearly a disconnect in Canada between the "sober second-thought champion of negotiation and compromise over bloodshed" and the bloody-mindedness of the national sport.

In a nation that puts peacekeepers on the currency, why are brawlers such as Todd Bertuzzi, Tie Domi, or Georges Laracque (each number one in team jersey sales in 2003–04) lionized for their aggression on-ice while many big-city mayors balk at decals on civic vehicles supporting the Canadian troops in Afghanistan? Canada—the nation that never shirked when the Empire called in two world wars and other adventures—now fancies itself as the nagging conscience of its southern neighbour, the Americans of Bush and Cheney—the Stern Daughter of the Voice of God in Dean Acheson's telling phrase. A tiger on the ice, Canada is often regarded as a political pussycat in the international sphere. Despite the cost in human lives in Afghanistan, modern Canada sees combat as the exception to its culture. Nothing underlined Canada's status as reluctant warrior in the international sphere more than the decision not to join the U.S. and Britain in the 2004 Iraq War (for more on Iraq see Chapter 7).

In a country of so many contradictions the disconnect between hockey values and the values characteristic of Canadian society in general is startling. Only hockey and lacrosse—both Canadian products—allow a player to fight and still remain in the game. No other popular team sport in the world does the same. Perversely, the resolve of other sports to eliminate violence has only reinforced the desire to keep the code of intimidation alive in hockey. It's as if fighting is kept as a poison pill to prevent other nations from stealing one of the few symbols left. Hockey has become a bulwark against multinational drift. To Don Cherry and likeminded souls, hockey is the only place where the Canadian fighting spirit of the two world wars and Korea is still alive. Thus, preserving hockey— in its traditional violent terms—is tantamount to preserving the warrior-proud Canadian history now being photoshopped by the forces of political correctness. Even if it means having to accept the brutality of Bertuzzis from time to time.

To Dave Schultz, the former Philadelphia goon who—following a brief mea culpa after his chaotic career—is now a poster boy for fighting again, the difference is something to be celebrated.

"Let's face it: respect is worth fighting for," says Schultz. "Players are supposed to stand up for something, build something and protect what is theirs. As far as I'm concerned, fighting is one of the more celebrated traditions of hockey. It is what keeps things civil, on a basic human level of understanding and respect in competition."

Freed from any law but its own by a timid judiciary and cowed politicians, Canadian hockey has enshrined the imported Scotish/ Irish tradition of the hard man, the unapologetic tough who dispensed and absorbed punishment in brooding silence. There's a famous Irish quip that sums up fighting as fun: "Is this a private fight or can anyone join in?" But "pleasure fighting" had a long tradition in the Celtic cultures that moved in their millions to Canada, one distinguished by clearly defined rules, willing participants, a sense of pleasure in the activity, and an absence of any real malicious intent (if you don't take into account that some fighters were killed or maimed). Often, the fighting was done with bats and shillelaghs but, many times, bare knuckles would do just as well. The other unique feature of such pleasure fighting was that those combatants left standing would often repair to the local bar for convivial drinking with men who, just moments before, had been trying to pummel them senseless. (Legendary linesman George Hayes probably spoke for almost everyone in the pleasure fighting culture of the NHL. "I liked everything about hockey," the Hall of Famer said after he retired. "But the fights were the best.")

Pleasure fighting was often the only means of status for poor Irish or Scots lads under the English yoke in small towns. It was only a short leap from the rowdy boy with a hurley in his hands in Ireland to his descendant, the robust defenceman, wielding a white ash hockey stick on the frozen ponds of the new country. (You can see the same pugnacious cultural traces in Australian Rules Football, a cross between ballet and attempted homicide.) The early NHL tough man was a loner like Eddie Shore with perfect recall of past treacheries, the hockey version of Clint Eastwood in *Unforgiven*. Reporter Elmer Ferguson provided a stark portrait of Shore in 1929, after a particularly nasty game against the Montreal Maroons:

> He gave no quarter and he asked none ... A long-reaching jab
> with a stick-blade tore open his cheek. Another sliced his chin.
> He was hammered, pounded, cut; and just at the end, a Maroon

player cut across Shore and deliberately gave a sickening smash to the mouth, which knocked out several teeth and felled the Bruin in his tracks. He was carried off and five minutes later, his wounds temporarily doctored, he was standing beneath the showers. Expecting an outburst, I said, "Rough going, Eddie." Through bloody, swollen lips he answered laconically, "It's all in the game. I'll pay off."

It's not that the originators of hockey intended Eddie Shore or Todd Bertuzzi to be the result of their labours. Lord Stanley and his blue-blooded sons intended hockey as a gentleman's game to be played within the British code of honour. Sportsmanship was meant to be part of the fabric of the game, as it was in other rugged sports such as rugby. "He never imagined that his gift would be a symbol of professionalism," wrote historian Henry Roxborough in 1967.

In his day, hockey was mainly the sport of society. It was played by gentlemen who had the time and the means to enjoy it as a pastime. But within a few years of the Cup's presentation, the rivalries of the clubs and the cities, the availability of mining and lumber money, the jealous pride of individual sponsors to prove that their players could buy the best players—all this soon turned the Stanley Cup from its original lofty purpose into an arena of bitter controversy.

While sports such as football and basketball were adopted and nurtured within an academic setting in the United States and Canada, hockey became the child of frontier capitalism and, later, American businessmen with empty calendar dates in their arena. The resource-based Canadian economy soon began exporting another natural product to the States—hockey players.

As the twentieth century dawned, for instance, the top hockey players were lured, not to tweedy college campuses, but to free-wheeling mining or forestry towns such as Ontario's Cobalt, New Liskeard, Haileybury, or Renfrew. (The most improbable Cup contender, Dawson City in 1905, was funded by Klondike Colonel Joe Boyle's mining riches that sent his team across the continent in the dead of winter via dogsled, train, boat, and foot to face the vaunted Ottawa Silver Seven.) From year to year, new millionaires such as M.J. O'Brien in Renfrew or the Timmins brothers in Haileybury would seek bragging rights by bringing the Stanley Cup to their new community. To assemble squads good enough to challenge for the Cup, owners needed top talent, and so future Hall of Famers such as Cyclone Taylor or Hooley Smith could jump from one town to the other in search of higher pay. This was not the stuff of gentlemen schooled at Upper Canada College or Bishops College School. Playing hockey had become a mercenary, not a gentlemanly, occupation. (Taylor, the quiet piano tuner who jumped as a free agent from team to team, wound up the best-paid player everywhere he went—the model of the contemporary player.)

Unlike the celebrated amateur values of football and basket-ball programs that (largely) flourished in American universities, hockey's concept of gentlemen's values and sport no longer mixed after the early 1900s. Instead of emulating the English sports-man's code, hockey found a model in lacrosse, the brutal Native game featuring nasty stick work and fighting, a game that occa-sionally saw players killed when tribes met. Because of their hand-eye coordination, many of the best hockey players into the present-day have been stars of lacrosse as well, comfortable in the game's mixture of speed, aggression, and stick work. The crossover of tactics and tolerances between the sports became natural. Watching a modern national lacrosse league game is a window into hockey's past, a primer on how and why hockey gained its warrior spirit.

With its rowdy decorum, the top level of hockey after 1900 became largely the domain of blue-collar boys looking to escape tough backgrounds, not a proving ground for sons of Canadian founding families. An education was not only unnecessary to hockey success, it was considered by most owners and managers to be an impediment for their boys to dwell too deeply on intellectual matters. ("Stop thinking, you're hurting the team," was the exhortation to players who asked too many questions.)

And while some "wannabe left wingers" in the 1890s were rankled by fighting and aggressive play, violent behaviour was quickly accepted and celebrated by the time Cobalt was making a run at the Cup in 1905. Cobalt's Harry Smith, "a notorious stick man," hacked his way through so many Haileybury players that year that the Haileybury police were called in to put him in jail. But when he returned to Cobalt, "Smith was welcomed by the town band...and there wasn't any favour too great for 'Battling Harry.'" And when Renfrew went into Haileybury, one local observer crowed, "They went in intact, but they came out on stretchers."

It was this encroachment of bare-knuckled force into what was meant by Lord Stanley to be a gentleman's game that led Stanely Cup trustee P.D. Ross to lament in 1904, "The finest game in the world to watch, hockey as our leading Canadian teams play it, is being made a byword and a disgrace by the manner in which matches are conducted and foul play tolerated. Unless a radical change occurs at once in the conduct of hockey matches, the noble Canadian winter sport must . . . sink in the public estimation to the level of pugilism." But as events would show, Ross was whistling in the wind when he tried to clean up the sport. (And he didn't have *Coach's Corner* to deal with.) Hockey had been kid-napped by commercial interests in the young country.

Contrast this rough culture with that of football and basketball in the United States. It was not till well after the Second World War that either professional league surpassed its college versions in either popularity or status. For much of their development, these sports were under the supervision of university presidents and educators who did their best to mix schooling and sport. Instead of boys moving down the social chain to become hockey pros, young American boys were lifted from humble means to college campuses. And where only the occasional Syl Apps elevated the collective IQ of the NHL, there were many future leaders of America who became sports heroes in football or basketball. Byron "Whizzer" White was considered the prototypical American sports hero. A Heisman Trophy winner as the best collegiate football player while at Colorado, White later went on to be appointed to a seat on the U.S. Supreme Court. Future president Ronald Reagan graduated from the football program at Eureka College to the White House. Even the fussy Richard Nixon tried out for the grid-iron at Whittier College. Then there was the Knute Rockne tradition at Notre Dame immortalized by Reagan's famous "Win one for the Gipper" deathbed plea. (Gipp came from the Upper Penin-sula of Michigan, where professional hockey was born, and grew up playing the game—cleanly, as it turned out.)

Even today, American sports movie sagas such as *Rudy*, *Remember the Titans*, *We Are Marshall*, and *Miracle* champion the noble tradition of winning by strength of character, not physical strength. And although the NCAA has been saturated by money scandals ever since the 1950s, fisticuffs and systematic intimidation are still considered unacceptable in their sports. Throwing punches in football or basketball—as well as baseball—is automatic grounds for expulsion from the game and, often, a suspension. (Sometimes just thinking of throwing punches can get you suspended, as Phoenix's Amare Stoudemire and Boris Diaw learned in the 2007 NBA playoffs when they were suspended for a crucial game against San Antonio for simply running a few metres from their bench during an on-court scuffle. Their punishment contributed to the Suns' loss in six games to the future NBA champs, the Spurs.)

"America also has a criminal element in many of its sports," writes longtime hockey writer Jim Kelley, an American, "but it seldom manifests itself on the playing surfaces of the NFL, Major League Baseball or the NBA. With a few notable exceptions, those despicable acts generally take place outside of the actual games, in large part because the leagues simply don't tolerate them. It's different in hockey, especially in Canadian hockey." And so whenever a fight does erupt in an NBA, MLB, or NFL game, some wag is bound to write, "... a hockey game broke out last night."

One further example serves to illustrate the contrasting attitudes of Canadians versus Americans when it comes to sports. In 2006, Albert Haynesworth, a brilliant but troubled defensive tackle on the NFL's Tennessee Titans used the exposed head of Dallas Cowboys centre Andre Gurode as a door mat during a game. With Gurode lying on the ground Haynesworth applied his football spikes to the face of the Cowboy centre, cutting him for 30 stitches and leaving Gurode's face looking like he'd lost a knife fight.

Haynesworth quickly issued a contrite and complete apology to Gurode and to the Titans. "It was just a moment, a blur, a big, big mistake," he said. "It's something I wish I could take back. I'd give anything to take it back. I don't know how to explain how sorry I am." Haynesworth said he will now enrol in anger management classes.

Although there was no apparent premeditation when the 320-pound Haynesworth rucked the visage of Gurode, he was suspended for five games by the NFL. The NFL Players Association—which famously appeals virtually any suspension given its members—turned its back on Haynesworth, allowing the suspension to stand. And the Titans' head coach Jeff Fisher pronounced, "We've turned the corner," cutting the cord with Haynesworth. More than that, they sought to have millions in bonus money paid to Haynesworth returned to the team. (The Titans later relaxed their demands, but the suspensions and condemnation were allowed to stand.)

Compare the NFL community's reaction to Haynesworth's attack to that of the hockey community when Bertuzzi famously mugged Moore in 2004. Bertuzzi's assault is unforgettable. Even in the United States, where hockey is on par with bass fishing and rock/paper/scissors, the video of Bertuzzi's assault received equal exposure to that of Haynesworth's cleating of Gurode. While Gurode was superficially damaged, Moore lost his career and his health to Bertuzzi's act.

Unlike the Haynesworth attack, the Bertuzzi mugging was premeditated. Three weeks passed between the Naslund hit and Bertuzzi exacting revenge. Payback was openly talked about by Canucks players, coaches, and management. The NHL itself was alert to the possibility and supposedly had referees monitor the situation. Did the Canucks use the Titans' model and walk away from Bertuzzi, expressing disgust and disappointment?

Quite the opposite.

The Canucks rallied around Bertuzzi, promising support and compassion for a player with a long history of violence in the NHL. Then-GM Brian Burke accused the media of a witch hunt for pursuing the issue. Bertuzzi was lionized by Canuck fans for defending a teammate. The NHL suspended Bertuzzi for the remainder of the season and playoffs, but quickly reinstated him for the start of the next season, despite the fact that Moore was still incapacitated. It dodged responsibility for not preventing the lynch mob for Moore. It scolded reporters who tried to link Bertuzzi's act with the acceptance of fighting and violence in the NHL.

Hockey Canada, which regularly lectures moms and dads about violence in minor hockey, instantly gave Bertuzzi an invitation to play for the national team at the 2006 Olympics when the NHL suspension was lifted after just 20 games. Moore's Colorado club then hired May, who'd issued the public threats against Moore when a member of the Canucks. The B.C. justice system cut hometown hero Bertuzzi a plea bargain without allowing Moore to personally address Bertuzzi and the court with a victim statement. Media maven Don Cherry said Bertuzzi's crime was hitting Moore from behind. "Do it face to face," advised Cherry. "That's the Canadian way." Seeing that, Albert Haynesworth might have wished he'd taken up hockey, not football, as his sport.

"Why do I fight?" former NHLer Rosaire Paiement asked in 1969. "To tell you the truth I just love it. What the heck, you know what you're doing, you can't get hurt . . . I did start one [fight]. In the first Toronto game I started the fight with Gary Monahan [of Toronto], but that's just because I figured we needed something to get us going. It's, you know, a challenge."

Hardly sounds like a man worried about a bad performance appraisal from the boss. Or worried that the folks back home will disapprove if a few haymakers bring home a win for the heroes. If you played hockey, you played it in the pleasure-fighting culture — whether your family came from Britain, France, Italy, Germany, Russia, or Ukraine. A look at the NHL's all-time penalty minute leaders shows how widespread the ethnic net became with names such as Schultz, Williams, Saleski, Kordic, Peluso, Ferguson,

Doernhoefer, Kypreos, and Semenko among the top penalty leaders of all time. In a nation that holds its newcomers to fewer and fewer of its traditions, hockey was the great melting pot.

The Canadian acceptance of bloody-mindedness in the national sport might have its inspiration in Canada's military tradition. It was no coincidence that men who embraced hockey were also the only troops to capture Vimy Ridge in 1917 after virtually every other army had failed. Or who helped to finally overtake the unassailable Monte Cassino in 1943. English author Robert Graves took note of the wild colonial boys in his First Word War memoir *Goodbye to All That*. According to the author who later made the treacherous Caligula famous, the Canadians who stormed Vimy Ridge were the most feared troops by the Germans. Stories abounded of Canadians putting hand grenades in the pockets of prisoners or shooting first and asking questions later. "How far this reputation for atrocities was deserved and how fair it can be ascribed to the overseas habit of bragging or leg-pulling, we could not decide." But it was clear to Graves and others that Canadians took their killing seriously.

The integration of toughs and bullies into a young business looking to sell tickets to non-hockey fans in Canada and the United States was a natural marriage. So, while soccer became a gentleman's game played by hooligans, and rugby became a hooligan's game played by gentlemen, hockey evolved into a hooligan's game played by hooligans. To suggest anything but a rough-and-tumble attitude was soon considered unmanly in the hockey culture. T. Emmitt Quinn, president of the National Hockey Association in 1910, mocked the advocates of sportsmanship over ticket sales when he, presaging Mr. Cherry decades later, proposed that "instead of giving a minor penalty, the referee should stop play, take the offender to one side for half-a-minute, talk to him and try to reform him." In short, hockey would not be for eggheads or sissies.

Only real men needed apply. "Hockey isn't for nice boys," wrote a
Duluth, Minnesota, sportswriter. "When players are disposed to
be ugly, there are many tricks to be used."

Like the Irish or Scottish pleasure fighters, however, there was
often little ongoing bitterness in the fighting. One incident in 1912
underlines the ambivalent attitude of players. During an exhibition game played in Toronto, Odie Cleghorn of the Montreal
Wanderers and Newsy Lalonde of the Canadiens ran into each
other at high speed, sending the pair to the ice. While Lalonde sat
stunned on the ice, Cleghorn's notorious brother Sprague skated
over and applied a two-hander to Lalonde's head, opening up a
bloody gash. Fights broke out and police were called. When the
melee had calmed down, Sprague Cleghorn was taken to jail for
assault; his brother and Lalonde were also taken to the jailhouse
as material witnesses. An agitated Wanderers boss, Charlie Querrie, rushed to the police precinct to bail out Lalonde and Odie
Cleghorn, the instigators of the brawl. When Querrie reached the
jail, however, he was shocked to find the two men, out for each
other's blood just hours before, sitting together in a cell, throwing
craps with the guard.

The cool ability to turn violence off and on at will was clearly
ingrained even before the NHL opened for business in 1917 and, as
Mel Angelstad proves, continues to this day. A career minor-
leaguer, he was signed by Washington to play his first (and only)
NHL game in the Caps' final game of the 2003–04 season. "I was
talking with (Rangers enforcer) Sandy McCarthy about fighting,"
Angelstad told CanWest news:

> We sat there for about a minute or two because it was a TV time-
> out. I said, "Sandy, let's get this done." He said, "You wanna fight
> tonight?" I said, "Yeah, let's do it." He goes: "I'm not fighting

tonight. It's the last game of the year. Why the hell would I wanna fight?" I was like, "C'mon, Sandy. I'm as old as you. I'm only going to get this one NHL game. Just do me a favour and let's get this done. You could beat the [bleep] out of me. I don't even care. I'll come out of this smiling and you can look like a king, but I'll be the happiest guy in the building."

McCarthy obliged Angelstad's request and the two men duked it out.

And for many Canadians, this tango between pain and danger is all right. "Some would love a comfort zone in which our game would be played," says retired NHL-tough-guy-turned-TV analyst Nick Kypreos.

It's not going happen. Players often scream at their opponents, "There's nowhere to hide tonight," and that couldn't be more true. Intimidation has been an art in the NHL for the last one hundred years . . . And you know why it's that way? It works. I've looked across a face-off circle and seen fear in an opponent's eyes. I knew he wasn't going to show up that night, and I didn't have to drop my gloves to find out. That's been part of the game for a long, long time. For whatever reason, Todd [Bertuzzi] made a point of designating himself as the one to get retribution. In terms of the suspension, he got what he deserved. Stuff like that shouldn't be tolerated by the league. But I don't see the correlation between this incident and the whole question of fighting. Take it out of the game, and guys will look for different ways to get their revenge.

Phil Esposito, the captain of Team Canada that year, described the MO of that legendary squad during an exhibition stop in Sweden during the 1972 series. "The Swedish press called us hooligans and the Canadian Mafia," Esposito wrote in his autobiography *Thunder and Lightning*. "To tell you the truth, we played as dirty as them, maybe dirtier . . . even though it was an exhibition game, boy, we went after them with both barrels. Beating them up was more important than winning."

Perry Berezan was a mild-mannered forward in his eight-year NHL career, totalling just 136 PIMs in 378 games. But in one game against Vancouver, he took a walk on hockey's wild side. "I got into fight with Jim Nill," recalls Berezan, now in the financial business in Calgary. "He wasn't a very rough player, either, but we went at it, and I broke his cheekbone. I kind of felt badly about it. But for the next few weeks," he said, "I was very popular with my team-mates. They called me 'Killer' and things like that. You never lose your standing within a hockey team by getting into a fight." The warrior runs deep in the mentality of hockey players.

Take legendary goalie Patrick Roy, winner of four Stanley Cups, the winningest netminder in NHL history, a fixture on Canada's national team. Roy, now the co-owner and general manager of the Quebec Major Junior Hockey League franchise in his hometown, is always looking to inspire the next generation of young players, offering them a role model. So what photo from his career adorns the Remparts dressing room? His first Cup win in 1986? His three wins as a member of the Colorado Avalanche? No, the photo in the Remparts room shows a bloodied Roy being shepherded off the ice by a linesman following his brawl with Detroit goalie Mike Vernon in a 1997 contest between the bitter rivals. Proving that even goalies feel that hockey passion and fighting go hand in hand.

Hammered home by the power of TV and the media, the glories and misconceptions of fighting remain a thorn in the side of teachers and educators in the game. And when events such as Bertuzzi emerge, ever more elaborate rationales are constructed for living as close to the edge of assault as possible. Detroit Red Wings veteran Brendan Shanahan tried to define that edge of hockey insanity in the days following the Bertuzzi assault. "As NHL players, we get fired up and sometimes do stupid things on the ice, but nobody wants to see injuries to the extent of Moore's." The problem in treading this line of violence is how do you know when to hold back? One noted political observer (and unabashed Senators fan) compared hockey's flirtation with anger to the political flirtation with graft. "These guys don't get it," wrote Jeffrey Simpson in the *Globe and Mail*, "It's like the Chrétien Liberals in Quebec. They, too, drew an imaginary line way out on the edge of acceptable behaviour and couldn't figure out why anybody would be upset as long as they didn't cross it. Except that, like Mr. Bertuzzi, they did."

So while you can take the boy away from the code, you can never take code out of the boy. The career of former Oiler and Ranger Jeff Beukeboom was ended by a Bertuzzi-like sucker punch—this one from Matt Johnson of the Kings. But such is the hardwiring of the Code that even Beukeboom, a victim of post-concussion syndrome, finds it hard to let go of the engrained messages about violence in the NHL. The ex-Ranger defenceman told *Maclean's* magazine in 2004 that he doesn't believe there's any unwritten code in hockey. "It's a competitive game," acknowledges Beukeboom, who retired in 1998 when he could no longer stand the headaches and other symptoms of PCS, "where you do what you can to get an edge, whether it's physical, being tough or being psychological—you do what you can to succeed. If you don't, someone else will come along and do it for you ... If Matt Johnson had tapped me on the shoulder and said, 'Let's fight,' I would've fought in a second. But I couldn't defend myself, and that's where you draw the line." Even a player who paid the ultimate price for the NHL's infatuation with intimidation believes that you can still draw a line on the edge of civilized behaviour and expect that people will respect it with millions of dollars on the line.

But intimidation-as-Canadian-mother's-milk is not to say that there haven't been challenges to the hegemony of intimidation and violence in Canada. For a number of years Father David Bauer offered a different message. Father Bauer understood that you can't stand too close to the fires of anger and intimidation without eventually getting burned, a lesson that the NHL and its players still haven't fathomed. Today, you rarely hear Father Bauer's name invoked, certainly not on Coach's Corner. The examples of how a team can be coached to play rugged, but not dirty, hockey do not fit the glitzy high-testosterone template produced by the NHL or *Hockey Night in Canada.* Father Bauer's amateur Canadian teams of the 1950s and '60s were filled with students, dreamers, and itinerant skaters who chose a different path.

"[Father Bauer] had the quaint [for hockey] notion that a player could be rugged without being dirty," wrote Scott Young in 1976, "and that mental discipline and development of the mind were as important as physical development and hockey skills. Even more galling to old-style hockey men was that much of the time his teams could beat their teams."

Bauer told his national team players "we will play to win, but not at any price." And though the Canadian national teams missed the gold at the Olympics or the World Championships, no one can argue that it was because they retained too much closeted tension and pent-up aggression from avoiding fights. Scott Young recalled one telling incident late in a tense international game in the '60s that underscored Bauer's message:

Sweden's Carl Oberg broke his stick during action on the ice and flung the broken end towards the Canadian bench. It hit Father Bauer on the face. Bleeding, he held back his enraged players and not only calmed them down, but kept two or three of the most furious on the bench for the last few minutes of the game fearing they would go out looking for blood.

Compare Father Bauer's example of restraint with that of an unkempt Alan Eagleson in 1972, when Canada's hockey leader flipped the bird to the crowd as he was escorted across the Luzhniki ice surface and away from the KGB.

Father Bauer's standard of restraint had its shining moments: only IOC chicanery kept Canada from an Olympic medal in 1964. There were inspirational wins against the Soviets and Czechs. But because Father Bauer's teams couldn't win the big one, the NHL and NHL Players Association director Eagleson eventually took over Canada's international program in 1972. Within months of NHL players, coaches, and managers putting on the maple leaf, Canada was being called a bully that threatened referees with sticks and flipped opponents the finger when things didn't go well for them. Which was often in the international game.

When the pros finally edged the Soviets in 1972, most hockey people quickly abandoned the lessons of Father Bauer as if they were flared lapels and paisley ties. To the plastic-pen-holder brigade, intimidation—fighting, a two-handed slash, or an elbow to the chin—won a respected place in the game on the ice surface of the Luzhniki Ice Palace in Moscow. It meant that testing the will of opponents *well* outside the rules was part of the game. Thus, Father Bauer is now thought of as a name on a Calgary arena or a quaint relic of the past, sort of like leather pads or ash hockey sticks.

Father Bauer would no doubt be happy to see that, since the

Bertuzzi assault, the NHL has made some attempts to rein in its endemic violence. Some forms of attack, such as checking from behind, shots to the head, and slashing, have been partly (although not satisfactorily) curtailed. Bench-clearing brawls have been completely eliminated. More of the opinion makers within the sport are moving to the conclusion that the Code of intimidation belongs in a museum, not a modern sports league. Boston Bruins legend Harry Sinden—who coached Bobby Clarke on Team Canada in 1972—has long contended that the game is diminished by fighting.

So what happened? How did mainstream Canada and the hockey culture diverge so dramatically since the days of Shore? Better yet, how did the ruling elites get so far in front of the people they represent that they couldn't connect hockey and policy? One explanation might suggest that, unlike Americans, average Canadians may be a repressed lot with good mothers who nagged them to wear clean underwear all the time in case of an untimely bus accident. So when the chance comes to get bloody and covered with saliva and sweat during a hockey game—and mothers don't object—well, it's almost like free sex to Canadians. Endorphins are released and much beer is consumed in the process. The release of endorphins has never characterized the political process from which the elites who hung Shane Doan out to dry have emerged. Power produces other hormones but none that might help you understand Eddie Shore or Dave Schultz. But, as I say, that would be a superficial view. There are other theories that have a more scholarly tinge.

The cloistered world of Ottawa, the nation's capital, has much to do with its disconnect. The values of a political hotbed whose living standards exceed many of those governed outside Ottawa is hardly a prescription for hockey zeitgeist. As Dwight Eisehnhower said of

Washington, "There are a lot of people who have been away from home for too long." As with nearly everything in Canada, it also comes down to the contrasting cultural epidemiologies of Canada and the Americans. This was not a nation forged by blood shed on domestic soil. While Americans have had everything from Bunker Hill to Gettysburg to Little Big Horn to Waco, Texas, on their native soil, Canadian domestic history has the unfortunate business with Louis Riel and then the St. Lawrence Seaway and a couple of shots fired at the Spanish fishing fleet. Likewise, Canada has gone from the third largest navy in the world following the Second World War to one that can't muster enough ships to patrol even the Arctic shores to which it lays claim. (When Prime Minister Harper asserted Canada's claims to the Northwest Passage at a meeting of the three North American leaders in August of 2007, U.S. president George Bush laughed off the claim as a case of Big Hat, No Navy.)

Bertuzzi's moment of ignominy coincided with a time in which successive Canadian governments had reduced its military to obsolescence. While the NHL brawled in the 1970s and '80s, Canada became more obsessed with projecting its values and sensitivity, not its best interests, to the world community. Consensus and conciliation became the way, not blunt-force diplomacy. The gentrification produced by years without war or international conflict—and America's willingness to protect Canada as a neighbourly courtesy—have lulled Canadians into a curious middle earth populated by environmental scolds and guardians of political correctness. Having not been asked to settle a bill in decades, many saw the meal as free. In a perverse way, hockey's violence is one of the few bracing reminders of a real, more brutal past. Lacking true examples of sacrifice and courage (outside the military and police) many turned to fighting in the national pastime as a dose of reality.

What's interesting about this transition from loyal sons of the Empire to politically correct vertical mosaic is that it has occurred even as Canada's sister dominion, Australia, moved in a remarkably different direction: more republican, yes ... but still at peace with its imperial past. Writer Mark Steyn captured the morphing of Canada in a 2006 article contrasting Canada and Australia though their respective Governors General, broadcaster Michaëlle Jean and soldier Michael Jeffrey respectively. "To the best of my knowledge, there's no *de jure* constitutional prohibition against a white male with a military background serving as Canada's governor general," wrote Steyn:

> ... but, if it hasn't been formally read into the Charter of Rights by Madame L'Heureux-Dubé, it might just as well have been. If you've got a name like Gord MacKinnon, don't hold your breath waiting for the nod to pack for Rideau Hall. And (Australia's G.G.) Major-General Michael Jeffery isn't just some blue-helmeted peacekeepy type. He led the Australian SAS—i.e., special forces, the toughest hombres on the squad. He won the Military Cross in Vietnam and still believes that that war was the right thing to do. He headed Australia's national counter-terrorism strategy team. In other words, if you wanted to devise the precise opposite of Michaëlle Jean, this is what he'd look like.

Which comes as little surprise in a nation where, says pollster Allan Gregg, "for good or ill, we continue to see ourselves as kind of the Baden-Powell of the world community, doing good deeds, not getting killed or killing others."

Now remind me again: Why do Canadians insist it's the American demand for violence that has ruined their national pastime? You can take all the time you need to answer that.

CHAPTER SIX

Cherry Bomb

"I enjoy being around hockey players. After all, I've always
enjoyed entertaining our fighting men."

—Bob Hope

T he stars-and-stripes tie blazed from beneath the starched
Edwardian collar. The face was flushed crimson. Pounding
the desk for emphasis, Don Cherry was in full rhetorical
flourish on the *Coach's Corner*, March 22, 2003. But instead of his
usual array of causes—visors, referees, floaters, his beloved Bobby
Orr—Cherry was into virgin territory: the newly minted war in
Iraq launched by U.S. President George W. Bush. Canada was consumed by the debate over the American-led coalition entering Iraq
for the second time in a dozen years. Not surprisingly, Quebec was
vehemently opposed. Left-wing sentiment in the rest of Canada
also felt that Bush had overstepped his authority in leading his
nation against the regime of Sadaam Hussein without the approval
of the United Nations. But a separate segment of Canadian
thought disagreed, feeling that, whatever Canada's qualms about
how the Americans had engineered the Iraq campaign, the nation's

best interests were served by joining the Americans and British in purging the brutal dictator's regime, not by siding with the dissenting French and Germans in the European Union.

Liberal prime minister Jean Chrétien had tried to walk the narrow line between his pacifist home province and pro-war American/British sentiment in the rest of Canada. He announced that Canada would not join the campaign in Iraq but instead would send troops to Afghanistan to help subdue the Taliban forces there and do a little nation building if there was time. (The idea being that the Afghanistan campaign was safer work. Guess again.) Naturally, passions ran high as the U.S. forces raced across Iraq in a swift assault that toppled Saddam in a few short weeks. Even as Bush prematurely declared "Mission accomplished" in the U.S., there were rallies, protests, stormy accusations in Parliament, and barbed insults from Liberal members such as Carolyn Parrish, who stomped on a George Bush doll on *This Hour Has 22 Minutes* and bitched about hating those "damn Americans" to a TV crew. Relations with Washington sank to an all-time low in Montreal when the crowd at the Bell Centre booed the American national anthem before the Canadiens game versus the Islanders in early 2003.

For Cherry, who had spent many of his working years as a player and coach in the United States, the show of boorish behaviour by the crowd at the Habs game was too much. "Years of pride went down the drain" when the Habs fans booed the "Star Spangled Banner," he proclaimed. Furthermore, Canada's refusal to join the American effort was a slap at an old friend. Cherry decried the "lack of support to our American friends ... I hate to see them go it alone. These guys are over there, they're over there giving it all ... we're just riding their coattails."

But Cherry's broadcast partner Ron MacLean came down on the opposite side of the debate. Looking pained, MacLean asked,

"Why attack Iraq if they haven't attacked you?" For approximately seven minutes the two friends sparred heatedly about Canada's place in the war. For a loosely scripted segment that typically causes a media sensation by debating referees' calls or touch-up icing, the segue into the politics of war created a whirlwind that lit up the CBC's phone lines. Some agreed with Cherry, some with MacLean. Others demanded to know what two hockey commentators were doing voicing opinions about Iraq on the public broadcaster that was supposed to be scrupulously unbiased. Perplexed executives at *Hockey Night in Canada* were torn between pulling the plug on the debate or allowing free speech to have its day—even with a puck-headed slant. In the end, they let the segment run its course.

"We thought that because Ron and Don are sports commentators and not political commentators there was no reason to put it anywhere else," CBC spokesperson Ruth-Ellen Soles told *The Globe and Mail*. While the CBC officially feigned approval, the March 22 segment of *Coach's Corner* vanished from the network's website shortly thereafter. And both Cherry and MacLean were later sternly reminded that in the future they were to limit themselves to items about hockey. But Cherry was hardly sated. The next day he appeared on the *Jim Rome Show*, a syndicated American radio program, to explain himself, the CBC, and the politics of his nation. "You have to realize the CBC is government owned... You have to say the government was against it [the war], and I'm for it, and I'm on a government program. I really thought this could be the end.

"Our media up here is totally left wing," he told an amused Rome:

> It's socialist, left wing, pinko, commies. I got ripped to shreds in the left-wing media. That's the chance you take. I don't regret it,

and if I had to I'd do it over again . . . The true Canadians do not feel the way they do in Quebec there. Believe me, the majority of the people in Canada love the United States. We know you'd be there to help us and don't think too bad of us. It's just a damn shame [Canadiens fans] had to boo the "Star Spangled Banner" in Quebec. You have to realize, it's Quebec and it's French Canadians.

Predictably, Cherry's second salvo was received with even less enthusiasm than was the first by the anti-war/anti-Bush clique in Canada. The requisite political voices demanded the CBC fire him. Internal voices at the Corporation were miffed that Cherry was free to express himself on the issues of the day but most of them were muzzled, forbidden from engaging in any outside political activity. "Mr. Cherry is an industry, namely himself," wrote *The Globe and Mail*'s Jeffrey Simpson:

> . . . and that industry depends, more than anything else, on the platform the country's public broadcaster accords him. Scrupulous about presenting opposing sides of issues, the CBC allows Mr. Cherry to rant and rave about hockey, the national sport, without anyone taking on his antediluvian views. If this were politics, or foreign policy or economics, the CBC would never get away with this kind of programming without creating a storm of protest. But hockey is a sport, and therefore entertainment, and Mr. Cherry can be considered entertainment in a manner of speaking.

If the CBC found itself caught in a tempest with Cherry then it was one of its own making. In exchange for the TV ratings and money that accompany Cherry's choleric performances each week on *Hockey Night in Canada* the Corporation has, in return, been obliged to perform damage control on a continuing basis when

THE MEANING OF PUCK 127

the former minor league journeyman brought the sensibilities of the dressing room to the tender ears of Canadians. Until the Iraq conflagration, the formula had worked exceedingly well for the two parties: CBC was able to advertise its blue collar bonafides on Parliament Hill while Cherry was burnished by the credibility of CBC's considerable journalistic reputation. (Cherry raging on TSN or Sportsnet would be considerably diminished without the appalled antagonism of the CBC crowd.) Questioning the ruling party's Iraq strategy was certainly Cherry's greatest challenge till that time. But after some turbulence from the usual suspects in the media and Parliament, Cherry survived to rage once more. Neither war nor civil strife nor insurrection seems to slow Grapes. (Although a remark about the visor-wearing tendencies of French Canadians and Euros did delay *Coach's Corner* by seven seconds for a time.)

Cherry understands the cardinal rule of broadcasting: Never be boring. And perhaps, a good offence is the best defence. I should know. I had the temerity to suggest in 2004 that:

He's perfected the evil villain routine better than any wrestler who ever pulled a foreign object from his trunks. In his guise as Everyman in a funny suit, Don utters something outrageous. The predictable parties recoil in disgust. The media goes into over-drive, quoting the hurt parties and Cherry's disbelieving response. Everyone tunes in the next Saturday for more. Instead, a damp-eyed Cherry sends out a greeting to a small boy with an incurable disease back in Blunderbuss, Saskatchewan. See, he's really a softy, folks.

Until the next week when he's back at Swedes and referees and French Canadians. And the whole sequence starts again. But as Henny Youngman proved, you don't need a lot of acts, just one good one to last a long time. So Cherry, like Youngman, endures with an act as old as the Rockies.

Cherry immediately leapt to his own defence on the airwaves of *Coach's Corner* during game three of the 2004 Flames–Sharks series (defying the maxim that only has a fool has himself as a client). There I was, minding my own business between periods in the press box at the Saddledome when I suddenly felt a burning sensation in my ears. I quickly looked to the TV monitor. In the din of the Dome, all I could see was lips flapping on the screen, eyes bulging and a stricken look on Ron MacLean's face.

Oh-oh. I was losing my Cherry on Coach's Corner. Cherry was telling the nation I hated kids with cancer!

Faster than you can say "Cesare Maniago," the cell phone on my belt began buzzing like a swarm of angry bees. Calls coming in from listeners far and wide. "Did you hear what *he* called you?" and "What was that all about?" And that was just my mother. Then my email in-tray filled up with missives from Canadians who hadn't read what I wrote, but were sure that it was some new low in journalism because Mr. C had told them so. What was a glib story detecting a certain pattern in how Cherry would swing between outrageous comment and playing Canada's favourite uncle had been inflated by Cherry into me bashing sick or injured kids. (I don't think he said I kick puppies, too, but you never know.) He was hopping mad that his MO was being scrutinized. I was lower than a bivalve on the evolutionary scale. My tongue was not worthy to lick the bottom of his shoe. As my emails quickly told me, you're never going to win against a guy who's allowed network airtime to conduct personal business. His rant also produced some clever writing from people who never read the offending column but are sure they knew all about it.

Here's a sample from a guy named Bob:

> What are you jealous your [sic] not on tv anymore, what kind of
> f*****n idiot, would say all Don has to do is mention a sick kids
> [sic] name and all is forgiven. I tried to read your column, but I
> ain't going to subscribe to some ****-*** newspaper to read some
> ignorant a******s comments. Someone should slap you in the
> mouth for being a mouthy p****."

Nice demographic.

Then there were the heartbreaking letters from parents who'd
lost kids to cancer or other diseases. In their eyes, I was worse than
Bin Laden for "attacking" terminally ill kids. Most relented somewhat when they read the context of the comments in the full column, but it was enough to discover the awesome weight of
Cherry's popularity and credibility with the hockey culture in
Canada. Needless to say *Hockey Night in Canada* never gave me a
chance at a rebuttal.

Cherry's longevity while operating on the knife's edge of political correctness has made him a hero to many in the conservative
political movement. Even as he chafed against the strictures of the
CBC and governmental elitism for almost two decades, right
wingers were being likewise savaged by the Liberal apparatus that
had ruled Canada for much of the past century. In a multicultural
Canada that seemingly has abandoned its imperial past in favour
of a pan-Canadian version of political Starbucks, Cherry at least
has stood for something. Settling it toe-to-toe. Lunch-pail values.
Canadians first—especially English Canadians. To the editorialists at the *National Post*, this code of hockey chivalry—however
dated—is preferable to an amorphous buffet of feel-good liberalism. "He is a moralist for the masses whose concepts of loyalty

and honour transcend the ice surface," wrote John Geiger in June of 2006.

> Like the motto of the Order of Canada, Don Cherry too 'desires a better country'—in fact in his way he has done much to bring it about—it's just that his concept of what constitutes a better country is at odds with what the professional Canadians think.

In an appeal for Cherry to be granted the Order of Canada, Geiger points out that in 2004, the former Boston and Colorado coach made the top 10 list on CBC television's *The Greatest Canadian* program, ranking seventh, ahead of Sir John A. Macdonald and even Wayne Gretzky. In 2005, he received the most votes in the *National Post*'s "Beautiful Minds" series, beating out Michael Ignatieff, Charles Taylor, and Naomi Klein as Canada's leading public intellectual. In short, the only ones not clued into Cherry's appeal are the keepers of the Canadian cultural establishment.

Famed Montreal author and Canadiens fan Mordecai Richler savaged him in *Macleans*:

> Here...was proof positive not only that man has descended from the baboon, but also in the case of one born in an obscure corner of Kingston, Ont, the evolutionary ascent was far from complete. (Cherry is) an inspirational figure. An appropriate model for cretins. He has established that a six-figure income is not beyond the dim-witted providing they are willing to act like a boor and dress like a harlequin.

But the haughty dismissals from the literati only enhanced Cherry's profile with his target audience. "Maybe my mind never got over eighteen," he once confided. "I relate to guys eighteen to twenty-five."

And they relate to Don.

If the voluble one didn't exist, it would have been necessary for the hockey culture to invent the bragging, bullying Cherry. As it was, *Hockey Night in Canada* did the next best thing, launching Cherry into low orbit where he might better be seen by the masses each Saturday night during the hockey season. As most minor hockey administrators will tell you, he saturates the debate on hockey in Canada at every level. NHL players report watching his *Coach's Corner* segments in the intermissions of their own games. To underestimate him is fatal; to ignore him, impossible. With the blessing of Canada's national broadcaster the CBC, Cherry and his brethren light a candle to the cause every Saturday night. No one is neutral about him and Cherry himself is never neutral.

It is easy to rage on about the outsized Cherry (Lord knows I've done my share) but considering his hardscrabble upbringing in the sport, it's difficult to see him turning out any other way. After all, when you are raised in a seminary, it's hard not think like a Catholic. So Cherry speaks confidently for the grunts such as Matthew Barnaby, an NHL journeyman tough guy who came up the hard way:

> In grade school, an older kid had me on my back with his knees holding my arms and shoulders down. He told me to 'give up,' and I refused. He punched me in the face. I still refused. He must have punched me ten times, and I kept spitting and laughing at him ... I never gave in, and they finally broke it up. I never had a father—I was an angry kid. I am stubborn over pain. It hurts, but I refuse to stop.

And here lies the irony of Cherry-as-public-barometer in the first decade of the twenty-first century. While his hockey insights grow less consequential (NHL players view his coaching clinics more as farce than fact), his significance on a cultural scale has surged. Having added tributes to Canada's fallen soldiers and police to his Saturday night repetoire in the past decade, Cherry has restored flag-waving patriotism to respectability. With Stephen Harper and the newly reconstituted Conservative party vaulting into power in 2005, Cherry's seeming political liabilities have become assets in the battle between Tim Horton's Canada and the Starbucks urban version in metropolitan areas such as Montreal, Toronto, and Vancouver. With voting polarity crystallized in the 2005 election, the minority Tories claimed precisely zero ridings in the 514, 416, and 604 area codes—and yet still ruled the nation. Increasingly, the hockey community in Canada regards urban Canadian culture with suspicion. Big cities have banded together to demand a larger share of the economic pie for infrastructure, and several recent leadership conventions have split between the big cities and the rural constituencies. There is also a cry for re-distributing ridings to better reflect the concentration of populations in Toronto, Calgary, Vancouver, and Montreal—at the expense of traditional rural ridings.

Seemingly progressive Quebec fractured along such lines in the 2007 provincial election, with conservative small-town mayors in towns such as Herouxville issuing codes of conduct aimed at preventing potential stonings and beheadings by radical Muslims should they take over their communities. Making the culture clash more edgy in rural Quebec was the controversial presence of André Boisclair, the openly gay leader of the separatist Parti Quebecois, who'd also admitted to snorting cocaine while a cabinet minister. The nationalist vote that typically went to the PQ in rural ridings deserted the party for Mario Dumont's ADQ, which played on the conservative nature of non-Montreal Quebecois who often view the big city as a godless stew of recent immigrants, gays, and out-of-control liberalism. The pitting of values in exchange for votes was too much for *The Globe and Mail* columnist John Ibbitson, who railed against:

> ... opinion leaders who single out a small group of immigrants, accusing them of refusing to fit in, condemning their culture, and ostracizing them from the mainstream, are nothing but bullies and bigots who contribute to the very radicalization they condemn ... So, to all the ADQ backbenchers and small-town mayors who disparage the latest batch of new arrivals, this message: Go ahead. You and your prejudices will fade away, and your towns will disappear, unless you can find a way to attract the very people you love to denigrate.

But *Maclean's* columnist Mark Steyn saw something entirely different at work in how the media viewed Boisclair's abject performance in the election.

> I was struck by the number of lifelong separatists who simply resented being subject to Queer Eye for the Separatist Guy and, even by the standards of the ever lamer bluff of Quebec "nationalism", couldn't buy the idea of a gay hedonist as their founding father. There's something a bit feeble about the media's refusal even to discuss this except through vague evasive allusions to the difficulty M. Boisclair had "connecting" with Quebec voters.

Similar schisms were revealed elsewhere in Canada. In the booming economy of Alberta, a resentment of conspicuously rich and urban Calgary was said to have played a part in the 2007 defeat of early favourite Jim Dinning when he ran to replace Ralph Klein as Progressive Conservative premier of the province. Vegreville farmer Ed Stelmach, a compromise candidate, instead took the leadership. In the federal Liberal leadership race of 2006, Liberals suspicious of the elite Toronto stylings of academic Michael Ignatieff and ex-Ontario premier Bob Rae turned instead to a compromise candidate, the unknown Stéphane Dion.

Across the country, resentment and values—those expressed by Cherry—played out in elections and controversies such as the Shane Doan parliamentary hearing. Like their oracle Cherry, people were frustrated at the "professional" class running politics and the subsuming guilt that erases many of their proudest national symbols. Governor General's Award winner David Adams Richards heard this frustration with elites that seemingly apologize for any success the country has in hockey. In his book *Hockey Dreams*, Richards laments, "hockey's where we got it right but we're not allowed to tell anyone that we have ... Somehow we permit ourselves the luxury of being the country without a face and allow others to tell us what face we should wear. Somehow we want it that way."

To the delight of his supporters and frustration of his opponents, Cherry proudly projects his own face onto the country and tells Canada to be proud of a past that many school districts wish to ignore or expunge. From the piercing eyes to the clenched fists to the testosterone-soaked jeremiads, Cherry is a living, breathing personification of the Tim Horton values. He projects the "chivalrous" codes of honour among the hard men of hockey onto a broader map. He unashamedly roots for the hapless Toronto Maple Leafs. At a time when Canadians are urged to adopt values of tolerance and multiculturalism, Cherry (a dedicated amateur historian) unapologetically plays favourites from the old days. So his support for old allies—such as the United States and Britain—over those of Belgium or Sweden when it came to the Iraq war. And his extension of the values of the grunts of hockey, the lunch pail guys, onto the military and police forces.

The more critics cringed at his rough-hewn strategies and cultural prejudices against the Europeans or French Canadians, the more Cherry embellished his Everyman-in-a-Gaudy-Suit persona. By 2004, he'd stretched his mandate on *Hockey Night in Canada* to include geopolitics, military affairs, police matters, and the medical challenges of Canadians from coast-to-coast. He expended valuable on-air time beating up on his media rivals and critics—including yours truly—with barely a whimper of complaint from the CBC. When there was doubt about him coming back to *Hockey Night*, Cherry shamelessly campaigned on-air to keep his job, raging like a hockey Lear each week at the hidden forces aligned against him in the country. He took great delight in publicly maligning the few CBC executives who threatened his tenure as spokesman for the masses in Canada.

Then there was his hockey philosophy. Ahem. In the guise of Pied Piper for people without a voice, Cherry became increasingly interested in promoting his version of "physical" hockey. Since he began his crusade to keep hockey a manly sport, the NHL game has taken his rock-'em, sock-'em style to heart, emphasizing hitting to a greater and greater extent. "You stick a tape in the VCR and you tell me how much hitting there was in a game from the old days compared to today," former NHL goalie John Davidson, now president of the St. Louis Blues, told *The Globe and Mail* during the 2004–05 lockout:

> Not 40 per cent, not even 30 per cent, and it takes away the flow
> of the game ... I hope people don't take this the wrong way, that

I'm a wimp and don't like hitting. That's not true. Hitting is one of the great spectacles of our sport. But when we eliminate every single player who has the puck along the boards, we eliminate him from the play. And a lot of time that's two or three steps after he's made a pass. A lot of times these are boarding plays and you wonder how the player can get himself off the ice. I honestly don't know how they do it. These are not small players any more. They're giants.

But to understand Cherry is to understand why and how hockey's rugged Code thrives in a time when we also debate eco-system threats to tree frogs and gender-neutral comic books. He comes by his faith in fighting naturally (his brother Dick was also a lifer in hockey—tougher than Don, say their contemporaries). A blue-collar product of the hockey machine, who'd have been at home in Haileybury or Renfrew at the dawn of the twentieth century, Cherry was the classic superannuated teenager in the body of an aging hockey warrior. (As the sardonic Dick Beddoes once wrote about hockey stars, "They reached adulthood, but they forgot to touch second base.") With a grade nine education and no skills other than hockey, Cherry burnished his working-class persona by toiling in manual labour in the construction industry when he wasn't playing hockey in the minors. After a peripatetic fifteen-year career—with just one NHL game to his credit—he made a comeback as the player/coach of the Rochester Americans. He found that he liked the idea of coaching. More than that, he liked the idea of the attention he got standing behind a bench. So he consciously dressed up like a dandy and fashioned himself as a crusader for keeping the traditional Canadian values of fighting and following in hockey. It worked out better than he ever could have wished.

Having played almost all his career among less-skilled players in the minors, where effort and sacrifice and the occasional dust-up won the day, he championed these traits as loyal "goodthink" and demeaned the intellectual approaches of people like Lloyd Percival or Father David Bauer. The American Hockey League's lunch-pail values of hard work and punching a guy from the front were the honest way to the big leagues. So was being suspicious of outsiders, be they "French guys," European players, or journalists who might disagree. He was never discouraged from these views by team owners, either, who have always used a little rock-'em, sock-'em as a gate attraction. (Something Cherry would profit handsomely from when it came to rock-'em, sock-'em video sales.)

Cherry's first shot at the big-time coaching came with the Boston Bruins in the fall of 1974. Bobby Orr's career was winding down due to knee problems (despite the image of longtime collaborators, Cherry coached Orr for just 93 games), and so Cherry reformed the team from one based on hockey's best defenceman of all time to a team-oriented approach that scrapped for its wins. While they possessed the offensive talent of Rick Middleton, Johnny Bucyk, and Brad Park, Cherry's Bruins were best known for tough guys who saw no problem in dropping the mitts (Stan Jonathan, Terry O'Reilly, John Wensink, Mike Milbury). While Cherry worshipped Orr, the greatest Canadian player till Gretzky, it was the Canadian lunch-pail values that he cited as the keys to the Bruins' success in the years from 1974 to 1979. Cherry's strategy came within a Guy Lafleur 1979 playoff goal of working, and though he made a series of coaching blunders in Game Seven against the Habs, the near-miss was sufficient to provide Cherry with a perch in the hockey world.

Executive producer Ralph Mellanby of *Hockey Night in Canada* liked the showmanship Cherry demonstrated behind the bench in Boston and took a flyer on the flamboyant Kingston, Ontario, product as his intermission analyst when Cherry was fired in Colorado. The conversion from journeyman hockey apprentice to lead singer for old-time Anglo-Canadian values was complete. The sport's bully pulpit was now occupied by a disciple of hockey without tears.

For the next seventeen years, The Don Cherry Fight Club became the symbol of the code he'd learned as a player and a coach for a generation of impressionable minds on *Hockey Night in Canada*, hockey's most influential sounding board. Coming to *Hockey Night* in the wake of gnome-like Howie Meeker, who was a stickler for detail and an advocate of progress and teaching in the sport, Cherry was seen as a refreshing, big-picture, speaks-his-mind kind of guy. His rough and unpolished diction—as foreign-sounding as Swahili to the gentrified CBC—came across as both honest and direct. His bloody-minded philosophy about how the game was played was translated as an "insider's view." His outlandish wardrobe completed the picture of the carny, the man out of time but not out of opinions. When he wasn't telling co-host Ron MacLean to shut up, he glorified the agitators, the fighters, the men who'd come up from tough backgrounds—just as he had done. He stumped heavily for friends and anything that wore a Boston B in the 1970s. The rest were visor-wearing wimps from Cue-bec or Europe.

In his smash-mouth philosophy, he much resembles John Madden, the legendary ex-NFL coach who has been the NFL's top TV analyst for two decades. But where Madden stuck exclusively to football, Cherry blew down that door to become a self-appointed critic on social, political, and cultural matters. In a Canada that was suddenly a melting pot (half the people in his beloved Toronto were born outside Canada), Cherry reassured millions of Canadians that their Anglo-Celtic roots were still very much alive in the NHL. His Canada apparently does not include modern Quebec, either. On a *Coach's Corner* segment, he said French players were prone to visor wearing (in other words, chicken) and said drug use in junior hockey was confined to the Quebec leagues. While continually wrapping himself in the Canadian flag, he once dismissed Nagano Olympic flag-bearer Jean-Luc Brassard, a mogul skiing champion in 1994, as "that French guy." (In his dotage he has taken a shine to Vincent Lecavalier of Tampa, however.)

Listening to his *Coach's Corner* homilies, it was possible to believe that there still existed a refuge in the sport from the massive changes raging outside the studio doors, before feminism and immigration changed Canada. Like Albert Finney in *Miller's Crossing*, Cherry could shed a tear for John McCormack singing "Danny Boy," even as he was emptying the chamber of a Tommy gun. In later years, when the Archie Bunker act grew stale and critics began denouncing his atavistic attitudes to visors, violence, and foreigners, Cherry ramped up his Common Man appeal by inserting florid tributes to the grunts in the Canadian military, the police, and to the sick or injured children across the country in his weekly rants.

Old-time hockey was linked to motherhood issues in an era of frightening change for Canada's founding cultures. Its mantra was Cherry's embrace of fighting and intimidation, the cornerstones of the Code. Anyone who disagreed with him was taunted or insulted—and identified by his ethnic or racial origins. He was anti-intellectual and proud of it.

If there exists a watershed moment for Cherry's TV career, it probably is the World Junior Hockey Championship brawl of 1987 in Piestany, Czechoslovakia. Canada, in contention for the gold medal with the Czechs, was leading the Soviet Union 4–2 in the final game of the tournament until a bench-clearing brawl erupted. The ice was quickly covered in helmets and gloves, and pairs of skaters—goalies included—engaged in a Cherryesque rock-'em sock-'em. When referees failed to get control of the melee on the ice, the panicked organizers shut off the lights in the arena. The players continued to fight in the dark, and organizers eventually cancelled the game. The decision cost Canada the gold medal. Cherry immediately leapt to the defence of the players, saying they'd had to fight to protect each other when "attacked" by the Russkies. When CBC TV host Brian Williams suggested the players had perhaps fallen into a trap concocted by the Czechs and Soviets, one they might have avoided by skating away from the provocation, Cherry went ballistic. We were Canadians, and Canadians don't back down, roared Cherry, who appeared ready to throttle Williams.

In the days following the debacle, I appeared with Cherry in a televised debate on the brawl, saying that the young Canadians should have simply skated away from the Russians and laughed all the way to the gold medal. Cherry, however, saw the brawl as a test of Canada's manhood that necessitated losing the gold to protect our hockey honour. As the debate got away from him, Cherry turned personal, asking me what I would do if my kids had gotten into a fight on the street. Would I help them or run away? It was a sucker question, I replied, fighting didn't have a real role in hockey. The fight shouldn't have started in the first place. But Cherry persisted in the parent/child analogy:

Cherry: If you were walking along the street and three guys
             attacked your son would you help your son?
Dowbiggin: I would call the police.
Cherry: Now let me get this right. If three guys had your

	son down putting the boots to him, you wouldn't
	wade in and help him?
Dowbiggin:	No, I would call the police.
Cherry:	I'll have nothing more to say to this coward who
	wouldn't help his son.

It was classic Cherry, of course, bullying and bombastic. In future derogatory reference, I was always called the coward who wouldn't defend his own kid. (Actually, that was one of the nicer things he's said about me.) With performances such as these, Cherry's popularity soared with his core audience; it became gospel to say that Canada stood still each Saturday when Cherry appeared as hockey sage. It's a reputation that doesn't bear much scrutiny after Cherry's own attempts to prolong old-time hockey with the Mississauga Ice Dogs of the Ontario Hockey league. With Cherry as either co-owner, GM, or coach, the Ice Dogs were the worst franchise in the history of the OHL. His clubs won just twenty-seven games in their first four seasons—in 2000–01, they won just three games the entire season. In his year as coach, 2001–02, they won just 11 of sixty-eight games (a .235 winning percentage). Then, within a brief period of his relinquishing a role in the club, Mississauga shot to the finals of the OHL in 2004. This record of futility is never mentioned on *Coach's Corner* (unlike almost any other of Cherry's commercial ventures) and the audience probably doesn't care. "He's good for shock therapy," Columbus head coach Ken Hitchcock says. "We don't necessarily listen for his ideas, but for his passion."

Despite his national mandate, Cherry openly cheers for the Maple Leafs on the national airwaves; when Calgary made the 2004 Stanley Cup finals, he spent much of the first intermission in the first game talking about his beloved Leafs, not the Flames.

When complaints were registered, Cherry scoffed about perpetually cranky westerners and told the Flames mascot Harvey the
Hound to "screw off" live on the air. CBC execs stayed silent. It
was a bravura, anachronistic performance in a post 9/11 world.

"I don't think that anybody could do what I do," he admitted to
Howard Berger of the *National Post*. "You'd have to be crazy to try it.
I've had a good run, and if they fire me, they fire me. There's nobody
else in TV who does what me and (Ron) MacLean do—not even in
the States. I don't think anybody else could get away with it." Wrote
Jeffrey Simpson, not a Cherry fan: "By allowing the Cherry industry uncontested access, the CBC not only abdicates its responsibility for balanced commentary, but becomes indirectly complicit in
the drawing of arbitrary lines that sustain the culture of violence."

While Cherry remains irreplaceable in Tim Horton's Canada,
his popularity remains something of a mystery to outsiders—the
Trailer Park Boy of hockey. Volker Nolte, a kinesiology professor
and an expert on coaching at the University of Western Ontario,
expresses the European view of Canada's fascination with pushing the envelope of violence:

> I'm looking at this from a European perspective, and I have no
> understanding of such violence. Sport is not a criminal event, nor
> is it war. Such a large segment of the population likes this violence
> but in reality, it is inhuman and disgraceful. On the other hand,
> what do you expect? We are surrounded by media that encourage
> these kinds of violent acts. The CBC pays Don Cherry a lot of
> money to make comments that support and foster such behaviour.

And, so long as he wants to vent, Cherry will likely find a
receptive audience in the Canadian terra incognito and with the
sponsors of *Hockey Night in Canada*.

CHAPTER SEVEN

Damn Yankees

Two lobstermen sit in a bar. One, an American, has a trap beside him with a top fastened on it. The other lobsterman, a Canadian, has a similar trap beside him. But the Canadian's trap has no top. "Tell me friend," says the American, "how can you keep your lobster from crawling out of the trap with no top on it?" The Canadian sips his beer and then says, "It's easy, b'y. These here are Canadian lobster. If any one of them should try to crawl out of the trap to escape, the rest would pull him right back in."

—allegedly a true story

They call it The Game. As in, "Don't hurt The Game" or "No one's bigger than The Game."

The Game is hockey.

Canadian hockey.

And in this country it is a sacred trust.

But at some point, no one is sure how, The Game became synonymous with the NHL. So now, when people warn incoming NHL Players Association executive director Paul Kelly of not messing with The Game by asking too much from those poor cash-strapped owners in Toronto and New York, they're really talking about not hurting the NHL. As if compelling the NHL to operate like something other than a Balkan shoe factory might in some way hurt hockey down at its grass roots on a Saturday morning.

How a for-profit operation run principally by real estate guys with an empty arena and an even emptier heart for hockey—and the people who love it—became the guardian of Canada's national pastime is baffling. But that didn't stop Canadian journalists and fans from telling Kelly that his loyalty lies not with the players who pay him to represent them, but with the Canadian myth of "Don't hurt The Game."

It was the same sucker play in the 1990s when Alan Eagleson's toadies said, "You're hurting The Game by doing a forensic audit of the union." Next thing you knew, Eagleson was off to jail. And when, in 2005, the same wise men told Chris Chelios and Dwayne Roloson, "Leave Ted Saskin alone, The Game's in enough trouble already." Then it was found that Saskin had been snooping the private email conversations of his members. Ah yes, the Canadian sucker play.

While Canadians may get the NHL and The Game confused, NHL commissioner Gary Bettman has no such affliction. And when the lockout started in September of 2004, he knew that those polite, order-taking, guileless, uncomplicated sons of the North would never be able to take the heat down at the grocery store or the garage when one of the boys—who couldn't run a 7/11—looked at him and said, "You're hurting The Game."

Oh, yes . . . the commissioner took that branch-plant colonial knowledge to the bank each night and kept it in a safe place for just the right moment when those hockey players couldn't stand any more heat. Bettman knew the Euros and the Yankees would hold out forever, because, for the boys from overseas, it was mostly about money, and for the American guys it was about the inalienable individual rights that are in every American's blood.

But the Canadian boys, they have The Game. Forget Trudeau's Charter of Rights and Freedoms, they serve a higher power. Brought up to ride a cold bus with a blocked head for fourteen hours and say, "Thank you sir, can I have fourteen more hours?" Schooled to keep their heads down, their mouths shut, and their injuries to themselves. Delighted just to pull on the sweater of some club owned by a guy looking for an easy tax loss. Poor things, they felt guilty for all those millions the league wanted to pay them. All to keep The Game alive.

And even though he looked like he'd faint at the first sign of blood—'specially his own—Bettman had the nice Canadian boys like Trevor Linden, Jarome Iginla, Tie Domi, and Chris Pronger pegged to cut and run when the lawyers' talk got too fancy. When their dads gave 'em the look at Christmas like, "What the hell you doin' here, boy? Get your butt on the plane to Pittsburgh and play. Here you are with your got-up attitude and your fancy union lawyer telling you to hold out. You're hurting The Game."

Bettman saw it all and told his owners, "Just hold on a few more months." And sure enough, when the going got tough in early 2005, the Canadians got going to their owner's office to see if a side deal couldn't be arranged to get around Goodenow and the no-surrender strategy they'd all agreed on months before. That's the reality that Kelly inherits: it was Canadians who turtled it when the pressure got too much. And no matter how much money they make, they can fold like a lawn chair again when the weight of The Game gets too heavy again.

Because they can't distinguish between the NHL and The Game. One's a business, the other's a myth perpetuated by endless *Hockey Night in Canada* tear-jerkers. One's a faded imitation of every scheme tried by the NFL, NBA, or major league baseball and the other's a column about protecting the sacred trust of The Game by pointing to the charade of the Levitt Report. One's a Saturday night money machine and the other's a Saturday morning game between eight-year-olds who just want to play. One's a way to make a living and the other is life itself for many in Canada.

And unless Paul Kelly can make his Canadian membership understand the difference between the two, you won't see the Conversion of Stan Mikita made into a movie anytime soon—at least, not in Canada. Conversion . . . what? For the first six years of his career, Mikita of the Chicago Blackhawks was among the best scorers in the league. The Czech-born centre was a gifted playmaker who scored at a clip surpassed only by his famed teammate Bobby Hull. Mikita was also the creator of the curved blade on the stick, a weapon so diabolical that, in his and Hull's hands, it revolutionized offence in the NHL.

But Mikita was more than just an offensive force early in his 1,394-game career. The 165-pounder was also a chippy, mouthy player whose name regularly topped the NHL's penalty leaders, too. In fact, Mikita accomplished the feat of leading the league in scoring and penalty minutes in the same year when he notched 89 points and 146 PIMs in 1963–64 (something never done before or since). There are plenty of tales that underscore Mikita's nasty side. In one game, Toronto defenceman Kent Douglas grew so annoyed with Mikita's yapping that the Leafs blueliner whacked Mikita over the head with his stick (the heaviest ever used in the NHL); Mikita needed forty stitches to close the wound. The Chicago centre also possessed a tongue as sharp as his stick, and he was tagged with many misconducts for his mouth.

If you'd taken a vote of players around the league in the fall of 1965, Mikita would have been voted among the most hated by

opponents (and maybe a few teammates, too). "When I first knew
Stan," wrote former Chicago teammate Phil Esposito, "he was a little
prick who never backed down from anyone. He used to get the
shit kicked out of him in fights on the ice. He always had an edge—
on or off the ice. He gave you the feeling he was better than you."

But then, one night early in the 1965-66 season, Mikita decided
enough was enough: he was going to mend his ways in the NHL.
The inspiration came after a chat with his young daughter, Jane,
who asked her dad why he was always being made to go sit by himself on the other side of the rink, away from his friends. The question from his daughter hit home with Mikita, who suddenly
understood how he was being perceived away from the confines of
hockey's culture. "I realized most of the penalties were additions
of ten minutes—misconducts," Mikita recalled. "I also tried to
knuckle down and stop the stupid, lazy penalties—the hooks, the
holds, the trips. I also realized that I couldn't talk referees out of
anything, so I just went to the penalty box if I was called for anything."

Virtually overnight, the man born Stanislav Guoth in the former Czechoslovakia transformed himself from a man with a major
anger problem on the ice into one of the most disciplined players
in the league. Critics of the reformed Mikita said he'd lose his fire
and his passion if he calmed down; he'd never be the same player
again. They were right. Mikita wasn't the same player again. He
was better. He went from 154 PIMS in 1964–65 down to just twelve
minutes in 1966–67. Yet he added a third and fourth Art Ross
Trophy as NHL's leading scorer in successive years from 1966 to
1968. He also captured the Hart Trophy in successive years where
he collected just twenty-six PIMS.

More than that, the former bad boy whose name was synonymous with dirty play was awarded the Lady Byng Trophy for gentlemanly play in 1967–68. It was a remarkable turnaround—and one

that The Game was apparently in no hurry to see emulated. Mikita was a non sequitur in a business that preached fighting as a safety valve for anger, living on the razor's edge of violence as the ultimate virtue in a player. If Mikita could take control of his demons and conquer them—all the while setting scoring records—then how could The Game still justify its hallowed myths about intimidation, violence, and the need for fighting? And how would coaches motivate their players without the weapon of violence on every shift? Mikita's example was a bald-faced challenge to all that was holy and accepted in NHL coaching and player development.

Luckily for the owners who market hockey's violent Code as a selling point, and coaches who use fighting and intimidation as a motivational technique for sleepy teams, Mikita was an exception in bucking The Game. Peer pressure is enormous within the closeted Canadian hockey community. And Mikita heard plenty from former antagonists when he played after his conversion. In part, he was protected by his status as an All-Star, but it was also a great act of will that defied conventional wisdom about hockey in Canada. He could play with passion but not always on the knife's edge of self-control where players are meant to exist. "Hey, these guys don't work in a bank," says former NHLer Al MacNeil, a teammate of Mikita's in Chicago for a time. "They're highly paid in their job, and part of that job is running the gauntlet and learning to survive. This is professional sports. In any professional sport, there is an intimidation factor involved."

Despite Mikita's example, few players after him could choose self-control over the approval of the dressing room, the bonding that bloody combat produced. The pressure of hurting The Game with some newfangled notion of not acting out your inner John Ferguson, no small matter in a business where one's standing with teammates in the dressing room is as important as your standing in the race for the playoffs. They risk being called out by the media pack that follows the NHL as if it were gang fights over turf. (There's the standard joke about guys who try to reform: "Crushers who become rushers soon become ushers.") One WHA enforcer, Jamie Bateman, who decided to go straight and ask embarrassing questions about his role, said he was locked inside a broiling sauna by his team's GM. Only when he agreed to brawl again and keep his mouth closed was he released by the GM from the suffocating heat of the sauna.

In short, The Game is a learned behaviour, reinforced at every step of the prodigy machine. And embraced by the unique Canadian culture that puts loyalty to team ahead of any personal gain. While America still extols its individualist mantra of "every man or woman can grow up to be president," the Canadian concept of team remains the template that shapes young hockey players even in the twenty-first century of multimillion-dollar contracts and free agency. ("I couldn't have done this without my teammates," is the well-worn interview staple.) Canadian hockey players are prized, above all, for their humility.

That humility extends to Canadian politics where—outside of the examples of Pierre Trudeau and René Lévesque—flashiness is considered a drawback in a politician. When former PC cabinet minister Elmer McKay described his son Peter's virtues upon entering politics, the elder McKay emphasized that the younger McKay was "not flamboyant." Jean Chretien was the "*p'tit gars de Shawinigan*." Prime Minister Stephen Harper's greatest selling point seems to be his stolid unflappability and generous tummy. By comparison, America elected an actor, Ronald Reagan, as president while politicians such as John McCain, Barack Obama, and Rudy Giuliani have been transformed into media superstars since the pervasive Fox TV News Channel and CNN made the 24-hour news cycle a staple of U.S. politics. And Bill Clinton ... well, the former president can't even spell humility, let alone display it.

The contrast between Canada and America is woven into the national psyche. "The Americans, always bumptious and aggressive, fought wars," wrote historian Jack Granatstein in *Who Killed the Canadian Military*, "but Canadians, nature's natural middlemen, kept the peace. The idea became a mantra, a powerful one that successive (Canadian) governments never challenged. War was foreign to Canadian thinking, but peacekeeping was the natural role for us."

Many will say that the same cockiness, the sense of self, also defines star American NHL players such as Jeremy Roenick, Keith Tkachuk, Mike Modano, or Chris Chelios. Canada knows best in hockey. But ask anyone who's to blame for hockey's problems and you'll get a stock answer: the Americans. Even the usually thoughtful Howie Meeker echoed this shopworn theme in a weak moment when he told a Canadian radio station, "American fans love the violence, they want the fights. They've been ruining the game for years, and we need to bring it back to Canada."

Sally Jenkins of the *Washington Post* eloquently summed up the Canadian sense of hockey supremacy in the wake of the 2004 Bertuzzi incident:

> You know what your problem is? You don't understand hockey...
> If you knew more about hockey, you'd understand the code of retribution, which says that bare-knuckled swinging is actually healthy because it prevents worse things, like, you know, cheap shots and high sticking.
>
> The people who really know hockey understand why Bertuzzi did what he did, and feel bad for the guy, and if you understood the game and all of its finer shadings, you'd feel bad

for him too. Instead, all NHL critics keep talking about is Moore's broken neck, and how yesterday he was moved to a hospital in Colorado that specializes in spinal cord injuries.

Real hockey people know Bertuzzi didn't mean to half-kill Moore, he only meant to catch him with a fist from behind and maybe give him a bad concussion and some payback, which is why he drove his forehead into the ice. A real hockey guy is a guy like Canucks Coach Marc Crawford, who's clearly unhappy with the NHL's suspension of Bertuzzi for the rest of the season and the $250,000 fine of the team, and who complains that Bertuzzi has been 'crucified' in the press . . .

Indeed, the encroachment of American values into the sport has long been used as a rallying point, whether it was Alan Eagleson blaming American influences within the NHLPA for exposing his criminal acts or traditionalists decrying the American influence at the NHL head office. ("He's a basketball guy," sneered Toronto's Bryan McCabe of Gary Bettman, the commissioner. "If he bumped into me on the street, he wouldn't know me. You could probably say that if he bumped into 95 per cent of the league".) The belated arrival of free agency in the NHL relative to their MLB, NBA, and NFL compatriots was attributable to the reluctance of many Canadian players to adopt American-style "salary disclosure"—in other words, revealing amongst themselves how much players actually made. It was thought too crass, too American, to talk about money among friends. Better to blend into the group, whether a hockey team or a political caucus or a military unit, as the ultimate homage to The Game.

So why does Canada still blame America for everything from its violence to afternoon games?

Because it works.

From Rick Mercer's jibes about American ignorance of Canadian geography, history, and culture to film maker Michael Moore's movie stereotypes about the peaceful northern neighbours, Canadians enjoy a smug superiority when it comes to their neighbours to the south. Even as Canadians flock across the border to shop in American stores or tan on American beaches, they reserve the right to correct their neighbours on their many failings. Wrote American Nora Jacobs, a medical sociologist living in Toronto: "In 'officially multicultural Canada' hostility to Americans is the last acceptable expression of bigotry or xenophobia. It would impossible to say the things about other nationalities that Canadians routinely say—both publicly and privately—about Americans."

Nurtured by centuries of menace over being swallowed by the United States (Trudeau compared it to a mouse sleeping with an elephant), this paranoia allows Canadians—with clear conscience—to trumpet a superior socialized medicine system even as they took a free ride on America's defence machine. (There would be scarce funds for Tommy Douglas' dream were Canada to provide and pay for real defence of its realm.) That sense of superiority has been abetted in recent years by the American provocateur Moore, whose films trash the U.S. on guns or medicine by contrasting it with trumped-up Canadian examples of kinder, gentler capitalism.

Whether it is Toronto mayor David Miller blaming the mean streets of America for his city's gun culture or NDP leader Jack Layton assailing the Conservative government for being in lockstep with the George Bush administration's "War" policies, playing the American card remains a staple of the Canadian condition. Paul Martin gave a bravura performance at the 2005 Kyoto conference held in Montreal. Canada was a signatory to the pact, the

Americans were not. Adopting an arch tone, Martin lectured the Americans on lacking "a global conscience" when it came to trimming greenhouse gas emissions. But the inconvenient facts were that, even as Martin tut-tutted U.S. officials, America's emissions had risen just 13 per cent since 1990 while Canada's own contributions to the atmosphere had spiked by 24 per cent. Being the stern contrarian works, as Jean Chrétien once casually remarked. "I make it my policy. It's popular."

Others have noted how "Blame America" has crept into hockey. While the Howie Meekers blame American commercial influences for coarsening their sport, the Buffalo, N.Y., writer Jim Kelley, who has covered the NHL for over a quarter century, saw the Bertuzzi episode as "in very large part, a Canadian thing:

> Look at the record. The list is seemingly endless, and Bertuzzi, a "good Canadian boy from Sudbury, Ontario" is only the most recent Canadian native to rise to the top of a rather lengthy list of infamous characters. There is of course Marty McSorley, lauded for serving as Wayne Gretzky's personal bodyguard, who committed the last unforgivable "stand alone" cheap shot four years ago when he whacked Donald Brashear across the side of the head—from behind—in the very same arena where Bertuzzi incapacitated Moore. It was Dale Hunter who separated Pierre Turgeon's shoulder with a hit from behind in 1993 and received a twenty-one-game suspension—the longest ever at the time— from new commissioner Gary Bettman.
>
> The list goes on and on and, for the most part, it's been a good ol' Canadian boys who have headed the cheap-shot parade. America has its share of dirty players, and certainly there are noteworthy Europeans who could be accused of the same, but clearly there is a trend here. Canadians and, I suspect, the NHL

itself will rail in protest at the charge, but not all of them. When you look at the numbers, you have to at least ask if there's some merit to the charge.

Well, let's look at the numbers: the NHL's top five leaders in career penalty minutes—Tiger Williams, Dale Hunter, Marty McSorley, Bob Probert, and Tie Domi—are all products of the Canadian system. Some will argue that Canadians have always comprised a higher percentage of NHL players (52.1 per cent in 2003–04, down from 66.2 per cent in 1992–93), but Kelley points out that "a significant number of other countries have been contributing an ever-growing number of players to the league and the vast majority of them simply don't play the game that way. After all, how do you explain that? The reason is simple: It's not in their culture."

If it's true that only your best friends will tell you the truth, then Kelley's analysis hit the mark. The schism in Canada's hockey's culture provoked an angry exchange between two figures who illustrate the parallel universes existing within the sport and its followers. "Hockey has always been dead-square, mainstream Canadiana," wrote Ken Dryden in *The Globe and Mail* just prior to his decision to leave the Maple Leafs to enter politics with the Liberal party.

> But hockey is at risk today of becoming an extreme sport, with excitement and danger, thrills and spills, but without the same emotional, in-the-bone connection. Something to watch, not something to do yourself. Something to be amazed about, not something to identify with. Something other, not something me.

Fired back Brian Burke, the American GM of Anaheim, who's a keeper of the Code's flame:

Ken tends to deliver lectures instead of answering questions. He likes to make bold statements. He prides himself as a spokesman for the game. Ken is entitled to his opinion but in no way, not even a little, do I agree with him.

As the exchange shows, anyone questioning intimidation and fighting is interpreted as attacking the Canadian way or the character of the players who made the sport. So when the supremacy of the NHL's retributive style of play was in doubt against disciplined Soviets (who did not fight), it was vital that Canadian values be seen at risk. Clarke's slash on Kharlamov preserved our culture.

And preserved a world view that is increasingly bunkered. Even as the globalized world moves further away from Canada's '70s-styled economy, the nation's government and business leaders still use investment-review agencies, supply-management policies, protectionist legislation, and all manner of industrial subsidies to ward off an American "threat" that harkens back to the failed fight against free trade in 1988. This denial of the forces outside our borders continues to resonate with economic nationalists who are, in the words of author Andrea Mandel-Campbell in her book *Why Mexicans Don't Drink Molson*, sending Canada to the "suds of global obscurity." Consider the title of the book by David Orchard, who ran for the leadership of the Conservative Party in 2004: *The Fight for Canada: Four Centuries of Resistance to American Expansionism*. "They are parochial Canadians," writes Jeffery Simpson of *The Globe and Mail* about the country's not-so-free traders, "who, like so many of their fellow citizens, seem to think that just being Canadian will be enough to impress the world."

Hello, Starbucks; goodbye Columbus.

But when challenged by real American influence in the sport

of hockey, that bold sense of self-determination melted like play-off ice in June. For years, all Canadian clubs except Toronto were dependent on the kindness of the U.S. teams as they paid most of their expenses using a 63-cent dollar. After losing Quebec and Winnipeg in 1997, Canadian assistance plans were used to keep the six remaining franchises alive. But the renewed power of a Canadian dollar at par is now in stark contrast to reduced influence of Canadian owners in the NHL. Despite providing more than a third of NHL revenues from only 20 per cent of the cities, Canadians have virtually disappeared from the key posts in the NHL hierarchy since the lockout ended in 2005. Loyalists to American commissioner Gary Bettman—such as Boston owner Jeremy Jacobs or Dallas owner Tom Hicks—now control the Board of Governors while no Canadian team representatives are on the key audit committee of the NHL. When RIM co-founder Jim Balsillie, based in Kitchener-Waterloo, Ontario, twice sought to buy floundering American franchises in 2006–07 with the goal of placing them in southern Ontario, he was not only rebuffed by Bettman but received no support from the six extant franchises north of the border. (Wayne Gretzky, God bless him, said he thought southern Ontario would be a great asset as a franchise.) Balsillie then asked when someone would stand up for Canadian interests in the NHL, the league employing so many Canadian players and floating on the loonie of late. The silence was deafening. Better to snipe from cover about American influence on fighting than take on the tougher question of who is paying the bills in a business faltering in its American branch plants.

The pushme-pullyou of Canadian hockey identity is why, more than a quarter century after the exhilaration of that final 1972 game in Moscow, Canada still hasn't come to grips with the drunken frat-boy behaviour of Team Canada '72. (Paul Henderson, a notable exception, now regards some of his teammate's undisciplined actions on the ice to have dimmed the lustre of the win.) We still see hockey as a passion play where questioning the tactics is akin to disloyalty. Team Canada director Wayne Gretzky upheld that Canadian value at the 2002 Olympics, when he pouted that everyone in hockey hates Canada. "It makes me ill to hear what's being said about Canadian hockey," Gretzky told the media after tying the Czechs 1–1.

> The whole world wants us to lose, except for Canada and Canadian fans. I don't think we dislike those other countries as much as they hate us. They don't like us, they want to see us fail; they love beating us. They may tell you something different, but when you're on the ice, that's what they say ... I'm tired of people taking shots at Canadian hockey. When the Europeans [play rough], it's OK. If we do something like that, we're hooligans.

Will Canada stop blaming Americans for everything that's wrong in hockey (and elsewhere) and accept that it's the Canadian thirst for violence—not the American—that drives the sport further from the mainstream of pro sports each week? Frankly, the attitude that Canadians are like art connoisseurs while watching hockey and that Americans are like ravenous dogs on a bone is condescending and out-of-touch. Edmonton playwright Ken Brown captured the huffy Canadian tone in a 1998 article for the *Edmonton Sun*.

"Unlike Americans," he wrote, "Canadians don't go to the game to see a fight break out. We understand it on a deeper level."

This *noblesse oblige* tone about the Yankees spoiling Canada's game moved American authors Jeff Z. Klein and Karl Reif to snort that:

> ... the traditional Canadian line about hockey fighting is just so
> much malarkey, a fable Canadians tell themselves so they won't
> have to face the fact that they are responsible for making hockey
> the world's only team sport (besides lacrosse) in which fighting
> does not result in immediate expulsion.

There might be much wrong with what the Gary Bettmans have done to the business (see: the flaming puck). Some Americans may have lapped up the Philly Flyers stuff. There are more American owners than Canadian owners in the NHL (Yanks currently own a Canadian franchise in Montreal). But the Code and all its attendant idiocy was dreamt up, developed, patented and then exported to the world by Canadians. Anyone who watched the crowds at a Montreal–Quebec or Edmonton–Calgary game in the '80s and then professes that it's American fans who demand fighting is patently lying. The bloodletting and revenge plot lines are as Canadian as the beer the players drink after the game. Okay, after the sales of Molson and Labatt maybe that's not such a good simile anymore. As Canadian as the bacon in a BLT. That's better. There's nothing comparable to our lust for Fight Club in other team sports.

As Jim Kelley pointed out, it takes a unique mindset to decide that you get three, count 'em, three fights in a single game before you're tossed out. Think of that. If you can physically stand the exertion, you get to fill your boots three times. That's one hell of a safety valve.

> America has much for which it has to answer to the world.
> George Bush. Michael Moore. Britney Spears. But the concept
> that it has fostered the Bertuzzi-style violence is delusional.
> American hockey doesn't allow fighting.

It chews up far fewer of its young people under the guise of development leagues like the Canadian Hockey League. It has traditionally a higher educational component than does Canadian hockey (although the CHL is trying to boost education through its scholarship program). In that respect, we have a lot to learn from, not to teach, the Americans.

And Americans perhaps have something to teach Canadians. Michael Claydon is a TV executive who also coaches AAA midget minor hockey in Toronto. His team travelled to Michigan for a tournament in 2004. Up against one of the top teams from the region, Claydon noticed how ferociously the American players hit his team with checks.

"We never faced such treatment at home," he notes. "They were relentless and hit hard. But a funny thing, the second the action was over and the whistle blew, they skated back to their bench. No pushing, no shoving after the whistle like Canadian kids. That's how they'd been taught to play. And so that's how they played." And that's how it's played in much of the American system. "In the Olympics and in college, if you fight, they throw you out of that game and the next game, so you don't fight," said Mike Eruzione, hero of the U.S. gold medal team in 1980. "The rules dictate you can't, so you don't. It's that simple. You become disciplined to turn the other cheek or get a good, solid, legal hit in later in the game."

That same discipline is also taught in football or rugby, games where players hammer each other all afternoon. Coaches in those sports instruct their players that the man who loses his temper loses his focus and thus loses the game. While players in both sports occasionally resort to throwing a punch, it is quickly discouraged by ejection for the player and severe punishment for the club. While coaches in other sports (deprived of the fighting card) must develop motivational techniques for getting players to play with emotion, the hockey coach has always been able to send a willing body over the boards to start a fight or intimidate an opponent and raise the temperature of his dressing room.

And there has never been a shortage of willing Canadian boys, short on skill, long on desire, to play a role described forty years ago by Toronto's GM/coach Punch Imlach:

> A coach has a chance to see a little deeper right into the soul of the game. And what I see at the heart of the game is a tough man who never backs up. You have to have enough of them on every team to give that team its aggressive character.

John Kordic became part of that cost of business. The former altar boy had never fought in a hockey game before joining the Portland Winter Hawks of the WHL in 1982. He and another future NHL star, Cam Neely, arrived in the Portland training camp, full of trepidation about life in major junior hockey. Kordic still saw himself as a skill player like his hero Darryl Sittler, bent on filling the net. But he and Neely sought out third-year defenceman Kelly Hubbard for a primer on what to expect. "We were wondering if there are a lot of on-ice fights?" Kordic asked Hubbard in Mark Zwolinski's *The John Kordic Story*. With that, Hubbard took the two young men in hand, literally, for some coaching on the art of throwing punches in hockey. Hubbard quickly noted that Kordic was a lefty. "That'll screw with a few guys' heads," he said approvingly. "Cause just about everybody throws with their right. So most guys look for that. They line up looking for it, they know they have to tie up your right hand so they can throw." Hubbard coached Kordic and Neely about tying up an opponent, throwing him off-balance and delivering a beating. "Now we separate the men from the boys," said Hubbard in a time-worn phrase.

By the opening game of the Portland season, Kordic was ready to rumble, getting into a savage fight in the second period—a fight he won decisively. Back in the dressing room after being tossed from the game, Kordic sat in trepidation, worried about how his rookie performance will be viewed by the team's management. He swallowed hard as the door banged open and Coach Ken Hodge and GM Brian Shaw entered the room. But instead of criticism, the two veteran executives of junior hockey were beaming, pleased beyond words that they had discovered a heavyweight fighter in their midst. They pounded Kordic on the back and shook his swollen hand. It was the same in the lobby of the arena as appreciative fans and available young women sidled up to the young Albertan. He'd made it in hockey through his fists.

Propelled by the cheers that night, Kordic went on to become one of the NHL's wildest brawlers in an era of unparalleled savagery on the ice. In 1988, he and Nordiques goon Gord Donnelly played up their status with a series of boxing-type posters, showing the two heavily muscled players, naked to the waist, standing back to back. In their first game after the release of the poster, Kordic and Donnelly dropped the gloves at the opening faceoff; in their next game they didn't even wait for the game to start before throwing the haymakers. (The pair was suspended for five games each; tellingly, their coaches who'd matched them on the opening lineup, were only fined.)

Kordic's behaviour was a product of more than simple coaching; there was also the tacit stimulus of drugs that allowed him to hang onto his piece of the Canadian hockey dream. Until it adopted a basic drug policy in 2005, the NHL's official stance on drugs was, "We were fortunate we hadn't been infected like basketball or baseball," according to NHL president John Ziegler. NHL Players' Association directors Alan Eagleson and later Bob Goodenow were also in no mood to blacken the reputations of their members, so they either ignored the threat posed by drugs or used it as a chip in collective bargaining. So, outside of players competing in international events, there was no record of any player positive testing for steroids, HGH (human growth hormone), or stimulants in this era.

But the example of Kordic, who died of an apparent drug overdose in 1992, gives a window into the use of performance enhancing drugs in this period. Kordic assembled a staggering 997 PIMS in just 244 NHL contests as he brawled his way through five NHL organizations. His own body ballooned in concert with his penalty statistics, till he was a chiseled, massive product of the weight room. But the personal toll for the former Edmonton altar boy was tallied in addictions to alcohol, drugs, and steroids. When he checked into a rehab centre in Tucson, Arizona, Kordic admitted to counsellors that he'd taken steroids in each of the previous three summers. He admitted to friends that he had had to take them to keep ahead of young challengers to his heavyweight title—men supposedly pumped up by steroids themselves. (Punch Imlach lamented the process by which players start to question their role: "I know one player who got into a fight one night in the penalty box, and he got told off by his wife for being a barroom brawler. He lost an awful lot of aggression from that one incident.")

He also told fellow players that he was getting his steroids through NHL teams—a charge that was never proven. Certainly his violent mood swings and rages bore the telltale indicators of steroid abuse. It defies credibility that Kordic was the only one using steroids to buff his fighter's physique or suffering the brutal tempers brought on by his drugs. (Tough guy Andrei Nazarov—

who played for seven different NHL clubs—reportedly said that drug use is "rampant" among NHLers, and that 99 per cent of enforcers are using some form of chemical assistance.) Yet, until Kordic's last days he was still being courted by NHL teams for his services, safe in the knowledge that, within hockey at least, he performed a marketable skill—one that could be blamed on Americans if necessary.

Anti-Americanism is an easy virtue in Canadian politics and culture these days, a smug way of pretending we're above all that. In hockey, U.S.-bashing has become a similar straw man whenever something goes wrong with the game. Too many teams, not enough fans. Too many playoff teams, not enough skill players. Damn Yankees. Instead of addressing the problems brought on by Bertuzzi, Canadians lament the American commercial influence on their game. Blame the TV money. Point fingers at the U.S. domination of the NHL's head office. Look everywhere but within.

There was a time when Wayne Gretzky looked as though he'd redeem Canadian hockey. "Did anybody do more for his sport than Gretzky did for hockey?" wrote his friend Rick Reilly in *Sports Illustrated* upon Number 99's retirement in 1999. "He snatched it from the bullies. He showed how ugly violence could be when set next to grace. He gave the game an imagination, passing off nets and skates and Gatorade bottles."

In 1994, Gretzky, still a player, was widely quoted as saying hockey had to get rid of fighting, that it was hurting the growth of the sport and was superfluous to winning. But ten years later, Gretzky the part-owner of the Phoenix Coyotes, appeared to have forgotten his convictions from a decade earlier. "I don't know what the NHL's going to do," he said plaintively in the wake of the Bertuzzi attack. If Gretzky, arguably the greatest Canadian of all time, goes silent, what chance is there for change?

CHAPTER EIGHT

Toronto *Uber Alles*

TORONTO—Once more, the world is focused on Canada's largest city, as Toronto has again given itself the title of Miss Centre of the Universe. For the twelfth consecutive year, the pretentious, narcissistic Canadian city declared itself the winner, beating out other self-serving cities such as Paris, Milan, and Rome.

"We just knew we were going to win," said Toronto, not even pretending to be surprised. "We were confident, almost to the point of arrogance. And it's great to be recognized for this achievement, but we know we got what we deserved." With this self-gratifying award, Toronto continues to portray itself as being the "only town that matters."

"We just knew that the best city won," said Toronto, amidst a large crowd of admiring Torontonians. "But really, it's the people of Toronto that make me as big as I am. Go Leafs!" In the event that Toronto cannot fulfill its aloofish duties, the first runner-up, Prague, will assume the title.

—The Touque

F or a Montreal Canadiens franchise that has seen more than
its share of dramatic moments, the ceremony marking the
retirement of Bernie "Boom Boom" Geoffrion's Number 5
jersey packed an emotional wallop. Geoffrion, the second man to
score fifty goals in a single season, a Hall of Famer who is widely
credited with developing the slapshot, was honoured by the Montreal franchise on March 11, 2006. The Number 5 *bleu-blanc-rouge*
jersey he wore from 1950 to 1964 was hoisted to the rafters to join
the great Habs of the past—including his father-in-law Howie
Morenz.

But Geoffrion was not at the Bell Centre that night with his
wife Marlene, his children, and grandchildren. On March 8,
Geoffrion had been diagnosed with stomach cancer. Despite his
debilitating illness, he vowed to make the trip to Montreal to see
his historic night. But when the pain would not let him travel,
Geoffrion insisted that his family go without him to see the day
through. Reluctantly they agreed. On the same day he was scheduled to be honoured in his hometown for his 393 career goals and
five Stanley Cups, Boom Boom died at the age of seventy-five in
Atlanta, Georgia—exactly sixty-nine years to the day after Morenz's
funeral at the Montreal Forum. In recognition of the special link
between the Morenz and Geoffrion families, the two numbers
were raised side by side (Morenz's banner was lowered halfway
and was raised back up to the rafters with Geoffrion's banner).

To add to the many coincidences of that day, the two numbers
on the banners of Morenz (7) and Geoffrion (5) formed the number 75, the age at which Geoffrion died. Dick Irvin, the broadcaster
and son of legendary coach Dick Irvin Sr., had seen many special

nights in his almost sixty years of watching Canadiens hockey. But seeing the weeping Geoffrion and Morenz families send Bernie's number to the roof of the Bell Centre—amidst an ovation from the 21,000 in the house—qualified as perhaps the most emotional scene Irvin had witnessed in his adopted hometown of Montreal. The moving scene captivated the province of Quebec—or those in the French-speaking audience.

Despite Geoffrion's historic career as a player and coach, very few in the rest of Canada saw the ceremony live, however. CBC's *Hockey Night in Canada* had instead chosen to broadcast the Toronto–Tampa Bay game to the national TV audience. The riveting ceremony in Montreal was given a brief mention in the pre-game show and a three-minute taped package at the first intermission. "CBC did the bare minimum in covering Bernie Geoffrion's banner-raising ceremony in Montreal," wrote Sam Mc-Caig in *The Hockey News* website. "This, despite the fact it was a long-overdue tribute to a Habs legend who had passed away earlier that morning. Geoffrion's family was on hand for the emotional forty-minute ceremony, and that (English) CBC all but ignored the event was an egregious error."

But what sent critics truly ballistic was that two Saturdays before, *Hockey Night*—the crucible of Canadian hockey—had dedicated its full half-hour pre-game show to ceremonies at the Air Canada Centre marking the 1,000th NHL game for Toronto tough guy Tie Domi. He of 104 career goals and 3,515 lifetime penalty minutes. The bile spilled from outside Toronto.

"Consider the ridiculous splash that rock-head Leafs player Tie Domi got the week before at the Air Canada Centre after playing his 1,000th game," wrote Allan Panzeri of the Ottawa Citizen. "Not showing the teary tribute to Bernie (Boom Boom) Geoffrion at the Bell Centre before Saturday's New York Rangers-Canadiens

game makes the disgrace even more embarrassing." Of course, ratings numbers favoured the Corporation's decision to cover southern Ontario's favourite team over a Canadiens game. Nationally, a
Leaf telecast—even of a poor team—can win the Corp as much as
half a million more viewers on a typical night. But that did little to
placate irate Geoffrion fans who once again saw what they thought
was the blunt instrument of Torontocentric influence blot their
sport. Whether it's the choice of games on Saturday or the choice
of announcers for those games, the weekly showpiece of hockey is
more political than a month of Question Periods in Parliament.

CBC is hardly alone in bearing the brunt of regional disaffec-
tion. To hockey fans outside southern Ontario who swallow a
heaping dose of Maple Leafs' news on Toronto-based TSN (The
Sports Network), the channel is bitterly known as The Toronto
Sport Network, where news of captain Mats Sundin's hip woes
trumped coverage of the national debate over Shane Doan's captaincy of the 2007 Team Canada. Or where, on any given night,
Rogers *Sportsnet* and *The Score* are populated with talking heads
from the Toronto area discussing the latest Leafs minutiae.

But then what else is new? Despite Toronto's position as
beneficent economic generator to much of the nation for over a
century, hating Toronto is as central to the Canadian identity as
NHL hockey on a winter Saturday night. Or, at least, hating that
part of Toronto that allegedly defines Canada by what happens between the 427 and Don Valley Parkway, the 401, and the Gardiner
Expressway. The latest movie star to park his fanny in Toronto, the
vagaries of Hogtown traffic, the endless fascination with Toronto's
unique multicultural makeup, the current weather either too hot
or too cold, a fatuous new political face, and, of course, the ex-
ploits and anxieties of T.O.'s sports teams, especially the Maple
Leafs. All are relayed to a reluctant nation via media giants em-

bedded squarely in Toronto. On a given day it can be easier to find traffic reports from Toronto's clogged arteries than on the circulation in your own town. No wonder Ottawa-based columnist Roy MacGregor delightedly reported:

> . . . a poll that finds Canadians who live in Ottawa to be far happier than those who have to live in Toronto. This particular survey, conducted online by Decima during the bitter cold of February (2007), merely asked respondents how they saw themselves. Ottawans said they consider themselves "happy" above all else. In second place, they think of themselves as "honest."
>
> Torontonians, on the other hand, see themselves first and foremost as "hardworking". And then "ambitious"—with "happy" somewhere down the scale. In wonderfully Canadian terms, it is impossible to determine a winner here. After all, since it involves Canadians living in both cities, it might easily be argued that the people of Toronto were actually far happier coming in second than first. Such a wonderful country, this. So long as you're not at the top.

Yes, loathing for Toronto takes on many forms—political, business, sporting, cultural—but in the end, it can almost always be reduced to a formula not found in the British North America Act: Tie Domi's 1,000th game in Toronto gets blanket coverage while Boom Boom Geoffrion's memorial service in Montreal is swept under the rug. Filmmaker Albert Nerenberg, who created the mockumentary *Let's All Hate Toronto*, says the central dynamic always comes down to hockey. "They feel the Leafs, a chronically underperforming team, are always being foisted on them. It seems superficial, but it's a metaphor for a larger thing—that this mediocre city is force-feeding its culture to the rest of the country."

Canadian cities vie to see which loathes Toronto with a more burning intensity. Montrealers have the benefit of seniority, having resented Toronto to their very atoms for the hundreds of years since Toronto was drained from the swamps of Muddy York while Montreal was already a thriving concern. Montreal's haughty attitude toward upstart Toronto can be summed up in the immortal "nice place to live but I wouldn't want to visit there." On the premise that everything in Canada comes back to hockey, Montreal feels a primacy based on its twenty-three Stanley Cups compared to Toronto's twelve (none in the past forty years)—a primacy that is not reflected in the airtime devoted to the Habs.

Montrealers also point out that Toronto copies everything they do. When Montreal staged Man and His World after Expo 67, Toronto constructed Ontario Place. When Montreal got the baseball Expos, Toronto later acquired the Blue Jays. When Montreal built Place Ville Marie, the tallest structure till then in Canada, Toronto came back with the TD Centre and later the CN Tower. Exacerbating Montreal's animus is the fact that most of the 200,000 Anglos and the corporate offices that fled Quebec's cultural revolution starting in the 1970s wound up in the Toronto region. Before the end of the twentieth century, seventy of Canada's two hundred biggest corporations were based in Toronto; fewer than half that number have made Montreal their home since Charles de Gaulle endorsed the liberation of Quebec in 1967.

You can hear the Hogtown resentment in the voice of Montreal-based author Neil Bissoondath, who related in the essay "Are we a nation of too many identities?" the impressions of Canadian cities from a West Indian man in London, England. "He had been impressed with Montreal," Bissoondah writes, "where he had seen the kind of cultural blending and crossbreeding he loved in London, but had not thought much of Toronto where he sensed a kind of isolationism, with the various ethnic groups too jealous of their specificities to offer themselves to others, to open up, to influence and be influenced . . . the city struck him as parochial . . . Montreal, in his view, was evolving into something new and unpredictable, while Toronto had, to a great extent, failed to profit from its even greater human possibilities."

Ouch. Unless you include the greater financial possibilities, of course, in which case Toronto has profited greatly while Montreal has plummeted from great heights. Only in fashion points can Montreal hold its own in a commercial sense with its brothers down the 401. While Vancouver can't claim to have resented Toronto's self-importance quite as long as has Montreal (and is a net importer of Torontonians), it's fair to say that Lotusland's hate burns with the bluest flame of neglect. Put simply, Vancouver sees no room for its destiny in the eternal George-and-Martha squabble between the founding entities in Ontario and Quebec. Author Naomi Klein summed up the frustration of getting a seat in the debate: "Canadians may be enthusiastic about political correctness, but once the newspapers have dealt with their Toronto bias, once the television producers have balanced their panels with someone from each coast, once the conference organizers have fussed over simultaneous French-English translation, there is little 'correctness' left over for anyone else."

Hidden behind its curtain of mountains and squeezed in by the Strait of Juan de Fuca, Vancouver has developed a bifurcated political entity pitting "tree-huggers" versus "clear-cutters," a multicultural stew that is rarely if ever reflected in the images beamed west from Toronto. (The local joke is that the Japanese want to buy Vancouver but the Chinese aren't selling.) To spite Toronto's self-obsession, Vancouver has developed itself into a convincing body double for American cities in U.S. films on the premise it's the only way Toronto will see them.

Whether it's the tyranny of those dismissive Pacific Time Zone references on *The National* or the temperate climate that sets it apart from the rest of the frozen country, Van city feels Toronto gives it no respect. Even winning the right to stage the 2010 Winter Olympics (after Toronto failed twice to lure the Summer Games) has not assuaged the feeling of the locals that they are somehow lacking in the trappings of a great metropolis compared to Hogtown.

But in Vancouver, as everywhere, the grievance can best be summed up in hockey terms. The concerted attempts of the Maple Leafs' owners to keep Vancouver out of the NHL for decades nurtured resentment on a monster scale on Granville and Robson. Even now, with the Canucks in the NHL for almost forty years (and in the Cup finals twice the past twenty years versus nada for the Leafs), Vancouverites chafe at the broadcast crews sent to cover their team, the starting times dictated by Eastern broadcasters, and amount of time dedicated to the Canucks on *Coach's Corner*. While the Canucks boasted superstars such as Pavel Bure, Mark Messier, and (now) Roberto Luongo, this rarely seemed to make a dent in the Wendel Clark/Doug Gilmour/Mats Sundin fascination delivered them from Toronto.

Even when CBC delivered the Canucks to their regional audience, it pissed off some of the locals. In 1970, the Maple Leafs employed Brian "Spinner" Spencer, native of Fort St. John, B.C., as their agitator. Spencer's number one fan was his father, Roy, who based his game-day schedule around his son's—eating at the same time as his son thousands of miles away, napping at the same time etc. On Saturday, March 14, Brian told his family he'd be interviewed during the intermission on *Hockey Night in Canada*. Roy

Spencer sat down to watch his son play on television—only to find that the Vancouver, not the Toronto, game was being broadcast in the Fort St. John area. Clearly unhinged, he grabbed his rifle and headed to the CBC transmitter to demand that the CBC switch over to his son's game and away from the Canucks contest. Tempers flared at the location, the RCMP was called, and, in a tragic show-down, Roy Spencer was shot and killed by the Mounties.

There have been less dramatic complaints about the starting times of Canucks games since that fateful day but none, appar-ently, about substituting Vancouver for the Leafs. If there is a just god for Vancouverites, he or she will deliver them a Stanley Cup before Toronto can luck into one.

The energy capital of Calgary, meanwhile, bridles at Toronto for a collection of indignities involving 1930s bankers, 1960s Trudeaupians, and 1980s National Energy schemes. With Quebec a perpetual recipient under the federal equalization scheme— spending $1500 per capita more than any other province on serv-ices such as $7 daycare, half-priced tuition, and a massive civil service—Albertans have complained that their oil wealth is being used by Toronto to bribe Quebec to stay in the federation. For that reason, Alberta has often mused about the idea of adopting the same separation strategy as Quebec in an effort to win back its money and influence in the federation.

The jealousies and resentments of how the Toronto Liberal establishment indulges the Quebec faction was a particular spur in launching the Reform Party movement in the 1980s. Preston Manning sought to restore fiscal conservatism and unintrusive government when he broke from the Progressive Conservatives. All of which is an anathema to the big-government proponents back east. Even when Conservatives elected Brian Mulroney in 1984 and Stephen Harper in 2005, cynical Calgarians noted that

petro dollars flowed to guarantee the election of professional political fixers on Bay Street, banker bogeys, and media managers of
the press barons. Former Ontario premier and Liberal Party candidate Bob Rae says Alberta's resentment is simply bucking history in Canada.

"Those who argue that Canada is made up of ten provinces
that must be treated exactly the same—a cookie-cutter approach
to equality—are arguing in defiance of Canadian history. Such an
approach might fit one person's theory of federalism, but we have
seen the dangers of governing in the name of a theory, whether it
is Lord Durham's, Pierre Trudeau's or Preston Manning's."

Needless to say, such views of federalism go over like a lead
balloon in Canada's energy capital, where asymmetrical federalism is about as popular as inquiries into the price of gas at the
pumps.

And then there's the hockey history between Toronto and the
cities that most covet its commercial ambitions. While it blisters
beneath the yoke of the federal dance of equal-but-not-equal,
Calgary hasn't recovered from another pillaging of the West: the
1993 deal that sent Doug Gilmour to Toronto for a bag of dried figs
and a roll of used electrical tape. Adding to the shame of the lopsided exchange was the fact that it was engineered on behalf of
the Maple Leafs by the Flames' former general manager Cliff
Fletcher. *Sic semper tyrannus.* The trade sped up a decade-long
descent into hockey mediocrity for the city in the Foothills. And
when the Flames finally flickered back to life with their Stanley
Cup final appearance in 2004, there was the snub from Don
Cherry during the Western final when he chose to talk Maple Leafs
over the hometown story. Editorialists raged, phone callers
protested, and Cherry merely shrugged.

"That's the inferiority complex they have in the West that the

East is always picking on them," Cherry told the *National Post*. "You think the people in Toronto care about Calgary? I have a tough time, myself, to tell you the truth. I love [the Flames]; they're lunch pail guys like my old Boston Bruins. They're a good, hard-working team and the people of Calgary should be proud of them. But it could never be like Toronto." To top the performance, Cherry the told the Flames' mascot Harvey the Hound to get lost when the man in the dog suit began upstaging the man in the horse-blanket suit.

Ottawa is perhaps the most visceral of the complainants, squeezed into the same province and time zone with the Maple Leafs. While francophone Montreal can easily be sloughed off to Radio Canada or RDS, there is simply no room for the Senators when they are scheduled opposite the Leafs. Referring to the four Stanley Cups won by the Senators before that unfortunate fifty-eight-year NHL hiatus, Ottawa has long believed that it has a pedigree that demands more respect. And if the second-class status on the TV schedule were not enough, there is the blue-and-white bias of the broadcast crew to inflame the Sens' faithful.

After Cherry made his Leaf allegiances crystal clear during a Toronto-Ottawa playoff series in 2003, an Ottawa city committee passed a resolution banning the wearing of Leafs jerseys in the Ottawa Senators home rink when Toronto played the Senators on April 3, 2004. The ban, while not official, required fans who insisted on wearing Leafs jerseys and paraphernalia to any 2004 playoff games to make a donation to the Ottawa Food Bank. "We want the Maple Leaf fans in the Corel Centre to realize the city is behind the Senators," said then-Ottawa mayor Bob Chiarelli. "Hopefully, they can take a joke better than Don Cherry or [Leafs coach] Pat Quinn."

The nation's capital experienced some measure of revenge when the Senators made the 2007 Stanley Cup final series against

Anaheim. That brought the national media to the national capital to take the temperature of the Sens (forgetting briefly that Ottawa's owner Eugene Melnyk is a Torontonian). But even that magic moment was sullied by the fact that Sens fell short of the Cup and that they didn't get to the final at the expense of the Maple Leafs in a playoff series (Toronto missed the postseason on the campaign's final day).

Canadians might be better disposed to Toronto's superior self image, but unfortunately there are the Maple Leafs as the symbol of all things Hogtown. As symbols go, the Leafs lack for something. Forty-plus years now since they won the Cup, Toronto's beloved team has not been even reasonably close to a repeat win since that cranky old crew of old-timers won in Centennial Year. There have been two Toronto teams that made the semifinal round—1978, 1993—but the rest of the time has been a parade of abject misery. Since that fateful year of 1967, Montreal has won ten Cups, Edmonton five, Calgary one (in three final series) and Vancouver has played in two final series. Ottawa, created in 1992, was about the only team Toronto could beat in the postseason in the past four decades, and then the Sens zoomed off to their own final in 2007.

The traditional grudges against Toronto are like a grey suit, portable for all occasions. Even as the numbers cease to add up to the old economic hegemony (according to author Andrew Coyne, "for 2007–08, Newfoundland's per capita revenues, equalization included, total $7,094, to Ontario's $6,631.") the bile still flows down Bay Street right to the doors of the Air Canada Centre. The list of grievances doesn't mean that hate blinds when it suits the rest of Canada to have Toronto on side for, say a few extra dates at their rinks in the West. So when the NHL changed its schedule to an unbalanced one in 2006—meaning Toronto would visit its three western Canadian cousins just once every three years—the

Oilers, Flames, and Canucks were suddenly in common cause with dreaded Toronto.

But when the eastern teams proved less than enthusiastic about changing the schedule to accommodate their western brothers, all hell broke loose. Edmonton's president Cal Nichols nearly had a cow over the tepid support his club had received in getting the eastern teams to play the Rexall Centre on a yearly basis.

Which met with little sympathy from one of Toronto's major sports columnists.

"Where western Canada teams really load up on the propaganda is when it comes to their interest in getting the Maple Leafs to town," noted *Toronto Star* columnist Damien Cox:

> On a 24/7 basis, you never hear the end of complaining from west of Kenora about how *Hockey Night In Canada* favours the Leafs (true), about how snooty old Toronto considers itself the Centre of the Universe and what a joke the Leafs are for failing to win a Stanley Cup for four decades. But for the good of the game, of course, the Leafs should appear in Alberta and British Columbia at least once a year. Patriotism and history and Pierre Berton and all that. Hogtown-wash. It's for the good of the coffers of those teams, period. As long as Toronto exists as the focal point of resentment, it's difficult for the disparate groups in (particularly) the English speaking elements of the country to get on with the business of finding what—outside hockey—binds them.

And that which binds Canadians—besides Leaf loathing—is not the blue-and-white of the hockey team, but the gold of the loonie. Not that this cuts any *fromage* with premiers in the rest of Canada, wrote Lorne Gunter in June of 2007 in the *National Post*:

Put simply, by 2008 or 2009, it is very likely Ontario will have ceased to be a "have" province in any meaningful sense. Meanwhile, Newfoundland and Nova Scotia, with their burgeoning oil and gas revenues, will have ceased to be "have-nots." Yet because of the perverse rules (and politics) surrounding federal-provincial funding in Canada, Ontarians will still be sending huge chunks of their incomes to Ottawa each year so the federal government can continue to pour rich equalization payments into Atlantic coffers.

And so we have the spectacle of premiers in Nova Scotia, Newfoundland, Saskatchewan, and anyone else with political points to score rounding on the federal government and its ally in Ontario about equalizing the pie of equalization.

All true, of course, but not likely to change minds about the bias of Toronto. And heaven forbid that the Maple Leafs ever summon the will to make an appearance in the finals—or even win the Stanley Cup. It will make a Danny Williams' rant look positively mild by comparison.

CHAPTER NINE

White Collar Black Magic

"I remember meeting a fellow in New York. He said, 'Bill, what's your area code?' I said '604.' He said, 'Oh, that's one of the area codes that I don't answer.'"
—Bill Majcher, former head of the Integrated Market Enforcement Team, in the *Toronto Star*, December 2007

When it comes to justice in Canada, the goalposts have a habit of moving. For instance, should some perp make an enforced withdrawal of $750 from a Mac's Milk store, Canadians would no doubt clap him in irons and throw away the key. Maybe spend a couple of billion on a handgun registry to stem gun crime, too. But should a nattily attired business thingy walk through the same door and rob the same store of the same $750 using a pen ... well, Canadians apparently draw a very different conclusion. In our cold-hearted neighbour to the south, they'd go all Dennis Kozlowski on the suit for embezzlement, extortion, fraud, the whole enchilada. He'd disappear into the federal prison system for a lifetime or two.

But we in Canada are made of more compassionate stuff—at least when it comes to suspects who sport the white collar.

Character references are cited, charitable work duly noted, and the perp usually gets off with a mild rebuke or—at worst—a few months in jail. We might even give him a national TV show on CBC just to placate any hard feelings and help pay the lawyer's bill.

A TV show? Exagerration, no? For your consideration...Garth Drabinsky, theatrical impresario, Broadway mogul, and all that jazz. Drabinsky and his Livent Corporation put Canada on the theatrical map in the 1990s with hit shows such as *Ragtime* and *Phantom of the Opera*. He was celebrated in the United States—which is to say he was legitimized in Canadian eyes. Along the way he and his partner Myron Gottlieb reportedly developed some curious ways of doing the books. Max Bialystock would have been proud to see how Garth and his friends, ahem, allegedly moved around zeroes as Livent went bankrupt.

While Max might have cooed, the American justice system took a dimmer view of Drabinsky's ciphering. They charged the mogul and partner Gottlieb with fraud for stiffing Livent investors of $125 million. (Those investors later won a $23.2 million judgement against Drabinsky and Co., which is still being appealed.) At the same time the Securities and Exchange Commission sued Drabinsky, Gottlieb, and six other former Livent executives for an alleged "multi-faceted accounting fraud spanning eight years." Owing to pressing business back in Canada, Drabinsky has, regrettably, been unable to travel to the New York courtroom where he was expected to answer those fraud charges, since 1999. The U.S. Justice system declared Drabinsky a fugitive from justice, and Canada's legal system of endless appeals and obfuscations swept in like a sheet of Arctic ice, slowing the process to a near standstill.

While the pair was charged in Canada in 2002, it took nine years after the Americans decided to act for Drabinsky and Gottlieb to make a curtain call in Canadian court facing fraud charges. The

Crown is alleging they raised $500 million for their company while covering up massive losses. Members of Livent staff were expected to say that Drabinsky ordered accounting staff to produce results where expenses were erased, balance sheets were altered to change losses to profits, and phoney invoices were prepared—all to fool investors about the health of the business.

None of which seems to have troubled the consciences of CBC executives or a host of theatrical luminaries who helped Drabinsky produce and star in a 2007 TV program entitled *Triple Sensation*—which apparently refers to Garth's performing skills on stage as opposed to his performing skills on the bottom line. "It's not a theatre event, it's a TV event," said Drabinsky of the show. As part of the promotion of the show, Drabinsky was also invited to visit theatre programs at several Canadian universities to counsel young thespians on . . . one hopes it wasn't accounting. Which begs the question: had Drabinsky robbed Broadway theatre-goers with a gun as opposed to a pen would the rapturous tone of his new show have been sustained very long? But Canadian critics and the performers enriched by Drabinsky in bygone days apparently glossed over this nagging detail. CBC's presumption of innocence clearly trumps the feelings of those viewers whose savings might have been mislaid in the Livent meltdown.

But why shouldn't Drabinsky bathe in the warmth of Canuck compassion? In his attempt to stay on the lam *chez nous* he is simply following in the noble Canadian tradition of another well-known white-collar fugitive from American justice: hockey felon/executive Alan Eagleson. To complete the picture, Gottlieb and Drabinsky decided to employ Brian Greenspan—the same lawyer who'd helped The Eagle avoid the long arm of U.S. justice—and his brother Eddie as their respective counsels. A nice dramatic arc there.

For those without a program, Eagleson (who conveniently squirreled away his savings in Yankee greenbacks) perched in Canada for almost five years while dodging American justice on embezzlement, fraud, and racketeering charges related to his running of the NHL Players Association, Hockey Canada's international tournaments, and his own player agency. Even as evidence emerged in the U.S. of how he cheated clients, players, and taxpayers, Eagleson was celebrated back home as a great Canadian patriot by former prime minister John Turner, a role model by Supreme Court justice Willard Estey, and a lovable rogue by many in Canada's sporting press.

For a man who claimed to never back down, Eagleson certainly made himself scarce from New Jersey when U.S. Justice Department officials indicted him on thirty-two charges in 1993. Hearing his name attached to the lengthy complaint, the Eagle reneged on a surrender agreement, caught the next plane back to his Toronto nest and there waited as the wheels of Canadian justice ground inexorably to a halt on his extradition. With his cheering section of politicians, business executives, and media apologists drowning out the sorry tales of hockey heroes Eagleson had bilked, the great man happily passed the time reading his media sycophants who produced reams of stories on his unique contributions to the sport and nation ("Sure he might have his faults, but look what he did for The Game!").

Comforting Eagleson in his safe perch in Canada were the slow-motion attempts by Canadian justice officials to come to grips with Eagleson's quarter century of self-dealing and ripping off players of their pension money and disability insurance. While U.S. justice officials and the FBI had been on the case since 1991, the Mounties had gotten out of the blocks a little later (1993)— perhaps hobbled by the reluctance of Eagleson's political pals to bring their buddy to answer for his crimes. (American justice officials would later say they had never had less cooperation on a cross-border case than they did on the Eagleson file.) Likewise, the Law Society of Upper Canada needed five years to wrap itself around charges of professional misconduct launched against Eagleson by Edmonton lawyer/player agent Ritch Winter. All seemingly stalled by the very Canadian reluctance to treat a crooked lawyer like any other thief.

But all good things must come to an end, and so it was for Eagleson, when Canadian justice finally got up to speed in 1998. Faced at last with a two-pronged prosecution, Eagleson claimed financial impoverishment and pleaded out to both Canadian and American officials. Even then he got the soft landing by agreeing to guilty pleas in the two countries on the condition that he served his time in the powder-puff Canadian system. Instead of the five years he would have served in the United States prison system after pleading guilty to three counts (encompassing all thirty-two charges), the man who'd lined his own pockets from NHLPA, international and Hockey Canada duties instead received an eighteen-month sentence in Canada—which, under the calculus of Canadian justice, translated into a mere four months in prison.

Not that Eagleson's admission of guilt did much to change minds in many quarters—particularly in Toronto. His character references at sentencing from former PM Turner and publishing executive Paul Godfrey described a cross between Albert Schweitzer and Mother Teresa instead of a man who'd stolen players' disability insurance, secretly lent players' retirement funds to his business partners, or turtled in collective bargaining against the NHL. The man celebrated by Turner as guided by "faith, friends and family" and by Philadelphia GM Bobby Clarke as "a decent man" was in fact described as a liar by an Ontario judge and as a corrupt union official by U.S. judge Nathaniel Gorton. As his plaque was taken down in the Hockey Hall of Fame and he was disbarred, the poster boy for greed and misplaced hope was still given preferential treatment in Canada: The convicted felon was spared being handcuffed leaving court in Toronto as he would not have been had he been a break-and-enter specialist. No wonder ex-player Carl Brewer—who led the pursuit of his former agent— got up in the Boston court room and said: "Thank God for America, because this never would have happened in Canada," (Eagleson, who knew the fix was in, started laughing when Brewer spoke).

The apologists for Eagleson were hardly silenced in the years after Eagleson emerged from his four-month prison stay. As the Eagleson's crimes faded from the public eye, the sentiment emerged that perhaps the disgraced union pioneer was being piled upon. One Toronto radio host made the case in 2007 that "trying to erase his name and forgetting his contributions to hockey is in itself a crime." In the fogginess of such memory, Eagleson was suddenly credited with starting the players' pension plan (false), starting the world junior tournament (false), and getting reluctant players to agree to salary disclosure (false). Revisionists claimed that for all the millions they spent, the U.S. justice officials "only" got Eagleson on three counts of fraud—even though the three counts included all thirty-two of the original charges from 1993 save racketeering. Some suggested incoming NHLPA executive director Paul Kelly had cut a "soft" deal in 1998 on behalf of U.S. justice when Kelly was the assistant district attorney responsible for the Eagleson case. When the revisionists were done, you'd have thought Eagleson was jailed for jaywalking, not systematically abusing the players' trust and money for a quarter century.

It's hard to envision anyone in the United States making the same arguments to mitigate the impact of what Kenneth Lay did at Enron or what Dennis Kozlowski did at Tyco International. "Sure Ken Lay cheated investors of billions, but let's not obscure how he changed the natural-gas business." Or "Yeah, Dennis misappropriated $400 million in assets, but he threw a hell of a party." Yet in Canada, Eagleson's consistent attempts to embezzle over decades—while always publicly declaring that neither himself, nor his family or businesses had made a cent from international hockey—are minimized while his parasitic association with Team Canada's wins are the stuff of legend. But the reluctance to treat white-collar thieves as thieves is in keeping with Canada's sheepishness in dealing with crime in the boardroom.

When the tech wreck hit North America in 2000, there was a steady stream of American corporate executives such as Lay, Ken Skilling, Kozlowski, John Rigas, and Bernie Ebbers (another Canadian) being sent to prison for lengthy prison terms. In Canada, however, few—if any—high-profile executives paid a price for the massive bilking of Canadian investors in phony investment schemes. Perhaps it was simply a coincidence.

The current Conservative government has made law and order a touchstone of its policy, but that applies almost exclusively to the crimes of drug dealing, gunplay, and property damage. On the issue of curbing Canada's reputation as a safe haven for fraudsters, grifters, and corporate criminals, Stephen Harper has been virtually mute. As proof, just look at sorry history of the Integrated Market Enforcement Team set up in 2003 to find slippery white-collar guys such as the people behind Bre-X and YBM Magnex Ltd. After a much-heralded debut, IMET proved a bust—mostly because of a lack of political will and funding. According to a *Toronto Star* report in 2007, after four years of operation, only five charges had been laid—one in Vancouver and four in Toronto. The four cases launched in Toronto were still working their way through the courts at the time of this writing. Not surprising when you consider that IMET didn't have subpoena power—as do investigators in the United States. Among the many other problems afflicting IMET was the inability to break through modest RCMP pay scales to hire the proper people who knew the street. At other times, its staff was pulled away from its duties to work on security for visiting dignitaries or to help with large drug busts. It was only in the summer of 2008—five years after its founding—that IMET finally got some traction with high-profile arrests in several cases.

Perhaps a properly funded IMET might have been able to resolve Canada's squeamishness when investigating Eagleson's old political chum, Brian Mulroney, the former prime minister of Canada. The tortured story of Mulroney and his shady dealings with Karlheinz Schreiber have both fascinated and repelled Canadians for a quarter century. Schreiber, a self-styled influence peddler and briber of the rich and famous in European and Canadian politics, hitched himself to Mulroney's star shortly before the Quebec lawyer became leader of the Progressive Conservatives in 1983. While Alberta premier Peter Lougheed warned his own cabinet against dealing with Schreiber, Mulroney and his circle apparently embraced the German wheeler-dealer. Schreiber claims he helped fly planeloads of Mulroney supporters to the PC convention that elected Mulroney that year. His money and influence were never far from the locus of power in the years after.

Even as he was charged in Germany with bribery, influence peddling, and tax evasion in cases that brought down the German chancellor Helmut Kohl, Schreiber still employed the contacts and information gained in dealings with Canadian politicians to avoid extradition to his native Germany. Such was Schreiber's influence in the inner sanctum that when he needed to post bond, his guarantee was assured by two former cabinet ministers Marc Lalonde

(Liberal) and Elmer McKay (PC). In the time-honoured tradition of Drabinsky and Eagleson, Schreiber used Canada's ponderous extradition legislation to stall all the way to the doors of the Canadian Supreme Court—a luxury afforded by his once-robust income as a briber of the rich and famous. (Imagine a bank robber delaying justice for so long.)

Because of his chumminess to many in the former Progressive Conservative party, Schreiber became the principal suspect when determining who had received $10 million in bribes paid after Air Canada's purchase of Airbus planes in 1988. His lengthy association with Mulroney and his closest advisors led to claims that the former PM had received some of Airbus' *Schmeirgeld* (bribe), a claim Mulroney vigorously defended by suing the Canadian government when the RCMP alleged the same in a 1995 letter to Swiss authorities. Under oath in 2004, Mulroney testified that he'd only ever had coffee with Schreiber and had never had business any dealings with the German operator. The ex-PM received $2.1 million in a settlement from the Liberal government (which was beset by its own tawdry white-collar shenanigans over federal loans that helped Prime Minister Jean Chretien sell a Quebec property for a handsome profit).

But when it appeared his endless stay at the pleasure of Canada's government was ending, Schreiber played his trump card. From the Toronto detention centre, where he awaited extradition to Germany, Schreiber created a national scandal by belatedly confessing that—contrary to Mulroney's sworn testimony of no business deals—he'd paid the former prime minister $300,000 in cash over three separate meetings in both Canada and the United States. (Mulroney says the figure is $225,000.) Schreiber told a 2007 Parliamentary committee that the payments had been agreed to in a meeting with Mulroney in the final days of his prime ministership—and that no one could say just what the payments were for. That confession and others that he'd been asked to perjure himself and send funds to Mulroney's Swiss banker sparked a federal inquiry into a fifteen-year-old story and yet another RCMP probe into the corruption charges. As questions were asked why an expensive inquiry was needed to establish facts that Mulroney himself could make clear in a press conference, a Mulroney spokesman admitted that the PM might have been a little short on change when he made his regrettable deal with Schreiber. (Mulroney hastily denied the penury story.) Calling the deal he'd tried to hush up "an enormous mistake," the former PM confidently predicted a full review of the Schreiber affair would vindicate him.

When he finally appeared in Ottawa to clear his name, that expected vindication took on a pyrrhic tone. The ex-PM was asked why a lawyer such as Mulroney would be dealing in large sums of unreported cash (any withdrawal of over $20,000 in cash needs to be documented at the bank), how he transported money given to him outside Canada back here, and why he delayed reporting the cash for income tax purposes for a number of years. Oh, and *why* he'd sworn that he'd had no significant dealings with Schreiber when the two had met on the three occasions in which the former PM received envelopes of cash. Mulroney didn't help his case before the MPs by blithely dropping the names of various (dead) world leaders as contacts he'd made on behalf of Schreiber's business.

After hours of extensive parliamentary hearings and testimony in 2007–08, the Schreiber episode was even more opaque than before. Prime Minister Harper warily inched toward a very restrictive public inquiry with little expectation that there might be any Eagleson-like resolution of the affair of the PM and The Bagman.

NDP MP Pat Martin summed up the Canadian perception on

the eve of Schreiber's testimony. If it comes down to who the people believe, said Martin: Will it be the man being "perpwalked in the orange jumpsuit and shackles" or "the man in the Hugo Boss suit with Gucci shoes who walks around the House of Commons as if he owns the place." You could tell from the look on Martin's face that Mulroney's white collar afforded him a benefit of the doubt that Schreiber, as the outsider and operator, could not match. As it had done for Alan Eagleson. And for Garth Drabinsky. Just call it the Canadian way. And keep your hand on your wallet.

CHAPTER TEN

The Bad Medicine Line

Should justice be race-neutral? A Montreal judge thinks not. Last week, she granted bail to a Mohawk named Davin Johnny, who was arrested during the post-hockey street brawl in Montreal. "We have to take into account the fact you are a Native American," she explained.

Mr. Johnny, who's on welfare, was caught on videotape trashing a police car. At his bail hearing, the police reported that he'd said he'd do it again, because he "hate[s] the pigs." He's got a criminal record for drug possession and theft, as well as a drinking problem. But hey! Why blame him? As the judge said, aboriginals are "disadvantaged in our society, and that is sometimes shown by the heavy rate of underemployment and alcohol abuse ..." The judge in question, Juanita Westmoreland-Traoré, is used to making waves. Before being appointed to the Quebec bench, she was a well-known human-rights activist who believed that in order to achieve equality, we had to treat people unequally.

In the case of aboriginals, this principle is enshrined in law. In 1996, a provision was added to the Criminal Code that instructed judges to give "particular attention to the circumstances of aboriginals" in sentencing. This instruction was later affirmed by the Supreme Court of Canada, which was alarmed by the heavy overrepresentation of aboriginals in the prison system. It urged the courts to find alternatives to prison and focus on "restorative justice."

—Margaret Wente, *The Globe and Mail*, May 1, 2008

I t was the simplest twist of fate. Had the puck skittered in the opposite direction from where Chris Simon was slowly getting to his feet. Had Ryan Hollweg of the Rangers headed away from the fallen Islander forward in pursuit of the puck. Had the mercurial Simon not been on the receiving end of several close calls from the referees—including one just seconds before when Hollweg rammed him headfirst into the boards. Had any of the above unfolded, what happened next might have been avoided. But, to Simon's eventual dismay, the fates mocked him. The puck stayed along the boards where Simon groggily raised himself after being run by the younger player. Hollweg was there in Simon's aim, available and tempting. Seeing no penalty called on Hollweg's borderline hit, Simon was steaming mad. In an instant Simon was on his feet. As Hollweg skated towards him, Simon took a full, chopping swing that landed in Hollweg's throat. Stunned, Hollweg fell to the ice, grasping the area where Simon's composite stick had struck him. Rangers teammates rushed to confront Simon and a meleé erupted between the bitter New York rivals. In short, an ugly scene in any sport.

But in a league still coping with the PR shock of the Todd Bertuzzi incident, Simon's brutal two-hander nearly decapitating Hollweg was the worst sort of news. Once again the NHL was subjected to a pummeling from its own supporters and those who never watch hockey but to criticize. Replays of the incident were replayed as often as sixteen or eighteen times in a one-hour high-light show on Canada's sports specialty channels. In the United States? Forget it, the news played as a video loop for hockey haters in the media. Simon's previous rap sheet for violence was not helping either. To its credit, the league reacted promptly to suspend Simon for the rest of the year—twenty-five games in total—for using his stick in such a vicious manner. Making the heavy suspension easier for the league to reconcile during the run for the playoffs was the checkered history of the six-foot-three, 240-pound Islander forward. Since coming to the league in 1992–93 with the Quebec Nordiques, Simon had amassed 1,765 penalty minutes and been known as one of the toughest of the tough guys in the league. In January 2004, he was suspended two games for an unprovoked attack in which "he cross-checked, jumped on and punched" Ruslan Fedotenko of Tampa Bay. He was also suspended during the 1997–98 NHL season when, during a game against the Edmonton Oilers, he allegedly addressed forward Mike Grier as a "nigger" to Grier's face in response to alleged comments about his own Native heritage. Simon was suspended three games as a result of the incident—one of eight times the league has suspended Simon.

In other words, Simon was a convenient target for the NHL's erratic justice system—as Don Cherry was quick to point out when he contrasted the twenty-five games in suspensions Simon gathered while his opponents received none for their parts in the violence. The veteran of six NHL clubs was made to order for a PR slam dunk. The bruising forward made little attempt to justify his vicious actions against Hollweg, which were the culmination of a chippy game during which referees had let much borderline play go unpenalized. Simon offered only that he was concussed by Hollweg's unpenalized hit and remembered little of what he did.

But Simon allowed there was "absolutely no place in hockey for what I did."

It was another black eye for the NHL and a serious setback for Simon, who has overcome much on his way to becoming a veteran player in the league. He'd become a consistent, if not dynamic, scorer at the NHL level and had played in three Stanley Cup finals, winning with Colorado in 1996 and losing with Washington (1998) and Calgary (2004). On his day with the Stanley Cup in 1996 he'd taken the Cup back to his hometown of Wawa, Ontario, to be with his family. He and his grandfather then took the famous trophy with them on a fishing trip. It was also a setback for a man who was trying to be a role model for Native youth. On the website Nativehockey.com, Simon's bio observes, "Since he broke into the league, Simon has been highly regarded by the Native American community, especially as a role model for Native youth. He...hopes that he is a positive example for Native kids to follow."

No one knew more precisely how far the Ojibwa had come than Simon's head coach on the Islanders, Ted Nolan, who had personally helped Simon overcome alcoholism back in 1992. As a young Native man in the fast-paced culture of the white world, Simon had fallen victim to addiction, but with Nolan's help he'd sobered up to make a career for himself in pro hockey. The two men shared a bond beyond hockey as well—Nolan is also Ojibwa, having grown up dirt poor on the Ojibwa First Nation reserve outside Sault Ste. Marie. One of twelve kids, Nolan used hockey to escape the poverty of his youth and find success—and bitter disappointment—in the NHL. The wounds—self-inflicted and undeserved—that both he and Simon experienced mirror those of the uneasy relationship that now exists between the First Nations of Canada and the rest of the nation. Wounds that were exacerbated when NHL disciplinarian Colin Campbell referred to "the actual help he's going to get and counselling he's going to get from the drug and the alcohol doctors"—a casual reference that seemed to say Simon might be drinking once again. That brought Phil Fontaine, the National Chief of the Assembly of First Nations, to demand that Campbell apologize to Simon for suggesting he is receiving drug and alcohol treatment following his suspension. The NHL replied by saying that Campbell was actually referring to the NHL's Substance Abuse and Behavioural Health Program, which is providing Simon counselling for behavioural management. Fontaine was not placated.

As such episodes show, Canada's two solitudes are now white and Native, not French and English. Despite a history far less bloody and imperial than that of the Americans with their Native populations, Canada's relations with its First Nations had seriously deteriorated by the summer of 2007. Decades of tension over land claims were reflected in the long-standing dispute between developers and local citizens against Six Nations people in Caledonia, Ontario—where a new sub-development was being challenged by the local Native group; at VIA rail—which cancelled trains on the heavily travelled Montreal-Toronto corridor for June 29, 2007, to avoid Native barricades on the National Day of Action; and at courts across the land, where fishing, mining, mineral, and logging rights were being debated on a weekly basis. Add to that list the continuing legal cases over residential schools, Native substance abuse, and abject poverty on reserves and you had a combustible equation. A communications-savvy group of Native leaders was taking its grievances to the general public in visible—and inflammatory—ways. "Poverty among Canada's first nation's peoples rivals Third World conditions," said Fontaine. "It's this country's dirty little secret."

If, as Fontaine argued, Native poverty on and off reserves was a secret to the general Canadian public in 2007, they would have had to have been in a coma to miss media outlets—particularly the CBC—which relentlessly pounded viewers and listeners with harrowing tales of abuse of alcohol or worse by kids in Davis Inlet, breakdowns in sanitary conditions at Kaschechewan, fraud in the Indian card system, and a life expectancy below that of other Canadians in virtually every Native community across the country. The flood of Natives off the reserves and to the cities has been another not-so-secret sign of many of the successes and failures of Canada's Native policy. (Fifty-one per cent of Canada's estimated one million aboriginals now live in cities, while 29 per cent live on the country's six hundred reserves. The rest live off-reserve in rural areas.)

If anything, the general public has been numbed, not shocked, by the horror stories of the seemingly intractable standoffs between Natives intent on preserving their traditional culture and the fast-changing urban outside communities. Native drunkenness, wife-beating, and child abuse are familiar themes running through the public consciousness whenever they read the paper or watch TV. At one time it seemed the solution was switching government policy from one of assimilation to self-determination, but that has done little to end the discord. If anything, empowered Natives have become more litigious, more confrontational, more willing to take their argument to the non-Native media. Which vexes the general population. Non-Native Canadians who see over $6 billion budgeted for Native issues and see lucrative Indian casinos dotting the landscape ask how can the almost one million who identify themselves as Natives argue they need more? What else can Canada do for Native groups who, in many cases, either can't or won't help themselves?

Margaret Wente of *The Globe and Mail* sought to explain the vicious cycle binding the solitudes on the Native issue. "Everyone is trapped in the narrative we've constructed to explain it," she wrote in June of 2007.

> The Europeans arrived, wiped out most of the Natives, stole their land and tried to stamp out their culture. All the dysfunction of aboriginal communities stems from the original sins of the conquerors. Only the restoration of their land and culture (plus more money) will restore their dignity and fortunes. We now have a vast Indian industry of chiefs, government bureaucrats, lawyers, consultants and academics that is heavily invested in this narrative. Many of these people are well-meaning. They are also the chief obstacles to change, because their remedies make the problems worse.

While white leaders create a tribunal to speed up land claims, and Natives such as Chief Clarence Louie or Calvin Helin are urging self-reliance—not handouts—for their fellow Natives, meaningful solutions seem far off at the moment. In a time when the face of Canada is rapidly morphing to black or yellow or brown, cooperating with the "white man" is still often seen as a sellout of the traditional ways of hunting and fishing. The vested grievance industries on both sides still have public profiles they wish to maintain and budgets they wish to control. And a non-Native population wonders when is enough enough in the game of writing cheques to assuage white guilt over Ipperwash or Akwesasne?

As with so many other issues in the painful dance of "white" and Native cultures in this country, Native participation in hockey also had a more promising beginning. Native Canadians in eastern Canada were involved in the birth of the sport, as the Native game of Ooochamkanutk merged with the Irish sport of bandy in the new country to produce hockey. Many of the best hockey sticks in the game's early days were hand-carved Mi'Kmaq models produced from the hornbeam and white ash trees of the Maritime and Quebec forests. Getting a Native player to the big time took a while longer but, once they were admitted to the NHL, a steady parade of Native Canadians and Métis played in the NHL and other pro hockey leagues.

Ironically, Natives were able to play in the NHL in the 1950s when other visible minorities—blacks, Asians—were effectively barred from playing. The first Native in the NHL was Fred Sasakamoose, who played one game for the Chicago Blackhawks in 1953–54. Although his career in the NHL was cut short by homesickness, Sasakamoose blazed the path for players such as George Armstrong, Jim Neilson, Bryan Trottier, and Reggie Leach to become stars in the league. As befitted the times, Native players were usually accompanied by the nickname "Chief." So pervasive was the handle that even Ukrainian Johnny Bucyk carried the nickname because of his dark complexion. Native images, always pervasive in sport, were rampant in hockey as well. The Chicago Blackhawks (Black Hawks as they were then spelled) were a seminal part of the original-six era of the NHL, and their superstar Bobby Hull used to joke about the thrill of playing for the Blackhawks, skating onto the ice at raucous Chicago Stadium with "a picture of Pierre Pilote on my chest." As with Bucyk, Pilote—a French Canadian from Quebec, "looked" Native enough to earn the nickname.

The stereotyping of Native players—or those who looked vaguely Native—spilled over into the roles that Natives and Métis could play in pro hockey. There have been high-skilled Natives in the NHL—Trottier, Leach, Grant Fuhr, Jonathan Cheechoo, Wade Redden, Sheldon Souray—but for the most part, Native players were told that their path to the big time lies in being a hockey "warrior." And so the long list of legendary NHL tough guys is punctuated with the names of Natives such as Stan Jonathan, Gino Odjick, Mike Peluso, Ron Delorme, Simon, Rocky Thompson, Jordin TooToo, and Nolan himself. Delorme, now an NHL scout who runs summer hockey schools for Native kids in western Canada, recalled how his path to the NHL was laid out before him. It was fight—be a fighter and agitator—or get lost in the system. Delorme fought for his place in the game with Colorado and Vancouver from 1976 to 1985—nine seasons, 667 penalty minutes. While the emergence of Cheechoo, Redden, Souray, and others shows that the typecasting is less pervasive than it was years ago. But as Chris Simon's story shows, adaptation for Natives is often still a shock filled with loneliness and dependency.

"Because of the fact that Native kids' upbringing is a little bit different on the reserves," Delorme told writer Marjorie Roden, "there's nobody to tell them to watch for the green light, the red light, the yellow light, as far as crossing the road, and that's just a little example. Our upbringing is a lot different than it is in the city. They have to understand [city] culture."

In many of the hockey examples, players thrust into the city culture to play the game have experienced similar demons as those faced by many Natives making the transition from the reserve or rural homes. The list of players such as Simon who have fought addiction to alcohol or drugs is depressingly long. Teammates of Leach's with Philadelphia in the 1970s recalled stories of pouring cups of coffee into the Flyers sniper after monumental drinking sessions so the semi-conscious player could function that night on the rink. (On one such occasion, Leach scored five goals after such a process.) It's hoped that the million-dollar salaries earned by today's stars might save the current crop of Native and Métis players—as well as enrich life on the reserve or in other Aboriginal communities.

Nolan's tangled experience with pro hockey is an apt metaphor for the Native experience within Canada. Having the talent and drive to make hockey his ticket out of the Native cycle of poverty, Nolan was drafted in the fifth round by the Detroit Red Wings in 1978 after an Ontario Hockey League career with the Sault Ste. Marie Greyhounds. Taunted by opponents and fans wherever he played, Nolan developed a thick hide to counter the abuse he received as a young Native player looking to fit into hockey's tight-knit white culture. With the Greyhounds and the Red Wings, Nolan was an energy guy with some scoring touch, a player willing to work in the corners. While not a fighter, the left-winger was not one to back down either. Still, there was a sense in hockey circles that Nolan did not tap his full potential as a pro player. That might be attributed to the Red Wings who were, at the time, a highly dysfunctional team at the bottom of the standings thanks to their alcoholic owner Bruce Norris and a series of ineffectual former Red Wings who came back to manage the team. From the time he turned pro in 1979 till his retirement in 1986, Nolan bounced back and forth from the minors to the NHL with Detroit and later Pittsburgh. In all he played seventy-eight NHL games and scored six goals, with sixteen assists and 106 penalty minutes.

By the time his playing career ended in 1985, Nolan had discovered that he enjoyed coaching and saw an outlet for his passionate outlook in being behind the bench. It was also a powerful underpinning to the message that he often delivered about Native confidence. If he could make it as an NHL coach, it could be an inspiration to Native youths who feel there's no chance of cracking the world outside the reserve. After coaching minor hockey in the area, Nolan got his big break with his old junior club in Sault Ste. Marie in 1988—where he'd been a fan favourite—when he came in as a mid-season replacement. Creating an up-tempo style that emphasized teamwork over grooming pampered stars for the NHL, Nolan eventually coached the Greyhounds to three consecutive Memorial Cup tournament berths, winning the national championship in 1993 with a team featuring future NHLers Steve Sullivan, Aaron Gavey, and Dan Cloutier. Once more he had to close his ears to the barbs and slurs that greeted him in opposing rinks. His high-energy, positive style finally attracted the attention of the NHL after his Memorial Cup win. After a season as an assistant coach in Hartford, Nolan became the second Native head coach (after George Armstrong) in the NHL when the Buffalo Sabres hired him in 1995. The success he'd enjoyed in Sault Ste. Marie followed him and within two seasons he was awarded the Jack Adams Trophy as the best coach in the NHL. The Sabres, meanwhile, won the Northeast Division title and were favourites to beat Ottawa in the opening round of the 1997 playoffs. It should have been the happiest of times, but Nolan's life was about to fall apart.

While the team appeared outwardly content, the self-possessed Nolan was actually at odds with his star goalie Dominik Hasek and his general manager John Muckler. Unfouned rumours of Nolan drinking or sleeping with one player's wife circulated through the NHL's gossip mill. So did tales of how he allegedly went behind Muckler's back to Sabres' ownership. (Nolan vigorously denied all the rumours, "I guess this stuff fits the stereotype," he told writer Tim Wharnsby.) What is undeniable is that in game three of the Buffalo–Ottawa series in 1997, Hasek pulled himself from the net, claiming a bad knee. But *Buffalo News* writer Jim Kelley wasn't buying Hasek's claim and wrote a column that accused Hasek of pulling the chute in a protest against Nolan. An incensed Hasek then attacked Kelley, which brought a three-game suspension from the NHL. Hasek didn't play another game in the series, and without their star goalie, the Sabres soon lost to Philadelphia in the next round. A power struggle between Nolan and Muckler seemed inevitable.

In the aftermath of the loss, Hasek told reporters that he supported Muckler, not Nolan, and it would be better for him if the emotional Nolan did not return. Certainly, the star goalie Hasek wasn't going away. In the end, neither manager made it to the fall. Muckler was fired by ownership and when new GM Darcy Regier offered coach-of-the-year Nolan a nominal one-year, $500,000 contract, Nolan angrily rejected the contract. As the best coach in 1996–97, he figured there would be no shortage of jobs. But when he was forced to reject an offer from the Tampa Bay Lightning due to family reasons, Nolan saw his last shot at coaching in the best hockey league in the world disappear for almost a decade. Muckler, who is well-connected in the hockey world from his long career, soon was hired by the New York Rangers as their coach. But Nolan's phone went largely silent. While he received perfunctory interviews for vacant head coaching positions the next decade with the New York Islanders and Calgary Flames, Nolan was not a candidate in any serious fashion while white coaches (with poorer records) were recycled once, twice, even three times in the same period. With each passing year, Nolan's reputation as a GM killer or a hothead or too proud to coach at the junior level grew. Nolan, it was said, was too impulsive, too stubborn; although that never kept the truculent Mike Keenan from finding work time after time. Rather than Nolan, better to hire someone more amenable, like Roger Neilson.

While Nolan occasionally coached his sons' team, did some motivational speaking, and ran his charity foundation that counsels Native kids, the notoriously clubby hockey community was happy to go on without the high-profile Native. In time, Nolan began to say that his disappearance was due to the colour of his skin. "I look different. I'm not one of them," Nolan told the *Globe and Mail* in 2006. While it might have been true, the candour did little to endear him to the men who run pro hockey. "Are you saying Natives have an inferiority complex?" replied Cherry when Nolan's quotes about racism were made public. "Go out and get your own fair shake in life and work for it. It wasn't racism that Ted Nolan didn't get the job. Him and (then-GM John) Muckler got at it, and that's why he didn't get the job. It wasn't racism; it was between him and the GM." The misapprehension between Nolan and the white hockey world was a perfect match for that existing between the Native and outside world.

In the fall of 2005, Nolan finally gave in to the demands from his hockey friends that he needed to resume coaching at the junior level to re-establish his bona fides for the NHL. Moncton Wildcats owner Robert Irving lured him to New Brunswick to coach his team. Once again, Nolan worked magic with his team, guiding the Wildcats—featuring Luc Bourdon and Brad Marchand—to the 2006 Memorial Cup final. But even then Nolan was forced to endure the casual racism of hockey fans. On December 16, 2005, fans of the Chicoutimi Sagueneens shouted racial slurs at him and performed the "tomahawk chop" as he stood behind the Moncton bench. Chicoutimi fans continued to taunt Nolan after the game. (Nolan later labelled the Saguenay as being the "Alabama" of the QMJHL.) Because of the Sagueneens' actions, the QMJHL launched a new anti-discrimination policy—but it couldn't change the underlying attitudes of its fans.

Nolan's success in Moncton renewed the calls for someone to break the unofficial sanction against him at the NHL level, but it took renegade owner Charles Wang of the New York Islanders to give Nolan a second chance in the fall of 2006. Ironically, Nolan's hiring precipitated the firing of another GM, this time Neil Smith. For a change, no one blamed Nolan. And despite the disappointment of the Simon incident, no one was critical of the job Nolan did with the unheralded Islanders in 2006–07. The team put up ninety-two points and qualified for its first playoffs with a dramatic shootout win on the final game of the season. Nolan was once again nominated for the Jack Adams Trophy as coach of the year— losing this time to Alain Vigneault of Vancouver.

Nolan showed he had mellowed somewhat. At his urging, legendary Islanders' coach Al Arbour came back for one night behind the Islanders' bench to reach the 1,500-game mark in the NHL. But it would be optimistic to say that both he and the hockey business were completely reconciled to each other. In July 2008, the Islanders fired Nolan following a season out of the playoffs. A difference of "philosophy" was cited for the dismissal. This time Nolan accepted the firing stoically, leading to the chance he'll get another post in the NHL. Like the government bureaucrats and radical Native leaders, Nolan and the conservative hockey world still eye each other with trepidation. They have learned a great deal about each other in the past decade—Nolan about self-reliance, the NHL about tolerance—but there remains a long way to go.

While Canadians congratulate themselves on their superiority over Americans in knowledge of world affairs, polls from education ministries show Canada at the bottom of most industrialized countries in knowledge of its own history. The absence of Natives (and members of other groups) from the NHL may help insulate many Canadians from the realities of their community, where large segments do not melt into the culture. Indeed, many of the new cultural communities actively choose not to assimilate.

While Nolan's story provides a warm spot for liberal guilt, it also points out the pitfalls of the multicultural experiment happening in Canada right now. As Harvard professor Robert Putnam has discovered, diversity and multiethnic blending are something less than the panacea promised by politicians. "In the presence of diversity, we hunker down," Putnam wrote in his study on diversity. "We act like turtles. The effect of diversity is worse than had been imagined. And it's not just that we don't trust people who are not like us. In diverse communities, we don't trust people who do look like us." That distrust causes neighbours, "regardless of the colour of their skin, to withdraw even from close friends, to expect the worst from their community and its leaders, to volunteer less, give less to charity and work on community projects less often, to register to vote less, to agitate for social reform more but have less faith that they can actually make a difference, and to huddle unhappily in front of the television." And lest you think Putnam some right-wing ideologue, he is, in fact, a liberal-minded academic who was hoping to find another message in his research. Still, he points out the dangers of extrapolating Nolan's success into a greater context. "It would be unfortunate if a politically correct progressivism were to deny the reality of the challenge to social solidarity posed by diversity," he wrote. While a successful immigrant society can make immigration and integration work, it is by no means as guaranteed as singing, "I'd like to buy the world a Coke."

And in Canada, it is not a slam dunk just because Ted Nolan is coaching again or Jarome Iginla—whose father is Nigerian—leads the NHL in scoring.

Owe Canada

C haracteristically, it took an American to tell Canadians that
they should be better served by the NHL. Paul Kelly, the
Boston lawyer who's now the executive director of the NHL
Players Association, believes that Canada should have at least
one—and perhaps more—NHL franchises if the league relocates a
team or expands.

"I think it would be a huge error not to relocate one of the
existing franchises to Hamilton or Winnipeg," Kelly told the
Toronto Star in May of 2008 when asked about where failing U.S.
franchises might move. Kelly (who was responsible in part for putting Alan Eagleson behind bars in 1998) pointed out the folly of the
league blackballing Research In Motion billionaire Jim Balsillie—
who tried twice to bring a failing American team to the southern
Ontario market now served exclusively by the Maple Leafs—while
the league embraced other investors who couldn't even get loans
from the bank.

"He built RIM from nothing into an $80-billion company. We
would be foolhardy not to see his efforts happen," Kelly said.

The inspiration for Kelly's remarks was the *Star*'s publication
of an internal NHL financial document that demonstrated that the
rise in the Canadian dollar and the bullish performance of Canadian

teams was obscuring major problems elsewhere in the league—problems not solved by the draconian lockout of 2004- '05. The report showed that the six Canadian-based teams (out of thirty NHL clubs) accounted for 31 per cent of the (U.S.) $1.1 billion in league ticket revenue during the 2007- '08 season. While the NHL trumpeted news that record attendance numbers and ticket revenue from Canadian sources had pushed total NHL revenues up by almost 10 per cent, eleven of the twenty-four U.S.-based clubs were either revenue-neutral or had experienced declines in ticket income over the same period.

In fact, in spite of the financial changes brought on by the new collective bargaining agreement (CBA), a number of teams are facing huge obstacles to survival in their markets. And that, ultimately, means less money for Kelly's membership.

According to the report, Phoenix had averaged a puny $450,000 per game that season. Atlanta, Miami, Nashville, Washington, St. Louis, the Islanders of New York, and Chicago generated less than half the ticket revenue per game as did the two least-profitable Canadian teams (Edmonton and Ottawa generate about $1.2 million per game). Despite NHL Commissioner Bettman's most tortured efforts, the sport was not growing financially in the U.S—except at the level of franchise equity. The book value of teams had remained relatively buoyant (in part thanks to Balsillie's efforts at purchasing a team at above-market value.) Franchise equity is the opiate of pro sports owners, of course, and the relative health of NHL values accounted for Bettman's continued support within the Board of Governors.

However, the release of the report—and Kelly's backing of more Canadian teams—during the much ballyhooed 2008 Detroit–Pittsburgh Stanley Cup Final was a major embarrassment to the NHL. As it tried to show improved American TV ratings as a sign of an American turnaround, the media instead jumped on the report like a fat kid on an Oreo. "Bettman Era a Total Disaster" was the *Globe*'s take. "Kelly Cranks Up the Heat on Bettman" said *The Calgary Herald*. "No matter what happens in terms of the future of the NHL," wrote the *National Post*'s Scott Taylor, "Winnipeg will ALWAYS be a better market for big-time hockey than the southern United States. Period. End of discussion."

Bettman raced onto the airwaves of *Hockey Night In Canada* before game four of the 2008 Final series to spin the story, but it was too late to reverse the perception that—despite having very little impact in the NHL inner sanctum—Canada had become the financial bedrock of his league. In fact, with the retirement of Harley Hotchkiss as chairman of the NHL's Board of Governors, virtually all the most influential posts within the league were held by Americans. It could be argued that, even as the Canadian dollar made the six teams in Canada more important than they'd been since 1967, the influence of Canadians in the direction of the league had rarely been more negligible. To quote Richard Rodier (Balsillie's spokesman) quoting the Blackberry dude himself, "We are becoming strangers in our own (hockey) house."

Which led many Canadians to ask: "Where are the Canadian NHL governors when it comes to boosting native content in the world's top hockey league? Why had no one (besides grandstanding politicians) come to the defence of more Canadian clubs?"

Where they are is keeping mum to avoid being fined by Bettman for opinions that cleave from the official NHL line that "there's a process going on" in the planned economy of the NHL. For instance, asking why Predators owner Craig Leipold got $50 million less to leave the Predators in Nashville—compared to what Balsillie offered to move the club to Ontario—would involve taking on Bettman. That's something no one in the Canadian Club wants to try with the commissioner insulated by Jeremy Jacobs as Board chairman and by an all-American audit committee. Besides, Bettman has cookies to dispense: Leipold's loyalty was subsequently rewarded with the juicy ownership of the Minnesota Wild.

Frankly, Canadian owners had no financial incentive to feel patriotic.

As it currently stood with the league, team owners were making piles of cash on ticket revenues and seat licenses—with waiting lists on season tickets a mile long and no turndown in sight—and they had no interest splitting up their lucrative national television market more than six ways if they didn't have to. The theology among owners was that the *uber*-rich Maple Leafs deserved hefty compensation should Balsillie land a team in southern Ontario— quite literally inside their own backyard. Even though Balsillie strenuously denied he would go the litigation route to win the day, the New Original Six were mortified at the prospect of Canadian courts scrutinizing NHL bylaws covering territorial monopolies.

So they held Bettman's coat while he shadow-boxed with Balsillie, hoping to get the benefits of a $240-million purchase price while making the loyalty noise go away. Problem is, unlike previous challengers who either disappeared or went to jail in due order, Balsille would not be going away anytime soon. With the NHL faceplanting in at least half a dozen U.S. markets, he understood that time was on his side. If he could exert steady pressure on the NHL's Canadian sponsors and media outlets, the day would eventually be his. If not Nashville, then Atlanta or Phoenix or whomever has a portable lease and a burning desire for $240 million in their pocket. "Either Jim will get a team, or he will shine a light on what's happening to hockey in this country," said Rodier.

The Canadian issue was a convenient tool for bludgeoning Bettman, who's never had great bona fides as a *vrai* Canadian (despite allowing a Canadian assistance program when the loonie was just 62 U.S. cents). Fairly or not, that perception wasn't helped by hosing CBC on Saturday night playoff dates in the spring of 2007. For all the equalization plans when the dollar was at par with Bhutan's ngultrum, Bettman has never been quite Tim Horton's enough for most folk north of the 49th.

But Bettman is less anti-Canadian than pro-Gary. The contemporary NHL is a sandbox where Bettman and his allies within the Board of Governors carefully dole out the fast-shrinking spoils to their pals, not to some hotshot Canadian businessman who happens to have revolutionized the communications history of the planet. It just so happens that Bettman's closest allies have a distinctly American tinge to them. As in, guys like Phil Anschutz and Ed Snider and Jeremy Jacobs who own or operate big arenas around the U.S. It's always worked like that in the NHL inner sanctum, where the only real loyalty is the care and feeding of owners.

But even the best-laid plans of mice and commissioners can get a reality check. So as Bettman spun the dire revenue numbers of his clubs he was blindsided by the financial miseries of owners he's championed around the league as saviours of the game in America. The league had vigourously promoted William "Boots" Del Biaggio as the rainmaker to keep hockey in Nashville and away from Balsillie's dreams of a Canadian team. Then Del Biaggio resigned abruptly in May of 2008 from the investment company he created. Seems the guy with deep pockets was being sued by everyone. There was also a federal probe into the finances of the forty-year old Bay Area socialite who'd been a minority partner in the San Jose Sharks at one point. According to the Tennessean newspaper, Bootsy had also—unbeknownst to Bettman—been loaned the money to purchase the Preds by two fellow owners, Anschutz of L.A. and Leipold of Minnesota. (Anschutz, who ran the worst team in the NHL, was clearly looking for Del Biaggio to move the Predators to his new arena in Kansas City.) Bettman was left with a choice: either he was complicit in this conniving or else he and his auditors deserved an F minus for due diligence.

None of the claims has been proven in court, of course. But it's hardly a ringing endorsement of the NHL's due diligence if Del Biaggio comes a cropper. Then there's Anaheim owner Henry Samueli, who resigned as chairman of Broadcom Corp. to fight a federal lawsuit alleging he conspired in a five-year scheme involving false accounting and lying to shareholders. (In June 2008, Samuel pleaded guilty to lying to U.S. Securities and Exchange Commission investigators.) To longtime NHL watchers, it all smacked of the 1996 John Spano fiasco, when the NHL's due diligence approved him as the new owner of the Islanders, only to see him carted to jail for fraud a short time later. And the conviction on fraud charges of Buffalo owner John Rigas and his son. Then there was Bruce McNall.... 'nuff said. But having alienated many in America's corporate community in his 15 years at the NHL's helm, marginal owners are probably the best Bettman can attract anymore. No wonder Tiger Woods dissed hockey when asked to handicap the 2008 Final. "I don't really care," Woods told reporters. "I don't think anybody really watches hockey any more, do they?"

Which brings us back to the purported unsuitability of Balsillie and his Canadian dream. The American leader of the NHLPA wanted the Blackberry Guy to add more Canadian content to the NHL. Wayne Gretzky—owner/ head coach of the Coyotes, added his voice, saying Hamilton is a bonafide NHL market. But voices in Canadian ownership remained silent on expanding the footprint of the NHL in their home country. It's self-evident that hockey is Canada's game and passion. Southern Ontario—at the very minimum—should have a team. But with Bettman seemingly more concerned with rescuing the deadbeats he brought into the league than with bringing real money, energy, and hockey passion to the sport, who was going to bring that message to NHL headquarters in Manhattan? Don't all queue up at once, Leafs, Flames, Canucks, Oilers, Habs and Senators.

It's a classic dilemma as Canada heads into the modern age. As David Adams Richards observed, hockey is where Canada got it right. But Canadians are not allowed to tell people about it. *Might be immodest.* (Like complaining about Canada's monopoly on cell phone rates.) *Might hurt The Game. Be like Gretz and hide the light beneath a bushel of self-effacement.* Sure, the Canadian teams underpin the economics of the business. But better let someone else run things. The acceptance of American executives and media people seems essential to affirming Canadian success. Besides, they seem happier doing the heavy lifting in these days of entitlement. Finding a champion within Canadian hockey is like finding a gun owner at an NDP convention.

Likewise, there seems no champion in the struggle for the Canadian hockey soul, between the rock 'em-sock 'em style of Don Cherry and the skilled, entertaining future of Sidney Crosby and Pavel Datsyuk. While *Hockey Night In Canada* celebrated the head punches and face washes of old pro Gary Roberts in the 2008 playoffs, media not embedded in the NHL's Code were focused on Henrik Zetterberg, Johann Franzen, Crosby, and the players doing the scoring and skating—the real work of hockey. While *Hockey Night* preached to the converted, others wondered if it was too much to hope that Detroit's unbridled skill—which eschewed the Code and its mandatory mayhem—meant that the long period of darkness in the thrall of Cherry's Lear-like rages ("I know what's going on. You don't," he snarled at his critics on air) about hockey was coming to an end.

The way Detroit's speed and grit and team play dominated the 2008 playoffs surely should have pointed the way for the rest of the twenty-nine teams in the NHL. The Red Wings were tough—who hit harder than Nicholas Kronwall?—and they had no trouble in the corners. (The artful Datsyuk led Game One in hits.) Outside of their dalliance with Darren McCarty, the Wings had no need for message senders to get across their simple point: skill wins. Whether Detroit's success would impress the Cherry cult enough to drop its affinity for the Roberts' routine is probably wishing upon a star.

The same might be said for Canada. Whether the onset of globalization, environmentalism, and the redistribution of wealth to the West is enough to break the template that has dominated Canada since the Trudeau era is hardly assured. Stephen Harper, for instance, headed from Calgary to Ottawa bound to recreate a new government paradigm but then found himself having to cut his cloth in the same old pattern, accommodating Quebec and the other traditional stakeholders in the political process. So as Canada heads into the second decade of the millenium, the rules keep changing but no one can say precisely what the game is anymore.

Symbolically leading the way backward was the ubiquitous Liberal MP Denis Coderre who understands the impact hockey has on the country—and on his own profile. Fresh from his triumph in tarring Shane Doan for sins he did not commit, Coderre found new ways to intrude upon sport. When a contractual dispute arose between the CBC and the composer of the iconic musical theme for *Hockey Night In Canada*, Coderre insisted that the Heritage minister Josee Verner intervene to force the Corporation to pay up for Delores Claman's ditty. "The *Hockey Night in Canada* theme is a part of Canada's culture that goes beyond sport," Coderre told reporters. "If the minister wants to show that she cares about

Canadian heritage, this is her chance." Coderre's prescription is wonderfully Liberal: populist, skeptical of the market, and promoting government intervention. It's also remarkably silly, but when has that ever discouraged the Coderres? As he well knows, when you mix the national pastime with the modern state apparatus, you can probably get hockey for a song. (Eat your heart out Ron MacLean.)

A Typical Shoot Out

Calgary Herald, May 8, 2007
by Bruce Dowbiggin

Oh dear. It's happening again. As if that unpleasantness with Edmonton last year wasn't enough—"City of champions, dude!"— it now appears we're going to be dragged into a glee club to cheer the Ottawa Senators to their first Stanley Cup since we last hit our Kyoto targets. Yeah...1927.

The telltale signs abound. Which is to say I got a phone call from a very pleasant young woman working for the CBC in Ottawa. "We're looking for some music suggestions to inspire the Senators on to the Stanley Cup," she said. "We heard you'd have some suggestions."

"How about 'Blame Ottawa!'" I riposted. The ensuing silence was sepulchral. I think I heard the Carillon in the Peace Tower perform the entire national anthem before another word came forth.

"You mean, you're not cheering for Ottawa?" she gasped.

"Er...there's no cheering in the press box," I replied. "Besides, if we didn't cheer for Edmonton last year, what in the name of Shane Doan makes you think we'll be losing our hearts to Ottawa's team?"

"Well, we're all Canadians aren't we?" she said.

Hey, Omar Khadr is Canadian, but that doesn't mean I'm in his corner either. But at this point, the young woman at the other end was sounding as if I was holding her puppy off a bridge over the Rideau. First hockey love can be emotional.

So rather than tell her I'd rather go camping in a two-man tent with Gilles Duceppe than have a vested interest in Ottawa winning the Stanley Cup, I pulled back a tad.

"Maybe some Tom Cochrane?" I offered.

This perked her up. "Good, good ... I'd heard you were the guy who'd know." (Let me get my hands on the person who'd told her that, and I'll filet him like a perch.) Fauré's *Requiem* would be a more appropriate ditty should the Sens succeed where the Flames had (barely) failed in 2004. "Funeral For A Friend." "Spring Can Really Hang You Up The Most." "Suicide Is Painless." "How Can You Mend A Broken Heart?" "Walking On Broken Glass." Anything by Kurt Cobain.

Stop me now, please. I mean, really ... I hope Ottawa has a blast with the Sens. May they party till the wee small hours on the Sparks Street Mall ... yeah, 7 p.m. ... and may they close down Bank Street (unless it's already closed). Party hearty, Bytown—in Gatineau where you always celebrate.

Just don't expect this Canadian to get all Vimy Ridge over it. The last time I looked, the Senators had a Trojan advertisement on their chest, not the maple leaf. Their every move is followed, not from coast to coast, but from Point Fortune in the east to that little village just east of Peterborough—Oompah Plevna, that's the one.

In fact, I have never quite understood why one Canadian living two time zones and several galaxies from Ottawa's reality is supposed to fall in line for the final remaining Canadian team at

Cup time. We didn't ask any of them to horn in on our Red Mile (and its ample amenities) in 2004, and we sure as heck weren't invited to Whyte Ave last spring to get all giggy with the Oil.

Get over it. When it comes to the other Canadian teams in hockey, our attitude is a lot like Quebec's within Canada. We're only in it for the money. The enemy of our enemy is our friend. Go Red Wings. Go Ducks.

C'mon Ottawa, don't sulk. When Los Angeles is in the World Series, do San Franciscans turn Dodger blue to support their fellow Californians? Do Seminole fans from Florida State don Gator jerseys when Florida plays for a nation title? Do Jets fans put on Giants blue when their NFL brothers in New York make the Super Bowl? Do Liberal senators have platinum Amex cards? It's nothing personal.

So, good luck to Ottawa. They don't need me. They don't need Alberta (except on pay day). We have Rob Anders. They have Jack Layton. We have Okotoks. They have Stittsville. We have Wild Rose Country. They have the Tulip Festival. We have Prairie Oysters. They have Beaver Tails. We have our oil money. They have our oil money.

As for the radio show, I probably won't say any of this. I'll play along and smile when they play The Bill Barilko Song by the Hip. I won't offend. After all, I am Canadian.

May 27, 2007
Doan, Senators have something in common
by Sheila Copps/Sun Newspaper Chain

Despots and dictators use anything to divide and conquer. Religion, oil, tribalism or just plain money. In Canada, it's hockey.

One only has to look at the Shane Doan story to see how sport can stir up hate and misunderstanding. Many Quebecers are still labouring under the misimpression, fuelled by Members of Parliament, that our World Cup Championship team was racist and francophobic.

Just read the email from Philip Landry complaining about a column I wrote for the Journal de Montreal in defence of Doan. He writes, "It wasn't long ago that when a player called another 'f—-ing n—-r or Indian,' they were suspended for several games and paid a fine. But in Doan's case, he was named team Canada's captain, a team without a single francophone, by the way...Would we have put up with a player who said, 'f—-ing Jews?' When I heard the cretin claim to be a great Christian, I wanted to vomit. Why is multiculturalism so important to English Canada as long as it is not Francophone."

Never let the facts stand in the way of a stupid argument. Landry ignores sworn parliamentary testimony exonerating Doan. The original slur actually came from a European player. Parliament learned that several francophone players were offered positions on the national team, but declined to play for personal reasons. Coming off tough NHL schedules, they chose family time. Obviously, you cannot blame the national team if invited players don't participate.

Landry believes Anglophone Canadians support everybody but Francophones. In fact, one of four young Anglophones now speaks fluent French. Hardly a sign of hate. He also writes, "One should never mix politics with sport. But YOU (his caps) do not have the right to say that. I remember a country with its ocean of flags at the Olympic Games who irritated the rest of the planet."

In reality, the planet couldn't care less about Canadian flag fights. They are simply fodder for domestic division. But using hockey to spew hate is not restricted to one language or region of Canada. Friendly competition is part of the game. But one just has to read a recent anti-Senator hockey rant by Calgary sportswriter Bruce Dowbiggin to see sport as code for regional divisions.

Dowbiggin slammed the Sens and their city, outlining multiple reasons why he would never cheer for the last Canadian team left in the Stanley Cup hunt.

His diatribe was more sophisticated than Mr. Landry's. Fewer expletives, but just as hate-filled. He made fun of Canada's tax capital, tulips, tourists and team.

His hockey vision is so narrow that last year he refused to cheer for Edmonton when the hometown Calgary Flames were knocked out.

GO DUCKS

Dowbiggin asked why any Canadian living two time zones and several galaxies away from the nation's capital should care about the fate of Canada's only team in the Stanley Cup. "Our attitude is a lot like Quebec's within Canada. We're only in it for the money... Go Ducks."

Just as the anti-Doan backlash was motivated by ill-informed nonsense, so the Sens trashing in the name of sport is equally divisive.

Dowbiggin's message was a lot more dangerous than that of the separatists.

Gussied up as a sport rant, he thinks it is perfectly OK to trash another part of Canada in the name of hockey. He claims Ottawa is only interested in Calgary's oil and money. He drags up every old peccadillo of West-East angst that he can muster. He spews a diatribe of regional epithets, couching their viciousness in a patina of jock talk.

In the end, he contributes to the same ignorance and unfounded accusations that Doan endured. Sports lynchers with a political agenda commit the worst kind of bigotry. In western backhand, Dowbiggin excretes the same bile that almost cost us our country twice. The last time I looked, the majority of Quebecers chose Canada. How many gut-wrenching referendums has he lived through?

Hockey as a tool for despots? In both official languages.

Calgary Herald, June 2, 2007
by Bruce Dowbiggin

Whether it's politics or hockey, you can always tell Sheila Copps, you just can't tell her much.

The erstwhile minister of A Million Flags Over Canada (cost: $45 million) has put on her size-17 waders and ventured into the realms of puck to decry the friable nature of the federation she so assiduously stewarded during her many years at the epicentre of power in Ottawa.

In plain English that even the former Hamilton ward heeler can understand: she's steamed over a column yours truly wrote urging Calgarians (and anyone else outside the 613 area code) to resist the urge to adopt the Ottawa Senators as Canada's team in this year's finals.

You may remember we opined, "The last time I looked, the Senators had a Trojan advertisement on their chest, not the maple leaf. Their every move is followed, not from coast to coast, but from Point Fortune in the east to that little village just east of Peterborough—Oompah Plevna, that's the one.

"In fact, I have never quite understood why one Canadian living two time zones and several galaxies from Ottawa's reality is supposed to fall in line for the final remaining Canadian team at

Cup time. We didn't ask any of them to horn in on our Red Mile (and its ample amenities) in 2004, and we sure as heck weren't invited to Whyte Ave last spring to get all giggy with the Oil.

"Get over it. When it comes to the other Canadian teams in hockey, our attitude is a lot like Quebec's within Canada. We're only in it for the money. The enemy of our enemy is our friend . . . Go Ducks."

More astute readers may have discerned a touch of sarcasm and mirth in the piece. Not our Ms. Copps. And boy, does the ex-deputy PM unload as only she can in her epistles to the Sun newspaper chain. "Hate filled" and "ill-informed nonsense" she steams about playing to regional interests in the nation. She even works up some dander over the shots about "Canada's tax capital, tulips, tourists and team."

"(Dowbiggin) claims Ottawa is only interested in Calgary's oil and money. He drags up every old peccadillo of West-East angst that he can muster. He spews a diatribe of regional epithets, couching their viciousness in a patina of jock talk."

Wait, wait, she's just warming up. "In the end, he contributes to the same ignorance and unfounded accusations that (Shane) Doan endured. Sports lynchers with a political agenda commit the worst kind of bigotry. In western backhand, Dowbiggin excretes the same bile that almost cost us our country twice. The last time I looked, the majority of Quebecers chose Canada. How many gut-wrenching referendums has he lived through?"

Uh, the same ones you lived through, Ms. Copps. The ones the Liberal Party did their best to blow through ineptitude and mismanagement? The ones that launched the Liberals' Sponsorship Scandal? The ones that have us facing a Quebec where 80 per cent stay as our brothers under the flag of convenience and financial stability?

As a born and bred Quebecker with French Canadian roots going back to the nineteenth century (who was living in Quebec in the 1980 referendum and voted no), I'm always amused by the Quebec parvenus such as Ms. Copps who believe that a French immersion course and particularly hot weekend at the Juste Pour Rire Festival make them experts on the culture of La Belle Province. But no matter, the parlous state of Quebec within Canada speaks to decades of Liberal vigilance on the separatist file.

When it comes to taking lessons on the culture and political agenda of Quebec, I'll take the guidance of another longtime Quebec resident (and former MNA) Reed Scowen, whose book *Time To Say Goodbye* catalogues how Ms. Copps and her generation of well-meaning friends did not heal the nation but instead opened an even wider divide between the province of my birth and the provinces I now call home. Scowen believes now is the time to file for separation ourselves, on our terms and on our timetable. I tend to concur.

In the end, it's hard to tell which is funnier: Ms. Copps' vitriolic defence of her record as a champion of Confederation or as a sudden convert to the culture of hockey in this country. But then Ms. Copps, like the rest of the Liberals, never were very good at getting a joke. Maybe because it was about them in the first place.

Index

PREFACE

ALTHOUGH any division of history into periods must be some-what arbitrary, there are good reasons for regarding either the Spanish-American War or the accession to the presidency of Theo-dore Roosevelt as the beginning of a new epoch in the United States. American development since those two events has been dominated by the same trends, and the American people have been confronted by the same basic problems. In internal affairs the chief factor has been the continued growth of machine technology and of the large corporation as the characteristic institution of machine civilization; during the twentieth century the American people have been largely occupied in the attempt to solve the economic, social and political problems which this growth has presented. In foreign relations the main factor has been the emergence of the United States into a world power and her consequent involvement in the affairs of Europe and of the Fast East.

The purpose of this book has been to describe the chief forces in the development of American society during the past forty years. While giving adequate space to political controversy and to legisla-tion, the author has endeavored to fill in the economic and social background and to place particular emphasis on those questions, both domestic and foreign, which are considered likely to be of greatest importance during the coming decade. The growth of in-dustrial corporations, the rise of trade unionism, the condition of agriculture, the problems of immigration and racial relationships, and intellectual and cultural changes have been examined in some detail. Believing that a history of the United States should be more than a history of the federal government, the author has also laid some emphasis on regional differentiation and on state and municipal government. In view of the importance which will certainly belong to foreign policy during the coming decade, considerable attention has been given to foreign relations, particularly to the causes of the American entry into the first World War, to relations with Europe during the twenties and thirties, and to relations with Latin America and with Japan.

The author is indebted to a number of persons for their kindness in reading the manuscript and suggesting improvements; particularly to Professor Thomas C. Cochran and to Miss Marian K. Pavlovich for reading the whole book; and to Professor Ralph B. Flanders, Professor Charles Hodges, Professor Lois MacDonald, Dr. Bernard Myers, and Professor Jonathan F. Scott for reading different sections of it. The author alone is, of course, responsible for expressions of opinion and for any factual errors.

Acknowledgements are due to the Brookings Institution for permission to quote from *America's Capacity to Consume* and from S. Bell, *Productivity, Wages and National Income;* to the Houghton Mifflin Company for permission to quote from P. H. Douglas, *Real Wages in the United States;* and to the Macmillan Company for permission to quote from A. A. Berle and G. C. Means, *The Modern Corporation and Private Property.*

HENRY BAMFORD PARKES

December, 1940

CONTENTS

PART THREE

THE WORLD WAR

PART FOUR

THE TWENTIES

PART FIVE

THE THIRTIES—THE FORTIES

The Heritage of the Nineteenth Century

PART ONE

I

PROBLEMS OF THE

TWENTIETH CENTURY

IN 1789, when Washington took office as first president under the Federal constitution, the United States covered an area of about 800,000 square miles and had a population of nearly 4 million. An overwhelming majority of the population was concentrated along the Atlantic seaboard; and, though the western boundary of the republic was the Mississippi River, colonization of the country between the Mississippi and the Appalachians had to face the hostility of savage Indian tribes, the British in Canada, and the Spaniards in Louisiana. There were only six cities with more than eight thousand inhabitants,[1] and their combined population amounted to only 3 per cent of the total population of the republic. Shipowners in New England, New York, and Pennsylvania had grown rich on trade with Europe and the West Indies and were beginning to establish contacts with India and China, but American manufacturing was still insignificant, and the Industrial Revolution had not yet commenced. There were only three banks in the whole country,[2] and none of them did business outside the state in which it was located.

Methods of communication were primitive; roads were merely dirt tracks. To travel from Massachusetts to Georgia required at

1. Philadelphia, Boston, New York, Baltimore, Charleston, and Salem.
2. The Bank of North America (at Philadelphia), the Bank of New York, and the Bank of Massachusetts.

least a month. Agriculture was the normal occupation of at least
nine-tenths of the population; and, except among the planters of
the southern states, it was practiced primarily for subsistence rather
than for trade. The typical American of that era was an independent
freeholder who produced almost all the necessities of life for himself and who was dependent upon marketing his crops for little
more than luxury articles and whatever money might be needed for
the payment of his taxes and the repayment of his debts.

By the year 1900 the United States had grown in size and wealth
with a rapidity unprecedented in history. Successive acquisitions
from France, Spain, Great Britain, and Mexico had extended her
territories westward as far as the Pacific, giving the republic a total
area of more than 3 million square miles. Every section of this vast
country had been colonized, so that it was no longer possible to
trace any continuous frontier line between inhabited and uninhabited
areas. The population amounted to nearly 76 million. One-third of
this population now lived in cities with more than 8,000 inhabitants, while there were nineteen cities each of which had more than
200,000 inhabitants and which had a combined population of more
than 11½ million. The application of science to technology and the
consequent development of mining and manufacturing had created
an industrial system with an extraordinary productivity and complexity. Agriculture was now the occupation of less than half the
population, and the American farmer now concentrated on raising
staple crops for sale to the cities and to Europe. There were more
than half a million factories and workshops, which employed more
than 5,300,000 workers and which turned out products with an
annual value of more than 13 billion dollars. 198,964 miles of
railroads had been built. There were 10,382 banks. And the annual
value of American foreign trade totaled nearly 2 billion dollars.
The national wealth amounted to 88 billion dollars, and the national income to nearly 18 billion dollars.

This vast growth had been accomplished without any fundamental
change in American institutions or in the American view of life. A
civil war had been fought to vindicate the authority of the Federal
union and to crush sectional independence. Nevertheless, the Fed-

eral constitution which had been drafted for the original thirteen states in 1787 had undergone only minor changes, and by the year 1913 thirty-five new states had been successfully incorporated into it. The Americans still cherished the doctrines of freedom and equality which had been proclaimed by their eighteenth-century predecessors; they still believed that society should encourage individual initiative, tolerate diversities of opinion, and allow no caste or class distinctions; they still felt that the United States had been destined to excel other nations in its devotion to democracy and in its youthful spirit of optimism and enterprise.

The material growth of the United States had, however, resulted in an economic and social structure fundamentally different from that of the eighteenth century. The industrial system had created a number of new problems which threatened, if ignored for too long, to undermine democratic institutions and to involve the country in dangerous and destructive conflicts. If the American people were to solve these problems, without doing violence to American traditions, they would be required to display political talents of a high order.

The typical American of 1789 gained his livelihood from his own land by his own labor and was almost independent of the market. The typical American of 1900 was dependent for his livelihood upon a complex economic system which was international in scope and the workings of which were beyond the control of any individual or group of individuals. Any sudden change or interruption in the delicate mechanisms of the world market might result in large-scale distress and unemployment. A sudden fall in values on the New York stock exchange meant that factories throughout the country closed their gates; a growth in the agricultural production of Asia and South America meant that farmers in the United States were unable to pay their mortgage obligations. This economic insecurity was to be, in every industrialized nation, the most acute problem of the twentieth century. There was, however, no agreement either among economic experts or among ordinary citizens as to what attitude should be adopted—whether industrial crises should be left to adjust themselves automatically, in accordance with the principles of laissez-faire economics, or whether governments should enforce some positive program of amelioration or control.

In the United States of 1789 there were no great extremes of wealth and poverty. With the exception of the Negro slaves, only a small fraction of the population was wholly without property, and there was no class of men so rich as to constitute a menace to democratic institutions. By 1900, on the other hand, the United States seemed to many persons to be in danger of falling under the rule of a small oligarchy. The leaders who had created and organized the new industrial system had acquired great wealth and economic power and were able to exercise a dangerous degree of control over the institutions of government. At the other end of the social scale a large urban proletariat had developed, whose earnings were insufficient to give them an adequate standard of living. Meanwhile the farmers, both in the South and in the West, were not receiving their fair share of the national income, and they believed that their economic difficulties were the result of privileges acquired by the big financiers and industrialists.

According to calculations made in 1890, one-eighth of the population owned seven-eighths of the wealth, and 1 per cent of the population, considered as a whole, owned more than did the other 99 per cent together. Champions of the existing order defended these conditions on the ground that the wealthy industrialists were, by their enterprise and organizing ability, increasing the productivity of the economic system and thereby benefiting all classes. Reformers, on the other hand, regarded this inequality as inconsistent with American democratic ideals and believed that, if it remained uncorrected, the result would be a growth of bitter class conflicts.

In the United States of 1789 there was an apparently limitless supply of cheap land and undeveloped natural resources. For a century thereafter America had remained a country of opportunity, where any individual, by going west, might hope to acquire economic security. By 1900 this safety valve against discontent had been almost closed. The most fertile lands and the most valuable mineral deposits had been transferred to private ownership; farming had become a precarious and often unprofitable occupation. The disappearance of the frontier tended to increase the dangers of class conflicts and to bring about a slow but considerable change in the national psychology. The people of the United States would, moreover, be required to husband their surviving natural resources with a care which had not hitherto been considered necessary. Unless future generations were to be condemned to poverty, a constructive program of conservation must be enforced.

The United States of 1789 had few political and economic ties with other countries. Europe was six weeks' voyage distant; and if the United States developed her own manufacturing system and prevented any European interference with the affairs of the western hemisphere, she could hope to isolate herself from the Old World and thereby to avoid destructive wars and alien political influences. By 1900 the United States had established important commercial connections with all parts of the world; both her farmers and her manufacturers exported an important proportion of their products; and American prosperity interlocked with that of Europe. Isolation was now impossible unless drastic changes were imposed upon the American economic system. Mechanical inventions were, moreover, bringing America steadily nearer to Europe and to the Far East; by the nineteen-thirties the Atlantic could be crossed within five days by sea, and within thirty-six hours by air; and happenings in Europe became known in the United States a few minutes after they occurred. The United States was therefore compelled to play a more active role in international politics and began to find herself more intimately affected by conflicts between European nations.

The American people of 1789, in spite of the differences of interest and viewpoint between the southern and the northern states, were remarkably homogeneous. With the exception of some 800,-000 Negroes, who had no political rights, Americans were predominantly Anglo Saxon in race and Protestant in religion. They had been educated into the political philosophy of the English Whig tradition, and their political disputes were normally provoked by its applications and not by any fundamental conflicts of principle. With few exceptions, they spoke the same language, professed similar beliefs, and cherished similar ideals.

The United States of 1900, on the other hand, had become a melting pot containing representatives of almost every race in the world. More than 20 million immigrants had entered the country during the nineteenth century, and during the last two decades of the century an increasing proportion of them had come from the countries of eastern and southern Europe, whose political and religious traditions were very dissimilar to those of native-born Americans. The Protestant Anglo-Saxon tradition was still predominant, but its control was no longer undisputed. Although the new racial groups could immeasurably broaden and enrich American culture, their growth was not always welcomed by the descendants of the earlier immigrants, and it threatened to provoke racial and religious conflicts. A similar problem was presented by the emancipation of the Negroes, who had become legally free as a result of the Civil War but who continued to suffer from economic, educational, and social disabilities. Meanwhile the traditions of eighteenth-century America were being modified by the growth of urbanization. While rural America remained faithful to her old mores, new attitudes—rationalistic, sceptical, and libertarian—developed in the cities. Two cultures, one traditionalistic and the other cosmopolitan, existed side by side; and it was becoming increasingly difficult for the adherents of one to understand or tolerate the other.

During the last thiry-five years of the nineteenth century, after the Civil War had terminated the great debate on the problem of slavery, the energy and intelligence of the nation were devoted primarily to economic development. Political conflicts rarely had any fundamental importance, and politics attracted few men of the highest ability. Nor did those thinkers who criticized American institutions, and who called attention to the questions which would require political solution, attract any considerable attention. The expansion of the industrial system took precedence over all other activities.

The turn of the century, however, marked the beginning of a new epoch in American history. The industrial system continued to expand, and the changes which it was causing in American society grew more widespread. But meanwhile political leaders were beginning to concern themselves more actively with the problems that industrialism presented and to undertake the task of reconciling the new economic order with American ideals and institutions. At the same time American intellectuals were becoming more critical of the traditional values and beliefs, and there gradually began a radical examination and revaluation of the American way of life. The twentieth century was to be a period of political reform and of intense self-criticism on the part of the American mind.

2

THE REGIONS

OF THE UNITED STATES

REGIONALISM

BEFORE considering the course of events after 1900, it is desirable
to describe the condition of the United States at the end of the nineteenth century, and to examine its economic, political, and cultural
structure.

Any discussion of American life should lay considerable emphasis
on the interplay between the forces of centralization and those making for regional separatism. The United States is a continental area
rather than a single country; and its government, unlike the governments of almost all European nations, has never been fully centralized. The various regions into which the country is divided have a
common language and similar institutions, but they differ from one
another in their geographical and economic characteristics and in
the psychology of their inhabitants. Political parties in the United
States have always been coalitions of different groups from different
regions, whose alliances have been based often on expediency or on
tradition rather than on common principles; and political conflicts
have defined themselves along regional lines at least as often as
along class lines.

Since the establishment of the Federal union, the strongest trend
has, however, been toward centralization. The different regions have
been drawn together by the building of the railroads, by the growth

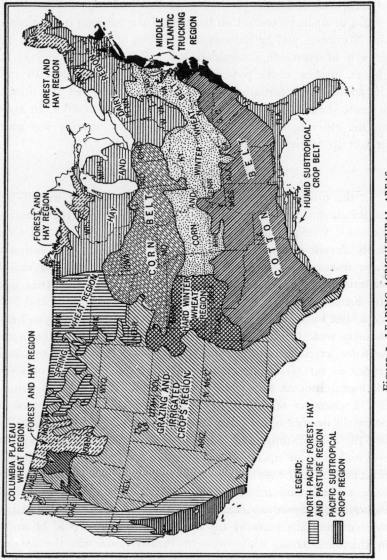

Figure 1. LEADING AGRICULTURAL AREAS

LEGEND:

NORTH PACIFIC FOREST, HAY
AND PASTURE REGION

PACIFIC SUBTROPICAL
CROPS REGION

COLUMBIA PLATEAU
WHEAT REGION

FOREST AND HAY REGION

FOREST AND
HAY REGION

SPRING WHEAT REGION

HARD WINTER
WHEAT REGION

UTAH, COL.
GRAZING AND
IRRIGATED
CROPS' REGION

CORN BELT

WINTER WHEAT AND CORN AND
WINTER WHEAT REGION

DAIRY
REGION

FOREST AND
HAY REGION

MIDDLE
ATLANTIC
TRUCKING
REGION

C O T T O N   B E L T

HUMID SUBTROPICAL
CROP BELT

of large-scale industries producing standardized commodities, by the spread of financial control on the part of the banking institutions of the Northeast, and by the migratory habits of the population. The growth of economic integration has led to a corresponding, but slower, increase in the powers of the Federal government. In 1789 the country was partially united by political ties, but the thirteen separate states had few economic bonds with one another. In 1900, on the other hand, the unity of the different sections was much greater economically than politically or psychologically.

THE INDUSTRIAL MIDDLE WEST

In the nineteenth century the allied occupations of mining and manufacturing had become the most important part of the American economic system and the chief source of American wealth. Originally developed in the Northeast close to the Atlantic seaboard, these industries had gradually moved westward into the middle western region across the Appalachians. Important industries were still located in southern New England and in New Jersey and New York; but by 1900 the most important branches of American heavy industry were to be found along the western slopes of the Appalachians, extending from Pennsylvania south along the mountain ranges as far as Alabama and west, through the states of Ohio, Michigan, Indiana, and Illinois, to the shores of the Great Lakes.

The character of this region was determined by its mineral deposits. In northeastern Pennsylvania, in the valleys of the Schuylkill and the Susquehanna, were 480 square miles of the hard smokeless coal known as anthracite. By 1920 more than a million persons were concentrated in the anthracite area. Deposits of soft bituminous coal were to be found throughout the whole Appalachian area from Pennsylvania down to Alabama and could often be dug out of hillsides without any necessity for sinking mines. Iron could be mined in the same areas, while western Pennsylvania was the original center of oil production. Pittsburgh, lying in the heart of the mining area, connected by river with the Gulf of Mexico and by canal with the Great Lakes, became in the later decades of the nineteenth century the chief center of heavy industry in the United States.

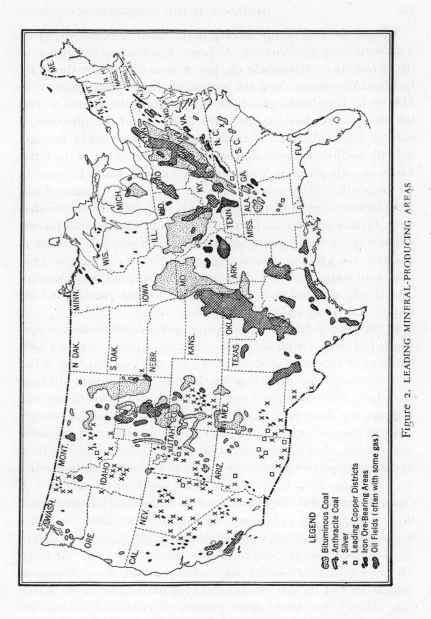

Figure 2. LEADING MINERAL-PRODUCING AREAS

LEGEND

Bituminous Coal
Anthracite Coal
Silver
Leading Copper Districts
Iron Ore-Bearing Areas
Oil Fields (often with some gas)

ME.
N.H.
VT.
MASS.
CONN. R.I.
N.Y.
PA.
N.J.
MD. DEL.
W. VA.
VA.
N.C.
S.C.
GA.
FLA.
ALA.
MISS.
TENN.
KY.
OHIO
IND.
ILL.
MICH.
WIS.
MINN.
IOWA
MO.
ARK.
OKLA.
TEXAS
KANS.
NEBR.
S. DAK.
N. DAK.
COLO.
N. MEX.
UTAH
ARIZ.
NEV.
CAL.
ORE.
WASH.
IDAHO
MONT.

Toward the end of the century heavy industry began to spread southward, and Birmingham, Alabama, became another center of steel production. Meanwhile the richest iron deposits in the world had been discovered along the western shores of Lake Superior, in Minnesota, lying in ranges above the surface of the ground so that the ore could be shoveled into cars without any of the apparatus of mining. The exploitation of these ranges drew branches of the steel industry northward, and industrial areas grew up closer to the Great Lakes, at such places as Youngstown, Ohio, and Gary, Indiana. In the twentieth century another industry, the making of automobiles, grew to enormous proportions; and this, with its affiliate manufactures, became centered at Detroit. Meanwhile Chicago had become the metropolis of the whole agricultural region which lay farther to the west; the greatest railroad terminal in the world, and the principal marketing center for grain and cattle, it specialized in industries closely affiliated with farming, such as meat packing and the manufacture of agricultural implements.

By the end of the nineteenth century this middle western region, which had grown with such overwhelming rapidity, was not only the heart of the new industrial economy; since the Civil War it had also dominated the politics of the country. Its economic development had given wealth and power to a group of industrialists who had, for the most part, started life without hereditary advantages and had risen to supremacy by their own ruthless energy and ambition. Closely allied to these industrial chieftains, and similar to them in character and viewpoint, were the political leaders who controlled the Republican Party in the Middle West; and from the accession of General Grant until the assassination of President McKinley (with the exception of the eight years of Cleveland's two administrations) it was the Middle West which provided the country with its presidents and which largely determined the policies of its majority party. The major characteristic of the middle western Republicans was their belief that the government should assist the growth of capitalistic industry but should never presume to regulate it or interfere with it.

At the same time, the laboring population of the Middle West

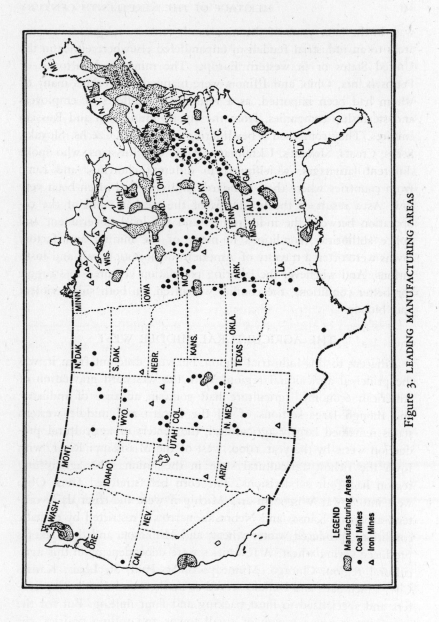

Figure 3. LEADING MANUFACTURING AREAS

LEGEND
Manufacturing Areas
● Coal Mines
△ Iron Mines

was, in the later years of the nineteenth century, subjected in some areas to an industrial feudalism unparalleled elsewhere either in the United States or in western Europe. The mines and factories of Pennsylvania, Ohio, and Illinois were manned by workers many of whom had been imported, as a result of the efforts of employers and steamship companies, from the Austro-Hungarian and Russian empires. They composed a bewildering mixture of Czechs, Slovaks, Serbs, Croats, Slovenes, Ukrainians, Poles, and Russians, who spoke different languages, worshipped in different churches, and came from countries where their standards of living had often been very low. As a result of the handicaps of the workers, and of the co-operation between the industrialists and the local government and police authorities, conditions in many of the mining and factory towns were often a travesty of American democratic ideals and institutions. And whenever the laboring population ventured to struggle for better conditions, the conflict was often, on both sides, violent and bloody.

THE AGRICULTURAL MIDDLE WEST

Adjacent to this industrial region, but very different from it, was the principal agricultural region. With the westward gravitation of American economy, agriculture had gone in advance of industry; and though large sections of all the eastern and middle western states remained largely agricultural, the centers of agricultural production were, by the year 1900, west of the Mississippi River, with Iowa the richest agricultural state in the union. The agricultural region had four subdivisions. The corn belt stretched from Ohio west into Iowa; Wisconsin and Michigan were the chief dairy centers; a part of Kansas and Nebraska, narrowly restricted by climatic conditions, produced winter wheat; and Minnesota and the Dakotas produced spring wheat. A few cities were dependent upon this agricultural region. Chicago, Minneapolis, St. Paul, St. Louis, Kansas City, Cincinnati, and Buffalo served as markets and distributing centers and specialized in meat packing and flour milling. But for the most part it was a region of small towns and rolling prairies, the monotony of which was almost unbroken by hill or forest.

The inhabitants of this vast area had a considerable uniformity of outlook. They were for the most part either of New England descent or of Scandinavian or German stock, with similar religious traditions and cultural traits. The typical farming unit was of less than 150 acres and was operated by a single family with the aid of a hired man and of the migratory laborers who came only for the harvest season. It was an area of a Protestantism which often became puritanical, and of a democracy which was perhaps more deeply rooted in economic and social conditions than elsewhere in the United States. It prided itself on its devotion to American ideals; and, having few direct economic or cultural ties with other parts of the world, it was in the twentieth century the chief center of the demand for an isolationist foreign policy.

The struggle to prevent any extension of slavery and to preserve the Union had caused this agricultural region to combine with the industrial sections in support of the Republican Party; but after the slavery issue had been settled, agriculture derived few advantages from the combination. Republican policies were devoted primarily to the benefit of industry and finance; and the farmers found themselves exploited by the railroads who transported their products, the merchants who bought those products, the industrialists who sold them machinery, and the bankers who loaned them money. After the Civil War there was never any permanent political realignment; but a series of waves of agrarian radical insurgency swept over the agricultural regions, some of which led to the formation of progressive blocs within the Republican Party, while others threatened to put an end to Republican predominance. In the eighteen-eighties Kansas, where the spirit of John Brown had perhaps a permanent influence, was particularly noted for a fanatical radicalism. In the twentieth century Wisconsin became the chief example in the United States of progressive ideals translated into practical politics; while the spring wheat section of Minnesota and the Dakotas, where the farmers had to contend with so many forms of natural catastrophe—with frost, drought, hail, rust, invasions of grasshoppers, and with a long five-month winter—became a new home of insurgency.

THE NORTHEAST

With the growth of the country the chief sources of wealth had moved west, but the ownership and control of that wealth had largely remained in the East. By 1900 the centers of industry were in the Middle West, and the chief agricultural region was west of the Mississippi River; but financial predominance still belonged to the banking institutions of the Atlantic seaboard cities. And as the industrial system developed, the powers of the eastern bankers tended to increase.

The northern and middle Atlantic seaboard had been predestined to greatness by its location, which enabled it to control the flow of commerce between Europe and the Middle West; and early in the nineteenth century its leading cities—Boston, New York, Philadelphia, and Baltimore—had become rivals for supremacy. Victory rested finally with New York, as a result of its superb natural harbor at the mouth of the Hudson River, of the building of the Erie Canal linking it with the Great Lakes, and subsequently of its railroad connections with the West. Commercial supremacy was followed by financial and cultural leadership; after the Civil War New York began to surpass Boston and Philadelphia as the headquarters of banking, and to become the intellectual capital of the nation. By the end of the century it was the home of America's leading financiers and industrialists, and the center of numerous economic empires whose properties extended into every state in the Union. It was the headquarters also of the publishing business, of the chief aesthetic and intellectual organizations, and of the numerous instrumentalities by which public opinion might be influenced or controlled.

Throughout the eastern states there were relics of the aristocratic traditions that had been created in the Colonial period, exemplified in the land-owning squirearchy of the Hudson valley and in the social leadership claimed by the older families in Philadelphia and Baltimore. It was, however, in New England, and especially in Boston, that these traditions were most powerful. In New England financial and industrial leadership had been retained by the Yankee families whose wealth had originally been created out of foreign trade in the eighteenth century and had afterward been increased by the development of textile manufacturing. These descendants of the Puritans, who now owned banks and factories and had investments in railroads and industries in other sections of the country, were characterized by their pride in their race and its traditions, their conscientious obedience to duty and moral obligation, and their patronage of learning and the arts. Animated at their best by a noble social idealism, they were too often rigidly conservative, intolerant toward alien races, unorthodox ideas, and more liberal customs. In New York, on the other hand, aristocratic traditions had been obliterated by the constant advent of new millionaire families from the West; and attempts to preserve social distinction based on inherited wealth had had little permanent success. The business leadership, which became concentrated in Wall Street and lower Broadway, was drawn from every part of the United States and from half a dozen different racial stocks.

Scattered over the eastern states were agricultural sections which had been settled during the Colonial period and where the inhabitants had retained strongly marked traditions and characteristics. In the New England countryside much of the old Yankee spirit had survived; New England farmers were still hardworking, frugal, self-reliant, and taciturn. The whole New England region, however, which in the early days of the republic had been the rival of the South for political predominance, which had led the way in the development of industrialism, and which had produced the most distinctive group of American writers, had since the Civil War been decreasing in relative importance. More than either of the other two Atlantic seaboard sections it had contributed its native sons and its traditions to the building of the West, and it had weakened itself in the process. Farming in this region, moreover, had ceased to be a profitable occupation, and between 1880 and 1920 the acreage of cultivated land in New England was cut in half. Southern New England became the most highly urbanized area in America. Similar to rural New England in the conservatism of its inhabitants, though more prosperous, were the agricultural sections of upper New York State and of New Jersey, while in the fertile valleys of central Penn-

sylvania the German communities which had been established early
in the eighteenth century still lived in isolation from the modern
world.

The great cities, however, dominated the whole northeastern region, and by the end of the nineteenth century they had become
conglomerations of all the innumerable races and religions in the
American melting pot. Important industries were still located along
the seaboard, in spite of the fact that almost all the materials for
them had to be imported from other sections. New England retained
its supremacy in textiles, in spite of increasing competition from the
South; the cities of northern New Jersey specialized in silk, leather,
and oil refining; while New York was the chief center of the clothing industry. These and other industries began before the end of the
nineteenth century to attract millions of immigrants from Italy and
eastern Europe and from French Canada, so that here, more than
in any other section of the United States, the Anglo-Saxon and Protestant traditions of the eighteenth century seemed to be in process
of obliteration. In New England, by 1920, one-quarter of the population was foreign-born, and nearly two-thirds had at least one
parent who had been born abroad. The immigrants did not attain
social or financial equality with the old Puritan families; but immigrant and Catholic influences soon began to predominate in the city
governments. In the City of New York the processes of the melting
pot were even more rapid. The most cosmopolitan city in the world,
it contained colonies of almost every racial group in existence. Restless, tolerant, and heterogeneous, New York epitomized all the
newer forces in American life.

THE SOUTH

These three regions, devoted respectively to industry, to agriculture, and to commerce and finance, were united by close economic
ties and, to a large degree, by a common allegiance to the Republican Party—an allegiance created by the Civil War and never fully
broken, though sometimes threatened by subsequent disagreements.
By contrast, the other sections of the United States—the South, the

Rocky Mountain region, and the Far West—were less integrated into the economic and political structure of the country.

The eleven states which had composed the Confederacy during the Civil War, along with the three or four border states—a section including nearly one-third of the area and nearly one-third of the population of the United States—differed markedly from every other part of the country. They were united by their bitter memories of the Civil War and of Reconstruction, by the poverty which had resulted from the war, by their preoccupation with the racial problem (about one-third of the population of the South being Negro), and by the common ancestry and traditions of their white inhabitants (in 1910 only 2.5 per cent of the population of the South was foreign born). The South contained, however, several clearly marked subdivisions. The heart of the whole section, and the location of its chief economic and racial problems, was the cotton belt which stretched from Georgia and South Carolina westward into Texas. The states farther to the north practised a more variegated agriculture and were less affected by the color question. Texas, an empire in itself, larger than, and potentially almost as rich as, any European nation except Russia, was as much western as southern in its psychology and economic conditions. The Appalachian and Ozark regions, comprising parts of almost every southern state, had scarcely been touched by any changes since the beginning of the nineteenth century.

Traditionally, the South was an agrarian section, putting the interests of agriculture above those of industry and priding itself on its gracious way of life and its freedom from the materialism and pecuniary standards which prevailed in the North. Defeat in war had, however, been followed by the decay of the southern tradition. Northern industrial corporations extended their operations to the South. At the same time, following the Reconstruction Period, leadership in the South was assumed by men who abandoned the traditions of the plantation aristocracy and believed that the South should now adopt the business methods of the North. In the latter part of the nineteenth century, under this "Bourbon" rule, the South began rapidly to be industrialized—a process accompanied by the low wages, the child labor, and the close connections between government and business that had characterized the earlier stages of the Industrial Revolution elsewhere.

A majority of the Southern population continued, however, to be agricultural; and they suffered, especially in the cotton belt, from a poverty rivaling that of the peasants of backward eastern European and Asiatic nations. Not only were the southern farmers, both white and Negro, exploited by the southern bankers, merchants, and landlords who had taken power after Reconstruction, but all classes in the South were the common victims of the results of the war—the destruction of southern economy in the war, northern control of the Federal government and of industry and transportation after the war, and the economic weaknesses of the system of cotton production itself. The poverty of the rural South meant, in turn, that it was severely handicapped with respect to health and public education; many of its inhabitants were physically weakened by hookworm, malaria, or pellagra, and were apt to follow the leadership of rabble-rousing demagogues. Any drastic reformation was rendered difficult by the pervasive and apparently insoluble problem of race. The white population of the South was united in its determination to keep the Negro in subordination. And though the decade of the nineties saw a widespread agrarian revolt against Bourbon control, it failed to achieve any real reorganization of southern society as a result of the belief of all white classes in the South that their racial unity must be preserved.

The South did not comprise merely the cotton belt and the new industrial sections in Alabama and the Carolinas; it included also the Appalachian and Ozark plateaus, the former of which was larger than all New England and New York. The population of these areas was wholly rural and wholly white. The small farmers of these secluded highlands, unaffected either by the plantation economy of the southern lowlands or by the growth of industrialism, still lived in the fashion of their eighteenth-century ancestors, preserving the customs, the forms of language, the superstitions, and the songs and dances which had died out almost everywhere else in the United States. They had a low standard of living, subsisting chiefly on pork, fried squirrel, corncakes, and corn whiskey; and their primitivism was often startling. Family feuds which had originated early in the nineteenth century occasionally resulted in killings as late as the nineteen-thirties. Such phenomena were a sign not of degeneracy but of backwardness; the Appalachian mountaineers were the contemporary ancestors of modern Americans. Whether their isolation would continue was, however, dubious; in the twentieth century they began to be drawn down into the cotton mills of North Carolina, and to find their ancestral homes in the Kentucky and Tennessee mountains transformed into coal-mining areas.

THE ROCKY MOUNTAIN REGION

Socially, the South differed markedly from the Northeast and the Middle West, but geographically the main dividing line in the United States was not that along which the Civil War had been fought but that which divided all the eastern sections from the West. Running through the Dakotas, Nebraska, Kansas, Oklahoma, and Texas was the line which separated the fertile lands of the East from the arid West. Here, for the first time, the Anglo Saxon race in its progress across the continent had met an environment which demanded fundamental changes in its economic methods. The plantation and the homestead were both unadapted to a country where the average rainfall was less than twenty inches a year.

The region of the Great Plains, the Rocky Mountains, and the western plateaus between the Rockies and the Pacific ranges, comprised nearly 30 per cent of the total area of the United States, but in 1900 it had only a little more than 2 per cent of the population. This proportion did not greatly increase during the next forty years. Successful agriculture required larger farms than the 160-acre homestead; and it required also a collective planning of irrigation, such as was alien to the laissez-faire individualism of nineteenth-century Americans. A number of homesteaders, tempted by an occasional year of heavy rainfall, had attempted farming in the Great Plains, but with disastrous results. And throughout the whole region the Mormons in Utah, thanks to a wise regulation of water rights, were almost the only white people who had developed a successful agriculture.

Except in Utah this was mainly a country of cattle ranches and mining camps. The eighties were the great age of cattle breeding, when herds could be driven almost freely across the plains from Texas as far as the Canadian border, and when the cowboy, borrowing his costume and his way of life from Mexico and living with a picturesqueness and a spaciousness rare in the annals of the Anglo Saxon pioneer, won for himself a permanent place in American legend. Subsequently barbed wire put an end to the open range; and overproduction, overcropping of the grass, and the severe winter of 1886–1887 ruined many of the cattle owners, though much of the country between the Great Plains and the Pacific was still devoted to cattle and sheep.

The other chief occupation of this region was the mining of silver, gold, copper, and lead. Exploitation of the mineral wealth of the western plateaus began during the Civil War; and prospectors, particularly in the silver mines of Nevada, occasionally became millionaires. But some of the mines were quickly exhausted; and ghost towns, built within a few months and deserted almost as rapidly, became a characteristic feature of the mining regions. The workers in these western mines were a nomadic people, often without family ties and habituated to the violence and the occasional lawlessness which flourished in this sparsely settled country. Their labor organizations, unlike those of the industrial East, were converted easily to revolutionary doctrines.

THE PACIFIC COAST

Almost all the West was arid, by contrast with the East—an aridity which culminated in the desert of Arizona, where the rainfall, over an area of nearly seventy thousand square miles, averaged less than three inches a year. The Indian tribes who still lived on the southern plateaus, in New Mexico and Arizona, had achieved a better permanent adaptation to their environment than had the more recently arrived Europeans. Close to the Pacific, however, along both sides of the coast ranges, water was more plentiful, although artificial irrigation was usually necessary; and the population of these areas, first settled by citizens of the United States in the eighteen-forties, continued to grow rapidly.

California, after the decline of its gold production in the fifties, found a more permanent basis for prosperity in fruit and vegetable farming. The coastal plain and the Imperial Valley east of the mountains in southern California, and the Great Valley in northern California, were as intensively cultivated as any part of the United States. Land ownership in the two valleys was monopolized by a few individuals and corporations—a relic of the Spanish heritage; and the work was performed by tenant farmers and by migratory laborers, many of whom were Japanese, Chinese, Hindu, or Mexican. The exploitation of agricultural labor, and the rivalry between white and colored farmers, created a complex agrarian problem which was peculiar to California. Meanwhile the state was becoming famous for its climate, and in the twentieth century hundreds of thousands of retired farmers and businessmen from the Middle West chose it as the home of their old age. California was at once the end of that march to the West,—begun three hundred years earlier at Jamestown and Plymouth—and the beginning, perhaps, of a new historic process which would make the Pacific the chief center of world civilization. Here everything was grandiose and both the idealisms and the eccentricities of the American race assumed exaggerated colors.

In the Pacific Northwest there was more sobriety. Washington and Oregon had a climate closely resembling that of northwestern Europe, the original home of the majority of the American people. Those states had been settled democratically, on the homestead principle. Potentially, through the development of water power, this was one of the richest areas in America, but in 1900 it could still consider itself as the last frontier. Prosperous farming regions were being developed in the Columbia basin, around Puget Sound in Washington, and in the Willamette Valley in Oregon. But lumbering, the first stage in the exploitation of virgin country, continued into the twentieth century to be the chief business of the region.

BIBLIOGRAPHY

D. Davidson, *The Attack on Leviathan* (1938)

H. H. McCarty, *The Geographic Basis of American Economic Life* (1940)

H. W. Odum and H. E. Moore, *American Regionalism* (1938)

* J. R. Smith and M. Phillips, *North America* (revised edition, 1940)

J. R. Smith, *Men and Resources* (1937)

N. B. Throughout the bibliographies at the end of each chapter books which students will find exceptionally useful, or which are of outstanding importance, are marked with an asterisk.

3

THE GROWTH OF

INDUSTRIAL CORPORATIONS

THE AGE OF THE CORPORATION

THE nineteenth century, more than any previous epoch in history, was a period of rapid change, especially in the economic field; and the structure of American society was, in certain respects, radically different in 1900 from what it had been in 1789. One of the most important results of these economic changes was the decrease in importance (except in agriculture) of individualistic private property and small-scale production. Largely responsible was the growth of great aggregations of capital, organized into corporations each of which was owned by thousands of stockholders and which gave employment to thousands of workers. By the end of the nineteenth century these large-scale corporations had acquired a dominant position in American economic life. In 1900 two-thirds of all manufacturing was done by corporations; and by 1940 the proportion had increased to nineteen-twentieths. Just as in Europe the twelfth and thirteenth centuries were the age of feudalism, and the seventeenth and eighteenth centuries were the age of absolutism, so in the United States the twentieth century will probably go down in history as the age of the corporation.

The characteristic feature of the new economic system was the mass production of standardized commodities. In place of small factories producing mainly for local markets, there developed large industrial organizations turning out goods in quantities sufficient for a nationwide market. This was made possible by new scientific inventions, by the growth of mechanization, and by the discovery of new sources of power, water power giving way to steam and later to oil and electricity. Every effort was made to discover more efficient and more economical methods of production. Industrialists encouraged scientific research and began finally to organize private research departments of their own; careful studies were made of methods for economizing labor; and the division of labor and the building of machinery with interchangeable parts were carried to almost fantastic extremes.

Since large capital investments were needed to build factories capable of using these new methods of production, it was inevitable that this economic development should result in the decline of small business units and the growth of large corporations, and in the achievement of economic power by the individual entrepreneurs who organized these corporations. The new methods of production meant, moreover, that the whole country began to be integrated into a single delicately adjusted economic system. The division of labor, which made possible an enormous increase in the national wealth and standard of living, meant also that individuals were no longer economically independent; the welfare of each section of the population became dependent upon that of every other section.

The development of the corporation system began in the northeast early in the nineteenth century; but before the Civil War its growth in other sections of the country was impeded by the opposition of the two agrarian sections, the South and the West. The war, however, gave supremacy to the North—a supremacy which was consolidated during the period of southern Reconstruction and was followed by a very rapid growth of industry. The war itself supplied a great stimulus to large-scale production, since the Union government gave orders for large supplies of clothing, food, and munitions for the Northern armies. After the war everything tended to favor further industrial growth. Industrialists enjoyed the support of a government which protected them both from opposition at home and from foreign competition. They found it easy to obtain labor, as a result first of the return of the soldiers to civilian life and afterward of large-scale immigration from Europe. They were often able to borrow capital from European investors. They could exploit the enormous natural resources of a continent still largely undeveloped. And for the sale of their products they had a larger internal market than any other industrialized nation in the world.

A corporation was, in theory, a co-operative enterprise, in which ownership was divided among a number of stockholders and management was entrusted to their elected representatives. Actually, however, most of the big industrial combinations of the post–Civil War period were created and dominated by single individuals, and it was not until after they had died or retired that the corporation passed beyond the stage of personal rule. Before the Civil War the chief sources of wealth had been foreign trade and the ownership of real estate. After the war the immense opportunities for industrial development were seized by a group of ambitious entrepreneurs —such men as Rockefeller in oil, Carnegie and Frick in steel, Vanderbilt, Hill, and Harriman in railroads, McCormick in agricultural machinery, Havemeyer in sugar, Duke in tobacco—almost all of whom had started life without hereditary advantages. They came to constitute a new plutocracy, whose wealth quickly surpassed that of the older mercantile and landowning aristocracies. Their less successful fellow-citizens were alternately dazzled by their triumphs, and alarmed by the power which they had acquired.

There were considerable variations in the methods by which these men achieved supremacy, and in their standards of economic morality. Some of them, like Andrew Carnegie and John D. Rockefeller, were genuine industrial entrepreneurs, whose wealth came primarily from the efficiency with which they organized production. Others were primarily financiers, who bought control over industries which others had created and who built their fortunes by combining corporations into more powerful units and by manipulating stock prices to their private advantage. All of them were alike, however, in the ruthlessness with which they sought power and crushed opposition, in their conviction that society had no right to interfere with their activities and that any methods, however unscrupulous, might justifiably be adopted for their protection, and in their belief that the pursuit of wealth was a noble activity, beneficial to society as well as to themselves. This attitude was an expression of the dominant ethos of nineteenth-century American civilization, derived partly from the Puritanism which had condemned pleasure and extravagance and had declared that devotion to one's work was pleasing to God, and partly from the doctrines of laissez-faire economics which had seen in the enlightened self-interest of each individual an instrument for promoting the common interests of all.

The building of huge industrial corporations was accompanied by an increase in the powers of the investment bankers, most of whom were located either in New York or in Boston. The investment bankers undertook to provide capital for industry by managing the sale of stocks—a function which industrial entrepreneurs could not easily undertake themselves at a period when a large proportion of the capital was supplied by European investors. And in order to protect the interests of the stockholders, the bankers gradually began to assume some degree of supervision over the management of corporations, and, in cases of bankruptcy, to undertake the responsibility for the necessary reorganization. Banking firms, particularly the most powerful of them, the House of Morgan, began to be represented on the directorates of an increasing number of railroads and manufacturing corporations; and this common banking supervision by means of "interlocking" directors was an important factor in checking competition and bringing about what the bankers described as a "community of interest."

The actual degree of control exercised by the banks was problematical. The younger Morgan insisted, before a Congressional committee in 1913, that it was "preposterous to suppose that every 'interlocking' director has full control in every organization with which he is connected and that the majority of directors who are not 'interlocking' are mere figureheads." But to many Americans, in the early years of the twentieth century, it seemed that the creation of these corporations in most of the leading industries was being followed by the integration of all such corporations into a single vast structure, and that the House of Morgan was in process of achieving a kind of economic dictatorship.

CORPORATIONS AND THE GOVERNMENT

The growth of the big corporations would have been impossible if they had not received legal protection and governmental assistance. The American Constitution had been planned largely for the protection of property rights, in accordance with the eighteenth-century theory that life, liberty, and property were the three natural rights of man and that the arbitrary deprivation of any one of them was tyranny. A series of judicial interpretations subsequently enlarged the conception of property rights, giving to corporations the same protection as to individuals and defining any drastic government regulation of corporate business as a violation of property rights. The growth of large-scale corporations could thus take place within a legal framework which had originally been created for the security of individual property owners.

The immunity of business from political interference received added justification from the economic theory of *laissez faire*. This theory, first elaborated by Adam Smith and subsequently built into a philosophical system by Herbert Spencer, whose writings had an enormous influence in the United States, declared that government should not meddle at all with economic activities, either to prohibit, to control, or to encourage, and that the mechanisms of the free market, regulated by the interplay of supply and demand, would guide the activities of each individual into the channels where they would be socially most useful. The doctrine of *laissez faire* was used by American businessmen to justify their freedom from political interference; continuous progress, they declared, was dependent upon unchecked freedom for individual enterprise. The successful entrepreneur must be protected from the envy of the poorer classes in the community, who lacked the industry and ability needed for acquiring wealth and who sought compensation for their economic failure through political action.

In reality, however, American businessmen never adopted the

doctrine of *laissez faire* completely or consistently; they used it as an instrument for repelling interference and opposition. The real attitude of American business was that it was the function of government to assist and encourage economic development. The prevalent belief was that if business entrepreneurs enjoyed freedom and protection, the benefits of their activities would percolate down to all sections of the population. The correct method of improving the condition of the workers and of other underprivileged classes was not to legislate directly for their benefit but to encourage business expansion.

A corporation was an artificial creation that came into existence through the granting of a charter by the government. Under the American federal system, however, it was the states and not the Federal government which gave corporation charters, although after a corporation had been created it could do business throughout the Union and enjoyed the protection of the Federal Constitution. Originally when a group of men wished to organize a corporation, they were required to apply to the legislature of their state, which would usually scrutinize carefully the terms of the proposed charter before granting it. In the course of the nineteenth century, however, all the states passed general incorporation laws—a process which began in Connecticut in 1836. Henceforth the organizers of a corporation could, to a considerable extent, write their own wishes into the charter. In the eighteen-eighties there was considerable alarm at the growth of monopoly, and a number of states passed antitrust laws limiting the powers granted through corporation charters.

In 1889, however, and again in 1893 and 1896, the State of New Jersey deliberately altered its corporation laws in order to encourage business entrepreneurs to apply for New Jersey charters. This step was taken at the suggestion of James B. Dill, who pointed out that the state could increase its revenues and solve its financial difficulties by going into the business of selling charters. Henceforth a group of businessmen could obtain a New Jersey charter for almost any purpose and with very few restrictions, in return for payment of a fee of twenty cents for every thousand dollars of capitalization.

Between 1889 and 1912, when the New Jersey laws were made stricter, almost all the big corporations obtained New Jersey charters; and by the year 1903 the state was making more than two million dollars a year from license fees. Other states which sold charters on easy terms were Delaware, which replaced New Jersey as the favorite home of big corporations after 1912, and West Virginia.

Once a corporation had been legally constituted it was protected from political interference by the Federal Constitution. In the establishment of freedom for business enterprise two amendments to the Constitution, the Fifth and the Fourteenth, were of particular importance. The Fifth Amendment prohibited the Federal government from depriving individuals of life, liberty, or property except by due process of law, while the Fourteenth Amendment, enacted after the Civil War, nominally to protect the Negro population in the South, extended the same prohibition to the state governments. Judicial interpretation of the Fourteenth Amendment, beginning in the year 1886, extended the due process clause, which had originally been intended merely as a ban on confiscation, to cover any regulation of corporations which might prevent them from earning what the judges considered to be a reasonable profit.

The same purpose was secured also through judicial interpretations of the commerce clause in the Constitution. According to the Constitution the Federal government might regulate interstate commerce, while commerce which was not interstate remained, it was implied, under the control of the state governments. A very narrow judicial definition of the word *interstate,* coupled with the fact that state governments were unable effectively to control corporations manufacturing products for a nationwide market, created a borderland between Federal and state authority, in which industrial corporations were able to enjoy almost complete independence. A similar freedom was not, however, granted to labor organizations. On the contrary, corporations were protected from attack by labor unions as well as by legislative bodies, in spite of the fact that this necessitated certain judicial inconsistencies. Laws forbidding actions tending to restrain trade, interpreted very loosely when the powers of corporations were involved, were used to restrict very severely the powers of labor unions.[1]

The rights of large corporations received additional confirmation from the patent laws. The granting of patents, running in most instances for seventeen-year periods, had been intended originally to protect and encourage individual inventors. But just as the rights of individual property owners had been extended to protect impersonal corporations, so the patent laws were applied to cover inventions made in the research departments of corporations and to allow the sale of patent rights from individuals to corporations and from one corporation to another. After 1896, moreover, as a result of court decisions, patent rights might be maintained even when they were not being utilized. The rapid increase in technical inventions after the Civil War greatly increased the importance of the patent system; and a number of the most powerful corporations in the country were built on the ownership of groups of patents, from the use of which competitors were legally excluded.

Industrial corporations not only enjoyed legal protection; they also expected and obtained direct assistance from the Federal government. The tariff, raised during the Civil War to increase revenues and left high in spite of treasury surpluses after the war, protected American industry from foreign competition and, by enabling corporations to charge higher prices, acted as an indirect subsidy. The tariff was a violation of the rules of laissez-faire economics; but economists who insisted that *laissez faire* should be applied consistently, and that free trade should therefore be established, were regarded by most businessmen with almost as much hostility as were the advocates of government ownership or control. The Federal government had at its disposal, moreover, all the natural resources of the undeveloped West, and until the end of the nineteenth century the dominant idea was that these resources should be transferred to private ownership quickly and on generous terms. Homesteads were given freely to farmers; but the major part of the mineral and timber resources of the West became the property of corporations,

1. See Chapter 10, page 132.

partly through gifts to the transcontinental railroads and partly through lax administration of the homestead regulations.

THE DECLINE OF COMPETITION

In the nineteenth century the majority of the American people believed in freedom for business enterprise, but they believed also in the preservation of competition. According to the laissez-faire doctrine, only constant competition could provide a stimulus for economic growth and guarantee the consumer against unjustly high prices. The growth of corporations led necessarily, however, to a decrease in competition. The need for aggregations of capital large enough to finance the building of the new large-scale machinery caused some industrial units to combine with one another, while others were driven into bankruptcy by cut-throat price-cutting. As the economic system developed, industrial organizations became larger and fewer; and the processes of combination seemed to be leading toward the creation of a few great monopolies which would enjoy absolute power over large areas of American life. Most businessmen disliked competition, which exposed them to the dangers of price wars, whereas by combining they could keep prices high and thereby increase their profits. With the decrease in the number of units in any branch of industry combinations became proportionately easier to arrange.

Combinations were effected in a number of different ways. Several corporations might be completely merged into one large corporation. Industrialists might make pooling and price agreements with one another, dividing the market and charging the same prices. A number of corporations might transfer their stock to a small committee, which was to hold it as trustees for the stockholders. (This device, invented in 1882 by the lawyers of Standard Oil, led to the original "trust," though the word "trust" was later applied, more loosely, to any industrial combination.) A single "holding company," dominated by one individual or group of partners, might own a majority of the stock in a number of other corporations. (The holding company appears to have been invented in Pennsylvania in 1868, and was definitely legalized in New Jersey in 1889.) One banking firm might secure sufficient power over several industrial corporations to enforce agreement and "community of interest." Interlocking directorates might place different corporations under the control of the same individuals. Or one corporation might acquire such a dominant position in a particular industry that it could dictate policies to its competitors and threaten them with a price war if they refused to comply.

In many ways the decline of competition was economically beneficial. Numerous small competing industrial units could not serve the public as effectively as could a few powerful corporations. In the eighteen-fifties and sixties, before the age of combinations, there were—to cite a few examples—50 different telegraph companies, 200 different companies making mowers and reapers, 450 different coal-mining companies, and several thousand oil producers; 30 different horsecar companies served the people of the City of New York, and persons traveling by railroad from New York to Chicago had to make seventeen changes. Competition, carried to this extent, resulted in obvious inconveniences, required much unnecessary duplication of equipment, led to a wastage of natural resources, and, by provoking cut-throat price wars, was accompanied by an instability which discouraged long-range industrial planning.

But although large-scale corporations were able to operate much more economically and efficiently, they did not always have sufficient inducements to share the benefits of combination with the consumer. The decline of competition meant that there was no longer automatic control over the price system; combination often made it possible for corporations to exploit the consumer through high prices. The evils of this situation were, moreover, intensified during periods of economic depression. Whereas competitive industries had to maintain production and cut their prices, the big corporations tended to maintain their prices and to restrict production, a policy which, by causing greater unemployment, increased the length and severity of the depression.

Public opinion was, in general, opposed to combination, the most vocal opponents of it being the small-scale producers who had to compete with the large corporations; and beginning in 1890, when the Sherman Anti-Trust Act was passed, the Federal government made a series of attempts to preserve competitive conditions. The various "trust-busting" campaigns, however, had little success. Some economic enterprises, such as the railroads and the public utilities that supplied electricity and telephone and telegraph services, were natural monopolies, where competition would involve wasteful duplication of equipment. In most branches of industry large-scale production appeared to be economically desirable; and it was difficult to decide at what point the disadvantages of combination began to outweigh the advantages of the increase in size. When, moreover, an industry had passed under the control of a small number of powerful corporations, legal prohibitions of combination became almost impossible to enforce; it was easy for corporation managers to make private price agreements with one another which were beyond the reach of the law. The general tendency of government action was toward public regulation of the rates and prices charged by railroads and public utilities and the enforcement of competition in other industries. But neither of these policies was conspicuously successful. The problem of preventing the big corporations from exploiting the public, without at the same time destroying the American system of free economic enterprise or losing the advantages of large-scale production, has remained until today as difficult as it was in the eighteen-eighties when it first presented itself.

THE GROWTH OF INEQUALITY

The building of the corporations was accompanied by a number of financial malpractices. By legal theory, a corporation was the common property of its stockholders, but in actuality the average small stockholder was incapable of exercising any effective supervision over corporation policies. Most corporations were, in the nineteenth century, dominated by individuals, who were apt to manipulate the finances of the institution for their own personal advantage. This domination might be secured through outright ownership of a majority of the stock; through such a wide diffusion of stock ownership that the various small stockholders were unable to unite in the protection of their interests; or through "pyramiding," building a structure of holding companies by which an individual might control one relatively small corporation which owned a majority of the stock in some larger corporation, which, in turn, might own stock in another and still larger corporation. This pyramiding of holding companies was to assume, in some cases, fantastic proportions in the nineteen-twenties. Thus, corporation directors could often secure for themselves an exorbitant share of the profits of the business by means, for example, of voting themselves excessive salaries, or of forming independent companies owned wholly by themselves, from which the corporations which they directed would then proceed to buy commodities at excessive prices.

The most prevalent of these financial abuses, and the most far-reaching in its consequences, was the watering of stock. When several small industrial units were merged into one large corporation, the owners who were being bought out would frequently receive an excessive price for their properties, and the bill would be paid by increasing the capitalization of the new corporation and persuading the general public to buy the newly issued stocks. It became customary to fix the capital value of a new corporation in terms not of the real cost of its properties but of the profits which it might be expected to make. As Andrew Carnegie once expressed it, "they throw cats and dogs together and call them elephants." The possibilities of profit by buying control of corporations, arranging mergers, watering the stock, and selling it to the public were, especially in the later decades of the nineteenth century, apparently almost limitless. A number of Wall Street financiers were able to weave an intricate course in and out of various corporations, accumulating private fortunes and leaving industries on the verge of bankruptcy behind them. Charles T. Yerkes, the Chicago street-railroad magnate, cynically explained that "the secret of success in my business is to buy old junk, fix it up a little, and unload it upon other fellows." The consequences of stock-watering were a large increase in the capital claims upon which profits must be earned, very much in excess of the actual increase in the capital equipment of industry. Unscrupulous financiers made gains at the expense of the small investors, whose stocks were decreased in value, and ultimately of the consuming public, whose purchases created the dividends which the newly created stocks were expected to earn.

This financial buccaneering, which usually conformed to the letter of the law but which occasionally crossed the line from legal to criminal, was perhaps the most spectacular feature in the building of the large corporations. And it would eventually necessitate more stringent government regulation of methods of corporate financing. But in spite of the indignation which it provoked, it was by no means the most important of the problems created by the new economic structure. To a large degree it was a symptom of growing pains, an accompaniment of rapid economic development, which ceased after an industry had reached its appropriate size and had become stabilized. Questions of greater permanent importance were presented by the status of the wage-earning classes in corporate industry.

The growth of large-scale industry led to a rapid increase in the numbers of the working class, and the decline of small-scale production and the completion of the settlement of the West made it increasingly difficult for even the more ambitious and enterprising of the workers to achieve economic independence. Urban society in the United States began to become stratified along class lines, with a clear line of demarcation between the salaried or property-owning business classes and the propertyless working class. That equality of social conditions and of opportunity upon which American society had traditionally prided itself seemed to be disappearing. Under such conditions the workers began to organize trade unions for the protection of their economic interests and to demand government regulation of industrial labor policies. Industrialists, however, continued to claim complete power to fix wage rates and to dismiss workers at their own discretion, opposing both trade union and government interference. According to the traditional conception of property rights the workers were merely hired employees, who had no rights in the corporation for which they worked.

This problem was intensified by the growth of absentee ownership. In the age of small-scale production the manager of a factory was usually its owner; and he often developed a sense of personal

responsibility for the welfare of his employees. But when owner-
managers gave place to large impersonal corporations, the primary
obligation of factory managers was to increase the profits of the
stockholders, while the stockholders and many of the directors rarely
had any direct knowledge of, or contact with, labor conditions in
the industry of which they were the owners. When a corporation
continued to adopt paternalistic attitudes towards its workers, it
was usually only in order to inculcate loyalty and to prevent them
from joining trade unions. The younger Morgan expressed the situation frankly when he told the Industrial Relations Commission, in
1915, that the directors of corporations were "not at all" "responsible for the labor conditions existing in the industries in which
they are the directing power." Under such conditions the workers
could have no security of employment or assurance of adequate
wages; and, as long as these rights were not recognized, there was
the danger of bitter class struggles.

The growth of corporate industry divided American society not
only along class lines but also along sectional lines. Ownership and
control of the big corporations was usually concentrated in the
Northeast, even when their material properties and equipment were
in the South or the West; and the development of corporate industry and of the powers of the investment bankers increased the relative wealth of the Northeast at the expense of that of other
sections of the country. The privileged position of the Northeast,
due originally to its priority in industrial and financial development,
was strengthened after the Civil War by the railroads, whose freight
rates tended to discriminate against the South and the West, and
by certain policies of the Federal government: in particular, by the
tariff, and by the payment of nearly 8 billion dollars in pensions,
raised by taxation on all sections of the country, to veterans of the
Grand Army of the Republic, most of whom were located in the
Northeast and the Middle West. The exploitation of the South and
the West by northeastern industry and finance resulted in enormous
disparities in the wealth and living standards of the different sections. By the nineteen-thirties sixteen northeastern and middle western states, with 57.6 per cent of the population and only 21.2 per

cent of the area of the United States, owned at least 80 per cent, and probably more than 90 per cent, of the total wealth of the country. The average Northerner owned nearly twice as much in bank deposits as the average Westerner, and more than five times as much as the average Southerner.

The growth in the national wealth and in standards of living which resulted from the new economic structure was thus counter-balanced by the growth of inequality and insecurity, by the power of corporation directors to exploit both the stockholders and the consuming public, and by the denial of economic rights to the working class. Meanwhile every decade gave the big corporations a more commanding position in American economic life. The individual entrepreneurs who played the dominant role in the later years of the nineteenth century had no comparable successors in the industries which they had created; the descendants who inherited their wealth tended to become a leisured *rentier* class, divorced from the actual management of industry. After a corporation had been built, it usually became an impersonal institution, controlled by a kind of corporation bureaucracy which tended to be self-perpetuating and to acquire an *esprit de corps* and an institutional loyalty of its own. But the fact that the salaried managers who took the places of the big entrepreneurs were not motivated, to the same degree, by a desire for personal wealth and power did not mean that the corporations which they controlled would cease to grow, nor did it necessarily mean that corporation policies would be in harmony with the interests of the public. Just as a statesman works primarily for his own country rather than for humanity as a whole, so the managers of a corporation were concerned primarily with the interests of the institution which they represented.

The giant corporation of the twentieth century, with its array of stockholders, directors, salaried executives, technicians, and wage earners, was a kind of economic empire, an *imperium in imperio,* endowed by American constitutional law with a semi-independence of the political authorities and enjoying enormous powers both over its own employees and over the general public. The position of these leviathans was in some ways comparable to that of the big feudal principalities in the kingdoms of the Middle Ages. And one of the primary problems of twentieth-century American society was to find some method of ensuring their subordination to democratic principles and to the interests of the general public.

BIBLIOGRAPHY

V. S. Clark, *History of Manufactures,* Vol. 3 (1928)

G. W. Edwards, *The Evolution of Finance Capitalism* (1938)

H. U. Faulkner, *American Economic History* (1924)

N. S. B. Gras, *Industrial Evolution* (1930)

N. S. B. Gras and H. M. Larson, *Case Book in American Business History* (1939)

L. Hacker, *The Triumph of American Capitalism* (1940)

B. J. Hendrick, *The Age of Big Business* (*Chronicles of America,* Vol. 39, 1919)

J. W. Jenks and W. E. Clark, *The Trust Problem* (1926)

E. Jones, *The Trust Problem* (1926)

M. Josephson, *The Robber Barons* (1934)

W. Kaempffert (ed.), *A Popular History of American Inventions* (1924)

W. I. King, *Wealth and Income of the People of the United States* (1915)

*E. C. Kirkland, *History of American Economic Life* (1933)

J. Moody, *The Truth about the Trusts* (1904)

G. Myers, *History of Great American Fortunes* (1909–11)

*A. Nevins, *The Emergence of Modern America* (*History of American Life,* Vol. 8, 1927)

W. Z. Ripley, *Trusts, Pools and Corporations* (1916)

*H. R. Seager and C. A. Gulick, *Trust and Corporation Problems* (1929)

F. A. Shannon, *Economic History of the People of the United States* (revised edition, 1940)

*I. M. Tarbell, *The Nationalizing of Business* (*History of American Life,* Vol. 9, 1936)

H. Thompson, *The Age of Invention* (*Chronicles of America,* Vol. 37, 1921)

M. W. Watkins, *Industrial Combinations and Public Policy* (1927)

4

SOME KEY INDUSTRIES

THE RAILROADS

FROM the Civil War to the end of the century the most important feature of American economic development was the building of the railroads. Before the Civil War a network of small competing lines had covered the Northeast and the Middle West. After the war these lines were consolidated into a few powerful systems; railroad facilities were extended through the South; and—with the aid of Federal subsidies and land-grants—the Pacific coast was connected with the East. The rapid growth of mileage was accompanied by an equally rapid increase in efficiency. The thirty-five years following the war saw the general introduction of the standard gauge, Bessemer steel rails, double tracks, steel bridges, Westinghouse air brakes, the block signaling system, and Pullman sleeping coaches. These improvements, coupled with the elimination of wasteful competition and the consolidation of small units into large systems, led to a great improvement in services and decrease in costs. Between 1860 and 1900 the average freight weight increased from 15,000 to 100,000 tons, the running time between New York and Chicago was reduced from fifty to twenty-four hours, and revenue per ton was cut from two dollars to seventy-three cents a mile.

The entrepreneurs who organized the building of the railroads, or who took control of them after they had been built, exhibited every possible variation, from scrupulous honesty and enlightened statesmanship to the most corrupt and fraudulent self-seeking. They included Henry Villard of the Northern Pacific, whose financial probity was above suspicion, and James J. Hill of the Great Northern, who devoted himself to building the prosperity of the regions which his railroad served; they included, at the other extreme, Jay Gould and Daniel Drew, who sought to control railroads merely for their personal profit and whose corrupt financial practices made them hated even on Wall Street. Most of the roads were tainted, to some degree, with fraud at the expense of the stockholders and with the corrupt manipulation of Federal congressmen or state legislatures. Yet there were many railroad builders, such as Cornelius Vanderbilt and Edward Harriman, who combined a lack of ethical scruples with a genuine passion to improve services and increase efficiency. This complex mixture of unscrupulous self-seeking and the pursuit of economic progress was typical of American society in the post–Civil War period.

Yet before the end of the century it seemed to a large proportion of the American people that the financial malpractices of the railroad builders outweighed their services to society. The offenses committed by some of them were undoubtedly numerous and varied. They cheated the stockholders by issuing watered stock and by forming dummy construction companies, owned by the financiers, with which the railroad corporations that they controlled would make contracts at exorbitant prices. They blackmailed towns and counties, refusing to give them railroad services unless they would buy their stock and give them land and subsidies. They gave stock to Federal congressmen, dominated state legislatures by wholesale bribery, and sought to avoid any legislative interference by distributing passes to all legislators. They imposed high freight rates and made discriminations between different businesses and different localities by collecting different rates, by giving rebates, or by charging more for a short haul than for a long one. And they combined with one another in pooling and price agreements. The general indignation against these practices led in 1887 to the establishment of the Interstate Commerce Commission, and it was to make the railroads the first branch of the American economic system which was subjected to Federal regulation.

In the Northeast the most important of the railroad builders was

Cornelius Vanderbilt. This semiliterate, domineering, and egotistical Dutchman, born in 1794, who had once been a Staten Island ferry boy, had made a fortune before the Civil War as a shipowner. In 1865 he began to buy control of the numerous small lines connecting New York with Chicago. By unscrupulous financing, corrupt control of the New York legislature, and a vast improvement in railroad services, he created the New York Central and, before his death in 1877, had increased his private fortune from 10 million to more than 100 million dollars. His holdings and policies were inherited by his son, William H. Vanderbilt. By 1900 the New York Central owned ten thousand miles of track, with terminals at New York, Boston, Chicago, St. Louis, and Cincinnati. Meanwhile the Pennsylvania Railroad, as a result partly of its domination over the Pennsylvania legislature and partly of the eagerness for progress exhibited by a series of able managers, J. Edgar Thomson, T. A. Scott, G. B. Roberts, and A. J. Cassatt, was extending its lines between Washington and the Great Lakes. Early in the twentieth century it tunneled under the Hudson River and built a terminal in New York City to rival that of the New York Central. Eventually it became the largest railroad corporation in the United States. The same eastern–middle-western areas were also served by three other lines: the Erie, which suffered for many years from the corrupt control of Jay Gould, but which was reorganized into an efficient system by the House of Morgan in 1894; the Baltimore and Ohio; and the Grand Trunk.

In the South few lines had been built before the Civil War. The seventies and eighties were a period of rapid building, with numerous small competing lines, many of which were corruptly financed and inefficiently managed. Some degree of order was created in 1894, when the House of Morgan plunged into the chaos and organized a number of the more important lines into the Southern Railway Company, linking the South Atlantic seaboard and the Gulf of Mexico with the Ohio River.

The most spectacular feats of the railroad era were, however, in the West, where before the end of the century five transcontinental lines were built to connect the Pacific coast with the East. The first link between East and West was established in 1869, in western Utah, when the Union Pacific, building westward from Nebraska, met the Central Pacific, which had built eastward from San Francisco. The four California magnates who controlled the Central Pacific—Stanford, Huntingdon, Hopkins, and Crocker—completed the Southern Pacific, connecting California with New Orleans, in 1883. In the next year the Atchison, Topeka, and Santa Fe was opened to traffic. In the Northwest the Northern Pacific, originally planned by the Philadelphia banker, Jay Cooke, who was bankrupted by the project, was carried to its conclusion in 1883 by Henry Villard, who himself lost control through another bankruptcy shortly afterward.

The ablest of the western railroad men was, however, James J. Hill, a Scotch-Irish Canadian, who until the age of forty was a small storekeeper in St. Paul. Taking control of a small Minnesota railroad in 1878 and entering into partnership with the builder of the Canadian Pacific, Lord Strathcona, Hill carried his Great Northern to the Pacific coast by 1893. His greatness lay chiefly in his realization that the prosperity of his railroad was dependent upon that of the people whom it served. He devoted himself to empire building on a grand scale throughout the Pacific Northwest, encouraging immigration, improving agriculture, building schools, and establishing steamboat connections between Seattle and the Orient.

The period of rapid railroad growth ended in the eighteen-nineties. Several years of economic depression reduced railroad earnings, and the railroad men now had to pay the penalty for their overcapitalization. In 1885 it had been estimated that one-third of all railroad stocks represented water. Between 1893 and 1898 no less than 67,000 miles of railroad, one-third of the total, passed through bankruptcies. Most of the bankrupt lines came under the control of the House of Morgan, which had handled the sale of railroad stocks to European investors and which now began to reorganize and supervise railroad practices in the interests of the stockholders. Morgan acquired control over the New York Central, the Erie, the Baltimore and Ohio, the Southern Railway, the Northern Pacific, and numerous smaller lines; and he entered into partnership with

Hill in the Great Northern. This was followed by a decrease in railroad competition, in accordance with Morgan's belief in establishing a "community of interest." In general, Morgan control meant improved efficiency and greater care for stockholders' interests although not necessarily for those of the general public. Not all Morgan financing could be considered honest, however. In 1903 Morgan acquired control of the New York, New Haven, and Hartford, placing Charles S. Mellen in charge as his personal representative. During the next ten years, in a campaign to monopolize the transportation facilities of New England, the capitalization of the railroad was increased, by extravagant watering, from 93 million to 417 million dollars.

The last of the great individualists in the railroad field was Edward H. Harriman, a nervous unimportant-looking little man who had begun life as a Wall Street clerk. Buying control of the Illinois Central, he made it one of the most efficient systems in the country; and in 1895, after entering into partnership with the banking firm of Kuhn, Loeb and with the Rockefeller-controlled National City Bank, New York rivals of the House of Morgan, he became owner of the Union Pacific. By 1901 he controlled also the Southern Pacific and a number of smaller lines in the Northwest and was beginning to compete with the Hill-Morgan combination. Foiled in an effort to capture the Chicago, Burlington, and Quincy, which would give his lines an independent connection with the Middle West, Harriman began to buy Northern Pacific stock in the hope of capturing it from Hill and Morgan. In one hour, on May 9, 1901, the value of the stock rose from $350 to $1,000. The rival groups found eventually that they had bought from speculators 78,000 more shares than actually existed; and, to save the speculators from ruin, they agreed to pool their interests in a gigantic holding company, the Northern Securities Company, chartered in New Jersey.

President Theodore Roosevelt promptly ordered that suit be brought against the Northern Securities Company as a violation of the Sherman Anti-Trust Act. This was the first time that the United States government had shown any serious desire to enforce the Sherman Act, and the resentment of the railroad men was extreme. "It really seems

hard," complained Hill, "when we look back on what we have
done—in opening the country and carrying at the lowest rates, that
we should be compelled to fight for our lives against the political
adventurers who have never done anything but pose and draw a
salary." In 1904, by Supreme Court decision, the Northern Securities Company was dissolved.[1] This verdict, although it affirmed the
supremacy of the Federal government over big business, did not
substantially alter the railroad situation; the Hill interests were left
in control of the Northern Pacific, but Hill and Harriman continued to act in accordance with the "community of interest"
theory. Harriman then turned his attention to the East, acquiring
control over the Baltimore and Ohio. His plan was not only to create a unified Atlantic-Pacific railroad but also to build lines in
Manchuria which would be the beginning of a world-wide system.
His death in 1909, however, put an end to these ambitious projects,
and resulted in a separation of his properties.

After 1900 few new railroads were built, although a sixth transcontinental line, the Chicago, Milwaukee, and St. Paul, was completed in 1909. The total mileage increased from 198,964 in 1900
to 263,821 in 1920. Big profits could no longer be made in the
railroad field. The railroad corporations ceased, for the most part,
to attract Wall Street promoters, and they passed under the control
of salaried managers, the ownership of stock being widely diffused.
There was also a rapid growth in the bonded debt of the railroads,
which increased from $4,462,000,000 in 1890 to $10,388,000,000
in 1910. By 1931 fourteen major systems owned most of the lines
in the country. This, together with the growth of a system of interlocking interests, by which one-quarter of all railroad stock was
owned by other railroads, and the enforcement by the House of
Morgan of community of interest, virtually ended effective competition between the various lines. Meanwhile the Federal government
had steadily extended its powers of supervision, a process which
culminated in 1920 when the Interstate Commerce Commission obtained full power to fix rates. The continued importance of the railroads in the economic life of the country was, however, indicated

1. See page 231.

by the facts that in 1920 the value of their properties amounted to $18,900,000,000, and their employ covered 1,700,000 workers.

OIL

Oil production was not a key industry until the development of the internal combustion engine in the twentieth century; but it had great importance as early as the eighteen-seventies and eighties because of its organization into the original "trust" and because of the enormous wealth acquired by those who promoted it.

Oil drilling began in 1859 in western Pennsylvania. The industry was at first violently competitive, with thousands of small producers, whose struggles with one another resulted in ruinous overproduction and wastefulness. John D. Rockefeller, the son of an itinerant medicine-seller, was at this period a produce commission merchant in Cleveland, Ohio. In 1862 Rockefeller went into the business of oil refining and set himself the task of organizing the oil industry into a single combine which would stabilize production, eliminate waste, and assure large profits to its owners. Rockefeller's methods were to enforce the strictest economy and efficiency; to organize alliances with his ablest competitors in order to monopolize the brains in the industry; to offer good terms to all who were willing to combine with him; to crush, by the most ruthless competition, those who refused to join him; and to accumulate reserves of capital which would enable him to do his own financing and to remain independent of the Wall Street bankers.

Rockefeller's complete success in establishing control over the industry and in destroying his competitors made him in the eighteen-eighties and nineties perhaps the most bitterly hated individual in the United States. Yet by contrast with many of the other business leaders of that epoch he had substantial merits. He was financially honest, never indulging in any watering of stock; he did not speculate on Wall Street; his labor policies were, considering the period in which he lived, relatively enlightened; and those who were willing to accept his terms and join his combine never had cause to regret it. His unpopularity was, in fact, due as much to his virtues as to his vices: his Puritan concentration on the single end of busi-

ness efficiency, his dislike of gambling, and the sobriety of his personal life. Of his business practices, the least venial were his secret
bargains with the railroads. He was able to compel the railroads not
only to give him rebates below their published rates for shipments
of large quantities of oil, but actually to pay him drawbacks on
shipments of oil of his competitors. These devices were, however,
not markedly below the ethical standards of the time. What made
Rockefeller hated was not so much the methods which he adopted
as the success with which he applied them.

Rockefeller realized that the way to dominate the oil business was
to monopolize not production but refining. In 1870, in combination
with Henry M. Flagler, Stephen V. Harkness, and his brother, William Rockefeller, he formed the Standard Oil Company of Ohio,
which obtained complete control of oil refining in the Cleveland
area. He then began to establish alliances with oil refiners elsewhere, most notably with Henry H. Rogers and John D. Archbold.
The first attempt to find a legal basis for a nationwide combination
of refiners was through purchase, in 1872, of the South Improvement Company, a corporation which had obtained a very vaguely
worded charter from the State of Pennsylvania. The oil producers,
who now had to accept whatever prices Rockefeller chose to offer
them and who were, in consequence, always his bitterest enemies,
secured a revocation of the charter, but the process of combination
continued.

By 1877 the Standard Oil group had a monopoly of refining;
they went on to establish control of pipe lines and of the selling of
oil. Several attempts by the oil producers to break the monopoly
were defeated. In the eighties and nineties Standard Oil began to
enter the European market and to fight European financiers for control of Russian and Asiatic oil fields. In 1882 the forty corporations controlled by the various members of the combination were
tied together by the device of turning over all their stock to nine
trustees. This original trust was the invention of the lawyer Samuel
C. T. Dodd. In 1892 the State of Ohio, under whose laws the
trust had been organized, ordered it to be dissolved. Big corporations could, however, always find hospitality in New Jersey; and

in 1899 the Standard Oil properties were combined through the organization of a holding company, the Standard Oil Company of New Jersey.

Rockefeller virtually retired from business in 1896. He devoted the remainder of his life to giving away a substantial part of his fortune. By 1928 his philanthropies had totaled, perhaps, $750,000,000, the chief beneficiaries being medical and educational institutions. Regarded throughout his business career as the embodiment of ruthless plutocracy, to later generations, who knew him only through his charities and through the skillful publicity of Ivy Lee, he seemed almost a saint. His philanthropic activities were inherited by his son, John D. Rockefeller, junior.

Meanwhile oil in its various forms, as fuel oil, gasoline, kerosene, lubricant, paraffin, and asphalt, was increasing in importance; and the development of the automobile industry, in particular, was swelling to enormous proportions the wealth of the Standard Oil group. Between 1897 and 1906 dividends on Standard Oil stock varied between 30 and 48 per cent a year. Before the end of the nineteenth century Standard Oil money began to spill over into other industries; and some of Rockefeller's partners, notably H. H. Rogers and William Rockefeller, did not share his aversion to Wall Street manipulation. J. D. Archbold became the political agent of the group and established connections with members of the United States Senate. The Standard Oil millionaires entered banking, became partners of James Stillman in the National City Bank, and began to acquire ownership of railroads, iron fields, copper mines, public utilities, and numerous other industries. The combined resources of the group represented an aggregation of financial power rivaled only by that of the House of Morgan.

The monopoly created by Rockefeller did not prove to be permanent. The rapid growth in the market for oil and the opening, in the twentieth century, of new fields, particularly those in Texas, Oklahoma, and Kansas, made it impossible for a single corporation to control the entire industry. Oil production, 63 million barrels in 1900, had risen by 1928 to 900 million barrels. In 1911, moreover, a Supreme Court decision under the Sherman Act ordered Standard

Oil to dissolve itself into thirty-three companies. Although the ownership of these companies remained at first with the same group, making this attempt to restore competition seem farcical, the various companies gradually began to grow apart from one another. In the nineteen-twenties the oil business was considerably more competitive than it had been at the beginning of the century. Whereas in 1897 the Standard Oil companies had done 87 per cent of the refining, in 1920 they were doing only 50 per cent.

STEEL

Probably the most important single industry in a mechanized society is the steel industry. All the key inventions in the process of steel manufacturing—the Bessemer process by which pig iron is cleansed of carbon and silica, the Thomas-Gilchrist process which made possible the cleansing of phosphorus-bearing iron, the Siemens and Martin open hearth method, and the development of the electric furnace—were made in Europe and not adopted in the United States until later. Nevertheless, the American steel industry by the end of the nineteenth century was the largest in the world as a result of both its unsurpassed mineral resources, particularly the Mesabi range in Minnesota, and the enormous market created by the needs of the railroads and factories.

The biggest figure in the development of the steel industry was Andrew Carnegie, whose character combined, in an extraordinary way, the most hard-headed business ruthlessness with an almost pathetic eagerness to promote democracy, education, and world peace. Brought to America from Scotland at the age of thirteen, Carnegie worked first in a cotton mill and then for the Pennsylvania Railroad. In 1864 he became an iron manufacturer at Pittsburgh and entered into partnership with Henry C. Frick, who provided him with coke from his Connellsville coal fields, with Charles Schwab, and with Henry Phipps, all of whom, like himself, had once been penniless. As a result of efficient business methods, a labor policy of low wages, long hours, and uncompromising hostility to unionization, and a close alliance with the Pennsylvania Railroad, the Carnegie Steel Corporation quickly outdistanced its competitors. By 1900 it was making one-quarter of all the steel in the United States and was the owner of coal fields, coke ovens, limestone deposits, iron mines, ore ships, and railroads. At this period the total annual production of steel in the United States was about 30 million tons, with 220,000 workers employed in the industry.

Morgan had meanwhile acquired an interest in some of the corporations competing with the Carnegie group and also in some of those making finished products, and the time seemed ripe for a consolidation. Carnegie, unlike most of the other business leaders of the epoch, had always preached competition rather than combination, but he was now eager to retire from business and devote the remainder of his life to philanthropy. In order to force the pace, he announced plans for enlarging the scale of his operations and entering into competition with the makers of finished products.

Morgan decided to act at once and to buy out Carnegie at whatever price he chose to ask. In 1901 eleven steel companies were combined into the United States Steel Corporation, which was to be headed by Morgan's nominee, Judge Elbert H. Gary. All the constituent units demanded an excessive price for their properties, Carnegie receiving bonds worth $429,000,000. The capitalization of the new corporation was nearly $1,400,000,000, more than half of which appears to have represented water. This was the first time that the capital value of any corporation had exceeded a billion dollars. In spite of the enormous quantity of water upon which dividends had to be paid, the investors who bought the stocks of United States Steel did not have cause to regret their purchases, since the total net profits of the corporation during the first twenty-five years of its existence amounted to more than $2,250,000,000.

At the time of its formation United States Steel controlled about 70 per cent of the industry, a proportion which afterwards declined to about 50 per cent. Bethlehem Steel, which was headed after 1903 by Charles Schwab, and several other steel corporations in different parts of the country remained independent. Judge Gary, however, applied the "community of interest" theory to the industry, organizing a series of "Gary dinners" at which the directors of the various corporations discussed their common problems. The Gary dinners ceased in 1911; but uniform price schedules, which sometimes remained unchanged for a dozen years, continued to be the rule in the steel industry. Gary also adopted plans for promoting the welfare of the workers and for assisting them to become stockholders in the industry, as a result of which he began to be regarded as a pioneer in the development of new and more enlightened industrial policies. It should be added, however, that the refusal of United States Steel to adopt competitive price-cutting meant that the public paid higher prices, that until 1937 the corporation was an uncompromising opponent of trade unionism, and that until 1923 its workers had a twelve-hour day and, in many cases, a seven-day week.

COAL

Coal mining is another important element in the industrial system. Its history, however, is less significant than that of steel.

The mining of bituminous coal, scattered over the Appalachian area from Pennsylvania down to Alabama, was always extremely competitive, with more than four thousand independent operators in the business. The lack of integration and the decline in the importance of coal as a result of the development of new sources of power in the twentieth century made this one of the most hazardous and most unstable occupations in the United States. The miners suffered from acutely low wages and from frequent unemployment; and their efforts to organize unions resulted in bloody struggles, in which the coal operators enjoyed the support of the local police authorities.

Anthracite mining, on the other hand, being concentrated in a single area in northeastern Pennsylvania, soon passed under the control of a small number of corporations. By 1900 half a dozen railroads, the chief of which was the Reading and Philadelphia, had a monopoly of the industry and had adopted community-of-interest policies. The Federal government, in the course of its anti-trust crusade, subsequently required the railroads to divorce themselves from the coal business. This measure did not, however, restore effective competition.

COPPER

Copper is a mineral of vital importance, particularly for the manufacture of electrical equipment and munitions. The copper-mining industry has, moreover, a most spectacular history.

The most valuable mines in the United States were at Butte, Montana, known as "the richest hill in the world," from which 2 billion dollars' worth of copper was extracted within thirty years. The leading figures in the early development of the industry were Marcus Daly and William A. Clark, both of them Irishmen who had gone to Montana as manual laborers in the eighteen-seventies. In 1899 H. H. Rogers of Standard Oil organized a number of copper mines, including Daly's Anaconda, into the Amalgamated Copper Company; and, by employing Thomas W. Lawson as his publicity agent, he achieved some remarkable speculative coups. The properties acquired by the Amalgamated cost Rogers and his associates 39 million dollars; but by watering the stock up to 75 million they made a profit of 26 million in cash and still retained enough stock to keep control of the corporation. During the next two years, by selling Amalgamated stock when it was high and buying it back when it was low, they made another 20 or 30 million. W. A. Clark had originally fought the Amalgamated; but in 1901, after he had bought his way into the United States Senate by spending $750,000 in bribes to the Montana legislature, he sold his properties.

Other copper mines in the Butte area were claimed by a young German immigrant, F. Augustus Heinze; and in 1900 there began a six-year struggle between Heinze and the Amalgamated for control of these mines. Heinze and Rogers fought each other with lawsuits and injunctions; they engaged in wholesale bribery of judges, newspaper owners, and members of the Montana legislature; and their employees waged pitched battles with dynamite in the tunnels of the mines. Heinze won popular support by giving his workers an eight-hour day and proclaiming that he was fighting the battle of the common people against the plutocrats of Standard Oil; but when the Amalgamated shut down all its properties and its seventy thousand employees were faced with starvation, the State of Montana capitulated, and Heinze lost the lawsuits. In 1906 Heinze sold his remaining properties to the Amalgamated and moved to New York to become a Wall Street operator. In 1907 the Standard Oil group succeeded in ruining him—an operation which has been alleged to have been one of the immediate causes of the financial crisis of that year. John D. Ryan was appointed head of Amalgamated, which subsequently changed its name to Anaconda Copper Company. Owning all the copper mines at Butte and later extending its operations to South America and to Europe, the Anaconda has remained the leading copper-mining company in the world.

Outside Montana the dominant figures in the copper industry were the Guggenheims. Meyer Guggenheim, an immigrant from Switzerland who had settled in Philadelphia in 1847, was first a manufacturer of stove polish and then a lace importer. In 1881 he acquired part ownership of a silver mine at Leadville, Colorado. Later he bought other mining properties, and in 1888 he began to buy control of smelting. The subsequent growth of the family fortune was the work of his seven sons, the leader of whom was Daniel Guggenheim. In 1899 a number of smelters organized the American Smelting and Refining Company. There followed a struggle between this corporation and the Guggenheims, which ended in 1901 in a merger by which the corporation passed under Guggenheim control.

The Guggenheims henceforth had a stranglehold over the smaller mining operators. They then went on to acquire ownership of many of the more valuable copper fields on the American continent. The Guggenheim Exploration Company hired John Hays Hammond, the mining expert, at a salary of $250,000 a year; and with Hammond's assistance the Guggenheims extended their properties through Utah and Nevada, into Alaska, Mexico, and Chile, and into the Belgian Congo. One aspect of the Guggenheim activities had political consequences. In 1907 they joined with the House of Morgan in organizing the Alaska Syndicate, which was to develop Kennecott copper, the cheapest in the world, open coal fields, and control the transportation services of the territory. The possibility that Alaska might become almost the private property of a group of financiers aroused the enemies of big business, who demanded that the Federal government retain control over Alaskan natural resources. The allegation (which was, in point of fact, untrue) that President Taft's administration was too friendly to the Alaska Syndicate was a leading factor in causing the attack on him by the Progressives and the split in the Republican Party in 1912.

ELECTRICITY

The development of electricity, with the consequent growth of the public utility industries, was one of the most important features of late nineteenth-century economic history. The potentialities of the new industry were immense, and the problems connected with it were peculiarly complex. Electrical power, manufactured from water power, promised to increase enormously the wealth of society, particularly in the Rocky Mountain and Pacific states, which contained nearly three-quarters of the potential water power of the United States. The use of electricity had, moreover, great advantages over the use of coal: it could be transmitted cheaply over long distances, allowing industry to be decentralized and the growth of unhealthy and congested urban areas to be checked; it could increase the comfort and lighten the labors of the rural population; and it could put an end to the ugliness and the dirt associated with industry in the age of coal. The electrical industries tended, however, to be natural monopolies, where competition would be wasteful and inconvenient. Hence some kind of public control over rates and services was necessary. The nature, degree, and purposes of this public control were a cause of bitter and prolonged controversies.

The use of electricity for lighting was due chiefly to the efforts of Thomas A. Edison, who solved in the eighteen-seventies the chief problem connected with it, the discovery of a satisfactory filament for use in bulbs. In 1878 the Edison Electric Company was formed, which in 1892 was amalgamated with the Thomson-Houston Company into the General Electric Company. Meanwhile an immigrant from what is now Yugoslavia, Nicholas Tesla, who was also working on the problems of electricity, invented alternating current, which proved to be superior to Edison's direct current. Tesla's patents were bought by George Westinghouse, who formed in 1891 the Westinghouse Electric and Manufacturing Company and began to use electricity to supply power for industry and transportation. General Electric and Westinghouse, by subsequently adopting a policy of pooling their patents, enjoyed almost complete control over the business of manufacturing electrical equipment.

The production of electrical power was, meanwhile, undertaken by a large number of small companies. The first waterpower plant was built at Appleton, Wisconsin, in 1882. Large plants were constructed at Niagara Falls in 1900, and at Keokuk, Iowa, in 1914. The number of power stations, two thousand in 1898, had increased to five thousand by 1914. The organization of large-scale combinations in the field of power production, however, scarcely began before the nineteen-twenties.

The electric telegraph had been invented by Samuel Morse in 1844. At first vigorously competitive, the telegraph business was consolidated after the Civil War by Western Union, which had obtained a complete monopoly by 1881. In 1886 there appeared a rival corporation, Postal Telegraph; but the two corporations agreed subsequently to charge similar rates and to divide the field with each other.

The telephone was the work of Alexander Graham Bell, a Scotch immigrant who, as a doctor, had specialized in the treatment of deafness. Bell's original telephone, completed in 1876, was subsequently improved by numerous other inventions, the most important of which were made by another Yugoslav immigrant, Michael Pupin. Bell's patents became the basis of the Bell Telephone Company, organized in 1879 by Theodore N. Vail. Vail subsequently lost control to a group of Boston financiers; but early in the twentieth century the company was taken over by the House of Morgan, which restored the management to Vail.

By this time the original Bell Telephone Company had grown into a network of Bell companies covering the whole country, which were tied together by means of a holding company, the American Telephone and Telegraph Company. The original Bell patents had expired, but American Telephone and Telegraph Company maintained an elaborate research department for investigating the whole field of acoustics and producing a steady stream of new inventions, the patenting of which enabled the corporation to maintain its leadership. The number of telephones in the United States, 1,355,-000 in 1900, increased to 8,730,000 in 1912 and to 19,453,000 in 1937, about 80 per cent of which belonged to the Bell system; and American Telephone and Telegraph grew into the biggest corporation in the country. The steady improvement of services under the management of Vail and his successors, and their financial integrity and scrupulous respect for the interests of the stockholders, caused American Telephone and Telegraph to be regarded by many persons as a model corporation. Less commendable were its struggles against rate-fixing regulations by the public utility commissions of state governments, its elaborately organized propaganda against government interference with private business, and its opposition to trade unionism.

OTHER TRUSTS

The formation of trusts and combinations was by no means restricted to the basic transportation, capital goods, and public utility industries. At the end of the nineteenth century the same monopolistic tendencies were equally apparent in a number of other branches of manufacturing.

The International Harvester Company, created in 1902 by the House of Morgan, acquired control over 85 per cent of the production of agricultural machinery. The principal constituent in this organization was the McCormick Company, located at Chicago, which had been making reapers since 1831 and had achieved a dominant position in the industry by selling them to farmers on the installment plan. An even larger proportion of control in their respective industries was enjoyed by the American Tobacco Company, organized in 1890 under the leadership of James B. Duke, and by the American Sugar Refining Company, formed in 1891 and headed by Henry O. Havemeyer. The latter owed its complete freedom from competition largely to the protective tariff. Other important combinations were the United States Rubber Company, the United

States Leather Company, the Pullman Company, and the Morgan-controlled International Mercantile Marine.

In the year 1904 John Moody calculated that 318 trusts had been formed, into which had been merged 5,300 formerly independent units, having a total capitalization of more than 7 billion dollars. Of these, 236 dated from the period 1898–1903.

INVESTMENT BANKING

Meanwhile the growth of combination in transportation and manufacturing seemed to many people to be accompanied by the development of another and even more important monopoly: a monopoly of money. A few New York and Boston banking firms, headed by the House of Morgan, appeared to be acquiring a control over the supply of capital and credit which might give them dangerously extensive powers over American industry.

J. P. Morgan, born in 1837, differed from most of the other leading personalities of his epoch in that he had inherited wealth and social position. His father had been the head of a banking firm which specialized in the sale of American securities to European investors. After the bankruptcy of Jay Cooke of Philadelphia in 1873, the House of Morgan became the leading investment banking firm in the United States; and J. P. Morgan gradually began to assume powers of supervision over the corporations whose stocks he sold. This he did in order to protect the interests of investors and to enforce his belief that if economic stability and high profits were to be maintained, competition must be replaced by a community of interest. In the eighties and nineties Morgan was principally occupied in the rescuing and reorganizing of bankrupt railroads. In the early years of the twentieth century he extended his interests into almost every important branch of American industry, selecting the managers of numerous corporations and appointing his partners to directorates in them. He owed his position at the apex of the American economic system partly to a financial integrity which (except in a few notorious cases, such as that of the New York, New Haven, and Hartford) made Morgan control synonymous with efficient management and high dividends, and partly to a personality so forceful and dominating that even the executives of the most powerful corporations rarely ventured to cross swords with him. Both in his financial activities and in his personal life he displayed a bent for the grandiose and the magnificent which recalled some of the despots of Renascence Italy.

It seemed for a period that the supremacy of Morgan might be challenged by the Standard Oil interests, through their control of the National City Bank. The possibility of a conflict between these two financial empires ended, however, in 1907 when the community-of-interest principle was applied to investment banking. The House of Morgan bought 1½ million dollars' worth of stock in the National City Bank, and the younger Morgan became one of its directors. Three other leading firms of investment bankers, Kuhn, Loeb in New York, and Kidder, Peabody and Lee, Higginson in Boston, were also brought into the combination. It was agreed that the members of the group would not compete with one another but would divide the market and share investments. During the next four years they conducted sixty-six joint operations, involving the sale of a billion dollars' worth of securities.

The situation was investigated in 1912 by a committee of the House of Representatives, headed by Arséne Pujo, which arrived at the conclusion that there was at least a possibility of a money monopoly. According to the Pujo Committee the three banks in the Morgan-Rockefeller combination—the First National, the Chase National, and the National City—had combined resources of $632,-000,000; the group also controlled other New York banks and trust companies with resources of $968,000,000, while the House of Morgan dominated the Equitable Life Assurance Society, whose assets amounted to an additional $504,000,000. The total supply of banking capital controlled by the group amounted, therefore, to $2,104,000,000. Members of the group, moreover, held 341 directorships in 112 different corporations, whose total capitalization was $22,245,000,000.

What deductions should be drawn from these discoveries was uncertain. The enemies of big business no doubt exaggerated the actual degree of power over the economic system which was exercised by the Morgan partners; the House of Morgan was a part of the system and not a controlling influence over it. However, it was evident that the New York banking combination had become the main channel by which the savings of the community flowed back into industry in the form of capital investments, and that the commissions which the bankers would earn on the sale of securities would continue to be large.

Unlike most of the other dominant figures of his epoch, Morgan passed on his powers to his son, the younger J. P. Morgan, who became head of the firm in 1913. He had, moreover, adopted the practice of inviting able financiers and corporation lawyers to become his partners, so that the House of Morgan had come to represent the ablest concentration of brains on Wall Street. It proved, therefore, to have considerable staying power, and in the nineteen-thirties its connections with corporate industry were substantially the same as they had been during the first decade of the century. Its role in the American economic system had, however, become less important. The vast increase in the buying and selling of stocks in the twenties caused the investment banking business to become more competitive—a development which had unfortunate consequences, since many of the newer banking firms did not adopt the Morgan policy of selling only securities that appeared to represent financially sound investments. The rapid growth of saving by corporations, moreover, shortcircuited the process of investment and made American business more independent of the Wall Street bankers.

FOREIGN TRADE AND INVESTMENTS

One other aspect of American industrial development remains to be discussed: its commercial relations with other parts of the world.

The economic dependence of the United States upon foreign markets was much less than that of any other industrial nation. The United States was far richer in raw materials and had a much larger internal market than did any European country. The American economic system was not, however, wholly self-sufficient, nor could it become so without considerable sacrifices.

Throughout the nineteenth century the United States imported many manufactured goods and much capital equipment from Europe. The most indispensable imports consisted, however, of raw materials not produced at home. The United States produced no rubber, tin, nickel, and a large number of other commodities which were vitally necessary to industry. Raw materials, such as silk, sugar, coffee, tea, and other products of tropical agriculture, were imported to meet the needs of the consumers' market. In the twentieth century, as American industrial resources increased, the general trend was toward a decrease in the proportion of imports from Europe and a greater dependence on the areas producing raw materials, such as South America and the East Indies.

Exports amounted in 1899 to 12.8 per cent of the total value of American production—a proportion which had decreased by 1914 to 9.7 per cent. The importance of the export trade was, however, very much greater in certain branches of production: more than half the cotton crop was exported, as were considerable proportions of the wheat and tobacco crops and of the products of several industries, particularly those making machinery and automobiles. In the twentieth century the most significant tendency in the export trade was the declining importance of agricultural products. Before 1900 about 75 per cent of American exports was usually agricultural; thirty years later 55 per cent was manufactured goods.

An overwhelming proportion of American foreign trade was carried in foreign-owned ships. American shipping had never recovered from the damages inflicted by Confederate privateering during the Civil War and from the failure to change from wood to steel and from sails to steam with sufficient rapidity. Between 1860 and 1900 the tonnage of American vessels engaged in foreign trade dropped from 2,500,000 to 800,000, and the proportion of goods carried in American ships dropped from 66.5 per cent to 9.3 per cent.

Until the World War the United States was a debtor nation, and European investors contributed heavily to the building of the American industrial system. In 1900 the total foreign investments in the United States amounted to about $3,300,000,000—a sum which had increased by 1914 to nearly $5,000,000,000. British and other European investors had especially large holdings in American railroads and in the steel industry; and they also owned about 30,000,000 acres of land in the South and West. Meanwhile, however, the United States was also beginning to export capital, especially to Canada, Mexico, and the Caribbean area. In 1897 about $635,000,000 of American money was invested abroad, and by 1914 the sum had increased to $3,314,000,000. American investments abroad remained small, however, by comparison with the immense holdings of the British; and British investors continued to hold the lead throughout most of South America.

It was predicted by many people that this growth of foreign investments would eventually cause the United States to adopt a policy of economic imperialism. The leading European nations were at this period pursuing a policy of acquiring ownership or control of colonial areas which contained valuable raw materials and opportunities for profitable investment and of excluding other nations from equal access to those areas, the resultant imperialist rivalries being one of the causes of the World War of 1914–1918. It was expected that the United States would follow a similar line, especially in the Caribbean and South America. Actually, however, her foreign policy was always less imperialistic than that of the European powers, although it developed strong tendencies in that direction at the end of the nineteenth century. Those persons who were economically interested in foreign trade and investments were never numerous or powerful enough to control the State Department. And although they were sometimes able to induce the United States government to put pressure on Latin American governments which were interfering with their properties, they were, in general, more interested in keeping world markets open to all competitors on a basis of equality than in building an American colonial empire from which their foreign competitors would be excluded. American foreign policy in the twentieth century, insofar as it reflected the interests of American foreign traders and investment bankers, was directed mainly toward the maintenance of the international free market—a policy which was, in some respects, the opposite of economic imperialism. The imperialist tendencies in American policy were due not so much to economic interests as to the growth of nationalist sentiment and to considerations of military and political security.

BIBLIOGRAPHY

L. D. Brandeis, *Other People's Money* (1914)
J. H. Bridge, *The Inside History of the Carnegie Steel Company* (1903)
J. I. Bogen, *The Anthracite Railroads* (1927)
E. G. Campbell, *The Reorganization of the American Railroad System, 1893–1900* (1909)
F. A. Cleveland and F. W. Powell, *Railroad Promotion and Capitalization* (1909)
H. Coon, *American Tel and Tel* (1939)
F. B. Copley, *Frederick W. Taylor* (1923)
L. Corey, *The House of Morgan* (1930)
N. R. Danielian, *A.T. and T.* (1939)
F. L. Dyer and T. C. Martin, *Edison* (1929)
J. T. Flynn, *God's Gold: The Story of John D. Rockefeller* (1932)
C. B. Glasscock, *The War of the Copper Kings* (1935)
W. H. Hamilton and H. R. Wright, *The Case of Bituminous Coal* (1925)
G. Harvey, *Henry Clay Frick* (1928)
J. B. Hedges, *Henry Villard and the Railways of the Northwest* (1930)
B. J. Hendrick, *Life of Andrew Carnegie* (1932)
W. T. Hutchinson, *Cyrus McCormick* (1930)
J. W. Jenkins, *James B. Duke* (1927)
E. R. Johnson, *History of Domestic and Foreign Commerce* (1915)
E. Jones, *The Anthracite Coal Combination* (1914)
G. Kennan, *E. H. Harriman* (1922)
T. Lamont, *Henry P. Davison* (1933)
H. Leech and J. Carroll, *Armour and his Times* (1938)
O. Lewis, *The Big Four: The Story of Huntingdon, Stanford, Crocker and Hopkins* (1938)
H. D. Lloyd, *Wealth against Commonwealth* (1894)
E. D. McCallum, *The Iron and Steel Industry* (1931)
J. Moody, *The Railroad Builders* (*Chronicles of America,* Vol. 38; 1919)
—— *The Masters of Capital* (*Chronicles of America,* Vol. 41; 1919)
*A. Nevins, *John D. Rockefeller* (1940)
H. O'Connor, *Steel—Dictator* (1935)
—— *The Guggenheims* (1938)
G. L. Parker, *The Coal Industry* (1940)
J. G. Pyle, *Life of James J. Hill* (1917)
H. G. Prout, *Life of George Westinghouse* (1921)

R. E. Riegel, *The Story of the Western Railroads* (1926)
W. Z. Ripley, *Railroads: Finance and Organization* (1915)
────── *Railway Problems* (1913)
T. A. Richard, *History of American Mining* (1932)
H. Satterlee, *J. Pierpont Morgan* (1939)
I. M. Tarbell, *History of the Standard Oil Company* (1904)
────── *Elbert H. Gary* (1928)
J. T. Winkler, *The First Billion: The Stillmans and the National City Bank* (1934)

5

LABOR

THE CONDITION OF THE WORKING CLASS

THE development of large-scale industry was accompanied by a rapid increase in the working class, who differed from other classes in that they normally owned no property and were wholly dependent upon their wages for a livelihood. This increase was brought about partly by a steady movement of young persons from farming areas into industry but chiefly by immigration from Europe. The growth of the national wealth resulted in a rise in the living standards of the workers, but their gains were much slower and less spectacular than those of the business classes. As the economic system developed, the ownership and control of property tended to become concentrated among relatively fewer persons, and the division between the richer and the poorer groups in the community grew greater.

At the end of the nineteenth century the number of wage earners in industry, mining, transportation, and commerce was about twelve million. According to the investigations of Paul Douglas, the average wage in 1900 was $490 a year, price levels being a little less than half what they were in 1940. Industry was employing an increasing number of women, whose average wage was considerably less than that received by men; while there were 1,700,000 child workers under sixteen years of age. At this period more than 50 per cent of the national wealth seems to have been owned by 1 per cent of the population, and there were 3,800 millionaires.

The general movement of both prices and wages was upward,

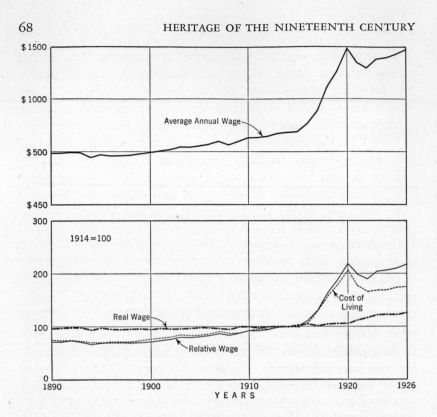

Figure 4. MOVEMENTS OF WAGES 1890–1926. (Based on figures in P. H. Douglas, *Real Wages in the United States,* published by Houghton Mifflin Company.)

with wages usually rising somewhat more quickly. Between 1890 and 1900, however, according to Paul Douglas, real wages, measured in terms of purchasing power, showed little change, while between 1900 and 1914 they increased about 6 per cent. It was not until after the World War that there was any considerable rise in the living standards of the wage-earning class. In 1899, hours of labor, according to Samuel Gompers, averaged nine and a half a day. Early in the twentieth century the workers in a number of different industries obtained an eight-hour day; but this reduction was by no means general.

These gains in wage and hour conditions were offset by a number of disadvantages. Labor, though concentrated into a shorter period, was becoming more intense. The function of the average factory worker was to tend a machine, the movements of which could be speeded up by the factory management; and his pace was no longer governed by the natural rhythms of the human body. Industrial accidents had become frequent, especially in mining and transportation. In the year 1913, for example, accidents caused 25,000 deaths and 700,000 disabilities of more than four weeks each. Between 1907 and 1920, deaths in the coal-mining industry were never less than 2,200 a year—a figure which, allowing for the difference in the number of workers, was three times as great as the rate in the coal mines of Great Britain.

The worker had no security of employment, and the impersonal processes of the economic system, with its alternation between booms and depressions, might at any moment deprive him of the wage which was his sole source of livelihood. During the economic crisis of the eighteen-nineties, for example, at least one-sixth of the working class were unemployed. The growth of absentee ownership, with factory managers becoming the salaried agents of stockholders, meant that there was no longer much personal contact or sense of mutual obligation between employer and employee. The workers were, moreover, crowded into the slum tenements of the rapidly growing cities, where poverty meant far more serious deprivations than it did in rural areas.

The dominant belief in the nineteenth century was that the state had no responsibility for the welfare of the working class. The owners of industry should have absolute power to hire and dismiss workers as they chose, and to decide what wages they could afford to offer. The standard of living of the working class should be regulated by the law of supply and demand. It was assumed that the processes of the economic system would sufficiently reward honesty, industry, sobriety, and intelligence; and the comforting idea that workers were themselves to blame for any misfortunes which they suffered and that even in times of depression deserving men could always find employment was very prevalent. This attitude v/?s applied not only to unemployment but also to industrial accidents. By common law doctrine, generally accepted until the twentieth century, an employer had no responsibility for injuries suffered by his workers if they were due to the ordinary hazards of the occupation, to contributory negligence, or to negligence on the part of fellow-workers.

Such an economic philosophy was too contrary to the realities of the situation to be accepted permanently. The interplay of supply and demand would not result in economic justice unless there were a reasonable degree of equality between the buyer and the seller of a commodity. There was no such equality between the employer who bought labor power and the individual worker who sold it. Unsanitary slum areas and low standards of living meant, moreover, that the health of all classes in the community might be endangered and the vitality of future generations undermined. Despite the belief of property owners that each individual should be held responsible for himself, the welfare of all social groups was, in the last resort, interdependent. Before the end of the nineteenth century a growing realization of this had caused a few states, most notably Massachusetts, to pass laws limiting hours of labor for women and children and prohibiting dangerous machinery and fire hazards. Such legislation was, however, always liable to be declared unconstitutional, as a violation of the rights of property and of freedom of contract, by both Federal and state courts. The United States remained, in general, two or three generations behind most of the European countries in its acceptance of the principle of social responsibility for individual welfare.

THE GROWTH OF TRADE UNIONISM

It was to be expected that the American workers, like those of the European countries, would organize trade unions in order to protect their interests and provide for collective, rather than individual, bargaining over wages and hours. The growth of trade unionism in the United States was, however, slower than in Europe, and until the nineteen-thirties the proportion of workers who belonged to unions remained considerably less. There were a number of reasons for this difference. Working-class wages and standards of living, although very low, were generally higher in America than in any European nation. American society was relatively democratic, without the rigid caste and social distinctions which prevailed in Europe. It was generally declared that there were no classes in America, and it was true that in the nineteenth century it was not unusual for able and ambitious workers to climb into the business and salaried groups. Most American industrialists were, moreover, bitterly opposed to unionism. They regarded it as an interference with the rights of property and represented it as a device by which agitators extracted dues from the workers and thus became salaried union officials—an attitude generally shared by the courts—and they used methods both of force and conciliation in order to crush the unions.

The organization of the working class was hampered also by the differences of interest between skilled and unskilled labor and by numerous racial, linguistic, and religious barriers. The stream of immigrants from Europe, continuing until the World War, was always liable to sweep away any trade union established among unskilled workers who could easily be replaced. Much of the immigration from eastern Europe in the late nineteenth century was, in fact, deliberately stimulated by employers who had been having labor troubles and who expected immigrant labor to be more docile and less responsive to union organizers.

For these reasons almost the only unions which achieved any permanent successes were those representing skilled workers, organized according to specialized crafts. Such unions were able to acquire a strong bargaining position by restricting their membership. A number of unions of this kind came into existence in the course of the nineteenth century. By the year 1870 there were already thirty-two unions organized on a national scale, although most of them were still very small.

After the Civil War the first important attempt to create a united working-class movement was the formation of the Knights of Labor, which was founded in 1869 by Uriah Stephens and headed after 1879 by Terence V. Powderly. The Knights of Labor was a loose organization, with vague purposes, professing a number of social ideals, varying from consumers' co-operatives to currency inflation, which had little connection with the immediate needs and interests of the working class. Although it was based on the craft unions, it invited into its ranks unskilled workers, farmers, and even members of the employing class. "For much of its membership," says Herbert Harris, "it was less a national union than a variety of religious experience." It had, nevertheless, a rapid growth, achieving by 1886 a membership of 729,000. Its decline was, however, equally rapid, and within half a dozen years it had virtually ceased to exist. It was killed by the incompetence and lack of realism of its leaders, by their tendency to adopt agrarian rather than working-class objectives, and by the discredit suffered by organized labor for some years after the Haymarket affair. The latter incident occurred in Chicago on May 4, 1886, when a group of men who professed anarchist ideals organized a public meeting at the Haymarket in support of the demand for an eight-hour day. When the police began to break up the meeting, some unknown person threw a bomb which killed seven people and injured sixty others. The anarchist leaders were tried on charges of incitement to murder, and seven of them received death sentences.[1] Although the anarchists appear to have had no connection with the unknown thrower of the bomb, and although the Knights of Labor had no connection with the anarchists, the incident was used by the enemies of the organized labor movement in order to arouse popular antagonism against it.

The lack of a strong trade union movement did not, however, mean that there were no conflicts between capital and labor. On a number of occasions in the seventies and eighties the workers, especially on the railroads, rebelled against intolerable conditions. These struggles were frequently accompanied by violence. In 1877 a wave of strikes spread across the country, assuming the proportions of a minor rebellion and resulting in the loss of scores of lives and property damage estimated at 10 million dollars. Pitched battles were fought between the militia and the strikers. There was a similar nationwide strike movement in 1884 and 1885, during which labor, by compelling Jay Gould to grant the demands of the workers

1. Five were executed; two were subsequently pardoned by Governor Altgeld.

on the southwestern railroads which he controlled, won its first important victory.

A new epoch in the history of American trade unionism began in 1881 when a number of unions seceded from the Knights of Labor and organized the American Federation of Labor. The guiding spirit in the new organization was Samuel Gompers, an immigrant from England, of Dutch-Jewish descent. Gompers and his friend Adolph Strasser controlled the cigar makers union, where for some years they had been putting into practice their belief in "pure and simple" trade unionism. This theory held that unions should abandon the vague and remote political idealisms that had ruined the Knights of Labor, should concentrate on the more humble objective of winning immediate gains in wages and hours, and should gain strength by strict discipline and the steady accumulation of financial reserves. As Strasser told a Senate committee in 1883: "We are all practical men. We have no ultimate ends. We are going on from day to day. We are fighting only for immediate objectives—objects which can be realized in a few years."

The new unionism insisted on centralized control by salaried officials, prohibited strikes which were not sanctioned by the central authorities, and required a regular payment of dues in order to build up strike funds and make possible the payment of sickness, accident, and death insurance benefits. The A. F. of L. had a steady growth, winning the adhesion of every important union except the four railroad brotherhoods. Its membership amounted in 1900 to 548,321, and in 1914 to 2,020,671. It never included, however, more than a relatively small proportion of the American working class. Gompers continued to act as president every year except one until his death in 1924.

Most of the unions belonging to the A. F. of L. represented only skilled workers, organized by crafts. The classification of workers according to their crafts often provoked controversies between different unions, each of which might claim jurisdiction over a particular group of workers. Thus, the officials of the A. F. of L. spent much of their time adjusting jurisdictional disputes. Each union was organized on a national scale and retained full autonomy within the federation. The local branches of the different unions also combined with one another to form state and city federations.

The primary object of every A. F. of L. union was to induce the employers to recognize the union as collective bargaining agent for the workers. The unions attempted to achieve this object by strikes, accompanied by picketing, and also by urging consumers to boycott firms which did not employ union labor. Most A. F. of L. unions hoped to establish a "closed shop," which meant that a person who was not a member of the union could not work in the factory in question and, hence, that any abandonment of collective bargaining would be impossible. Employers, on the other hand, demanded the preservation of the "open shop," which they often preferred to call euphemistically the "American plan." The A. F. of L. disliked strikes, except when they were necessary to win union recognition; and it declared itself opposed to the use of any form of violence. This repudiation of violence was, however, not always respected by some of its constituent unions.

Unlike the trade union movement in Europe, the A. F. of L. never joined forces with any political organization. It formally repudiated Socialism in 1894. Gompers and his leading lieutenants accepted the capitalist system, but at the same time they insisted that there were inevitable conflicts of interest between the capitalist class and the working class. The political program of the A. F. of L. was to fight for social reforms which would be of benefit to the workers. In 1906 it declared that its policy was to support its friends, whether in the Republican or in the Democratic parties, and to punish its enemies. It also carried on lobbying activities which were intended to counteract the lobbying of the industrialists. Although the A. F. of L. usually leaned more toward the Democratic Party, some of its leaders preferred to support the Republicans.

The A. F. of L. had considerable success in winning benefits for its members in the form of higher wages, the eight-hour day, and establishment of collective bargaining. Representing, however, only the "labor aristocracy," it had little concern for the welfare of the masses of unskilled workers who remained outside its ranks. Its "closed shop" policy, although necessary as a safeguard of collective bargaining, could easily lead to abuses, since it meant that union officials virtually had the right to supply factories with new workers when they were needed and to decide who could, or could not, obtain employment. The A. F. of L. was, in fact, endeavoring to establish a series of labor monopolies—a policy exemplified also in the attempt of certain unions which had won the closed shop to restrict their membership by means of strict apprenticeship rules and high initiation fees. The officials of the A. F. of L., moreover, receiving large salaries and elevated above the class to which they had originally belonged, tended to develop into a privileged bureaucracy, whose interests were in some respects different from those of the workers whom they supposedly represented. A labor monopoly could thus be as opposed to the general welfare as could a capitalist monopoly.

After the rise of the A. F. of L. a number of employers were willing to accept collective bargaining, realizing that the workers had genuine grievances and that, if they could voice their grievances through a responsible trade union organization, the result might be an increase in industrial efficiency. Mark Hanna, the chief representative in national politics of big business interests and the close friend of President McKinley, was sympathetic to the A. F. of L. In 1901 he helped to found the National Civic Federation, which was intended to bring together employers and labor leaders. A majority of the big industrialists, however, including the directors of all the basic mass-production industries, remained uncompromisingly opposed to unionism. They formed a number of associations, including notably the National Association of Manufacturers and the National Metal Trades Association, to provide for common action in their fight against the unions. These associations maintained lobbies in order to prevent any legislation which might threaten the absolute control of the employer over his business, and they organized propaganda campaigns in defence of the open shop.

A number of manufacturers adopted the practice of hiring labor spies who would watch the workers and enable the employers to dismiss at once any advocates of unionism. Several agencies, notably Pinkerton's National Detective Agency, went into the business of supplying manufacturers with spies and strikebreakers. Since the spies owed their living to the prevalence of labor troubles, they were likely to become *agents provocateurs* and foment troubles deliberately where none existed. In some industrial areas, especially in the mine fields of Pennsylvania, West Virginia, and Kentucky, the workers were little better than feudal serfs. Their employers controlled the local police and maintained private police forces of their own. When there were disturbances, order was enforced by deputy sheriffs, who were sworn in by the local authorities but paid by the employers. The workers, moreover, frequently lived in company houses, from which they could be evicted if they ventured to strike; they bought at a company store; and they received medical attention from a company doctor. In such areas workers were often required to sign a "yellow dog" contract, pledging themselves not to join unions. Any union organizer who ventured to enter the district did so at the peril of his life.

The powers of the unions were, moreover, narrowly restricted by the courts, particularly through the use of the injunction to limit or prohibit picketing and to forbid any public appeal to boycott firms employing nonunion labor. An injunction was a court order forbidding certain actions on the ground that they would cause loss or damage to individuals of a kind which could not afterwards be remedied through legal procedure. Persons who disobeyed an injunction were liable to prosecution for contempt of court and were not allowed the right to a jury trial. Possibly the most famous injunction in United States history was issued in connection with the Pullman strike of 1894. When the employees of the Pullman car works near Chicago went on strike against a wage cut, the American Railway Union, headed by Eugene V. Debs, supported them by refusing to handle Pullman cars. President Cleveland, informed that the mail trains were being held up, ordered Attorney General Olney to intervene; and Olney's representative, Edwin Walker, secured from the Federal Circuit Court at Chicago a blanket injunction forbidding the officers of the union to take any measures, including peaceful persuasion of the workers, likely to obstruct the railroads or hold up the mail. Debs defied the injunction and was sentenced to six months' imprisonment. The broad uses to which the injunction could be put were shown in the Bucks' Stove and Range Company Case of 1907 and the Danbury Hatters' Case of 1908, in which the officials of the A. F. of L. were forbidden to include these firms in their "We Don't Patronize" list or to make any reference either in print or by word of mouth to their refusal to employ union labor.[2]

SOME IMPORTANT UNIONS

The strongest A. F. of L. unions were in the building trades with one-third of the total membership of the Federation belonging to the building unions in the nineteen-twenties. It was these unions that typified some of the abuses connected with the labor movement. Building was carried on by small-scale contractors, whose market was local and not national. Since this type of work required skill, could be only partially mechanized, was done during only part of the year, and usually had to be completed by a certain date, the building unions were able to achieve a strong position. The result was an increase in building costs, at the expense not so much of the contractors as of the general public. The building unions, moreover, sometimes found it desirable, where possible, to establish close connections with those municipal officials who had authority over the awarding of contracts for public buildings. They likewise established close relations with those who, through their power to manipulate real estate taxes and to formulate conditions for the issuing of building permits, had some degree of supervision over private building. These connections occasionally involved corruption and racketeering.

The use of violence and sabotage against contractors who refused to employ union labor was not unknown. This practice involved the A. F. of L. officials in a *cause célèbre* which had damaging consequences. On October 1, 1910, the building of the Los Angeles *Times,* whose proprietor was a bitter enemy of unionization, was destroyed by dynamite, causing the death of twenty-one persons. Three members of the International Association of Bridge and Iron Workers, John I. and James B. McNamara and Ortie McManigal, were arrested. The two McNamaras protested their innocence and

2. See page 139.

were vigorously supported by the leaders of the A. F. of L. During the trial, however, the McNamaras admitted their guilt; and the A. F. of L. officials, although they had defended the McNamaras only because they had believed in their innocence, were widely attacked for having implicated themselves in the case.

By contrast, two of the most ably managed unions in the country were in the clothing industry. The workers in this industry were largely Jewish and Italian immigrant women who had suffered from excessively long hours, low wages, and insanitary conditions of labor. In 1909 and 1910 there occurred a series of strikes in the New York sweatshops, which publicized the grievances of the strikers and attracted wide sympathy. The employers agreed finally to the establishment of regular machinery for the arbitration of disputes, the details of which were worked out chiefly by Louis D. Brandeis, at that time a lawyer in Boston and widely known—through his activities on behalf of underprivileged classes—as the "people's counsel." The International Ladies Garment Workers Union, founded in 1900, was able to win a strong position in the industry.

At the same time there was a strike in Chicago among the men's clothing workers of Hart, Schaffner, and Marx, who were led by an immigrant from Lithuania, Sidney Hillman. This strike also was settled by the adoption of arbitration, which it was agreed should thereafter be the normal method of settling disputes. In 1914 Hillman and his followers founded the Amalgamated Clothing Workers of America, which remained outside the A. F. of L. These two needle-trades unions were pioneers in their sponsorship of arbitration; in their belief that, once collective bargaining had been accepted, the unions should co-operate with the employers in efforts to improve the methods of the industry and increase its efficiency; and in the numerous cultural and social services which they provided for their members.

The largest single union in the A. F. of L., the United Mine Workers of America, was founded in 1890 and was organized as an industrial union, comprising all the workers in the industry, rather than as a craft union. The union began among the workers in the bituminous mines, and in 1902 it organized a strike in the anthra-cite area. The able leadership of John Mitchell and the arrogance of the mine owners won for the strikers much public sympathy and some support from the administration of President Theodore Roosevelt. Although the union did not win formal recognition as bargaining agent for its members, it secured higher wages and a large increase in membership.[3] During the next eighteen years the United Mine Workers steadily gained in strength, and by 1920 it had a membership of 370,000, about half the total number of miners in the country. After 1920, however, it failed to hold these gains, and until 1933 its membership steadily declined.

Coal was the only basic industry where the A. F. of L. met with any successes. Steel, for example, remained a stronghold of the "open shop." The National Amalgamated Association of Iron and Steel Workers had been formed in 1876, but it could make no headway against the bitter hostility of the industrialists. In 1892 the workers in a Carnegie plant at Homestead, Pennsylvania, refused to accept a wage reduction and took possession of the factory. Frick, who had been left in charge by Carnegie, hired three hundred Pinkerton detectives to drive out the workers, and a pitched battle ensued, in which the Pinkertons were defeated. The governor of Pennsylvania then sent eight thousand state militia to the aid of the Carnegie Company. The workers were expelled from the factory and replaced by nonunion labor. Other attempts to unionize the steel industry were defeated in 1901 and in 1919; and steel remained "open shop" until 1937. With the exception of the railroads, where the four craft unions—the brotherhoods of locomotive engineers, firemen, conductors, and railway trainmen—won a strong position but remained outside the A. F. of L., every other large-scale corporation was equally successful in resisting unionization.

THE INDUSTRIAL WORKERS OF THE WORLD

Unskilled labor, excluded from the craft unions of the A. F. of L., was scarcely touched by the growth of unionization until the nineteen-thirties. There was, however, one earlier attempt to create a

3. See page 233.

labor movement which would include all categories of workers. This was the organization of the Industrial Workers of the World.

The I. W. W. was an outgrowth of the Western Federation of Miners, a militant union which had seceded from the A. F. of L. in 1898 and had organized a number of strikes in the mining camps of the Rocky Mountain area. The western miners, mostly migratory and without family ties and living in frontier communities where there was little respect for established law and order, responded quickly to revolutionary doctrine and a belief not in reforming the capitalist system but in overthrowing it. Labor struggles in the West frequently became violent on the part of both the workers and the mine owners. The head of the Federation, William D. Haywood, one of the ablest and most genuinely idealistic radical leaders in American labor history, was idolized by his followers.

Haywood's revolutionary sentiments became widely publicized in 1906 when he was put on trial as accessory to the murder of Frank Steunenberg, Governor of Idaho. In 1899 Steunenberg had called in Federal troops to break a strike in the lead mines of Coeur d'Alene, and six years later he was killed by a member of the Federation, Harry Orchard. Orchard declared after his arrest that he had acted on Haywood's orders. The trial of Haywood caused two well-known lawyers to confront each other, William E. Borah for the prosecution and Clarence Darrow for the defence. Contrary to the expectations of labor leaders and radicals throughout the country, the trial was scrupulously fair; and Haywood was acquitted for lack of evidence, although the members of the jury declared later that they had believed him to be guilty.

In 1905 Haywood joined a number of other left-wing leaders in organizing the I. W. W., which was to unite all sections of the working class into one big union and to revolutionize the economic system. The I. W. W. contained at first radicals of all varieties, but in 1908 the Socialists left it and its official viewpoint became syndicalist; that is, it believed that the capitalist class should be overthrown by the working class, but it was opposed to state ownership or to any extension of state power. Bitterly hated by the owners of industry, the I. W. W. won a number of strikes and struggles for free speech in the West; and in 1912 it came east and organized a successful strike in the textile factories of Lawrence, Massachusetts. The following year, however, it was defeated in an attempt to unionize the silk mills at Paterson, New Jersey; and during the World War the wave of anti-radical hysteria enabled its enemies to crush it by the enactment of laws against "criminal syndicalism."

The I. W. W. included some of the ablest left-wing leaders in the country, Haywood, Carlo Tresca, Arturo Giovanitti, and Elizabeth Gurley Flynn being outstanding. During its career it conducted 150 strikes and issued more than a million membership cards. Its membership, however, was very transitory, and its strength at any one time was much less than this figure would imply.

BIBLIOGRAPHY

L. Adamic, *Dynamite: The Story of Class Violence in America* (1931)
E. Berman, *Labor and the Sherman Act* (1930)
C. E. Bonnett, *Employers' Associations in the United States* (1922)
P. F. Brissenden, *The I.W.W.* (1919)
M. R. Clark and S. F. Simon, *The Labor Movement in America* (1938)
*J. R. Commons and others, *History of Labor in the United States* (4 vols., 1918–35)
H. David, *History of the Haymarket Affair* (1936)
P. H. Douglas, *Real Wages in the United States, 1890–1926* (1931)
F. Frankfurter and N. Greene, *The Labor Injunction* (1930)
S. Gompers, *Seventy Years of Life and Labor* (1925)
G. G. Groat, *The Attitude of American Courts in Labor Cases* (1911)
C. A. Gulick, *The Labor Policy of United States Steel Corporation* (1924)
H. Harris, *American Labor* (1939)
R. H. Harvey, *Samuel Gompers* (1935)
W. Haywood, *Bill Haywood's Book, An Autobiography* (1929)
L. Levine, *The Women's Garment Workers* (1924)
L. L. Lorwin and J. A. Flexner, *The American Federation of Labor* (1933)
L. MacDonald, *Labor Problems and the American Scene* (1938)
A. T. Mason, *Organized Labor and the Law* (1925)
John Mitchell, *Organized Labor* (1903)
S. Perlman, *History of Trade Unionism in the United States* (1923)
T. V. Powderly, *Thirty Years of Labor* (1889)
*E. Stein and others, *Labor Problems in America* (1940)
J. M. Viau, *Hours and Wages in American Organized Labor* (1939)

N. J. Ware, *The Labor Movement in the United States, 1860–1895* (1929)

G. S. Watkins and P. A. Dodd, *Labor Problems* (1940)

E. E. Witte, *The Government in Labor Disputes* (1932)

L. Wolman, *The Growth of American Trade Unionism* (1924)

S. Yellen, *American Labor Struggles* (1936)

6

AGRICULTURE

IN THE WEST

THE GROWTH OF PRODUCTION

THE decades after the Civil War, which saw the growth of large-scale industry, brought an equally remarkable development of agriculture. The colonization of the West and the application of science to farming resulted in a great increase in production and a corresponding decrease in the need for human labor. This agricultural progress, without which the growth of industry would have been impossible, did not, however, bring prosperity to the farmers who were responsible for it; on the contrary, the farm population suffered during the later years of the nineteenth century, and again after the World War, from a depression which constituted one of the most serious weaknesses of the American economic system.

The rapid expansion of agriculture after 1865 was due to a number of different factors: the need both of European countries and of the new urban areas in America for American agricultural products; the opening of the West by the railroads; and the Homestead Act of 1862 and the large number of Civil War veterans, native Americans from the eastern states, and immigrants from northern Europe, who were eager to take advantage of it. During the next thirty years vast areas in the states west of the Mississippi were transformed into farm land. Between 1860 and 1900 the total acreage of American farms increased from 407 million to 840 million, and the total value of farm properties increased from 8 billion to 20 billion dollars. In 1900 there were 5¾ million farms and 10¼ million persons engaged in agriculture as either owners, tenants, or hired laborers.

Equally remarkable was the progress in agricultural methods. Seeds and animals were steadily improved by a series of importations, blendings, and breedings. Such artificial fertilizers as nitrogen, potash, and phosphate began to be used for improving the quality of the soil. The knowledge of scientific agricultural methods was diffused among the farm population through the land-grant colleges set up under the Morrill Act of 1862, the agricultural experiment stations established by the Hatch Act of 1887, and the itinerant farmers' institutes financed by the state governments and supervised by the U. S. Department of Agriculture.

Meanwhile the successive inventions of the mechanical reaper, the binder, and the threshing machine had, by the eighteen-eighties, mechanized the whole process of harvesting, from cutting the grain to bagging the kernels; and in the twentieth century the development of the tractor made the horse almost unnecessary. Between 1830 and 1900 the total amount of labor needed for producing a bushel of wheat was reduced from 183 minutes to 10 minutes. Between 1850 and 1895 production per labor unit increased 500 per cent. In the twentieth century other developments—the telephone, the automobile, good roads, electric lighting and electric apparatus, and the radio—along with the great expansion of selling by such mail-order houses as Sears Roebuck and Montgomery Ward, greatly increased the amenities of farm life and destroyed much of its traditional isolation.

THE ECONOMIC CONDITION OF THE FARMERS

To the farmers themselves the growth of mechanization was by no means wholly beneficial. It meant that they had sacrificed their economic security and independence. In the eighteenth century farmers fed and clothed themselves and made their own houses and implements. If they were free from debt, they needed money for nothing except the payment of their taxes and the purchase of salt, gunpowder, and a few luxuries. The twentieth-century farmer, on the other hand, is a part of an intricate economic structure. His higher standards of living greatly increase his need for money, so that he now has to find markets for a much larger proportion of his products. Furthermore, in order to obtain the harvesters and the tractors which promise to reduce his labors, he very frequently has to go into debt. The farmer has tended increasingly to concentrate on the production of a single staple crop, all of which he sells, and to buy all his necessities rather than raise them himself. Instead of grinding his own grain and baking his own bread, he now sells his wheat and buys his bread. His life is, in consequence, more leisurely but also much more precarious. The insecurity of it is, moreover, increased by the extension of his market to Europe. The total annual value of American agricultural exports in the eighteen-nineties averaged about 660 million dollars. One-third of the American wheat crop was exported. It was, indeed, the American farmer who, by producing this surplus beyond domestic needs, enabled the American economic system to pay the interest on the capital invested in it by Europeans and who thus made possible the rapid expansion of industry.

The economic difficulties from which the American farmer so frequently suffered were due, in the first place, to international competition. In the later years of the nineteenth century there was a rapid growth of agricultural efficiency in Russia, in India, and in South America, which resulted in falling prices and a tendency toward the overproduction of basic foodstuffs. At this period American industry was producing mainly for the domestic market, so that it was possible for Congress to give it protection by means of tariff duties. The tariff could, however, be of no assistance to the farmer, and its effect was to raise the prices of the manufactured products which he bought.

In the second place, the farmers were in a much weaker position than the industrialists because they were unable to form combinations to limit the effects of competition. Except among the California fruit and vegetable growers, there was no important tendency toward large-scale methods in farming. Large-scale farming was economically unnecessary, since the most improved scientific methods needed no great outlay of capital and could profitably be applied on relatively small farms. At the end of the century the size of the average farm was 146.6 acres. Since the farmers were unable to unite with one another to limit production but were forced to compete with one another, they found themselves caught in a vicious circle, in which greater production meant lower prices and lower prices led to further increases in production. Between 1870 and 1900, for example, American wheat production increased 250 per cent while the price of wheat per bushel dropped from 105.3 cents to 62 cents. Increased production and lower prices were, in themselves, socially desirable; but unfortunately American large-scale industry had been able to escape from the cycle of competition by adopting monopolistic practices of restricted production and high prices. The decrease in farm prices was thus not compensated by any equivalent decrease in industrial prices, the result being that the farmers' share in the national income tended to grow smaller. The ultimate result, which was reached in the nineteen-twenties, was an absolute overproduction of farm products.

In the third place, the farmer was constantly victimized by other groups in the community who had been able to escape the effects of competition, or who enjoyed political or legal protection. His grain was stored first in elevators which were—in the nineteenth century—largely owned by a small group of men who combined to keep their charges high. It was shipped to market by the railroads, whose charges were also high. Finally it was sold to the terminal elevator operators at the big grain markets, who were further likely to exploit the farmers. As the crowning touch to the grievances of the farm population, many of these operators were in the habit of speculating on "futures" in the Chicago wheat pit and could sometimes make millions by doing so. Moreover, the agricultural machinery used by the farmers was, after 1902, usually bought from the International Harvester Company, one of the most powerful trusts in the country. When the farmers needed credit—and they frequently required short-term loans in anticipation of their harvests

—they had to go to local merchants, who frequently charged interest rates of from 15 to 20 per cent.

The grievances of the farm population were especially acute during the seventies, eighties, and nineties. This was a period of deflation, which appears to have been caused chiefly by the failure of gold production to keep pace with the growth of the economic system. The main burden of the consequent fall in prices was borne by the farmers, since industry was able to protect itself through combination. Meanwhile there was no reduction in rates of interest. The result was a steady growth in farm indebtedness and in tenancy. By 1900, 31 per cent of all farms carried mortgages, the proportion being even higher in such rich agricultural states as Iowa and Wisconsin. Since national banks were forbidden under the National Bank Act of 1863 to lend on farm mortgages, this function was assumed principally by investment trusts, which were owned mostly by Easterners and which, especially in the eighties, carried on elaborate advertizing campaigns to persuade farmers to borrow. The proportion of farms operated by tenants in 1900 was 35.3 per cent. This figure included the South, where the problems of agriculture were complicated by the evil heritage of slave and Civil War problems, but the rate of tenancy was also high in the states west of the Mississippi. The landlords were, in many cases, themselves farmers; and many of the tenants were sons, brothers, or former hired men of their landlords, who expected eventually to become owners.

But if the tenure ladder often led upward, it could also lead downward, causing owners to lose their properties through mortgage foreclosures. An appreciable part of the farm population lived migratory lives, renting farms for two or three years only and then, unable to pay their landlords, moving elsewhere with little hope of finding permanent homes. The only bright feature in the farm situation was that, as a result of the growth of population and the march of industry westward, real estate values were steadily rising. There were, for example, lands in Iowa, worth $7 an acre in 1877, which by 1914 were selling at $200. Owners could normally expect, therefore, to be able to sell at a profit, thus providing for their old age.

The grievances of the farmers found expression in a series of waves of agrarian insurgency, which culminated in the campaign of Bryan for the presidency in 1896. After 1896, however, the position of the farmers began to improve, and until the World War it seemed possible that the agricultural problem might be gradually solving itself. The opening of the Transvaal gold mines and the use of the new cyanide process for mining precious metals increased the amount of money in circulation. State governments and, finally, the Federal government established stricter control over the railway and public utility corporations and made it more difficult for them to exploit the farm population. The farmers themselves organized co-operatives which acquired ownership of county elevators and which, though more slowly, began to handle the marketing of farm products.

There was, moreover, a decline in the rate of growth both of the farm population and of farm production, the result being an increase in farm prices. Between 1900 and 1910 3 million persons left the rural areas to seek employment in the cities. The number of persons employed in agriculture reached its peak in the census of 1910, with a figure of 10,415,000, and then began to decrease. Crop production per capita declined after 1906. Between 1900 and 1910 the production of grain increased by only 1.7 per cent, while the value of the grain crop rose by 79.8 per cent. During the same period the number of cattle dropped from 41 million to 36 million, while their value rose by 42 per cent. The result was that between 1900 and 1914 the real income of the farm population, measured in terms of purchasing power, was increasing at the rate of 1.3 per cent a year.

Unfortunately this steady improvement was ended by the World War. The demand of Europe for almost unlimited supplies of American foodstuffs led to a sudden expansion of crop production, millions of new acres being put under the plough. For a period the farmers enjoyed high prices and were encouraged to borrow heavily. The restoration of peace in Europe and the subsequent growth of economic nationalism abruptly ended this agricultural boom and during the twenties and thirties the plight of the farmers was even worse than it had been before 1896.

SOIL EROSION

The economic difficulties of the farmers were only a part of the American agricultural problem. Underlying the dilemma of the farmers was another factor, the long-range consequences of which were of incalculable importance: the growth of soil erosion. The significance of soil erosion had been grasped by the great Virginians of the eighteenth century, particularly by Washington and Patrick Henry; and it had been studied scientifically in Marsh's *The Earth as Modified by Human Action,* published in 1874. Yet it was not until the nineteen-thirties, when irreparable damage had already been done, that there was any general recognition of the need for action to prevent it.

Before the coming of man, topsoil was held in place by forests and grass, which prevented rain and wind from carrying it away. On the American continent the arrival of the European races disturbed this natural economy; and there began a reckless despoliation of timber and grassland with little attempt to replace what was being destroyed. Enormous natural resources, the fruit of tens of thousands of years of slow accumulation, were wasted within a few generations.

There had originally been, within the area of the United States, 800 million acres of virgin forest. By the nineteen-thirties 90 per cent of this had been destroyed, and such replanting as had been undertaken was wholly inadequate to repair the damage. During the first 250 years of white colonization, the timber resources of the Northeast were mostly exhausted. In the later decades of the nineteenth century the lumbermen attacked the forests of Michigan, Wisconsin, and Minnesota, moved thence to Louisiana and other southern states, and turned finally to the last large areas of untouched timber, in Washington and Oregon.

By the nineteen-thirties only 60 million acres of forest land existed in the East and only 77 million in the West. The peak of timber production was reached in 1907, after which—in spite of the continued use of timber for building and the rapidly growing demand for paper to supply the needs of the newspapers—production declined and prices began to rise. The growing scarcity of timber was increased by the prevalence of forest fires, which sometimes consumed as much as 10 million acres in a year. The government began gradually to assume the duty of reforestation, but no obligation was laid upon the lumber companies to replace what they used— an attitude contrasting with that of several European countries, such as Sweden, where the law required a tree to be planted for every one that was cut down. This wholesale exploitation of the forests not only meant that future generations would be confronted by a timber shortage, it also weakened the topsoil and made it easy for rain water to carry it away. The weakening of the topsoil was increased by the generally prevalent practice of burning areas where trees had been cut down, the result being to destroy the humus content in the soil.

Equally harmful was the destruction of grass on sloping land where there was nothing else to hold the soil. Millions of acres which should have been left to grass were made into arable land by American farmers. Whether farm prices were high or low, there was an equal stimulus to sacrifice the future to the present. During boom times the grass was ploughed in order to take advantage of prosperity, during slumps, in order to pay debts. The destruction of grass was especially serious in the Great Plains, a region several thousand feet up, whence rain water had an uninterrupted flow down into the Mississippi and the Gulf of Mexico. The grass of the Great Plains was initially damaged in the eighteen-eighties through overcropping by cattle. By 1885, on land where forty acres per head would have been the correct proportion, the ratio was ten acres per head. The severe winter of 1886, which decimated the cattle, gave a respite to the grass; but in the World War the demand of Europe for wheat caused much of this land to be put under the plough.

The result of this cutting of timber and ploughing under of the grass was that rain water, instead of sinking into the ground, flowed off it and carried the topsoil along. Soil erosion was most noticeable where it took the form of steadily expanding gullies. More widespread and more dangerous was sheet erosion, the importance of which was first shown in 1903 by Hugh Bennett, then a surveyor for the Department of Agriculture. Land with an 8 per cent slope might lose as much as an inch of soil a year through sheet erosion. On one recorded occasion a farm in California, situated on a heavy slope, lost three inches of soil in a single cloudburst. Careless farming might ruin land irreparably within a generation. The total loss of topsoil through erosion by water has been calculated at 3 billion tons a year; and since it requires six hundred years for a single inch of soil to be recreated by the processes of nature, this loss is, for all human purposes, irreplaceable. By 1934, according to the Soil Conservation Service of the Federal government, 50 million acres of land in the United States had been totally ruined, another 50 million had been almost ruined, 100 million had been seriously damaged, and another 100 million was losing soil at an alarming rate. Thus, out of the 610 million acres of land where agriculture was possible, the people of the United States in their relatively brief career had already destroyed or damaged nearly half.

The most spectacular consequences of soil erosion were floods and dust storms. Since the ground could no longer hold water, it flowed down into the rivers, which then began—at the end of wet winters—to rise far above their normal levels. Floods in the Mississippi valley grew steadily worse throughout the whole period since the beginning of white settlement, and by the nineteen-twenties flood control required large-scale projects of government engineering. By the nineteen-thirties floods on other rivers were becoming almost as catastrophic. Dust storms, which carried clouds of topsoil for hundreds of miles, were less destructive than water erosion, but the spectacle of the nation's natural wealth being blown out into the ocean dramatized the problem of soil erosion even more vividly. It has been calculated that in the great storm of May 11, 1934, three hundred million tons of soil were carried from Texas, Oklahoma, Colorado, and Kansas out into the Atlantic. The inescapable meaning of these events was that large areas of the United States were in danger of becoming as barren as the Sahara Desert. Morris Cooke, head of the Water Section of the Natural Resources Board, declared in 1936: "As the matter now stands, and with continuance of the manner in which the soil is now being squandered, this country of ours has less than one hundred years of virile national existence."

The solution of this problem—in its long-range effects perhaps the most important of all American problems—required a drastic reorganization of American agriculture. The farmers themselves were not to blame for the wastage of the soil, since they were caught in an economic system which did not promise them secure prosperity and which encouraged the wastage of natural resources at the expense of future generations. To guarantee effective soil conservation, several conditions were necessary. The farmers must enjoy prosperity, since otherwise they might be compelled to cut their timber and plough their grass; the drift toward tenancy must be checked, since tenants rarely preserve the soil as carefully as do owners; and farming must be regarded not as a business, in which a man might make money in a few years by mining the soil and then retire or move elsewhere, but as a way of life which farmers would transmit to their descendants. A check was needed, moreover, upon the individualism hitherto characteristic of American life; floods and dust storms often damaged the good farmer as well as the bad, and only co-operative action could prevent this. The question was whether the necessary degree of co-operation could be secured by democratic methods, without unduly restricting individual freedom or enlarging the area of government control.

BIBLIOGRAPHY

*O. E. Baker, R. Borsodi, and M. L. Wilson, *Agriculture in Modern Life* (1939)
E. L. Bogart, *Economic History of American Agriculture* (1923)
D. E. Clark, *The West in American History* (1937)
Paul De Kruif, *Hunger-Fighters* (1928)
H. U. Faulkner, *American Economic History* (1924)
H. Garland, *A Son of the Middle Border* (1917)
N. S. B. Gras, *History of Agriculture in Europe and America* (1925)
B. H. Hibbard, *History of the Public Land Policies* (1924)
*E. C. Kirkland, *History of American Economic Life* (1933)
R. Lord, *Behold Our Land* (1938)
F. L. Paxson, *History of the American Frontier* (1924)
H. Quick, *One Man's Life* (1925)

J. Schafer, *Social History of American Agriculture* (1936)

L. B. Schmidt and E. E. Ross, *Readings in the Economic History of American Agriculture* (1925)

E. R. A. Seligman, *Economics of Farm Relief* (1929)

F. A. Shannon, *Economic History of the People of the United States* (revised edition, 1940)

W. P. Webb, *The Great Plains* (1931)

W. A. White, *Our Changing West* (1939)

7

AGRICULTURE AND INDUSTRY

IN THE SOUTH

AGRICULTURE

IF AGRICULTURE in the West was handicapped by being an individualistic economy in a society increasingly dominated by big corporations, agriculture in the South was suffering not only from this same disadvantage but also from the crushing damages, both material and psychological, which had been inflicted during the Civil War and the period of Reconstruction. Although southern leaders devoted themselves to rebuilding their society with an extraordinary energy, the South was to remain for a long period the victim of extreme poverty and of all the physical and cultural ills in which poverty results.

Cotton continued to be the basis of southern economy, tobacco and sugar being the only other important commercial crops. The production of cotton remained unmechanized, and the labor which it required was almost as great in the twentieth century as before the Civil War. Nor would the introduction of new technical methods have been altogether welcome; the development of a mechanical cotton-picker, which began to seem possible in the nineteen-thirties, would have meant a sudden loss of livelihood for hundreds of thousands of tenant farmers. More than half the cotton crop was sold to Europe, cotton being the largest single item in the American export trade, so that the South had to face the growing competition of India and the Sudan.

The steady exhaustion of the soil, one of the chief causes of that demand for the extension of the slave system which had provoked the Civil War, continued at an alarming rate. After the war the chief centers of cotton production tended to move westward from the Deep South into Texas or, as a result of the use of chemical fertilizers, to return to the Atlantic states. The difficulties of the South were, moreover, increased by the spread of parasites, in particular the pink boll worm and the Mexican boll weevil. The boll weevil crossed the Rio Grande in 1892 and moved northward at the rate of from 40 to 140 miles a year, inflicting damage which sometimes reached 300 million dollars a year. Nevertheless the cotton crop steadily increased. By 1876 it was again as large as in 1859; between 1876 and 1914 it increased by 300 per cent, a process inevitably accompanied by steadily falling prices. On several occasions southern leaders discussed proposals for limiting production by means of an agreement among the producers; but such a project could not be successfully carried out without the aid of the Federal government, which was not forthcoming until 1933.

Before the Civil War cotton for world trade had been grown principally on big slave plantations. The financial losses incurred during the war, the abolition of slavery, and the crushing taxation of the Reconstruction Period destroyed the plantation system and led to the parceling of the plantations into small farms. Between 1860 and 1900 the number of separate farm properties in the South increased from 700,000 to 2,500,000. In 1900 about 55 per cent of these farms were operated by owners, roughly 1,200,000 of them being white, and 180,000 Negro. Of the tenant farmers, who numbered about 1,125,000, slightly more than half were Negro. The size of the average farm was smaller in the South than in the West; the tenant, moreover, operated less than the owner, and the Negro farmer less than the white. The average holding of the white tenant farmer was 84 acres; that of a Negro tenant farmer only 40 acres.

Both the tenant farmers in the cotton belt and also many of the smaller owners suffered from a crushing poverty unequaled among any other group in the United States. They operated almost universally without capital, on a basis of indebtedness to their landlords or to the local merchants. Nearly half the tenant farmers were sharecroppers, who used tools, animals, and seeds supplied by their landlords and were required, in return, to give him half their crop. A majority of the remainder operated on a basis of share-tenancy, under which the tenant owned the tools and animals but the landlord supplied the seeds and received from one-quarter to one-third of the crop. A large number of both the tenants and the owners were, moreover, compelled to take goods on credit every spring from the local merchants, who acquired, in return, liens on their crops. The interest rates were excessive, sometimes reaching 40 per cent, and there was also a large difference in price between goods sold for cash and goods advanced on credit.

The viciousness of the system was increased by the insistence of the landlords and the merchants that farmers concentrate on a single cash crop, in order that they might be better able to pay their debts. In the cotton belt, therefore, little was cultivated except cotton, and the farmers were unable to grow their own food or to improve the quality of the soil by introducing a more variegated agriculture. In this respect the boll weevil proved to be a blessing in disguise, since after about 1915 its ravages caused the South to rely less completely on cotton and to adopt other forms of agriculture.

Yet if the landlords and local merchants victimized the farmers, it was not because they themselves were, by choice, an exploiting class. Equally with the farmers they were the victims of southern poverty and of the uncertainties of the single-crop system. Bad debts were frequent; and the local merchants and landlords were themselves usually in debt to wholesalers, who, in turn, were usually in debt to northern bankers and manufacturers. The result was that the average income of the southern farmer was less than half that of farmers elsewhere and that the number of tenant farmers steadily increased both relatively and absolutely. By 1930 the proportion of tenancy in the South had risen from 45 to 55 per cent, and the number of tenant farmers to 1,790,000.

INDUSTRY

Many Southerners after the Civil War believed that the South could save herself by building her own industry in imitation of the

North—a viewpoint of which the most vigorous champion was Henry Grady, editor of the *Atlanta Constitution*. In the eighties and nineties there was, therefore, a rapid industrial development. Many of the steel mills, coal mines, and railroads which were built in this "New South" were financed mainly by Northerners; hence, the profits from them did not remain in the South. There were, however, a number of industries that were southern-owned, of which the most important was the textile industry, located especially in North Carolina. Established in the eighteen-eighties, this industry had a steady growth, competing successfully with the factories of Massachusetts and Rhode Island. By 1927 more than half the textile industry of the United States was located in the South. At this date the total number of wage earners in all southern industries was more than 1,300,000.

The capital for the southern textile industry was at first raised locally, Northern investors not entering the field until the twentieth century, and the ownership of it was widely diffused. The factories were small, numerous, and fiercely competitive. Labor was obtained chiefly among the small white farmers of the hill country. These conditions created labor problems of peculiar difficulty. The workers had been accustomed, before they entered the factories, to long hours, low earnings, and child labor; long hours, low wages, and child labor continued, therefore, to be the rule in the industry. Since they worked at first more slowly and less efficiently than Northerners, who were more accustomed to factory labor, their lower earnings had some economic justification. In 1900 the average hours of labor were from 72 to 75 a week, and the average family wage (earned jointly by father, mother, and children) was from $15 to $25 a week. Thirty years later hours were still from 55 to 60 a week, and wages were still less than two-thirds of those paid in New England.

The wide diffusion of stock ownership and the patriotic enthusiasm of southern public opinion made the amelioration of labor conditions extraordinarily difficult. The growth of trade unionism or the enactment of laws limiting hours or protecting women and children might handicap southern factories in their competition with those of the North and deprive the South of that ultimate salvation from sectional poverty and inferiority which it hoped to achieve through the building of industry. Particularly did Southerners resent any attempt by northern labor organizers, sociologists, or politicians to meddle with southern labor conditions. Such interferences were frequently regarded as due to sectional jealousy and caused by the desire of the North to retain its industrial supremacy. The belief that the South had a right to compensate herself for her many handicaps by paying low wages to her workers remained prevalent even after the southern textile factories had begun to surpass their New England competitors and to drive many of them out of business.

BIBLIOGRAPHY

P. Blanshard, *Labor in Southern Cotton Mills* (1927)
R. P. Brooks, *The Agrarian Revolution in Georgia, 1865–1912* (1914)
P. H. Buck, *The Road to Reunion, 1865–1900* (1937)
*W. T. Couch (ed.), *Culture in the South* (1934)
J. Daniels, *A Southerner Discovers the South* (1938)
B. B. Kendrick and A. M. Arnett, *The South Looks at its Past* (1935)
B. Mitchell and G. S. Mitchell, *The Industrial Revolution in the South* (1930)
H. W. Odum, *Southern Regions of the United States* (1936)
——— *An American Epoch* (1930)
M. A. Potwin, *Cotton Mill People of the Piedmont* (1927)
W. S. Robertson, *The Changing South* (1927)
H. Thompson, *The New South* (*Chronicles of America,* Vol. 42, 1919)
R. B. Vance, *Human Factors in Cotton Culture* (1929)
——— *Human Geography of the South* (1932)
W. P. Webb, *Divided We Stand* (1937)

8

THE POLITICAL SYSTEM

THE PARTY STRUCTURE

THE party system, which had not been foreseen by the makers of the constitution, became in the nineteenth century the dominant factor in American politics. Effective democratic government is probably impossible without it. A legislative body cannot carry out a coherent program unless a majority of its members belong to the same party organization and have agreed to support the same objectives. And only where there are two such parties, capable of giving each other effective criticism and opposition, can the electorate maintain adequate control over their representatives. Certain features of the American form of government make the party system even more necessary in the United States than in the democracies of Europe. Whereas in most European countries the leaders of the majority party in the legislature constitute the executive, in the United States, in both the Federal and the state governments, executive and legislature are separated from each other. This is liable to cause a conflict between the two authorities, resulting in a deadlock. Co-operation can, however, be maintained as long as the executive and the majority of the legislature belong to the same party and are pledged to the same program. In the local governments the party system is rendered necessary also by the large number of positions filled by popular election. The need for co-operation among the various officeholders makes it desirable that they belong to a single political party.

The danger of the party system is that, ceasing to be merely a means by which the will of the electorate can be translated into action, it may become an end in itself. Parties may maintain the loyalty of their members and endeavor to win elections not in order to carry into action a body of political ideals but merely for the sake of the rewards of office. A degeneration of this kind was very apparent in the United States after the Civil War. The differences of principle which had originally separated the Republicans and the Democrats began to be forgotten or to become unimportant, and each party tended to become a body of professional politicians primarily interested in patronage and offices. Party regularity was the chief political virtue, even when it involved dishonesty; and to become a "mugwump" and "bolt" one's party was a political crime. Political leaders tended to degenerate into political bosses, and political parties into political machines.

The Republicans were normally the majority party, winning the presidential elections of 1868, 1872, 1876, 1880, 1888, 1896, and 1900. The Democrats were always, however, a formidable opposition, winning control of Congress occasionally and electing Grover Cleveland to the presidency in 1884 and again in 1892. The party system thus justified itself by ensuring that officeholders were never exempt from criticism and could not afford to ignore the wishes of the electorate. Party rivalries, however, rarely reflected any of the fundamental political divisions in American life, and there was little difference in the policies which each party adopted when it was in office.

Probably the most important political division in the United States was the conflict of interest between business and agriculture —a division which had led, immediately after the establishment of the Federal government, to the opposition between Hamilton and Jefferson. This natural line of division had been destroyed by the Civil War. The attempt of the southern planters to extend slavery to the western territories, and their subsequent secession from the Union, had separated the two agrarian sections, the South and the West, and had brought about the alliance of eastern industrialists and western farmers in the Republican Party. This realignment of forces continued long after its original cause—slavery—had been abolished. The Republican Party, although it was dominated by the eastern industrialists and financiers, was able to retain its western agrarian supporters by appealing to their memories of the Civil War —a political tactic known as "waving the bloody shirt"—and by generous distributions of pensions to veterans of the Grand Army of the Republic.

If, however, the Republican Party continued to be a heterogeneous combination of conservative eastern bankers and corporation magnates, radical western farmers, and idealists originally attracted to it by the crusade against slavery, it could claim to be relatively coherent by contrast with the Democratic Party. After the Civil War the Democrats became the party of white supremacy in the South, including both conservative Bourbon leaders who represented the interests of southern industrialists and landlords, and agrarian radicals who championed the cause of the southern farmers. To these mutually hostile southern groups were added a number of corrupt city machines in the North, particularly the Tammany machine in New York, a few northern financiers and industrialists whose viewpoint was little different from that of the conservative Republicans, and a number of western farmers whose interests were identical with those of their Republican neighbors.

In theory, the two parties advocated different principles. The Republicans, for example, were traditionally in favor of a strong Federal government and a high tariff; the Democrats were the party of states' rights and a low tariff. After the Civil War, however, these differences had little reality. The states' rights question lost its importance; and, while the Democrats still professed to believe in a low tariff, Democratic congressmen were usually willing to support a high tariff when it gave protection to industries in which their constituents were interested. Actually, each party was a coalition of different sectional groups with discordant interests, held together by the doctrine of party regularity. The party allegiance of individuals was frequently determined not by political principle but by the traditions of their family, by the section in which they lived, and in many cases by their race. The vote of the northern Negroes, for example, was almost solidly Republican; the Irish vote, on the other hand, went mainly to the Democrats. In the North and

West the Republican Party was usually the party of respectability, whereas the Democrats were the party of revolt; in the South, on the other hand, the reverse was true. Each party had a conservative wing and a radical wing and could swing in one direction or the other to conform to the tendencies of the electorate. The two parties differed from each other in character and tradition. They were, however, able to compete with each other in winning the favor of the electorate by putting forward similar programs. And the fact that each of them covered almost the whole range of political thought had certain advantages; it meant that American politics was usually free from that fanatical bitterness which becomes inevitable when political divisions are formed purely along class or sectional lines.

PARTY ORGANIZATION

The methods of party organization had been worked out during the Jackson-Clay period and had not been radically changed since that time. Each party consisted of a hierarchy of committees and conventions, which were bound together by a system of indirect elections. At the base of the party pyramid were the ward and precinct committees in the cities, and the village and township committees in the rural areas. Above these came, first, the city and county committees and conventions, then the state committees and conventions, and finally the national committee and convention. Party candidates and party platforms were adopted by the appropriate convention, which consisted of delegates nominated by the organizations immediately below it in the party pyramid. The task of winning elections and supervising the party policies belonged to the appropriate committees.

In theory, therefore, each party was organized on a democratic basis, and the party leaders were ultimately responsible to the rank and file of the party members. Actually, however, each party was largely controlled by groups of political bosses. The rank and file of the membership, who composed the local committees upon which the party pyramids were based, consisted mainly of professional politicians whose main interest was to secure the rewards of office.

In return for party regularity and skill in securing votes for the party candidates, they expected to obtain places on the government payrolls, either Federal or local. This pecuniary interest in political success necessarily made them subservient to the local bosses, whose power was based on their capacity to distribute patronage; and most of the decisions made by the various committees and conventions were, in practice, dictated by bosses, who controlled the proceedings from behind the scenes. The contrast between the theory and the reality of the party system was perhaps most evident in the national conventions, which met every four years to choose presidential nominees. The rank and file of the party delegates were gathered together to listen to speeches and to applaud their chosen candidates, the number of minutes of applause which greeted each name being measured and regarded as of great significance. The real work of the convention was, however, done in private by the party leaders from the different states. Speeches delivered in the convention itself rarely had much influence upon the decisions which it made.

In matters of organization there was little difference between the two parties, though there were some variations in the rules governing the two national conventions. The Democrats, for example, had a unit rule, by which all the delegates of a state had to vote for the same candidate; and no candidate was made the party nominee until he had secured a two-thirds majority in the convention. A peculiarity of the Republican convention, on the other hand, was that the delegations from the southern states consisted mainly of Negro officeholders, with no real party organization behind them. When the Republican Party was in power, these delegations were usually controlled by the administration—a fact which made it easy for a Republican president to nominate his own successor.

The powers of the political bosses, the dependence of each party on the patronage system, and the lack of principle displayed in much political activity were deplored by idealists; yet to some degree they were probably necessary features of the American form of government. The boss system arose because of the need for responsible leadership; and if some bosses were primarily concerned with securing personal advantages, there were others who achieved power by similar methods but who used it to promote the public interests. The patronage system was a recognition of the need of a party organization for paid workers and regular subscriptions; and its abolition would have made political parties more dependent upon outside contributions, and hence more subservient to the interests of those who had wealth to contribute. Practical reformers in the twentieth century generally found it advisable to accept the party system and to work from inside it. It was only by doing so that they were able to secure results.

LOCAL GOVERNMENT

The various units of local government—the states, counties, cities, and townships—were from some points of view even more important than the Federal government. Local government, having control over such matters as public health, education, protection against crime, and regulation of economic activity, affected the ordinary citizen more intimately and in more varied ways than did the Federal government. Although the issues which were decided at Washington were of more fundamental importance, national political parties were based on the local organizations; hence, when local politics was corrupt, Federal politics could not wholly escape contagion.

In the latter part of the nineteenth century the degree of corruption in many of the local governments was very great. Political bosses and political machines exercised great powers and rarely used them to promote the general welfare. The electorate was frequently unable or unwilling to maintain effective control over the officeholders. For the prevalence of corrupt machine politics there were a number of different reasons. In the first place, local questions were entangled with national questions with which they had no real connection. While the local machines might be Republican or Democratic, in their actual organization and policies they were almost indistinguishable. Many voters would support a local machine because of its national party affiliation instead of judging it by its performances in local government. In the second place, there were an enormous number of different elective officials, and voters were wholly incapable of judging their qualifications separately. A machine could, therefore, nominate its candidates for office with the assurance that the average voter would support all the nominees of his party without discriminating against those who were incompetent or corrupt.

Third, there were a large number of different overlapping jurisdictions—county governments, city governments, and independent organizations controlling such matters as education, sanitation, roads, public parks, water, and so on—each of which had its own elective officials. In Cook County, Illinois, to cite an extreme example, there were 392 separate units of government, all of which were legally independent of one another, and 2,537 different elective officials. Within a nine-year period each voter was required to decide as to the qualifications of nearly two hundred of these officials. Under such conditions the voter was obviously unable to maintain control over the activities of his officials. Fourth, many persons did not pay sufficient attention to questions of local government. This was particularly true of the county governments, whose activities often went entirely unnoticed. As late as 1917, after the reforms of the Progressive Era, the National Municipal League could declare that "county government is the most backward of all our political units, the most neglected by the public, the most boss-ridden, the least efficiently organized and most corrupt and incompetent, and, by reason of constitutional complications, the most difficult to reform."

Fifth, many of the local governments, particularly those of the cities, did not have sufficient power; their rights of self-government were narrowly limited by the state constitutions and by the state legislatures, and the legislatures usually exercised their control in the interests of political partisanship rather than of good administration. Sixth, there was in most of the larger cities a considerable immigrant vote, which could easily be controlled by machine politicians. The importance of this factor, however, was probably exaggerated. Rural districts, inhabited by families of Anglo-Saxon stock, were sometimes as politically corrupt as the cities. But the greater wealth of the cities, and the consequently larger opportunities for graft, caused the city machines to receive much more publicity.

The best local government was probably in rural New England, where the town meeting had retained its vitality. The township system had spread also to parts of the Middle West but had not acquired much importance there. Outside New England the chief units of local government, below the state governments, were the counties and cities, of which the latter, owing to their greater wealth and population, were the more important. New York City, for example, had by the end of the nineteenth century a budget larger than those of London, Paris, and Berlin combined, and larger also than those of the central governments of some of the smaller European countries. A city government consisted usually of a mayor and a council or a board of aldermen. In the latter part of the nineteenth century the powers of the councilmen and aldermen had been steadily decreasing, and those of the mayors had been growing larger. The legal forms of city government, however, did not usually correspond to the real situation. At the end of the century almost every city in the United States was controlled by a political machine.

THE CITY MACHINES

The rank and file of a city machine consisted of party workers, whose duty was to secure votes for their party in the districts for which they were responsible, and who expected, in return, to receive jobs on the city pay roll. The boss who controlled a city machine did not usually hold any official position himself; he was usually a self-made man, with little education, who controlled the city government from behind the scenes. The mayor was often a mere figurehead, put forward by the machine because of his vote-catching powers and apparent respectability. Some city bosses enriched themselves at the public expense, but most of them cared for power rather than for money. And although they could never afford to be scrupulous in the methods by which they kept their machines in office, some of them were genuinely anxious to provide good government in return.

The votes which elected a city machine into office, apart from those which came to it because of its party label or as a reward for whatever genuine services to the city it might have performed, were obtained chiefly by two methods. There were, first, much ballot-box stuffing, intimidation or bribery of voters, and numerous other kinds of fraud. In the second place, however, a machine also obtained votes by protecting the poorer families in the city from starvation, by finding jobs for them, and by giving them assistance when they were accused of violating the law. Social services of this kind, although they might better have been performed by the government or by philanthropic organizations, supplied a genuine need, especially among the immigrant population; and it was not surprising that city politicians could thereby win in slum areas a loyal support which was scarcely weakened by proofs of corruption or bad administration.

In addition to votes, a machine also needed money, much of which was obtained corruptly. City officeholders were required to contribute a part of their earnings to the machine, in return for which they could usually augment their official salaries by various forms of petty graft. The chief opportunities for petty graft arose through laws and regulations which reflected the moral principles of the community rather than its practices. Laws limiting the sale of liquor or prohibiting prostitution could, for example, usually be evaded by paying graft to the appropriate local authorities. Occasionally this condonation of activities which society regarded as immoral, developed into an alliance with definitely criminal elements.

Besides the petty graft obtained from lawbreakers, city machines also gathered money from wealthy businessmen. A machine, through its ability to grant contracts for official buildings and supplies, to change tax assessments, and to impose police regulations of numerous kinds, could easily be extortionate. Businessmen, moreover, often wanted favors. The money which passed between business interests and city machines could be regarded either as blackmail or as bribery, and in many cases it was probably both. The accepted idea in the nineteenth century was that such payments were purely blackmail and that all the dishonesty was usually on the side of the politicians. This idea was challenged, early in the twentieth century, by Lincoln Steffens and other "muckrakers," who insisted that the businessman who gave money was as guilty as the politician who took it.

The tendency to condone those who paid bribes did not, however, extend to the most notorious of the numerous corrupt relations between business and city politics. In the eighteen-eighties and nineties a group of financiers, headed by Charles T. Yerkes, William L. Elkins, P. A. B. Widener, William C. Whitney, and Thomas Fortune Ryan, obtained control over the street railroads of New York, Chicago, Philadelphia, and nearly a hundred other cities. The creation of this monopoly, which was based on the acquisition of franchises given by city governments, would have been impossible if the city officials had not been open to bribery. Once the monopoly had been created, the financiers who controlled it were able to make enormous profits by the usual method of watering the stock and unloading it upon the public.

There were occasional revolts against a city machine. Machines were likely to grow too confident, to allow too many criminals to escape punishment, and to increase excessively the costs of city government. Under such conditions a reform administration might be elected to office. Almost invariably, however, the machine returned to power at the next election, chastened by its temporary separation from the city pay roll but not fundamentally changed. Reform administrations were likely to alienate businessmen by being too honest, the poorer classes by failing to give them that protection from individual misfortune which they had received from the machine, and the general public by insisting on a strict enforcement of puritanical legislation. The members of a reform party were, moreover, amateurs, who lacked the skill of the professional politicians of the machine and who were apt to grow tired of political activity. Experience showed that reforms were temporary but that the machine was permanent.

THE STATE MACHINES

In most of the state governments conditions were similar. The state machines were, however, less carefully organized than the city machines and more likely to disintegrate. The state bosses were usually men of a very different type from the city bosses, although they exercised similar functions. The state boss was usually a man of old American stock, wealthy and well-educated. He did not have the preference displayed by the city bosses for remaining in the background, being very frequently a member of the United States Senate. Probably the strongest of the state machines was the Republican machine in Pennsylvania which, under a succession of able leaders, Simon Cameron, Matthew Quay, and Boies Penrose, controlled the state from the Civil War until after the World War. The fraudulent methods by which this machine gathered votes were notorious.

The Republican Party in New York State was similarly boss-controlled, although it had to face a strong Democratic opposition, based on the Tammany machine in New York City, which could occasionally win control of the governorship. In 1915, at the New York State constitutional convention, Elihu Root recalled how "for many years Conkling was the supreme ruler in this state; the governor did not count, the legislature did not count; comptrollers and secretaries of state and what not did not count. It was what Mr. Conkling said; and in a great outburst of public rage he was pulled down. Then Mr. Platt ruled the state; for nigh upon twenty years he ruled it. . . . I don't criticize the men of the invisible government. . . . But it is all wrong." What Root said of New York might, at the turn of the century, have been said with equal truth of a majority of the other states in the Union.

The state governments resembled the city governments also in the prevalence of corrupt financial connections between government and business. Businessmen insisted, with much justice, that the payments which they made to state legislators were a form of blackmail. Moorfield Storey declared in 1894 that "when a state legislature meets, each large corporation within its reach prepares for self-defence, knowing by bitter experience how hospitably attacks upon its property are received in committee and on the floor." State legislators would introduce what were known as "strike bills" limiting the rights of business corporations. These were not intended to pass.

but they would frighten corporation directors into distributing bribes. In Indiana, for example, it was customary to introduce bills prohibiting the sale of cigarettes; the tobacco companies were then compelled to safeguard themselves by buying off the members of the legislature.

On the other hand, the powers enjoyed by the corporations were often excessive. In the eighties and nineties a number of state governments, from New Hampshire in the East to California in the West, were virtually the property of railroad corporations. In Pennsylvania the representative of the Pennsylvania Railroad actually sat alongside the legislators in the state capitol and instructed them how to vote. Corporation magnates were frequently indifferent to party distinctions and were willing to do business with whatever party happened to be in power. As Jay Gould expressed it, during the period when he controlled the Erie Railroad, "In a Republican district, I was Republican; in a Democratic district, I was Democratic; and in a doubtful district, I was doubtful; but I was always Erie."

The American people were, for a long period, remarkably indifferent to the vices of machine government. As long as they felt that the nation was making progress, as was proved by its industrial growth, they were willing to tolerate official corruption, accepting fatalistically the idea that most politicians were self-seeking. Yet they paid a heavy price for their indifference; they suffered not only directly, through the extravagance of machine government, but also indirectly, through the lack of honest and efficient administration of such vital matters as public health, housing, and education. Some of the evil effects of local misgovernment, such as the failure to plan city growth with a view to eliminating slums, creating public parks and playgrounds, and avoiding traffic congestion, would prove to be very difficult to remedy later.

THE FEDERAL GOVERNMENT

The Federal government was always considerably more honest than the local governments, yet in the latter part of the nineteenth century it exhibited similar tendencies toward boss and machine rule and corrupt connections between politics and business. The dishonesty of local politics inevitably infected Federal politics. There were, moreover, certain features of the American form of government which tended to encourage irresponsibility and inefficiency.

A student of American politics, who was subsequently to turn from theory to action, Woodrow Wilson, declared in a book published in 1885: "The Federal government lacks strength because its powers are divided, lacks promptness because its authorities are multiplied, lacks wieldiness because its processes are roundabout, lacks efficiency because its responsibility is indirect and its action without competent direction." Of any policy adopted by the Federal government, Wilson continued, it could usually be said that "a dozen men originate it; a dozen compromises twist and alter it; a dozen officers whose names are scarcely known outside Washington put it into execution."

One reason for the inefficiency of the Federal government was that most congressmen regarded themselves as being primarily the representatives of special local interests and not of the national interest. This was perhaps a consequence of the constitutional rule that a congressman must be a resident of the state from which he was elected. The result of this rule was that politics was a precarious profession, since a man who was unable to secure election from his own state was permanently excluded from Congress—a fact which discouraged men of ability from adopting politics as a profession. And since every congressman had to retain the support of his own state, it was necessary that he secure special benefits for his constituents. He must endeavor to get tariff protection for commodities produced in his state, to arrange that Federal money be spent in the state, and to obtain appointments to the Federal pay roll for his supporters. Much congressional activity took the form of bargaining between various congressmen, who would agree to support one another in the furthering of their various local interests. The most notorious example of this system was the annual Rivers and Harbors Bill, under which Federal money was appropriated for making improvements in different parts of the Union. Such distributions of Federal money were known as the "pork barrel."

A result of the system was that few congressmen, especially in the House of Representatives, could afford to oppose the party leaders; they would be punished for their independence when the party was in power by being deprived of their share of Federal "pork" and Federal patronage. The powers of the party machine were thereby enhanced; and meanwhile the national interests suffered. All the local interests taken together as a whole did not necessarily create the national interest. The combination of local interests, for example, might result in a tariff bill which gave protection to every local industry and result also in large Federal expenditures on internal improvements, whereas the national interest might require a low tariff and a reduction of expenditures.

Another weakness of the American government was the separation of the legislature and the executive. In practice, it was difficult to distinguish legislative and executive functions from each other, and efficient administration was impossible unless the two branches of the government were willing to co-operate with each other. This difficulty was partially surmounted by the party system. During the first two years of a presidential term the President and the majority of the Congress usually belonged to the same party and were pledged to the same program. Even under these circumstances, however, there was always the danger of a conflict, and the President would frequently use his control of Federal patronage as a weapon for retaining the support of congressmen—a practice which, however necessary, did not encourage political honesty. When, moreover, the President and the congressional majority belonged to opposite parties, as often happened during the last half of a presidential term, there was liable to be a complete deadlock; and the government had to remain almost inactive until the time arrived for the next election.

Woodrow Wilson recommended strong leadership by the President, the only elected authority who represented the national interest and not merely a local interest, as the most appropriate remedy for the weaknesses of the Federal government. Between 1865 and 1901, however, only one President, Grover Cleveland, was willing to exercise such leadership. The Republican Presidents were generally willing to allow the party leaders in Congress to determine government policies. Before 1901, when Theodore Roosevelt began to reassert presidential initiative, the real authority in Washington was divided among the President, the Speaker of the House of Representatives, and a small group of senators.

The House of Representatives was the weaker of the two houses of Congress, chiefly because the two-year term of its members, as contrasted with the six-year term of the senators, made it more difficult for them to assert their independence of their party leaders. Most of the real work of the House was not done in its public debates but in the committees, which considered bills before they were submitted to the House as a whole and which were virtually able to kill any proposals of which they disapproved. The Speaker, who was nominated by the caucus of the majority party and then elected at the beginning of each term by the House, was able after 1889 to exercise virtually dictatorial powers. In that year the Republican Speaker, Thomas B. Reed, confronted by a strong Democratic opposition, carried through a revision of the rules. Henceforth the Speaker made all the committee appointments given to members of the majority party, being able to punish opponents by giving them unimportant assignments; through his control of the Committee on Rules he could decide what business the House was to discuss; and by refusing to recognize members who wished to speak or to entertain motions which he chose to regard as "dilatory," he could guide all proceedings on the floor of the House. Reed, generally known as "Czar Reed," dominated the House until his retirement in 1899. Similar powers were exercised by Joseph G. Cannon, Speaker from 1901 until 1911, a convinced conservative of great political shrewdness, whose general attitude was that any change was likely to be for the worse.

The Senate, on the other hand, was one of the ablest legislative bodies in the world. The six-year term of the senators, the prestige of many of them, and their jealously guarded right of unlimited debate gave them a personal independence not enjoyed by members of the House. Although, however, the Senate always contained men of great ability, it was, at the end of the nineteenth century, dangerously out of contact with popular sentiment. The system of election by state legislatures made the senators the nominees of the party bosses and of powerful business corporations rather than of the people. It contained so many men of great wealth that it was sometimes referred to as the millionaires' club. Many of its members were themselves business magnates, and others were corporation lawyers, who continued to receive regular retainers from their employers after their election to the Senate. Chauncey Depew of New York, for example, was a director of seventy different corporations, from which he derived fifty thousand dollars a year in fees alone. Such men spoke as the political agents of economic interests, of railroads or steel or oil, rather than as representatives of the states.

The two leading senators at the end of the century were Nelson W. Aldrich of Rhode Island, the Republican floor leader, and Mark Hanna of Ohio, the friend and adviser of President McKinley. Both these men had qualities of statesmanship, and Hanna at least believed that business magnates should develop a stronger sense of responsibility for the welfare of the workers. Both of them, however, were essentially aristocratic in their political philosophy, distrusting democracy and advocating government by and for men of wealth. Both of them, moreover, were millionaires, with numerous interests in street railroads, mines, and other industries. Their attitude was reflected in a remark which Hanna was said to have made in 1890. "You have been in politics long enough," Hanna had told an associate, "to know that no man in public office owes the public anything."

The evils of the division of responsibility between President and Congress were particularly evident in matters of foreign policy and of finance. The rule that treaties should be made by the executive and ratified by the Senate made it virtually impossible for the United States to pursue any consistent long-range foreign policy, of the kind adopted by European governments. From some points of view this may have had its advantages, one of which was that it helped to preserve the American tradition of freedom from entangling alliances. The lack of a foreign policy was, however, a luxury which the United States could maintain only as long as the American hemisphere was immune from attack across either the Atlantic or the Pacific. The lack of any coherent financial program and the power of Congress to appropriate money contrary to the wishes of the executive were, on the other hand, wholly bad. That the bad effects were not more obvious was due only to the fact that in the nineteenth century there was almost always a treasury surplus. In theory, financial questions were controlled by the Ways and Means Committee of the House of Representatives and by the Senate Finance Committee; but in practice, after 1880, nine committees of the House of Representatives could initiate appropriations of money directly, and five others could do so indirectly.

FEDERAL FINANCE

Between the Civil War and the end of the century financial questions probably occupied more of the time and attention of Congress than did any others; and the tariff and veterans' pensions were the two pivots of Republican Party strategy.

The tariff, raised to provide revenue during the Civil War, remained high after the war on the theory that the manufacturing costs of European industry must be equalized with those of American industry; free trade, it was claimed, would compel American producers to reduce wages to the lower levels prevalent in Europe. Actually, however, the tariff was generally higher than was needed to achieve this purpose; it enabled American industry not only to pay higher wages than were paid in Europe but also to charge high prices from American consumers. Some American industries, such as steel, continued to receive tariff protection long after they had begun to compete successfully with European industries in European markets. No coherent national tariff policy was ever adopted; the tariff was a local question, tariff bills being constructed by means of trading between congressmen, each of whom wanted protection for the industries in the district which he represented. And although the Democratic Party was, in theory, in favor of tariff reductions, chiefly because of the influence of the cotton planters, whose prosperity depended on foreign markets, Democratic congressmen would often vote for tariff bills which gave protection to their own constituents.

In 1866 the average tariff duty was 40.3 per cent ad valorem. In 1876 and 1878 and again in 1884 and 1886 the Democrats controlled the House of Representatives. The Democratic leadership proposed tariff reductions, but bills providing for lower tariffs were always defeated in the House by combinations of Republicans and insurgent Democrats. In 1888 Grover Cleveland forced a lower tariff through the House of Representatives; but it was then rejected by the Senate. The next election gave the Republicans a majority in Congress, and in 1890 the McKinley Tariff Act was passed. This raised the schedules and also gave tariff protection to a number of farm commodities, although the farmers, producing largely for export, had little need for this kind of protection. In 1893, with the Democrats again in control of Congress, the Wilson Bill, lowering the tariff, passed the House; but in the Senate assistance from the Democrats enabled the Republicans to raise the schedules, and in 1894 Cleveland allowed the Gorman-Wilson Tariff to become law without his signature. Finally, after the Republican victory of 1896, the Dingley Tariff Act of 1897 became law. The Dingley Tariff raised the schedules to an average of from 49⅞ to 52 per cent, and gave especially high protection to steel, wool, hides, and sugar. There was no further change in the tariff until 1909.

The revenues derived from the tariff were spent in the same manner as they were collected, each congressman being anxious that Federal money be distributed in his district. Although the debt of the Federal government was reduced from $2,678,000,000 in 1865 to $1,097,000,000 in 1895, there was a treasury surplus almost every year; and considerable sums were therefore available for appropriation. Some 11 or 12 million was spent each year through the annual Rivers and Harbors Bill; but when the Republicans were in power, the preferred method of distributing money was through veterans' pensions. The political advantage, everywhere except in the South, of giving pensions to veterans of the Northern armies was obvious;

and by 1937 a total of $7,934,171,000 had been spent on this purpose. In 1862 service-disability pensions were voted, and the benefits paid were later steadily increased. By 1889 there were 489,725 pensioners, who were receiving about 89 million dollars a year. In 1890 a Republican Congress passed the Dependent Pension Act, which gave pensions to all veterans who were disabled for manual labor, whether the disability had been acquired during the Civil War or not, and also to all veterans' widows who had been married before 1890. By 1893 this measure had increased the number of pensioners to 966,012 and the amount paid to nearly $157,000,000 a year. In 1904 Theodore Roosevelt ordered that pensions be paid to all veterans past the age of sixty-two, his action being ratified by Congress in 1907. In 1908 Congress increased the benefits paid to widows, and in 1912 all pensions were again raised. In 1913 Civil War veterans and their widows received a total of $174,171,000, and as late as 1929 they were still costing the Federal government about $125,000,000 a year.

BIBLIOGRAPHY

C. A. and W. Beard, *The American Leviathan* (1930)
*D. W. Brogan, *Government of the People* (1933)
R. C. Brooks, *Corruption in American Politics and Life* (1910)
H. R. Bruce, *American Parties and Politics* (revised edition, 1932)
*J. Bryce, *The American Commonwealth* (1888)
H. Croly, *Marcus Alonzo Hanna* (1912)
D. R. Dewey, *Financial History of the United States* (revised edition, 1938)
W. Y. Elliot, *The Need for Constitutional Reform* (1935)
W. H. Glasson, *Federal Military Pensions in the United States* (1918)
H. F. Gosnell, *Boss Platt and his New York Machine* (1924)
P. Herring, *The Politics of Democracy* (1940)
C. O. Johnson, *Government in the United States* (1937)
H. J. Laski, *The American Presidency* (1940)
A. F. Macdonald, *American City Government and Administration* (1941)
J. M. Mathews, *The American Constitutional System* (1940)
A. McLaughlin, *Constitutional History of the United States* (1935)
C. E. Merriam, *The American Party System* (1922)
S. P. Orth, *The Boss and the Machine* (*Chronicles of America*, Vol. 43, 1919)

M. Ostrogorski, *Democracy and the Organization of Political Parties* (1902)

J. T. Salter (ed.), *The American Politician* (1938)

L. Steffens, *The Shame of the Cities* (1904)

———— *Autobiography* (1931)

N. W. Stephenson, *Nelson W. Aldrich* (1930)

F. W. Taussig, *Tariff History of the United States* (revised edition, 1931)

Woodrow Wilson, *Congressional Government* (1885)

H. Zink, *City Bosses in the United States* (1930)

———— *Government of Cities in the United States* (1939)

9

POLITICAL CONTROVERSIES

OF THE EIGHTIES

AND NINETIES

THE AGRARIAN CRUSADE

AFTER this general discussion of the functioning of the American government, it is desirable to consider certain political controversies of the late nineteenth century which were to have an important effect on American political development in the twentieth century. The most important of these was the agrarian crusade.

The most fundamental division in American politics has usually been that between the western agrarian debtor interests and the creditor interests of eastern business and finance—a division which originated before the American Revolution. After the Civil War this division was no longer represented by the party rivalry between Republicans and Democrats, both parties usually being dominated by creditor interests. The conflict between debtor and creditor interests continued, but it ran counter to the line of demarcation between Republicans and Democrats. The insurgent agrarians constituted a radical wing to both the major parties and also made several attempts to form a farmer-labor combination which would be the basis of a third party.

In the eighteen-seventies farmers' organizations known as Granges had spread throughout the Middle West and had been mainly responsible for a series of laws regulating the railroads, which laws were finally destroyed by a Supreme Court decision of 1886. There also was a short-lived Greenback movement for currency inflation, which ran General James B. Weaver as its presidential candidate in 1880. The early eighteen-eighties was a period of greater prosperity, but for a decade following 1887 the prairies were parched by droughts and swept by hot dry winds, and a series of bad harvests revived the movement of agrarian insurgency with greater vigor. Two farmers' organizations, the Southern Alliance and the Northwestern Alliance, grew rapidly; and in 1889 and for several following years representatives of the two alliances held political conventions and put forward political programs. They demanded government ownership of railroads, telephones, and telegraphs; control of currency by the government instead of by the banks; and currency inflation both by the coinage of silver and by an increase in paper money. For the relief of their credit difficulties they put forward a subtreasury plan under which the government was to establish warehouses where farm products could be held for a year, producers meanwhile receiving loans up to 80 per cent of the value of their products. They proposed also the popular election of senators, the initiative, and the referendum; and, in the hope of attracting labor support, they urged an eight-hour day for government employees and the abolition of such private detective agencies as the Pinkertons.

The Southern Alliance worked in some states inside the Democratic Party and in others with the Republicans. In 1890 it won control of Georgia and South Carolina, and elected a number of congressmen elsewhere. The Northwestern Alliance was strongest in Kansas, where the movement had all the fervor of a religious crusade. The Alliance there was led by Mary Lease, who told the farmers to "raise less corn and more hell"; "Sockless" Jerry Simpson; and the long-whiskered W. A. Peffer—figures who provoked the contempt of wealthy Easterners because of the crudity of their manners and who filled them with alarm because of the radicalism of their sentiments. In 1892, after both the major parties had nominated conservatives, the two alliances held a convention at Omaha, at which they named General Weaver as candidate of the People's *Populist* Party. Weaver won a popular vote of 1,041,600 and an electoral vote of 22. Two years later the Populist vote in the congressiona! elections increased to 1,471,600, and it seemed that it might become a permanent factor in American politics.

These expectations were frustrated in 1896, when the Democratic Party adopted the issue of free silver and captured the bulk of the Populist vote. Gold had been made the sole basis of the American currency in 1873. The Bland-Allison Act of 1878, which was superseded in 1890 by the Sherman Act, had provided for the purchase and coinage by the government of limited quantities of silver; but in 1893 Grover Cleveland had induced Congress to repeal the Sherman Act. The abandonment of silver was opposed by the owners of western silver mines, who wanted to raise silver prices, and also by western agrarians, who believed that an increase in the quantity of money in circulation would raise farm prices and lighten the burdens of debtors. A combination of the two groups persuaded the Democratic convention of 1896 to repudiate Cleveland and to adopt as the chief proposal of its platform the free and unlimited coinage of silver at a ratio to gold of sixteen to one.

William J. Bryan, a thirty-six-year-old lawyer and newspaper editor from Nebraska, who had served one term in Congress and had for two years been preaching the gospel of free silver throughout the South and West, swept the convention with his famous "cross of gold" speech and was nominated for the presidency on the fifth ballot. The Democratic platform contained few of the other demands of the Populists, but the free silver issue and the eloquence of Bryan were sufficient to win them to the Democratic standard. The leaders of the People's Party tried to retain their independence by repudiating the vice-presidential candidate of the Democrats and nominating instead Tom Watson of Georgia, but most Populists preferred to vote the full Democratic ticket.

The Republican convention of that year was dominated by Mark Hanna, who secured the nomination for his friend, William McKinley of Ohio. The campaign aroused a bitterness of class feeling such as had been equaled only in 1800 and in 1828. The issue of free silver became merely a symbol of the hostility between agrarianism and big business. Bryan, tall, handsome, eloquent, and magnetic, too simple to be ranked as a statesman but too honest to be condemned as a demagogue, traveled 18,000 miles and delivered 600 speeches, arousing everywhere a crusading fervor among his agrarian supporters. He was the spokesman of those egalitarian aspirations which had formerly been championed by Jefferson and by Jackson. The business classes, on the other hand, saw in Bryan a dangerous and anarchical revolutionary and rallied round McKinley as the representative of business prosperity and economic sanity. Hanna raised a huge campaign chest; and his supporters threatened that if Bryan were elected, farm mortgages would not be renewed, business orders would be canceled, and factories would be closed. McKinley was elected president by a popular vote of 7,107,000 and an electoral vote of 271, as against 6,533,000 and 176 for Bryan. The silver issue was afterward buried by the Gold Standard Act of 1900.

After 1896 agrarian insurgency assumed milder forms. The merger of the Populists with the Democrats and the defeat of Bryan ended agrarian hopes of winning control of the Federal government, and a period of rising farm prices and greater prosperity caused the discontent of the farmers to become less bitter and fanatical. Twentieth-century Progressivism, however, developed out of Populism; and, under the leadership first of Theodore Roosevelt and later of Woodrow Wilson, reforms were enacted which realized many of the Populist aspirations.

REGULATION OF BIG BUSINESS

The grievances of the farmers and of small businessmen against the big corporations could not be altogether ignored by Congress, in spite of the generally conservative sentiments of that body. The economic theory of *laissez faire* prohibited government regulation of business, but it declared also that competition must be maintained; and the growth of the trusts meant that many economic enterprises were ceasing to be competitive. Railroad practices and the methods used in building such corporations as Standard Oil were, moreover, causing great indignation not only among agrarian radicals but also among conservatives. In the eighteen-eighties, therefore, Congress began to take the first hesitating steps toward regulation of big business. It established a mild degree of government control over the railroads, appointing a special commission for that purpose; and it endeavored to preserve competition between industries which were not naturally monopolistic.

The Supreme Court invalidation of the Granger Laws in 1886 made it plain that only the Federal government could regulate the railroads, and in 1887 Congress passed the Interstate Commerce Act. The act declared that railroad rates must be published and must be reasonable, endeavored to preserve some degree of competition by forbidding the railroads to make pooling arrangements for the division of traffic, and prohibited rebates, drawbacks, rate discriminations between long and short hauls, and other devices for giving advantages to certain businesses or localities. An Interstate Commerce Commission of five members was appointed to supervise railroad practices and prosecute violations of the act, and shippers who had been charged unjust rates were to appeal to the Commission for redress.

The Interstate Commerce Commission was, however, a futile body until it was invigorated by President Theodore Roosevelt. The membership of the Commission was conservative, and it was denied adequate power by the courts. In the Maximum Freight Case of 1897 the Supreme Court declared that it could not fix maximum rates, and in the Alabama Midland Case of the same year the Court prevented it from exercising effective control over long and short haul discriminations. Out of sixteen cases which were brought before the Supreme Court under the Interstate Commerce Act before 1901, fifteen were won by the railroads.

The function of preserving competition was undertaken by the Federal government in 1890. A number of state governments had already enacted antitrust laws and established stricter supervision over the issuance of corporation charters; but since other states had failed to take action or, like New Jersey, were deliberately making themselves refuges for corporations, these state laws could not be very effective. The Sherman Anti-Trust Act, enacted in 1890, de-clared that "every contract, combination in the form of trust or otherwise, or conspiracy, in restraint of trade or commerce among the several states, or with foreign nations" was illegal. Persons who conspired to monopolize any branch of commerce were to be fined or imprisoned. The Federal district attorneys were to see that the act was enforced, and persons who had been injured by combina-tions in restraint of trade were to sue for damages. Congress did not intend that the act should apply to labor unions but decided that it was unnecessary to make this exemption a part of the law.

During the administrations of Harrison, Cleveland, and McKin-ley the government made no serious attempt to enforce the Sherman Act against the trusts; it did, however, pervert the act into a weapon against trade unionism, most notably in the injunction which it ob-tained against the American Railway Union during the Pullman strike of 1894. In eleven years Federal law officers brought eighteen suits under the Sherman Act, and succeeded in winning ten of them. These ten victories were scored not against any of the big trusts but against the Addyston Pipe Company, two railroad asso-ciations, three local associations of coal dealers, and four trade unions. Twenty-two suits were brought by private persons, of which only three were successful.

During this period the two most important Supreme Court de-cisions under the Sherman Act were in the E. C. Knight Company Case of 1895 and the Trans-Missouri Freight Association Case of 1897. The Knight Case was an attack on the sugar trust. The gov-ernment showed that the sugar trust controlled 95 per cent of the sugar refining business; it failed, however, to prove that a monopoly of manufacturing was also a monopoly of interstate commerce, and on this ground the trust was acquitted by the Supreme Court. In the Freight Association Case, on the other hand, the Court agreed that any combination in restraint of interstate trade was illegal, even though it could be argued that such a combination was "reason-able." This case suggested that the Court would be willing to en-force the act if the government would act vigorously and present its evidence adequately.

Before the accession of Theodore Roosevelt to the presidency, therefore, Federal action to curb business abuses remained wholly futile. Certain processes had been initiated, however, which twentieth-century administrations would make more effective. A division had been made between those economic enterprises that were naturally monopolistic and should, therefore, be under direct government regulation, and those that were naturally competitive and in which the government should act to enforce competition. The principle had been established that, where regulation was necessary, it should be performed by a commission with partly administrative and partly judicial functions. A number of legal difficulties to effective regulation had also become apparent. It was almost impossible to define clearly what was included in "interstate" commerce, what was meant by the rule that railroad rates must be "reasonable," or what was meant by the prohibition of combinations in "restraint of trade." In practice the concrete meaning of these phrases depended on the attitude of the courts, which thus acquired increased powers.

CIVIL SERVICE REFORM

One other reform movement of the late nineteenth century must be given brief mention—namely, the attempt to abolish the traditional system of making appointments to the civil service on the basis of political partisanship. The civil service reformers were, for the most part, men who were conservative on all other questions. They wished to weaken the powers of political bosses and political machines and to establish a merit system similar to that of Great Britain and France. This was particularly necessary at a time when the growing complexity of the economic system was compelling the government to assume new functions which could be performed only by men with specialized skill and training.

The assassination of President Garfield by a disappointed office-seeker publicized the need for reform, and in 1883 the Pendleton Act was passed by Congress. Certain civil service positions might be placed on the classified list either by executive order of the President or by act of Congress, and these positions were then to be filled by competitive examinations, which were to be supervised by a Civil Service Commission. It was also provided that positions at Washington should be fairly distributed among the different states, and that no officeholder should be assessed for political campaign funds. Sixteen thousand positions, out of a total of 116,000, were placed immediately on the classified list by President Arthur; and the number was steadily increased by all later presidents. By 1932, 461,231 Federal employees, 79 per cent of the total number, were under civil service rules. In 1938 the number under civil service rules had risen to 582,604; but there had meanwhile been a rapid increase in the total number of Federal employees, so that the proportion had decreased to 67 per cent. Of the state governments, New York and Massachusetts adopted civil service reforms in 1883 and 1884, and a number of others followed their example in the twentieth century.

Politics, however, was by no means eliminated from the civil service. A number of important government departments remained wholly unaffected by the reforms; and even the positions included on the classified list were not put wholly on a merit basis. In making appointments on the basis of competitive examinations, the government was permitted to choose among the top three candidates. After an appointment had been made, promotion might depend on political considerations, and officials could sometimes be dismissed arbitrarily and without appeal. Wage schedules, moreover, tended to be inflexible and generally low; and the examination system was designed to test specialized technical training rather than, as in Great Britain, general ability and education. For these reasons the American civil service had difficulty in attracting and keeping men of great ability and probably remained inferior to the civil services of some of the European nations.

POLITICAL CHANGES IN THE SOUTH

Populism had especially important consequences in the South, where it began as a revolt against an oligarchy of landlords and industrialists and ended by espousing the cause of white supremacy.

The Bourbons who dominated the South in the eighteen-eighties controlled the Democratic Party through a number of devices, such as taxation and literacy qualifications for voting, and heavy representation for the black belt, which enabled them to out-vote the small farmers who constituted a majority of the white population. The Republican Party, consisting partly of white farmers in the mountains and partly of Negroes who held Federal offices, was unimportant everywhere except in North Carolina. The Negroes were not legally disfranchised, but few of them dared to exercise their right to vote unless they were encouraged to do so by white politicians. Genuine political conflicts were, however, possible through the institution of primary elections for the choice of Democratic Party candidates.

The rapid growth of the Southern Alliance in the late eighteen-eighties was due not only to grievances which the farmers of the South shared with those of the West—falling agricultural prices and the growth of mortgages and of tenancy—but also to their indignation against Bourbon control. In addition to easier credit and regulation of the railroads and other corporations, they wanted a more democratic form of government and a greater expenditure of money on public education. These aspirations were, however, complicated by their hostility to the Negroes. The low living standards of the colored population resulted in economic antagonisms between white and Negro farmers, since the landlords were likely to prefer Negro tenants to white ones because the former were more easily exploited. The white farmers believed, moreover, often with good reason, that if the Negroes were allowed to exercise political rights, their votes would be controlled by the landlords. Some of the Populists advocated an alliance of white and colored farmers against their common enemies, but the majority, led by such men as Ben Tillman of South Carolina and Jeff Davis of Arkansas, were fanatically opposed to racial equality. The attitude of these men is illustrated by the complaint of Tillman in 1901, when President Roosevelt entertained Booker T. Washington at the White House. "The action of President Roosevelt in entertaining that nigger," declared Tillman, "will necessitate our killing a thousand niggers in the South before they will learn their place again." This obsession with the color question, the ancestral curse of the South, tended to transform the Southern agrarian leaders into demagogues and to frustrate their democratic aspirations.

In 1890 the Southern Alliance captured the Democratic Party in South Carolina, Georgia, and Tennessee, and made an alliance with the Republicans in North Carolina. For several years there were bitter political conflicts throughout the South. Both sides employed bribery and intimidation to capture Negro votes; but the Bourbon landlords, who could often bring their Negro tenants and share-croppers to the polls in gangs, were more successful in this competition than were their agrarian opponents. This increase in the political importance of the colored population alarmed both sides, and they finally agreed to unite with each other in adopting legal methods for permanently disfranchising the Negroes.

Devices by which this might be accomplished were adopted first in Mississippi. In 1890 that state enacted a law that nobody could vote unless he had paid a poll tax eight months before the election and had resided in the same district for at least a year. In 1892 a literacy test was added, requiring every voter to be able to read and interpret part of the Federal constitution. Similar laws were subsequently adopted in all southern states. These regulations were likely to disfranchise white as well as colored citizens; so Louisiana in 1898 added a grandfather clause, giving the vote to anybody whose father or grandfather had been a voter before 1867.

The grandfather clause was subsequently invalidated by the United States Supreme Court, but the purpose of these regulations—defined by Carter Glass at the Virginia Constitutional Convention of 1901 as "discrimination within the letter of the law"—was achieved through their administration by white Boards of Registry. It was easy for these boards to declare all Negroes—even when, as occasionally happened, they were professors in Negro colleges—to be illiterate and all whites to be literate. The bulk of the colored population was thus effectively disfranchised. In Louisiana, for example, there were 130,344 Negro voters in 1896 and only 5,320 in 1900. In the twentieth century there was a slow increase in Negro voting in the southern cities, where the Negro population often had able leaders and the white population was relatively liberal; but throughout the rural areas the Negroes remained disfranchised and, in general, accepted their exclusion apathetically. In 1930 the highest proportion of Negro voters was in Virginia, where 18,000 Negroes, 5.2 per cent of the Negro adult population, were permitted to vote. By this date the rate of real illiteracy among southern Negroes was less than 20 per cent.

After 1900 many of the Populist leaders retained office and authority in the South; but the anti-Negro movement had diverted them from their primary intentions and killed their originally liberal aspirations. Agrarian leaders in the South tended to degenerate into rabble-rousing demagogues, who accomplished little for their followers when they achieved power, while the Bourbon landlords and industrialists retained their control over the economic system. The power of conservatism was increased by the poll tax laws, which had the effect of disfranchising many of the poorer white farmers as well as the Negroes. There were occasional conflicts between conservatives and radicals; but these were usually antagonisms between rival personalities rather than between opposed political philosophies.

The tragedy of the South was, perhaps, best exemplified in the career of Tom Watson, Populist candidate for the vice presidency in 1896 and for the presidency in 1904 and 1908. Watson began as a champion of agrarian democracy; but he subsequently convinced himself that the overthrow of the Bourbons required the permanent disfranchisement of the Negroes. He gradually degenerated into a virulent advocate of racial and religious hatreds—anti-Negro, anti-Catholic, and anti-Semitic—and the spiritual father of the Ku Klux Klan. Yet Watson never wholly abandoned his Jeffersonian convictions; he remained an enemy of Bourbonism, a defender of civil liberties, and a friend of the Socialist leader Eugene Debs. During the World War he fought the draft act and the suppression of free speech. Such an apparently paradoxical combination of opinions is illustrative of the extraordinary complexity of the political problems of the South.

Nevertheless the early twentieth century was a period of steady progress in the South. Despite the poverty of the entire section, southern states enormously increased their appropriations for education, public health, road-building, and other improvements. Salaries in southern schools were low and terms were short; by 1930 per capita expenditure on education in most of the southern states was only one-third as large as in New York and New Jersey; and the rate of illiteracy in the South was still about 8 per cent as contrasted with 4.3 per cent for the United States as a whole. Yet most southern states devoted a larger proportion of their state budgets to education than did most northern states. Southern colleges were similarly handicapped by poverty. In 1903, out of a total of $157,000,000 of endowments owned by all United States colleges, only $15,000,000 was held in the South. But thirty years later such institutions as Duke, Vanderbilt, North Carolina, and Louisiana were among the most important centers of cultural activity in the United States. Great progress has also been made in stamping out such diseases as hookworm, malaria, and pellagra, which had devitalized a considerable section of the southern rural population. Northerners do not always appreciate the handicaps from which the South has suffered since the Civil War, or the herculean efforts which it has been making to overcome them.

BIBLIOGRAPHY

A. M. Arnett, *The Populist Movement in Georgia* (1922)
W. J. Bryan, *Memoirs* (1925)
P. H. Buck, *The Road to Reunion, 1865–1900* (1937)
S. J. Buck, *The Granger Movement* (1913)
────*The Agrarian Crusade* (*Chronicles of America,* Vol. 45, 1921)
J. B. Clark, *Populism in Alabama* (1927)
C. R. Fish, *The Civil Service and the Patronage* (1905)
F. E. Haynes, *Third Party Movements since the Civil War* (1916)
A. B. Hepburn, *History of Coinage and Currency in the United States* (1924)
*J. D. Hicks, *The Populist Revolt* (1931)
P. Hibben, *The Peerless Leader: William Jennings Bryan* (1929)
*P. Lewinson, *Race, Class and Party* (1932)
J. C. Long, *W. J. Bryan* (1928)
L. Mayers, *The Federal Service* (1922)
W. Z. Ripley, *Railroads: Rates and Regulations* (1912)
W. D. Sheldon, *Populism in the Old Dominion* (1935)

F. B. Simkins, *The Tillman Movement in South Carolina* (1926)
D. H. Smith, *The United States Civil Service Commission* (1928)
F. M. Stewart, *The National Civil Service Reform League* (1929)
A. H. Walker, *History of the Sherman Law* (1910)
M. R. Werner, *Bryan* (1929)
W. C. Williams, *William Jennings Bryan* (1936)
*C. V. Woodward, *Tom Watson* (1938)

IO

THE FEDERAL JUDICIARY

JUDICIAL REVIEW

THE chief weaknesses of the American legislative and executive system at the end of the nineteenth century were that its checks and balances encouraged irresponsibility and impeded efficient action, and that it was unduly deferential to the interests of big business. Similar criticisms might be made of the functioning of the judicial branch of the Federal government.

The system of judicial review, which gave to the judiciary the right to declare acts of Congress unconstitutional, and which therefore limited the sovereignty of the legislature, was perhaps the chief peculiarity of the American form of government. Judicial review had become a necessary feature of the American government for two reasons. In the first place, government functions were divided between the Federal government and the state governments; and, in order to preserve the balance of power between these two authorities and to prevent either of them from encroaching upon the rights of the other, an impartial judicial body must be given a right of veto. In the second place, one of the primary purposes of the makers of the constitution had been to protect minorities and individuals from arbitrary governmental interference; they wished to guard against the tyranny of a majority as much as against the tyranny of an individual despot. The judiciary acquired the function, therefore, of prohibiting legislation which might violate the rights of individuals.

In the last two decades of the nineteenth century both these judicial functions were exercised in such a way as to give excessive protection to business activities and to impose excessive limitations upon legislative powers, both Federal and state. The courts restricted both Federal and state powers in a manner which created a kind of borderland where neither of the two forms of government had jurisdiction. As Theodore Roosevelt declared in 1910: "There has grown up a neutral land—a borderland in the spheres of action of the national and state governments—a borderland over which each government tends to claim that it has the power, and as to which the action of the courts unfortunately has usually been such as to deny to both the power." This borderland, it was sometimes said, was inhabited chiefly by large corporations. In interpreting individual rights, moreover, the courts tended to pay excessive regard to the rights of property and to interpret government regulation of economic activities as a violation of those rights. In this respect the state courts often went further than the Federal courts, although the decisions of the Federal courts attracted more attention and had more far-reaching consequences.

THE FOURTEENTH AMENDMENT

According to eighteenth-century liberal theory, the three natural rights of individuals were the rights of life, liberty, and property; and governments should not be permitted to deprive men of those rights in an arbitrary manner. By the Fifth Amendment to the constitution the Federal government was forbidden to deprive men of life, liberty, or property except by due process of law. In 1868 the Fourteenth Amendment, enacted primarily to protect the Negro population in the South, extended a similar prohibition to the state governments. "No state," it was stated, "shall make or enforce any law which shall abridge the privileges or immunities of citizens of the United States; nor shall any state deprive any person of life, liberty or property without due process of law; nor deny any person within its jurisdiction the equal protection of the laws." These two amendments, therefore, guaranteed American citizens from arbitrary violations of their rights by any governmental authority. The original meaning of "due process," according to the definition of Daniel Webster, was that the law "hears before it condemns, . . . proceeds upon inquiry, and renders judgment only after trial."

In the course of the nineteenth century a series of court interpretations made the Fifth and Fourteenth Amendments not only a legitimate protection of individual rights but also a barrier against government regulation of business. In the first place, since the time of Chief Justice John Marshall a corporation had been defined as a legal person, so that its property was protected in the same manner as the property of individuals. In the second place, in the eighteen-eighties and nineties the "due process" clause was extended to prohibit not only confiscation but also any regulation which might prevent a corporation from making a "reasonable" profit on its investments; and the function of deciding how much profit was "reasonable" was assumed by the courts.

The general tendency of the judiciary was to identify the principles of the United States constitution with the rules of laissez-faire economics. The faith of the judges in *laissez faire* was derived from the prevalent tendencies of nineteenth-century thought, which believed that freedom of business enterprise was the only method by which progress might be ensured. These principles derived particularly from the writings of Herbert Spencer. The belief in *laissez faire* was combined with the eighteenth-century doctrine of natural rights. The proper functions of the state, the judges believed, were negative rather than positive, and its principal duty was to protect the liberty of individuals. Liberty, as Justice Peckham declared in the case of *Allgeyer v. Louisiana* in 1897, included "the right [of the individual] . . . to pursue any livelihood or avocation, and for that purpose to enter into all contracts which may be proper, necessary and essential to his carrying out to a successful conclusion the purpose above mentioned."

In the opinion of the judges, there was always danger that this individual liberty might be violated by legislative bodies which were under the control of radical demagogues representing the envy of the poorer classes—a tendency which, if unchecked, would end in socialism or anarchism. It was therefore the duty of the judiciary to restrict the powers of legislatures in order to preserve the rights of individuals.

Many people believed, however, that such an attitude was a perversion of the original meaning of the constitution and that the judges were motivated not so much by abstract principles of justice as by a desire to protect the economic interests of the class to which they belonged. Certainly, these judicial interpretations of the constitution were at least open to dispute, as was proved by the tendency of the judges to disagree among themselves and to reverse their own decisions. While state powers were restricted under the due process clause, they might be enlarged under the conception of "police power." And when the Supreme Court considered any particular state law regulating economic activities, it was often difficult to predict whether it would invalidate it as a violation of "due process" or uphold it as a legitimate exercise of the "police power."

For twenty years after its enactment, the Fourteenth Amendment seemed to be of small importance. The Federal courts declined to use it for its original purpose—the protection of the Negro population in the South. In a series of decisions in the seventies and eighties they declared that Negroes must seek remedy for oppression in the state courts, and they threw out Federal laws giving them protection, as violations of state's rights. They did not, however, apply the Fourteenth Amendment to the protection of business. In 1872, in the Slaughterhouse Cases, the Supreme Court refused to void a Louisiana state law which, by giving a monopoly of the slaughtering business in New Orleans to a single corporation, had driven a thousand persons out of business. The Fourteenth Amendment, declared the Court, did not abridge the police power, by virtue of which state governments could regulate business, and the due process clause "has never been supposed to have any bearing upon or inhibit laws that indirectly work harm or loss to individuals." In an important dissenting opinion, however, Stephen J. Field foreshadowed the later attitude of the Court, declaring that the Fourteenth Amendment guaranteed the natural rights of the individual.

Similarly in the Granger Cases of 1876 the Supreme Court allowed state governments to regulate the rates charged by railroads and grain elevators, declaring that it was the right of the legislature and not of the judiciary to determine what rate of profit was reasonable. The Court agreed that "property does become clothed with public interest when used in a manner to make it of public consequence. When, therefore, one devotes his property to a use in which the public has an interest, he, in effect, grants to the public an interest in that use, and must submit to be controlled by the public for the common good." "In countries where the common law prevails, it has been customary from time immemorial for the legislature to declare what shall be a reasonable compensation. . . . We know that this is a power which may be abused, but this is no argument against its existence. For protection against abuses by legislatures, the people must resort to the polls, not to the courts."

In the eighties, however, these decisions were reversed, and the Court accepted the doctrine of Justice Field, as we shall see later. The growth of Populism in the western farming states and of labor militancy in the East were causing general alarm among the wealthier classes, and the appointment of several former railroad lawyers to the Supreme Court gave it a more conservative character.

The new interpretation of the Fourteenth Amendment was foreshadowed in 1882, in the case of *San Mateo County v. Southern Pacific Railroad,* in which Roscoe Conkling appeared as lawyer for the railroad. Conkling had been a member of the congressional committee which had drafted the Fourteenth Amendment, and he argued that protection of business corporations had been one of its purposes. "At the time the Fourteenth Amendment was ratified," he explained, "individuals and joint stock companies were appealing for congressional and administrative protection against invidious and discriminatory state and local taxes." "Those who devised the Fourteenth Amendment wrought in grave sincerity. . . . They planted in the Constitution a monumental truth to stand four square to whatever wind might blow. That truth is but the golden rule, so extended as to curb the many who would do to the few as they would not have the few do to them." In this case the Court ruled against the railroad.

Four years later, on the other hand, in the case of *Santa Clara County v. Southern Pacific Railroad,* the Court adopted Field's and Conkling's interpretation of the Fourteenth Amendment, agreeing that it gave protection to corporations as well as to individuals. And in 1890, in the case of *Chicago, Milwaukee and St. Paul Railroad v. Minnesota,* the Court extended the due process clause to prohibit "unreasonable" regulation and declared, contrary to its opinion in the Granger Cases, that the decision as to reasonableness of rates was "eminently a question for judicial investigation, requiring due process of law for its determination." In 1898 these judicial doctrines were reaffirmed in the case of *Smyth v. Ames.* A corporation, it was stated, was a legal person; a corporation must be allowed a "reasonable" return on its investments; and rate-fixing regulations were subject to judicial review. The Court declared, moreover, that the reasonableness of such regulations depended on "the fair value of the property," and that in estimating this value various factors must be considered, among which was "reproduction cost new."

This new interpretation of the Fourteenth Amendment proved to be of enormous importance. Between 1872 and 1888 there had been only 70 cases involving the amendment; between 1890 and 1910, on the other hand, there were 528, of which 289 referred to corporations and only 19 to Negroes. How the Court would interpret the amendment in any given case was, however, often unpredictable. In cases involving the "reasonableness" of rate-fixing regulations the Court was unable to say conclusively what rate of profit was reasonable or how the value of the investment upon which the profit must be earned should be determined. As the Court had declared in the Granger Cases, these were, in reality, matters for legislative and not judicial decision.

In matters of labor legislation, similarly, the views of the Court were apt to vary. Minimum hour laws were sometimes upheld under the police power and sometimes voided on the ground that they interfered with the right of workers to contract for as many hours of labor as they and their employers might choose. In 1898, in the case of *Holden v. Hardy,* the Court allowed the State of Utah to enact an eight-hour day for miners. In 1905, on the other hand, in the case of *Lochner v. New York,* a ten-hour day for bakery workers was ruled out as unreasonably "interfering with the liberty of person or the right of free contract." "The limit of the police power has been reached and passed in this case," declared the Court; bakery workers were "able to assert their rights and care for themselves without the protecting arm of the State interfering with their independence of judgment and action." In a dissenting opinion Justice Holmes retorted that "this case is decided upon an economic theory which a large part of the country does not entertain. . . . State constitutions and State laws may regulate life in many ways which we, as legislators, might think as injudicious or if you like as tyrannical as this. . . . The liberty of the citizen to do as he likes so long as he does not interfere with the liberty of others to do the same . . . is interfered with by school laws, by the Post-office, by every state or municipal institution which takes his money for purposes thought desirable, whether he likes it or not. The Fourteenth Amendment does not enact Mr. Herbert Spencer's Social Statics." *Lochner v. New York* was subsequently reversed by *Muller v. Oregon* in 1910, in which the Court allowed a ten-hour day for women factory workers, and by *Bunting v. Oregon* in 1917, in which the Court allowed a ten-hour day for men.

THE COMMERCE CLAUSE

A similar trend was exhibited by the Court in its interpretations of the commerce clause in the constitution, particularly with reference to the Interstate Commerce Act and the Sherman Anti-Trust Act. In 1886, in the case of *Wabash, St. Louis and Pacific Railroad v. Illinois,* the Court abandoned its tolerant attitude in the Granger Cases ten years earlier and declared that the states had no power to regulate railroads engaged in interstate commerce. The result was that nine-tenths of the state railroad laws were rendered inoperative. When, moreover, the Federal government undertook the function of railroad regulation, the powers of the Interstate Commerce Commission were narrowly restricted by the Court; in the Maximum Freight Rate Case of 1897 the Commission was denied the power to fix rates on the ground that this was properly the function of the

legislature, not of an administrative body. Court definitions of interstate commerce served, similarly, to limit the application of the
Sherman Act when, in the E. C. Knight Company Case of 1895, a
monopoly of manufacturing was declared to be not a monopoly of
interstate commerce and the sugar trust was, on this ground,
acquitted. Another example of the suspicion with which the Court
regarded attempts by Congress to extend the sphere of interstate
commerce was afforded in 1917 when, in the case of *Hammer v.
Dagenhart,* the Court threw out the Keatings-Owen Act which had
attempted to abolish child labor by prohibiting products made by
child labor from entering interstate commerce.

Although, however, the Court interpreted interstate commerce
strictly when it considered laws regulating business, it adopted a
much broader definition with reference to the activities of labor
unions. The Court viewed the unions with disfavor, regarding the
closed shop as a violation of the freedom of contract of the individual worker. It was inclined to regard such union tactics as picketing and the boycotting of firms employing nonunion labor as actions
tending to the restraint of trade, and hence as coming within the
scope of the Sherman Act.

The chief weapon employed by the courts against the unions was
the injunction. The first use of the injunction in labor disputes
appears to have been in the railroad strike of 1877. Since certain
railroads were in receivership and the Federal courts were temporarily responsible for their management, Walter Q. Gresham,
a Federal judge at Indianapolis i,ssued an injunction forbidding their
employees from striking. When the strike leaders disobeyed the
injunction, they were arrested for contempt of court, which meant
that they would be denied the right to a jury trial. Judge Thomas
Drummond, who tried the strikers, upheld the injunction and
declared that a strike was a violation of the freedom of contract of
individual workers. This doctrine made injunctions possible in
virtually all labor disputes.

After the passage of the Sherman Act, however, most injunctions
were issued on the ground that union activities were restraining
trade. This interpretation of the Sherman Act was accepted by the

Supreme Court in 1894 when it upheld the injunction obtained by the Federal government against the American Railway Union in the Pullman strike. The Sherman Act was subsequently used to prohibit union boycotts, as in the Bucks' Stove and Range Company Case of 1907 and the Danbury Hatters' Case (*Loewe v. Lawlor*) of 1908. With reference to the former of these cases, the Supreme Court declared in 1911 that "any act, however peaceful, which was part of a conspiracy to restrain interstate trade unlawfully, itself partook of the illegal nature of the conspiracy." In the latter case an employer who was being boycotted for not employing union labor sued the union for damages and was awarded $252,200.

Another example of the conservative tendencies of the Supreme Court was afforded in 1895, when the income tax law of 1894 was declared unconstitutional. The ground given for the decision was that, according to the constitution, direct taxes must be apportioned among the states according to their population. During the hearings, however, Joseph Choate argued that such a tax was confiscatory and communistic, and at least one of the justices reflected this viewpoint in his decision.

THE RESULTS OF JUDICIAL CONSERVATISM

The result of these decisions was to create a legal structure very favorable to the large corporations. In the doing of this, the Court had restricted the powers of the legislatures much more narrowly than in the past. Between 1789 and 1870 a number of state laws had been declared unconstitutional; but there had been only two Supreme Court invalidations of acts of the Federal Congress, one being in the otherwise unimportant case of *Marbury v. Madison,* and the other being in the Dred Scott Case which had helped to provoke the Civil War. Between 1870 and 1920, on the other hand, the Court invalidated thirty-nine acts of Congress, in addition to a large number of state laws. And although the Court showed liberal tendencies for about a decade after the Lochner Case, under the influence of the Progressive movement, there was no decisive abandonment of conservatism until 1937. A few justices were inclined to allow more freedom to the legislatures and to regard human rights as more important than property rights, the most notable of these being Holmes (appointed in 1902), Brandeis (appointed in 1916), Stone (appointed in 1925), and Cardozo (who succeeded Holmes in 1930). But prior to 1937 the liberalism which these men represented was in a minority.

The conservative attitude of the judiciary had obvious dangers. A growing proportion of the American people believed that a society dominated by big corporations could not be governed in accordance with the rules which had originally been formulated for a society of individual property owners, and they believed that the government must have more power to regulate economic activity than had been necessary in the past. Regardless of whether the laws voided by the Supreme Court were good or bad, its attempts to restrict legislative power might eventually cause the popular demand for business regulation to take a revolutionary rather than a reformist direction and to end in an attack on the American form of government. And although defenders of the judiciary maintained that the Supreme Court was merely interpreting the plain words of the constitution, it appeared that the constitution meant different things at different times, its meaning in the eighteen-seventies being, for example, different from its meaning in the eighteen-nineties.

BIBLIOGRAPHY

E. S. Bates, *The Story of the Supreme Court* (1936)

C. A. Beard, *The Supreme Court and the Constitution* (1931)

L. B. Boudin, *Government by Judiciary* (1932)

B. N. Cardozo, *The Nature of Judicial Process* (1925)

E. S. Corwin, *The Twilight of the Supreme Court* (1934)

———— *The Commerce Power versus States Rights* (1936)

F. Frankfurter (ed.), *Mr. Justice Holmes and the Constitution* (1927)

———— *Mr. Justice Brandeis* (1932)

F. Frankfurter and J. M. Landis, *Business of the Supreme Court* (1928)

R. H. Gabriel, *The Course of American Democratic Thought* (1940)

R. G. Gettell, *History of American Political Thought* (1928)

C. G. Haines, *The American Doctrine of Judicial Supremacy* (1932)

C. E. Hughes, *The Supreme Court of the United States* (1928)

E. R. Lewis, *American Political Thought from the Civil War to the World War* (1937)

A. Lief (ed.), *Dissenting Opinions of Mr. Justice Holmes* (1929)

———— *Social and Economic Views of Mr. Justice Brandeis* (1930)

———— *Public Control of Business: Opinions of Justice Stone* (1940)

C. E. Merriam, *American Political Ideas, 1867–1917* (1920)

J. P. Pollard, *Mr. Justice Cardozo* (1935)

D. Richardson, *Constitutional Doctrines of Justice Holmes* (1924)

*C. Warren, *The Supreme Court in United States History* (revised edition, 1926)

———— *Congress, the Constitution and the Supreme Court* (1930)

II

THE UNITED STATES

BECOMES A WORLD POWER

THE GROWTH OF POWER POLITICS

THE last two decades of the nineteenth century were marked by one further important political development. The United States began to play a more important part in world politics as a great power and to show a tendency towards imperialist expansion.

Throughout the earlier decades of the century American foreign policy had been generally isolationist. With the exception of such interludes as the War of 1812, the war with Mexico, and an occasional outbreak of nationalistic excitement, it had also usually been pacifistic. With vast undeveloped territories at home, the United States had no economic motives for expansion abroad and little reason for taking any active part in the affairs of Europe. American diplomacy was conducted mostly by amateurs and never acquired the professional traditions of European foreign offices. Until 1882 the United States navy was inferior not only to the navies of all the European great powers but even to that of Chile. As late as 1898, at the outbreak of the war with Spain, the United States army contained only 28,000 men.

The one permanent feature of American foreign policy was the Monroe Doctrine. The United States would always oppose any attempt by a European power to acquire new possessions in the western hemisphere. Prior to 1895, however, the Monroe Doctrine was not interpreted as meaning more than opposition to European conquest or colonization; it did not imply any claim that the United States should exercise suzerainty over the foreign relations of Latin American republics. The United States, prior to that time, had not intervened in diplomatic disputes between Latin American republics and European powers, even when such disputes involved the use of force. On several occasions when European powers had despatched warships to Central or South America to enforce payment of debts or respect for the rights of their citizens, the United States had not thought it necessary to interfere. On one occasion, after the French had taken advantage of the American Civil War to occupy Mexico, the United States had taken action to preserve the independence of a Latin American republic. But the fact that the Latin American countries had not at other times been threatened by European conquest was owing, in reality, not so much to the Monroe Doctrine as to the sea power of Great Britain. From the time that those countries had won their independence from Spain, Great Britain had established close economic connections with them and had consistently been interested in preventing her European rivals from acquiring control of them. It was, in fact, British control of the Atlantic which had been their principal guarantee against reconquest in the eighteen-twenties. The dependence of the Monroe Doctrine on British sea power was not, however, generally appreciated in the United States.

During the last two decades of the nineteenth century there was a growing sentiment in the United States in favor of a more aggressive foreign policy. American foreign trade was rapidly increasing; and, although American industrialists were, in general, opposed to policies of war and imperialism, American politicians believed that it was their duty to capture new foreign markets for American exports. The leading European powers, Great Britain, France, and Germany, were rapidly building or increasing their empires and beginning to engage in competition for military and naval supremacy. Americans were both infected by their example and alarmed lest their own security be threatened by this growth of aggressive power politics. The writings of such English imperialists as Rudyard Kipling had great influence in the United States; and such men as

John Hay, Senator Henry Cabot Lodge, Theodore Roosevelt, and Whitelaw Reid of the New York *Herald Tribune* were eager that their own country assert herself as a competitor of the European imperialisms. Similar ideas of nationalistic greatness were propagated by the popular newspapers developed by Joseph Pulitzer and William Randolph Hearst. The first result of these new attitudes was the building, after 1882, of a new American navy, for which the doctrines of A. T. Mahan, lecturer in naval history at the Naval War College at Newport, Rhode Island, was largely responsible. By 1900, with sixteen battleships completed or under construction, the navy of the United States was surpassed only by those of Great Britain and France.

In the eighties and nineties the United States government began to evince greater interest in Latin America, largely in the hope of increasing trade. Attempts were made to promote pan-American unity under the leadership of the United States. The chief prophet of pan-Americanism was James G. Blaine, Secretary of State under President Harrison, who organized the first Pan-American Congress in 1889. Such advances, however, received little response south of the Rio Grande. The Latin American republics were generally suspicious of the United States, fearing her superior strength, remembering such episodes as the war with Mexico, and believing that their own Catholic and Hispanic traditions might be endangered by Yankee economic penetration. Most of them preferred to cultivate closer relations with Europe rather than with the United States; and the only kind of unity which they favored was Latin American unity against Yankee encroachments. The first Pan-American Congress had few results; and, although similar meetings were held at five-year intervals in the twentieth century, most of them were equally disappointing to the advocates of New World union.

The fears of the Latin American countries were increased in 1895, when the United States made a most challenging assertion of her leadership in the western hemisphere. After Great Britain had refused to allow a boundary dispute between Venezuela and British Guiana to be settled by arbitration, Richard Olney, Secretary of State under President Cleveland, informed the British Prime

Minister, Lord Salisbury: "Today the United States is practically sovereign on this continent, and its fiat is law upon the subjects to which it confines its intervention. Why? . . . It is not because of the pure friendship or good will felt for it. . . . It is because, in addition to all other grounds, its infinite resources combined with its isolated position render it master of the situation and practically invulnerable as against any or all other powers." The dispute was finally settled peacefully, with Great Britain submitting to arbitration. This incident was followed by a marked growth of Anglo-American friendship, owing largely to the growing power of Germany, which alarmed the governments of both nations.

Salisbury had, however, pointed out in reply to Olney that if the United States were to claim the right to settle all disputes between Europe and the Latin American countries, then it must assume the function of supervising the behavior of those countries. "Such a claim," he said, "would have imposed upon the United States the duty of answering for the conduct of those states, and consequently the responsibility of controlling it. It follows of necessity that if the Government of the United States will not control the conduct of these communities, neither can it undertake to protect them from the consequences attaching to any misconduct of which they may be guilty towards other nations." This corollary, which meant that the weaker and more disorderly of the Latin American republics would virtually become dependencies of the United States and which threatened to transform the Monroe Doctrine into an instrument of United States imperialism, was subsequently accepted and put into practice by President Theodore Roosevelt.

THE WAR WITH SPAIN

The growing imperialist psychology of the American people found overt expression in 1898, in the war with Spain. In 1895 a rebellion against Spanish rule broke out in Cuba. At that time 50 million dollars of American capital was invested in Cuba, but American business interests had no sympathy with the movement for Cuban independence and little desire that the United States become involved in the conflict. There developed, however, a considerable popular sentiment in favor of United States intervention on behalf of the rebels. This sentiment was stimulated by stories of atrocities committed by the Spanish authorities—stories which were circulated by agents of the Cuban nationalists and by the newspapers of Pulitzer and Hearst, who were then engaged in a fierce circulation rivalry. The battleship *Maine* was sent to Havana to protect United States citizens, and on February 15, 1898, the *Maine* was blown up, apparently by a mine.

The Spanish authorities were accused, wholly without evidence, of having caused the explosion; and President McKinley demanded that Spain agree to an armistice and accept United States mediation. The Spanish government was willing to comply, but it could not do so immediately because of Spanish public opinion. Meanwhile popular sentiment in the United States was demanding war; and McKinley, who wanted peace but who also had to consider the next election, was not strong enough to resist it. On April 11 McKinley sent a message to Congress, in which he minimized the fact that Spain was preparing to accept the American demands and hinted that war had become necessary. On April 19 Congress declared war and pledged itself that Cuba should be liberated. The main cause of the war was the crusading ardor of the American people, in which motives of idealism and of self-aggrandizement were curiously mingled. It was a popular war and not a capitalist war, since most of the leaders of American business were opposed to it.

The war was being fought to free Cuba, but its first episode was an attack on another Spanish possession, of which most Americans had never heard. Theodore Roosevelt, Assistant Secretary of the Navy, had been left in charge of the Navy Department for a single afternoon in February, and he had seized the opportunity to send orders to the Asiatic fleet that if war came it should proceed at once to the Philippines. On May 1 Admiral Dewey won the battle of Manila Bay. In June American troops arrived, subsequently capturing the city of Manila, while elsewhere Filipino nationalists under Emilio Aguinaldo expelled Spanish officials and declared the Philippines an independent republic.

Meanwhile there had been a naval and military invasion of Cuba.

On July 1 the American army won the battle of San Juan Hill; on July 3 a Spanish fleet was destroyed outside Santiago; and on July 15 the Spanish army in Santiago surrendered. The American troops then proceeded to Puerto Rico, which was occupied without serious fighting. On August 12 Spain sued for peace. In spite of the rapidity of the victory, the war revealed gross confusion and incompetence in the administration of the American army. Against only 287 American soldiers killed in battle were 2,639 who died of disease. Theodore Roosevelt, who had resigned from the government to become second-in-command of a volunteer regiment of Rough Riders, and whose presence at the battle of San Juan Hill received considerable publicity, was—apart from Admiral Dewey—the most popular hero created by the war.

By the Treaty of Paris, signed on December 10, 1898, Cuba was to become independent and the United States acquired Puerto Rico, the Philippines, and the island of Guam in the Pacific, paying 20 million dollars to Spain in compensation for the Philippines. This adoption of an imperialist policy, which meant that for the first time the United States was assuming dominion over colonial peoples not easy of assimilation and Americanization, was opposed by the Democrats and by a number of New England Republicans. When the treaty was submitted to the Senate, it obtained the necessary two-thirds majority by only one vote. In the presidential election of 1900, Bryan, who was again nominated against McKinley, based his campaign on the issue of imperialism, demanding that the Philippines be immediately freed. McKinley was, however, elected by a slightly increased majority, receiving 7,219,530 popular votes and 292 electoral votes, as against 6,358,071 and 155 for Bryan.

AMERICAN COLONIAL POLICY

The elaboration of an American colonial policy was largely the work of Elihu Root who, after a long career as a New York lawyer, was appointed Secretary of War in 1899. Root's primary task was to make those drastic reforms in the organization of the army which the war had shown to be necessary, but he also took charge of over-seas possessions. The primary purposes of American colonial administration were to improve education and public health, and to train the colonial peoples for self-government on the American model. It was never unduly deferential to American business interests. But although the colonial policy of the United States was probably more liberal and enlightened than that of any other imperialist power, it could never overcome the natural preference of the subject races for independence. The dislike of the Filipinos and the Puerto Ricans for alien rule, however efficient that rule might be, was, moreover, stimulated by the Nordic color prejudice of many American officials.

Cuba remained under American control for three and a half years, with General Leonard Wood as governor. Wood separated church and state, built schools, and reorganized the finances. Yellow fever, the causes of which had been discovered by Dr. Walter Reed and by the Cuban physician Carlos Finlay, was stamped out by Major William C. Gorgas. Meanwhile a Cuban constitutional convention was meeting; and the future relations between Cuba and the United States were defined in an amendment to the military appropriations bill of 1901, which was written by Root and introduced into Congress by Senator Platt. By the Platt Amendment the United States was to have the right to intervene in Cuba, when necessary, in order to maintain order and preserve Cuban independence. The Cuban government was not to permit any foreign power to secure control over the island or to acquire debts in excess of its capacity to pay. On May 20, 1902, Cuba became independent. Since the island was primarily dependent on the sugar industry, President Roosevelt negotiated a treaty by which Cuban sugar was admitted into the United States at 20 per cent less than the regular tariff schedule. Congress gave a somewhat reluctant assent in December, 1903. Cuban independence, however, never seemed to have much reality. American capital poured into the island, especially after 1914. By 1928 the total American investment was more than 1½ billion dollars, and the island was little more than an economic dependency of the National City Bank of New York. The Cubans themselves, it was said, retained only a national flag, a national anthem, and the duty of paying taxes. On two occasions danger of revolution or civil war caused American troops or marines to be landed; and from

1906 until 1909 and again from 1917 until 1922 Cuba was partially controlled by officials appointed by the United States.

Puerto Rico and the Philippines, under the Organic Acts passed by Congress, were to be similar in status to the thirteen colonies before 1776. Each was to have a governor and a council appointed by the President and an elected legislature. A legal formula defining their status was worked out by the Supreme Court in the Insular Cases. They were to be dependencies of the United States and not a part of it, their native inhabitants being American nationals but not American citizens. They did not have the full protection of the Bill of Rights; and, unless Congress decided otherwise, they would be outside the American tariff wall. According to the Supreme Court the "fundamental" provisions of the constitution, but not its "formal" provisions, applied to them. The chief "fundamental" provision was the right not to be deprived of life, liberty, or property except by due process of law, while the "formal" provisions included such rights as that to trial by jury.

Puerto Rico had an area of 3,670 square miles; its population amounted in 1898 to about a million and in 1930 to more than a million and a half. Its government was established by the Foraker Act of 1900. Under American rule the death rate was cut in half; and by 1930, with one-third of the total government expenditures devoted to the school system, half the children of the island were being educated. There were, however, frequent conflicts between the government and the legislature; and American control intensified the island's economic problems. After 1902 Puerto Rico was inside the American tariff wall, and American capitalists began to acquire ownership of sugar and tobacco plantations. By 1928 the total foreign investment, owned mostly in the United States, was 176 million dollars and 89 per cent of Puerto Rican foreign trade was with the United States. The result was that land ownership became concentrated, four-fifths of the population being without land in 1930, and that the island was dependent for its livelihood on the export of sugar, tobacco, coffee, and fruit. In 1929 the average rural family in Puerto Rico was earning only $6.71 a week; and in the following year, when the depression cut down its export trade, 60 per cent of the population were unemployed and without means of support.

In the Philippines, American rule was more beneficial. These islands, more than 3,000 in number, had an area of 114,400 square miles, and a population amounting in 1903 to 7,635,426 and in 1930 to 12,082,000. The decision to retain them, rather than to allow them to become independent, was due partly to a well-founded belief that their inhabitants were unfitted for self-government and partly to economic considerations. President McKinley explained to a group of Methodist ministers that "there was nothing left for us to do but to take them all, and to educate the Filipinos, and to uplift and civilize and Christianize them, and by God's grace do the very best we could by them as our fellow men for whom Christ also died." Other members of the government were more impressed by the suggestion that the Philippines would be a convenient base for trade with China and also by the probability that, if the United States surrendered them, they would be annexed by Germany.

A number of the Filipinos, headed by Aguinaldo, had expected independence; and for three years, from 1899 until 1902, an American army of 70,000 men—four times as large as that which had invaded Cuba—was engaged in crushing the Filipino nationalists. This prolonged guerrilla warfare cost 4,300 lives, and was accompanied by numerous atrocities committed by both sides. In 1899 a commission headed by Jacob Gould Schurman was sent to prepare the way for the establishment of civilian government; in 1900 a second commission was sent under the presidency of William Howard Taft. The same year Taft was appointed the first civil governor. Congress passed the Organic Act in 1902, and the first legislature was elected in 1907.

The success of American rule was due largely to the work of Taft, who served as governor until December, 1903, and who became extremely popular among the Filipinos. By 1921 the rate of illiteracy had dropped from 85 to 37 per cent, and the number of school children had risen from 5,000 to more than 1,000,000. Cholera and smallpox were wiped out, and the infantile death rate in Manila was cut from 80 to 20 per cent. The government encouraged the growth of small landholdings and restricted the right of corporations to acquire land. Taft solved one of the most difficult problems of the islands, the wealth and power of the Catholic clergy, by visiting Rome and arranging for the purchase by the government of 400,000 acres of church lands and their sale to Filipino farmers on easy terms. In preparation for self-government, the number of Filipinos in the government service was steadily increased.

Progress toward independence became much more rapid in 1913, when the Democratic Party came into power in the United States. President Wilson appointed Francis Burton Harrison governor of the islands; and Harrison increased the number of Filipinos in the civil service, reducing the number of Americans from 2,623 in 1913 to 614 in 1921. He also gave the Filipinos a majority on the appointive commission and established government ownership of railroads and other economic enterprises. In 1913, moreover, the Underwood Tariff established complete free trade between the Philippines and the United States. In 1916 the Jones Act promised independence as soon as the Filipinos seemed to be ready for it, gave the suffrage to all literate males, and substituted an elective senate for the appointive commission. Many Americans in the islands believed that the growth of Filipino influence in the government was proceeding too rapidly and that the honesty and efficiency of the government were decreasing. In 1921 these policies were reversed by the Harding administration.

The liberality of American rule did not prevent the Filipinos— or at least the more vocal of them—from wanting to govern themselves; and their desire for independence won increasing support in the United States. The United States derived few economic benefits from possession of the islands, either directly or through the development of trade with China; and American statesmen soon began to realize that they were a military liability. They were more than 6,000 miles from the American coast, and in the event of war with Japan it would be almost impossible to defend them. By the year 1907 Theodore Roosevelt, who had been more responsible than any other American for the conquest of the Philippines, had come to the conclusion that it had been a mistake.

In addition to Puerto Rico and the Philippines, the United States also owned the island of Guam, taken from Spain in 1898; a part of the island of Samoa, known as Tutuila, taken by agreement with Great Britain and Germany in 1899; and the more important possessions of Alaska and the Hawaiian Islands. Alaska, with an area of 590,000 square miles, had been purchased in 1867; but until the end of the century it remained unimportant. The discovery, first, of gold and, subsequently, of copper, coal, and iron, then gave it a new value. It was given the status of a territory in 1912. The eight Hawaiian islands, having an area of 6,406 square miles, had come under the control of immigrants from the United States, who set up a government in 1893, secured annexation by the United States in 1898, and were given territorial status in 1900. By 1930 Hawaii had a population of 368,336; but nearly two-thirds of them were immigrants from China, Japan, and the Philippines, who worked on sugar and fruit plantations owned by Americans.

THE OPEN DOOR IN CHINA

Another indication of America's growing interest in world politics was the promulgation by John Hay of the "Open Door" policy in China. At the end of the nineteenth century the Chinese Empire was beginning to dissolve, and its territories were being carved into spheres of influence by the European powers and by Japan. In the Open Door policy the United States expressed her opposition to this process; she wished to preserve the territorial integrity of China, in the interests both of the Chinese themselves and of Americans who had commercial interests in the Far East.

The Open Door policy was of British origin. Great Britain handled 65 per cent of China's foreign trade and had large investments in the Yangste Valley. Her government was alarmed by French, Russian, and Japanese encroachments upon Chinese territory. In 1898 Great Britain suggested that the United States join her in demanding equal commercial opportunity for all nations in all parts of China. The United States refused this proposal; and Great Britain then adopted a different policy. Alarmed by the growing power of Germany, she proceeded to make agreements with her leading rivals in the Far East, with Japan in 1902, France in 1904, and Russia in 1907. John Hay had, however, been impressed by the British suggestion; and, when he became Secretary of State, he resolved to make it the American policy.

In 1899, in the first of the Open Door notes, Hay asked the leading European powers to adopt the principle of commercial equality for all nations within the spheres of influence which they controlled in China. In 1900 a group of fanatical Chinese, the Boxers, began to attack foreigners; and the leading white powers, including the United States, sent a joint military expedition to protect their citizens and suppress the Boxers, subsequently levying a heavy indemnity on the Chinese government. Fearing that the European powers might take advantage of the situation to annex part of China, Hay issued in July, 1900, the second of the Open Door notes, in which he urged not only commercial equality for all nations in China but also the territorial integrity of the Chinese Empire. Finally, in February, 1902, after Russia had begun to acquire industrial privileges for her citizens in the Chinese province of Manchuria, Hay circulated a third note, in which he extended the Open Door to include equality in industrial development and in the investment of capital.

In theory the Open Door policy, like the Monroe Doctrine, represented an admirable combination of idealism and self-interest. It would benefit the Chinese by protecting them from foreign conquest; it would benefit the Americans by enabling them to share in the commercial and industrial development of the Far East; and it would check the growth of imperialist rivalries and hostilities by preventing the European powers from excluding one another from any part of China. Unfortunately the United States was not strong enough to enforce the Open Door by herself, nor were the American people sufficiently interested in Far Eastern affairs to undertake the responsibilities of carrying out a positive policy. And although the European powers professed respect for the principles of the

Open Door, they adopted qualifications and limitations which deprived their adherence of any practical reality. The United States hoped on several occasions that Great Britain would join her in defending the Open Door; but, once the British had come to terms with their leading rivals, their primary interest in the Far East was to protect their own holdings in the Yangste Valley. Successive administrations were to attempt for forty years to uphold the Open Door, which began to acquire the sanctity of a tradition; but their successes were dubious and their failures frequent.

BIBLIOGRAPHY

W. H. Anderson, *The Philippines* (1939)
*T. A. Bailey, *Diplomatic History of the United States* (1940)
M. J. Bau, *The Open Door Doctrine in Relation to China* (1923)
*S. F. Bemis, *Diplomatic History of the United States* (1936)
Brookings Institution, *Puerto Rico and its Problems* (1930)
J. M. Callahan, *American Relations in the Pacific* (1901)
F. E. Chadwick, *Relations of the United States and Spain* (1909–11)
A. C. Coolidge, *America as a World Power* (1907)
T. Dennett, *Americans in Eastern Asia* (1922)
——— *John Hay* (1933)
R. A. Fitzgibbon, *Cuba and the United States, 1910–35* (1935)
W. C. Forbes, *The Philippine Islands* (1928)
L. M. Gelber, *The Rise of Anglo-American Friendship, 1898–1906* (1938)
*A. W. Griswold, *The Far Eastern Policy of the United States* (1938)
W. H. Haas (ed.), *The American Empire* (1940)
H. Hagedorn, *Leonard Wood* (1931)
L. H. Jenks, *Our Cuban Colony* (1928)
*P. C. Jessup, *Elihu Root* (1938)
W. Millis, *The Martial Spirit* (1931)
*D. Perkins, *The Monroe Doctrine, 1867–1907* (1937)
R. F. Pettigrew, *The Course of Empire* (1920)
J. W. Pratt, *Expansionists of 1898* (1936)
*H. F. Pringle, *William Howard Taft* (1939)
J. S. Reyes, *Legislative History of America's Economic Policy toward the Philippines* (1923)
E. Root, *Military and Colonial Policy of the United States* (1916)
L. M. Sears, *A History of American Foreign Relations* (1936)
M. Storey and M. P. Lichauco, *The Conquest of the Philippines* (1926)

G. H. Stuart, *Latin America and the United States* (Revised edition, 1938)
W. R. Thayer, *Life of John Hay* (1915)
A. K. Weinberg, *Manifest Destiny* (1935)
M. Wilkerson, *Public Opinion and the Spanish-American War* (1932)
*B. H. Williams, *Economic Foreign Policy of the United States* (1929)
W. W. Willoughby, *Territories and Dependencies of the United States* (1905)
——— *Foreign Rights and Interests in China* (1920)
D. C. Worcester and R. Hayden, *The Philippines* (1930)

12

THE MINORITY RACES

IMMIGRATION

THE economic development of the United States through the nineteenth century was accompanied and made possible by a large-scale immigration which fundamentally altered the racial composition of the American people. Before the Civil War there was no restriction whatever upon the entry of immigrants, and such regulations as existed were made by the state, and not by the Federal government. Until 1921 there was no limitation upon the number of immigrants who might be admitted. The United States, it was believed, had room for all who wished to come; it could offer freedom and opportunity to all victims of political, religious, or economic oppression. Special efforts to stimulate immigration were made by the steamship companies who sold berths in Atlantic liners, by the railroad corporations who owned western lands which they wished to populate, and by industrialists, particularly in coal and steel, who were troubled by strikes and wanted workers who would be more docile and would accept a low standard of living.

Between 1820 and 1936 more than 38 million immigrants entered the United States, although not all of them remained in the country permanently. This constituted the largest movement of peoples of which history has record. Before 1900 the majority of the immigrants came from northern and western Europe, especially from Germany, Scandinavia, Great Britain, and Ireland, the largest number being reached in the eighteen-eighties. With the exception of the Irish, these immigrant stocks were mainly Protestant and were accustomed to a relatively high standard of living. They settled in the rural areas of the United States.

After 1900 the stream of immigrants changed its character and began to flow mainly from southern and eastern Europe, from Italy and the Austrian and Russian empires, and also from French Canada. These later immigrants were Catholic, Greek Orthodox, or Jewish by religion. Coming from relatively backward countries, they were frequently illiterate; and, although they had come mostly from rural areas in their homelands, they settled in the cities when they reached the United States. The two highest points were in 1907 and 1914, more than 1,200,000 immigrants being admitted in each of these years.

By 1921, when the door to immigration began to be closed, the United States was no longer a predominantly Anglo-Saxon nation. It had become a combination of almost every people in the world. In 1790, although there was already greater racial variety than is usually realized, more than 90 per cent of the white population was either English or Scotch-Irish. By 1920, according to the national origins quota, the English and Scotch-Irish element in the population had been reduced to 42.7 per cent, while some other estimates made it as low as 33 per cent. In 1937, after sixteen years of restriction, there were still 10 million residents who had been born abroad, and 25 million whose parents were foreign-born. Every part of the country except the South had large immigrant colonies, but the greatest concentrations were in the cities of the Northeast and the Middle West. In 1920 more than 30 per cent of the populations of New York, Boston, Chicago, and Cleveland were foreign-born; in 1937, 73.3 per cent of the population of New York were either foreign-born or the children of foreign-born.

The immigrant races supplied the bulk of the manual labor for the building of the railroads and for mining and manufacturing. They could often contribute to the American scene a color and an emotional warmth and vitality that was lacking among the more dour and reserved Anglo-Saxons. And although relatively few of their members acquired leadership in Federal politics or in industry and finance, they made large contributions, in spite of economic and educational handicaps, to science and technology and to learning and the arts. Their arrival made the United States a new kind of nation—a nation bound together, not by community of race and history and tradition, but by common hopes for the future and common allegiance to the principles of freedom and human equality. Idealists saw the United States as a country where the representatives of every racial group, with their different aptitudes and cultural inheritances, could for the first time in history live together and co-operate with one another in mutual tolerance and respect.

This hope, unfortunately, was not always realized. The natural distrust of most human beings for people who are unlike themselves could not easily be conquered, and the older racial stocks were apt to regard the newcomers as a potential menace to American institutions. There were periodic outbreaks of racial and religious intolerance; and the prevalent belief was that the immigrants must, as rapidly as possible, be assimilated and Americanized. The languages and customs of the immigrants were treated as signs of inferiority; and they were encouraged to abandon their native traditions and to adopt the mores and beliefs of the dominant Anglo-Saxon Protestant and capitalistic culture.

It was the excessive rapidity of this Americanizing process, as imposed in the schools and by public opinion, which created most of the problems of racial adjustment. The majority of the immigrants were, in reality, only too eager to become Americanized; they felt inferior as long as they remained unassimilated. They often had good reasons for repudiating their previous national attachments, for they were liable to be penalized for misdeeds committed by the governments of the countries where they had been born, as happened to the Germans during the World War. Yet relatively few of them retained any sense of political allegiance to those countries.

In the process of Americanization, however, they were apt to abandon much that was valuable and to acquire only those American characteristics which were bad. This was particularly true of the children of immigrants. Becoming habituated in the public schools to the use of the English language and to the idea that immigrant customs were signs of inferiority, they often became psychologically separated from, and contemptuous of, their parents. Growing up with little religious or family discipline, they came in contact only with the worst aspects of American urban life—with its acquisitiveness, its emphasis on pecuniary standards of value, and its frequent lawlessness. The prison rate among the foreign-born was only one-third of the national average; but it was higher than the average among their children. Crime and gangsterism flourished especially in those urban areas where one racial community intermingled with another and where the disintegration of cultural traditions was therefore especially rapid. The growth of these lawless and acquisitive urban populations, living with few religious or cultural ties or standards of manners and morals, was a most alarming phenomenon of twentieth-century life. The cause of it was not, as was too often assumed, the unrestricted admission of immigrants but the imposition upon them of a forced and superficial process of Americanization.

THE BEGINNING OF RESTRICTION

Hostility to the unrestricted admission of immigrants appeared before the end of the nineteenth century. The most justifiable reasons for restriction were those presented by the American labor movement. The flow of immigrants made it difficult to establish trade unions and to maintain high wage levels; immigrants had, moreover, often been used as strikebreakers. Some employers, on the other hand, maintained that anarchism and communism were prevalent among the immigrants, an accusation for which the factual basis was very small—surprisingly so in view of the economic exploitation to which many of the immigrants were subjected. Other factors in the demand for restriction were the strong prejudice against the Roman Catholic Church and the growth of the Nordic myth among the Anglo-Saxon elements. The anti-Catholic prejudice, especially strong in the rural areas, gave birth to the powerful American Protective Association. The Nordic myth, which was invented by Gobineau and popularized in the United States by Lothrop Stoddard and Madison Grant, taught that the races of northwestern Europe were congenitally superior to all others. These beliefs resulted in the formation in 1894 of the Immigration Restriction League, with headquarters in Boston.

In 1875 the Federal government forbade the entry of convicts and prostitutes. In 1882 idiots and persons likely to become public charges were excluded; and a small head tax was imposed to finance the immigration service. In 1891 the Federal government assumed complete control of immigration. A Bureau of Immigration was established in 1894, and the law was extended to exclude polygamists and persons suffering from serious diseases. Subsequent laws, passed in 1903, 1907, and 1910, excluded anarchists and persons engaged in the white slave trade. In 1897, 1913, and 1915 Congress passed bills imposing literacy tests; but these were all killed by Presidential vetoes on the ground that they would discriminate unfairly against the natives of backward countries. Presidential opposition to the literacy test was overridden by Congress in 1917. It was not until 1921, however, that the United States completely abandoned its traditional policy and imposed limitations upon the number of immigrants.

Special problems were presented by immigrants from Asia, owing to the strength of the popular prejudice against the colored races. Chinese labor began to be introduced into California in 1848, and was used extensively in the building of the Central Pacific Railroad in the sixties. White workers were bitterly opposed to the Chinese, who were willing to accept a standard of living far below that of any white race. In 1862 American ships were forbidden to bring Chinese coolies to the United States. Any immigration of Chinese workers was temporarily forbidden in 1882, and the ban was made permanent in 1902. Chinese immigrants were not allowed to be naturalized, but Chinese who were born in the United States ranked as American citizens. More complicated was the question of the Japanese, a few of whom began to enter California in the eighteen-eighties. Many of them became tenant farmers and antagonized their white competitors by their industry and their low standards of living. When, however, the California state legislature began to pass laws discriminating against them, the government of Japan protested. The problem was partially settled by the Gentlemen's Agreement of 1907, under which the Japanese government promised not to allow Japanese laborers to go to the United States; but Japan continued to feel insulted by the racial prejudice of which her natives were made victims.

THE IMMIGRANT RACES

The largest of the immigrant groups was the German. More than 5 million immigrants entered the United States from Germany, the two chief waves of German immigration coming after the failure of the 1848 revolutions and in the eighteen-eighties. The German element in the American population amounted in 1920 to 16.8 per cent according to the national origins quota. Some other estimates placed it as high as 25 per cent. The earlier German immigration was mostly Protestant and rural, the later mostly Catholic and urban. Considerable areas in the rural Middle West were settled by the Germans; they also dominated the cities of Milwaukee and St. Louis, and settled strongly in Chicago and New York. In the twentieth century the World War and the subsequent rise of the Nazi dictatorship made their position peculiarly difficult; yet the majority of them had left Germany because of their liberalism and their antagonism to the traditions of Prussian militarism. Liberal convictions made the German immigrants of the eighteen-fifties strong supporters of the antislavery movement and, hence, of the Republican Party, and this political allegiance continued to be important.

The total Irish immigration amounted to more than 4 million, the majority of whom came to the United States after the famine of the eighteen-forties. According to the national origins quota they composed 11.6 per cent of the American population; by other estimates, as much as 15 per cent. They were to be found mainly in the cities; by the nineteen-thirties only 8 per cent of them were engaged in agriculture. Their sense of racial loyalty and their devotion to Catholicism made them remarkably cohesive. The hatred of Great Britain which persisted among the Irish in America was sometimes an influential factor in American foreign policy. The Irish began very early to display an especial talent for politics, and by the end of the nineteenth century they controlled a large number of the local political machines. In 1894, when their influence was greatest, Irish politicians dominated the city governments of New York, Brooklyn, Hoboken, Jersey City, Boston, Chicago, Buffalo, Albany, Troy, Pittsburgh, St. Paul, St. Louis, Kansas City, Omaha, New Orleans, and San Francisco. Since the Irish vote went by tradition to the Democratic Party, their political talents were an important factor in maintaining the party strength after the Civil War.

A third important group among the nineteenth-century immigrants were the Scandinavians, of whom there were more than 2 million. Most of them were small peasant farmers, who had left their homelands mostly in the eighteen-eighties because of economic oppression and religious discrimination. About 80 per cent of them remained agricultural in the United States and settled especially in Illinois, Wisconsin, Minnesota, and the Dakotas. The Scandinavian influence was often strong in the various movements of agrarian insurgency.

Among the twentieth-century immigrants the largest national group was the Italians, of whom there were more than 4 million. Coming mainly from southern Italy, where their ancestors had been peasant farmers, they settled in cities when they reached the United States. A few of them adopted truck farming in New England, where they cultivated land which had been abandoned by the descendants of the Puritans; others took up grape farming in California. But the majority became industrial workers in Boston and other New England cities and in New York. Their political influence was relatively small.

The later immigration included representatives of numerous Slavic races—Czechs, Slovaks, Serbs, Croats, and Slovenes from the Austro-Hungarian Empire, and Poles, Ukrainians, and Lithuanians from Russia—about 5½ million in all. Some of the Czechs adopted agriculture in Texas and the Middle West, and parts of the New England countryside became Polish; but the majority of the Slavic immigrants entered industry. They supplied much of the labor for the steel mills and the coal mines in Pennsylvania, Ohio, and Illinois, and for the automobile factories in Detroit.

The flow of peoples from eastern Europe also brought a considerable Jewish immigration. The Jewish population in the United States included three separate groups. About 3,000 Sephardic Jews settled in the country before the Revolution, mainly in Rhode Island and New York. The German immigration after 1848 included about 230,000 German Jews. Finally, in the late nineteenth and early twentieth centuries, about 1,500,000 Jewish immigrants entered the country from Poland, Lithuania, Galicia, and Rumania. In 1927 the total Jewish population numbered about 4,250,000, of whom 1,750,000 were in New York City.

In Europe, where the Jewish communities had been separated by race and religion from their Christian neighbors, the Jews had traditionally been the victims of anti-Semitic prejudice. In the United States, where the Jewish community was merely one among many alien races and where all white inhabitants were descended from immigrants and refugees, the Jews did not wholly escape the curse of anti-Semitism. Anti-Semitic feeling existed in certain social circles and occasionally took political form, as in the Ku Klux Klan of the nineteen-twenties. The advent of the Nazi dictatorship, and the efforts of Nazi agents to win support in the United States, were to make this form of intolerance peculiarly dangerous to American ideals. Contrary to the accusations made by anti-Semitic propagandists, a large majority of the Jewish population in the United States belonged to the working class, chiefly in the clothing industries. With the exception of a small number of German-Jewish families, they were not prominent in business and finance, and the proportion of wage earners among them was higher than for the population as a whole.

One of their most prominent characteristics was their eagerness to see their children educated, and the proportion of Jewish college students, despite the poverty of many Jewish families, was higher than the national average. In consequence, they were able to make important contributions to law, medicine, scholarship, and the arts, while they also became especially prominent in the entertainment industries. Their racial and religious identity had been preserved in Europe for two thousand years chiefly because of the constant intolerance to which they had been subjected; however, in the relatively liberal atmosphere of the United States the disappearance of the traditional Jewish rituals and beliefs among the younger generation was rapid. In the nineteen-thirties the Jewish religious congregations had only about 750,000 members, and a number of these belonged to liberal or reformed synagogues whose beliefs and practices differed little from those of Christian Unitarianism.

Almost every other country in the world contributed representatives to the American nation. There were steady additions to the British and Scotch-Irish stocks, the total immigration from Great Britain and Northern Ireland after 1820 amounting to about 2 million—very much more than the total ˙immigration before 1776. There were also more than 500,000 immigrants from France, more than 400,000 from Greece, and more than 200,000 each from Portugal, Holland, Switzerland, and the Turkish Empire. Of the Asiatic races there were, in 1930, 138,000 permanent residents of Japanese ancestry, mainly in California, and 75,000 Chinese.

THE NEGROES

Far more difficult than any of the problems of adjustment between the different white races were those confronting the Negro population. We must, therefore, examine these problems in more detail. The position of the Negro in American civilization presented questions of peculiar complexity as a result of the low economic and cultural level of most of the Negro population, the barriers created by color prejudice, and the heritage of slavery, Civil War, and Reconstruction.

The total number of Negroes in the United States was 8,833,994 in 1900 and 11,891,143 in 1930. The proportion of Negroes in the total population had been steadily decreasing, amounting to 19.3 per cent in 1790, 11.6 per cent in 1900, and 9.4 per cent in 1930. The decrease did not, however, continue after the restriction of immigration from Europe, since the birth-death ratio of the Negroes differed little from that of the whites. The bulk of the Negroes were concentrated in the South, although they began to migrate northward in the twentieth century. In 1900, 90 per cent of them were in the South, and they constituted 32.3 per cent of the total southern population; in 1930, 78.7 per cent of them were in the South, and the ratio had decreased to 24.7 per cent. The states where the proportion of colored people was largest were South Carolina, Mississippi, Alabama, Florida, Georgia, and Louisiana. Apparently about one-fifth of the Negroes were Mulatto. Many mulattoes were predominantly white, but any colored ancestry, however small, caused a person to be classified as Negro.

Whites and Negroes differ in their racial traits and aptitudes, but, despite popular prejudice to the contrary, there is no scientific evidence for the doctrine of Negro inferiority. The Negroes were, however, handicapped by their background of slavery. At the close of the Civil War they had been suddenly set free without property, without education or technical skill, and without training in habits of responsibility and family life. Their handicaps had been intensified by the fiasco of Reconstruction. After attempting for ten years to force Negro suffrage upon the South, the North had ended by washing its hands of the whole problem, leaving the white race in the South determined to prevent any recurrence of Negro and carpetbagger domination.

The burden of educating the Negro population was left to the South and to private philanthropy; and, since the southern states were too poor even to provide adequate education and social services for their white inhabitants, it was understandable that little should be done for the Negroes.[1] The whole South, white as well as colored, suffered because of the poverty and ignorance of the Negro population and the prevalence of disease among them. In the twentieth century preventable death and disease caused an economic loss to the South estimated at $300,000,000 a year. But the realization that the South could not regenerate herself without also regenerating her colored population was inevitably slow.

The problem was, moreover, complicated by a tendency toward self-righteousness on the part of Northerners, who were apt to regard color prejudice as a peculiarly southern characteristic. Yet, if the Southern whites were determined that the Negro race should

1. In 1930 the cost of public education in the South was $45.63 for each white child and $14.95 for each Negro child; in South Carolina, where the greatest discrimination occurred, the figures were $52.89 and $5.20.

remain inferior, their attitude was often paternalistic. On the other hand, such phenomena as the race riots which broke out in a number of northern cities in 1919, and the severe repression of Negro rights in Florida towns, such as Miami, which were inhabited mainly by Northerners, showed that anti-Negro feeling could be even more virulent in the North than it was in the South.

In 1900, 82.8 per cent of the southern Negroes were engaged in agriculture; 25.2 per cent of them were owners; the remainder, mostly sharecroppers. Standards of living were extremely low, 40 per cent of the Negro families living in one-room cabins. The landlords of the Negro sharecroppers often prided themselves on caring for the welfare of their dependents, like the slave-owning planters before the Civil War, and they would help them when they suffered from sickness or from a bad harvest. But the possibilities of fraud in such a relation were great. Most of the sharecroppers were in debt to their landlords and were bound to the soil until the debt was paid off. When a Negro was sentenced to pay a fine, it was customary for a white landlord to pay it, the Negro becoming his debtor and tenant. The increase in Negro ownership, which had been remarkably rapid in the last two decades of the nineteenth century, was, moreover, not maintained after 1920. By 1935 the proportion of owners among the Negro farmers had decreased to 20.5 per cent. In that year there were 186,665 southern Negro owners and 629,301 Negro tenants.

In the South it was difficult for the Negroes to find occupations outside agriculture and personal service. Most forms of wage labor were pre-empted by white workers, and the southern trade unions were mostly hostile to the Negroes. The North, however, offered more opportunities, particularly when there was a scarcity of labor. Through the twentieth century there was a steady movement among the Negro population from agriculture into the cities and from the South to the North, the shift being particularly rapid in 1917 and in 1923. By 1930, 43.7 per cent of the Negroes were urban, as contrasted with 22.7 per cent in 1900; and the cities of New York, Chicago, Baltimore, Washington, and New Orleans each had more than 100,000 Negro residents. Economic depressions were, however, liable to affect the Negroes with particular severity, since Negro workers were usually the first to be dismissed. In 1935, for example, one-quarter of the entire Negro population was living on relief.

The color barrier meant that contacts between white and Negro society were reduced to a minimum; and, as Negro society progressed toward higher economic and cultural levels, these contacts tended to become even smaller. The Negro population in the United States seemed to be developing into a self-sufficient colored community, paralleling the white community but sharply separated from it. In the twentieth century a Negro business and professional class, serving only the Negro population, began to appear. By 1936 there were 73 Negro banks with total assets of $6,250,000, a number of Negro insurance companies with assets worth $25,000,000, and 250 Negro newspapers. Negroes operated some 70,000 independent businesses and owned property worth $2,500,000,000. There were, moreover, 4,000 Negro doctors, 2,000 dentists, and 1,200 lawyers. Negro professionals were, however, often handicapped by their inability to secure adequate training and were far too few for the needs of the Negro population.

The educational development of the Negroes in the South was largely at the mercy of the white officials on the county boards of education. They received help, however, from private philanthropy, especially from the Rosenwald and Peabody foundations, while Congress passed an amendment to the Morrill Act in 1890 which resulted in the establishment of seventeen Negro land-grant colleges. The rate of Negro literacy steadily increased from 20.1 per cent in 1880 to 83.7 per cent in 1930. By 1937 there were 2 million Negro children in elementary schools and 150,000 in high schools, and there were 56,000 Negro teachers. Most of the schools, however, were overcrowded and underequipped, and most of the teachers were inadequately trained. In 1927 there were 68 Negro colleges, with 28,556 students and 1,752 instructors; and there were about 10,000 Negro college graduates. But most of the colleges were either theological or mechanical institutes, and the work was rarely above high school standards. Even the best Negro colleges, such as Howard, Fisk, Atlanta, and Dillard, were severely handicapped by lack of money and by inability to buy books and to secure access to research materials.

These low educational standards necessarily affected the Negro churches, which had a most important influence among the Negro population. In 1936 there were 45,000 Negro churches and 25,000 Negro ministers. Nearly half the Negro population were church members, two-thirds being Baptists and most of the remainder Methodists. Very few of the Negro religious organizations had any contacts at all with the white churches. The majority of the Negro ministers were men of little education, and the religion which they preached was usually revivalistic and highly emotional. From time to time there appeared preachers who made messianic claims, the most notable being Father Divine, who won a large body of adherents in New York City in the nineteen-thirties.

The economic handicaps of the Negro population were most clearly exemplified in their death statistics. In 1900, in certain typical areas, the Negro death rate was 30.2, as contrasted with 17.3 for the whites; the Negro infant mortality rate was 344.5 per thousand. During the twentieth century there was a steady improvement in Negro standards of health; but since white standards were also improving, the ratio between the two races did not greatly change. Certain diseases were especially frequent among Negroes; tuberculosis seems to have been three times as prevalent and venereal diseases five times as prevalent as among the white population.

The most spectacular illustration of the inferior status of the Negro race was the prevalence of lynching. Originating in frontier communities where there was no adequate police protection, lynching had spread to the black belt in the South after the Civil War as a method of keeping the Negro population in its place. Since the police and the courts could always be trusted to deal severely with Negro offenders, the practice had no justification. According to the figures compiled by Tuskegee Institute there were 4,697 lynchings in the United States between 1882 and 1939, 3,408 being Negro men and 84 Negro women. Nearly 90 per cent of all cases were in the South, especially in Mississippi, Georgia, and Texas.

The Negroes lynched were accused of a large variety of crimes, rape being the alleged cause in less than one-third of all cases. The worst year was 1892, when there were 292 lynchings. The growth of a more enlightened social conscience among officials and leaders of public opinion resulted subsequently in a steady decrease. The year 1901 was the last year in which there were more than 100 cases, and 1926 was the last year in which there were more than 30. Between 1927 and 1936, lynchings averaged 15 a year; in 1939 there were only 3; and during the twelve-month period ending May, 1940, for perhaps the first time since the Civil War, there was none.

After the Civil War the Negro population had been encouraged by northern politicians to expect full equality with the white race and rapid political, economic, and cultural progress. The failure of Reconstruction was followed by disillusionment and by the formulation of more modest aspirations. The chief Negro leader of this period was Booker T. Washington, who founded Tuskegee Institute in 1881. Washington declared that the Negroes could solve their racial problems only by winning the respect of the white race through hard work, sober conduct, and skill in agriculture and mechanics; they must make themselves, by their own efforts, an indispensable element in American civilization. Until the early years of the twentieth century Washington was regarded as the outstanding leader of the Negro population. Negro intellectuals of the next generation, however, tended to repudiate Washington's program as too humble and too passive, and to preach a militant Negro nationalism. The Negro race, they declared, was as gifted as any other, and it could win full social and legal equality only by struggling for it. The chief spokesman of this point of view was W. E. Burghardt Du Bois, a Harvard Ph.D. who became a professor at Atlanta. Whereas Washington had argued that "the race, like the individual, that makes itself indispensable, has solved many of its problems," Du Bois insisted that "persistent manly agitation is the way to liberty." Symptomatic of this change of attitude was the foundation, in 1910, of the National Association for the Advancement of Col-

ored People. The growth of nationalistic attitudes among the Negroes was illustrated also, on a much lower intellectual plane, by
the rise of the Negro Improvement Association, founded in 1917
by the West Indian Negro Marcus Garvey, who proposed to build
a great Negro empire in Africa. Before its collapse the Negro Improvement Association had received contributions from one million
Negroes in the United States and was estimated to have won support from nearly half the Negro population.

In view of the handicaps from which they suffered, the Negro
race made remarkable progress in twentieth-century America. Such
Negro intellectuals as George Washington Carver and W. E. B.
Du Bois made important contributions to science and scholarship;
there was a rapid growth in the number and quality of Negro poets
and novelists; and the share of the Negroes in the development of
American music exceeded that of any other racial group. James
Weldon Johnson, the Negro writer, once declared that "the only
things artistic that have sprung from American soil, permeated
American life, and been acknowledged the world over as being dis-
tinctively American have been the creations of the Negro Americans"—a statement which he afterward modified by excluding skyscraper architecture. Few white persons would accept this claim; yet
undoubtedly the aesthetic talents of the Negro race had a pervasive
influence on much American culture, especially in some of the popular arts; and their primitivistic capacity for enjoyment provided an
often refreshing contrast to the rapid tempo and the utilitarian
standards of twentieth-century white civilization.

THE INDIANS

One other minority group remains to be mentioned—the Indians,
whose ancestors had been the original occupants of the country. In
1780 the total number of Indians in the area subsequently included
in the United States was probably about 850,000. War and disease
steadily reduced their numbers until 1880, when the white conquest
was completed, after which the cessation of war led to some increase.
In 1930 the total Indian population amounted to 234,792, although

only about half of these were of pure Indian descent. They were located, as wards of the Federal government, on 135 reservations, the majority being in the Southwest.

Until the last two decades of the nineteenth century the Indian tribes in the West were still too dangerous to white settlers to win any sympathy, and the traditional frontier attitude that "a good Indian is a dead Indian" was generally prevalent. As late as 1876 the Sioux Indians, led by Sitting Bull, were strong enough to defeat General Custer in the battle of Little Big Horn. Once the Indian tribes had been effectively conquered, however, the white race began to develop a more sensitive conscience as to the fate of the original occupants of the North American continent. The writings of Helen Hunt Jackson aroused public opinion; and in 1887 Congress passed the Dawes Act, which was intended to promote the assimilation of the Indians into white civilization. The Indian community lands were to be broken up into private properties; the Indians were to receive homesteads and citizenship rights; and money was appropriated for their education.

The Dawes Act, however, led in practice to the transference of Indian lands to white ownership at the rate of 2 million acres a year; and, except in Oklahoma, where a number of Indians were enriched through the discovery of oil, few of them derived much benefit from it. Most of them did not accept assimilation with any enthusiasm, and their attitude was often one of passive hostility and contempt for the practices of the race that had conquered them. Among the tribes in New Mexico and Arizona the traditional customs and religious rituals retained much of their vitality, although they were in considerable danger of degenerating into spectacles for tourists. To a number of intellectuals it seemed that the Indian way of life and the Indian religious outlook embodied much of unique value, from which the white race might profit. After 1933, under the leadership of John Collier, as Commissioner for Indian Affairs, the Indian policy of the Federal government was reversed. The attempt to assimilate the Indians was abandoned, and the government undertook instead to protect their communal way of life and to preserve their native traditions.

BIBLIOGRAPHY

L. Adamic, *From Many lands* (1940)

American Academy of Political and Social Science, *The American Negro* (November, 1928)

*F. J. Brown and J. S. Roucek, *Our Racial and National Minorities* (1937)

J. H. Chadbourn, *Lynching and the Law* (1933)

J. R. Commons, *Races and Immigrants in America* (1920)

D. Dutcher, *The Negro in Modern Industrial Society* (1930)

W. E. B. DuBois, *Black Folk* (1939)

E. R. Embree, *Brown America* (1931)

H. P. Fairchild, *Immigration* (1925)

H. Feldman, *Racial Factors in American Industry* (1931)

R. L. Garis, *Immigration Restriction* (1929)

L. J. Greene and C. G. Woodson, *The Negro Wage Earner* (1930)

A. L. Harris and S. D. Spero, *The Black Worker* (1931)

I. A. Hourwich, *Immigration and Labor* (1912)

J. W. Jenks and W. J. Lauck, *The Immigration Problem* (1926)

C. S. Johnson, *The Negro in American Civilization* (1930)

L. V. Kennedy, *The Negro Peasant Turns Cityward* (1930)

E. G. Mears, *Resident Orientals on the American Pacific Coast* (1928)

R. Moton, *What the Negro Thinks* (1929)

S. Nearing, *Black America* (1929)

A. F. Raper, *The Tragedy of Lynching* (1933)

—— *Preface to Peasantry* (1936)

E. B. Reuter, *The American Race Problem* (1938)

B. Schrieke, *Alien America* (1936)

W. C. Smith, *Americans in the Making* (1939)

G. M. Stephenson, *History of American Immigration* (1926)

A. H. Verrill, *Our Indians* (1935)

B. T. Washington, *Up From Slavery* (1909)

C. H. Wesley, *Negro Labor in the United States* (1927)

W. White, *Rope and Faggot* (1929)

C. Wissler, *The American Indian* (1922)

C. Wittke, *We Who Built America* (1939)

13

THE FORMATION

OF PUBLIC OPINION

THE PROTESTANT CHURCHES

THE three agencies which have had most influence on the formation of public opinion in modern society are the church, the school, and the press (to which have been added, in the twentieth century, the motion picture and the radio). In the United States of the eighteenth and nineteenth centuries the most important of these was the church, particularly the Protestant church. The twentieth century, however, saw a marked decline in the influence and prestige of American Protestantism, its place as the principal moulder of public sentiment being taken, perhaps, by the public school system.

There were in the United States about 150 different Protestant denominations, with membership amounting in 1900 to about 18 million and in 1926 to about 32 million. More than half of the Protestant church members were Methodists or Baptists, while the remainder were (in order of numbers) Lutheran, Presbyterian, Episcopalian, and Congregationalist. In earlier periods these different organizations had emphasized their theological disagreements with one another, but in the twentieth century most of them began to associate in support of their common ideals. The chief indication of this trend toward Protestant union was the formation, in 1908, of the Federal Council of Churches of Christ in America.

In addition to these denominations which had originated in Europe, there were a number of cults that were native to the United

States, the most important being the Latter Day Saints, commonly known as the Mormons, and the Christian Scientists. The Mormon Church flourished in Utah and spread into other western states. Abandoning polygamy in 1896, it lost the aura of scandal that had surrounded its early history. Although it gave its primary allegiance to Joseph Smith rather than to Jesus Christ, it was clearly, in its doctrines and practices, an offshoot of Protestant Christianity. It laid more emphasis, however, on social regulation of individual economic activities than was customary in other Protestant churches. In 1926 it claimed a membership of about 600,000. Christian Science was founded by Mary Baker Eddy in 1876. At the time of Mrs. Eddy's death in 1910, it had about 1,000 churches and a membership variously estimated at from 300,000 to 1,000,000.

The main traditional tendencies of the Protestant churches (with the exception of Episcopalianism) were toward fundamentalism, evangelicalism, and individualism. Abandoning the Catholic belief in the authority of the organized Church, they preached the Bible as the inspired Word of God; and their main effort was to secure conversions, often by highly emotional forms of revivalism, and to induce men to live honest, sober, and chaste lives. They paid little attention to social and economic questions, apart from urging men to work conscientiously at their daily tasks; and they were inclined to regard success in business as a reward of virtue and a proof of divine favor. The declining influence of Protestantism in the twentieth century was chiefly due to the fact that these three tendencies were no longer in harmony with prevalent intellectual and social conditions. Protestantism failed to adapt itself to a changed society with sufficient speed.

Protestant fundamentalism was weakened by the development, in the nineteenth century, of scientific biblical criticism and of the Darwinian theory of evolution. The more liberal Protestant leaders, such as Henry Ward Beecher, accepted the findings of the scientists and endeavored to reinterpret Christian doctrine in scientific terms, but for a long period they were likely to be accused of heresy by their more conservative colleagues. The slowness and reluctance with which the churches adapted their teachings to the new scientific outlook deprived them of much of their prestige among the laity. Nor were Protestant theologians conspicuously successful in reconciling science and dogma. When they adopted a scientific view of life, they frequently abandoned the most significant features of traditional religion, substituting for it a vague evolutionary optimism which did not arouse enthusiasm or stimulate to self-discipline and self-sacrifice.

Meanwhile revivalistic methods were gradually falling into disrepute among the better educated classes; and such generally respected figures as Moody and Sankey, the leading revivalists of the late nineteenth century, were followed in the twentieth century by sensationalistic exhibitionists of the type of Billy Sunday and Aimee Semple MacPherson. The Protestant churches continued, however, to be associated with ethical puritanism; but their moralism was often legalistic and unimaginative. They were active in the movement for the prohibition of alcoholic liquors and in the censorship of books and pictures which were regarded as likely to encourage breaches of the seventh commandment of the Decalogue. This latter activity was undertaken especially by the Society for the Suppression of Vice, which was headed from 1873 to 1915 by Anthony Comstock. Comstock had considerable success in persuading states and municipalities to suppress immoral books and plays and in inducing the Federal government to prohibit the sending of immoral literature through the mail and the importation of immoral books and pictures from abroad. The inability of such men as Comstock to distinguish between art and pornography, and the dangers of attempting to make men virtuous by legislation, provoked ridicule and resentment among persons who valued intellectual freedom.

Many of the Protestant clergy appeared to regard sobriety and chastity as the most important of all the virtues. Meanwhile they were often tolerant of unscrupulous business practices which appeared to many people to be more far-reaching in their consequences and more deserving of condemnation. Protestantism had always been closely associated with the ethics of individualistic capitalism; and many of the more ruthless economic buccaneers of the late nineteenth century, including figures as disreputable as Daniel Drew, were pillars of the Protestant churches and generous contributors to Protestant finances. Before the end of the century certain Protestant leaders, such as Washington Gladden, of Columbus, Ohio, and George D. Herron, Professor of Applied Christianity at Iowa College, began to develop a more sensitive conscience toward economic exploitation and to preach a social, and not merely an individual, gospel. In 1907 Walter Rauschenbusch, of the Rochester Theological Seminary, published his *Christianity and the Social Crisis,* which proclaimed the duty of the Christian churches to be the working toward a new and more humane social system. By the nineteen-thirties the associations of Protestantism with movements for economic reform had become close and numerous, and such influential Protestant theologians as Reinhold Niebuhr and Harry F. Ward, of Union Theological Seminary of New York, were active supporters of radical political movements. This change of attitude, however, came perhaps too late to save the prestige of the churches among intellectuals. The financial dependence of many of the Protestant clergy on the wealthier members of their congregations, moreover, made it difficult for all of them to follow this example.

During the twentieth century the Protestant churches continued to increase their membership not only absolutely but also relatively to the growth of population. Church membership, however, involved fewer responsibilities and moral obligations than in the past. Protestantism did not produce leaders who exercised as much influence on national life as had, in the nineteenth century, such men as Henry Ward Beecher and Phillips Brooks; and it had difficulty in maintaining the intellectual and cultural standards of its ministry on a sufficiently high level. An increasing proportion of its activity was devoted to winning support by making the churches attractive centers of social life, conforming to the prevalent tendencies of secular society instead of preaching a new way of life. It was only in the more conservative rural areas, especially in the South, that it continued to be a really vital and dominating social force; and in these areas it continued to be associated with a fundamentalist view of the Bible, with revivalism, and to a large degree with economic individualism.

THE ROMAN CATHOLIC CHURCH

The Roman Catholic Church, on the other hand, grew rapidly in size and importance. Its membership in the United States amounted in 1900 to between 9 and 10 million, and in 1938 to more than 21 million. Three of the largest immigrant groups, the Irish, the Italians, and the Poles, were predominantly Catholic; and of these it was the Irish who exercised the greatest influence and who filled most of the leading clerical positions. Partly by its elaborate educational program, which included the establishment of a number of parochial schools for Catholic children and of colleges and universities for higher education, and partly by adapting itself to American life, professing allegiance, for example, to the American ideals of democracy, intellectual freedom, and separation of church and state, it had great success in retaining the support of the younger generations. It met with vigorous opposition in the rural areas of the South and the Middle West. By 1896 the anti-Catholic American Protective Association had a million members, and similar attitudes were represented after the World War by the Ku Klux Klan. Catholicism became, however, a major influence in the cities of the Northeast, and its leading spokesmen, such as Cardinal Gibbons of Baltimore in the first two decades of the twentieth century and Cardinal Hayes of New York in the twenties and thirties, acquired an authority unequalled by any of the Protestant clergy. The logical rigor of the doctrines of the Church, its ability to give plausible answers to the questions raised by science, and the aesthetic beauty of its ritual made it, moreover, more attractive than any branch of Protestantism to some American intellectuals.

The growing political influence of Catholicism was exercised to inculcate a conservative attitude toward individual morality and, with considerable reservations, a mainly liberal attitude toward economics. Emphasizing the importance of the family, it opposed birth control and divorce; and, although it gave no support to the prohibition movement, it was as active as the Protestant churches in the suppression of books and plays which it regarded as immoral. On the other hand, its official economic program, as laid down in the nineteenth century by Pope Leo XIII and after the World War by Pope Pius XI, condemned many of the unscrupulous practices of powerful financiers, insisted that workers had a right to receive a living wage and to form trade unions, and proclaimed the responsibility of the state to regulate industry in the interests of social justice. Most American Catholics belonged to the working class, and the Church had considerable influence in the American Federation of Labor.

In practice, however, American Catholic leaders were by no means in agreement in their attitude toward economic questions. The clergy of the Atlantic seaboard tended to be more conservative than those in the industrial and mining regions of the Middle West. The position of the Church was complicated by its uncompromising hostility to socialism and communism, and by its international affiliations. In certain other countries, especially in Spain and Mexico, the Church tended to support political and economic reaction; and its opposition to radicalism in those countries sometimes seemed to have more influence on its American policies than its liberal economic principles. In the nineteen-twenties and thirties there were some Catholic leaders, such as Father John A. Ryan, and the editors of the weekly magazine, *The Commonweal,* who adopted a liberal approach to political and economic problems; but there were others, probably having more influence on the Catholic lay population, who were strongly conservative.

THE PUBLIC SCHOOL SYSTEM

The function of determining the ideals and attitudes of the younger generation, which had formerly been performed chiefly by the church, was now assumed to an increasing extent by the public school. State-provided education underwent an enormous expansion after the Civil War. Universal free education had always been an American ideal; and, with the increase of national wealth, this ideal was extended to include a high school and college education as well as the more rudimentary education supplied by the grammar schools. Most Americans believed (to quote from the Iowa State Constitution of 1846) in "a general system of education, ascending in regular gradation from township high schools to a State University, where tuition shall be gratis and equally open to all."

By 1900 universal elementary education was established everywhere except in the South. At that date there were about 15,500,000 pupils in grammar schools and 695,903 in high schools. Seventy-eight per cent of all children between the ages of five and seventeen were attending school, as contrasted with 57 per cent in 1870. The average period of schooling was five years; and the money spent for each child, which had averaged $9.23 a year in 1870, had risen to $48.02 a year. Teachers' salaries, however, were still low, averaging $42.14 a month for men and $38.14 a month for women.

After 1900 there was an improvement in educational facilities in the South, and a further expansion of the high school system everywhere. By 1936 grammar school pupils totaled 22,706,806; high school pupils totaled 6,424,968; the proportion of children between five and seventeen who were at school had risen to 84 per cent; the cost per child had risen to $74.38 a year; and there were 870,963 school teachers. Facilities varied considerably, however, in different parts of the country. Whereas New York was spending $25.32 a year per capita on education, Arkansas was able to spend only $5.15; and whereas in New York the average school teacher received a salary of $2,414 a year, in Mississippi the average salary was only $571 a year. The national rate of illiteracy among persons above the age of ten amounted to 17 per cent in 1880, 11 per cent in 1900, and 4.3 per cent in 1930.

Accompanying the quantitative growth of the public school system, there was a general attempt to improve its standards. Supervision was entrusted to state and municipal boards or commissions of education; and professionally trained teachers were secured through the establishment of numerous normal schools and schools of education. The school system was made more genuinely democratic through such changes as the provision of free textbooks (which conservatives denounced as a step toward communism) and free lunches. And there was a widespread movement, largely stimulated by the philosophy of John Dewey and by the influence of

Teachers College at Columbia University, for abandoning the dogmatic inculcation of fixed principles and ideas, for encouraging school children to participate more actively in the educational process through "learning by doing," and for connecting the schools more intimately with society through the study of contemporary social and cultural changes.

The quantitative development of the American educational system was amazing, and there was nothing comparable to it, for size and wealth, in any other country in the world. Its quality, however, left more to be desired, and in the twentieth century there was a growing feeling that its methods and standards were in need of considerable revision.

The cardinal characteristic of the school system was that it was democratic, giving no encouragement to class distinctions and being based on the principle that every child had an equal right to an education. A large majority of the population passed through the same public school system. In 1936 there were only 270,128 pupils in private high schools, 4 per cent of the number in the public high schools. The average educational level of the whole population was probably higher in the United States than elsewhere. On the other hand, there had been a considerable leveling-down as well as a leveling-up; the educational standards of high schools and colleges were generally lower than in the leading European countries; and the whole system was vitiated by a too dogmatic application of egalitarian ideals. Little was done to segregate and encourage children of above-average ability or to provide an appropriate training for that considerable section of the population who were too unintelligent to profit by any kind of cultural education. At one extreme, talented children were likely to be held back by the necessity for keeping pace with the majority; at the other extreme, there were throughout the system a number of schools attended mainly by children of low-grade intelligence where the lack of discipline and the illiteracy were appalling.

The schools were liable to suffer also from too much political interference, which manifested itself in a suspicion of teachers and of ideas regarded as radical, a belief that the principal function of the school system was to inculcate a mechanistic loyalty to Anglo-Saxon American traditions, and occasional campaigns against "unpatriotic" textbooks. The difficulties of American schoolteachers were further complicated by the decline of family discipline, the increasingly numerous distractions of twentieth-century urban life, and the low prestige of the teaching profession, which was indicated by the fact that it was regarded as mainly an occupation for women. The proportion of women teachers was 70 per cent in 1900 and 85 per cent in 1920, but had decreased to 80 per cent by 1936.

In the opinion of many educational reformers the school system generally failed to accomplish its primary task: that of teaching how to think logically, to read understandingly, and to write lucidly.

HIGHER EDUCATION

The development of the college system paralleled that of the public schools. After the Civil War the financial resources of the colleges were enormously increased through the growth of tax-supported state universities, through the grant of 13 million acres of public land to 69 colleges under the Morrill Act of 1862, and through gifts by rich men. In 1900 there were 500 colleges, with a total enrollment of 237,000. By 1931 the number of colleges and universities of all kinds had increased to 931, of which 262 were public, 205 private, and 464 denominational. Eighty-two had enrollments of more than 2,500. The total number of college students was 1,024,-739; the membership of college faculties amounted to 90,232; the money spent on higher education approached $500,000,000 a year; and the total value of the endowments and properties of colleges and universities was $3,691,859,000. Other features of the growth of the college system were the development of higher education for women through the establishment of co-education in the state universities and the founding of numerous women's colleges (in 1931 two-fifths of all college students were women), and the foundation and improvement of schools for professional training, particularly in the fields of medicine, law, and engineering. The increase of higher education was especially rapid in the decade 1920–1930, during which the number of college students more than doubled.

The older American colleges had emphasized the study of classics and theology, one of their primary purposes being to provide the Protestant churches with a learned ministry. A large number of them had been controlled by religious denominations. After the Civil War, with the decline in clerical influence and the growing importance of science and technology, college curricula and methods of instruction were revolutionized. The leader of the educational reformers was Charles W. Eliot, president of Harvard from 1869 to 1909. Eliot, who was himself a scientist, broadened the college curriculum by introducing numerous new subjects in the fields of the sciences, history, literature, and languages; and he established the elective system, under which undergraduates, instead of confining themselves to a single restricted course of study, were allowed to exercise considerable freedom of choice among different subjects. He also vitalized the professional schools of law and medicine and made them an integral part of the university. Almost as influential as the work of Eliot was that of Daniel Coit Gilman, president of the newly founded Johns Hopkins University from 1875 until 1912. German methods of higher education were beginning to exercise a dominating influence upon the American system, and Gilman established a graduate school on the German model, in which students participated with professors in the work of a seminar and were expected to devote themselves to research in order to obtain a doctorate.

The innovations made by Eliot and Gilman spread through the American college system, and were adopted and extended by a number of other college presidents, among whom were Andrew D. White of Cornell, F. A. P. Barnard of Columbia, James B. Angell of Michigan, William R. Harper of Chicago, and G. Stanley Hall of Clark. Learning and research were also stimulated through the establishment of associations of scholars in all the major fields of knowledge, beginning with the American Historical Association in 1884 and the American Economic Association in 1885, and through the endowment by rich men of numerous libraries, museums, laboratories, research institutes, and research fellowships.

The criticisms most frequently directed against American higher education in the twentieth century were that too much importance and prestige were attached to nonacademic college activities, particularly to athletics, and that cultural standards were being debased through the introduction of numerous technical and commercial subjects into the college curricula. The elective system, which had originally been a useful instrument for undermining the supremacy of the classics and broadening the range of studies, caused considerable dissatisfaction, since it encouraged undergraduates to pick up a smattering of knowledge in a very varied range of subjects without acquiring a mastery of any of them. There was little dissent when Professor Morison, historian of Harvard University, where the system had originated, called it the "greatest educational crime of the century." Among college faculties the emphasis on research and on the acquisition of a Ph.D. degree caused the American academic world to make increasingly numerous and important contributions to all branches of knowledge; but it was criticized as having a narrowing effect and as impelling college teachers to become specialists who knew more and more about less and less. Although, moreover, there was considerably less political interference in the colleges than in the public schools, the powers of state legislatures over the state universities and the eagerness of many presidents of private colleges to extract endowments from rich men endangered academic freedom, as was shown by the occasional dismissals of instructors with radical opinions. In the American universities, unlike those of Europe, control was vested not in the faculty but in a body of trustees, and administration was largely divorced from teaching.

Implicated in these weaknesses of the educational system was a more fundamental factor: the decay of the traditional conception of a liberal education. The modern technological environment encouraged specialization, and the most successful branches of the educational system were probably the schools, such as those of law, medicine, and engineering, which provided specialized training for the professions. A broad cultural discipline in the liberal arts had ceased to have any great immediate social or economic utility. A large majority of the undergraduates of the leading American universities expected to become businessmen or to go on to the professional schools, and for them the chief utility of an education in a liberal arts college was in its social contacts rather than in anything learned in classrooms. The decreasing value attached to liberal education could be regarded only as very alarming by those who hoped to see the United States assume a cultural world leadership comparable to its economic supremacy, and who realized that a satisfactory solution of the pressing social and economic problems of the twentieth century would be impossible unless a sufficient number of citizens were broadly educated, trained to understand political and social movements, and sensitive to cultural values.

THE PRESS

The people of the United States derived their viewpoint mainly from the church and the school; but for their knowledge of day-by-day events they were dependent on the press. American democracy could not function successfully without accurate and unbiased news reporting.

The press of the United States, unlike that of most other countries, remained local and never became national. Each city of any size relied primarily for its news on papers which were published locally and which gave considerable attention to events of local importance. In 1900 there were in the United States 2,226 daily newspapers with a total circulation of 15 million and 14,000 weeklies with a total circulation of 42½ million. Half of all the world's newspapers were published in the United States.

The nineteenth century had been an age of personal journalism, in which the leading newspapers expressed the tastes and opinions of individual editors. The most prominent representatives of this kind of journalism were Horace Greeley of the New York *Tribune* and William Cullen Bryant of the New York *Post*, both of whom flourished in the middle decades of the century. The tradition was continued into the eighteen-nineties by Charles A. Dana of the New York *Sun* and Edwin L. Godkin of the *Post* and the *Nation*. Outside New York a similar influence was exercised by the Bowles family, who edited the Springfield *Republican* through three generations, ending in 1917, and by numerous editors of local dailies who never became nationally famous. Perhaps the last notable example of this personalistic tradition was William Allen White, who assumed editorship of the Emporia *Gazette* in Kansas in 1895 and was still editing it in 1940.

In the twentieth century the American press started to become a big business and to pass through the same development as other branches of the economic system. There was a decrease in competition and a tendency toward the concentration of ownership. National newspaper chains were created by such men as Hearst and Scripps; and, although the press remained local, different newspapers in different parts of the country, passing under the ownership of one man, began to propagate the same opinions and to print the same syndicated articles. In some cities competition ceased altogether with the entire newspaper service passing under the same ownership. At the same time the financial resources of the press increased as a result of larger circulations and of a rapid growth of advertising, and this made possible a considerable improvement in the mechanism of production and in the efficiency with which news was gathered. Newspapers became larger, were printed more attractively, and contained better illustrations. A more comprehensive news service was provided through the establishment of the Associated Press and of other independent news-gathering agencies, and through a considerable increase in the number of foreign correspondents. By 1926 the number of daily newspapers had decreased to 2,001, but their circulation had increased to 36 million.

The growth of a popular daily press, which acquired an enormous circulation by the most sensationalist methods, was the result mainly of the work of two individual proprietors: Joseph Pulitzer and William Randolph Hearst. Pulitzer, of Hungarian-Jewish ancestry, arrived in the United States in 1864 without a penny. He settled in St. Louis and achieved such success as a journalist that he was able to acquire the St. Louis *Post-Despatch* and, in 1883, to buy the New York *World*. Pulitzer built up the circulation of the *World* by printing the most lurid news stories; but in its editorial columns he crusaded for liberalism, reform, and political honesty, and he was able to perform a number of valuable public services by exposing cases of corruption and injustice. Hearst, on the other hand, inherited his wealth from his father, a California mining millionaire, and used his power mainly for self-advertisement. After being expelled from Harvard, he bought the San Francisco *Call* in 1887, became owner of the New York *Journal* in 1896, and went on to build up a national chain of newspapers covering every section of the country. The *Journal* and the *World* became bitter rivals; and their fight for circulation caused them to compete with each other in printing stories of Spanish atrocities in Cuba and in stirring up the war fever—an activity which caused the circulation of both newspapers to pass the million mark, but which Pulitzer later regretted. In the early years of the twentieth century Hearst campaigned against big business, advocated reforms which verged on socialism, and was regarded by all conservatives as a dangerous demagogue. He also made a series of attempts to be elected to public office, running at various times for the presidency of the United States, the governorship of New York State, and the mayoralty of New York City; but he was successful only in securing one term in the House of Representatives. After the World War he swung over to the opposite extreme and became a complete reactionary, preaching a foreign policy that was both imperialistic and isolationist and denouncing any progressive tendency in internal affairs as Communistic and inspired by Moscow. The *World,* on the other hand, continued to champion progressivism until its demise in 1931, while its news columns, after Pulitzer's death in 1911, became much more sober.

The growth of journalism into a big business meant that newspaper proprietors were usually rich men who might be expected to have conservative opinions, and that these papers had acquired considerable power to misrepresent events and to mould public opinion to suit their own political and economic interests. The dangers of such a situation were illustrated most vividly in the postwar activities of the Hearst press. To what extent the newspapers could really control public opinion was, however, dubious, especially after the invention of the radio. The most overwhelming electoral victory in recent American history, that of Roosevelt in 1936, was won in spite of opposition from a majority of the press. It should be remembered that the dependence of the press on large circulations meant that, to some extent at least, it must follow public opinion instead of leading it.

The dangers of unscrupulous editorial policies were partially counterbalanced by the growth of professional standards of ethics, which was stimulated by the foundation, in association with a number of universities, of schools of journalism. Another compensating factor was the revival, in a new form, of the personalistic tradition of the nineteenth century. Prominent individual journalists began to write syndicated columns of personal comment, in which they were usually allowed considerable freedom of expression and which probably acquired more influence on public opinion than any other part of the newspaper.

There were always certain newspapers which were conducted on the principle that their primary responsibility was to provide the public with accurate news. *The New York Times,* owned after 1896 by Adolph Simon Ochs, generally lived up to its slogan of giving all the news that was fit to print. Equally high standards were maintained by such organs as the New York *Herald-Tribune,* the Baltimore *Sun,* the Chicago *Daily News,* the St. Louis *Post-Despatch,* the Springfield *Republican,* and the *Christian Science Monitor.* None of these papers was completely innocent of coloring news to suit its editorial policies; but the careful reader of any of them could derive a reasonably full and accurate account of world events. The American metropolitan public was better served by its newspapers than was the public of any other nation in the world; and in the nineteen-twenties and thirties, with the appearance of a number of remarkably gifted and well-informed foreign correspondents, American readers had a much clearer view of European affairs than did the public of any European nation. Unfortunately the leading American newspapers did not circulate widely outside the metropolitan areas; and the various local papers that served the majority of the population continued to give little attention to international affairs and to present unreliable reports of them.

MAGAZINES
The most influential magazines of the nineteenth century generally had small circulations, were sober in tone, and reflected the genteel and conservative tendencies of the cultural tradition of Boston. The leading weeklies were the *Nation,* edited by E. L. Godkin; the *Independent,* edited by Henry Ward Beecher; and *Harper's,* edited by George W. Curtis; and the leading monthlies were the *Atlantic* and the *North American.*

In the eighteen-nineties, however, there began to appear a number of magazines of a new kind, which printed good fiction and accurate news stories but which were sold at a low price and aimed at a wide circulation. The pioneers in this field were Edward Bok, Frank A. Munsey, and John Brisben Walker; but the most vigorous of the new publishers was S. S. McClure, who, in 1893, began to issue a popular magazine named after himself, which forced down the price to ten cents. During the first decade of the twentieth century these new cheap magazines continued to maintain high standards and to exercise a most valuable influence on public opinion. They made possible the work of the muckrakers, who provided the stimulus for many of the reforms of the progressive era.

After about 1910, however, there was a marked degeneration. Business interests began to exercise a deleterious influence on the magazines, chiefly through advertising pressure; their attitude toward contemporary events became much more conservative; and their fiction grew less realistic. The large-selling magazines of the twenties and thirties were little better than drugs, catering to all the prejudices of middle-class readers and supplying them with sentimental and escapist fiction. Equally harmful were the cheaper and more sensationalist magazines, specializing in sex or adventure stories, which appeared in increasing numbers for more unsophisticated readers.

A number of high-priced commercial monthlies, such as *Harper's, Scribner's,* the *Forum,* and the *Atlantic,* continued, however, to present a more realistic attitude toward the contemporary scene; and an influence out of proportion to their small circulations was exercised by two subsidized liberal weeklies, the *Nation,* which was acquired in 1918 by Oswald Garrison Villard and edited by him until 1933, and the *New Republic,* which was founded in 1914 and of which the principal editor, until his death in 1930, was Herbert Croly.

BIBLIOGRAPHY

H. K. Beale, *Are American Teachers Free?* (1936)

W. G. Bleyer, *Main Currents in the History of American Journalism* (1927)

E. Bok, *The Americanization of Edward Bok* (1922)

O. Carlson and E. S. Bates, *Hearst* (1936)

E. P. Cubberly, *Public Education in the United States* (1934)

*M. E. Curti, *Social Ideas of American Educators* (1935)

R. L. Duffus, *Democracy Enters College* (1936)

F. Franklin, *Life of Daniel Coit Gilman* (1910)

R. H. Gabriel, *The Course of American Democratic Thought* (1940)

G. Gardner, *Lusty Scripps* (1932)

W. E. Garrison, *The March of Faith* (1933)

T. C. Hall, *Religious Background of American Culture* (1930)

H. James, Jr., *Charles W. Eliot* (1930)

E. W. Knight, *Public Education in the South* (1922)

A. M. Lee, *The Daily Newspaper in America* (1936)

J. M. Lee, *History of American Journalism* (1923)

F. Lundberg, *Imperial Hearst* (1936)

F. J. McConnell, *Humanism and Christianity* (1928)

S. E. Morison, *Three Centuries of Harvard* (1936)

F. L. Mott, *History of American Magazines* (1930–38)

Mrs. Fremont Older, *William Randolph Hearst* (1936)

B. Raup, *Education and Organized Interests* (1936)

W. Raushenbush, *Christianity and the Social Crisis* (1907)

H. K. Rowe, *History of Religion in the United States* (1930)

*A. M. Schlesinger, *The Rise of the City* (*History of American Life,* Vol. 10, 1933)

G. Seldes, *Freedom of the Press* (1935)

D. C. Seitz, *Joseph Pulitzer* (1924)

E. E. Slosson, *The American Spirit in Education* (*Chronicles of America,* Vol. 33, 1921)

W. W. Sweet, *The Story of Religion in America* (1930)

C. F. Thwing, *History of Higher Education in the United States since the Civil War* (1910)

H. F. Ward, *The Social Creed and the Churches* (1914)

J. K. Winkler, *Hearst* (1928)

T. Woody, *History of Women's Education in the United States* (1929)

14

NEW CULTURAL TENDENCIES

URBANIZATION

THE revolutionary changes in the economic system necessarily caused an enormous transformation in the habits and outlook of the ordinary citizen. Traditional standards of value, which tended to disintegrate under the impact of the new technology, were not immediately replaced by new standards more appropriate to the new ways of life. The process of mental adaptation to the changes in the economic and social structure was slow and painful and was responsible for much of the bitterness and sense of frustration that characterized American intellectual activity in the twentieth century.

Many of the changes in the way of life of the ordinary citizen can be summarized in the word "urbanization." In 1900 about two-fifths of the American people lived in towns and cities with more than 4,000 inhabitants. By 1930 the proportion had risen to three-fifths, and more than one-quarter of the total population was concentrated in seven urban areas—those of New York, Chicago, Philadelphia, Boston, Detroit, Los Angeles, and Cleveland. Urban habits and ideas were, moreover, spreading rapidly throughout the rural areas.

The older rural America had been a country of independent farmers and small businessmen. It had encouraged the qualities of self-reliance, industry, and versatility, and had stimulated a strong sense of private property. In such a society the prosperity of each individual depended mainly on his own efforts, and when men failed to prosper it was usually because of their own weaknesses.

The new society that was developing in the cities stimulated traits of a different kind. The typical city dweller did not own private property of the old kind; he was usually a wage earner or salary earner in a large organization. Even when he had property, it was frequently in the form of paper securities which entitled him to interest or dividend payments but which gave him little real control over any branch of economic activity. Instead of living in his own house, he often lived in a rented apartment; and instead of performing himself all the varied activities needed for the maintenance of life, he devoted himself to a single task and relied for everything else on the paid labor of other people. Since this specialized function could not satisfy all his physical and emotional needs, it became necessary for him to find physical exercise and recreation outside his work.

The growth of urban society brought with it both gains and losses. Its chief characteristics can best be summarized, perhaps, in four words: rationalism, standardization, specialization, and interdependence.

The rationalism of urban society meant that it tended to judge ideas and habits by the tests of logic and utility and to abandon those which could not be justified in these terms. The virtues of rationalism were most obviously exemplified in the triumphs of science and technology. Mankind steadily advanced toward a scientific control of the material world and was thereby able to make human life infinitely richer, safer, more leisurely, and less arduous. The growth of medical knowledge—perhaps the most clearly beneficial, and the least capable of being put to wrong uses, of all branches of science—resulted in a steady lowering of the death rate (which fell from 15.8 to 10.9 per thousand between 1900 and 1933), in the conquering of epidemic diseases, and in the alleviation of innumerable physical discomforts.

Along with the superstitions of rural society, however, scientific rationalism appeared to be undermining also its religious beliefs and the bases of its ethical values. Nineteenth-century science, which seemed to leave man a stranger in a godless universe, frequently resulted in an extremely pessimistic outlook. When the tests of logic and utility were applied to the moral standards and beliefs that had formerly impelled men to sacrifice themselves for one another and for the sake of posterity, it was often difficult to find any convincing justification for them. Men were therefore in danger of using the vast powers that science had given them mainly for personal power and pleasure. This fact was tragically illustrated in the history of twentieth-century Europe and—on a less alarming scale—in many symptoms of social disintegration in the United States.

Standardization was a device which increased man's power over the material universe. It was a necessary feature of machine production, making possible greater economy and efficiency of labor. And although it was at first denounced as causing a degradation of aesthetic standards, this accusation proved finally to be unjustified. In the twentieth century the application of art to industrial processes led to a rapid aesthetic improvement in machine-made goods. Standardization tended, moreover, to promote equality and to weaken class differences (in clothing, for example). Its dangers lay in its extension to cultural and intellectual processes. In the twentieth century one could plausibly look forward to a time when local and individual peculiarities would be largely obliterated and when the population of the entire country would be responding to the same advertisements, eating the same food, wearing the same kind of clothes, reading the same books, listening to the same entertainments, and—presumably—thinking the same thoughts. In such a society the individual would have become merely a regimented and devitalized cog in a vast machine, and this machine—as shown by European experience in the totalitarian states—could easily be controlled to their own advantage by a few power-loving bureaucrats.

Specialization was another necessary feature of machine production. It was carried to its furthest extreme during the nineteen-twenties in the assembly lines of the automobile factories, where the function of each individual worker was limited to the adjustment of a single sheet of metal or the tightening of a single bolt. Under such conditions the individual could find no real pleasure or emotional fulfillment in his work and, in compensation, there was a rapid growth of organized amusements. Games began to be an important feature of American life before the end of the nineteenth century. The first professional baseball league was founded in 1871; football was introduced from Great Britain in 1875; basketball was invented in 1891; golf, tennis, and organized athletics appeared a few years later. A similar development occurred in such mass entertainment industries as the theater and vaudeville, the publication of novels and magazines, the writing of songs and dance tunes, and eventually the motion picture and the radio.

These popular arts occasionally display a liveliness and a technical competence which are genuinely aesthetic; but their tone is, for the most part, sentimental, escapist, and nostalgic. They enable men and women to forget the monotony of their daily lives and to pass into a dream world where all men are successful, all women beautiful, and all desires satisfied. The most undesirable feature of the growth of organized amusements has been the loss of individual participation. Outside the schools, games are played mainly by paid professionals or by amateur specialists, and the ordinary individual has the role of merely a spectator and a partisan. The popular arts of earlier periods were popular in the sense that all individuals participated in them; they sang the songs, played the music, and performed the dances. The popular arts of the machine age, on the other hand, are usually the work of professionals.

The growth of standardization and specialization has meant a corresponding growth of interdependence. Each person has become a part of a very complex system, dependent for his security upon the performance by other people of their appointed duties and upon the smooth functioning of the system as a whole. The extraordinarily elaborate organization of urban life, providing food, clothing, shelter, light, water, heat, and recreation for millions of different individuals in the same restricted area, is a triumph of human ingenuity; but the consequences of any breakdown in the system would be catastrophic. There has been inevitably a loss in personal freedom and independence and a need for much greater social control than in the past. The old individualistic viewpoint of rural America has had to be drastically modified.

For optimists the growth of the cities is the prelude of a new civilization in which man will be the master of nature and in which collective regulation of individual activities will make possible a universal security and well-being. Pessimists, on the other hand, believe that the decline of individual independence and initiative and the growth of regimentation and specialization will devitalize the masses of mankind and make them instruments of a dictatorship exercised either by financiers or by bureaucrats.

Whatever validity there may be in either of these predictions, it is certain that the American people have not yet successfully adjusted their ideas and institutions to the new urban society, and that the old rural society had a greater permanent vitality. Whether, however, it is the ideas and institutions that are at fault, or whether urban life itself is harmful, is a matter for controversy.

THE BIRTH RATE

The clearest indication that human society has not adapted itself to urban life is the disintegration of the family and the decline of the birth rate. Rural society was based on the family. The family rather than the individual was the economic unit, the wife and the older children participating with the husband and father in the work of the farm. Children were usually economic assets. In the cities, on the other hand, the individual wage earner is the economic unit. Women, released from many of their traditional duties in the home, frequently become wage earners themselves; and children involve considerable expense and inconvenience. The tendency of urban society is toward the weakening of family ties, with a rapid increase in the number of divorces, and the gradual assumption by the state of much of the responsibility for training and educating children which were formerly undertaken by the parents.

Urban society means everywhere a decrease in the birth rate, particularly among the professional and business classes. This is due to economic insecurity, to the desire to maintain a high standard of living, to the difficulties of rearing children in an urban environment, and to the growth of rationalistic and sceptical attitudes which cause individuals to prefer personal satisfactions to family and social continuity. The birth rate in the United States, which had been extraordinarily high throughout the colonial period, reached its peak in 1810, at which date there were 976 children under five years for every thousand women of child-bearing age. By 1900, with the gradual spread of urban society and urban standards of value, the figure had dropped to 541, and by 1930 to 407. In that year, in cities with more than 100,000 inhabitants, every ten adults had an average of only seven children. In all urban areas the deficit of children was 8 per cent, and among the professional classes, who presumably included the most gifted members of society, the deficit was 40 per cent. Urban society was thus failing to reproduce itself. Among the farm population, on the other hand, every ten adults had an average of fourteen children.

Statisticians have deduced from these figures, first, that the American population will probably reach its peak in 1960, with a figure of 140 million, and will begin to decline after 1980; and, second, (a possibility which has some startling implications), that a large majority of the future inhabitants of the United States will be descended from the inhabitants of the more conservative rural areas, which have been least affected by modern civilization and which, in consequence, have the highest birth rates—from the southern tenant farmers, the Appalachian mountaineers, and the members of certain old-fashioned religious sects in the Middle and Far West.

Such figures do not mean that urbanization will be a passing phase in history since there will presumably continue to be migration into the cities from those rural areas that continue to be reservoirs of population. Nor do they necessarily mean that urban life is inherently decadent and degenerative. Obviously, however, conditions under which the more talented and enterprising stocks steadily become extinct cannot be regarded as healthy.

THE DOCTRINE OF SOCIAL RESPONSIBILITY

Men's mental attitudes frequently change more slowly than the economic and social conditions in which they live; and in periods of rapid social transformation people are apt to cling even more firmly than usual to their traditional beliefs. The reaffirmation of accepted ideas becomes a ritual, which gives a sense of emotional security but which has no practical efficacy. The changes in American society after the Civil War were not, therefore, immediately accompanied by any corresponding revolution in intellectual viewpoints. Eventually, however, the American people were compelled to undertake the task of adapting their ideas and their institutions to each other, of changing their ideas so that they would be in harmony with their institutions, and of changing their institutions in order to preserve what was permanently valuable in their traditional ideas. Certain new intellectual tendencies, which reflected the transformation of the social and economic system, began to appear before the end of the nineteenth century. The most important of these was a new emphasis on social responsibility for individual welfare.

Traditionally, the American people believed that individuals should be responsible for their own welfare, both spiritual and economic, and that paternalism was likely to undermine their morale. This belief in individualism, which originally had been derived partly from the religious doctrines of Protestantism and partly from the theories of eighteenth-century liberal politics and laissez-faire economics, was strengthened by the influences of the American environment with its abundance of cheap land, its enormous opportunities, and its freedom from the social, racial, and religious tyrannies of the Old World. Throughout most of the nineteenth century it was in harmony with American conditions.

By the end of the century, however, there was need for a change of attitude. As a result of the growing complexity of the economic system men often suffered from poverty and unemployment through causes wholly outside their own control, and the simple individualistic moral code of earlier generations was no longer an adequate guide to right living. Thinkers in the fields of economics and sociology began to argue, therefore, that social organization should make it possible for individuals to satisfy their economic and cultural needs, and that individual behavior should be judged not only by its conformity to a code of moral principles but also by its social consequences. Among the most influential exponents of this new social philosophy were Lester Frank Ward, who published his

Dynamic Sociology in 1883, and two professors of economics, Simon Patten and Richard T. Ely, who appear to have been influenced by the growth of state paternalism in Germany, and who were largely responsible for the founding, in 1885, of the American Economic Association. The Association declared in its statement of principles: "We regard the state as an agency whose positive assistance is one of the indispensable conditions of human progress."

In its extreme form the new attitude became Socialism—the doctrine that all economic enterprises should be transferred, either by revolution or by peaceful reform, to public ownership. Socialist doctrines were first brought to the United States in the eighteen-fifties by German immigrants who were disciples of Karl Marx. In 1876 the Socialist Labor Party was organized. In the eighties the Party passed under the leadership of Daniel DeLeon, an immigrant from the West Indies who had been a lecturer at Columbia University. DeLeon's advocacy of revolution was, however, opposed by a number of Socialists who believed in constitutional methods. The reformists seceded from the Socialist Labor Party in 1899, and in 1901 they formed the Socialist Party.

The leader of the Socialist Party for the next twenty years was Eugene Debs, who had become converted during his imprisonment after the Pullman strike; and his principal lieutenants were Victor Berger of Milwaukee and Morris Hillquit of New York. Debs's attractive personality won a number of converts, and the party vote steadily increased, reaching nearly 900,000 in the election of 1912. By that date there were thirteen Socialist daily newspapers, 298 weeklies, and 12 monthlies; while the Socialist *Appeal to Reason,* published from Girard, Kansas, had a circulation of 500,000. In spite of this rapid growth, however, organized Socialism never achieved any real influence on American political development; it made little progress inside the trade union movement; and its chief strength was among recent immigrants and among middle-class intellectuals and professionals.

Socialist ideas were also advocated in a number of novels describing imaginary Socialist utopias. The most important of these were Edward Bellamy's *Looking Backward,* published in 1888, and W. D.

Howells's *A Traveller from Altruria*. *Looking Backward,* which depicted the United States as it might be in the year 2000, sold 350,000 copies within two years of its publication, and resulted in the formation of a chain of clubs to establish the social system recommended in it. In spite of its popularity, however, the permanent effects of the book were very small.

Much more influential were those thinkers who analyzed in more concrete detail the evils of the existing social system. The most important of these were Henry George and Thorstein Veblen.

Henry George (1839–1897), by occupation a printer, was born in Philadelphia and in 1868 settled in San Francisco. He was struck by the prevalence of poverty in a state so rich and new and by the fact that landowners were becoming wealthy through the increase in real estate values. He concluded that the unearned increment which accrued to the owners of land was the primary evil of the social system. Private ownership of industry and private enterprise should be preserved, but this unearned increment should be transferred to society by means of a "single tax" on land. Meanwhile monopolistic tendencies in industry should be checked by the abolition of the tariff and patent rights. These ideas were set forth in *Progress and Poverty,* published in 1879.

George's ideas have been criticized on the ground that the private ownership of capital is a more important cause of economic injustice than the private ownership of land, and his doctrine of the single tax has had little effect on legislation. Nevertheless the lucid style and the humanitarian fervor of *Progress and Poverty* influenced numerous readers; and a large number of the twentieth-century Progressives first became aware of economic injustice as a result of studying the book.

Thorstein Veblen (1857–1929) attracted attention much more slowly. Born in Wisconsin of Norwegian parentage, he taught economics at the University of Chicago, Leland Stanford University, and the Missouri School of Commerce. His personal eccentricities and inability to conform to the accepted social and marital conventions, and his involved and ironical manner of writing, with its lack of crusading fervor and moral indignation, prevented him from winning any wide recognition during his lifetime. It was not until after his death that he was generally accepted as one of the most important of American thinkers. Veblen's cardinal idea was the distinction between industry and business. Industry made goods, while business was a series of money-making devices which enabled predatory financiers, stock promoters, and absentee owners to extract tribute from the remainder of the population. In a series of books Veblen analyzed the American economic system and concluded that the parasitical activities of business would eventually become incompatible with the existing social structure. Either business would be overthrown, or else society would pass under some kind of militaristic dictatorship.

Much of the opposition to the new doctrines of social responsibility was clearly a reflection either of a blind conservatism, which refused to recognize the incompatibility of eighteenth-century ideas with the twentieth-century economic system, or of the private interests of wealthy men. For this reason it was easy for liberal intellectuals to assume that the growth of state paternalism was a healthy and progressive tendency. More acute observers, however, while recognizing that this tendency was to a considerable extent inevitable, realized that its benefits were by no means unmixed and that it constituted a genuine threat to individual liberty. This attitude was exemplified by the sociologist William Graham Sumner of Yale and the economist John Bates Clark. These men believed that freedom was possible only in a laissez-faire economic system, but they recognized that *laissez faire* was being destroyed as much by the tariff policies and monopolistic tendencies of big business as by the social reforms sponsored by liberals and radicals. Sumner declared in 1907 that the twentieth century would be an age of socialism, militarism, and imperialism, all of which were equally hostile to the freedom of the individual.

PRAGMATISM

Contemporary with these new tendencies in social theory was a new philosophical movement, which was of equal importance in changing traditional ideas. This was the movement known as pragmatism or instrumentalism.

Throughout the nineteenth century American philosophers had been adherents either of the "common sense" school which had originated with John Locke, according to which all ideas were deductions from sense impressions, or of the German idealist school, which regarded the material universe as an expression of the divine mind. Both of these schools, however, believed in the capacity of the human mind to formulate absolute truths and immutable moral principles. Most Americans held that there were certain fixed ethical rules which individuals must obey if they wished to prosper and, similarly, that there were permanent political and legal principles by conformity to which a nation would prosper and which had been understood by the fathers of the American republic and were embodied in the American constitution.

Pragmatism, on the other hand, declared that thinking was subordinate to action, that the real function of the mind was to serve as a guide for successful behavior, and that all ideas should be judged by their practical consequences. The true significance of any general proposition was to be discovered by inquiring what it meant in terms of human action. The principles of pragmatism were first suggested in the eighteen-seventies by the mathematician and philosopher Charles Sanders Peirce. Their best-known exponent, however, was William James (1842–1910), who turned to philosophy late in life, after devoting himself primarily to psychology. These principles, under the name of instrumentalism, were subsequently elaborated in more detail and with more philosophical precision in the writings of John Dewey (1859——).

Pragmatism included two different principles: first, that the meaning of an idea could be determined only by considering its practical consequences; and second, that there were no absolute truths and that an idea should be judged as true or false according to whether its consequences were good or bad. The second of these propositions was open to criticism on the ground that, by undermining all general principles and by failing to set up criteria as to what constituted goodness and badness, it tended to weaken traditional ethical and intellectual standards without putting any sufficiently definite new standards in their place. It thus gave some encouragement to the belief that power and pleasure were the only valid ends of human activity and that ideas should be judged by their utility in increasing individual power and pleasure. In Europe pragmatist doctrines had an influence on the development of Fascism. These deductions were, however, repudiated by the American pragmatists, both James and Dewey being vigorous champions of democracy and enemies of imperialism.

The most valuable consequence of pragmatism was to encourage a critical examination of traditional beliefs. By applying to general principles the test of practical efficacy, it made both their virtues and their deficiencies more evident. The influence of pragmatism was especially important in education, where it resulted in the theory of "learning by doing." Instead of inculcating ideas dogmatically, teachers should encourage their pupils to discover ideas themselves through practical experiment. Even more significant was the effect of pragmatism on jurisprudence. In this field it caused students of the law to abandon the belief that the courts were engaged in interpreting immutable constitutional principles and to inquire instead into the actual social consequences of court decisions. William James's friend, Justice Oliver Wendell Holmes, viewed the pretensions of the judiciary with a wholesome scepticism, declaring that "the prophecies of what the courts will do in fact, and nothing more pretentious, are what I mean by the law." His conclusion was that the courts should allow Federal and state governments more freedom to experiment with new kinds of legislation. Meanwhile Roscoe Pound, of the Harvard Law School, was teaching that jurisprudence "must be judged by the results it achieves, not by the niceties of its internal structure; it must be valued by the extent to which it meets its ends, not by the beauty of its logical process"; he advocated "putting the human factor in the central place and relegating logic to its true position as an instrument." This pragmatist approach to the law was exemplified by Louis Brandeis, whose practice was to show the real meaning of judicial decisions by examining in detail their economic and social consequences. Legal pragmatism thus brought American constitutional theory into closer contact with the realities of twentieth-century American life.

REALISM IN LITERATURE

The social and philosophical reformers, while recognizing the evils of existing conditions, were optimistic about the possibility of changing them. In literature, on the other hand, the most significant new tendency was the growth of a profound pessimism. This was a marked contrast with the attitude of most nineteenth-century Americans, who had believed that American society was more fortunate than that of other nations and, in the words of W. D. Howells, that "the more smiling aspects of life . . . are the more American."

Prevalent literary and aesthetic standards were never lower than in the period between 1860 and the end of the century. Of the great pre–Civil War writers, Melville survived until 1891 and Whitman until 1892; but the best work of both of them had been done before the war, and neither of them received the recognition which he deserved. Popular taste demanded conformity with conventional beliefs rather than criticism, and sentimental romanticism rather than realism. At the end of the century the accepted leaders of American poetry were such figures as R. H. Stoddard, E. C. Stedman, T. B. Aldrich, and R. W. Gilder, who produced diluted imitations of Tennyson; while the chief tendency in the novel was toward historical romance, as exemplified in the works of T. N. Page, Winston Churchill, S. Weir Mitchell, F. Marion Crawford, and Mary Johnston, and—on a lower aesthetic level—in those of G. B. McCutcheon, R. W. Chambers, and Charles Major. Considerable popularity was enjoyed also by sentimental portrayals of American rural and small-town life, as in the poetry of James Whitcomb Riley and the novals of Owen Wister and John Fox, Jr.

The United States was not lacking in important writers, but they found it difficult to secure attention. The greatest poet of the period, Emily Dickinson, lived in complete obscurity at Amherst, Massachusetts, and remained generally unknown until long after her death; and its greatest novelist, Henry James, made his permanent home in England. Of those novelists who received popular recognition there were two—Mark Twain (1835–1910) and William Dean Howells (1837–1920)—whose work was of permanent literary value, but the development of both of them was impeded by the lack of an audience with adequate critical standards. Mark Twain's novels based on his early life on the Mississippi rank among the greatest achievements of American literature, but the reticence of American middle-class society prevented him from growing into real maturity. When in his later life he wrote sincerely, it was to express a rather naïve disgust with human nature.

Howells, a writer whose permanent importance was less than that of Mark Twain, was a more significant figure in American literary history in that he initiated the movement toward realism. He was also the first American novelist to deal with industrial conflicts from a somewhat radical viewpoint. However, his creed of "reticent realism" prevented him from describing social conditions with genuine frankness.

In the nineties new literary influences began to become important. Younger writers began to abandon the conventions of English and German romanticism, which had dominated American literature since the transcendentalist movement, and to imitate the French and Russian realists, particularly Zola and Tolstoy. They were strongly affected by the materialistic and anti-religious doctrines of nineteenth-century scientists and by the gloom provoked by the evils of nineteenth-century industrialism. They began to repudiate the genteel tradition of the New England school of writers and to describe the society in which they lived with a realistic frankness, a lack of respect for accepted moral standards, and a pessimism which shocked most of their readers.

In poetry the most important new figure was Edwin Arlington Robinson, who published his first book in 1896, but who remained wholly unknown until he was discovered by Theodore Roosevelt in 1906. He did not achieve wide recognition until 1920. In the novel the nineties produced three important realistic writers. Two of them, Stephen Crane (1871–1900), author of *The Red Badge of Courage,* and Frank Norris (1870–1902), author of *The Octopus* and *The Pit,* died young; but the third, Theodore Dreiser (1871——), survived to become a major figure of the twentieth century. Dreiser's *Sister Carrie* appeared in 1900; but the book's irreverent attitude toward traditional morality caused such antagonism that he was unable to publish his next novel until 1911. Other writers had meanwhile begun to deal realistically with American rural society, emphasizing the hardships of the pioneer farmers and abandoning that sentimental idealization of rural life which had become an American tradition. The most important example of agrarian realism was Hamlin Garland's *Main-Travelled Roads,* published in 1890. although similar tendencies had been exhibited earlier in Edward Eggleston's *The Hoosier Schoolmaster* (1871), in Ed Howe's *The Story of a Country Town* (1883), and in Joseph Kirkland's *Zurj* (1887).

The new literary tendencies for a long time had a kind of underground existence, and they did not begin to dominate the cultural scene until after the World War. The accepted intellectual leaders of American society, in the universities and in journalism, paid little attention to this growth of realism and continued to preach optimism, respectability, and political and ethical conservatism. There was, however, one figure, born into the highest social position and exhibiting great intellectual talents and wide scholarship, whose attitude toward modern society was fully as pessimistic as that of the realistic novelists. After a lifetime divided between teaching at Harvard and associating with the nation's political leaders at Washington, Henry Adams (1838–1918) concluded in his *Education* that the high moral and political standards bequeathed to him by his ancestors had no place in the chaotic and predatory world of late nineteenth-century industrialism, that the changes which had befallen America might fairly be measured by the differences between President Washington and President Grant, and that the transition from the organic unity of the society of the Middle Ages to the disintegrated multiplicity of modern society should be regarded as decay rather than as progress.

BIBLIOGRAPHY

*O. E. Baker, R. Borsodi, and M. L. Wilson, *Agriculture in Modern Life* (1939)
R. Blankenship, *American Literature* (1931)
F. S. Chapin, *Contemporary American Institutions* (1935)

J. Dewey, *Democracy and Education* (1921)
—— *Characters and Events* (1929)
*J. Dorfman, *Thorstein Veblen and his America* (1934)
D. Dudley, *Forgotten Frontiers: Dreiser and the Land of the Free* (1932)
G. H. Geiger, *Philosophy of Henry George* (1931)
M Hillquit, *History of Socialism in the United States* (1910)
H. W. Laidler, *American Socialism* (1937)
—— *History of Socialist Thought* (1933)
R. Lindquist, *The Family in the Present Social Order* (1931)
*R. S. and H. M. Lynd, *Middletown* (1929)
C. E. Merriam, *American Political Ideas, 1865–1917* (1920)
L. Mumford, *The Brown Decades* (1931)
H. W. Odum (ed.), *American Masters of Social Science* (1927)
*V. L. Parrington, *Main Currents in American Thought,* Vol. III (1930)
*R. B. Perry, *Thought and Character of William James* (1936)
R. Pound, *Introduction to the Philosophy of Law* (1925)
President's Committee, *Recent Social Trends* (1933)
I. W. Riley, *American Thought* (1923)
E. A. Ross, *Sin and Society* (1907)
*A. M. Schlesinger, *Rise of the City* (*History of American Life,* Vol. 10, 1933)
H. E. Starr, *William Graham Sumner* (1925)
L. Symes and T. Clement, *Rebel America* (1934)
J. G. Thompson, *Urbanization* (1927)
W. S. Thompson and P. K. Whelpton, *Population Trends in the United States* (1933)
H. G. Townsend, *Philosophical Ideas in the United States* (1934)
D. Wecter, *The Saga of American Society* (1937)

The Progressive Era

PART TWO

15

INTELLECTUAL INFLUENCES

PROGRESSIVE IDEALS

THE thirteen years between the accession to the presidency of Theodore Roosevelt in 1901 and the outbreak of the World War in 1914 were a period of political and economic reform, generally known as the Progressive Era. The growing discontent of large sections of the American people with political corruption and economic oligarchy, which had found expression during the eighties and nineties in the agrarian crusade, in the trade union movement, and in the attempts to curb the powers of the trusts, now began to find more statesmanlike leaders and more concrete objectives and to achieve practical results in state and Federal legislation.

The Progressive leaders accepted American traditions; they believed in individual freedom, in democracy, and in private property; and, although they advocated public supervision of business practices, they were opposed to any thorough-going form of socialism. But they felt that the realization of American ideals required an extension of government activities. Whereas the dominant idea of the nineteenth century had been that freedom and democracy could best be achieved by leaving men alone and restricting the government to the negative function of preventing men from injuring one another, the Progressives argued that the achievement of freedom and democracy now required positive action by the government. Most of the Progressives began by viewing social evils in moral terms; they were horrified by the dishonesty of individual politicians and business leaders. They were, however, gradually forced to recognize that the causes of this dishonesty were to be found in social and economic conditions as well as in individual corruption and that the remedy was social and economic reform.

The chief purposes of the Progressive reforms were: in politics, to revitalize democratic institutions by destroying the powers of bosses and machines and by making government officials more directly responsible to the people; and, in economics, to establish public control over big business in the interests of the farmer, the worker, and the small businessman and in the interests of the general welfare, present and future, of the American nation.

THE MUCKRAKERS

In arousing public opinion to the need for reform, an important part was played by a group of journalists who are generally known as the muckrakers—a word first applied to them by Theodore Roosevelt in a moment of irritation in 1906. The muckraking movement began almost by accident. S. S. McClure, one of the ablest of the group of publishers who had begun to produce low-priced popular magazines in the nineties, printed in October, 1902, an article exposing political corruption in St. Louis, which had been written by Lincoln Steffens in collaboration with Claude H. Wetmore. In the following month appeared the first installment of Ida Tarbell's *History of the Standard Oil Company,* which had been contracted for two years earlier. These two articles attracted wide attention and showed McClure that there was now a large audience for documented and accurate exposés of political and economic abuses. Similar work had been done earlier by Benjamin O. Flower, editor of *The Arena* since 1889, and by Henry Demarest Lloyd, whose study of Standard Oil, *Wealth against Commonwealth,* had appeared in 1894. But these earlier publications had caused relatively little excitement.

Having discovered the commercial possibilities of muckraking, McClure went on to publish a number of similar articles, of which the most important were a series of analyses of political corruption in different city and state governments by Lincoln Steffens, and a study of railroad practices by Ray Stannard Baker. The circulation of *McClure's* eventually reached 500,000. Meanwhile other popular

magazines quickly began to imitate *McClure's*. *Everybody's* joined
the muckraking movement in 1903, *Collier's* in 1905, *The American*
and *The Cosmopolitan* in 1906, and *Hampton's* in 1907. The
supremacy of *McClure's* did not survive the secession of its leading
contributors in 1906; and in the later stages of the muckraking movement the leadership belonged to *Collier's*, which was ably edited by
Robert J. Collier with the assistance of Norman Hapgood and Mark
Sullivan and which had achieved by 1912 a circulation of more than
a million.

Among the most important works of the muckrakers were:
Thomas W. Lawson's *Frenzied Finance*, Charles E. Russell's exposé
of the beef trust, and Ben Lindsay's study of crime among young
people, all of which were published in *Everybody's;* Samuel Hopkins
Adams's analysis of the patent medicine business in *Collier's;* and
David Graham Phillips's articles on *The Treason of the Senate* in
The Cosmopolitan. Not all the muckrakers were equally conscientious. Lawson was a Wall Street operator who had been associated
with H. H. Rogers in his copper manipulations and who was anxious
to advertise his own activities. Phillips's articles were more sensational than accurate. But the majority of the muckrakers, particularly
those who wrote for *McClure's*, were scrupulously careful to tell
the truth and to base everything that they wrote on lengthy and
detailed researches.

The muckraking movement ended before 1914. The public
eventually began to become tired of it; and their confidence in the
reliability of the muckrakers was weakened by a growth of sensa-
tionalism. A more important factor, however, was advertising pressure. Business leaders began to refuse to buy advertising space in
magazines whose editorial policies they disliked; and since the average low-priced magazine was sold for less than its cost of production,
it could not survive without advertisements. After 1912 or 1913
popular magazines very rarely printed anything offensive to big
business.

Of the muckrakers themselves, a number grew more conservative.
After the World War Mark Sullivan developed into a champion of
business freedom and an enemy of state regulation, and Ida Tarbell

turned from excoriating John D. Rockefeller to glorifying a new kind of business leadership represented by Judge Gary and Owen D. Young. Lincoln Steffens, on the other hand, concluded that it was society rather than individuals which needed to be changed and that in capitalist society corrupt politicians were often less hypocritical and more realistic than those who prided themselves on their honesty. Believing that what was needed was a union of political and economic leadership which would make corruption unnecessary, he became in the thirties one of the most influential of the American "fellow travellers" of the Communist Party.

Contemporary with the muckraking journalists were a number of writers who exposed similar abuses through the medium of fiction. Their work rarely had any great literary value and was quickly forgotten; but much of it exercised considerable influence on public opinion. The best-known of the muckraking novels was Upton Sinclair's *The Jungle,* published in 1906. *The Jungle* was written to advocate socialism; but what caught public attention was a section describing the filth of the meat-packing factories in Chicago. The book sold 150,000 copies within a year of publication and helped to bring about the Meat Inspection Act of that year. Another best-selling socialist novelist was Jack London, whose studies of the class struggle and prophecies of proletarian revolution were incongruously mingled with Nietzschean doctrines of the superman and with a belief in the supremacy of the Aryan race. Among other muckraking novels were Winston Churchhill's *Coniston,* Robert Herrick's *Memoirs of an American Citizen,* Booth Tarkington's *In the Arena,* Brand Whitlock's *The 13th District,* and William Allen White's *The Old Order Changeth,* the majority of which were published in 1905 and 1906.

POLITICAL THEORY

The muckraking journalists and novelists were concerned primarily with specific abuses. The formulation of more general historical and sociological theories, which would provide the Progressive movement with a theoretical basis and help to define its ultimate purposes, came more slowly, although the groundwork had already been done by some of the academic economists, sociologists, and philosophers.

In the later years of the Progressive Era writers began to reinterpret American history, with a view to emphasizing the influence of economic forces and stripping American traditions of much of the aura of sanctity with which they were surrounded. This new approach to the American past was foreshadowed in J. A. Smith's *Spirit of American Government,* and in Gustavus Myers's *History of the Great American Fortunes,* both of which were published in 1907. The most important of the historical iconoclasts, however, was Charles A. Beard, who published his *Economic Interpretation of the Constitution* in 1913. Beard's book showed in detail the precise economic interests of the members of the Constitutional Convention of 1787 and deduced that their primary intention had been to protect property owners from radical legislation. Beard probably overestimated the importance of economic motivations; yet it might be said that since the exposure of the Donation of Constantine by Lorenzo Valla in the fifteenth century, no single work of historical research has had such an important political influence.

Writers who attempted to guide future political development included Walter Weyl, whose *New Democracy* appeared in 1912, and a younger man, at this period a moderate socialist but subsequently a champion of *laissez faire,* Walter Lippmann, who published his *Preface to Politics* in 1912. The most influential work of this kind, however, was Herbert Croly's *Promise of American Life,* published in 1909. Croly, adapting the Hamiltonian belief in a strong Federal government to twentieth century conditions, argued that large business corporations must be accepted as economically desirable but that they must be subjected to Federal control. The Sherman Act should be repealed, but at the same time the powers of big business should be counteracted through the growth of a strong trade union movement. In other words, the correct policy was not to abolish special privilege but to give privileges to everybody. Croly's thesis had considerable influence on Theodore Roosevelt and foreshadowed the first phase of the New Deal of Franklin Roosevelt.

This semisocialist point of view was supported by one section of the Progressive movement but was opposed by others who believed that the growth of large corporations was caused not by their superior economic efficiency but merely by the superior opportunities for self-enrichment which they offered to unscrupulous financiers. The most influential exponent of this second point of view was the Boston lawyer, Louis D. Brandeis. Brandeis argued that beyond a certain point the growth of centralization, both in politics and in economics, resulted in inefficient administration and was incompatible with individual freedom and initiative. Brandeis wished to prevent the "curse of bigness" by prohibiting, through Federal regulation, any corporation from controlling more than 30 per cent of any industry, thus restoring effective competition. The political leaders of the Progressive movement were divided between these two conflicting economic philosophies, Theodore Roosevelt, for example, inclining more to the Croly thesis, and Wilson and La Follette to that of Brandeis.

BIBLIOGRAPHY

J. Addams, *Forty Years at Hull House* (1910)
L. D. Brandeis, *Other People's Money* (1914)
——— *The Curse of Bigness* (1934)
J. Chamberlain, *Farewell to Reform* (1932)
H. Croly, *The Promise of American Life* (1909)
B. P. De Witt, *The Progressive Movement* (1915)
*H. U. Faulkner, *The Quest for Social Justice* (*History of American Life*, Vol. 11, 1931)
*L. Filler, *Crusaders for American Liberalism* (1939)
*R. H. Gabriel, *The Course of American Democratic Thought* (1940)
N. Hapgood, *The Changing Years* (1930)
E. R. Lewis, *American Political Thought from the Civil War to the World War* (1937)
W. Lippmann, *Preface to Politics* (1914)
C. E. Merriam, *American Political Ideas, 1867–1917* (1920)
C. C. Regier, *Era of the Muckrakers* (1932)

T. Roosevelt, *The New Nationalism* (1910)
*L. Steffens, *Autobiography* (1931)
M. Sullivan, *The Education of an American* (1938)
O. G. Villard, *Fighting Years* (1939)
W. Weyl, *The New Democracy* (1912)

16

PROGRESSIVISM

IN LOCAL GOVERNMENT

MUNICIPAL REFORMERS

MANY of the more important achievements of the Progressive movement were in city and state politics. All over the country, in the early years of the twentieth century, there appeared reform movements which endeavored to destroy manifestations of political and economic corruption that were becoming intolerable. Since many of the reformers began by attacking corruption in local government and were later drawn into national politics, and since the degree of honesty in national politics was partially dependent upon conditions in local politics, it is appropriate to discuss local reform movements first.

The leadership of these movements was assumed by disinterested citizens, usually lawyers by profession or more rarely newspaper editors or businessmen, who belonged to each of the two major parties but were alike in their opposition to machine politics. The pressure which carried them to success was supplied by groups of middle class citizens. An important part, particularly in the enactment of social welfare legislation, was played by women's organizations, which were rapidly growing in size and influence. The General Federation of Women's Clubs had been formed in 1889; and the membership of the organizations affiliated with it increased from 50,000 in 1898 to more than a million in 1914. Also of great importance was the growth of social work, which made many middle

class citizens aware for the first time of the darker side of industrial
society. Settlement houses for social work in slum areas, modeled
after Toynbee Hall in the East End of London, began to be established in the eighteen-eighties. By 1900 there were about a hundred
such projects, the most prominent being Hull House in Chicago,
founded by Jane Addams in 1889, and the Henry Street Settlement
in New York, founded by Lillian D. Wald in 1893. Much of the
local legislation of the Progressive Era was due largely to the efforts
of social workers.

In the city governments the main purposes of the Progressives
were to destroy the powers of the political bosses and machines and
to end the corrupt influences of business interests, particularly of the
street railroad, gas, and electric companies. They were, however,
constantly hampered by the lack of complete municipal home rule
and by the fact that many of the public utility corporations were too
large for municipal control. Finding that cities could not achieve
good government as long as the state legislatures remained corrupt,
many of the municipal reformers were gradually compelled to extend
their activities to state politics.

The most famous of the city reformers was Tom Johnson of
Cleveland. Johnson had himself been a street railroad magnate, who
had made money by the usual corrupt methods. A porter on a train
induced him to read a book by Henry George; and Johnson found
George's arguments unanswerable. As a result he became converted
to the reform movement. He thus had the advantage of possessing
an intimate knowledge of business practices. He also had a capacity
for winning popularity and affection, and a freedom from fanaticism,
which were equally unusual among reformers. Johnson served as
mayor of Cleveland from 1901 until 1909. His primary objective—
municipal ownership of public utilities—was vetoed by the Ohio
government, and the state authorities also prevented him from
increasing the taxes paid by the street railroad corporations and from
building municipal lines to compete with them. When Johnson ran
as candidate for the state governorship, he was defeated. In spite
of these failures, however, Cleveland under his rule won the reputation of being the best-governed city in the United States. Johnson

gathered round him able disciples, notably Newton D. Baker, who succeeded him as mayor, and Frederick C. Howe; and he publicized and dramatized all the problems of municipal government. Reformers from all over the United States visited Cleveland to study Johnson's methods.

During the same period there were a number of other municipal reformers who attracted national attention, most notable of whom was, perhaps, Joseph W. Folk of St. Louis. Elected district attorney in 1901, Folk secured twenty convictions against those responsible for a particularly reprehensible street railroad manipulation. Under the rule of the city boss, Edward R. Butler, a group of financiers had bought a railroad franchise from the city council with a bribe of $250,000, and then sold their franchise to the existing railroad corporation for $1,250,000.

Equally spectacular was the crusade against the boss of San Francisco, Abe Ruef. Ruef was finally convicted in 1909 through the efforts of the newspaper editor, Fremont Older, and of two lawyers, Francis J. Heney and Hiram Johnson, although the business leaders behind Ruef, the owners of the street railroads and of the Southern Pacific Railroad, proved to be beyond the reach of the law. Among other cities which had notable reform administrations were Toledo and Milwaukee. The former was governed from 1897 to 1904 by "Golden Rule" Jones and from 1904 to 1913 by Brand Whitlock. Milwaukee elected a socialist mayor in 1910 and continued until 1939 to keep socialists at the head of its government because of their honesty and in spite of their political ideals.

NEW IDEAS IN MUNICIPAL GOVERNMENT

The chief new ideas in municipal government were the commission and city manager plans. The advantages of these plans were that they avoided the division of responsibility between the mayor and the council or board of aldermen, got rid of the numerous elective positions upon which the powers of political machines had been largely based, and made possible a nonpartisan administration concerned merely with municipal needs and divorced from national party politics. Commission government originated at Galveston,

Texas, in 1901, when a destructive flood made efficient administration more necessary than usual. In 1907 the plan was adopted, with improvements, by Des Moines, Iowa, which henceforth took a leading place in the movement for better city government. In 1913 Dayton, Ohio, adopted the commission system, and added a city manager, who was to act as executive and to be responsible to the commission. By 1921 there were perhaps five hundred cities that had adopted some form of commission government, most of them having commissions with five members. Other improvements in city government were the growth of municipal ownership of public utilities, the public letting of contracts, and city planning.

Few cities were wholly unaffected by these municipal reforms, but there were a number which continued to be dominated by machines. The three largest cities in the country, New York, Chicago, and Philadelphia, continued to suffer from corruption and misgovernment; and even in the nineteen-thirties there were still some city machines, such as the Hague machine in Jersey City and the Pendergast machine in Kansas City, which exhibited all the vices that had been characteristic of municipal government in the eighteen-eighties and nineties.

STATE REFORMERS

In the state governments the Progressives endeavored to make changes in the electoral system which would make officials more directly responsible to the people. Likewise, they attempted to destroy the corrupt powers of business corporations, particularly the big railroads, and to enact social legislation protecting the working class from insecurity and exploitation. They were, however, constantly impeded by the judiciary, both state and Federal, which was likely to regard reforms as violations of the rights of property.

The outstanding Progressive leader in state politics was Robert M. La Follette of Wisconsin. After a prolonged struggle with the railroad and lumber interests, who twice prevented him from securing the Republican nomination for governor by bribing the convention, La Follette won the nomination and the election in 1900, and was re-elected in 1902 and 1904. In order to prevent the old Republican machine from regaining control of the state, La Follette built up a powerful organization of his own, which continued to dominate the State of Wisconsin long after his own death. He sought advice constantly from intellectuals and social scientists and received effective collaboration from the staff of the state university. As governor, La Follette succeeded in enacting a long series of reforms, which became known as the Wisconsin Idea and made Wisconsin the chief example of Progressivism in the United States. The Wisconsin Idea included taxation of the railroads, fixing of railroad rates on a basis not of the capitalization of the railroad corporations but of the real physical value of their properties, income and inheritance taxes, laws regulating insurance and banking practices, laws limiting hours of labor for women and children, a workmen's compensation law, creation of a state forest reserve, and establishment of primary elections for the choice of party candidates for office. In 1906 La Follette went on to the United States Senate. Denounced by his enemies as a self-righteous fanatic, he was regarded by his friends as the greatest champion of liberalism in the United States.

No other state governor achieved such an imposing series of reforms as did La Follette; but there were a number who adopted at least part of the Wisconsin Idea. Two municipal reformers became state governors, Folk governing Missouri from 1904 to 1908 and Johnson governing California from 1910 to 1916. Each of them was able to rescue the state administration from control by the railroads, Missouri having hitherto been dominated by the Missouri Pacific and the Burlington, and California by the Harriman-controlled Southern Pacific. Another notable Progressive administration was that of Woodrow Wilson, who was elected Governor of New Jersey in 1910 as a preliminary to a presidential nomination and who used his two years in office to put through a number of laws limiting the powers of the political machines and regulating corporation charters, thereby driving the holding companies out of New Jersey and forcing them to find a new sanctuary in the State of Delaware.

Another Progressive achievement in state politics, which helped to create two national reputations, was regulation of the insurance companies. The insurance business had hitherto been conducted purely for private profit, at great expense to the policyholders and with little security. In Massachusetts Louis D. Brandeis showed that between 1890 and 1905 the insurance companies had received more than 61 million dollars from policyholders, had paid out less than 22 million dollars, and had retained less than 10 million dollars in reserve. The balance had been taken in salaries by the directors of the companies. Brandeis was able to secure rigid state regulation of insurance practices and to make possible the transfer of much of the business to the savings banks, which sold insurance at relatively low cost. This achievement, along with his prolonged fight against the corrupt financing of the Morgan-controlled New York, New Haven, and Hartford, his services in settling the garment workers' strikes, and his numerous other activities as the "people's counsel," caused Brandeis to be regarded by all conservatives as a dangerous radical and led to his appointment to the Supreme Court in 1916 by Woodrow Wilson.

In New York insurance practices were even more scandalous. The funds of the three big companies were used by their directors for Wall Street speculation, salaries of $150,000 a year were paid, and each company was accustomed to set aside- nearly $1,000,000 a year for bribing officials. The situation became public knowledge in 1905, when there was a struggle for control of the Equitable among a number of financiers, chiefly the railroad magnate Edward H. Harriman and the street railroad manipulator Thomas Fortune Ryan. The New York *World* started a campaign against the companies, forced the governor to appoint the Armstrong Committee to investigate them, and secured as counsel for the committee a forty-three year old lawyer, hitherto unknown to the general public, Charles Evans Hughes. Hughes's success in exposing the practices of high finance led to his election to the governorship in 1906. As governor, Hughes secured several changes in the insurance laws. The new law mutualized the insurance companies, made the directors responsible to the policyholders, prohibited speculation in insurance company funds, and limited directors' salaries. These changes did not end abuses since the policyholders had no real control over the directors, and

222 THE PROGRESSIVE ERA

they were less drastic than the measures enacted in Massachusetts. However, these and other reforms caused Hughes to be regarded as a presidential possibility. His honesty won support from Progressives, while his generally conservative opinions and his legal connections with big corporations made him acceptable to the standpat Republicans.

NEW IDEAS IN STATE GOVERNMENT

The Progressive movement was responsible for a number of new political devices, of varying utility, which were intended to strengthen popular control over the state governments. Most of these originated in the West and had originally been suggested by the Populists in the eighteen-nineties. The leading crusader for reforms of this kind was a citizen of the state of Oregon, William S. U'Ren.

The initiative, which allowed 5 per cent of the citizens of a state to demand consideration of a proposal for a new law, and the referendum, which allowed such proposals to be submitted to direct popular vote, were adopted by South Dakota in 1898 and by Oregon in 1902. They were ultimately established in twenty states. The recall of elected officials by popular vote was adopted by Oregon in 1908 and subsequently by ten other states. Eight states, moreover, allowed the recall of judges, and Colorado made it possible for a popular vote to overrule certain judicial decisions. The results of the initiative, the referendum, and the recall, however, in spite of the violent controversy which these measures excited, proved to be insignificant.

More important was the adoption of the direct primary allowing popular choice of party candidates and thereby restricting the powers of the party conventions, which had so often been controlled by bosses and open to bribery by business interests. The primary had originated with the Democratic Party in the South, and it began to spread into the North after 1903, when it was adopted in Wisconsin. By 1915 it had been established in thirty-seven states. The use of the primary for the choice of presidential candidates began in Oregon in 1910 and had been adopted in twenty states by 1920. Since, however, the final choice had to be made by the national convention, the party members of each state could only indicate their preference and must allow considerable discretion to their delegates. Presidential primaries, therefore, had little value. The primary system was also extended to the choice of senatorial candidates. By 1912 twenty-nine states had compelled their state legislatures, in the choice of senators, to follow the popular decision indicated in the primaries. This led in 1913 to the Seventeenth Amendment, which established direct election of senators.

The results were at first disappointing to the Progressives, since a number of big business representatives, who had become senators as a result of business control of the state legislatures, were able to win popular majorities. The Senate, however, gradually changed its character. During the administration of Theodore Roosevelt it had been known as the millionaires' club, but thirty years later a large number of its outstanding members were Progressives.

In order to curb the powers of business interests, most of the states established public utility commissions which regulated, with varying and often dubious effectiveness, the rates and practices of railroad, telephone, and electric corporations. They also imposed legal restrictions on the granting of public utility franchises. Bribery of state officials was diminished by anti-lobbying and corrupt practice laws, by the reduction of the number of elective positions, and by the adoption of civil service rules; and more efficient use of state revenues was achieved by the establishment of budget systems.

In the protection of workers, the most important advance was represented by Workmen's Compensation Acts establishing insurance systems for the benefit of injured workers, to which employers were compelled to contribute. The first such law was passed in Maryland in 1902, and similar laws had been adopted in forty-two other states by 1920. A number of states also established safety and health codes for the protection of industrial workers and adopted old age pension and mothers' assistance plans. More controversial were the attempts to impose maximum hours and minimum wages. The Supreme Court decision in the Lochner Case of 1905 appeared to prohibit wage and hour legislation; but in 1910 and 1917 Oregon laws fixing maximum hours first for women and later for male factory workers were upheld. In 1912 a minimum wage law for women was enacted in Massachusetts, and by 1923 this example had been followed by fourteen other states and in the District of Columbia. In 1923, however, the District of Columbia law was invalidated by the Court in *Adkins v. Children's Hospital,* and in 1925 and 1927 the Court also voided the Arizona and Arkansas laws. The attitude of the Court toward wage and hour laws continued to be very uncertain, and it reversed itself on these questions several times.

Supreme Court opposition also prevented any effective prohibition of child labor. A number of states passed laws restricting child labor and appointed Departments of Labor or Industrial Boards to supervise enforcement; but prohibition of child labor by any one state would handicap its industries in competition with those of other states. In 1916 Congress passed the Keating-Owen Act which —on the analogy of Federal laws directed against the white slave and narcotics traffics—prohibited the entry into interstate commerce of products made by child labor. This law was voided by the Court the following year in the case of *Hammer v. Dagenhart.* Opponents of child labor then turned to constitutional amendment as the only method of reform, but in the nineteen-thirties they were still unable to secure ratification by a sufficient number of states.

THE EIGHTEENTH AMENDMENT

Associated with Progressivism in local politics were two movements which eventually resulted in amendments to the Federal constitution and which, therefore, deserve special mention: the prohibition movement, and the woman suffrage movement. Both of these had originated in the middle of the nineteenth century, but both of them gained impetus from the swing toward reform in the Progressive Era, although only the second of them was clearly in harmony with progressive ideals.

The attack on alcoholic liquors began in New England and the Middle West. The State of Maine adopted a prohibition law before the Civil War. From the beginning prohibition was closely associated with the Protestant churches. The Women's Christian Temperance Union was founded in 1879 under the leadership of Frances

Willard; and the Anti-Saloon League was founded in 1895. These two organizations, working in co-operation with the Methodist, Baptist, and Presbyterian churches, became the chief forces in the movement.

The prohibitionists publicized the very real evils of the saloon, especially its associations with prostitution and with vote-buying by corrupt political machines. Their cause was strengthened by the rapid increase in the consumption of liquor in the latter decades of the nineteenth century. Between 1878 and 1898 per capita consumption more than doubled.

The Anti-Saloon League was, however, not content with legitimate propaganda against the abuse of liquor. Under the leadership of Wayne B. Wheeler and W. H. Anderson it organized the prohibitionists into a pressure group with lobbies in Washington and in the state capitals. By 1908 it had a hundred offices and was spending $400,000 a year. Through asking only that politicians vote as Drys, without inquiring whether they lived as Wets, it carried the movement to eventual victory, but it also contributed considerably to the growth of political hypocrisy.

The areas of rural Protestantism, in the South and the Middle West, were most responsive to prohibitionist propaganda. In the South the movement was strengthened by the desire of the white race to enforce temperance upon the Negroes. The cities, on the other hand, where immigrant and Catholic influences were strong, remained hostile. The movement also received considerable support from wealthy businessmen, who were anxious to increase the efficiency of their employees.

Five states—Maine, New Hampshire, Vermont, Kansas, and North Dakota—adopted prohibition before 1900. Between 1907 and 1916 fourteen other states, eight of them in the South and six in the West, followed their example. In March, 1913, Congress adopted the Webb-Kenyon Act which prohibited the shipment of liquor into dry territory. Other states passed local option rules, which enabled counties and municipalities to adopt prohibition; and every state except two introduced propaganda against liquor into its school system. By 1916 three-quarters of the area of the United States, containing half the population, was legally dry; and only the cities still resisted the movement.

A prohibition amendment was first submitted to Congress in 1913; but it was not until the World War, which necessitated the economizing of foodstuffs and the greatest possible industrial efficiency, that Congress capitulated. The Eighteenth Amendment passed Congress in 1917, was ratified by every state except Connecticut and Rhode Island, and was declared a part of the constitution in January, 1919. Congress passed, over Wilson's veto, the Volstead Act in October, 1919, which defined liquor prohibited by the terms of the Eighteenth Amendment as containing more than 0.5 per cent alcohol. Enforcement began on January 1, 1920.

THE NINETEENTH AMENDMENT

The abolition of legal and economic differences between the sexes was everywhere an accompaniment of the growth of industrialism, which made it possible for many women to become independent wage earners. This movement was particularly rapid in America, especially in the West, where pioneering conditions had resulted from the beginning in a greater degree of sexual equality than existed in Europe.

After the Civil War there was a steady increase in the number of women employed outside their own homes. In 1870, 1,321,000 women, 11.8 per cent of the total number, were gainfully employed in nonagricultural occupations, but about half of these were in domestic service. By 1920 the number employed had increased to 7,306,000, 21.3 per cent of the total number. More than one-fifth were married, and only one-quarter were in domestic service. The average wage of women was still, however, only about three-quarters that received by men.

In spite of considerable opposition, women began to assert their right to enter any of the professions and to combine marriage with a professional career. As a result the states began to pass laws giving women control over their own property and removing other legal restrictions. The independence of married women was also greatly increased by two movements, which many people opposed on moral and religious grounds: the increase of divorce, and of the use of contraceptives. Divorce laws differed considerably in various states, but it was always possible for wealthier persons to secure a divorce by establishing residence in a state with easy laws. For every 1,000 marriages there were 62 divorces in 1890, 81 in 1900, and 164 in 1935.

The sale of contraceptives was generally banned by state laws. Despite this, their use gradually became widespread among the wealthier classes, and the only effect of these laws was to make it difficult for working class women to obtain birth control information. The legalizing of birth control was advocated by The American Birth Control League, which was founded in 1912 under the leadership of Margaret Sanger and Mary Ware Dennett. Although the Catholic Church remained opposed to birth control on religious grounds, the opposition of the Protestant churches gradually diminished. By 1940 South Carolina was operating birth control clinics for working class wives; and other states seemed likely to follow this example.

The suffrage was the most important right from which women were excluded, since the vote would bring with it the possibility of remedying other grievances through legislation. The first woman suffrage association was founded in 1869 by Elizabeth Cady Stanton and Susan B. Anthony, who argued that the emancipation of the Negroes should logically be followed by the emancipation of women and that the Fourteenth Amendment should be applied to both sexes. The National American Woman's Suffrage Association was founded in 1890. In the twentieth century the chief leaders of the movement were Carrie Chapman Catt and Dr. Anna Howard Shaw. These leaders adopted methods of peaceful persuasion; but in 1912 another section of the movement, headed by Alice Paul, began to introduce into America the militancy practiced by Mrs. Pankhurst and the suffragettes in Great Britain.

Four states—Colorado, Idaho, Wyoming, and Utah—adopted woman suffrage before 1900. Between 1910 and 1914 eight more states, all of them west of the Mississippi, followed their example; and in 1916 a woman, Jeanette Rankin of Montana, was elected to

Congress. The leaders of the movement demanded a Federal amendment; and in the campaign of 1912 they won the support of Theodore Roosevelt, while Wilson expressed sympathy but recommended
that the question be left to the individual states. Congress rejected
the proposed amendment in 1914; but the woman suffrage leaders
campaigned against all those who had voted against it when the
latter ran for re-election. They claimed to have secured the defeat
of forty-three of them. The World War weakened the opposition,
and the Nineteenth Amendment was added to the constitution in
1919.

BIBLIOGRAPHY

American Academy of Political and Social Science, *Women in Public
    Life* (1914)
J. Chamberlain, *Farewell to Reform* (1932)
E. H. Cherrington, *The Evolution of Prohibition in the United States*
    (1920)
A. H. Eaton, *The Oregon System* (1912)
*L. Filler, *Crusaders for American Liberalism* (1939)
R. G. Fuller, *Child Labor and the Constitution* (1923)
E. A. Hecker, *Short History of Women's Rights* (1914)
F. C. Howe, *The City, The Hope of Democracy* (1905)
———— *Wisconsin, An Experiment in Democracy* (1912)
———— *Confessions of a Reformer* (1925)
T. Johnson, *My Story* (1911)
J. A. Krout, *Origins of Prohibition* (1925)
A. Lief, *Brandeis* (1936)
R. M. LaFollette, *Autobiography* (1913)
C. C. McCarthy, *The Wisconsin Idea* (1912)
W. B. Munro, *The Initiative, The Referendum, and the Recall* (1912)
F. Older, *My Own Story* (1926)
P. H. Odegard, *Pressure Politics: The Story of the Anti-Saloon League*
    (1928)
*F. L. Paxson, *Pre-War Years* (1936)
L. Steffens, *Autobiography* (1931)
B. Whitlock, *Forty Years of it* (1925)

17

THE ADMINISTRATION

OF THEODORE ROOSEVELT

PRESIDENTIAL LEADERSHIP

PROGRESSIVISM began to be a force in national politics in 1901. On September 14 of that year President McKinley, who represented a close alliance between government and big business, died as a result of wounds inflicted by a demented anarchist, Leon Czolgosz, at the Pan-American Exposition in Buffalo; and he was succeeded by Theodore Roosevelt.

Born on October 27, 1858, of a prosperous and long-established New York family, Roosevelt had gone to Harvard, had served one term in the New York State legislature, had spent parts of the years 1884–1887 cattle-ranching in Dakota, and had subsequently been a member of the United States Civil Service Commission, president of the New York City Police Commission, and Assistant Secretary of the Navy. After his performances in Cuba he had been elected governor of New York State and had annoyed the Republican Party boss, Senator Platt, by imposing taxes on corporation franchises and by changing the state superintendent of insurance. In order to get rid of him, Platt boosted him for the vice presidency in 1900; and his candidacy was supported by other state bosses who wished to annoy Mark Hanna, the real leader of the Republican Party. It also evoked wide popular enthusiasm. Hanna, who suspected that Roosevelt did not share McKinley's reverence for big business, accepted

Roosevelt as Vice President with reluctance, referring to him as "that damned cowboy" and asking his fellow bosses if they did not realize that there would be "only one life between that madman and the presidency." Roosevelt himself, expecting to be shelved by the party leaders after his term was over, planned to start a new career by reading law with the Chief Justice.

Czolgosz's bullet put into the White House the youngest President that the United States had ever had and the first President since Lincoln who was capable of real statesmanship. Roosevelt believed that the powers of the President should be greatly increased, declaring that "it was not only his right but his duty to do anything that the needs of the Nation demanded, unless such action was forbidden by the Constitution or by the laws." He was able to win popular support for his activities by his talent for dramatizing them and coining singularly vivid phrases. Fundamentally a conservative, with no desire to change the existing system of property relations, he was shocked by the low ethical standards prevalent in business and by the apparent conviction of the corporation magnates that they should be independent of the laws and the government. He believed that if business were not compelled to conform to higher standards, American capitalism would be endangered by a growth of revolutionary sentiments. Roosevelt's real conservatism, his ability to work with and through the old-guard Republican leaders, and the frequent discrepancy between his words and his deeds—the former often being much more radical than the latter—caused many of the Progressives, particularly Robert La Follette, to denounce him as dishonest and insincere. Such accusations derived support from two factors—Roosevelt's capacity for self-deception, which sometimes caused him to violate promises and change policies without admitting it, and the egotism which prevented him from being just to men against whom he cherished personal grudges.

The changes made by Roosevelt in the functioning of the economic system were, in fact, meager; but his real importance was that he was the first President since the Civil War to insist on the principle of government supremacy over business. By his varied intellectual and aesthetic interests, moreover, which had been equaled among American Presidents only by Thomas Jefferson, and by the energy with which he both preached and practiced the strenuous life, he did much to elevate the tone of American politics. His most dangerous weaknesses were his passion for militarism and his leaning toward imperialism.

Roosevelt's accession to the presidency caused considerable alarm in business circles, but Roosevelt declared at once that he proposed to follow in the footsteps of his predecessor and to co-operate with Hanna and with the old-guard Republican leaders in Congress, Senator Aldrich and Speaker Cannon. He retained the somewhat mediocre cabinet inherited from McKinley, which was headed by Secretary of State John Hay. Hay, however, was now old and feeble, and Roosevelt relied for advice chiefly on Elihu Root, the Secretary of War, recognizing that Root's capacity for dispassionate analysis provided a valuable check on his own impulsiveness. In 1904 William H. Taft returned from the Philippines to succeed Root, and in the following year Root succeeded Hay. During Roosevelt's second term, he, Root, and Taft, who were united by close friendship as well as by political agreement, liked to regard themselves as "the three musketeers."

THE TRUSTS

Public opinion regarded the growth of the trusts as the most important national problem; and big business quickly discovered that in spite of Roosevelt's promise to follow McKinley, he intended to interpret his duties as President in a different spirit. Roosevelt's first message to Congress was a lengthy and studiously moderate document, the most important feature of which was a statement that "in dealing with the big corporations we call trusts we must resolutely purpose to proceed by evolution and not by revolution." "We do not wish to destroy corporations; but we do wish to make them subserve the public good." "The biggest corporation like the humblest private citizen must be held to strict compliance with the will of the people as expressed in the fundamental law."

It soon appeared that Roosevelt intended these phrases as more than soothing generalities. In March, 1902, he ordered Attorney General Knox to bring suit under the Sherman Act, hitherto almost a dead letter, against the Northern Securities Company, which had been established by Hill, Harriman, and Morgan in order to monopolize the railroad facilities of the Northwest. This sudden action caused great indignation on Wall Street; and Morgan, regarding Roosevelt as a kind of rival rather than as a superior authority, urged him to send "your man to my man" to arrange a settlement. The Supreme Court eventually decided against the Northern Securities Company by a vote of five to four. Roosevelt then went on to attack a number of other trusts, among them being Standard Oil, the American Tobacco Company, the Du Pont powder trust, and the meat-packing trust; and he secured in all, during his seven and a half years in office, twenty-five indictments and eighteen bills in equity.

The economic results of this trust-busting crusade, however, scarcely justified the furore which it excited. Court decisions compelled the trusts to dissolve themselves into their component parts, but it could not transfer these parts to new ownership. Hence, there was no real revival of competition. "Community of interest" arrangements, beyond the reach of court action, took the place of legal ties as the method by which business magnates maintained high prices and limited production. The Sherman Act, moreover, was gradually weakened by the Supreme Court. The act had originally defined combination in restraint of trade as a criminal action; but in the Northern Securities Case both the government and the Court agreed that the defendants should be immune from criminal penalties—a step which caused Oliver Wendell Holmes, recently appointed a justice by Roosevelt, to vote with the minority. Although, moreover, the Court originally agreed that the Sherman Act forbade all combinations, it subsequently decided that it should apply only to those which were "unreasonable." In the Standard Oil and American Tobacco Cases, which did not reach the Court until 1911 and 1912, the justices declared that only "undue" restraint of trade was forbidden. This adoption of the rule of reason meant that the ultimate authority over business now belonged to the Court rather than to the government.

Roosevelt recognized the inadequacy of trust-busting as a method for reforming the economic system. Making a distinction between good trusts and bad trusts, he declared that "we draw the line against misconduct, not against wealth." Unlike Bryan and the Democratic Party leaders, who wished to prevent any corporation from controlling more than 50 per cent of an industry, Roosevelt believed that big business should be accepted, but that it should be subordinated to the public interest. During his second term he urged that corporations be licensed and regulated by the Federal government instead of by the state governments and that various specific malpractices be prohibited, but bills to that effect were rejected by the Senate. He believed, however, that the most important questions involved were not so much economic as political and legal. "When I became President," he declared in his *Autobiography*, "the question of the method by which the United States Government was to control the corporations was not yet important. The absolutely vital question was whether the Government had power to control them at all." "These men demanded for themselves an immunity from governmental control which, if granted, would be as wicked and as foolish as immunity to the barons of the twelfth century."

OTHER ACTIVITIES OF ROOSEVELT'S FIRST TERM

Roosevelt's next intervention in the workings of the economic system was equally unprecedented. The miners of anthracite coal were one of the most exploited groups in the United States. Their wages averaged $560 a year; their employment was very irregular; their families received no compensation in cases of death or injury; and they lived in company houses and had to buy at company stores. The railroad magnates who operated the coal fields had a feudal attitude toward their workers which shocked even Mark Hanna and J. P. Morgan. A remarkably able and dynamic young labor leader, John Mitchell, succeeded in recruiting the miners into the United Mine Workers' Union; and in the summer of 1900 they struck for higher wages. Since a coal shortage might endanger the re-election of McKinley, Mark Hanna persuaded the operators to grant a 10 per cent increase in wages.

In 1902 the United Mine Workers asked for union recognition,

a nine-hour day, guarantees that the coal dug would be accurately
weighed, and a 20 per cent increase in wages. In March, 1902,
after the operators had refused to negotiate, 150 thousand miners
went on strike. There was considerable popular sympathy for the
miners, and this was increased when the principal employer, George
F. Baer of the Reading and Philadelphia, declared in reply to a
letter urging him to end the strike, that "the rights and interests of the
laboring man will be protected and cared for—not by the labor agitators, but by the Christian men to whom God in His infinite wisdom
has given the control of the property interests of this country."

By the autumn there was danger of a scarcity of coal, and Roosevelt resolved to intervene—not, as Cleveland had done in the Pullman strike, to support the employers but to enforce negotiation. He
called representatives of both sides to a conference at the White
House, but the operators refused to negotiate with Mitchell, whom
they regarded as no better than a criminal. Roosevelt then made
plans to send the army into the coal fields to dig coal, and meanwhile Elihu Root induced J. P. Morgan to support arbitration and
to put pressure on the mine owners. The owners finally consented
to arbitration by a government commission; and, although they
would not allow labor to be officially represented on the commission, they made no objection when Roosevelt appointed a trade
union leader but called him an "eminent sociologist."

The decisions of the commission were that the union should not
win recognition, but that the workers should receive a nine-hour
day and a 10 per cent increase in wages, they should have their own
checkweighman at the scales, and a board of conciliation should be
established to negotiate future disputes. The settlement was followed by ten years of peace in the coal fields. In 1912 the workers
won another wage increase after a month's strike, and in 1916 they
secured an eight-hour day and union recognition.

Legislation during Roosevelt's first term was relatively unimportant. Congress passed only three acts that deserve mention. In 1902
the Newlands Act established the Reclamation Service and provided
for the establishment of irrigation projects by the Federal government with money derived from public land sales. By 1915 a million

and a quarter acres of arid land in the West had thus been opened to agriculture. In 1903 Roosevelt secured the creation of a Department of Commerce and Labor, which included a Bureau of Corporations. Congressional opposition to this measure was overcome when Roosevelt made public a series of telegrams sent by Archbold of Standard Oil, which revealed the corrupt connections between big business and certain senators. Also in 1903 there was passed, with the approval of the railroads, the Elkins Act which forbade the giving of rebates on freight rates and declared that corporations receiving rebates were to be fined for each offence. How strictly the act would be enforced, however, remained to be seen. In 1907 Judge Kenesaw Mountain Landis condemned a Standard Oil affiliate in Indiana to pay a fine of $29,240,000 for accepting a series of rebates; but this decision was reversed by a higher court, and the company was acquitted.

Roosevelt's relative caution during his first term was due mainly to his fear that he might not be renominated. His leadership of the Republican Party was, however, strengthened by the death of Hanna in February, 1904; and in the summer he secured the party nomination for a second term without opposition. The Democrats, abandoning Bryan, adopted as their presidential candidate a conservative Easterner, Judge Alton B. Parker of New York. They no longer demanded coinage of silver or an income tax, and thus they hoped to secure business support. The corporation magnates, however, still preferred the Republicans and contributed lavishly to Roosevelt's campaign fund, Harriman giving a quarter of a million dollars and Standard Oil a hundred thousand. Roosevelt was re-elected by a popular vote of 7,628,834 to 5,084,491 and an electoral vote of 336 to 140. Debs as Socialist nominee received 402,283 votes; and Watson, nominated by the surviving Populists, received 114,753. The Republicans also won large majorities in both houses of Congress. Immediately after the election Roosevelt made a statement which he afterwards regretted. "Under no circumstances," he declared, "will I be a candidate for or accept another nomination." Henceforth he was much more outspoken in his denunciations of big business.

THE RAILROADS, PURE FOOD, AND CONSERVATION

The most important achievement of Roosevelt's second term was the Hepburn Act, passed in 1906, which revitalized the Interstate Commerce Commission and gave it real authority over the railroads. Roosevelt's original proposals, which were more drastic than the act as finally passed, were accepted by the House of Representatives, where Speaker Cannon, in spite of his own conservatism, considered it his duty to co-operate with the administration; but they were vigorously opposed by the old-guard Republicans in the Senate. Roosevelt had to allow a Democrat, Tillman of South Carolina, to take charge of the bill and to agree to compromises.

In its final form the Hepburn Act extended the authority of the Commission over all forms of transportation, forbade the giving of railroad passes except to railroad employees, required the railroad corporations to divorce themselves from their ownership of coal fields, and gave the Commission power, when there were complaints by shippers, to reduce unreasonable rates. Rate reductions were, however, to be subject to judicial review and were not to go into effect until the courts had agreed that they were reasonable, although the burden of proof was placed on the railroads and not on the Commission. The authority thus given to the courts was denounced by Progressives, who wanted some clearer definition of what constituted a reasonable rate; and La Follette urged that the Commission be empowered to assess the physical value of the railroad properties, so that the rates might be judged in relation to the capital really invested in them rather than to their nominal capitalization, which included so much watered stock.

The Hepburn Act proved to be more effective than the Progressives had anticipated, and within two years of its enactment there were nine thousand complaints by shippers against unreasonable railroad practices. But few of these related to rates, and it was dubious whether the Commission had acquired effective power to force reductions. In 1910, however, the powers of the Commission were further extended by the Mann-Elkins Act, which gave the Commission authority over the telephone and telegraph systems, and allowed the Commission to suspend rate increases until it had been decided whether they were reasonable. Passage of the act was hastened by an announcement on the part of the railroad companies that they proposed to increase rates, and in 1911 this increase was prohibited by the Commission. La Follette's proposal for a physical valuation of railroad properties was accepted by Congress in 1913. Finally, in 1920, the Esch-Cummins Act gave the Commission full power to fix all railroad rates and to regulate the finances of the railroad corporations.

Two other important laws passed in 1906 were the Meat Inspection Act and the Pure Food and Drug Act. Chemical experts in the pay of the state and Federal governments, originally appointed to serve the interests of the farmers, had for some years been investigating the widespread adulteration of foods by manufacturers and the selling of harmful patent medicines; and popular indignation had also been provoked by a number of startling disclosures, particularly those made by Harvey W. Wiley of the U. S. Department of Agriculture. However, the Senate had previously rejected several pure food bills on the old principle of "caveat emptor." The patent medicine interests, moreover, were well protected from newspaper criticism by means of an unscrupulous use of advertising pressure.

The pure food crusaders won Roosevelt's support in 1905, but Congress again refused to take action. In the spring of 1906, however, Roosevelt read Upton Sinclair's *The Jungle*. He appointed a commission to investigate conditions in the packing houses, and the commission reported that the reality was even worse than Sinclair's lurid descriptions of it. When the meat-packing interests succeeded in blocking a bill providing for government inspection of the packing houses, Roosevelt made public some of the findings of the commission, with the result that the sales of canned meat immediately dropped by one-half. In June, 1906, popular indignation forced Congress to accept the Meat Inspection Bill and, at the same time, a Pure Food and Drug Bill which prohibited the sale of harmful foods and ordered that foods and medicines be correctly labeled. This was a step in the right direction, although as a result partly of weaknesses in the act and partly of inadequate enforcement it by no means ended the selling of adulterated or harmful products. In the nineteen-thirties the patent medicine interests were still fighting against stronger legislation, and it was not until 1938 that Congress passed a more effective Pure Food, Drug, and Cosmetic Act.

Another and even more vital national problem to which Roosevelt drew attention was the need for conservation of natural resources. Roosevelt was the first President to realize the importance of preventing the unchecked exploitation of timber and mineral supplies by business interests concerned merely with immediate profits. A United States Geological Survey had been established in 1879, and under the directorship of F. H. Newell it had been studying the surviving natural wealth on the public lands. In 1891 followed the Forest Reserve Act, which authorized the President to retain public ownership of timber lands. Some 36 million acres had been so reserved by Harrison, Cleveland, and McKinley, and had been placed in charge of a United States Forest Service. Among government officials, however, in Roosevelt's opinion, "the habit of deciding, wherever possible, in favor of private interests against the public welfare was firmly fixed." Roosevelt endeavored to inculcate a different point of view, in which he was assisted by James R. Garfield, who became Secretary of the Interior in 1907, and by the director of the Forest Service, Gifford Pinchot, who devoted himself to the cause of conservation with a zeal which approached fanaticism. Between 1906 and 1908 Roosevelt added about 150 million acres to the forest reserves. In this he included not only genuine timber lands but also—with dubious legality and in spite of protests in Congress—lands which contained coal, phosphates, and water-power sites. Roosevelt's interest in public ownership of water power was indicated also by his veto of a bill which would have allowed a private power company to build a dam at Muscle Shoals on the Tennessee River.

Roosevelt was anxious that the state governments co-operate with the Federal government in conservation, and in 1908 he called a White House Conference of state governors. The Conference recommended that the Federal government retain ownership of all public lands containing minerals and that ownership of the surface of the soil be separated from ownership of the subsoil. Roosevelt failed to secure supporting legislation from Congress, though his activity had an important effect in awakening public opinion to the seriousness of the problem and led to the appointment of conservation commissions in forty-one of the states.

Roosevelt's denunciations of the "malefactors of great wealth" grew steadily more bitter throughout his second term; and when, in October, 1907, the stock market suddenly slumped and there were numerous bankruptcies, the financiers accused the President of having provoked it by undermining business confidence. The aftermath of the panic was, however, chiefly notable for an episode which showed how far Roosevelt was from being an economic radical. The brokerage house of Moore and Schley was in financial difficulties, and its collapse threatened to cause further bankruptcies on Wall Street. The house owned 5 million dollars' worth of stock in the Tennessee Coal and Iron Company, for which it was unable to find purchasers; and J. P. Morgan decided that the situation could be saved if Tennessee Coal and Iron was purchased by United States Steel. He sent Gary and Frick to ask Roosevelt for a guarantee that the purchase would not be followed by a prosecution under the Sherman Act; and without learning all the details Roosevelt gave his assent. United States Steel thereupon added Tennessee Coal and Iron to its properties at a price of 45 million dollars. Enemies of big business declared that Morgan and Gary had deliberately made use of the crisis in order to acquire Tennessee Coal and Iron for much less than its real value and that they had misled Roosevelt as to the facts of the situation. That Roosevelt later came to suspect that Morgan had outwitted him was suggested by the extraordinary vehemence with which he defended what he had done.

During his last year in office Roosevelt sent a long series of messages to Congress, attacking the misdeeds of business, denouncing the conservatism of the courts, and demanding income and inheritance taxes. His approaching retirement, however, deprived him of any effective control over legislation, and the Republican leaders ignored almost all his recommendations. Roosevelt was, however, in a position to nominate his successor, because of the control always enjoyed by a Republican President over the southern delegates to the Republican convention. His own preference was Elihu Root; but Root was liable to attack on account of his long career as a wealthy corporation lawyer. After considering and rejecting the claims of Charles Evans Hughes, Governor of New York, Roosevelt secured the nomination for William Howard Taft. The Democratic Party, for the third and last time, nominated Bryan. Taft was elected President by a popular vote of 7,679,006 to 6,409,106, and an electoral vote of 321 to 162; and the Republicans retained substantial majorities in both houses of Congress. The popular vote for Debs was 420,890, and for Watson 29,146. In 1909, at the age of only fifty-one, Roosevelt left office and departed for a long visit to Africa and Europe.

BIBLIOGRAPHY

L. F. Abbott (ed.), *Letters of Archie Butt* (1924)
J. B. Bishop, *Roosevelt and His Time* (1920)
C. G. Bowers, *Beveridge and the Progressive Era* (1932)
L. D. Einstein, *Roosevelt: His Mind in Action* (1930)
*P. C. Jessup, *Elihu Root* (1938)
E. Jones, *The Trust Problem* (1926)
M. Josephson, *The President-Makers* (1940)
J. Ise, *United States Forest Policy* (1920)
H. C. Lodge, *Selections from the Correspondence of Theodore Roosevelt and Henry Cabot Lodge* (1925)
W. F. McCaleb, *Theodore Roosevelt* (1931)
B. H. Meyer, *History of the Northern Securities Case* (1906)
F. G. Newlands, *Public Papers* (edited by A. B. Darling, 1932)
*H. F. Pringle, *Theodore Roosevelt* (1931)
*——— *William Howard Taft* (1939)
W. Z. Ripley, *Railroads: Rates and Regulations* (1912)
——— *Trusts, Pools and Corporations* (1916)
T. Roosevelt, *Autobiography* (1913)
*H. R. Seager and C. A. Gulick, *Trust and Corporation Problems* (1929)
N. W. Stephenson, *Nelson W. Aldrich* (1930)
M. Sullivan, *Our Times*, Vols. I–III (1926–30)
W. R. Thayer, *Theodore Roosevelt* (1919)
C. R. Van Hise and L. Havemeyer, *Conservation of our Natural Resources* (1930)
H. W. Wiley, *Autobiography* (1930)
O. Wister, *Roosevelt: The Story of a Friendship* (1930)

18

THE TAFT ADMINISTRATION

ROOSEVELT'S energy and versatility, and his talent for inspiring newspaper headlines, had made him for seven and a half years the focus of public attention. Almost any successor would have seemed, by contrast, to be tame and uninspiring. Taft therefore began his administration under a severe handicap; nor did he have the political cleverness or the capacity for leadership needed to surmount it. Honest, good humored, placid, and likeable, he had been a capable, industrious, and loyal subordinate; but he had too little force and subtlety of character to fill the highest place. By temperament he was better suited for a judicial than for an executive position.

Born in Ohio in 1857, Taft had been in public office since a year after his graduation from Yale; but of the nine posts which he had filled, eight had been appointive and only one elective. He had been Solicitor General under Harrison, a Federal judge, Governor of the Philippines, and Secretary of War. His own strongest wish was to serve on the Supreme Court, to which Roosevelt had three times offered to appoint him; but he had allowed himself to be persuaded by his wife and his brother to aim instead at the presidency. He shared Roosevelt's progressive inclinations, and endeavored to follow in Roosevelt's footsteps; but he differed from Roosevelt in his greater respect for the letter of the constitution and for the legal rights of property. Instead of extending presidential initiative, as Roosevelt had done, he preferred to follow the constitutional principle that Congress should make the laws and the President should enforce them. In reality, his administration was perhaps more fruitful in progressive legislation than was Roosevelt's; but Taft received little of the credit for it and finally found himself branded by public opinion as a champion of conservatism.

Taft was, moreover, unfortunate in assuming the presidency at a time when the Republican Party was beginning to split into two factions, one conservative and the other insurgent. Under Roosevelt the conservatives had dominated Congress, and Roosevelt had worked in co-operation with the conservative leaders, Aldrich and Cannon. By 1909, however, the growth of Progressivism in the state governments had led to the formation of a Progressive bloc in Congress. There was now a group of Progressive Republicans, headed by La Follette in the Senate and by George W. Norris of Nebraska in the House, who were bitterly opposed to Aldrich and Cannon and were hoping for presidential support. Confronted by a dilemma which only a man of the greatest political subtlety could have overcome, Taft continued to co-operate with the conservatives. He was thereupon denounced by the Progressives as a tool of predatory business interests.

The Taft administration, nevertheless, was marked by numerous reforms. The Progressive movement derived its impetus from the work of the reformers in the states and from the doctrines preached by Theodore Roosevelt; but Taft loyally supported it, except in those instances when he believed that Progressive demands were blocked by legal obstacles or that the President had no power to act. Aldrich and the Senate conservatives, moreover, were astute enough to understand the growing power of Progressivism and to realize the need for making concessions.

The Taft administration brought ninety suits against the large corporations under the Sherman Act, as contrasted with Roosevelt's record of forty-four. Among the trusts attacked were the American Sugar Refining Company, the International Harvester Company, the National Cash Register Company, General Electric, and United States Steel. The suit against United States Steel was based on its purchase of Tennessee Coal and Iron—a procedure which, however justifiable, was politically unfortunate since it was bitterly resented by Theodore Roosevelt. This case did not reach the Supreme Court until 1920, by which time the trust-busting crusade had been obliterated by the World War; and it ended in a legal victory for United States Steel.

Other measures passed during Taft's presidency were the Mann-Elkins Act of 1910 strengthening the powers of the Interstate Commerce Commission; the creation of a separate Department of Labor and a Children's Bureau; the establishment in 1910 of a Postal Savings Bank and in 1912 of the parcel post; and two laws, enacted in 1910 and 1911, requiring that expenditures in Federal political campaigns, and the sources from which the parties derived financial support, be made public. In 1913 Alaska was organized as a territory, and New Mexico and Arizona were admitted as states, the latter episode being notable for an unsuccessful attempt by Taft to prevent Arizona from adopting in her constitution a clause providing for the recall of judges. The Sixteenth Amendment, authorizing an income tax, and the Seventeenth Amendment, providing for the popular election of senators, were, moreover, passed by Congress with Taft's support in 1909 and 1910, and were ratified in 1913.

The problem that brought out into the open the split in Congress between the conservative and the Progressive Republicans was that of the tariff. There had been no change in the schedules since the Dingley Act of 1897, which popular sentiment now felt to be too high and too favorable to big business. Roosevelt had not dared to handle the question, partly because he knew the difficulty of securing reductions and partly because he felt that he did not sufficiently understand financial questions. He therefore bequeathed the problem to his successor. The Republican platform of 1908 promised that the tariff would be revised; and Taft made it plain that, in his opinion, revision meant reduction. He thereupon called a special session of Congress immediately after his inauguration to undertake the task. The House of Representatives quickly passed a bill providing for considerably lower schedules; but when the bill reached the Senate, Aldrich and the Senate Finance Committee proceeded to insert some six hundred increases. For eleven weeks Aldrich's proposals were attacked by a group of Progressives, including La Follette of Wisconsin, Dolliver and Cummins of Iowa, Beveridge of Indiana, and Bristow of Kansas. It became very ap-

parent during the debates that whereas the Progressives had genuinely studied the question, the conservatives had merely written
into the bill the wishes of the manufacturers and did not understand their own proposals. The Progressives had been hoping for
support from Taft; but apart from persuading the Senate Finance
Committee to adopt a 1 per cent tax on the earnings of corporations, to support the income tax, and to make some extensions in
the free list, Taft left the question in Aldrich's hands.

Aldrich's bill finally passed the Senate, and most of his proposals
were subsequently accepted by the House. Taft again disappointed
the Progressives by refusing to veto the bill; and the Aldrich-Payne
tariff became law on August 5, 1909. Whether the tariff had actually been raised or lowered it is almost impossible to say. Of the
schedules in the Dingley Tariff, 650 had been lowered, 220 had
been raised, and 1,150 had been left unchanged. The Progressives
maintained, however, that the reductions had been made only on
such commodities as coal, lumber, iron, and steel where there was
no possibility of foreign competition and that many of the increases
would enable big business to exact higher prices from the consumer.
The schedules for wool and sugar were particularly resented. Other
features of the act were the corporation tax and the establishment
of a commission which was to study the tariff scientifically and,
when necessary, recommend changes. Taft particularly approved of
the latter measure, but the commission proved to be of little value
and was abolished by the Democratic majority in Congress in 1912.

The unpopularity which Taft had incurred by failing to put
pressure on the conservatives was increased when, in a most unfortunate speech at Winona, Minnesota, he described the act as
"the best tariff bill that the Republican Party has ever passed."
There was wide agreement when Senator Dolliver described the
president as "an amiable man, completely surrounded by men who
know exactly what they want."

Another of Taft's misfortunes was a controversy over conservation. Roosevelt had withdrawn lands from public entry by executive
order. Taft regarded this method as of doubtful legality and preferred to act through Congress, which in 1910 passed a series of

nine laws, separating ownership of the surface from ownership of the subsoil and adding a number of timber, mineral, oil, and water-power sites to the lands reserved for permanent government ownership. After promising to reappoint Garfield as Secretary of the Interior, Taft replaced him by Richard A. Ballinger, of Seattle, who was distrusted by the Progressives because he had formerly been a corporation lawyer. Ballinger, because he believed that Roosevelt had acted illegally, restored to public entry certain water-power sites in Montana and Wyoming which had been included by Roosevelt among the lands placed in reserve. His action was bitterly opposed by Gifford Pinchot, who regarded the cause of conservation as more important than obedience to the letter of the law.

Ballinger also incurred the enmity of Louis R. Glavis, an official of the General Land Office. Some 5,280 acres of coal land in Alaska were claimed by the Cunningham syndicate, which was supposed to be affiliated with the Morgan and Guggenheim interests. Glavis was investigating this claim, and he came to believe that Ballinger, who had formerly served as attorney for the Cunningham syndicate, was trying to have the claim validated without sufficient inquiry. Pinchot supported Glavis' accusation. Taft and Attorney General Wickersham examined the charges made against Ballinger by Pinchot and Glavis and came to the conclusion that Ballinger was entirely honest—a verdict with which later students of the question have usually agreed.

Instead of accepting Taft's decision, however, Pinchot and Glavis proceeded to make their suspicions public, initiating a series of violent attacks on Ballinger by progressive journalists and congressmen, who declared that the Department of the Interior had been turned over to the Guggenheims. Taft then had no alternative but to dismiss Pinchot and Glavis for breaking the rules of official discipline. Ballinger was exonerated by a congressional investigation, but he resigned shortly after. The episode strengthened the belief of the Progressives that the administration was controlled by big business.

The growing strength of the Republican insurgents was exhibited in March, 1910, when they succeeded in stripping Speaker

Cannon of the semidictatorial powers which he exercised over the House of Representatives. The Progressives had always regarded Cannon as one of their particular enemies, and the journalist Mark Sullivan organized a press campaign to arouse public opinion against him. The revolt against Cannon was headed by George W. Norris, who had come to Congress in 1902 at the age of forty-one as an orthodox Republican but had rapidly been disillusioned by what he saw there. Norris succeeded in winning a majority vote for a proposal that the Rules Committee, which determined what business should be discussed by the House, be enlarged to fifteen and be elected by the members of the House instead of nominated by the Speaker and the minority leader. The power of the Speaker to control legislation was further diminished the following year, when the appointment of all other committees was transferred to the Ways and Means Committee.

The elections of 1910 resulted in Democratic and insurgent victories. The Democrats won a majority in the House of Representatives and elected governors in New York, New Jersey, Ohio, Massachusetts, and Connecticut. Progressive Republicans controlled Michigan, Wisconsin, Indiana, and most of the states west of the Mississippi. The remainder of Taft's term was occupied chiefly by constant conflict between President and Congress.

Taft suffered yet another disappointment through the failure of a reciprocity agreement that he negotiated with Canada, which provided for free trade in food products and for reductions in the duties on manufactured articles. Although it was denounced by the Progressives as favoring American industry at the expense of American agriculture, this measure was accepted by the Senate. However, Champ Clark, the new Democratic Speaker of the House, declared that he was for it because he hoped "to see the day when the American flag will float over every square foot of the British North American possessions clear to the North Pole," and similar pronouncements were made in the newspapers of William Randolph Hearst. These imperialistic sentiments enabled the Canadian manufacturers to secure a rejection of the treaty by the Canadian Parliament.

BIBLIOGRAPHY

L. W. Busbey, *Uncle Joe Cannon* (1927)
C. G. Bowers, *Beveridge and the Progressive Era* (1932)
C. Clark, *My Quarter-Century of American Politics* (1920)
K. W. Hechsler, *Insurgency* (1940)
E. Jones, *The Trust Problem* (1926)
M. Josephson, *The President-Makers* (1940)
R. M. LaFollette, *Autobiography* (1913)
R. L. Neuberger and S. B. Kahn, *Integrity: The Life of George W. Norris*
    (1937)
G. Pinchot, *The Fight for Conservation* (1910)
*H. F. Pringle, *William Howard Taft* (1939)
W. Z. Ripley, *Trusts, Pools and Corporations* (1916)
*H. R. Seager and C. A. Gulick, *Trust and Corporation Problems* (1929)
R. M. Stahl, *The Ballinger-Pinchot Controversy (Smith College Studies
    in History,* Vol. 11, 1926)
N. W. Stephenson, *Nelson W. Aldrich* (1930)
M Sullivan, *Our Times,* Vol. IV (1932)
———— *The Education of an American* (1938)
I. M. Tarbell, *The Tariff in our Times* (1931)
F. W. Taussig, *Tariff History of the United States* (revised edition, 1931)

19

THE ELECTION OF 1912

PREPARATIONS for the presidential campaign of 1912 began on January 21, 1911, when the National Progressive Republican League was organized. The Progressives planned to capture the Republican Party and to prevent Taft from being nominated for a second term. La Follette hoped to become the beneficiary of a Progressive victory, and in the summer he launched a campaign for the Republican nomination.

Meanwhile Theodore Roosevelt, still vigorous and relatively young, was finding the position of an unemployed ex-president, with no political future, exceedingly irksome. He had returned to the United States in June, 1910, resolved, in fairness to Taft, to avoid political controversies; but he was immediately surrounded by men, such as Gifford Pinchot, who believed that Taft was betraying the cause of Progressivism and that it was Roosevelt's duty to return to active politics. Nor was Roosevelt sufficiently magnanimous to recognize that Taft might have had good reasons for adopting different methods and choosing different advisors; whatever innovations Taft had made in the presidential policies he interpreted as an implied rebuke to himself. The two men had begun to move apart on the day when Taft took office. Taft had angered Roosevelt by failing to reappoint more than two members of Roosevelt's cabinet; and many of the friends of both men had encouraged them to feel suspicious of each other. After returning to America, Roosevelt continued for eighteen months to give Taft at least nominal support. He was, however, unable to remain in retirement, and his utterances became increasingly radical.

In the summer of 1910 Governor Hughes persuaded him to support a proposal for adopting primary elections in New York; and, when the proposal was defeated by the conservative Republicans, Roosevelt's irritation caused him to swing further to the left. In August he made a speaking tour of the country, nominally in order to support the Republican Party in the congressional elections; but the doctrines which he advocated were almost identical with those of La Follette and the insurgents. In a speech at Osawatomie, Kansas, he proclaimed what he called the "new nationalism" and the "square deal." "I mean," he explained, "not merely that I stand for fair play under the present rules of the game but that I stand for having the rules changed so as to work for a more substantial equality of opportunity and of reward for equally good services." The changes of the rules which Roosevelt specified as necessary included not only such economic reforms as he had supported when President—Federal regulation of corporations, conservation, revision of the tariff, income and inheritance taxes, labor codes, child labor regulation, and publicity for contributions to campaign funds—but also the whole Western program of political reform—primaries, the initiative, the referendum, the recall, and the recall of judicial decisions. The inclusion of this last item, which Roosevelt supported by vigorously denouncing the conservatism of the judiciary, was especially alarming to the conservatives. After the elections of 1910, Roosevelt still refrained from directly attacking Taft; but he gave general support to the Progressive Republican League and seemed favorably disposed to La Follette's campaign for the nomination. And as late as December 20, 1911, he declared that he did not want to be president again and that he had not the slightest idea of becoming a candidate.

Many of the Progressives, however, preferred Roosevelt to La Follette. The glamour of Roosevelt's personality and his immense personal popularity made him a much stronger candidate, and his relatively conservative record as president attracted many moderate reformers who regarded La Follette as too radical and too doctrinaire. While Roosevelt's recent speeches had won the approval of the Western insurgents, he continued also to have close associations with certain wealthy Easterners who were willing to give him financial support—particularly George W. Perkins of the House of Morgan and the newspaper publisher, Frank Munsey. La Follette's presidential hopes collapsed on February 2, 1912, when—as a result of overwork and his daughter's serious illness—he lost control of himself during a speech at Philadelphia and continued talking, with complete incoherence, until most of his audience had gone. Meanwhile Roosevelt's personal resentment against Taft broke all bounds when the government instituted suit against United States Steel for absorbing Tennessee Coal and Iron and when Taft made a speech (which Roosevelt interpreted as a personal reference) denouncing the more radical reformers as "political emotionalists" and "neurotics." On February 10, by arrangement with Roosevelt, a group of Republican state governors invited him to become a candidate, and two weeks later Roosevelt declared that his hat was in the ring.

The fight between Roosevelt and Taft for the Republican nomination was a deplorable exhibition of mudslinging. Roosevelt bitterly denounced the man whom he himself had selected for the presidency as feeble, incompetent, and ungrateful, and implied that Taft's primary obligations were not to the American people but to himself. Taft, with more sense of personal decency but equal lack of dignity, apologized for attacking Roosevelt by telling the public that "even a rat in a corner will fight." The party convention met at Chicago in June, 1912. From those states, thirteen in number, which had adopted the presidential primary, three-quarters of the delegates were for Roosevelt. The conservatives, however, had a majority of the delegates from the other states; and the administration could, as usual, count on the support of the delegations from the South. There were rival delegations from Indiana, Michigan, and Wisconsin; and the credentials committee, which had been appointed in 1908 and was controlled by the conservatives, decided these disputes in favor of the Taft delegations.

At the first meeting of the convention Elihu Root, the candidate of the conservatives, was elected chairman; and it became obvious that the Progressives had failed in their effort to capture the party. Roosevelt ordered his supporters to leave the convention, and Taft

was then renominated on the first ballot. Whether a different decision in the case of the disputed delegations would have given
Roosevelt a majority is doubtful. And although Roosevelt was
unquestionably supported by a majority of the rank and file of the
Republican voters, it would be unjust to accuse the conservatives of
having deprived him of the nomination by fraud. They had merely
used the traditional methods of manipulating the party machinery,
which had been employed by Roosevelt himself in securing the
nomination for Taft in 1908. Roosevelt, however, declared that Taft
was a beneficiary of a "successful fraud," that he had "no claim to
the support of any Republican on party grounds," and that he had
"forfeited the right to win the support of any honest man on moral
grounds."

Roosevelt's supporters met again at Chicago on August 5 to
launch the Progressive Party. The convention was a curious mixture
of Western insurgents who liked Roosevelt's principles, wealthy
Easterners who liked his personality, and social reformers of all
kinds, including many from what Roosevelt had once called the
"lunatic fringe." After a keynote speech by Senator Beveridge of
Indiana, Roosevelt was nominated for the presidency, with Hiram
Johnson of California as his running mate. When Roosevelt arrived
in Chicago to accept the nomination, he told reporters that he felt
like a bull moose; and the bull moose was adopted as an appropriate
symbol for the new party. The proceedings ended in a spirit of religious enthusiasm. Roosevelt concluded his speech of acceptance by
declaring that "we stand at Armageddon, and we battle for the
Lord," and the convention then sang *Onward, Christian Soldiers*.

From the viewpoint of Progressivism the Bull Moose movement
was a disastrous mistake. Its only results were to make it inevitable
that the Democrats would win the 1912 election and to leave the
conservatives in complete control of the Republican Party. Being
primarily the expression of a single man's ambition, the Bull Moose
Party had no permanent vitality; and, after failing to recapture the
presidency, Roosevelt proceeded to desert his followers and kill his
party. The Progressives then had no alternative but to return to
Republicanism. They had lost influence and prestige through their

temporary desertion and were further than before from capturing
the party machinery.

The Democrats met at Baltimore on June 25. The two leading
candidates were Champ Clark of Missouri, Speaker of the House of
Representatives, and Woodrow Wilson of New Jersey. Bryan, present as a member of the Nebraska delegation, was still the leading
figure in the party; and his attitude would largely determine the
final decision of the convention.

Wilson had first been suggested as a presidential possibility in
1906 by George Harvey, a New York publisher with Wall Street
connections. Although he came from Vermont, Harvey happened
to be a Democrat; and he was looking for a conservative leader who
could oust Bryan and the western radicals from control of the party
machinery. Wilson was born in Virginia in 1856, studied at Princeton and Johns Hopkins, taught and wrote on American history and
politics, and in 1902 was appointed president of Princeton University. In this position Wilson's forceful personality and eloquent
speeches began to attract national attention. He was uninterested in
economic questions at this period; and, although his democratic
sentiments were unimpeachable, he was hostile to Bryanism and
showed little understanding of the need for the kind of reform which
the Progressives were advocating. Admiring the type of leadership
produced by the English parliamentary system, Wilson proclaimed,
in a rhetoric that was stirring but often vague, the importance of
political honesty and idealism.

Meanwhile he was endeavoring to destroy the powers of the
aristocratic clubs which dominated Princeton undergraduate society,
and in so doing he came into conflict with Andrew F. West, dean
of the Graduate School. West's desire for a Graduate School separated from the remainder of the university interfered with Wilson's
plans for reorganization; and in 1910, when West defeated him by
securing a lavish endowment, Wilson resigned from the presidency.
Harvey then persuaded the Democratic Party bosses in New Jersey
to nominate Wilson for the governorship. Elected governor by the
party machine, Wilson proceeded to assert his independence. He
broke with Harvey, who considered Wilson his protégé and tried to

dictate his policies; and with remarkable political ability he succeeded in forcing through the New Jersey legislature a series of reforms which won the applause of liberals throughout the country. Contact with practical politics had changed Wilson from a preacher of rhetorical generalities into a leader of Progressivism.

When the Democratic convention began to ballot for the presidential nomination, Clark was at first in the lead. Bryan, however, had determined that no candidate should win the nomination who was supported by Tammany or by such Wall Street Democrats as the banker, August Belmont, and the street railroad magnate, Thomas Fortune Ryan. After the fourteenth ballot, when the New York delegation gave its votes to Clark, Bryan set out to swing the convention to Wilson. Wilson secured the nomination on the forty-sixth ballot.

The sentiment of the electorate was predominantly Progressive, and the campaign was mainly a contest between Roosevelt and Wilson. Alike in their conviction that democracy must be revitalized by limiting the powers of the big corporations and of the political bosses, the two men differed in their remedies. Roosevelt's New Nationalism would accept the big corporations as economic necessities but would establish Federal regulation over them and, in so doing, greatly extend the powers of the Federal government. Wilson, on the other hand, preached a New Freedom; the growth of the big corporations must be limited, competition re-established, the rights of the small businessmen protected, and the powers of the state governments preserved.

From the election figures it does not appear that many voters changed their party allegiance; Wilson received the regular Democratic vote, while the Republican vote was divided between Roosevelt and Taft. With a popular vote of 6,286,214, 42 per cent of the electorate, Wilson won 40 states with an electoral vote of 435; in only 14 of these states, however, did he have a clear majority over both his opponents. Roosevelt had a popular vote of 4,126,020 and an electoral vote of 88, carrying Pennsylvania, Michigan, Minnesota, South Dakota, Washington, and 11 out of the 13 California votes. Taft, with a popular vote of 3,483,922, won only 8 electoral votes, those of Utah and Vermont. The election also marked a big increase in the Socialist vote, with Debs securing a popular vote of 926,090. In addition to carrying the presidency, the Democrats also elected twenty-one state governors and won majorities in both houses of Congress.

BIBLIOGRAPHY

*R. S. Baker, *Woodrow Wilson: Life and Letters,* Vols. I–III (1927–31)
R. S. Baker and W. E. Dodd (eds.), *Public Papers of Woodrow Wilson* (1925–27)
C. G. Bowers, *Beveridge and the Progressive Era* (1932)
A. Butt, *Taft and Roosevelt: Intimate Letters* (1930)
O. K. Davis, *Released for Publication* (1925)
*P. C. Jessup, *Elihu Root* (1938)
W. F. Johnson, *George Harvey* (1929)
M. Josephson, *The President-Makers* (1940)
J. Kerney, *The Political Education of Woodrow Wilson* (1926)
W. F. McCombs, *Making Woodrow Wilson President* (1921)
*H. F. Pringle, *Theodore Roosevelt* (1931)
*——— *William Howard Taft* (1939)
V. Rosewater, *Backstage in 1912* (1932)
M. Sullivan, *Our Times,* Vol. IV (1932)

20

THE WILSON ADMINISTRATION

WOODROW WILSON

WILSON entered the White House with only two years of experience in active politics behind him; and many of his supporters scarcely expected that he would be a strong president. He was, nevertheless, to dominate Congress and to dictate the policies of the government even more decisively than Theodore Roosevelt had done. From 1913 until 1919 the political history of the United States was determined mainly by the personality and mental development of Woodrow Wilson.

The descendant of Presbyterian ministers on both sides of his family, Wilson inherited a character marked chiefly by strength of will, a gift for eloquence, and a moral idealism which caused him to view the world in terms of a battle between good and evil. He could dominate men from his study or from the platform by inspiring them with his own faith in justice, freedom, and democracy and his own uncompromising hatred of whatever obstructed the forces of righteousness. He had, however, the defects of his qualities. Narrow both in his intellectual interests and in his sympathies, he was often lacking in the detailed social and economic understanding needed for making his ideals effective. Although he was capable of warm affection for a few intimate friends, he appeared reserved and coldblooded to others, and he was often ineffectual in handling individuals by personal contact. And his faith in the justice of his own ideals was apt to degenerate into obstinacy and self-righteousness and to make him feel that those who opposed him were opposing God. Preferring to break rather than to bend, he had strength but little subtlety. This combination of qualities predestined him to tragedy.

Bryan was still the most influential personality in the Democratic Party, and his support would be necessary if Wilson were to retain control over Congress. Wilson therefore appointed him Secretary of State. He had, however, little confidence in Bryan's capacity to handle foreign affairs, and he acted as his own Secretary of State whenever any important crisis occurred. Of the remainder of the cabinet, the most important members were William G. McAdoo, of Georgia and New York, who became Secretary of the Treasury, and Franklin K. Lane of California, Secretary of the Interior. The chief diplomatic posts mostly went to minor literary figures. Wilson left the less important appointments to his private secretary, Joseph P. Tumulty, who also supervised most of the contacts between Wilson and the American people outside Washington—a responsibility which he performed with complete loyalty and integrity. More influential than any holder of public office, however, was Colonel Edward M. House, a wealthy Texan and an amateur in politics, who had met Wilson in 1912 and had quickly become his closest personal friend and confidant.

In April Congress was summoned for a special session, with revision of the tariff as its first responsibility. For more than a quarter of a century Wilson had been declaring that the influence of pressure groups and private interests over the legislature could be checked by means of strong executive leadership; and his resolution to put his own doctrines into practice became apparent when he reverted to the old custom, abandoned in 1801, of the President's addressing Congress in person. In his inaugural he had restated the ideals of Progressivism with that solemn and deeply moving eloquence characteristic of all his major speeches, and he went on to specify, as subjects where reform was most needed, the tariff, banking and currency, conditions of labor, conservation, and public health.

THE TARIFF

The tariff had been conspicuously a subject over which presidential leadership and party discipline had often proved ineffectual and in which private interests had prevailed over the public welfare. The success with which Wilson forced a genuine reduction through Congress was, therefore, unprecedented. Believing that previous tariffs had served to strengthen the trusts by guaranteeing them against foreign competition, Wilson proposed to restore "effective competition." "We must," he declared, "abolish everything that bears even the semblance of privilege or of any kind of artificial advantage and put our business men and producers under the stimulus of a constant necessity to be efficient, economical and enterprising." A bill providing for drastic reductions, drafted primarily by Oscar Underwood of Alabama, passed the House of Representatives in May. Its acceptance by the Senate was endangered by the lobbyists of the manufacturing interests; but Wilson rallied popular support by denouncing their activities, and he succeeded in preventing individual Democratic senators from deserting the program of the party. In September the bill passed the Senate with only minor changes, and in October the Underwood Tariff became law.

As compared with the schedules of the Payne-Aldrich Tariff, there were 958 reductions and only 86 increases, and the average duty was lowered from 36.86 per cent to 26.67 per cent. More than 100 articles, many of which were of daily necessity, were transferred to the free list. A considerable loss of revenue was anticipated, and in compensation the act included an income tax, which had recently been legalized by the Sixteenth Amendment. Unmarried persons earning more than $3,000 and married persons earning more than $4,000 were to pay 1 per cent; on incomes above $20,000 the rates were increased, 6 per cent being levied on incomes above $500,000. The number of persons who paid income taxes was 357,515. These details were, in the main, the work of a young congressman from Tennessee, Cordell Hull. Thus, for the first time since the Civil War the tariff had been genuinely reduced. What effect tariff reductions would have on the American economic system was, however, never revealed, since shortly after the Underwood Tariff became law international trade was disrupted by the World War.

THE FEDERAL RESERVE SYSTEM

The second duty that Wilson assigned to Congress was a revision of the banking and currency system. The need for reform had been generally admitted since the financial crisis of 1907. The currency system was regulated by the National Bank Act of 1863, under which the quantity of notes that a bank might issue depended on the quantity of government bonds that it held.

This system had two cardinal weaknesses. In the first place, the supply of currency had no relation to the need for it. No provision was made for increasing the supply of notes when there was an increase in the volume of business, despite the greater need for currency both in prosperous years than in years of depression and in the autumn, when the volume of business was normally greater with the harvesting of crops. To a considerable degree, in fact, prosperity caused the supply of currency to contract instead of expand, since the prices of government bonds increased when business was good and at such times the banks preferred to sell them rather than to buy them. The second weakness was that no provision was made for mobilizing the nation's bank resources to save any particular bank which found itself in danger. The United States contained approximately 30,000 separate and independent banking institutions, each of which had to maintain its own reserve and, at a time of crisis, to rely on its own resources.

In 1908 Congress had passed the Aldrich-Vreeland Act, which permitted banks to issue notes on certain other kinds of securities in addition to government bonds, and which set up a National Monetary Commission, with Senator Aldrich as chairman. After devoting four years to a study of banking practices and issuing forty volumes of reports, the Commission recommended the establishment of a central bank that would be controlled by the bankers and would be independent of the government. The Democratic Party, however, faithful to its Jacksonian and agrarian traditions, insisted that any reform of the banking system must provide for decentralization, so that financial power would not be concentrated in the Northeast, and must also provide for some degree of government supervision. The need for reform was further demonstrated in 1912 by a congressional committee under the chairmanship of Arsène Pujo, which investigated Wall Street financial practices.

In June, 1913, Congress began consideration of the Federal Reserve Bill. The details of this measure were the work of various individuals, but its chief authors appear to have been Carter Glass of Virginia, Chairman of the House Committee on Banking and Currency, and President Wilson, while valuable advice was contributed by—among others—H. Parker Willis of Columbia University. The bill was vigorously opposed by many of the bankers, who objected to the powers of control which it gave to the Federal government and predicted that it would ruin the financial system of the country; but it passed both houses of Congress with only minor amendments and became law on December 23.

By the Federal Reserve Act all national banks were required, and state banks were invited, to become members of the Federal Reserve System. The country was to be divided into twelve regions, in each of which a Federal Reserve Bank was to be established. The stock of these Federal Reserve Banks was to be subscribed by the member banks, and each of the Reserve Banks was to be governed by nine directors. Three of these directors were to be appointed by the Federal Reserve Board, and the remainder were to be elected by the member banks. The Federal Reserve Board, which supervised the whole system, was to consist of the Secretary of the Treasury, the Comptroller of the Currency, and five other members, one of whom was to be Governor. The latter five were to be appointed by the President for ten-year terms.

The Federal Reserve Banks were given two duties of special importance. In the first place, they were to hold all the reserves of the member banks. Various devices were provided by which these reserves might be transferred in case of need from one region of the country to another. The Federal Reserve System thus made possible the mobilization of bank reserves at times and places where they were most needed. In the second place, the Reserve Banks were to obtain Federal Reserve Notes from the Federal Reserve Board in return for either gold certificates, eligible commercial paper, or United States government bonds. The latter required the consent of a majority of the Board; and, according to the original act, it was allowable only until 1933. The Reserve Banks could then pass these notes on to the member banks, in return for collateral of the same kind. These Federal Reserve Notes were to take the place of the bank notes that had circulated under the previous system; and, since their number was determined not merely by the holdings of the banks in government bonds but also by the quantity of gold certificates and commercial paper which they might acquire, it was hoped that the supply of notes would expand or contract in proportion to the volume of business.

In addition to mobilizing reserves and providing for an elastic currency, a sound banking system must also perform one other function: it must provide for a check on excessive loan expansion during boom periods, in order to prevent a dangerous credit inflation. The directors of the Federal Reserve System could curb inflation in two ways. First, they could raise the rediscount rate on the commercial paper given them in return for notes by the member banks. This would be the equivalent of charging the member banks a higher rate of interest and would thus, it was hoped, compel the member banks in turn to raise the interest rates charged for their own loans to businessmen and also compel them to stop expanding the quantity of notes in circulation. Second, the directors could sell government bonds and commercial paper in the open market and then withdraw from circulation the money which they obtained by these sales. These two powers in combination would make it possible, if sound banking practices were followed, for the directors of the system to exert a considerable degree of control over the movements of the business cycle.

By 1915, 7,615 banks, with about half of the total banking resources of the nation, had become members of the Federal Reserve System. By 1928 the proportion of the banking resources controlled by the system had risen to 80 per cent, and by 1938 it was 87 per cent. A large number of the smaller state banks preferred, nevertheless, to remain independent; even in 1938 only 11 per cent of the state banks had become members. The system proved to be a considerable improvement over previous banking practices and was especially valuable during the World War. It did not, however, prevent bank failures, even of member banks, nor did it succeed in evening out the business cycle.

The chief weakness of the system, perhaps, was that a proper functioning of it depended primarily on the wisdom and integrity of the Federal Reserve Board. If its members were to perform their function of checking inflation by raising discount rates and selling bonds during a boom period, they must be capable of resisting political and business pressure in favor of continued easy money. The events of 1927–1928 showed that to expect this might be to demand too much of human nature. Another deficiency of the Federal Reserve Act was that, in spite of recommendations by the Pujo Committee, nothing was done to regulate the stock exchange and investment banking.

ANTITRUST LEGISLATION

The third principal measure that Wilson asked of Congress was legislation to curb monopoly and protect the rights of labor. Consideration of these problems began in January, 1914, and resulted in the Federal Trade Commission Act, signed on September 26, and the Clayton Anti-Trust Act, signed on October 15.

The Federal Trade Commission, superseding Roosevelt's Bureau of Corporations, consisted of five members, appointed for seven-year terms. Its functions were to investigate and publicize the business practices of corporations engaged in interstate commerce; to hear complaints of unfair methods of competition; and, when necessary, to issue "cease and desist" orders, the corporations having in these cases the right of appeal to the courts.

The Clayton Act specified as illegal a number of practices which tended to prevent competition, among them being price discrimination, interlocking directorates in large industrial corporations which had previously been competitive, and "tying" contracts by which manufacturers prohibited dealers from handling commodities of rival firms. The act also provided methods by which injured persons might obtain redress and—unlike the Sherman Act in its original form—declared that the penalties for violation were to be civil and not criminal. Section 6 exempted labor unions from the antitrust laws, and Section 20 restricted the use of injunctions in labor disputes and declared that strikes, boycotts, and picketing were not contrary to any Federal law. Gompers, who had thrown the support of the A. F. of L. to Wilson during the presidential campaign, declared that these two sections constituted the Magna Carta of labor. They were, however, considerably weakened by judicial interpretation after the World War, and throughout the nineteen-twenties employers continued to obtain injunctions against numerous trade union activities.

Under the Sherman Act the Wilson administration in eight years instituted legal proceedings in ninety-two cases, as contrasted with about the same number brought by the Taft administration in only four years. This decrease in trust-busting was a result of the adoption of the rule of reason by the Supreme Court, the avoidance by corporations of practices that might open them to legal attack, the fact that the chief trusts had already been attacked by Roosevelt and Taft, and the World War. Meanwhile, however, the Federal Trade Commission was active in checking illegal practices and monopolistic tendencies. Between 1915 and 1921 it issued 788 formal complaints and 379 "cease and desist" orders. The problem of the trusts, it was hoped, would in this manner be solved by prevention rather than by cure.

After August, 1914, the process of reform was abruptly checked by the outbreak of the War in Europe, and attention was concentrated on the economic disturbances caused by the War and on the problems of American foreign policy. The latter years of the Wilson administration were not, however, completely devoid of progressive legislation. In 1915 was passed the La Follette Seaman's Act regulating conditions of labor on board ship, and in 1916 the Adamson Act, which averted a railroad strike by establishing an eight-hour day for the employees of interstate railroads. In the same year, as a result of renewed agrarian discontent, which found expression in the Non-Partisan League of North Dakota, an attempt was made to provide easier credit facilities for farmers. Under the Federal Farm Loan Act twelve Federal Land Banks were established, which were to raise money by selling bonds to the public and were to lend it to co-operative farm associations. The latter were to be formed and controlled by farmers and were to make mortgage loans, at from 5 to 6 per cent, to individual members. By 1930 there were 4,659 such associations, which had loaned to farmers a total of $1,630,000,000.

BIBLIOGRAPHY

W. G. McAdoo, *Crowded Years* (1931)

*R. S. Baker, *Woodrow Wilson: Life and Letters,* Vol. IV (1931)

R. S. Baker and W. E. Dodd (eds.), *Public Papers of Woodrow Wilson* (1925–27)

T. C. Blaisdell, *The Federal Trade Commission* (1932)

D. R. Dewey, *Financial History of the United States* (revised edition, 1938)

W. E. Dodd, *Woodrow Wilson and his Work* (1926)

C. Eliot, *The Farmer's Campaign for Credit* (1927)

C. Glass, *An Adventure in Constructive Finance* (1927)

G. C. Henderson, *The Federal Trade Commission* (1924)

D. F. Houston, *Eight Years with Wilson's Cabinet* (1926)

E. Jones, *The Trust Problem* (1926)

E. W. Kemmerer, *The A.B.C. of the Federal Reserve System* (revised edition, 1938)

J. M. Laughlin, *The Federal Reserve Act* (1933)

A. D. Noyes, *War Period of American Finance* (1926)

*F. L. Paxson, *Pre-War Years* (1936)

W. Z. Ripley, *Trusts, Pools and Corporations* (1916)

*H. R. Seager and C. A. Gulick, *Trust and Corporation Problems* (1929)

C. Seymour (ed.), *Intimate Papers of Colonel House* (1926)

E. S. Spahr, *History and Theory of Agricultural Credit in the United States* (1932)

I. M. Tarbell, *The Tariff in our Times* (1931)

F. W. Taussig, *Tariff History of the United States* (revised edition, 1931)

J. P. Tumulty, *Woodrow Wilson as I knew him* (1921)

P. M. Warburg, *The Federal Reserve System* (1930)

H. P. Willis, *The Federal Reserve System* (1923)

21

THE RESULTS

OF PROGRESSIVISM

THE fact that the Progressive movement was interrupted by the World War, before it had fully achieved its objectives, makes it difficult to judge it fairly and has often caused it to be underestimated. It is true that its leaders were too prone to moral exhortation and denunciation, their diagnoses of economic abuses were often superficial, and the effect of many of their reforms was relatively small. Evils which were checked in one direction often reappeared in new forms. The Progressives were, nevertheless, responsible for real achievements; they did much to create a healthy and vigorous public opinion, and they made genuine advances toward political and economic democracy.

Democratic control over the government was strengthened by the Progressive campaign against the political bosses and by such devices as the primary, publicity for campaign funds, and popular election of senators. The boss and the machine by no means disappeared; certain city governments, such as those in New York and Chicago, were almost as corrupt in the twenties as they had been in the nineteenth century. But it was now easier for the public to control its officials, and the influence of machine politics became much less conspicuous in the state and Federal governments. The result was that seekers after privilege had to win popular support instead of negotiating with politicians behind the scenes. The raising of standards was not always obvious, since the mass of the people could sometimes be swayed by unscrupulous propaganda. The oligarch was sometimes replaced by the demagogue. But the opinion of the public could never, henceforth, be ignored.

Business interests, similarly, now had to win the approval of the people for their activities. The "public-be-damned" attitude of the eighties and nineties disappeared. Business henceforth sought to present its activities in a favorable light, and "public relations" became an important branch of its activities. Business leaders endeavored to prove that they were engaged in serving the public and that they had an enlightened attitude toward labor. Indicative of this change of viewpoint were the policies pursued by Judge Gary, head of United States Steel. Gary continued to oppose trade unionism, but he spent considerable sums on promoting the welfare of his employees. He encouraged them to become stockholders in the corporation; he tried to defend the twelve-hour day on the ground that the workers themselves desired it; and he conducted the financial affairs of the corporation with scrupulous integrity.

Another symptom of a new attitude was the policy adopted in 1914 by the Rockefellers. In that year one of the outlying dependencies of the Rockefeller empire, Colorado Coal and Iron, was the scene of a strike. The manager of the company resorted to the traditional methods of crushing the strikers; and on April 20 company police attacked a strikers' camp at Ludlow, with the result that twenty-five persons, including twelve women and eleven children, were killed. The Ludlow massacre caused widespread indignation throughout the entire country, and it also shocked John D. Rockefeller, junior, who had hitherto paid little attention to the affairs of Colorado Coal and Iron. In order to prevent any repetition of such incidents, Rockefeller instituted a plan which he described—somewhat euphemistically—as "industrial democracy." The workers were to be allowed to voice their grievances through a "work's council"—an institution which became better known later by the name of "company union." Rockefeller also hired Ivy Lee as a "Public Relations Counsellor." Lee's task was to win good will for the Rockefeller interests, and this involved, in Lee's words, "shaping the affairs of the corporation, so that when placed before the public they will be approved."

Welfare capitalism by no means remedied all the grievances of the working class. Company unions could deal with minor complaints, but they were never allowed any control over the basic questions of wages and hours. Radicals, indeed, bitterly attacked these new tendencies, declaring that the employers were trying to appease their workers by means of palliatives and thus trying to prevent them from becoming militant. But from any other point of view welfare capitalism marked a distinct improvement over the practices of the eighties and nineties.

The Progressive movement won definite acceptance of the principle that business could be regulated by the government. The large corporations were compelled to recognize that they must obey the law of the land. Regulation was to be performed by appointive commissions, such as the I. C. C., the F. T. C., and the state utility commissions, which had broad powers but which were subject to judicial review. The spirit of such regulation would, however, depend upon the attitude of the party in control of the Federal government. In the twenties the Federal government used its powers mainly to assist big business rather than to maintain its subordination to the public interest. Although, moreover, the campaign against monopoly had achieved considerable success, it had not removed the basic evil. The drive toward business consolidation had been checked, and in many branches of industry there was more competition in the twenties than there had been earlier in the century. Combination, however, tended to assume new forms. Trade associations and other more or less hidden devices for fixing prices replaced open trusts and mergers. The chief evil of monopoly—the lack of any mechanism for ensuring price reductions—therefore remained unremedied.

Progressivism considerably extended the functions of the government, both Federal and local, in order to prevent bad conditions of labor, protect women and children, and conserve natural resources. The state began to acquire positive functions instead of being regarded merely as an instrument for maintaining peace and order. The development of these new activities was, however, impeded by the courts, which continued to regard much welfare legislation as a violation of the individual rights guaranteed by the Fourteenth

Amendment. Although the courts slowly retreated from the extreme position which they had assumed in the eighties and nineties, they continued to claim extensive powers of supervision. To what extent they would exercise these powers in any particular instance remained very uncertain. Measures of business regulation were not upheld as constitutional unless the courts regarded them as "reasonable." Many state laws might be either accepted as legitimate exercises of the police power or rejected on the ground that they violated the due process clause. As a result of the Federal system and of judicial review the United States was much slower than the European countries in accepting such measures as old age, unemployment, and health insurance.

The economic system during the Progressive Era seemed to be developing in a generally healthy direction. The currency problem of the seventies and eighties had been solved as a result of a considerable increase in the supply of gold. Production increased faster than population; the increase of production between 1901 and 1913 was 3.1 per cent a year, that of population was 2.0 per cent a year. A larger share of the national income went to the farmers as a result of a rise in the prices of farm products and a fall in the prices of other commodities. The working class increased its average annual wage from $490 in 1900 to $675 in 1913, and wages rose a little more rapidly than the cost of living, so that the real earnings of the average worker increased by about 6.0 per cent. The business classes, on the other hand, acquired a slightly smaller share of the national income. In the price of each unit of industrial production (calculated in terms of constant purchasing power), the share represented by wages decreased from 1899 to 1914 by 15.6 per cent, while the share represented by profits decreased by 22.3 per cent. Thus, the general economic results of the period were that the farmers and workers were somewhat better off and the owners of capital were not acquiring an unhealthily large proportion of the total income.

22

FOREIGN POLICY, 1901-1914

IMPERIALIST TENDENCIES

THE foreign policy of the Progressive Era seems, from some points of view, to be inconsistent with the dominant tendencies of domestic politics. At home the period from 1901 to 1914 was marked by liberal reforms intended to protect democracy from the powers of big business; but in foreign affairs the United States played the part of a great power and developed imperialist tendencies which often appeared to be serving the interests of American industry and finance. Some of the leading Progressives, such as President Roosevelt and Senator Beveridge, were among the most ardent champions of United States imperialism. These two tendencies had, however, one thing in common: both of them were marked by an extension of the powers of the Federal government, which assumed more positive functions than in the past.

The three Presidents of the Progressive Era pursued quite different objectives in their foreign policy. Roosevelt was a believer in the leadership of the Anglo-Saxon race, in the need for the use of force in settling international disputes, and in the therapeutic value of war; in foreign affairs he thought primarily of increasing the military strength and security of the United States. During the Taft administration economic considerations predominated; the government advocated "dollar diplomacy" and endeavored to secure new foreign markets for American trade and investments. Wilson, on the other hand, was a moralist, who deplored the influence of commercial and financial interests on foreign policy and believed that the United

States should use its strength to promote democracy, peace, and the rule of law in international affairs.

Yet in spite of these marked differences in viewpoint, the policies actually adopted by the Roosevelt, Taft, and Wilson administrations differed little from one another. Throughout the whole of the Progressive Era the United States claimed certain rights of suzerainty over the Caribbean region and was actively concerned with the affairs of Europe and the Far East. The main consideration dominating American foreign policy appears to have been the growth of both power politics and imperialist rivalries in other parts of the world. For this reason the United States had to consider her national security more carefully than in the past, and, in particular, she had to strengthen the Monroe Doctrine in order to prevent European powers from acquiring a dangerous position in the Caribbean region.

The most significant development of American foreign policy in the Progressive Era—the growth of the practice of intervention in the Caribbean republics—has been attacked as a form of economic imperialism. It is true that it often served the interests of American bankers and industrialists; but the chief reason that caused Roosevelt, Taft, and Wilson to adopt this policy, in spite of the differences in their ideals, was the fear of encroachment by European powers, particularly Germany. This policy had, however, the unfortunate result of antagonizing and alarming all the Latin American nations, South American as well as Caribbean. What the United States lost by this policy, through the growth of Latin American hostility, may have been more important than what she gained by it.

THE PANAMA CANAL

During the Roosevelt administration the most important episode in American foreign policy was the construction of the Panama Canal. The building of a canal across Central America was of vital importance to American security since it would enable the navy to move quickly between the Atlantic and the Pacific. Without a canal the United States would be compelled to maintain a first-class navy on both oceans. The need for it had been dramatized by the voyage of the battleship *Oregon* around Cape Horn during the Spanish-American War. Although, however, Roosevelt deserves credit for the building of the canal, his handling of the diplomatic problems involved showed a marked disregard for the rights of weaker nations and caused bitter resentment throughout Latin America.

The building of a canal across Central America had been considered at the time of the acquisition of California; and in 1850, by the Clayton-Bulwer Treaty, the United States and Great Britain had agreed that the proposed canal should be jointly controlled by the two countries and should not be fortified. The project subsequently was dropped until after the war with Spain. Secretary of State John Hay then opened negotiations with Great Britain for a revision of the Clayton-Bulwer Treaty; and in 1901, by the Hay-Pauncefote Treaty, it was agreed that the United States might construct, control, and fortify a canal, but that ships of all nations should use it on equal terms. A commission thereafter surveyed the ground and decided that the canal should be built across Nicaragua.

Meanwhile there was in existence a French corporation, the New Panama Company, which held a concession from the government of Colombia for the building of a canal across the isthmus of Panama. This concession would expire in 1904. The concession had originally been acquired in the eighties by Ferdinand de Lesseps, who had begun to dig a canal but had gone bankrupt. The New Panama Company, which had taken over de Lesseps's properties, was headed by Philippe Bunau-Varilla and employed as its American representative a New York lawyer, William Nelson Cromwell. The holdings of the company would become worthless if the Nicaragua canal were built, and it was therefore anxious to sell out to the United States government, at a price which it finally fixed at $40,000,000. Cromwell and Bunau-Varilla therefore set out to advertise the superior merits of Panama over Nicaragua. After dilating on the dangers of volcanic eruptions in Nicaragua and contributing $60,000 to the Republican campaign fund, they converted Roosevelt and, in June, 1902, persuaded Congress to pass the Spooner Act. The canal was to be built across Panama, and the New Panama Company was to receive the $40,000,000; but if the government of Colombia refused its consent, the Nicaraguan route was to be substituted.

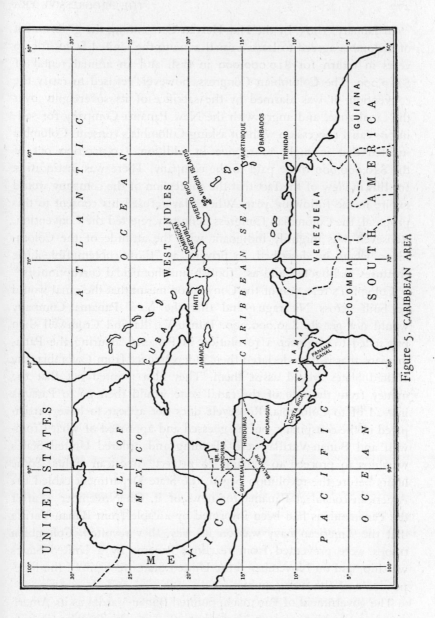

Figure 5. CARIBBEAN AREA

In January, 1903, by the Hay-Herran Convention, the government of Colombia agreed to lease a canal zone to the United States for 99 years in return for $10,000,000 in cash and an annual rental of $250,000. The Colombian Congress, however, refused to ratify the convention. It was alarmed by the sacrifice of its sovereignty over the canal zone, and angry with the New Panama Company for selling its canal concession without asking Colombia's consent. Colombia insisted that it ought to receive in addition $10,000,000 out of the $40,000,000 to be paid to the company. There was justification for this in view of the fact that the concession of the company would expire in the following year. When Hay refused his consent to this proposal, the Colombian Congress definitely rejected the Convention. Roosevelt was mightily indignant with the attitude of the Colombians, whom he described, in private, as "those contemptible little creatures in Bogota" and as "foolish and homicidal corruptionists."

Colombia's rejection of the Convention meant that the canal would be built across Nicaragua and that the New Panama Company would not get its $40,000,000. Bunau-Varilla and Cromwell then proceeded to engineer a revolution in Panama, assuring the Panamanians that if they declared their independence from Colombia, the United States would assist them. They also pointed out that the money from the sale of the canal zone would then go to Panama instead of to Colombia. Roosevelt does not appear to have participated in the conspiracy; but he guessed and approved of what Cromwell and Bunau-Varilla were planning and ordered United States warships to proceed to Panama to protect American rights. Some hours before the revolution began, the State Department cabled the American consul at Panama for news of it. On November 3, after the Panamanians had been informed by a cable from Bunau-Varilla that the American navy was on its way, they revolted. Colombian troops were prevented from reaching Panama by a United States warship, and on November 6 the United States recognized the independence of the new republic.

The government of Panama appointed Bunau-Varilla as its American representative; and on November 18, 1903, by the Hay–Bunau-Varilla Treaty, the United States leased the canal zone in perpetuity for $10,000,000 in cash and an annual rental of $250,000. The New Panama Company thereupon obtained the $40,000,000. The identity of the stockholders to whom the money was paid has never been revealed. Roosevelt insisted that they were French citizens, but there were persistent accusations, which have never been disproved, that the rights of the New Panama Company had been acquired by Wall Street financiers.

The behavior of the United States government caused indignation throughout Latin America. There was little justification for the support given by Roosevelt to the Panamanians since there was no pressing reason either for beginning the canal before 1904, when the concession held by the New Panama Company would expire, or for choosing Panama in preference to Nicaragua. Cromwell and Bunau-Varilla had succeeded in maneuvering Roosevelt into a violation of the rights of Colombia for the benefit of the unknown stockholders whom they represented. Roosevelt, moreover, increased the resentment of Colombia when, in a speech at Berkeley, California, in 1911, he declared flatly: "I took the Canal Zone." In 1914 Secretary of State Bryan negotiated a treaty with Colombia by which the United States government agreed to pay $30,000,000 in compensation and expressed "sincere regret that anything should have occurred to interrupt or mar the relations of cordial friendship." However, the Republicans in the Senate succeeded in defeating ratification, as a slur on Roosevelt. Colombia's continued hostility proved, however, to be harmful to American commercial interests; and in 1921, when American businessmen were anxious to obtain oil concessions from the Colombian government, a new treaty was negotiated and ratified. The United States government made no expression of regret but paid Colombia $25,000,000.

Construction of the canal by the United States Army Engineers Corps began in 1904. Progress was at first disappointingly slow; but the primary difficulty—the prevalence of tropical diseases—was finally removed by the work of Dr. William E. Gorgas. Building proceeded rapidly after 1908, when Colonel George W. Goethals was given sole authority. The first ocean vessel passed through the canal in 1914, and the work was completed in 1920, the cost being $275,-

000,000 for the canal itself and $113,000,000 for the fortifications. In 1912 Congress decided that United States ships engaged in coastal trade should be exempt from paying taxes; but this measure was attacked by the railroads and denounced by Great Britain as a violation of the Hay-Pauncefote Treaty. President Wilson persuaded Congress to repeal it in 1914.

INTERVENTION IN THE CARIBBEAN

The importance of the Panama Canal to American security made it necessary for the United States to guard the approaches to the Canal and to prevent European powers from acquiring positions in the Caribbean. The Caribbean republics suffered from frequent revolutions, which were likely to endanger the lives and properties of foreign citizens. Also, they often defaulted on their foreign debts. There was, therefore, danger that European powers might intervene to protect their commercial and financial interests. Roosevelt concluded that, in order to avert the possibility of such intervention, the United States must, when necessary, intervene herself. As the British government had pointed out, this was a logical deduction from the claims made by Secretary of State Olney during the Venezuela boundary dispute of 1895.

In his message to Congress of December 2, 1904, Roosevelt declared that: "Chronic wrongdoing, or an impotence which results in a general loosening of the ties of civilized society may in America, as elsewhere, ultimately require intervention by some civilized nation, and in the Western hemisphere the adherence of the United States to the Monroe Doctrine may force the United States, however reluctantly, in flagrant cases of such wrongdoing or impotence, to the exercise of an international police power." This assertion that the United States ought to police the western hemisphere, which became known as the Roosevelt Corollary, had never, in the nineteenth century, been regarded as justified by the terms of the Monroe Doctrine. The Latin American nations generally disliked it and put forward an alternative doctrine, named after Luis Drago, Minister of Foreign Affairs for the Argentine. According to the Drago Doctrine, any kind of armed intervention for the collection of debts and the protection of foreigners, whether by the European powers or by the United States, should not be tolerated.

Defenders of the practice of intervention have argued that it was justifiable not only on grounds of national security but also because it brought good government and economic and social improvement to the Caribbean area. There appears to be considerable truth in this assertion, but it should be added that the good government was not always appreciated by the natives of the Caribbean republics and that intervention was generally accompanied by the use of force. And, although economic and financial imperialism was not the original cause of interventionism, it was certainly one of its consequences. Debts due by Caribbean republics to European investors were frequently transferred to American bankers, who acquired a dominating position in the Caribbean area; and United States intervention was likely to result in the maintenance of conservative governments and in the suppression of radical movements which were hostile to foreign capitalists. Opponents of the Roosevelt Corollary had, therefore, some reason for believing that it had perverted the Monroe Doctrine into an instrument of United States financial hegemony.

Roosevelt's practices, in foreign policy as in internal affairs, were milder than his public utterances, and it was not until after he had left the White House that intervention became a habit. Roosevelt's moderation was partly due to the influence of Elihu Root, who became Secretary of State in 1905 and who had a strong appreciation of the value of Latin American good will.

In 1902, when Venezuela refused to compensate foreigners for losses which they had suffered during a civil war, British, German, and Italian warships blockaded the Venezuelan coast. Roosevelt, however, merely urged the different governments to submit to arbitration, and he expressed approval when the dispute was settled by the Hague Tribunal. During the World War Roosevelt alleged that the attitude of Germany had been particularly intransigent and that he had forced the German government to give way by threatening to go to war. However, there is no documentary evidence in support of this assertion.

In 1905, on the other hand, Roosevelt intervened in the Dominican Republic. Unable to pay its debts to European bondholders and threatened by attack from European powers, the Dominican government was persuaded to sign a treaty by which an American receiver-general was to collect its customs duties and supervise the spending of them. The United States Senate refused for two years to ratify the treaty, but Roosevelt ignored this rebuke. American marines took charge of the republic until 1907. By that date its revenues had been doubled, and the claims of its foreign creditors had been almost halved. Roosevelt then withdrew the marines, declaring that he had "put the affairs of the island on a better basis than they had been for a century." This may have been true; but it should also be pointed out that the claims of the European creditors had been transferred to New York bankers, who henceforth controlled the economic development of the republic, and that the Dominicans themselves continued to prefer self-government, however bad, to government by the United States. Again in 1906 Roosevelt sent American troops to Cuba, in accordance with the Platt Amendment, to prevent civil war, and the island remained under American rule until 1909.

The imperialistic implications of Roosevelt's Caribbean policy became more explicit during the Taft administration. Taft's Secretary of State, Philander C. Knox, a believer in what he himself called "dollar diplomacy," set out to secure economic opportunities for American financiers. This was most evident in Central America. In 1909, when a revolution in Nicaragua, which was supported by United States mining interests, overthrew President Zelaya, Knox was quick to recognize the new regime. In 1911 he negotiated treaties providing for United States control over the finances of Nicaragua and Honduras, but he was unable to persuade the Senate to ratify them. Finally in 1912, when there was another revolutionary movement in Nicaragua, which threatened to overthrow a president friendly to the United States, the Taft administration sent marines to assist in maintaining order. An American citizen was appointed to supervise the finances of Nicaragua, and American bankers took control of its national bank. The marines did not finally leave Nicaragua until 1933.

Woodrow Wilson came into office as a convinced opponent of imperialism. He believed that the United States should not use force to protect the economic interests of its citizens in foreign countries, and that the Latin American republics should enjoy complete independence and self-government. In an address at Mobile, Alabama, on October 27, 1913, he declared that "morality and not expediency is the thing that must guide us." "It is a very perilous thing to determine the foreign policy of a nation in the terms of material interest." He added that "the United States will never again seek one additional foot of territory by conquest." Unfortunately it was easier to preach these idealistic sentiments than to practice them. As a result both of considerations of national security and of pressure from financial interests, Wilson found it impossible to abandon the Roosevelt corollary, and his administration was actually responsible for more interventions than the Roosevelt and Taft administrations combined. Wilson endeavored to reconcile his policies with his ideals by intervening not in the interests of the United States but for the sake of the Latin Americans themselves and in order to promote democratic government. Actually, however, the moral imperialism of Wilson differed little from the military and economic imperialism of his predecessors, and it was equally unpopular in Latin America.

The Haitian republic was unable to pay its debts, and in 1915 there were revolutionary disorders. President Sam massacred 160 of his political opponents and he was then seized by a mob and literally torn limb from limb. American marines thereupon landed on the island and forced the Haitians to accept a treaty which made the republic virtually a United States protectorate. Haiti was allowed to elect a new president, but the marines stayed to enforce order. While they brought an unprecedented peace and prosperity, they also shot more than 2,000 of the Haitians in the process.

A similar situation occurred the following year in the Dominican Republic. A new president, after taking power by revolution, refused to obey the Convention of 1905. Marines took control of the republic for five years. During this period the American officials increased Dominican revenues from $700,000 to $4,500,000, reduced the cost of collection from 15 per cent to 5 per cent, and built schools and roads. They also imposed a strict press censorship and meted out justice sternly through naval courts.

Cuba again saw American marines in 1917, when a disputed election resulted in civil war. The marines stayed until 1922, although until 1920 native officials were free to govern the republic. During this period there was a rapid increase in American investments and in the sugar crop, while Cuban officials took advantage of the prosperity of the republic to enrich themselves. In 1920 the price of sugar fell from 22½ cents a pound to 3¾ cents; and the danger of economic collapse caused General Enoch H. Crowder to be sent as financial advisor. Crowder supervised Cuban finances until 1922, when the island resumed full self-government.

The Wilson administration was also responsible for the purchase of the Virgin Islands from Denmark in 1916, at a price of $25,000,-000, in order to strengthen United States control over the approaches to Panama.

THE MEXICAN REVOLUTION

The most difficult problems which confronted Wilson in Latin American affairs were those presented by the outbreak of revolution in Mexico. From 1876 until 1910, except for one four-year interlude, Mexico had been governed by Porfirio Díaz. In theory Díaz was merely president of the republic, and his powers were limited by a constitution, but actually he had ruled as a dictator. Díaz had given Mexico a long respite from civil war and revolution and had brought about an enormous economic development. Most of the capital had been supplied by foreign investors, chiefly citizens of the United States, who by 1910 had acquired ownership of mines, oil fields, railroads, public utilities, plantations, and cattle ranches with a total value of perhaps a billion dollars. After 1900 Díaz had become alarmed by the growth of American interests and had given preference, whenever possible, to British financiers, who became owners of a number of oil fields which Americans had hoped to acquire.

The bulk of the Mexican people had, however, failed to benefit from Díaz's policies. The peasants had been expropriated for the benefit of a small group of aristocratic *hacendados,* so that by 1910 at least 95 per cent of the rural population owned no land. The working class suffered from excessively long hours and low wages, and they were crushed by government troops if they ventured to strike. All classes of Mexicans were angered and alarmed by the powers and privileges acquired by foreigners. Díaz, moreover, in spite of the fact that in 1910 he was eighty years of age, had refused to provide Mexico with a successor.

In November, 1910, there began an insurrection against Díaz, which was headed by Francisco Madero, an idealistic liberal of a wealthy family, who hoped to make constitutional government a reality. American financial interests, irritated by Díaz's pro-British policy, were sympathetic to Madero, and the United States government allowed him for several months to use Texas as his base of operations. In May, 1911, Díaz was overthrown and Madero became president. American businessmen, however, quickly began to oppose Madero partly because he began to restrict the privileges enjoyed by foreign capitalists and partly because the Mexican workers and peasants were allowed to organize and to demand reforms. The United States minister in Mexico, Henry Lane Wilson, became a fanatical enemy of Madero, telling the State Department that Mexico was in a state of anarchy. In February, 1913, Madero was overthrown by a group of reactionary generals, headed by Victoriano Huerta, and was subsequently murdered. Minister Wilson had been informed in advance of Huerta's plans; and, when Huerta seized power, he hailed him publicly as "the savior of Mexico" and urged that the new government at once be officially recognized. Wilson also refused to intercede with Huerta to spare Madero's life.

Huerta's government was tyrannical and corrupt, and Huerta himself was a dipsomaniac. He was, however, quickly recognized by the European powers. He followed Díaz's later policy of giving preference to British interests, and he was on friendly terms with the British minister in Mexico. Meanwhile movements to avenge Madero and to restore constitutional government had been initiated in several parts of the country. In the north these movements were led

by Venustiano Carranza and Pancho Villa, and in the south by
Emiliano Zapata. Thus, when Wilson assumed office Mexico was in
a state of civil war.

Considerations both of economic interest and of morality caused
the United States to be hostile to Huerta. Wilson proposed, however,
to allow the Mexican people to settle their own affairs without interference, and he recognized that they could never achieve permanent peace without fundamental changes in their economic system.
He refused to recognize Huerta, recalled Henry Lane Wilson from
the American embassy in Mexico, and imposed an embargo on shipments of munitions. In the summer he sent John Lind, former
Governor of Minnesota, to Mexico as his personal representative;
Lind endeavored, without success, to persuade Huerta to resign and
to allow a free election to be held to determine his successor. The
danger of a clash with Great Britain over Mexican affairs was
averted by negotiation. In return for repeal of the law exempting
American coastal ships using the Panama Canal from paying tolls,
the British foreign office agreed to give no support to Huerta and
to follow the lead of the United States.

Wilson's policy of "watchful waiting" proved increasingly irksome to American businessmen. They wanted peace in Mexico and
demanded that the United States government intervene to end the
civil war. Wilson was therefore unable to leave Mexico to work out
its own salvation. On December 3 the embargo was lifted for the
benefit of the constitutionalists. Huerta was not overthrown so
quickly as Wilson had hoped, and Wilson then adopted more forceful measures. When some American marines who had landed at
Tampico were placed under temporary arrest by one of Huerta's
generals, the American admiral demanded that, by way of apology,
the American flag be saluted. When Huerta refused, Wilson decided
to resort to force. Informed that a German ship was on its way to
Vera Cruz with munitions for Huerta, Wilson ordered the American fleet to seize the town. On April 21 American marines occupied
Vera Cruz, an episode which cost the lives of eighteen Americans
and nearly two hundred Mexicans. This act was denounced by the
constitutionalists, whom Wilson was trying to help, as vigorously

as by Huerta. The marines stayed in Vera Cruz until November, by which time Huerta had gone into exile, Carranza had been installed as provisional president, and Wilson could hope that peace was returning to Mexico.

Unfortunately the different constitutionalist factions now proceeded to fight one another. Villa and Zapata refused to accept the leadership of Carranza; and it was not until the end of 1915 that Carranza's victory was assured. Wilson recognized Carranza as president and prohibited the sale of American munitions to Villa. Carranza, however, showed little consideration for the rights and interests of Americans in Mexico and strongly resented Wilson's suggestions that he make some return for the support which the United States was giving him. Villa, moreover, regarded the United States as primarily responsible for Carranza's victory. After he had been defeated by Carranza's generals, he proceeded to exact vengeance. On January 10, 1916, a band of Villistas killed sixteen American citizens at Santa Ysabel, in northern Mexico; and on March 9 they raided the town of Columbus, New Mexico, and killed sixteen more Americans. Wilson ordered American militia to guard the border and sent General Pershing with sixteen thousand troops into Mexico to capture Villa. Villa succeeded in evading his pursuers, while Carranza, though reluctantly consenting to the Pershing expedition, expressed great resentment. Numerous incidents and border clashes, in which both Mexicans and Americans lost their lives, appeared to be bringing the two countries to the brink of open war; and there were numerous demands in the United States for occupation of the entire country. The danger was, however, averted by the approach of the American entry into the war in Europe. Pershing left Mexico in February, 1917, without having captured Villa.

Later in the year Mexico adopted a new constitution, under which the rights of aliens to own land were restricted and the subsoil was declared to be the inalienable property of the nation. These provisions were not put into force, but they represented a threat to Americans who owned estates and oil fields in Mexico. Carranza, moreover, had failed to restore order, and large parts of the country were virtually in a state of anarchy. American oil interests organized an Association for the Protection of American Rights in Mexico; and Senator Fall of New Mexico, a close friend of the oil magnate Edward L. Doheny, took the lead in demanding intervention. In the autumn of 1919, when an American consular officer at Puebla was seized by bandits, Secretary of State Lansing sent vigorous protests, and war again seemed imminent. Wilson was in virtual retirement as a result of his physical collapse during the League of Nations controversy; but he emerged to silence Lansing and work for peace; and after the consular officer had been released, the crisis ended. In the following spring Carranza was overthrown by forces headed by General Obregón. The new regime had considerable success in restoring order and appeared to be more friendly to American interests.

THE FAR EAST

In the Far East Roosevelt, Taft, and Wilson all continued to support the policy, first enunciated by John Hay, of preserving the Open Door in China and protecting her territorial integrity. American diplomacy in the Far East was, however, not conspicuously successful, partly because the American people were not sufficiently concerned about the independence of China to use force in its defence and partly because China was now threatened not merely by European powers but by a new and aggressive Asiatic imperialism, that of Japan. The United States was, moreover, in no position to invite Japanese hostility, owing to the fact that she possessed hostages to fortune in the Far East in the shape of the Philippine Islands.

In February, 1904, began the Russo-Japanese War. Russia was regarded in the United States as the more aggressive and imperialistic of the two powers, and American sympathy was with Japan. The Japanese won a series of naval and military victories; but it was doubtful whether their resources would be sufficient for a long war, and Roosevelt was anxious that peace be concluded before they were exhausted. Russia consented to accept American mediation, and the delegates of Russia and Japan conferred at Portsmouth, New Hampshire. With Roosevelt's assistance a treaty was agreed upon in September, 1905, by which Japan acquired control over

Korea and made other territorial gains. Roosevelt later asserted that in the course of the war he had warned France and Germany against intervening in order to deprive the Japanese of the fruits of their victory, but no record of such a warning has survived.

The war left Japan the dominant power in the Far East, and it was followed by Japanese economic control of a large part of southern Manchuria, which was legally a part of China. It began to seem that if the United States wished to maintain the Open Door, she had made a mistake in supporting Japan against Russia. After the war there was, moreover, a growth of bad feeling between the two nations. The Japanese decided that they ought to have received better terms at the Treaty of Portsmouth and blamed the United States, and they resented the outspoken opposition of the white population of California to Japanese immigration.

There was an outburst of indignation in Japan when, in October, 1906, the San Francisco Board of Education issued an order segregating Oriental children in the public schools of the city. Roosevelt met the danger in a realistic spirit. As a demonstration of the power of the United States, he sent the sixteen battleships of the American navy on a tour round the world. Although he had no legal power over the school system of San Francisco, he summoned the municipal authorities to Washington and persuaded them to rescind the segregation order. He induced the Japanese government, by the Gentlemen's Agreement of 1907, to pledge itself to issue no more passports for laborers to come to the United States. Finally, by the Root-Takahira Agreement of 1908, Japan and the United States agreed to maintain the status quo in the Pacific area, to respect each other's territorial possessions, and to uphold the Open Door. The agreement tacitly accepted Japan's control over Manchuria, and to that extent, in the opinion of some students, it marked a retreat from the policy of John Hay, Japan's promise to obey the Open Door being more academic than real. If this opinion is correct, then Roosevelt had decided to accept Japanese penetration into China in return for security for the Philippines.

The Taft administration reversed Roosevelt's policy of coming to terms with Japan and attempted to make the Open Door a reality.

Largely as a result of the influence of Willard Straight, an American diplomat who had served for some years as consul in Manchuria, Taft and Knox attempted for four years to secure opportunities for American capital in the Chinese Empire, including Manchuria. They challenged the control exercised by Japan and by the European powers over different parts of China by insisting that American bankers should participate in loans to the Chinese government and in investments in Chinese railroads. This policy antagonized the various powers who were already entrenched in China, and it did not result in any considerable American investments, chiefly because American bankers were very reluctant to risk their money in the Far East. Dollar diplomacy was intended to serve the interests of American industry and finance. However, in this instance its motivations were political and not economic, and it was not supported by those interests which were expected to benefit by it. The policy was abandoned by Woodrow Wilson, who declared in 1913 that the United States government would not give support to American bankers' loans to the Chinese government. Wilson's decision was in line with his general program of refusing to allow the United States government to be used to defend the material interests of private citizens in foreign countries; but this abandonment of economic imperialism was—paradoxically enough—received with satisfaction on Wall Street.

During the World War Japan took advantage of the preoccupations of the European powers to enlarge her holdings in the Chinese Empire. The Wilson administration continued to support the Open Door, and in the hope of checking Japanese expansion it finally returned to the Taft-Knox policy which Wilson had repudiated. Relations between Japan and the United States suffered also as a result of laws, enacted after 1913 by a number of state governments, which prohibited Japanese from acquiring ownership of land. This policy of racial discrimination caused constant resentment in Japan, but under the American federal system the United States government had no power to prevent it.

In 1914 Japan, as the ally of Great Britain, declared war on Germany and proceeded to seize the German possessions in the Far

East, including a number of islands and certain economic and political rights in the Shantung peninsula, which was legally a part of China. Great Britain was compelled to accept this growth of Japanese imperialism, and in February, 1917, the British government formally consented to the Japanese control of Shantung. In 1915 Japan took further advantage of the war by presenting China with her Twenty-One Demands. Japan wanted complete control of Manchuria and Shantung, and far-reaching rights in the remainder of China. The United States protested against the demands, but it was in no position to check Japan. In November, 1917, after the United States and Japan had technically become associates in the war with Germany, the Japanese diplomat Viscount Ishii visited Washington; and by the Ishii-Lansing Agreement the Open Door and the territorial integrity of China were—on paper—reaffirmed; but Japan's special interests in Manchuria and Shantung were admitted in suitably vague terms.

As soon as possible, however, the Wilson administration took more forceful measures to check Japanese expansion. In 1918 Wilson insisted that American bankers should participate in a new loan to the Chinese government. In the same year the Allied powers sent troops to various parts of Russia, which had now, under its new Bolshevik government, concluded a separate peace with Germany. The original purpose of these troops was to prevent military stores from being seized by the German armies, although they stayed until 1919 in order to assist Russian monarchists in their war with the Bolsheviks. The United States participated in the Allied expedition to Siberia primarily in order to watch the Japanese and prevent them from seizing Russian territories. Nine thousand Americans under General Graves landed in Siberia in August, 1918, and stayed until April, 1920. At Wilson's orders they gave no support to the Russian monarchists. Wilson succeeded in preventing any Japanese annexation of eastern Siberia, though Japanese troops remained in Russian territory until 1922. At the peace conference of Versailles he was, however, compelled to allow Japan to retain the German islands in the Pacific and—at least temporarily—her control over Shantung.

EUROPE

Prior to 1914 direct relations with Europe were unimportant, except insofar as they foreshadowed the events of the World War. During the war with Spain Great Britain was friendly to the United States, while Germany was sympathetic to Spain. Between 1901 and 1914 several minor controversies with Great Britain were settled amicably—notably a dispute over the boundary line between Canada and Alaska in 1903, a dispute over American use of the Newfoundland fisheries in 1909, and the Panama Canal tolls question in 1914. Meanwhile German ambitions in the West Indies and in the Far East and the aggressive speeches of the German Kaiser caused slowly increasing alarm in the United States. American statesmen were no longer so convinced as in the nineteenth century that the United States could safely remain neutral in European conflicts; and in 1905, when a dispute between Germany and France about the economic control of Morocco threatened to provoke war, Theodore Roosevelt used his influence to bring about a settlement by negotiation. A conference met at Algeciras in 1906, at which two American representatives were present. The conference ended in a diplomatic defeat for Germany—a result to which the United States had not contributed but by which she was by no means displeased.

Meanwhile the United States was attempting to encourage the settlement of international disputes by arbitration. In 1908 and 1909 Elihu Root negotiated treaties with twenty-five nations for the arbitration of any controversies about minor questions. In 1911 Taft negotiated treaties with Great Britain and France for the arbitration of all disputes, major or minor; but the Senate, under the leadership of Henry Cabot Lodge, amended them so thoroughly that they became meaningless. Finally Bryan in 1913 and 1914 negotiated thirty "cooling off" treaties, according to which all disputes should be submitted to commissions of investigation, and there should be no resort to war for twelve months after the beginning of a dispute.

BIBLIOGRAPHY

T. A. Bailey, *Theodore Roosevelt and the Japanese-American Crisis* (1934)
*——— *Diplomatic History of the United States* (1940)

*R. S. Baker, *Woodrow Wilson: Life and Letters,* Vols. IV–VI (1931–37)
*S. F. Bemis, *Diplomatic History of the United States* (1936)
J. B. and F. Bishop, *Goethals, Genius of the Panama Canal* (1930)
J. M. Callahan, *American Foreign Policy in Mexican Relations* (1932)
P. H. Clyde, *International Rivalries in Manchuria* (1928)
I. J. Cox, *Nicaragua and the United States, 1910–27* (1927)
H. Croly, *Willard Straight* (1924)
T. Dennett, *Roosevelt and the Russo-Japanese War* (1925)
L. M. Gelber, *The Rise of Anglo-American Friendship, 1898–1906* (1938)
*A. W. Griswold, *The Far Eastern Policy of the United States* (1938)
E. Gruening, *Mexico and its Heritage* (1928)
C. W. Hackett, *The Mexican Revolution and the United States* (1926)
H. C. Hill, *Roosevelt and the Caribbean* (1927)
*P. C. Jessup, *Elihu Root* (1938)
C. L. Jones, *Caribbean Interests of the United States* (1919)
——— *The Caribbean since 1900* (1936)
C. L. Jones, H. K. Norton, and P. T. Moon, *The United States and the Caribbean* (1929)
C. Kelsey, *American Intervention in Haiti and the Dominican Republic* (1922)
M. M. Knight, *Americans in Santo Domingo* (1928)
W. D. McCain, *The United States and the Republic of Panama* (1937)
H. G. Miller, *The Isthmian Highway* (1929)
A. C. Millspaugh, *Haiti under American Control* (1931)
D. G. Munro, *The United States and the Caribbean Area* (1934)
A. Nevins, *Henry White* (1930)
E. T. Parks and W. D. McCain, *Colombia and the United States* (1935)
*D. Perkins, *The Monroe Doctrine, 1867–1907* (1937)
*H. F. Pringle, *Theodore Roosevelt* (1931)
C. F. Remer, *Foreign Investments in China* (1933)
J. F. Rippy, *The United States and Mexico* (1926)
G. H. Stuart, *Latin America and the United States* (revised edition, 1938)
C. C. Tansill, *The Purchase of the Danish West Indies* (1932)
E. Tupper and G. E. McReynolds, *Japan in American Public Opinion* (1928)
S. Welles, *Naboth's Vineyard: The Dominican Republic* (1928)
*B. M. Williams, *The Economic Foreign Policy of the United States* (1929)
M. W. Williams, *Anglo-American Isthmian Diplomacy, 1818–1915* (1916)

The World War

PART THREE

23

THE OUTBREAK

OF THE WAR

THE World War, which ended the American Progressive move-ment, upset the balance of the American economic system, and eventually drew America out of her traditional isolation, was the result of historic rivalries between European nations which had originated many generations earlier. With these questions most Americans believed, at first, that they had no concern.

Having failed to achieve any kind of unity, Europe had become divided into six great powers and a number of smaller nations. The great powers all maintained large armies or navies; they feared and suspected one another; and each of them was afraid lest it be crushed by a combination of more powerful rivals. Under such con-ditions the sentiment of nationality, both among the independent peoples and among the minority races who did not enjoy self-gov-ernment, had developed into an explosive passion capable of de-stroying tolerance and rationality. The great powers were, moreover, competing with one another for the control of colonial areas where they could obtain raw materials, invest capital, and find profitable markets for their surplus products. Another important factor in the growth of hostility was that several of them had semidespotic gov-ernments which had to pursue aggressive and successful foreign policies in order to maintain their prestige, as well as privileged military and naval castes who wanted the opportunity to win glory.

Of the various international rivalries, two were of especial importance: that of Russia against Austria, and that of Germany against Great Britain and France. Austria and Russia, the former of which included a number of discontented minority races, had for a long period been competing with each other for influence over the Slavic peoples in the Balkan peninsula. Meanwhile Germany, having defeated France in the War of 1870, had developed into the strongest military and industrial power in Europe. Her government was eager that she should acquire the dominating position and the prestige which her strength warranted, and that she should deprive Great Britain of her traditional naval and commercial supremacy. The British and French were, however, unwilling to allow Germany to become too powerful. They had succeeded in winning control of the most profitable colonial areas, and did not wish to share them with Germany. And they feared the aggressive methods of German diplomacy and the influence exercised over the German government by the military caste.

Early in the twentieth century the European powers had become grouped into two hostile and approximately equal combinations—a situation which always makes war probable. Russia had allied herself with France in the eighteen-nineties. Then Great Britain, faithful to her traditional policy of preventing any one power from becoming strong enough to dominate the continent, had formed an entente with the Franco-Russian combination and had supported the French in several disputes with Germany. In opposition to this triple entente was the triple alliance of Germany, Austria, and Italy. Italy's loyalty to the alliance was, however, very dubious, so that Austria was Germany's only reliable friend.

On June 28, 1914, the heir to the Austrian throne was murdered at Serajevo by a young student, a believer in the liberation of the Slavic races from Austrian rule. Since the activities of the Slav nationalists were being encouraged by officials of the Servian government, Austria proceeded to make demands upon Servia which the Servians regarded as incompatible with their independence. Russia supported Servia; Germany, fearful of alienating her only friend, supported Austria, and until July 27 she did not ask for any modification in the Austrian demands on Servia. On July 28 war began between Austria and Servia, and on the next day Russia began to mobilize her army. Since the war plans of the German army were based on the assumption that France could be crushed before Russia was ready, the Russian mobilization meant that Germany must either attack France without delay or—unless war were averted —face a war on two fronts and probable defeat. Rather than gamble on the chances of peace, the high command of the German army insisted on immediate action. Germany attacked France, and its army proceeded to violate the neutrality of Belgium. Meanwhile Great Britain had promised to protect the French coast against a German naval attack; but British public opinion was not at first convinced of the necessity of British participation in the war. These doubts were ended by the German invasion of Belgium, and on August 4 Great Britain declared war on Germany. British participation, really necessitated by considerations of national security, appeared to the British people as due also to a desire to protect the rights of small nations and the sanctity of international law. For British public opinion, therefore, the war became an idealistic crusade. Subsequently a number of other nations, swayed by the hope of territorial gains, which were promised to them in a number of secret treaties, entered the war. Turkey and Bulgaria became allies of Germany. Japan, Italy, Rumania, and Greece, whose nationalistic and imperialistic ambitions could best be satisfied at the expense of the central powers, joined Great Britain, France, and Russia.

The war took most Americans by surprise, and the belief that the United States should and could remain neutral was, at first, almost universal. Even Theodore Roosevelt, who was soon to urge American participation on the side of the Allies, declared in September that he was in favor of neutrality. Wilson issued a neutrality proclamation on August 4, and two weeks later he urged Americans to remain "impartial in thought as well as in action." In December, in his message to Congress, he referred to the European conflict as "a war with which we have nothing to do, whose causes cannot touch us." Wilson was no advocate of isolation; on the contrary, he hoped from the beginning that the United States would eventually be able to act as mediator in the European conflict and to bring both sides together in an enduring peace. He declared, however, at least in his public utterances, that there were rights and wrongs on both sides of the European struggle, that a lasting peace must be a peace without victory, and that the United States could not serve the interests of humanity unless she preserved her impartiality.

The train of events which finally caused Wilson to abandon this position and to become convinced that there could be no real peace without an Allied victory, will probably be a subject of controversy for many generations. As to the immediate cause of American entry into the war, there can be no dispute. The United States went to war with Germany on the ground that the German submarine campaign constituted a violation of the traditional right of neutrals and noncombatants to the freedom of the seas. In retrospect, however, it has seemed to many people that this was an inadequate reason for war. In the first place, Wilson's protests against the German submarine campaign appear to have been based both on a misreading of international law and also on a refusal to recognize that conditions had changed since the law had been formulated. And in the second place, the British blockade of Germany was also a definite violation of traditional neutral rights. It has therefore been argued that the submarine campaign was merely a pretext for war, and that the decision of the American government was due, in reality, to the influence of bankers, munition manufacturers, and other persons who had acquired an economic interest in an Allied victory. A further cause has been held to have been initial prejudices in favor of Great Britain which had been strengthened by British propaganda. These factors may have been of considerable importance; but they do not provide an answer to the fundamental question at issue. The real problem is to determine, not what various motives may have contributed to the American decision, but whether the decision itself was wise. Would a German victory in Europe have endangered the security of the United States, her system of democratic government, and the independence of the western hemisphere? Was it of vital interest to the American people to prevent the British and French from being crushed by Germany?

In spite of his public professions of neutrality, Wilson believed from the beginning of the war that a German victory would present a threat to the United States. Great Britain was an imperialist nation; but her policy was defensive and basically pacific; and on all major questions, and except when her own security was threatened, she respected international law and the rights of other nations. The United States had generally found it easy to co-operate with Great Britain; and the maintenance of the Monroe Doctrine had always depended on the control of the Atlantic by British sea power. Germany, on the other hand, was an ambitious and aggressive power; her violation of Belgian neutrality seemed to indicate that she had little regard for treaty obligations and neutral rights; and if she succeeded in destroying British naval supremacy, she might possibly extend her ambitions to the western hemisphere. The United States would then be compelled, in self-defence, to become a militaristic nation.

As early as September, 1914, Wilson had come to the conclusion that, as he told the British ambassador, a German victory would compel the United States to "give up its present ideals and devote all its energies to defence, which would mean the end of its present system of government." "England," he said to Joseph Tumulty, "is fighting our fight." Wilson's leading advisers on European affairs, Colonel House, Robert Lansing, and Walter Hines Page, were even more strongly convinced that the security of the United States required that Germany should not be allowed to crush the Allies. For this reason American policy, from the beginning of the war, was never genuinely neutral. Wilson was as lenient as American public opinion would allow to British violations of American rights and interests, declaring, as he told Tumulty, that he would never "take any action to embarrass England when she is fighting for her life and the life of the world." German violations of American rights, on the other hand, he treated with much greater severity. Eventually the majority of the American people, as a result of the submarine campaign and of sabotage activities of German agents in the United States, came to accept Wilson's private belief that Germany must not be allowed to win the war; and the United States then joined the Allies.

It is possible that the American decision was a mistake; but the wisdom of it must be judged in relation to the interests and security of the United States as a world power. The American people were not, as some recent commentators have suggested, tricked by bankers, munitions manufacturers, and Allied propagandists into a war with which they had no concern.

BIBLIOGRAPHY

A. M. Arnett, *Claude Kitchin and the Wilson War Policies* (1937)
*R. S. Baker, *Woodrow Wilson: Life and Letters,* Vols. V–VI (1935–37)
J. von Bernstorff, *My Three Years in America* (1920)
E. Borchard and W. Lage, *Neutrality for the United States* (1937)
M. E. Curti, *Bryan and World Peace* (1931)
———— *Peace or War: The American Struggle* (1936)
C. Dumba, *Memoirs of a Diplomat* (1932)
S. B. Fay, *Origins of the World War* (1928)
R. H. Gibson and M. Prendergast, *German Submarine War* (1931)
C. H. Grattan, *Why We Fought* (1929)
Lord Grey, *Twenty-five Years* (1925)
S. Gwynn (ed.), *Letters and Friendships of Sir Cecil Spring-Rice* (1929)
B. J. Hendrick, *Life and Letters of Walter Hines Page* (1922)
D. F. Houston, *Eight Years with Wilson's Cabinet* (1926)
J. P. Jones and P. M. Hollister, *The German Secret Service in America* (1918)
F. K. Lane, *Letters* (1922)
R. Lansing, *War Memoirs* (1935)
A. M. Morrissey, *The American Defence of Neutral Rights* (1939)
W. Millis, *The Road to War* (1935)
H. Notter, *Origins of the Foreign Policy of Woodrow Wilson* (1937)
*F. L. Paxson, *Pre-War Years* (1936)
H. C. Peterson, *Propaganda for War* (1939)
B. E. Schmitt, *The Coming of the War* (1930)
J. B. Scott, *Survey of International Relations between the United States and Germany* (1917)
C. Seymour, *Woodrow Wilson and the World War* (*Chronicles of America,* Vol. 48, 1921)
———— *American Diplomacy during the World War* (1933)

———— *American Neutrality, 1914–17* (1935)
C. Seymour (ed.), *Intimate Papers of Colonel House* (1928)
M. Sullivan, *Our Times,* Vol. V (1933)
*C. C. Tansill, *America Goes to War* (1938)
C. Wittke, *German-Americans and the World War* (1936)
G. S. Viereck, *Spreading Germs of Hate* (1930)

24

PSYCHOLOGICAL AND

ECONOMIC TIES

WITH THE ALLIES

INITIAL SYMPATHIES

ALTHOUGH the attitude of the American government toward the European war, and the final decision of Congress to abandon neutrality, were determined by American national interests, there is no doubt that the American people were influenced also by emotional and economic factors. It must not be assumed, however, that these factors were the decisive ones, or that they were, by themselves, strong enough to cause the American entry into the war.

At the outset of the war the attitude of many individual Americans depended on their ancestry. Those of German and Irish descent were generally opposed to American assistance for the Allies, and they were frequently inclined to sympathize with Germany. The Allies, however, had a strong initial advantage in the United States in that the British Americans, though they composed less than half the population of the country, outweighed all other groups in their economic and political influence. Most Americans of whatever descent were, moreover, predisposed to sympathize with Great Britain by reason of ties of language and literature and of common political and legal traditions. There was also a strong initial sympathy for France, due both to admiration for French civilization and to memories of the War of Independence. On the other hand the aggressive methods of German diplomacy and the bellicose utterances of the German Kaiser had offended and alarmed American opinion ever since the beginning of the century.

Pro-British feeling was stronger among the wealthy and intellectual classes—in Wall Street and in the universities—than among the farmers and workers; it was stronger along the Atlantic coast than in the Middle and Far West. This was due partly to factors of racial origin, and partly to the fact that men of wealth and education, especially in the East, were more aware of the economic and cultural ties between the United States and Europe and less inclined to believe that the United States could safely remain isolated. Among business magnates, sympathy for Germany was confined almost entirely to those of German descent. The House of Morgan, for example, according to Thomas Lamont in 1920, "had never for one moment been neutral; we didn't know how to be. From the very start we did everything we could to contribute to the cause of the Allies." In the administration the only individual who was genuinely and consistently neutral in thought as well as in action was William Jennings Bryan. In Congress, on the other hand, neutral opinion was considerably stronger, most of its leading spokesmen being the representatives of middle western states where there was a strong German element in the population.

BELLIGERENT AGENCIES

The initial advantage enjoyed by the Allies was ably cultivated by the British government. Controlling the Atlantic cables, and censoring all mail between Germany and America, the British were able to make it difficult for the Germans to state their case to Americans. Sir Gilbert Parker took charge of a British propaganda campaign, in which well-known British writers made lecture tours in America, a weekly newssheet presenting the British case was distributed to American newspapers, American libraries and clubs were supplied with British books and documents, and prominent Americans in every profession received letters from individual Englishmen. Particularly influential were the efforts to publicize the atrocities

allegedly committed by the German army in Belgium. The appointment of Lord Bryce, student of American government and former
British ambassador in Washington, to head the British committee
which gathered evidence against the Germans counted heavily with
American public opinion. Much of this British propaganda, particularly that relating to the German atrocities, was not wholly honest,
and it undoubtedly helped to convince many Americans that it was
their duty to enter the war. Its influence should, however, not be
overestimated; it was not British propaganda alone which caused
most Americans to desire an Allied victory.

The German government also subsidized propaganda agencies in
the United States, spending a total of $35,000,000 in the United
States during the period of American neutrality. German money
was spent to buy or establish newspapers in the United States, particularly *The Fatherland,* which was edited by George Silvester
Viereck. Such money was also contributed to various pro-German
and pacifist committees. German propaganda was, however, very
inept, and it was handicapped by the intrinsic weakness of the German case. German agents could not deny that Germany had initiated the war in western Europe, that her armies had invaded
Belgium and were fighting on foreign soil, and that German statesmen sometimes spoke about treaties and rules of international law
with a most injudicious cynicism.

When, moreover, the United States developed into a source of
supply for Allied war needs, German agents began to meddle in
American internal affairs; and they also committed the error of being found out. These German subversive activities had great influence in convincing Americans that the German government had
no proper regard for the rights of other nations and that a German
victory in Europe would therefore endanger American security. As
early as May, 1915, the United States secret service began to investigate the activities of German agents; and on July 24 a secret
service officer succeeded in stealing a brief case belonging to Dr.
Heinrich Albert, which had been left by its owner on the Sixth
Avenue Elevated Railroad in New York. From the contents of the
brief case, which were turned over by the government for publica-

tion in the New York *World,* it was discovered not only that the German government was spending large sums on propaganda but also that its agents were interested in promoting strikes and organizing sabotage in American munitions factories.

In August the British intercepted letters which the Austrian ambassador Dumba had sent to Vienna, from which it appeared that the Austrian government also was encouraging strikes. Dumba's recall was requested in September; and in December the German military and naval attaches, Von Papen and Boy-Ed, were asked to leave because they had tried to buy American supply ships for the use of German raiders. These revelations caused widespread alarm, and many people began to think that the United States was honeycombed with German secret service agents. Two serious fires in munition plants, the Black Tom fire of July, 1916, and the Kingsland fire of January, 1917, were generally attributed to German agents.

German activities, moreover, not only provoked antagonism against Germany; they also succeeded in weakening the pacifist movement. In addition to two avowedly anti-Ally groups—the National German-American Alliance and the American Truth Society (an Irish organization)—there also came into existence a number of committees for the preservation of American neutrality, particularly the Friends of Peace, which was supported by W. J. Bryan, and Labor's National Peace Council. Pro-Germans, however, promptly joined these organizations and provided them with money, thereby creating in the public mind a conviction that pro-Germanism and pacifism were the same thing.

Discredited by German propagandists, the pacifist movement was then made ridiculous by the fiasco of the Ford peace ship. In 1915 an Emergency Peace Conference, headed by Jane Addams and David Starr Jordan, made plans to create an international organization at The Hague which would endeavor to mediate between the two groups of powers. In November a member of the Conference, Rosika Schwimmer, asked Henry Ford for financial assistance; and Ford promptly chartered a ship for transporting various pacifist leaders to Europe. A publicity man employed by Ford informed the press that they would "get the boys out of the trenches by Christmas," and this absurd suggestion made the whole enterprise seem laughable. Serious leaders refused to join the Ford Peace Ship, which eventually left Hoboken with a party of eccentrics on December 4 and brought most of them home again after they had spent five days in Europe. Opponents of war thus became branded in the public mind as both pro-German and impractical. The result was that, after being defeated in their attempt to preserve neutrality, they were to be regarded as a public menace and deprived of their rights of free speech during the period of American participation in the war.

EXPORTS TO THE ALLIES

Meanwhile close economic connections between the United States and the Allies were being created through the export of munitions and foodstuffs. Thanks to the British blockade, American sales to Germany were negligible. Sales to Great Britain and France, on the other hand, steadily increased throughout the whole period of the war. The business was handled by the House of Morgan who, at their own suggestion, were in December, 1914, appointed commercial agents for the British government, with a commission of 2 per cent on the first $10,000,000 worth of purchases and 1 per cent on all subsequent purchases.

Exports of munitions were especially important. Between August, 1914, and December, 1915, the Allies spent $508,269,245 on munitions in the United States; between January, 1916, and March, 1917, the value of their purchases amounted to $1,679,679,554. Nearly one-third of these sums was used for explosives, most of which were supplied by E. I. Du Pont de Nemours. The firm of Du Pont, in fact, manufactured 40 per cent of all the ammunition used by the Allies during the war. The Allies, however, relied on their own factories for artillery and for airplanes, the result being that these industries were not developed in the United States and that America's own war preparations after she entered the war were severely handicapped.

The result of these purchases was to create business prosperity.

The year 1914 was a period of depression, and in August there were more than a million unemployed. A year later most branches of American economic activity were booming. The excess of exports over imports, which had amounted to $438,800,000 for the year 1913–1914, had risen to $3,567,800,000 by the year 1916–1917. And although the financiers and munitions makers may have benefited most from this war prosperity, it is important to realize that all classes of the population were affected by it. If the average profits of American steel companies rose from 7.4 per cent in 1913 to 28.7 per cent in 1917, the total profits of American wheat farmers rose from $56,713,000 in 1913 to $642,837,000 in 1917. It was not the bankers alone who had economic motives for desiring American entry into the war.

Pacifists and pro-Germans denounced the munitions traffic as unneutral. In refusing to interfere with it, however, the administration had good legal and practical justification. In August, 1915, Secretary of State Robert Lansing, replying to protests by the German government, pointed out that to change the rules of international law by embargoing munitions in the middle of a war would be unfair to the Allies, and that a general policy of embargoing munitions would benefit militaristic nations, discriminate against pacifistic nations, and compel each country to increase its own munitions manufactures. What the administration apparently failed to realize, however, was that the munitions traffic gave the United States a weapon with which it might have induced the British government to abandon those features of its blockade policy that were unduly damaging to American interests. As the British themselves realized, an embargo on munitions by the United States would have compelled them to make almost any concession that might have been asked. The American government, however, saw the situation in reverse. If the British reduced their purchases of munitions, the result would be a trade depression in America. Thus the British government was actually able to put pressure on the United States by threatening to buy a larger portion of its munitions from some other part of the world and to cut off supplies of raw material, such as rubber and tin, which were under its control.

LOANS TO THE ALLIES

Almost as influential as the purchase of American munitions by the Allies was their borrowing of American money. At the outset of the war the Allies were able to buy for cash, partly by shipping gold to the United States, partly by selling American securities owned by their citizens. Altogether they sent about 1 billion dollars in gold, and sold about 2 billion dollars' worth of securities. The United States government, moreover, refused at first to countenance loans to the Allies. Approached by the House of Morgan in August, 1914, Secretary of State Bryan declared that the floating of an Allied war loan would be unneutral.

It was, however, difficult to organize large-scale sales without short-term credits. The opposition of the administration to credits soon began to weaken; and once credits were allowed, it was the logical next step to tolerate loans. By that time American prosperity had become dependent on Allied purchases; and when the cash reserves of the Allies began to be exhausted, loans became the only method by which it could be maintained.

In October, 1914, President Wilson agreed that American banks might make short-term credits to the Allies. Credits then began to accumulate, with no provision made for their liquidation; and by August, 1915, this financial problem had become acute. Pressed by Lansing and McAdoo and by the Wall Street bankers, Wilson then agreed not to oppose loans to the Allies. An Anglo-French mission arrived in September and proceeded to float a loan of $500,000,000, which was to run for five years at 5 per cent. After this there were no more large loans for nearly a year. By August, 1916, however, the financial resources of the Allies were near exhaustion. Between that date and April, 1917, Allied borrowings in the United States totalled $1,072,000,000 by Great Britain, $267,000,000 by France, $250,000,000 by Canada, and $50,000,000 by Russia. These loans were floated by American bankers, who collected commissions; but the money was contributed by perhaps as many as 500,000 American citizens. These 500,000 individuals, and not merely the Wall Street bankers, were now financially interested in the success of the Allies.

By the beginning of 1917 it was becoming more difficult to sell

Allied bonds in America. Should, however, the credit of the Allies be exhausted, the result would be not only that they would probably lose the war but also that they would be unable to make further purchases from American factories and farms; the United States would therefore suffer from an acute economic depression. Some of Wilson's advisers were aware of this fact, and they urged American entry into the war as the only way out of the dilemma. This point of view was put forward, in particular, by Walter Hines Page, who sent a cable to Wilson in March, 1917, in which he declared that "the pressure of this approaching crisis has gone beyond the financial ability of the Morgan financial agency for the British and French governments. The need is becoming too great and urgent for any private agency to meet. . . . Our going to war is the only way in which our present pre-eminent trade position can be maintained and a panic averted."

There is no evidence that Wilson was influenced in any degree by these economic considerations, nor were they the real reasons why Page wanted America to enter the war. Page had been a strong partisan of the Allied cause since the beginning of the war. The United States favored the Allies for reasons of national interest, and she entered the war because of the German submarine campaign. It is, however, obvious that if the German government had abandoned the use of the submarine, the economic pressure in favor of American entry into the war would have become increasingly strong. What the United States would have done if the German government had not made its fateful decision of January, 1917, to adopt unrestricted submarine warfare is a question about which one can only speculate.

BIBLIOGRAPHY

The same as for Chapter 23.

25

AMERICAN DIPLOMACY, 1914-1916

CONTROVERSIES WITH GREAT BRITAIN

THE primary official responsibility of the United States government after the outbreak of the war was to protect the rights of neutrals under international law against the warring powers. These rights had been codified in the Declaration of London of 1909. The Declaration had not been ratified by the British Parliament, but the differences between the Declaration and previous international law were of small importance. The Declaration of London declared, first, that "paper" blockades were illegal. To be legal a blockade of an enemy seaport must be effectively maintained by an adequate naval force. Second, the doctrine of "continuous voyage" was denied. In other words, goods other than war material could be shipped freely to neutral ports even if they were ultimately destined for a blockaded country. Third, goods were divided into absolute contraband, conditional contraband, and noncontraband, and the only goods which could be seized by a blockading force were war material (absolute contraband) and goods for the use of armed forces (conditional contraband). All goods destined for civilian use were exempt from seizure. By international law, therefore, the United States had the right to trade freely with the civilian populations of both Great Britain and Germany.

At the outset of the war the British government established a blockade of Germany, which grew steadily more comprehensive, and which violated several rules of international law. The United States government, however, made no serious attempt to secure a modification of the British blockade policies. Wilson did not wish to prevent the British from taking action which they believed necessary to win the war. Of his chief advisers on foreign policy, Colonel House and Robert Lansing, who was then Counsellor to the State Department, were even more definitely pro-Ally, while the American ambassador in London, Walter Hines Page, was from the beginning an enthusiastic partisan of the Allied cause. These pro-Ally sympathies were ably cultivated by the English Foreign Secretary, Sir Edward Grey, whose personality was particularly sympathetic to the Americans.

Although, therefore, the United States officials made frequent protests against the British blockade policies, they never threatened to resort to action. Robert Lansing afterward declared that "there was always in my mind the conviction that we would ultimately become an ally of Great Britain and that it would not do, therefore, to let our controversies reach a point where diplomatic correspondence gave place to action." "The notes that were sent were long and exhaustive treatises which opened up new subjects of discussion rather than closing those in controversy. Short and emphatic notes were dangerous. Everything was submerged in verbosity. It was done with deliberate purpose. It insured continuance of the controversies and left the questions unsettled." The primary purpose of these notes was, in fact, to satisfy American public opinion; and both Page and House occasionally gave advice to the British government as to how the notes might most effectively be answered and what measures would both enable the British to maintain their blockade and at the same time appease American traders whose goods were being confiscated. Sir Edward Grey recorded later that "Page's advice and suggestions were of the greatest value in warning us when to be careful or encouraging us when we could safely be firm." The British realized quickly that the United States would never support its protests by action; and throughout the whole course of the war they did not make a single important concession. In certain respects, in fact, they appear to have abused the friendly attitude of the United States in order to secure illegitimate commercial advantages for themselves.

At the beginning of the war the United States asked the warring powers if they would obey the Declaration of London. Germany agreed, but Great Britain declared that the Declaration must be modified. In a series of Orders in Council the British steadily extended their contraband lists to include many raw materials, such as foodstuffs and cotton, declaring that almost all commodities were potentially war materials. They began to seize commodities being shipped to the neutral countries of northern Europe, except when the shipper could prove that they were not destined for German use; they declared that the whole of the North Sea was a military area and that all neutral vessels must stop at British ports for inspection; and finally, on March 11, 1915, they extended the blockade regulations to cover all commodities entering or leaving Germany. The blockade now completely prohibited all imports into Germany and northern Europe except when they could be proved to be for neutral consumption. Supplies shipped to neutral countries were limited to their normal peace-time needs, and all cargoes consigned to firms which traded with Germany were seized. These orders violated the rules of international law which had declared that a blockade must be effective, that the theory of "continuous voyage" could be applied only to war materials, and that goods not destined for military use were exempt from seizure.

The United States government sent protests against these Orders in Council in September and December, 1914, and in March, 1915. These protests, however, were not worded in a manner likely to win concessions. That of December, for example, requested the British not to interfere with American trade "unless such interference is manifestly an imperative necessity to protect their national safety, and then only to the extent that it is a necessity." In February, 1915, moreover, in retaliation for the British blockade, the German submarine campaign had commenced; and the British government could then time its replies to the American protests so that they arrived during periods of controversy between the United States and Germany. The British reply to the American note of March, 1915, for example, arrived in July, in the middle of the *Lusitania* controversy.

Apart from the blockade itself, the necessity for which the United States government finally accepted, there were a number of minor matters which provoked American complaints. American ships bound for neutral ports in northern Europe were often detained in British ports for months before they were finally searched and allowed to proceed. Meanwhile British trade with those same neutral countries was increasing. The United States sent a note of protest in October, 1915, to which the British did not reply until April, 1916, during the controversy with Germany over the sinking of the *Sussex*. The British searched all mail passing between the United States and Germany and northern Europe; and it was suspected that they used this practice in order to obtain American trade secrets for the benefit of their own traders. Controversy on this subject continued through 1916. The British made a black list of neutral firms suspected of trading with Germany and attempted to prevent all other firms, British or neutral, from doing business with them. In July, 1916, the black list was extended to cover about thirty American firms. American protests, however, caused this order to be modified. Finally, the British held up shipments of German exports which were needed by American industry, and they offered to supply goods of their own manufacture in their place. A controversy about a consignment of German machine knitting needles continued from May, 1916, until February, 1917. It was then discovered that the British manufacturers were themselves importing German knitting needles of the same brand without interference by the British government.

The British attitude to these questions finally extorted from President Wilson, in October, 1916, the complaint, "How difficult it is to be friends with Great Britain without doing whatever she wants us to do."

CONTROVERSIES WITH GERMANY

Meanwhile the United States government, having tolerated violations of international law by the British, was insisting that the Germans obey it. This difference reflected the pro-Ally sympathies of Wilson and his advisers, though Wilson himself does not appear to have been consciously inconsistent.

On February 4, 1915, the Kaiser signed an order for submarine warfare on all enemy merchant ships in British waters. On February 10 the United States government declared that Germany would be held to "strict accountability" if any American ships or lives were lost; and when the submarines finally commenced action, on February 22, they were given strict orders not to attack neutral ships. The first American life was lost on March 28. On that date the British passenger ship *Falaba* was torpedoed after the passengers had been allowed twenty-three minutes in which to disembark, and one American, Leon C. Thrasher, was among the drowned. On April 28 the American ship *Cushing* was attacked by a German seaplane, and on May 1 the American tanker *Gulflight* was torpedoed with a loss of three Americans. These two attacks were accidental, and Germany at once apologized and offered compensation. Finally, on May 7, 1915, the British liner *Lusitania* was torpedoed off the Irish coast. The ship sank in eighteen minutes, and of 1,959 persons on board, 1,198 were drowned, 128 of these being Americans. This episode, which aroused widespread indignation in the United States, brought matters to a head. More than any other single event it was to be the cause of American participation in the war two years later.

During the controversy with Germany over the use of the submarine, the United States government made two contentions, both of which appear to have been legally faulty. It was maintained, in the first place, that American citizens were under American protection even when they chose to travel on enemy ships. This attitude seems to have been contrary to the accepted rules of international law, and it was opposed by Secretary of State Bryan, who declared that an American who lost his life while traveling on a British ship was guilty of contributory negligence and that it was wrong for "one man, acting purely for himself and his own interests, and without consulting his government" to create an international crisis. Wilson, however, preferred to follow the advice of Robert Lansing. In contending that American citizens traveling on British passenger ships should be immune from German attacks, the United States government also failed to take account of the fact that those ships sometimes carried munitions. On board the *Lusitania* were 4,200 cases of cartridges and 1,250 cases of shrapnel; and, although the liner appears not to have been equipped as an auxiliary warship, the Germans had reason for believing that she was. Another significant feature of the episode was the failure of the ship's officers to take even the most elementary precautions to avoid a submarine attack. In the case of the *Lusitania,* therefore, Germany was not the only guilty party; the British were to blame for transporting munitions on a passenger ship, and the American government was at fault for failing to warn American citizens that if they traveled on enemy ships it was at their own risk.

In the second place, the American government insisted that submarines must search merchant ships and provide for the safety of the passengers and crew before torpedoing them. This was an established rule of international law; but it did not apply to the existing situation. From the beginning of the war the British government armed its merchant ships and ordered them, whenever possible, to ram submarines rather than submit to seizure; it also made a practice of luring submarines to their destruction by flying American flags on British vessels. For German submarines to conform to international law was, therefore, to invite their own destruction. Nor was such procedure legally necessary, since a merchant ship armed with offensive weapons—and against the submarine all weapons were offensive —lost its peaceful character and became legally a warship. The American government, nevertheless, continued to insist that the weapons carried by British merchant ships were purely defensive and that no such ships might be torpedoed without warning. In support of this claim it quoted the opinion of Chief Justice John Marshall in the *Nereide* Case, declaring that merchant ships might legitimately arm themselves. Wilson's legal advisers, however, omitted a paragraph from Marshall's opinion in which the Chief Justice had added that an armed merchant ship must be regarded as "an open and declared belligerent" and "subject to all the dangers of the belligerent character."

The only sound legal reason for protesting against the submarine campaign was that it violated the American right, under international law, to ship noncontraband articles to the Allies. The United States, had, however, weakened its case by waiving that right in the case of the British blockade of Germany. There was a strong feeling in the United States that the German submarine campaign differed from the British blockade in that it involved the destruction of lives and not merely of property. As Wilson declared in April, 1917, "property can be paid for; the lives of peaceful and innocent people cannot be." Such a distinction was, perhaps, not strictly fair to Germany, who was unable to adopt any other method of retaliating against the blockade. Nor could the blockade, which set out to starve the German population into submission, be regarded in its ultimate consequences as a particularly humane method of warfare. The truth was that the American government was never strictly neutral or impartial; and its attitude, which must be condemned if it is judged in purely legalistic terms, can be justified only in terms of national policy and interest. American diplomacy was helping to prevent Germany from winning the war.

The first *Lusitania* note was sent on May 13. Germany replied by defending the sinking and, in July, by offering not to attack passenger ships if the United States would guarantee that they did not carry contraband. Meanwhile, submarine commanders were secretly given orders not to attack large passenger ships. Wilson regarded the German replies as unsatisfactory and further notes were sent on June 9 and July 21. Bryan believed that the American position was legally unsound and that it would inevitably lead to war, and on June 8 he resigned from the State Department and was succeeded by the pro-Ally Robert Lansing.

On August 19 a German submarine, disobeying orders, sank the British passenger ship *Arabic* without warning, two Americans being drowned. On September 4 another British passenger ship, the *Hesperia*, was torpedoed; and on November 7 an Austrian submarine sank an Italian passenger ship, the *Ancona*, with the loss of about twenty American lives. Meanwhile the controversy about the *Lusitania* continued; and although, in February, 1916, Germany admitted her liability for the loss of American lives and expressed her regret, she still refused to accept Wilson's contention that the sinking had been illegal. In the same month the German government ordered that all passenger ships should be spared but that armed merchant ships might still be sunk without warning. These orders were violated on March 24, when the French steamer *Sussex* was sunk without warning, the submarine commander having failed to recognize it as a passenger ship.

Wilson replied, on April 18, by threatening to break off diplomatic relations unless Germany would agree that neither merchant ships nor passenger ships should henceforth be torpedoed without warning. The German government decided to give way, and on May 4, 1916, it gave the required pledge. It added, however, that unless the United States induced Great Britain to relax her blockade, it might be compelled to reconsider this decision. This ended the controversy. Wilson had forced Germany to abandon unlimited submarine warfare and, by so doing, had made a considerable contribution to an Allied victory. He had, however, placed the United States in a position where, if Germany decided to abandon the agreement, the United States would have no alternative but to go to war.

In the course of the controversy Wilson and Lansing had realized that the arming of merchant ships by the British was the crux of the matter and that they could not fairly ask the Germans not to torpedo ships without warning unless they also asked the British not to arm their ships. A note to this effect was sent to the British government in January, 1916; but when Great Britain refused to agree the matter was dropped.

Meanwhile the stand taken by the American government was beginning to cause alarm in Congress. Many congressmen, believing that American interests were not involved in the European struggle, felt that the United States should not go to war with Germany in order to defend the claim that American citizens traveling on British ships should be immune from attack. In February, 1916, resolutions in repudiation of this claim were introduced by Senator Gore and Congressman McLemore. Wilson protested against these resolutions in a letter to Senator Stone, chairman of the Senate Foreign Relations Committee, in which he insisted that Americans had a right, under international law, to travel safely on British passenger ships. "No nation, no group of nations," he declared, "has the right while the war is in progress to alter or disregard the principles which all nations have agreed upon in mitigation of the horrors and sufferings of war. . . . For my own part I cannot consent to any abridgement of the rights of American citizens in any respect. . . . What we are contending for in this matter is of the very essence of the things which have made America a sovereign nation." As a result of administration pressure Congress was induced to reject the Gore-McLemore resolutions.

While the debate on these resolutions was in progress, Colonel House was in Europe exploring the possibility of American mediation between the two sides. At the same time he was bringing the United States appreciably nearer to entering the war. Wilson had already sent House to Europe in January, 1915; but this visit had been fruitless apart from a suggestion by Sir Edward Grey that after the war a world parliament must be established to maintain peace and that the United States ought surely to exercise leadership in such an organization. House returned to Europe in January, 1916; and, after a visit to Berlin, he joined Grey in drafting a memorandum, which was signed on February 22. The memorandum declared that when the Allied powers should so request, President Wilson would invite both sides to a peace conference, and that if Germany refused the invitation, or if the conference failed to bring peace, the United States would probably enter the war on the side of the Allies. Wilson himself was now almost convinced that the United States ought to join the Allies; and some time in the early months of 1916, in the so-called Sunrise Conference, he made the suggestion to the Democratic leaders in the House of Representatives. At this period, while the Allied armies were unable to break through the German lines in France and Flanders, Germany was winning victories over Russia and in the Balkans; and if the United States remained neutral, it seemed quite possible that Germany might eventually win the war.

When, however, the Allies failed to respond to the House-Grey memorandum, Wilson became considerably disillusioned. In spite of his conviction that the Allies were fighting America's battle, he still believed that only a negotiated peace would make possible a lasting settlement. The Allied peoples, however, were so convinced of Germany's guilt in starting the war and so resentful of the deaths and sufferings which they had endured, that they would not consider peace until after Germany had been decisively defeated. They continued to hope, moreover, that their armies would win real victories in Flanders. They refused, therefore, to suggest a conference. Disappointed at his failure to bring about peace, and increasingly angered by the British violations of American rights of trade, Wilson began to turn in the direction of a genuine neutrality. At the end of 1916 he was more nearly impartial toward the war than at any time since it had started.

BIBLIOGRAPHY

The same as for Chapter 23.

26

THE UNITED STATES

ENTERS THE WAR

PREPAREDNESS

DURING the first two and a half years of the war, public opinion in the United States continued to be undecided on the question of American participation. Many people, particularly in the East, believed that war should have been declared after the sinking of the *Lusitania*. The most prominent and the most aggressive of these was Theodore Roosevelt, whose contempt for Wilson's pacifistic inclinations was unbounded. The advocates of neutrality, however, although they made considerably less noise than the interventionists, probably had a majority of the people on their side.

The most conspicuous result of the war on American politics was the crusade for preparedness. It was predicted that if Germany won the war in Europe and destroyed the British naval supremacy, she would proceed next to intervene in Latin America in violation of the Monroe Doctrine, and might even attack the United States. These possibilities caused widespread alarm. A number of organizations were established to advocate preparedness, among them being the Military Training Camp Association, the Junior American Guard, the National Society for Patriotic Education, the National Security League, the American Defence Society, the American Legion, and the American Rights Committee. The most prominent champions of the movement were Theodore Roosevelt and General Leonard Wood.

There was also a growing tendency to be intolerant toward the more recent immigrants and toward the use of foreign languages. A National Americanization Committee was formed to inculate patriotism among the so-called "hyphenated Americans." In the summer of 1916 a number of preparedness parades were organized. During one such parade, held in San Francisco on July 22, a bomb was exploded, and two California labor leaders, Thomas J. Mooney and Warren K. Billings, were convicted and sentenced to life imprisonment on what appeared later to have been fabricated evidence. This *cause célèbre* continued to excite controversy until the release of both men in 1939 and 1940.

Wilson opposed the preparedness movement as long as he dared. He apparently felt that even if the United States should finally enter the war, she must prove her pacifistic inclinations by being unready for it. He finally decided, however, that it was necessary for political reasons that he support moderate measures of preparedness, and in June, 1916, he marched in a preparedness parade in Washington. The same month Congress passed a National Defence Act, providing for an increase in the army to 175,000 men and the creation of a Reserve Corps for training civilians and officers. In August, in the Naval Appropriation Act, a billion and a half dollars was voted for increases in the navy; and the Army Appropriation Act provided for the creation of a Council of National Defence, composed of six cabinet members and seven civilian experts, to regulate civilian life during war. In September Wilson secured the creation of a United States Shipping Board, with an appropriation of $50,000,000 for building merchant ships. This measure, obviously necessary in view of the scarcity of American ships and the diminution of Allied ships as a result of the submarine campaign, had been advocated by Wilson since the autumn of 1914; but private shipping interests had hitherto succeeded in blocking it on the ground that it was socialistic.

THE ELECTION OF 1916

Meanwhile the presidential election was approaching. The Democratic convention was notable for a speech by Governor Glynn of New York, in which he provoked enormous enthusiasm by praising

Wilson for avoiding war. "He kept us out of war," became the chief campaign slogan of the Democrats. Wilson was careful to make no commitments for the future. "I know that you are depending upon me to keep this nation out of the war," he had declared in a speech in January. "But you have laid another duty upon me. You have bidden me see to it that nothing stains or impairs the honor of the United States. . . . There may at any moment come a time when I cannot preserve both the honor and the peace of the United States. Do not exact of me an impossible and contradictory thing." Nevertheless many people voted for Wilson in the belief that the Democratic slogan was a promise as well as a statement of fact.

The Republican convention was notable chiefly for the return of Theodore Roosevelt to the fold. The nomination was given to Charles Evans Hughes, who had been an Associate Justice of the Supreme Court since 1910, and who was acceptable to both wings of the party. When Roosevelt was nominated by a separate Progressive convention, he refused to be a candidate and urged the Progressives to vote for Hughes—a desertion which caused bitter resentment among many of those who had followed him out of the Republican Party in 1912. The Republicans then proceeded to try to carry water on both shoulders. While some of their orators, headed by Roosevelt, demanded immediate war with Germany, others appealed to the pro-German vote on the ground that Wilson had supported the Allies. Hughes himself, unable to reconcile these contradictory attitudes, made speeches about the tariff, a question which excited no enthusiasm.

The election, nevertheless, was close, Wilson winning by an electoral vote of 277 to 254 and a popular vote of 9,129,000 to 8,538,200. The vote of California, which went to Wilson by a majority of only 4,000, was enough to decide the election; and it appeared that Hughes would probably have won the state if he had not been misled by the conservative Republicans into snubbing Hiram Johnson, leader of the California Progressives, who had won the Republican nomination for the Senate.

WAR

After the election Wilson made another, and more serious, effort to bring about a negotiated peace in Europe—a move which was the more necessary in view of the likelihood that Germany would resume unlimited submarine warfare. In December he invited all the belligerents to formulate their peace terms, declaring that their war aims, as stated hitherto, appeared to be "virtually the same"—a statement which caused considerable indignation in Great Britain and France.

The replies of the belligerents showed, however, that peace was wholly impossible. The Allied peace terms, which included not only the evacuation of all conquered territories and the restoration of Belgium and northern France but also the dismemberment of Austria-Hungary and payment by Germany of compensation for the damages which her armies had inflicted, would never be accepted by Germany unless she were defeated. Germany, who had hitherto been victorious in military operations, was genuinely hopeful for peace, but only for a peace advantageous to herself, to which the Allied powers would never agree. On January 22, in an address to the Senate, Wilson stated his own conception of a satisfactory peace settlement. The peace terms must be arranged by mutual agreement and without a victory for either side; they must recognize the right of all nationalities to self-government; they must give every great nation access to the sea and must guarantee the freedom of the seas; and armaments must be limited and entangling alliances forbidden. The settlement must, moreover, be maintained by a system of collective security which would make aggression impossible. Wilson summarized his ideals by demanding a universal Monroe Doctrine.

Nine days later, on January 31, the German government announced that on the next day it would adopt unlimited submarine warfare. The seas around Great Britain and France were declared to be a war zone, and all ships, both neutral and belligerent, which entered the zone were liable to be sunk without warning. The United States was to be allowed to send one passenger ship a week to the British port of Falmouth, provided that the ship was clearly marked with red and white stripes and that it carried no contraband. The German civilian government had consistently opposed submarine warfare, but it had now been overruled by the military leaders, who were convinced that they could starve Great Britain into submission and that, even if the United States entered the war, her military assistance to the Allies would be negligible and her economic assistance could not be greater than it was already.

At a meeting of his cabinet Wilson found that all his advisers felt that there was now only one course open to the United States and that, in the words of Secretary of Agriculture Houston, "nothing worse can ever befall us than what Germany proposes and no greater insult can be offered to any people." On February 3 diplomatic relations with Germany were broken, and the German ambassador was dismissed.

During the next two months Wilson slowly and reluctantly arrived at the conviction that war was unavoidable. On February 24 the Zimmermann note, sent by the German Foreign Secretary on January 19 and intercepted and decoded by the British, was made public. In case the United States should declare war, Mexico was invited by Germany to become her ally and to regain the territories taken from her in 1848; and the Mexican government was urged to invite help from Japan. This fantastic suggestion caused widespread indignation and alarm in the Southwest and along the Pacific coast.

On February 26 Wilson asked Congress to appropriate money for arming American merchant ships. The United States was to adopt a policy of armed neutrality and await overt action by Germany before taking more drastic steps. A large majority of Congress was in favor of the proposal, but a small group of western senators, headed by La Follette, succeeded in killing it by filibustering until March 4, when the session ended. Wilson denounced the filibusterers as "a little group of wilful men, representing no opinion but their own," who had "rendered the great government of the United States helpless and contemptible." On March 12 he ordered merchant ships to be armed even without congressional assent.

The overt action which Wilson expected came on March 12, when a submarine sank the *Algonquin* by gunfire. During the following three weeks five other American vessels were sunk, the loss of life amounting to twenty-five Americans and thirty-nine of other nationalities. On March 20 Wilson found that his cabinet was unanimous for war, and Congress was summoned to meet on April 2. Wilson was still reluctant to accept the necessity of war. He realized how much harm it would do to American democratic ideals. On the evening before the meeting of Congress he told Frank Cobb, of the New York *World:* "Once lead this people into war, and they'll forget there ever was such a thing as tolerance; to fight you must be brutal and ruthless, and the very spirit of ruthless brutality will enter into the very fiber of our national life." He sought justification for America's entry into the war in the belief that only American influence could bring about a just peace, without revenge, and that the Allies would not listen to America if she remained neutral. Unless the United States joined the Allies, he told Jane Addams, she could "only call through a crack in the door" when the peace conference was held. Further support for the belief that Wilson's ideals could be achieved through an Allied victory was provided by the Russian Revolution, which overthrew the Czar in February, 1917. Wilson could now claim what had formerly been impossible—that this was a war of the democracies against the autocracies.

Wilson's war message, read to Congress on April 2, declared that the submarine campaign, the sabotage plots of German agents in the United States, and the Zimmermann note left no alternative but war. "It is a fearful thing," he declared, "to lead this great peaceful people into war, into the most terrible and disastrous of all wars, civilization itself seeming to be in the balance. But the right is more precious than peace, and we shall fight for the things which we have always carried nearest our hearts—for democracy, for the right of those who submit to authority to have a voice in their own governments, for the rights and liberties of small nations, for a universal dominion of right by such a concert of free people as shall bring peace and safety to all nations and make the world itself at last free. To such a task we can dedicate our lives and our fortunes, everything that we are and everything that we have, with the pride of those who know that the day has come when America is privileged to spend her blood and her might for the principles that gave her birth and happiness and the peace which she has treasured. God helping her, she can do no other."

There was never any doubt that Congress would decide for war,

and the only question was the size of the majority. In view of the
inflamed state of public opinion, a vote against war required considerable courage. In the Senate the vote was 82 against 6, the dis-
senters being La Follette of Wisconsin, Norris of Nebraska, Stone of
Missouri, Vardaman of Mississippi, Gronna of North Dakota, and
Lane of Oregon. The viewpoint expressed by these men was that the
British violations of American rights were as deserving of condemnation as those committed by the Germans, and that the United States
was being drawn into the war on the Allied side by the economic
interests of bankers and munitions manufacturers. In the House
of Representatives the vote was 373 to 50. War was declared on
April 6.

The outcome was to show that Wilson's idealistic aspirations could
not be achieved by means of an Allied victory, and to this extent it
justified the small group of men who had voted against war. As
Wilson himself had realized, a peace dictated by the victors, at the
end of four and a half years of bitter conflict, could be a peace only
of revenge and not of conciliation. It is plain, moreover, that the
United States had finally been driven into the war by the German
government because she had never been genuinely neutral and had
asked from Germany an obedience to international law which she
had not required of the Allies. Realization of these facts was eventually to cause many Americans to feel that their entry into the war
had been an error and that they had been tricked into it by the propaganda of the Allies and by those Americans who were financially
interested in an Allied victory. Although, however, the United States
may have gone to war for mistaken reasons, one must not conclude
that entrance into the war was itself a mistake. The cardinal question
at issue was neither the rights and wrongs of the submarine campaign nor the relative honesty and idealism of the Allied and German
governments, but whether it was desirable that the United States, as
a democratic nation, interested both in her own security and in the
maintenance of international order and world peace, should prevent
a German victory. Whether the United States acted wisely or not
can be determined only by comparing what actually happened after

1918 with what might have happened if the Allied nations, deprived of American assistance, had been compelled to capitulate to the German army.

BIBLIOGRAPHY

The same as for Chapter 23.

27

THE WAR AT HOME

THE TASK OF PREPARATION

ONCE the United States had abandoned neutrality, the overwhelming majority of the population loyally supported the government, and only a very small number of individuals dared to oppose the war. The task of placing American life on a war footing was, nevertheless, one of enormous difficulties. Modern war is not merely a war between armies and navies; it is also a war between economic systems, and the victory goes to the side which can command the greater economic resources and can more effectively mobilize the efforts of its civilian population and maintain their morale. After the United States entered the war, the government was compelled to assume dictatorial powers over industry, regiment the lives and thoughts of the American people, and place restrictions on civil liberties. The United States became, for the duration of the war, a totalitarian state.

In spite of the measures of preparedness which had been adopted in 1916, the country was unready for immediate participation in the war. The army, owing mainly to the reforms that had been made by Elihu Root between 1899 and 1904, was a much more efficient body than it had been at the time of the war with Spain; but it was too small to be of any immediate service to the Allies. Before the United States could reinforce the British and French in France, hundreds of thousands of civilians had to be drafted and trained. The army, moreover, had also to be equipped and transported; and the United States was deficient in many important branches of the munitions industry and lacked an adequate supply of both ships and yards for building them. The economic needs of the Allies had meanwhile to be supplied—a task which the German submarine campaign made both vitally important and exceedingly difficult.

Hence, while the United States was drafting into the army a large part of the civilian population, she must also increase the productiveness both of agriculture and of industry. It was therefore not surprising that the American war preparation should proceed so slowly that critics began to accuse the government of criminal negligence, and also that it was not until May, 1918—nearly fourteen months after the United States had officially entered the war—that American troops began to participate in serious fighting on the Western Front.

The chief responsibility for war preparation belonged, under Wilson, to Newton D. Baker, a disciple of Tom Johnson of Cleveland, who had become Secretary of War in March, 1916. As chairman of the Committee of National Defence Baker had the task not only of organizing the army but also of putting the American economic system on a war basis. Of the twenty months during which the United States was at war, the first six were unavoidably devoted mainly to formulating policies, the second six to organization and preparation, and only the last eight to action. At the outbreak of the war whatever suspicions the administration may have entertained against big business were abandoned; and leading industrialists were invited to come to Washington to serve the government at nominal salaries of a dollar a year.

The tasks of organization were at first entrusted to a number of committees, which were responsible to the Committee of National Defence. Washington at this period has been described as "a patriotic madhouse." It gradually became apparent that divided responsibility was incompatible with efficiency; and single individuals, responsible to the President, were gradually given sole authority over the various branches of the American war effort. This process was hastened by the growth of discontent with the apparent slowness of the war preparation, which came to a head in January, 1918. Many Republican leaders denounced the government as inefficient, and they were supported by the Democratic Senator Chamberlain, chairman of the Senate Committee on Military Affairs, who told a New York audience that "the military establishment of America has broken down. . . . It has almost ceased functioning." Instead of consenting to the Republican demand for a coalition, Wilson replied by asking that the government be given virtually dictatorial powers over industry. These were granted by Congress in the Overman Act, which was passed in May.

Subsequent investigators have generally absolved Wilson and Baker of any charges of being dilatory or inadequate, and they have concluded that the government acted with a most impressive efficiency. Equally remarkable, perhaps, was its freedom from corruption. The Republican administration which followed that of Wilson spent more than $3,000,000 in an effort to prove that its predecessor had been dishonest; and, although not all the dollar-a-year men were blameless, it was unable to find any evidence of misconduct on the part of the regular government officials.

As it turned out, however, America's war preparations were on a much more elaborate scale than was necessary. The administration made its plans on the assumption that the war would continue at least until the end of 1919, and that in its final stages the United States would bear the main burden of the struggle with Germany. The unforeseen collapse of German resistance in November, 1918, made much of the American preparation unnecessary and caused the war to be much more costly than it need have been. The United States drafted at least four times as many soldiers as were needed and spent vast sums unnecessarily on ships, munitions, and equipment. The cost of the war was further increased by the sale after the war, particularly by the Harding administration, of ships, factories, and supplies for a small fraction of what the government had originally paid for them.

THE DRAFT

Soon after the declaration of war, it was decided that an army should be sent to France and that it should be raised mainly by conscription. There was considerable opposition to conscription in Congress, but the experience of Great Britain showed that it was necessary—not because of any lack of enthusiasm but because it would enable the government to choose which persons could be spared for service in France and which were needed at home.

The Selective Service Act became law on May 18. The War Department had already made preparations for the draft, the officials mainly responsible being General Enoch H. Crowder, the Provost Marshal–General, and Captain Hugh S. Johnson. On June 5 all men between the ages of twenty-one and thirty, inclusive, were required to register. A year's imprisonment was the penalty for refusal, but every effort was made to treat the registration day as an occasion for patriotic enthusiasm and to avoid any emphasis on compulsion. In 1918 the registration ages were extended to from eighteen to forty-five. The total number who registered was 23,908,576. Local draft boards then gave exemption to men who had families dependent on them, who were physically incapacitated, who were needed for duties at home, or who belonged to religious organizations with pacifistic principles. This left 6,373,414 persons available for service. The final choice was then made by lottery.

In June, 1917, 687,000 persons were called for service, and more than two million were called at later dates. Altogether more than 4,750,000 persons served in the armed forces. Of these about 750,000 were in the army, navy, and national guard at the outset of the war; more than 1,250,000 were accepted as volunteers; and the remainder were drafted.

Draft evaders numbered 337,649, only 163,738 being caught. Of those who, after being drafted, refused war service, a number, whose objections were based on religious principles, were assigned to noncombatant service; but 450, who refused service on political grounds, were condemned to imprisonment. Some of these objectors were not released until November, 1920.

FINANCE

The total ultimate cost of the war to the United States government has approached 50 billion dollars. About 32 billion was spent during 1917, 1918, and 1919. Of this sum $10,338,000,000 represented credits to the Allies for purchases in the United States, of which $2,606,000,000 was subsequently repaid. About one-third of the cost was paid for immediately by means of taxes; the remainder became part of the national debt.

Taxes were steadily increased by successive acts of Congress. By the end of the war there was an income tax of 2 per cent on all incomes above $1,000 and surtaxes on larger incomes. Incomes above $4,000 paid a surtax of 12 per cent; those above $500,000 paid 65 per cent. The corporation income tax was increased to 6 per cent, and special excess profits taxes were imposed in order to check profiteering. Firms earning a profit of more than 15 per cent paid an excess profits tax of 20 per cent; those earning more than 33 per cent paid 60 per cent. In addition to these direct taxes, Congress also voted a large number of excise duties on luxury articles.

Five war loans were raised, the last of them in April, 1919. The total amount of money subscribed was nearly 21 billion dollars. The interest rates varied from 3½ per cent on the first loan to 4¾ per cent on the last. The government sold its bonds directly instead of acting through the banks; and every effort was made to arouse popular enthusiasm, including some intimidation of those who seemed reluctant to subscribe. The results of this high-pressure salesmanship were remarkable. It was estimated that previously not more than 300,000 persons had been in the habit of buying stocks or bonds, yet the total number of subscribers to the fourth government war loan amounted to 21 million.

WAR INDUSTRIES

The measures for the control of industry involved a direct reversal of previous government policies. Whereas the government had previously been endeavoring to maintain competition, it was now necessary to enforce co-ordination and combination. In the early months of the war the Council for National Defence appointed seven major committees composed chiefly of dollar-a-year men, which were to take charge of the more vital branches of economic activity. These committees were responsible for war industries, shipping, food, transportation, fuel, foreign trade, and labor.

The most important of the committees was the War Industries Board. Composed at first of a number of prominent businessmen,

it was reorganized in March, 1918, and placed under the sole
authority of Bernard M. Baruch, who henceforth functioned as a
kind of economic dictator. A free-lance Wall Street operator who
had made a fortune by speculation, Baruch was qualified for his
position not only because of his great ability but also because he combined an intimate knowledge of business practices with personal
independence. He was, moreover, personally congenial to President
Wilson.

The first function of the War Industries Board was to determine
priorities. With both the Allied governments and the various
branches of the American government all competing with one
another for supplies, it was necessary to decide in what order their
different needs should be satisfied. The powers of the War Industries Board steadily increased. It finally took charge of all purchases
by the government; and it could order that the production of some
raw materials be expanded and others conserved, could standardize
products (an activity which had a permanent effect on the American
industrial system), and could fix prices.

The general policy of the government in buying supplies and in
making contracts for construction was to avoid too much haggling
about prices and to allow a rate of profit that would stimulate production and bring marginal mines and factories into operation. Such
a policy had the additional advantage that it enabled manufacturers
to pay higher wages, thereby avoiding labor disputes. It resulted also
in a rapid increase in both prices and profits, although it was hoped
that much of the latter would be recaptured by the government
through taxation. Baruch did, however, force down a number of
prices. Steel plates, for example, were reduced from 4.25 cents to
3.25 cents a pound, and copper from 32.5 cents to 22.5 cents a
pound, still leaving the manufacturers of these commodities a substantial profit. In making construction contracts the traditional
method of competitive bidding was abandoned, and the government
agreed to pay the cost of production—however much that might be—
plus a reasonable profit. The profits allowed by the government
under the cost-plus contracts varied between 2½ per cent and 15 per
cent according to the size of the contract; but some manufacturers

appear to have been able to increase their earnings illegitimately by
exaggerating their costs of production. Between 1916 and 1919 the
number of persons reporting incomes of more than $25,000 in-
creased from 38,382 to 56,323. The large war profits caused much
criticism, especially since many of the individuals responsible for
the government's economic policies were dollar-a-year men who
could hardly be expected to view the claims of business impartially.

Control over War Department purchases was given to General
Goethals, builder of the Panama Canal, who was appointed in April,
1918, as head of the Purchase, Storage, and Traffic division of the
General Staff. There was no serious difficulty in obtaining supplies
of rifles, machine guns, and ammunition, although the government
was compelled to build plants of its own in addition to relying on
private industry. It constructed the 60-million-dollar powder plant
at Nitro, West Virginia (subsequently sold for $8,551,000), the
90-million-dollar Old Hickory plant at Nashville, Tennessee (subsequently sold for $3,500,000), and a plant at Muscle Shoals on
the Tennessee River, which became the subject of one of the major
political controversies of the twenties and thirties. On the other hand,
for its heavy artillery and tanks the American army was compelled
to rely mainly on the British and French, and in one branch of
production—aircraft—there was serious mismanagement.

At the outset of the war the American army possessed fifty-five
planes, of which fifty-one were described as obsolete and the
remainder as obsolescent. Since there was no aviation industry in
the United States, one had to be created. Progress was exceedingly
slow as a result of disagreement over policies, shortage of materials,
and misconduct by those in charge of both the government program
and the contracting corporations. The navy spent $143,000,000 on
aviation and succeeded in acquiring 570 airplanes in time for service
in Europe.

The army, on the other hand, spent more than a billion dollars
on aviation. It shipped its first airplane to France in March, 1918,
and by the time of the armistice it had in active service in France
no bombers and only 196 observation planes of a type which was

officially described as "exceptionally dangerous to pilots and observers because of its defective construction." American aviators were compelled to use British and French airplanes. The individual mainly responsible for this fiasco was a dollar-a-year man who had been placed in charge of the War Department program. Apparently he was more interested in giving large contracts to corporations with which his friends and family were connected than in obtaining airplanes. A committee headed by Charles Evans Hughes investigated his activities. After deciding that there was not sufficient evidence for a criminal prosecution, the committee recommended that, since he had accepted a commission as a colonel, he might appropriately be court-martialled.[1] In May, 1918, he was replaced by John D. Ryan, of the Anaconda Copper Corporation, and by November, 1918, 11,754 airplanes had been completed. Almost all of these, however, were too late to be shipped to France, and most of them were subsequently scrapped.

SHIPPING

The most vital of all the needs of the Allied powers was for shipping. In the spring of 1917 the German submarine campaign was so successful that Great Britain was in imminent danger of being starved into surrender. By June of that year the British had lost 5,360,000 tons of shipping, and sinkings were continuing at the rate of about 600,000 tons a month. Ships were being sunk more than twice as fast as they could be built, and at one point the British had supplies of food enough for only six or seven weeks. Later in the year the situation was still so serious that the British Food Controller cabled to the American government that the war was lost.

In 1914 the United States had had less than 1 million tons of shipping engaged in foreign trade. In 1916 Wilson had secured from Congress permission to create the United States Shipping Board, whose chairman in the latter stages of the war was Edward M. Hurley. The Shipping Board created the Emergency Fleet Corpora-

1. See the Report of the Aircraft Inquiry, issued by the Department of Justice in 1918.

tion, with the function of purchasing and building merchant ships. In April, 1918, Charles M. Schwab was placed in charge of the program. This corporation, though government-owned, took out a charter in the District of Columbia and was thereby freed from much red tape and congressional interference—a legal device which was imitated by other government agencies and which was to be of considerable importance. The Emergency Fleet Corporation confiscated German ships interned in American ports, purchased a number of neutral ships, built four great shipyards with ninety-four launching ways, and contracted for the construction of millions of tons of shipping. Ten months after the United States entered the war the number of shipyard workers had increased from 50,000 to 350,000. On one day—July 4, 1918—one hundred ships were launched. In the year 1918 533 ships, totaling more than 3 million tons, were built; and by August 31 of that year the Emergency Fleet Corporation controlled more than 8,500,000 tons.

Most of this gigantic effort was, however, too late to be of service to the Allies. It was not until close to the end of the war that the dockyards built by the corporation began delivering ships in any quantity. The total new tonnage completed before September, 1918, amounted to less than half a million, the remainder of the ships controlled by the corporation having been confiscated or purchased from neutrals. The Hog Island yards near Philadelphia, for example, where the Emergency Fleet Corporation created a new city of 150,000 inhabitants, with eighty miles of railroads and fifty launching ways, did not deliver a single ship until December, 1918. Most of these new ships were subsequently sold to private companies for very much less than their cost, or they were left to rot. It was therefore fortunate that the British navy had meanwhile discovered how to conquer the submarine. Sinkings of merchant ships began to decrease in the summer of 1917, and throughout 1918 they averaged only 200,000 tons a month. The British merchant fleet was able not only to keep Great Britain supplied with food but also to transport to France about half the American Expeditionary Force.

FOOD PRODUCTION

Another vital necessity resulting from the submarine campaign was for an increase in food production. Herbert Hoover, who had earned a great reputation by his control of Belgian relief earlier in the war, was placed in charge of the problem in May, 1917, and was given legal authority by Congress in August. Hoover supervised food imports and exports, arranged transportation priorities. was allowed (within limits) to fix prices, and organized a publicity campaign for strict economy, with meatless and wheatless days.

The problem of wheat was especially serious, since production had decreased from more than 1 billion bushels in 1915 to only 636 million bushels in 1916. By May, 1917, the price had risen to $3.45 a bushel. Congress therefore created a Grain Corporation, which promised to buy the total wheat crop. The price for 1917 was fixed at $2.20 a bushel. The Grain Corporation also bought the 1918 and 1919 crops at similar prices. Assured of a market and urged to do their patriotic duty by the government, the farmers increased their wheat acreage from 45 million in 1917 to 75 million in 1919.

Total agricultural production increased during the war years by 24 per cent over 1913. As a result of greater production and decreased consumption, there was an enormous increase in the export of food. Exports of breadstuffs averaged 3,320,000 tons before the war and 10,566,165 tons for the year 1918–1919; exports of meats and fats rose from 645,000 tons to 2,369,630 tons; exports of sugar rose from 618,000 tons to 1,704,523 tons. American farmers thus helped to defeat the German submarine campaign. The ultimate consequences to the farmers themselves were, however, disastrous. For a period they made big profits, which encouraged them to buy more land at swollen prices and to increase their mortgages. They also ploughed up millions of acres in the Great Plains which should have been left to grass. In 1920, when Europe resumed normal peacetime production, the agricultural boom collapsed; and the farmers found themselves caught between wartime debts and peacetime prices. The problem remained unsolved throughout the twenties and was one of the causes of the general depression of the thirties.

TRANSPORTATION, FUEL, AND FOREIGN TRADE

The railroads were at first placed under a board of railroad men, which was supposed to co-ordinate their operations. This measure proved to be inadequate, and by the end of the year the roads were seriously congested. In December, 1917, the government leased the railroads from their owners, agreeing to pay them their average earnings during the previous three years, and began to operate them as a single system. William G. McAdoo, the Secretary of the Treasury, was placed at the head of the Railroad Administration. In August of 1918 the telephone and telegraph services were also taken over by the government on similar terms and were entrusted to the Post Office.

The Fuel Administration was created in August, 1917, with Harry A. Garfield as its chairman. The domestic use of fuel was severely curtailed, daylight saving was introduced, and a number of submarginal bituminous coal mines were opened, the result being a 37 per cent increase in production.

Foreign trade was supervised by the War Trade Board, headed by Vance C. McCormick. The War Trade Board controlled all imports and exports, prohibiting those which it regarded as unnecessary. Under the Trading-with-the-Enemy Act of October, 1917, the Board helped to enforce the British blockade regulations, prohibited trade with neutral countries which might be of assistance to Germany, and adopted the British practice of black-listing certain neutral firms. All enemy properties in the United States, the total value of which was estimated at about 500 million dollars, were entrusted for the duration of the war to an Alien Property Custodian.

LABOR

The government paid special attention to the interests of the working class both because of the liberal sympathies of Wilson and Baker and because of the need for increasing production and preventing strikes. At the beginning of the war labor was restless as a result of the rapid increase in the cost of living. In 1916 there were 3,789 strikes involving 2,275,000 workers; and in 1917 the numbers increased to 4,450 and 2,349,600. While Gompers and the other A. F. of L. leaders supported the war policies of the government, believing that the defeat of Germany was necessary for the preservation of democracy, the more radical branches of the labor movement, including especially the I. W. W., opposed the war as the work of bankers and munitions makers. In the Far West there were labor disputes accompanied by violence on both sides. In July, 1917, during a strike in a copper mine at Bisbee, Arizona, the employers kidnaped 1,186 of the strikers, transported them into the deserts of New Mexico, and left them there. In August an I. W. W. organizer, Frank Little, was lynched in Montana. And in September the U. S. Department of Justice arrested 113 I. W. W. leaders. These men were put on trial for sedition before Judge Kenesaw Mountain Landis in April, 1918, and 93 of them were given prison sentences, W. D. Haywood being condemned to twenty years.

Although, however, there was some danger that the war might be used as an excuse for crushing the labor movement, the administration maintained its sense of justice; nor did Gompers and the A. F. of L. leaders regret the suppression of the radicals. In 1917 the Council for National Defence appointed a Committee on Labor under the chairmanship of Gompers. Later in the year a National War Labor Conference Board worked out a program that proved to be very advantageous to the more conservative branches of the labor movement. The labor leaders agreed that there should be no more strikes; and in return they were promised an eight-hour day, a raise in wages to keep pace with the rise in prices, collective bargaining, and the right of all workers to belong to unions. A National War Labor Board, headed by ex-president Taft and Frank P. Walsh, was appointed to arbitrate labor disputes; and a War Labor Policies Board, headed by Felix Frankfurter of Harvard University, supervised the details of the program.

The final result was that wages actually rose as quickly as prices. In 1916 average real wages had been 5 per cent greater than in

1913. In 1917 they decreased by 4 per cent, but in 1918 they began to increase; and by the end of the war, although prices were almost double what they had been in 1913, real wages were as high as in 1916. After the war, prices fell sharply while wage rates remained relatively stable, with the result that by 1922 real wages were 16 per cent above the 1913 level. This was the most rapid rise in real wages in American history. The chief sufferers from wartime prices were not the working class but the middle classes, whose money earnings were slower to change.

There was, moreover, a decrease in hours of labor during the war years, which proved to be no impediment to an increase in production. Industrial production in 1918 was 38 per cent higher than in 1913, yet the proportion of workers who had gained a forty-eight hour week had increased from 11.8 per cent to 48.6 per cent. There was also a rapid increase in unionization, which for the first time was receiving the support of the Federal government. In 1914, 2,716,000 workers had belonged to unions. By 1920 the number had risen to 5,111,000, about 4 million of whom belonged to the A. F. of L.

THE CONTROL OF PUBLIC OPINION

The control of public opinion and the maintenance of popular enthusiasm were regarded by all the belligerent governments as vital parts of their war policies. In the United States this function was entrusted to the Committee on Public Information, which was headed by a progressive journalist of a remarkably colorful and exuberant personality, George Creel. Creel declared that his object was not censorship but "unparalleled openness"; he set out to acquaint the American people with every aspect of America's war effort. The Committee on Public Information distributed 75,000,000 pamphlets, sent out 75,000 "four-minute men" who made 7,500,000 four-minute speeches to audiences totaling more than 300,000,000, gave news to 16,000 local and foreign-language newspapers, and published a daily *Official Bulletin of the United States*. Having thus popularized the war in the United States, Creel went on, in 1918, to advertise the personality and ideals of Woodrow Wilson to the entire world—a publicity effort which has never been equaled in history and which had extraordinary and in some ways tragic consequences. By contrast with the propaganda agencies of the other belligerent governments, Creel displayed considerable integrity. He never indulged in conscious lying, and he did not allow atrocity stories unless he had reason for believing that they were true.

Creel's activities, however, helped to increase the popular hysteria, and this was the most lamentable feature of the whole war period in the United States. The intolerance displayed by the American public was, with much less excuse, fully as great as that which prevailed in any of the other belligerent nations. The number of Americans who opposed the war or who sympathized with Germany was far too small to be dangerous. Of that large body of Americans who were of German descent, the overwhelming majority were wholly loyal to the United States government. A few radicals opposed the war for political reasons, but they won no support. In April, 1917, the Socialist Party, in a convention at St. Louis, voted against the war; but a considerable number both of the leaders and of the rank and file refused to accept this decision, and the party began to disintegrate. These radical opponents of the war were, however, generally regarded as pro-Germans—an identification which was due partly to the support given by German agents to pacifism and to labor sabotage in 1915 and 1916.

In November, 1917, moreover, the Russian Revolution passed into a more radical phase, with the Bolshevik seizure of power. The Bolsheviks were believed by many Americans to be agents of the German government, and those American radicals who approved of them came under the same condemnation. Popular opinion, therefore, failed to discriminate between pro-Germanism and political radicalism; and the result was a wave of intolerance which threatened to destroy all the traditional guarantees of civil liberty. Journalists, businessmen, college professors, and ministers of religion vied with one another in propagating hatred; and they began to condemn not only pacifism and radicalism but also the use of foreign languages, the publication of foreign-language newspapers, and the most harmless deviations from orthodox customs and beliefs.

Congress retained rather more sanity than the remainder of the population; and the limitations which it imposed on civil liberties were due at least partly to a desire to restrain the popular hysteria. If the government had not undertaken to restrict the liberties of those who opposed the war, many of them might have been lynched. In June, 1917, Congress passed an Espionage Act, which imposed penalties for interfering with recruiting or making false statements that might obstruct the successful prosecution of the war and also prohibited the use of the mails for treasonable literature. In May, 1918, these limitations on free speech were increased by the Sedition Act; the penalties were made more severe, and the list of offences was extended, including, for example, the uttering of abusive language about the government, constitution, armed forces, or flag of the United States.

These laws, relatively moderate in themselves, were enforced with excessive severity by the officials of the Post Office Department and the Department of Justice and by judges and juries who had totally lost their capacity for giving impartial verdicts. Albert Sidney Burleson, Postmaster General, forbade the use of the mails to a large number of Socialist periodicals, including particularly *The Masses* and *The Milwaukee Leader;* and the Department of Justice arrested persons suspected of radicalism almost indiscriminately and demanded that they be given prison sentences which would far exceed the duration of the war. To assist the government in protecting the country from radicalism and pro-Germanism, the Department organized 250,000 volunteer patriots into an American Protective League. There were 1,597 arrests under the Sedition Act. Twenty-year prison sentences were given to 24 persons, including Victor Berger, formerly Socialist congressman from Milwaukee; fifteen-year sentences were given to 6 persons; and ten-year sentences were given to 11 persons, including the presidential candidate of the Socialist Party, Eugene Debs. The repressive activities of the Department of Justice continued, moreover, for more than a year after the armistice, long after all excuse for them had disappeared. The harm thereby done to the American traditions of liberty and democracy became one of the permanent legacies of the World War.

BIBLIOGRAPHY

*R. S. Baker, *Woodrow Wilson: Life and Letters,* Vols. VII–VIII (1939)

E. Berman, *Labor Disputes and the President of the United States* (1924)

E. L. Bogart, *War Costs and their Financing* (1921)

Z. Chafee, *Freedom of Speech* (1920)

J. M. Clark, *Costs of the World War* (1931)

*G. B. Clarkson, *Industrial America in the World War* (1923)

G. Creel, *How We Advertized America* (1920)

B. Crowell and R. F. Wilson, *How America Went To War* (1921)

F. H. Dixon, *The Railroads and Government* (1922)

A. R. Ellingwood and W. Coombs, *The Government and Railroad Transportation* (1930)

E. L. Hurley, *The Bridge to France* (1927)

H. D. Lasswell, *Propaganda Technique in the World War* (1927)

J. R. Mock and C. Larson, *Words that Won the War* (1939)

W. G. McAdoo, *Crowded Years* (1931)

A. D. Noyes, *The War Period in American Finance* (1926)

F. Palmer, *Newton D. Baker: America at War* (1931)

*F. L. Paxson, *America at War* (1939)

G. Seldes, *Iron, Blood and Profits* (1934)

M. Sullivan, *Our Times,* Vol. v (1933)

Norman Thomas, *The Conscientious Objector in America* (1923)

W. F. Willoughby, *Government Organization in War Time and After* (1919)

28

THE SURRENDER

OF GERMANY

AMERICAN NAVAL AND MILITARY ACTIVITIES

THE most valuable contributions of the United States to the cause of the Allies were economic and political rather than military. It is probable that the Allies would have been unable to defeat the Central Powers if they had not been allowed to rely on the United States, both before and after April, 1917, as a source of supplies and financial assistance. The American government aided them also by inducing the German government not to adopt unlimited submarine warfare during the first two and a half years of the war, and—after April, 1917—by representing the war as a crusade for a better world and thereby helping to break down the morale of the German people.

By contrast the military contributions of the United States were less important. Without American reinforcements the Allied armies would probably have been unable to end the war in 1918; but it is at least possible that they would eventually have been victorious if no American troops had been sent to France. Certainly it was unnecessary for the United States to raise an army of more than four million men. The military preparations of the American government, like its industrial policies, were based on the assumption that the war would last at least a year longer than it actually did.

The importance of the economic contributions of the United States is shown by the fact that of the total direct cost of the war to all the countries engaged in it, which is calculated at 186 billion dollars, about one-sixth was paid by the United States. Of the lives lost in the war, on the other hand, only one in every eighty-nine was American. The total loss of life to all countries was about 10 million. Of these, 1,385,300 were French, and 947,023 were British. American military losses amounted to only 48,909 killed in action, and 63,513 dying from other causes.

The American navy began to co-operate with that of Great Britain soon after the American declaration of war. Three hundred ships and 75,000 men, under the command of Admiral W. S. Sims, served in European waters, where they assisted the British in defeating the submarine campaign. Their most important activity was the laying of an enormous mine barrage, 245 miles long and 20 miles wide, across the northern end of the North Sea. This project, the inception of which was partly due to Assistant Secretary of the Navy Franklin D. Roosevelt, was an important factor in the defeat of the submarine. The American navy was also responsible for convoying American troops across the Atlantic. The remarkable success of this activity is shown by the fact that about 2 million American soldiers were successfully transported to France before the end of the war and that only one ship and one hundred lives were lost on the eastbound passage.

American military assistance, on the other hand, was much slower in reaching the Allies. It was on May 28, 1917, that the first American troops left the United States, and on October 21 that Americans for the first time occupied frontline trenches in a quiet sector of the Western Front, near Toul. But during the first eleven months after the United States entered the war American troops sent to France averaged only about 700 a day. By March, 1918, there were in France only 300,000 Americans, inadequately equipped. The delay was due not only to the fact that the Americans had first to receive military training but also to the scarcity of ships. This was a problem not merely of transporting men but also of bringing to France the equipment, munitions, and food supplies needed to support them.

General John J. Pershing had been selected to command the American armies in France. Pershing's qualifications were generally admitted; although it was felt in some circles that General Leonard

Wood had a better claim and that he had been rejected because of his political activities as an adherent of the Republican Party. Other generals who occupied important positions were Peyton C. Marsh, who became chief of the General Staff in Washington in December, 1917, and J. G. Harbord, who assisted Pershing as head of the Services of Supply, with headquarters at Tours. A general who was also a banker, Charles G. Dawes, took charge of the General Purchasing Board in France. Wilson and Baker gave Pershing complete freedom of action; he was to have full responsibility for American activities in France, and the function of the War Department in Washington was, as far as possible, to carry out his recommendations. Baker told Pershing on his departure that he was giving him only two orders: to go to France, and to come home again. Until March, 1918, when American troops began to arrive in large numbers, Pershing's most prominent activity was to insist, in opposition to the British and French, that the Americans should eventually constitute a separate army, fighting independently under their own commanders, and that they should not be used merely as reserves and reinforcements, wherever they might be needed, by the British and French generals. Believing that the British and French were too exhausted ever to take the offensive, Pershing decided that it would be the task of the Americans to win the war, and he trained his troops for attack.

Since the autumn of 1914 the fighting on the Western Front had become a matter of trench warfare, the advantages being with the defense rather than with the attack. The Germans had taken the offensive in 1916, and the Allies in both 1916 and 1917. Gains of a few miles had been purchased with enormously heavy losses, and it seemed impossible for either side to win a decisive victory. The rival armies faced each other in lines extending from the North Sea to the Swiss border, and each of them hoped to wear down the other by a slow and very costly process of attrition.

The Germans, however, were capable in 1918 of one last effort. They had made peace with the Bolshevik government of Russia, had forced Rumania out of the war and occupied most of the Balkans, and had inflicted a crushing defeat on Italy at Caporetto. In March,

1918, they brought all their available men to the Western Front in the hope of winning a decisive victory before American reinforcements should arrive in large numbers and before the morale of the German people should begin to crack under the strain of the Allied blockade. The German offensive began on March 21, with a crushing attack on the British Fifth Army which drove a deep salient into the Allied line in the region of the Somme. This was followed by other and equally vigorous German attacks in Flanders and in the region of the Aisne and Marne. The initiative remained with the Germans until July 17; and the Allies, driven back in three different areas, seemed in imminent danger of defeat.

The crisis compelled the Allies, for the first time, to adopt unity of command. In April the British consented to accept French leadership, and General Foch was appointed to command all the Allied armies in France. Pershing assented to this decision; and, although he still insisted that the Americans should finally become a separate army, he agreed on March 28 that during the crisis they might be used as reinforcements by the British and French. The transportation of American troops was hastened, with the British supplying the majority of the ships; and for the next six months American arrivals averaged 263,000 a month. Wilson promised that by June of 1919 there should be 3,200,000 American soldiers in France.

The Americans saw their first real fighting on May 28, when the American First Division, brigaded with the British in the region of the Somme, captured Cantigny. The success of this operation convinced the British and French generals, hitherto sceptical, of the fighting capacity of the Americans. In June the Second and Third Divisions were used to reinforce the French in the region of the Aisne and Marne, which was now the scene of the main German offensive. The Americans stopped the German advance to Château Thierry, thereby checking a movement which threatened to capture Paris, and subsequently drove the Germans out of Belleau Wood.

The German offensive was exhausted by July 17. The initiative then passed to the Allies, and Foch immediately ordered a series of counterattacks. At this period the American troops were scattered along the whole Allied line from Ypres to near the Swiss border.

An American army corps had been organized around Château Thierry, under the command of Hunter Liggett, and on July 18 this First Army Corps participated with the French in a successful offensive. In August the Allied offensive became general; the British under Haig attacked along the Somme, and French troops under Mangin advanced up the Oise, a number of American divisions taking part in both these operations. Meanwhile the bulk of the American troops were being concentrated further east, between Verdun and the Moselle, where on August 30 Pershing took command of a First American Army.

Contrary to the wishes of Foch, who believed that the Allied attacks should be concentrated on the regions further west, Pershing insisted that the Americans should undertake an independent operation under their own leaders and that it should take the form of an attack on the German salient at St. Mihiel. The attack took place on September 12, with complete success; and it might perhaps have been followed by an advance upon Metz and the Rhineland and the cutting of the German lines of communication if Foch had allowed Pershing to follow up his advantage.

Subsequently the American troops were moved somewhat farther to the west, into the region of the Argonne and the Meuse, where they launched an attack on September 26—an operation notable for the episode of the "lost battalion." This region was the main scene of American operations for the remainder of the war, two separate armies, under Hunter Liggett and Robert Lee Bullard, being organized on October 12. The terrain was singularly difficult, owing—as Pershing described it—to "the vast network of uncut barbwire, the deep ravines, dense woods, myriads of shell craters and a heavy fog." In this region the American armies made a series of attacks and continued slowly to advance throughout October, threatening finally to cut the railroads by which the Germans in Flanders maintained contact with their sources of supply. At the same time the British and French armies farther to the west, with American divisions participating, were also advancing; and by the second week in November the retreat of the Germans had become a rout.

WILSON'S WAR AIMS

Meanwhile services equal in importance to those of the American armies were being performed by Woodrow Wilson, whose eloquent advocacy of a just peace helped to convince the German people that they ought to surrender. In a series of speeches Wilson insisted that the United States was not fighting against the people of Germany but only against their government, that the war ought not to be followed by punitive annexations or indemnities, and that peace should henceforth be maintained by the establishment of the rule of law in international affairs and of a League of Nations to enforce it. Wilson's war aims had never been accepted by the British and French; Wilson had probably made a mistake in not requiring that the British and French governments formally adopt these aims as a condition of America's entrance into the war. But most people assumed that Wilson was speaking for all the Allies.

On January 8, 1918, in a message to Congress, Wilson outlined the war aims of the United States in a series of fourteen points. This was done at the suggestion of George Creel, who pointed out that a brief and concrete summary of Wilson's program could effectively be publicized inside Germany. The fourteen points were as follows: open covenants of peace, openly arrived at; freedom of the seas, both in peace and in war; no economic barriers between nations; the reduction of armaments to the lowest point consistent with domestic safety; an impartial settlement of claims to colonies, in which the interests of the colonial populations would be considered equally with those of the great powers; evacuation of the Russian territory held by the Germans; evacuation and restoration of the Belgian territory held by the Germans; evacuation and restoration of the French territory held by the Germans, with the return to France of Alsace-Lorraine; an adjustment of the frontiers of Italy in accordance with the lines of nationality; autonomous development of the peoples comprising the Austro-Hungarian Empire; a reorganization of frontiers in the Balkans along ethnic lines, with access to the sea for Serbia; self-determination for the peoples comprising the Turkish Empire; independence and access to the sea for Poland;

and a "general association of nations." In another speech, delivered on July 4, Wilson summarized his international ideals as including the destruction of arbitrary power everywhere, the right of all peoples to self-determination, the rule of law in international affairs, and the organization of peace.

Wilson's speeches and war aims were then publicized throughout the world by George Creel and the Committee for Public Information. By the end of the war Creel had agents in every Allied and neutral capital in the world, and he was supplying news not only to the belligerents but to all the leading neutrals. Wilson's speeches were translated into every major language within twenty-four hours of delivery, and Wilson began to be regarded by the peoples of the war-torn countries as a kind of world saviour, endowed with a wisdom and a sanctity that were more than human. Peasants in Catholic countries put up pictures of Wilson beside the images of their local saints. Extracts from Wilson's speeches and information about America's war preparations were, moreover, distributed by airplane throughout Germany.

By October the German High Command knew that they had lost the war and that the only way to prevent an Allied invasion of Germany was to sue for peace immediately. There was a change in the German government, and a liberal, Prince Max of Baden, became chancellor. On October 5 Germany informed Wilson that she was willing to accept a peace based on the Fourteen Points. On October 8 Wilson asked if the German acceptance was unconditional and if the German armies would evacuate all invaded territories. On October 14 he declared that the Allied military leaders would fix armistice terms and that submarine warfare must end immediately, and he asked for further confirmation that the new German government was genuinely representative of the German people. Germany agreed to these conditions, and on October 23 Wilson gave the correspondence to the Allied governments. The Allies now declared that they were willing to accept the Fourteen Points with two amendments: the doctrine of the freedom of the seas must be modified, and Germany must agree to pay reparations for all the damage done to the civilian populations of the Allied countries by land, sea, and air. Foch was then appointed to arrange terms of armistice. Meanwhile Bulgaria had sued for peace in September, and Austria on November 3; and there were beginning to be revolutionary disturbances inside Germany. On November 9 the Kaiser abdicated and the Social Democrats took over the government. On November 11 Foch's armistice terms were accepted, and fighting ceased.

BIBLIOGRAPHY

L. P. Ayres, *The War with Germany* (1919)
*R. S. Baker, *Woodrow Wilson: Life and Letters,* Vols. VII–VIII (1939)
T. G. Frothingham, *Naval History of the World War,* Vol. III (1926)
——— *American Reinforcement in the World War* (1927)
J. G. Harbord, *The American Army in France* (1936)
——— *America in the World War* (1933)
B. H. Liddell Hart, *History of the World War* (1934)
H. D. Lasswell, *Propaganda Technique in the World War* (1927)
*F. L. Paxson, *America at War* (1939)
J. J. Pershing, *My Experiences in the World War* (1931)
S. Thomas, *History of the A.E.F.* (1920)

29

THE TREATY

AND THE LEAGUE

WILSON'S TASK

WILSON had led the United States into the war hoping that American influence would induce Great Britain and France to accept a just peace, one which would satisfy the legitimate interests of both the victorious and the conquered countries. But after the victory of the Allies a just peace was impossible. The peoples of Great Britain and France, convinced that Germany had deliberately started the war, and embittered by the sufferings and deaths of the past four and a half years, were determined on vengeance. No government which attempted to treat Germany leniently could have stayed in office. The governments of Great Britain, France, Italy, Rumania, and Japan had, moreover, made a series of secret treaties by which they had promised one another certain territorial gains at the expense of Germany and Austria. The Allied governments had never fully accepted Wilson's war aims, and it was natural that they should resent any attempt on the part of the United States to dictate the details of the settlement in Europe. It was the Allied powers, and not the United States, that had borne the brunt of the conflict and had suffered most of the losses; and it was their right, they believed, to draft the peace treaty. During the peace negotiations Wilson was therefore compelled to concede most of the Allied demands, even when they conflicted with his Fourteen Points. In compensation, he could insist that the establishment of a League of Nations should be an integral part of the peace treaty, and he could hope that the benefits of the League would outweigh the injustices of the remainder of the treaty.

Wilson was, moreover, handicapped in his negotiations with the British and French by the fact that the Republicans had won control of Congress. Before the congressional elections of 1918 Wilson had been attacked by certain prominent Republicans, notably by Theodore Roosevelt, whose desertion of the party in 1912 had now been forgiven and forgotten, and by Henry Cabot Lodge, Republican leader in the Senate. Wilson had retaliated by issuing, on October 25, a request that a Democratic congress be elected as an expression of confidence in his own leadership. This intervention in party politics was a tactical mistake, of which the Republicans made good use; and in the elections of November the Democrats lost control of Congress. The Republican Party captured the Senate, and with it the Foreign Relations Committee, by 49 to 47 and the House of Representatives by 239 to 194.

During the campaign, moreover, it had become apparent that the Republicans were planning to oppose Wilson's peace aims. Earlier in the war it had seemed that almost all groups in America were in favor of a League of Nations. In 1915 a League to Enforce Peace had been formed, under the presidency of ex-President Taft, in order to work for the creation of a League of Nations; and a number of prominent Republicans, including Henry Cabot Lodge, had made speeches in support of it. In 1918, however, some of the Republican leaders decided that the most effective method of attacking Wilson and winning the election was to demand vengeance on Germany and to denounce the League as a superstate that would deprive America of her independence.

Wilson resolved to go to Europe himself, and he failed to take with him any prominent Republican or any member of the Senate—an error of judgment which would strengthen the opposition to the peace treaty. The American delegates, in addition to Wilson himself, were House, Lansing, General Tasker H. Bliss, and Henry White. White, who was qualified for appointment by his very wide experience of European diplomacy, belonged to the Republican

Party, but he had not for a long time been active in American politics. Wilson reached Europe on December 13. During the next month he made visits to Paris, London, and Rome, during which he was received with a popular enthusiasm which probably surpassed that given to any other figure in human experience. The people of the Allied countries might not share Wilson's belief in fair treatment for their enemies, but they felt, nevertheless, that he was the embodiment of a new world-order in which war would somehow be made impossible. Liberals in all countries, moreover, recognized that all their hopes for a just settlement depended upon him. The moral leadership which Wilson exercised at this period has no parallel in all history.

THE PEACE CONFERENCE

The peace negotiations began on January 18 at Versailles. Wilson's belief in open diplomacy was abandoned at the outset, and the more important decisions were made in secret conclaves by a council of four, consisting of Wilson, Clemenceau of France, Lloyd George of Great Britain, and Orlando of Italy. Clemenceau, representing a nation whose soil had been invaded by the German army twice within half a century, was determined to achieve security for France; and he believed that this could not be accomplished unless Germany was weakened and humiliated. The negotiations were largely a conflict between the realism of Clemenceau and the idealism of Wilson. Orlando's primary concern was to win territorial gains for Italy. Lloyd George was more sympathetic to Wilson, but his hands were tied by his Tory supporters and by the fact that the government which he headed had just won a general election by promising to hang the Kaiser and to make Germany pay. German delegates were not invited to the peace conference until the treaty had been drafted and it was time for them to sign it.

At the beginning of the conference Wilson won two victories by insisting that the German colonies should not be annexed by the Allied powers but should be held by them as mandates, under international supervision, and that the Covenant of the League of Nations should be drafted immediately. Wilson became chairman of a League

commission, which finished its work on February 13. Liberal leaders
in Great Britain and France, as well as in the United States, had been
advocating a League since the early months of the war; and the
League commission had several different drafts upon which to work.
The Covenant of the League, as finally agreed upon, provided for an
Assembly representing all member-nations and a Council containing
representatives of the United States, Great Britain, France, Italy,
Japan, and four other nations to be elected by the Assembly. Most
decisions of the Council were to be unanimous. The articles of
greatest importance in the Covenant were Article 10, which guaranteed all member-nations against loss of territorial integrity and
political independence through external aggression; Article 11,
which declared that a war was a matter of concern to the whole
League and that any circumstance which seemed likely to result in
war might be brought up for discussion; Article 12, which provided
that all disputes should be submitted either to decision by a Permanent Court of International Justice or to investigation by the
Council; and Article 16, which declared that economic sanctions
should automatically be applied by all League members against any
nation resorting to war in violation of the Covenant, and also that,
if the Council so recommended, economic sanctions might be followed by military action.

When the details of the Covenant became known in the United
States, it was immediately denounced by a number of Republican
senators, and thirty-nine of them—enough to prevent ratification—
signed a statement declaring that they would vote against it. Wilson
returned to the United States for a two-weeks visit; and, after meeting a number of senators and receiving advice from two Republicans
who favored some kind of League, Taft and Root, he concluded
that four amendments to the Covenant were needed in order to
ensure the support of American public opinion. Maintenance of the
Monroe Doctrine must be guaranteed; domestic questions such as
immigration and the tariff must be specifically excluded from League
control; and nations must be assured of freedom to withdraw from
the League and to refuse to accept colonial mandates. After having
returned to France on March 14, Wilson persuaded the other powers

to agree to these amendments. In return for these concessions, however, France, Italy, and Japan demanded that Wilson yield to some of their territorial ambitions.

The details of the peace were worked out in April. Wilson, who was suffering at the time from a severe attack of influenza, engaged in a prolonged struggle to save his Fourteen Points and to prevent the secret treaties from becoming the basis of the settlement. By threatening to withdraw from the conference, he won three important victories. France abandoned her demand that Germany be deprived of the Rhineland, accepting in return a joint guarantee from Great Britain and the United States to protect her from German aggression. Italy was not allowed to annex Fiume, and she did not receive the African colonies which the secret treaties had encouraged her to expect. Japan, while acquiring the economic suzerainty which Germany had exercised in the Shantung peninsular, was not allowed to annex this area, which remained under Chinese sovereignty. With these exceptions, however, the treaty was punitive, and designed to maintain Franco-British supremacy over Europe.

Germany was stripped of her colonies and her navy, forbidden to maintain an army larger than 100,000 men, deprived of Alsace-Lorraine in the west and the Polish territories in the east, declared to be guilty of having caused the war, and condemned to pay the Allied powers the full cost of it. The amount of reparations was fixed two years later at 33 billion dollars, payment of which was to continue for generations. Allied armies were, moreover, to occupy the Rhineland for fifteen years. The Austrian Empire was dismantled, and four new or newly enlarged "succession states"— Czechoslovakia, Rumania, Jugo-Slavia, and Poland—became the guardians of Franco-British supremacy in eastern Europe. All these countries contained large minority groups, whose rights to self-determination were denied and whose discontent constituted a perpetual threat to the stability of the peace settlement. The Turkish Empire was similarly broken up, and much of its territory, along with the former German colonies, became British and French mandates.

Clemenceau and Lloyd George should not be blamed too severely for the treaty. Its two most indefensible features were the exaction of reparations and the fixing of the frontier lines in eastern Europe. Payment of reparations, however, was demanded by an enraged public opinion in the Allied nations, and the swollen boundaries of such countries as Poland and Rumania were largely due to the fact that the governments of those states were already seizing what they wanted and could not be dislodged except by force. The primary error here lay with Wilson's own principle of self-determination. In eastern Europe races were so intermingled that to fix frontiers along ethnic lines was impossible; any kind of settlement must create a minorities problem. Permanent peace in this area was impossible unless nationalistic hatreds were forgotten, armaments and trade barriers abandoned, and some form of political and economic confederation created. After the World War, however, this was totally impossible. The Fourteen Points had promised disarmament and the abolition of trade barriers, but Wilson had no practical scheme for accomplishing these objectives.

The effect of the Versailles settlement was to divide Europe into satisfied and dissatisfied powers. In the former category were Great Britain, France, and some of the states in eastern Europe; in the latter were three defeated countries, Germany, Austria, and Hungary, and one of the victorious countries, Italy. Peace under such conditions would endure only as long as the satisfied powers retained decisive military supremacy. And Wilson's intervention, which deprived France of permanent control of the Rhineland in return for a guarantee of military protection that the United States Senate subsequently refused to accept, actually had the effect of hastening the next war.

Peace might have been maintained permanently if the European powers had accepted Wilson's ideals of just treatment for all nationalities, disarmament, abolition of trade barriers, freedom of the seas, and collective security through the League of Nations. Peace might have been maintained longer than proved to be the case if the peace conference had accepted Clemenceau's thesis that nothing but force could prevent German aggression and if the makers of the settlement had therefore set out to give an overwhelming military superiority to those powers who had profited by it. Actually, however, the Treaty of Versailles was neither one thing nor the other; and unless the United States were prepared to intervene constantly in Europe to maintain the settlement, it made another war almost inevitable.

Nor did the League of Nations, which Wilson hoped would outweigh the injustices of the remainder of the treaty, prove to be a remedy. Germany was excluded from membership until 1926. Any revision of the treaty by peaceful negotiation proved to be impossible, and the dissatisfied powers and minority races soon came to believe that they could obtain their demands only by force or the threat of it. The League settled a number of minor disputes and provided for valuable international co-operation on nonpolitical matters, but on the major political questions it functioned primarily as an instrument for maintaining the Versailles settlement. Nor did the British and French governments give much support to its ideals except where they coincided with their own political interests.

THE FIGHT FOR RATIFICATION

The treaty was signed by the German delegates on June 28, and Wilson left for the United States on the next day. The treaty and the League were submitted to the United States Senate on July 10. Wilson had deliberately seen to it that the League Covenant should be a part of the Versailles treaty, so that the Senate could not reject one without rejecting the other.

Of the members of the Senate, there were forty, all Democrats, who were for ratification. Thirteen or fourteen, headed by Borah of Idaho and Johnson of California, were for unconditional repudiation. The remainder were for ratification with reservations.

The viewpoint of Borah and Johnson was that Article 10 of the League Covenant committed the United States to defense of the existing territorial arrangements throughout the world, and that these territorial arrangements contained many injustices and must inevitably cause future wars. The United States, they believed, should not commit herself to perpetual involvement in European conflicts, nor should she pledge herself, as would in fact be the case, to go to the defense of the British and French empires. This isolationist attitude represented a sincere conviction, but it might be condemned as impractical. Experience had shown that the United States did become involved in European wars even against her will (neither Borah nor Johnson had voted against war in 1917).

The attitude of the reservationists was more complex. Their chief objections to the Covenant were that it might limit the independence of the United States by requiring her to go to war with aggressor nations against her will, and that it might deprive her of the suzerainty she exercised over the weaker Latin American countries under the Monroe Doctrine. Some of the reservationists felt that the Versailles Treaty had been too severe, and inclined toward isolation; others denounced Wilson for not having yielded to all the demands of the Allied powers, indicating that they would have been willing to substitute for the League a pledge on the part of the United States to go, when necessary, to the defense of Great Britain and France. Elihu Root criticized the Covenant as impractical. He argued that nations would not, in practice, be willing to obey Article 16 requiring them to apply economic sanctions against any aggressor, and that this article would, by raising false hopes, do more harm than good. Subsequent history has shown that Root's objections to the Covenant were well-founded.

Mingled with these legitimate considerations of foreign policy were a desire to assert the powers of the Senate over the Presidency, much personal dislike of Woodrow Wilson, and a willingness to use a vital international question as a football of party politics. If the Republicans were to win the next election, Wilson must be discredited; Republican politicians who wanted office, and business leaders who wanted to end Progressive legislation and return to the practices of the McKinley era, therefore set out to destroy Wilson-ism by defeating the League which Wilson had created. Throughout the spring there had been an elaborate anti-League campaign, financed chiefly by two Pennsylvania business magnates, Henry Clay Frick and Andrew Mellon. The American people had been told that the League would be a superstate which might compel them to accept unrestricted Japanese and Chinese immigration, which might deprive them of their army and navy and put them at the mercy of Mexican bandits, which might enable the colored races of the world to out-vote and dominate the white races, and which might cause the whole world to become subjected to the Roman Catholic Church. The anti-League propagandists omitted to point out that according to the Covenant of the League important decisions of the Council had to be unanimous and that the United States would be a per-petual member of the Council. The campaign soon began to take effect; and public sentiment, which—in the opinion even of the enemies of the League—had been strongly in favor of it in 1918, swung slowly toward isolationism.

The isolationists and the reservationists, with their conflicting views, were marshaled for common action with consummate politi-cal cleverness by Henry Cabot Lodge, who was himself a reservation-ist but whose principal motive seems to have been hatred of Wilson. Of the other Republican leaders, Roosevelt had died in January, and Taft, as head of the League to Enforce Peace, continued to support Wilson and to urge American entry into the League. Lodge worked in close co-operation with George Harvey, who nine years before had started Wilson on his political career but who had now become one of his bitterest enemies. The Senate debate on the treaty con-tinued through the summer and autumn of 1919, and every possible objection to the Versailles settlement was thoroughly aired.

Meanwhile Wilson determined to carry his case to the American people. On September 3 he left Washington for the West, and in twenty-two days he delivered thirty-seven speeches and traveled eight thousand miles. Warning the American people of the pos-sible consequences of isolation, he declared that: "To play a lone hand now means that we must always be ready to play by ourselves. It means that we must always be armed, that we must be always ready to mobilize the man strength and the manufacturing resources of the country. That means that we must continue to live under not diminishing but increasing taxes and be strong enough to beat any nation in the world." His audiences, at first apathetic, grew steadily more enthusiastic; and it seemed possible that he would finally be victorious. These hopes, however, were destroyed by a physical breakdown. Never a man of strong physique, Wilson had endured in succession the responsibilities of war leadership, the struggle to achieve his ideals at Versailles, and now the fight with the Senate. On September 26 he had a paralytic stroke while his train was crossing Kansas; and for the remainder of his presidency he was compelled to remain inactive.

In November the Foreign Relations Committee adopted fifteen reservations to the League Covenant, the most important of which were that the United States would not undertake to employ economic or military sanctions by order of the League Council unless Congress consented, and that the United States alone could interpret its powers and responsibilities under the Monroe Doctrine. Other reservations condemned the Japanese control over Shantung and (with Lodge dissenting) urged independence for Ireland. Taft and the League to Enforce Peace advocated acceptance of the reservations as the only method of bringing the United States into the League. Wilson, however, believed that the reservations would fatally weaken the League's authority and that, if the United States refused to enter the League except on its own terms, every other power would claim similar privileges. He recommended the Democratic senators to vote against them. This decision was probably a mistake.

When a vote was taken, thirty-nine senators voted for the treaty with the reservations; fifty-five, including both Democrats and isolationists, voted against it. In a second vote thirty-eight senators voted for the treaty without the reservations; fifty-three voted against. The question was then adjourned until March, by which time some of the Democrats had decided that the treaty with the reservations was better than no treaty at all. In a final vote, on March 19, 1920, forty-nine voted for the treaty with the reservations; thirty-five voted against. The treaty with the reservations thus failed by seven votes to secure the necessary two-thirds majority. Rejection of the treaty meant that the United States was still legally at war with Germany, and a resolution by Congress declaring that the war was ended was vetoed by Wilson. It was not until July, 1921, after Harding had become president, that the war was officially ended.

Whether the American people in 1920 were for the League or

against it cannot be determined. The Republican victory in the election of the autumn was due to many causes other than hostility to
the League, and many persons who voted for Harding did so in
the belief that they were voting not against the League but for the
League with the reservations. The defeat of Wilson proved, however, to be a victory for the isolationists, and throughout the twenties
and thirties they continued to be strong enough to prevent any intimate participation by the United States in the affairs of Europe.

Time will show whether this attitude was wise. That the United
States could remain aloof from future European conflicts and could
preserve her freedom and her democracy no matter what happened
in other parts of the world was a dubious proposition. If this proposition proves to be untrue, then one must conclude that the United
States ought at least to have attempted, by supporting the League,
to reinforce those elements in Europe which were working for a
permanent peace. The enemies of the League were wrong in
declaring that it would become a superstate which would deprive
America of her independence. Although their suspicions of British
and French diplomacy may have had some justification, it is probable
that continued American participation in European affairs would
have strengthened those groups in Europe who believed in justice
and in collective security against aggression.

One of the most significant features of world politics in the
twenties and thirties was the manner in which isolationists in the
United States and conservatives in Great Britain and France played
into each others' hands. America's refusal to support the League
served to justify those European statesmen who believed that a new
world order was impossible and that international affairs must be
conducted by the old methods of power politics and secret diplomacy.
And on every occasion when the British and French governments
acted in terms of power politics rather than of Wilsonian idealism,
the American isolationists had a new argument for urging that the
United States had been right in not supporting the League. The
United States had enabled the Allies to win the war; but by refusing
—after Wilson's defeat at Versailles—to use her influence in behalf
of a new world order and shirking her responsibilities as a great

power, she lost the peace and—in the final outcome—sacrificed all the objectives which she had professedly entered the war to achieve.

BIBLIOGRAPHY

R. S. Baker, *What Wilson Did at Paris* (1919)
———— *Woodrow Wilson and the World Settlement* (1922)
D. F. Fleming, *The United States and the League of Nations* (1932)
D. Lloyd George, *Memoirs of the Peace Conference* (1939)
W. S. Holt, *Treaties Defeated by the Senate* (1933)
E. M. House and S. Seymour (eds.), *What Really Happened at Paris* (1921)
R. Lansing, *The Big Four* (1921)
———— *The Peace Negotiations* (1921)
H. C. Lodge, *The Senate and the League of Nations* (1925)
D. H. Miller, *The Drafting of the Covenant* (1928)
A. Nevins, *Henry White* (1930)
*H. Nicholson, *Peace Making, 1919* (1933)
G. B. Noble, *Policies and Opinions at Paris, 1919* (1935)
F. Palmer, *Bliss, Peacemaker* (1934)
J. T. Shotwell, *At the Paris Peace Conference* (1937)
H. W. V. Temperley, *History of the Peace Conference of Paris* (1920–24)
Mrs. E. B. Wilson, *My Memoirs* (1939)

30

THE RETURN

TO NORMALCY

POSTWAR HYSTERIA

FROM September, 1919, until March, 1921, the United States was virtually without a president. Wilson continued to be the head of the administration, and he occasionally asserted his will on important issues; but he was incapable of performing most of the functions of his office and, at the same time, unwilling to allow them to be performed by anybody else. Throughout this most important period, when the adjustment from wartime to peacetime conditions had to be made, the United States therefore had no leadership. Congress relaxed the war regulations, and industry returned to production for civilian needs; but little attempt was made to plan the transition. Meanwhile there was a continuance of the war hysteria which constitutes one of the most shameful episodes in American history.

The popular fear of alien influences which had developed during the war now expressed itself in hostility to any form of liberalism or radicalism. The crusading idealism which Wilson had infused into America's war preparations was replaced by cynicism and conservatism. Meanwhile the working class was becoming restless, and some members were affected by the radical tendencies that flourished for a short period in postwar Europe. The Bolshevik government in Russia was maintaining itself in power, despite efforts to overthrow it by Russian reactionaries and Allied armies. And while conservatives regarded Bolshevism as a menace to civilization, radical idealists saw in it the promise of a new and better social order. In 1919 a number of former members of the Socialist Party, the best-known of whom was the journalist John Reed, organized the Communist Party on a basis of co-operating with the Russian government in the Communist International and working for a proletarian revolution in the United States. And although the Communists were far too few to constitute any real danger to American capitalism, they provoked hysterical alarm among many American conservatives.

Throughout 1919 there were many conflicts between capital and labor, and in the course of the year more than 4,000,000 workers participated in strikes. From September, 1919, until January, 1920, 300,000 steel workers were on strike, under the leadership of William Z. Foster, demanding union recognition, higher wages, and the abolition of the twelve-hour day. In spite of much popular sympathy for the strikers, Judge Gary and the other steel magnates made no concessions. They imported Negro strikebreakers and played upon nationalistic antagonisms among the workers, such as that between Serbs and Italians, and the strike was defeated. It was not until 1923 that, as a result of a personal request by President Harding, the steel corporations finally conceded the eight-hour day. During the same period a coal strike, involving 450,000 workers, was defeated by means of an injunction obtained by the Federal government. On the west coast the I. W. W. was again active in labor conflicts, and in February, 1919, there was a five-day general strike in Seattle.

The growth of labor militancy even began to infect city employees, such as policemen and firemen; and at Boston there occurred a police strike, which gave the United States a future president. The cause of the strike was the refusal of the Boston Police Commission to allow the men to join a union. On the third day of the strike, following much rioting, the governor of Massachusetts, Calvin Coolidge, called out the State Guard to restore order. After the strike had been broken, he upheld the Police Commissioner in refusing to reinstate the strikers. Samuel Gompers intervened on their behalf, whereupon Coolidge defended his attitude in a singularly forceful telegram, one sentence of which—"There is no right to strike against the public safety by anybody, anywhere, any time"—was widely applauded. As to the wisdom of Coolidge's actions there has been considerable controversy; but the political effectiveness of his message to Gompers was indisputable.

The authorities reacted to this wave of labor militancy by adopting sternly repressive measures. A. Mitchell Palmer, Wilson's Attorney General, arrested numerous individuals suspected of radicalism, often with little or no legal justification, and expelled from the country those of them who were not American citizens. In December, 1919, 249 alien radicals were deported to Russia. On New Year's Day, 1920, the offices of the Communist Party throughout the United States were raided, and 6,000 Communists were arrested, most of them being subsequently released for lack of evidence of any criminal activity. A number of state governments enacted criminal syndicalism laws, under which the Communist and I. W. W. organizations were declared illegal and many of their leaders were given long prison sentences. Under these laws it became illegal to make statements which tend to provoke violence, or to believe in the desirability of a proletarian dictatorship. Although such laws appeared to be inconsistent with the Bill of Rights, they were upheld in a number of cases by the Supreme Court. Meanwhile radical meetings were frequently broken up, and radical leaders were attacked and occasionally lynched by mob action, in which ex-soldiers frequently took the leading part. Socialists, as well as Communists and members of the I. W. W., were attacked, despite the belief of the former in peaceful and constitutional methods of change. Five regularly elected Socialist assemblymen were expelled from the New York State legislature.

One episode of this period was to become particularly notorious. On April 15, 1920, two men were murdered at South Braintree, Massachusetts, and $150,000 which they were carrying was stolen. Two Italians who held radical opinions, Nicola Sacco and Bartolomeo Vanzetti, were accused of the crime, convicted, and sentenced to death. Many people believed that the evidence against them was wholly inadequate and that their conviction had been due to their radicalism, which had been emphasized during the trial both by the prosecution and by the judge. Sacco and Vanzetti were finally put to death on August 23, 1927, after their conviction had provoked bitter controversies and had been denounced as judicial murder by liberal, radical, and labor organizations not only in the United States but throughout the civilized world.

THE ELECTION OF 1920

The presidential election of 1920 registered the general desire of the American people to abandon crusading idealism, both in foreign policy and at home, to forget that they lived in a world of change to which their ideas and institutions must constantly be readjusted, and to return to an earlier and simpler age. It was a rejection not only of Wilsonism but of the whole movement of twentieth-century Progressivism.

The Republican convention met at Chicago on June 8. The two leading candidates were General Leonard Wood, who had been a close friend of Theodore Roosevelt, and Governor Frank Lowden of Illinois, whose support came chiefly from the agricultural regions. Hiram Johnson of California also controlled a number of delegates. Since neither Wood nor Lowden would yield to the other, it became necessary to find a compromise candidate; and during the evening of June 11 this task was undertaken by a group of senators and party bosses, who were anxious to weaken presidential authority and to restore to Congress much of the power which, under Roosevelt and Wilson, had been assumed by the executive. With this end in view they agreed to swing the nomination to Warren Gamaliel Harding of Ohio.

Harding had been for most of his life the editor of a small-town newspaper in Marion, Ohio; he had served as lieutenant governor of Ohio, and had been in the United States Senate since 1914. Harding was good-natured, well-meaning, warm-hearted, and very likeable, but totally lacking in both the intelligence and the strength of will needed for the presidency. He was in many ways a typical citizen of a middle western small town; and if he had never entered politics, he would have lived and died with the affection of all his neighbors. Unambitious himself and aware of his own limitations,

Harding had been pushed into politics partly by his wife and partly
by his friend, Harry M. Daugherty, an Ohio lawyer with a dubious
reputation. Daugherty was Harding's manager at the Chicago convention; and, having sized up the situation very shrewdly, he had
predicted to newspapermen what might happen. A journalist,
paraphrasing Daugherty, had announced that Harding's friends
expected him to be nominated for the presidency by fifteen men in
a smoke-filled hotel room at eleven minutes past two in the morning. This was substantially what happened. On the day after the
party leaders made their decision, the convention began to turn to
Harding, and he was nominated on the tenth ballot. In retaliation
for obeying their leaders as to the presidential nomination, the rank
and file of the convention insisted on making their own choice for
the vice presidency. Ignoring the senatorial cabal, who had picked
Lenroot of Wisconsin, they gave the nomination to Calvin Coolidge.

The Democratic convention, which met at San Francisco three
weeks later, was deadlocked for an even longer period. The leading
candidates were W. G. McAdoo and A. Mitchell Palmer, both of
Wilson's cabinet, and James A. Cox, a newspaper publisher who
had been governor of Ohio. Cox was finally nominated on the
forty-fourth ballot, with Franklin D. Roosevelt, Wilson's Assistant
Secretary of the Navy, as vice presidential candidate.

The only issue in the campaign was Wilsonism. Little was said
about domestic questions, and attention was concentrated on the
League of Nations. The Democratic convention declared that the
election was a "solemn referendum," and Cox and Roosevelt toured
the country advocating unconditional adherence to the League. The
Republican position, however, was much less clear cut. The Republican Party included both isolationists and reservationists; and in
order to retain the support of both groups, the platform had
deliberately been made vague. The Republicans were opposed to
Wilson's League, but they declared that they were not opposed to
every kind of League; their platform promised support for an
"association of nations" which would fulfill the same purposes as
Wilson's League but which would safeguard American sovereignty.
While Johnson and Borah urged the election of Harding on isola-

tionist grounds, a group of thirty-one Republican supporters of the League (including Root, Hughes, Herbert Hoover, and Nicholas Murray Butler) declared that they would vote for Harding because he would take America into the League on the basis laid down by the Senate reservationists. From the viewpoint of reconciling these contradictory attitudes, Harding was an ideal candidate. He had such a fondness for soothing, sonorous, and empty phraseology, and his mental processes were so cloudy and so imprecise, that it was possible to interpret his speeches as meaning almost anything one wished. The strongest impression to be derived from his utterances was that he would give the country an era of placid conservatism. "America's present need," he declared, "is not heroics but healing; not nostrums but normalcy; not revolution but restoration; . . . not surgery but serenity."

The result was a landslide for the Republicans. Supporting Harding were conservative Republicans who wanted to return to McKinleyism, war-weary citizens who were disillusioned by the outcome of the crusade in Europe and wanted to forget about the world outside America, representatives of the racial groups—German, Italian, and Irish—who resented the Treaty of Versailles, and all those who for one reason or another had come to dislike Woodrow Wilson. Harding was elected president by a popular vote of 16,152,-000 to 9,147,000 and an electoral vote of 404 to 127, and the Republicans strengthened their control of both Houses of Congress. The vote for Debs, running as Socialist candidate from prison, was 919,799.

BIBLIOGRAPHY

S. H. Adams, *The Incredible Era* (1939)
J. R. Commons and others, *History of Labor in the United States,* Vols. III and IV (1935)
W. Z. Foster, *From Bryan to Stalin* (1937)
F. Frankfurter, *The Case of Sacco and Vanzetti* (1927)
C. M. Fuess, *Calvin Coolidge* (1940)
J. S. Gambs, *The Decline of the I.W.W.* (1932)
B. Gitlow, *I Confess* (1939)
G. Hicks, *John Reed* (1936)

366 THE WORLD WAR

W. F. Johnson, *George Harvey* (1929)
J. Oneal, *American Communism* (1927)
M. Sullivan, *Our Times,* Vol. VI (1935)
W. A. White, *A Puritan in Babylon: The Story of Calvin Coolidge* (1938)
S. Yellen, *American Labor Struggles* (1936)

The Twenties

PART FOUR

31

GENERAL ECONOMIC TRENDS

AN ERA OF PROSPERITY

THE end of the World War and the return to power of conservative Republicanism inaugurated a period which in many respects resembled the epoch of McKinley. By the year 1920 war conditions were ending and business was able to return to peacetime methods. The war had raised all prices; and, when it ended, the prices of raw materials fell much more sharply than those of manufactured goods. Hence, the manufacturers' margin of profit was larger. Industry, moreover, had a large market for its goods owing to the numerous needs, both in the United States and in Europe, which had been left unsatisfied during the war years. There was an acute but brief economic depression in 1921; but the years from 1922 until 1929 were, with the exception of a minor setback in 1925, a period characterized by a business prosperity unexampled in the previous history of the United States. The average profit of the 2,046 leading manufacturing corporations during these years was 11.25 per cent a year.

Throughout this period business leaders enjoyed the admiration and applause of the general public; government officials held that their chief function was not to police business but to assist it and co-operate with it; and critics of the economic system were few in number and exercised little influence. It was widely believed that business had reformed itself and had abandoned the antisocial practices characteristic of the age of the trusts, that prosperity would continue indefinitely without any of the cyclic periods of depression which had recurred throughout the nineteenth century, and that poverty was steadily being abolished. These hopes ended abruptly in the autumn of 1929, when the American economic system entered the most acute depression in its history. It then became apparent that throughout the twenties the system had many weaknesses which were overlooked. In the opinion of many economists the most important of these weaknesses were the prevalence of monopolistic practices resulting in price rigidities, the relatively restricted purchasing power of the farmers and of many sections of the working class, the rapid growth of savings as contrasted with the relatively slower growth of consumption, the increase in debts, and the dependence of important branches of production on an export trade which was largely financed by American loans.

The most remarkable feature of the twenties, and the chief cause for the prevalent spirit of optimism, was the rapid growth of the national wealth and the national income. Between 1920 and 1929 production in all branches of the economic system increased by no less than 46 per cent. The total national income, which had been about 27 billion dollars in 1909, had risen to 66 billion dollars in 1922 and to 82 billion dollars in 1929. If allowance is made for the decreased value of money, the real increase was 44 per cent between 1909 and 1922, and an additional 31 per cent between 1922 and 1929. Throughout the whole period from 1900 to 1929 population rose from nearly 76 million to nearly 123 million, while the national wealth increased from 88 billion dollars to 361 billion dollars. In 1929 the per capita wealth was $2,977, and the per capita income was $692.

The chief cause for the growth of wealth was the increase in the productivity of labor, brought about by new mechanical inventions, the development of new sources of power, and the application of new techniques for promoting efficiency. Between 1922 and 1929 population increased by 1.4 per cent a year, production increased by 3.8 per cent a year, and production per capita increased by 2.4 per cent a year. The growth of productivity was especially great in manufacturing. According to the National Resources Board the output of American factories increased between 1920 and 1929 by 40.6 per cent, while the man-hours worked decreased by 1.9 per cent and the unit-labor requirement decreased by 30.2 per cent. The result was that, in spite of the growth of population, the number of factory workers decreased during the decade by a figure variously estimated at between 200,000 and 600,000. Sixty-nine workers in 1929, and fifty-five workers in 1934, could produce as much as a hundred workers could in 1920. In mining and transportation there were similar tendencies. Between 1920 and 1929 the number of miners decreased by about 250,000, whereas the output of the mines increased by 5.5 per cent; and on the railroads the number of workers decreased by about 100,000, while output decreased by only 0.8 per cent.

THE DEVELOPMENT OF THE CORPORATION

In spite of the trust-busting activities of the Progressive Era, the giant corporations which had been formed a quarter of a century earlier continued to dominate the economic system. Such industrial empires as United States Steel, American Telephone and Telegraph, the various Standard Oil companies, General Electric, and the leading railroads retained leadership in their respective fields. And although the House of Morgan exercised less control over the business of selling securities than it had in 1913, it still occupied its position at the apex of the economic pyramid; in 1932 it was estimated to have connections with one-quarter of all corporate wealth. Meanwhile a number of new monster corporations had appeared in new fields of activity. Some of the most notable were General Motors and the Ford Motor Company in automobiles, Du Pont in chemicals, and Commonwealth and Southern, Electric Bond and Share, United States Electric Power, and Samuel Insull's Middle West Utilities in the production of electricity.

A few figures will illustrate the dominance of the large corporations. In 1929, according to figures compiled by the Bureau of Internal Revenue, there were 456,000 corporations actively engaged in business. These did about 95 per cent of all manufacturing, and their total net income was $8,740,000,000. No less than 80 per cent of this sum was earned by those corporations, only 1,349 in number, whose incomes exceeded $1,000,000 each. According to

Berle and Means the 200 largest nonfinancial corporations owned
49.2 per cent of all corporate wealth and 22 per cent of the total
national wealth. The combined assets of these 200 corporations
amounted to 26 billion dollars in 1909, 43 billion dollars in 1919,
and 81 billion dollars in 1929. Their growth had thus kept pace
with the growth of the national wealth.

The internal organization of these great industrial empires was,
however, undergoing important changes. The individual entrepreneurs of the age of the trusts, who had combined ownership with
management, were disappearing; and the corporations were developing into collective enterprises in which ownership and management
were divorced from each other. Ownership was becoming diffused
among a considerable number of stockholders, while effective control was frequently assumed by salaried executives. The trend toward
the increase of stockholders was constant; and the larger the corporation, the more widely diffused was its ownership. It was, however, during the years from 1916 until 1921 that the most rapid
extension of ownership occurred. In 1909 nearly three-fifths of all
stocks were the property of the 25,000 richest individuals; by 1927
the proportion had decreased to a little over one-third. Of the 200
largest corporations, only 11 per cent by number and 6 per cent by
wealth were, in 1930, controlled by single stockholders who owned
a majority of the stock. At least 71 of them, on the other hand, had
more than 20,000 stockholders each.

The most conspicuous example of this trend was American Telephone and Telegraph Company, the largest corporation in the
country, whose assets amounted in 1930 to more than 4 billion
dollars and whose employees numbered more than 450,000. In
1901 A. T. and T. had 10,000 stockholders; by 1930 the number
had increased to nearly 570,000, none of whom owned as much as
1 per cent of the stock. The second and third largest corporations,
United States Steel and the Pennsylvania Railroad, also had no
stockholder owning more than 1 per cent.

Similar tendencies prevailed in the smaller corporations. In 1925,
according to the Federal Trade Commission, the officers and directors of more than four thousand typical medium-sized corporations

owned, on an average, only 10.7 per cent of their firm's common stock and 5.8 per cent of its preferred stock.

The diffusion of ownership, important as it was, did not, however, mean that the American people were becoming a nation of capitalists. The total number of stockholders, variously estimated at between 3 and 12 million, was probably closer to the former figure; and the bulk of the dividends were paid to a relatively small group. According to the Bureau of Internal Revenue, total dividend payments amounted in 1929 to $5,750,000,000. More than one-third of this sum went to about 17,000 individuals, and more than three-fifths of it to about 150,000 individuals. The profits of American corporate enterprise were thus going, in a large degree, to a small body of absentee owners who constituted a privileged leisure class.

There were still in the twenties a few outstanding entrepreneurs who combined ownership with control, among them being Henry Ford and the three Du Pont brothers. In general, however, the control of corporate business was exercised either by financial promoters or by salaried managers. Financial promoters were able to dominate corporations in which they owned a minority of the stock by means of various legal devices, such as control of proxy votes and voting trusts, and the pyramiding of holding companies. Notable examples of the holding company technique were afforded by the Van Sweringen brothers, who controlled railroads worth more than 2 billion dollars by means of an investment of less than twenty million, and by Samuel Insull, who constructed a system in which one dollar invested in Middle West Utilities controlled $1,750 invested in the Georgia Power Company.

The most significant development, however, was toward management control. This prevailed in 44 per cent by number and 58 per cent by wealth of the two hundred largest corporations. Management control was rendered possible by the large diffusion of stock holdings. Individual stockholders rarely had detailed information as to the policies pursued by the management; and, even when some of them disapproved of those policies, it was almost impossible for them to gather enough support to demand a change. The management thus had almost complete power and tended to become self-perpetuating. The state laws regulating incorporation were, moreover, becoming laxer, especially in Delaware, which had become the chief source of corporation charters after 1912, when Woodrow Wilson reformed the New Jersey corporation laws. The executives of some corporations used their freedom from control to develop a sense of responsibility to the interests of the general public, but there were others who did not resist the temptation to secure financial advantages for themselves at the expense of the stockholders.

In the opinion of Berle and Means the substitution of management control for ownership control constituted a minor revolution. "There has resulted," they declared, "the dissolution of the old atom of ownership into its component parts, control and beneficial ownership. This dissolution of the atom of property destroys the very foundation on which the economic order of the past three centuries has rested." "Those who control the destinies of the typical modern corporation own so insignificant a fraction of the company's stock that the returns from running the corporation profitably accrue to them in only a very minor degree. The stockholders, on the other hand, to whom the profits of the corporation go, cannot be motivated by those profits to a more efficient use of the property, since they have surrendered all disposition of it to those in control of the enterprise. The explosion of the atom of property destroys the basis of the old assumption that the quest for profits will spur the owner of industrial property to its effective use. It consequently challenges the fundamental economic principle of individual initiative in industrial enterprise."

Other observers felt that the closest analogies to the position held by corporation managers were to be found in the sphere of politics. The executives of a big corporation resembled the rulers of an empire in that the principal motive which determined their policies was not primarily the quest for personal profits, as in the individualistic capitalism of earlier periods, but rather the ambition to win greater power and prestige both for themselves and also for the enterprises to which they belonged. The big corporations, both in their impetus toward expansion and in their alliances and hostilities with one another, resembled independent political entities.

MONOPOLY

There was less monopoly, in the strict sense of the word, in the twenties than there had been at the beginning of the century. This was a result not only of the trust-busting of the Progressive Era but also of the rapid growth of production, which made it more difficult for any one corporation to acquire complete control of any branch of industry. Thus, for example, the various Standard Oil companies, which had controlled 80 per cent of the oil business in 1911, controlled only 43.1 per cent in 1926; the share of International Harvester in the agricultural machine industry dropped from 80 to 64 per cent; the proportion of the steel industry controlled by United States Steel declined from 70 to 40 per cent.

One monopolistic practice, however, of the greatest importance, tended to increase. Rival corporations adopted the habit of maintaining uniform prices and of competing with one another not by reducing prices but by improving quality and by advertising. When an industry was controlled by a small number of corporations, it was easy for them to agree on uniform price schedules; and none of them had any sufficient motive for resorting to price competition, which would result only in a price war and no profits for any of them. Uniform price schedules, which sometimes remained unchanged for a decade, became the rule in many of the more important branches of industry. These were sometimes achieved by means of trade associations, of which there were about two thousand, although only about a hundred seem to have adopted effective price-control policies. More frequent was price leadership by a large corporation, the price policies of which were imitated by its smaller competitors. Among the firms exercising price leadership were United States Steel, Standard Oil, International Harvester, Philadelphia and Reading (in anthracite), American Can Company, International Paper Company, and National Biscuit Company.

Even in many industries in which there was neither a trade association nor a price leader it became customary for prices to be uniform. This was conspicuously the case with cigarettes and with milk. Businessmen in general strongly favored price stability and felt that any resort to price-cutting was an unfair form of competition. Although, however, price stability tended to stabilize business conditions during prosperity periods, the prices appear often to have been made unduly high, thus restricting production and consumption for the sake of higher profits. The results during periods of depression were disastrous. Another incidental consequence was an excessive growth of advertising. In 1929 the money spent on advertising amounted to about 2 billion dollars, representing an increase of nearly 500 per cent since 1915.

ATTITUDE OF THE FEDERAL GOVERNMENT

The Federal government, under Republican control, made little attempt to restrict monopoly practices and pursued policies designed to assist business development. The tariff was raised in order to protect American industries, and taxation was lowered in order to provide capital for expansion. The Department of Commerce, under Herbert Hoover, promoted industrial efficiency and encouraged the standardization of products in accordance with the methods first adopted during the war. In ten years, by diminishing unnecessary variations in different commodities, it enabled business to make economies amounting to 250 million dollars a year. Hoover also encouraged the growth of trade associations, and sponsored two hundred "codes of fair practice" drawn up by the associations and other groups of businessmen. Big business was no longer regarded with suspicion, and trust-busting was not revived. The Federal Trade Commission attempted to prohibit certain unfair forms of competition, such as fraudulent advertising and the misbranding of commodities, but the more important provisions of the Sherman and Clayton Acts became almost a dead letter. The Commission took no action against holding companies or against interlocking directorates, nor did it interfere with the various devices by which corporation managers protected themselves from stockholder interference.

Similar policies were adopted by the courts. Former President Taft became Chief Justice of the Supreme Court in 1921, and he was succeeded in 1930 by Charles Evans Hughes. The Court abandoned the mild tendency toward liberalism which it had shown between 1905 and the World War; and throughout the twenties a

majority of the justices were conservative, liberalism being represented only by a minority consisting of Holmes, Brandeis, and (after 1925) Stone. The acquittal of United States Steel in 1920 meant
that bigness was no longer regarded as a violation of the Sherman
Act. Since the Court decided for acquittal on the ground, among
others, that the dissolution of the corporation would injure the public interests and the development of foreign trade, it seemed to
some observers that the "rule of reason" had been replaced by a
"doctrine of business expediency." In 1925 the Court further weakened the Sherman Act by declaring, in the cases of the Maple Floor-
ing Manufacturers' Association and the Cement Manufacturers'
Protective Association, that trade associations were not illegal.
Meanwhile the courts were again granting injunctions against labor
unions, in spite of the apparent prohibition of this practice by the
Clayton Act; and they were again using the Fourteenth Amendment
to protect business against interference by state legislatures and
public utility commissions.

It was widely believed that government regulation of business
had become unnecessary because business had reformed itself. Business, it was said, had become a profession, and its primary purpose
was to serve the public. Numerous organizations of businessmen,
particularly the Rotary Clubs, preached the ideal of service, and in
1925 the United States Chamber of Commerce adopted fifteen "principles of business conduct" which businessmen were supposed to
follow. This attitude was accepted by many former muckrakers,
especially by Ida Tarbell. It is true that a number of the forms of
unfair competition which had prevailed in the late nineteenth century had almost disappeared; and it is true also that businessmen
now realized the need for conciliating public opinion and that they
devoted considerable money and attention to securing popular approval. Business, nevertheless, was still carried on in order to make
profits, and the quest for profits was still liable to result in activities
contrary to the public interests.

Numerous episodes during the twenties suggested that the reform
of business had been relatively superficial. Many corporations still
pursued oppressive and tyrannical labor policies. The telephone and

power corporations carried on extravagant and unscrupulous propaganda campaigns against government regulation. Businessmen condoned the bribery of government officials, as was shown when Sinclair and Doheny were elected directors of the American Petroleum Institute after it had been proved that they had obtained oilfields from the Federal government by bribing the Secretary of the Interior. There were certain wealthy financiers who enriched themselves at the expense of the stockholders of the corporations which they controlled. And the belief that rich men were justified in taking advantage of loopholes in the income tax laws in order to evade payment was widely prevalent.

Nor was the maintenance of honesty and of obedience to the law the only problem presented by the new economic structure. The most significant feature of business development was that in a number of industries, as a result of managed prices, laissez-faire principles were no longer fully operative. There were corporation executives who were scrupulously honest but who, nevertheless, adopted price and wage policies which were probably detrimental to the public interest.

CHANGES IN THE CHARACTER OF ECONOMIC ACTIVITY

Another important aspect of economic development was the increasing importance of durable and semidurable commodities. The production of basic necessities, such as food and clothing, was becoming relatively less important, while there was a rapid growth in the production of articles which had formerly been considered luxuries, such as automobiles, refrigerators, telephones, electrical equipment, and plumbing fixtures. There was also a marked increase in the production of capital equipment—of machinery, factories, and office buildings. Between 1922 and 1929 (according to F. C. Mills) the production of nondurable consumption goods increased by 24 per cent; on the other hand, durable consumption goods (housing excluded) grew by 72 per cent, and capital equipment (buildings included) grew by 70 per cent. In 1899 food and clothing constituted 57.9 per cent by value of all production, while durable goods amounted to only 26.5 per cent. By 1929, on the other hand, food

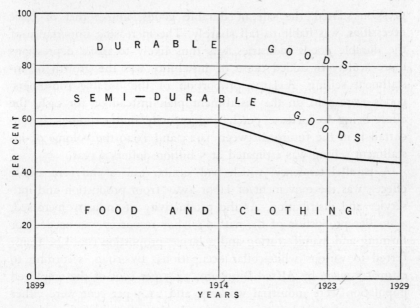

Figure 6. PERCENTAGES OF DURABLE, SEMI-DURABLE, AND NON-DURABLE GOODS IN TOTAL PRODUCTION. (Based on figures from F. C. Mills, *Economic Tendencies in the United States,* published by the National Bureau of Economic Research.)

and clothing had dropped to 43.6 per cent, and durable goods had risen to 35.21 per cent.

Such a tendency was a sign of economic progress; it indicated a rapid rise in the general standard of living. Unfortunately it also increased the instability of the economic system. The market for durable consumption goods, unlike that for basic necessities, could easily become glutted; and the attempt of manufacturers to maintain sales by means of constant changes in style—by, for example, urging the public to buy a new car every year—could not wholly surmount this problem. Nor could the production of new capital equipment continue indefinitely. The building of new factories required a constantly expanding consumers' market for the commodities which these factories would produce. When, moreover, a depression started, the sale of durable goods, unlike that of basic necessities, was liable to fall sharply. The increasing importance of the durable goods industries was thus likely to make depressions more acute. An added cause of instability was the growth of installment selling. A large proportion of the durable consumers' goods were sold on the installment plan instead of for cash, the effect being to increase purchasing capacity in the present but to curtail it in the future. Between 1923 and 1929 the volume of installment selling was estimated at 5 billion dollars a year.

A parallel tendency, which had similar causes and comparable effects, was the movement of labor away from production and into service and distribution. As the productivity of industry increased, a smaller proportion of the nation's labor resources was needed for farming and manufacturing and a larger proportion could be transferred to various white-collar occupations. By 1930, according to estimates made by Alfred Bingham, 34.5 per cent of the employed population were industrial workers, and 21.5 per cent were either farmers or farm laborers; professional, clerical and service occupations accounted for 30.5 per cent, while 8 per cent were businessmen and 5.5 per cent were in domestic service. Thus only 58 per cent were engaged directly in production, whereas in 1920 the proportion had been 65 per cent.

The growth in the number of clerical workers (nearly half of whom were women) and of workers engaged in retail trade was particularly rapid. The result was that consumers received better service; but on the other hand there was an excessively rapid growth of distribution costs and an increasing price spread between what the producer received and what the consumer paid. According to estimates made by R. R. Doane, persons engaged in distribution received 3 per cent of the national income in 1860, 7.6 per cent in 1904, 9.5 per cent in 1922, and 12.6 per cent in 1929. Between 1913 and 1929 the cost of distributing food rose by 90 per cent. In 1929, according to the Department of Agriculture, consumers paid $21,199,000,000 for articles of food, and of this sum only $8,792,000,000 was received by the farmers who produced them. Paul D. Converse estimated that in the same year more than half of the total retail prices of all commodities was represented by distribution costs. The growth of chain-store systems was an important feature of economic development in the twenties. In 1909 chain stores were responsible for perhaps 15 per cent of all retail sales, and in 1925 for 30 per cent. This development made distribution more efficient, but it does not appear to have reduced its costs as much as might have been expected. It had, moreover, the disadvantage that profits from retail selling did not remain in the communities where they were made but were diverted to stockholders living elsewhere.

The high cost of distribution was responsible for one of the more significant economic developments of the twenties and thirties—the growth of consumer co-operatives. The co-operative movement originated in Great Britain, and it was also strongly established in the Scandinavian countries. Under the leadership of J. P. Warbasse, it was introduced into the United States in 1915 and began to grow rapidly after 1926. It was strongest among the farm populations, especially those of Scandinavian descent, in the Middle and Far West. By 1936 there were 20 wholesale co-operatives and 3,600 retail co-operatives; they had 677,750 members and were doing an annual business of $182,685,000. The leaders of the movement preached co-operation with great fervor and believed that its general adoption would remedy most of the economic weaknesses of capitalism.

INEQUALITY AND DEBT

Monopolistic price-fixing, the growth of the durable goods industries, and the increase of distribution costs could not be regarded as altogether healthy tendencies. Economic weaknesses of more fundamental importance, however, were the prevalence of inequalities of income and the growth of debt.

Throughout the twenties the wage-earning class made substantial gains; and it was widely believed that a new economic order was being created, characterized by high wages and a large-scale consumers' market. Actually, however, poverty and inequality continued to a much greater extent than most observers realized, the result being that the purchasing power of the American people remained considerably smaller than the productive capacity of American agriculture and industry. It might perhaps be considered that $2,500 was the minimum annual income on which an urban family of normal size could enjoy an adequate standard of living; but in 1929 71.2 per cent of the employed population were receiving less than this figure, and 42 per cent of all American families were earning less than $1,500 a year. In that year, according to estimates made by the Brookings Institution, the income distribution was as follows:

INCOME GROUP	FAMILIES IN THOUSANDS	PER CENT	INCOME IN MILLIONS	PER CENT
Under $1000	5,899	21.5	$ 2,900	3.8
$1000–1999	10,455	38.0	$15,364	19.9
2000–2999	5,192	18.9	$12,586	16.3
3000–4999	3,672	13.4	$13,866	18.0
5000–9999	1,625	5.9	$10,820	14.0
10,000 and over	631	2.3	$21,580	28.0

Thus the 631,000 richest families were receiving a total income substantially greater than that of the 16,000,000 families at the bottom of the scale.[1]

The tendency throughout the twenties, moreover, was toward an increase in inequality. The prices of raw materials tended to fall, thus decreasing the earnings of the farm population; the prices of consumers' goods tended to rise, thus lowering the living standards of persons with fixed incomes. This divergence in price movements meant larger gross earnings per unit for the industrial corporations. The bulk of the increase went to profits rather than to wages. Between 1922 and 1929 the real wages of industrial workers increased, on an average, by 1.4 per cent a year. Since, however, production per capita was increasing by 2.4 per cent a year, the gains of the workers were not proportionate to the increase in what they produced. Certain sections of the working class, moreover, especially in bituminous coal and in textiles, were receiving wages very much below the national average.

The largest gains were made by salaried executives and by stock-

1. See *America's Capacity to Consume*, page 54.

holders. Whereas the money wages of all industrial workers increased between 1922 and 1929 by 33 per cent, salaries increased by 42 per cent, corporation net profits by 76 per cent, and dividends paid to stockholders by 108 per cent. Labor costs per unit (estimated in dollars of constant purchasing power) fell by 9.5 per cent, but overhead expenses and profits rose by 10.6 per cent. Out of the value added by manufacturing, the proportion received by all wage and salary earners dropped from 58.7 per cent in 1921 to 47.7 per cent in 1929. While, therefore, the wage earners were receiving larger incomes, their share in the total national income was decreasing.

Another unhealthy tendency was the growth of debt. Between 1912 and 1930 long-term debts, both public and private, increased at the rate of 12.2 per cent a year, considerably faster than the national wealth and the national income. During the period of the war, for example, there was a rapid growth of farm mortgages, which totaled 3.8 billion dollars in 1912, 8.9 billion dollars in 1922, and 9.2 billion dollars in 1930. There was also a steady increase in the indebtedness of state, county, and municipal governments, which were expending large sums on roads, public buildings, and other improvements, and financing them by borrowing. The net public debt (excluding that of the Federal government) amounted to 4.3 billion dollars in 1912, 9.9 billion dollars in 1922, and 17.6 billion dollars in 1932. By 1930, according to the estimates of John Blair, the total private long-term debt was 84.5 billion dollars, and the total public debt was 31.9 billion dollars. If to these sums are added the debt of financial institutions (21.9 billion dollars), all short-term debts (112.4 billion dollars), and the value of all corporation stocks (86 billion dollars), the total invested capital upon which interest and dividend payments were being made amounted to 336.7 billion dollars. Interest payments (not including dividends to stockholders) totaled 2.1 billion dollars in 1913 and 7.6 billion dollars in 1929.

This disproportionate growth of debt tended to increase economic inequality since it meant that the rentier class was receiving a larger share of the national income; and it made the economic system less able to withstand the effects of a depression. The development of a complicated structure of interlocking debt obligations, in which farmers, businessmen, railroads, industrial corporations, banks, insurance companies, and government bodies were all dependent on one another, meant that if any of these groups became unable to make their interest payments, the chain of bankruptcies was liable to spread with the speed of a forest fire.

SURPLUS MONEY AND IDLE MEN

The primary economic justification for inequality was that the richer families would save a large proportion of their incomes and would thus provide capital for industrial expansion. Almost all saving was done by the richer families. Those who earned more than $300,000 a year saved, on an average, more than half their incomes. Two-thirds of all saving (according to H. G. Moulton) was done by the 2.3 per cent of the families with incomes above $10,000. On the other hand, 59 per cent of the families having incomes below $2,000 were responsible for only 1.6 per cent of all saving. The 60,000 richest families saved as much as the 25,000,000 poorest families. There was also a rapid growth during the twenties in the savings made by corporations. Corporation executives began to set aside considerable surpluses for expansion and for security against depression, in preference to distributing them among stockholders. Between 1922 and 1927 the big corporations saved 29.4 per cent of their profits, and it was estimated that 40 per cent of all saving was done by corporations.

During the twenties it appears that the supply of savings was in excess of the economic need for it. According to H. G. Moulton the total savings available for investment amounted to 8 or 9 billion dollars in 1923 and had risen to 15 billion by 1929. Between 1922 and 1929 the rate of increase in savings was 4.7 per cent a year, whereas production was increasing by only 3.8 per cent a year. Of these savings, however, only about 5 billion dollars a year was invested in industrial expansion or in mortgages. Of the remainder, part was loaned to foreign countries and the remainder was diverted into investment trusts or holding companies or used for speculation.

on the stock exchange. There was consequently a very rapid rise in the prices of stocks, amounting to an average of 19.4 per cent a year. After stocks had been pushed far above their real values (as measured by their capacity to earn dividends), a sudden and catastrophic fall became inevitable.

Meanwhile the fact that these large sums were being diverted into speculation, instead of being used to buy new consumers' goods or invested in new capital equipment, meant that the system of production was unable to operate at its full capacity. Throughout the twenties a part of the nation's industrial equipment and of its labor resources was lying idle. Even in 1929, at the height of prosperity, it would have been possible (according to the estimates of the Brookings Institution) for production to have been 19 per cent greater than it actually was. Unemployment existed throughout the twenties; and, although there are no exact figures, it has been generally estimated that there were never less than about 2 million men looking for work. The mobility of labor was increasing, and workers were constantly being displaced by machinery. Although eventually such workers were usually able to find employment elsewhere, they frequently had to move from one part of the country to another or to adopt occupations for which they had not been trained, so that the interval of unemployment was liable to be unduly long. It was, moreover, increasingly difficult for men past the age of forty-five, once they had been displaced, to find jobs of any kind.

The combination of surplus savings, idle factory equipment, and unemployed workers proved that the economic system was not functioning as it should. Although it was not until the nineteen-thirties that the problem became acute, it was present on a smaller scale throughout the twenties. Considered from the viewpoint of human needs, the economic system was still capable of great expansion. Very much more wealth was required by the American people than was actually being produced. A large number of American families lacked basic necessities. In 1929 only one American family in six owned an automobile; only one in five (exclusive of farm families, where the proportion was even smaller) had a fixed bathtub or electricity; and only one in ten had a telephone. If these needs were to be satisfied, idle money, factories, and men must be kept at work, and the purchasing power of the mass of the people must be increased. Although, however, the nature of the problem was evident, there was no agreement as to its solution. While defenders of capitalism maintained that business leaders, if left free from political interference, would continue to increase the national income, reformers argued that the government must intervene directly in order to regulate the investment of capital and increase mass purchasing power. Certainly statesmanship of the highest order would be required from both the political and the industrial leaders of the nation.

BIBLIOGRAPHY

F. L. Allen, *The Lords of Creation* (1935)
T. Arnold, *The Folklore of Capitalism* (1937)
S. Bell, *Production, Wages and National Income* (1940)
*A. A. Berle and G. C. Means, *The Modern Corporation and Private Property* (1932)
*J. M. Blair, *Seeds of Destruction* (1938)
J. C. Bonbright and G. C. Means, *The Holding Company* (1932)
*A. R. Burns, *The Decline of Competition* (1936)
T. N. Carver, *The Present Economic Revolution in the United States* (1925)
E. Clark (ed.), *Internal Debts of the United States* (1933)
L. Corey, *The Decline of American Capitalism* (1934)
L. Dennis, *Is Capitalism Doomed?* (1932)
W. J. A. Donald, *Trade Associations* (1933)
P. H. Douglas and A. Director, *The Problem of Unemployment* (1931)
Federal Trade Commission, *Open-Price Trade Associations* (1929)
F. A. Fetter, *The Masquerade of Monopoly* (1931)
J. H. Foth, *Trade Associations* (1930)
*L. Hacker, *American Problems of Today* (1938)
E. L. Heermance, *Ethics of Business* (1926)
E. D. Kennedy, *Dividends to Pay* (1939)
W. I. King, *The National Income and its Purchasing Power* (1930)
*E. C. Kirkland, *History of American Economic Life* (1933)
H. W. Laidler, *Concentration of Control in American Industry* (1931)
*M. Leven and others (Brookings Institution), *America's Capacity to Consume* (1934)
H. A. Marquard, *Dynamics of Industrial Combination* (1931)
P. M. Mazur, *American Prosperity* (1928)

*F. C. Mills, *Economic Tendencies in the United States* (1933)
*H. G. Moulton, *Income and Economic Progress* (1935)
*———— *The Formation of Capital* (1935)
National Industrial Conference Board, *Trade Associations* (1925)
———— *Mergers and the Law* (1929)
*E. G. Nourse and others (Brookings Institution), *America's Capacity to Produce* (1934)
B. S. Kirsh, *Trade Associations: The Legal Aspects* (1928)
President's Committee on Recent Economic Changes, *Recent Economic Changes* (1929)
W. Z. Ripley, *Main Street and Wall Street* (1927)
J. Rorty, *Our Master's Voice: Advertizing* (1934)
F. A. Shannon, *Economic History of the People of the United States* (revised edition, 1940)
Norman Thomas, *Human Exploitation in the United States* (1934)
R. G. Tugwell, *Industry's Coming of Age* (1927)

32

SOME NEW INDUSTRIES

AUTOMOBILES

UNQUESTIONABLY the most important industry of the postwar period was the manufacturing of automobiles. Originating near the end of the nineteenth century, it developed into spectacular proportions in the twenties. By 1928 it was giving direct employment to 5 per cent of all industrial workers and paying 6 per cent of all industrial wages. It had, moreover, stimulated the gasoline, leather, plate glass, rubber, steel, paint, and cement industries; and it had created jobs for thousands of mechanics, chauffeurs, and filling-station attendants. The number of cars that had been manufactured was 24,500,000, and the total number of workers directly or indirectly dependent upon the industry was probably close to 4,000,000. The growth of this industry was the most important single factor in creating the prosperity of the twenties.

The first gasoline-driven vehicles were made in Europe in the eighteen-seventies and eighties. The most important pioneers there were Jean Lenoir, Carl Bery, and the Daimler brothers. Until 1905 there were more automobiles in Great Britain than in the United States. The first Americans to make automobiles were Charles Duryea, Elward Haynes and the Apperson brothers, and Henry Ford, all of them in the eighteen-nineties. Ford's first car, made in 1893, traveled twenty-five miles an hour, had a wooden flywheel and a cylinder made of a piece of gas pipe, and was mounted on a carriage with bicycle wheels. The period of experimentation lasted until 1910. After that date the standard cheap car was of four cylinders, shaft-driven, magneto-equipped, and water-cooled; and it had a three-speed sliding-gear transmission. In 1912 appeared the electric starter, first adopted by Cadillac. The chief subsequent improvements were the adoption of stronger bodies and tires.

The growth of the industry would have been impossible without the building of hard-surfaced roads. Roads were at first built by the county governments. Starting with New Jersey in 1892, the state governments began to assume responsibility. Finally, by acts of Congress passed in 1916 and 1921, the Federal government entered the field. The Department of Agriculture began to organize a national system of numbered highways, the cost of which was to be divided equally between the Federal government and the states. After 1920 Federal expenditures on roads varied between $65,000,-000 and $100,000,000 a year. This sum, however, was only a small fraction of the total amount spent on roads. The increase of automobiles made it necessary for roads to be built at least partly of cement, for automobiles quickly ruined roads made merely of water-bound macadam. The cost of a cement highway was from $33,000 to $44,000 a mile, and the upkeep also was expensive. By 1922 there were about 200,000 miles of cement roads. The cost in 1921 was $1,140,000,000, most of which was paid by the state governments. Only a small proportion of this sum was raised by automobile fees and gasoline taxes. In other words, the whole community was virtually being taxed to subsidize the automobile industry. Whereas the railroads had been required to construct their own lines of track, the automobile industry received roads as a gift from the state.

The development of the industry exhibited the usual transition from competition to combination. Altogether nearly 200 independent firms undertook, at one time or another, to manufacture automobiles, of which 44 were still in existence in 1927. By that date, however, at least 60 per cent of the industry was controlled by two corporations, General Motors Corporation and Ford Motor Company. Some of the evils of competition had, moreover, been avoided by the standardization of thousands of the small parts of which automobiles were composed. The industry had at first been impeded by patent rights which had been acquired in 1879 and 1895 by G. B. Selden; but Selden's claims were dismissed by the courts in 1911, after he had sued Ford for infringement. Subsequent to 1915 the automobile manufacturers adopted the policy of pooling all patents.

General Motors was the creation of William C. Durant, who began his career as a drugstore clerk and was subsequently a patent medicine salesman and a wagon manufacturer. Winning control of the Buick Company, Durant expanded it into General Motors, but lost control of it to a group of bankers in 1910. He then organized the Chevrolet Company and was able to recapture General Motors in 1915. In the postwar depression he lost control again, this time permanently, and General Motors became a subsidiary of the Du Pont and Morgan empires, which had formed an alliance. Effective control remained henceforth with the Du Pont family, who owned about 30 per cent of the stock. Throughout the twenties General Motors was the most spectacular money-maker of all American corporations. Anyone who had invested $25,000 in it in 1921 was a millionaire by 1929; and during 1927, 1928, and 1929 its profits exceeded $200,000,000 a year. The corporation not only manufactured cars of all prices, but it also extended its activities into the fields of radio, aviation, electric refrigeration, and power and light production. Ranking eighth among all corporations in capital value, it was exceeded in the average volume of its profits only by American Telephone and Telegraph.

Henry Ford was almost the last survivor of the kind of individual entrepreneur who had dominated American industry in the eighteen-seventies and eighties. In 1903 he entered into partnership with the Dodge brothers and with James Couzens. In 1907, however, he bought out his associates and became the owner of a majority of the stock in the Ford Motor Company. His policy henceforth was to retain personal control and not to surrender his independence to bankers or stockholders. More fully, perhaps, than any of his contemporaries, he grasped the essential elements of the new industrial system—standardization, division of labor, high wages, and mass production at low prices for a popular market. From 1909 until

1927 he made only one type of car, the famous Model T. By adopting the assembly line, on which division of labor was carried to an
almost fantastic extreme, he reduced the time required for making
the chassis from 12 hours 28 minutes to 1 hour 33 minutes. Starting
in 1908, he set out to sell his car at a price which the average
middle-class American could meet. He paid, moreover, wages considerably above the average. On January 5, 1914, he created a sensation by announcing that henceforth Ford workers would receive five
dollars a day for an eight-hour day. For a number of years his profits
reached 100 per cent a year. As a result of these policies Ford was
regarded in Europe as the principal spokesman and symbol of American industrial civilization. In America, on the other hand, he incurred considerable antagonism on account of his paternalistic attitude to his employees, his stubborn opposition to trade unionism,
and the naïve eccentricity of many of his pronouncements on political and social questions.

AVIATION

Human beings had dreamed of flying for thousands of years; but
the first persons who actually constructed a successful flying machine
were Wilbur and Orville Wright, the owners of a bicycle shop at
Dayton, Ohio. The Wrights began to study flying in 1896; and they
chose as the scene of their experiments the desolate and inaccessible
sand dunes of Kitty Hawk, on Roanoake Island in North Carolina.
By 1902 they had built a successful glider, after which they proceeded to the application of power. They made their first successful
flight on December 17, 1903, traveling 852 feet and staying in the
air for 59 seconds. Two years later they could travel a distance of
24 miles. So successfully had they solved the problems involved
that the machine of today is, in essentials, identical with that built
by the Wrights. The Wrights discouraged publicity; and because of
the general scarcity of news regarding their achievement, those reports that did appear in the papers were received with scepticism.
It was not until 1908 that the public became aware that flight had
become possible.

The aviation industry remained backward in the United States un-

til 1927. Ninety per cent of the factories built during the war were
scrapped in 1919, and the government made little effort to develop
military aviation. Brigadier General William Mitchell, who had
commanded the American air force in France, insisted that future
wars would be won by aviation, but his superior officers paid no
attention to him. When his protests became disrespectful, he was—
in 1926—court-martialled and dismissed. During the early twenties
aviation was carried on by numerous small companies and by independent barnstormers who sold rides to persons who were interested in the experience.

The development of aviation into a major industry began with
the Air Mail Act of 1925, by which the government was empowered to subsidize the industry through the granting of contracts for
carrying mail. Lindbergh's flight across the Atlantic in May, 1927,
further aroused popular enthusiasm. These events were followed by
a boom in aviation stocks, which had reached a value of a billion
dollars by the autumn of 1929. One individual, who had invested
$40 in an aviation company in 1926, found that three years later
his stocks had a value of $5,624,640. The industry rapidly became
consolidated. Although there were in the thirties thirty-four different companies manufacturing airplanes, the bulk of the business
was controlled by three major groups: North American Aviation,
which was connected with General Motors; Curtiss-Wright; and
United Aircraft and Transport Corporation. Most of the leading
transportation lines were connected with these three groups. The
process of consolidation was assisted by the Federal government. In
1930, under the Air Mail Act, Walter F. Brown, Postmaster General under President Hoover, allotted 90 per cent of the air mail
contracts to the three major groups without competitive bidding,
thereby eliminating many of the smaller companies which lacked
political influence. The War Department also made three-quarters
of its purchases from the same groups. In spite of lavish subsidies,
however, the companies reported small profits, chiefly because they
paid high salaries and were milked by holding companies. A congressional committee commented in 1933 that: "although the air
transport industry is a very young one its intercorporate relationships

have rapidly assumed a degree of complexity which would do credit to long established industries such as the utilities and the railroads."

The Roosevelt administration attempted, by the Air Mail Act of 1934 and the Civil Aeronautics Act of 1938, to cleanse the industry of its financial abuses. The air mail subsidies were reduced, and an effort was made to separate manufacturing from transportation and to prevent interlocking directorates. Meanwhile there was a steady growth in air transportation services, particularly those of Pan American Airways, which covered 63,000 miles in 1939. There was also a growth in sales of airplanes, the majority of which were to the United States government or to foreign governments for war purposes.

E. I. DU PONT DE NEMOURS

Ranking third among all American corporations in the postwar period with respect to net profits, surpassed only by American Telephone and Telegraph and General Motors, was the original Du Pont corporation of E. I. Du Pont de Nemours, which was unique in that it had been controlled by the same family for more than a century. The Du Pont firm originated as early as 1802, when a French immigrant, Eleuthère Irenée du Pont, built a gunpowder factory on the Brandywine in Delaware. Exactly one hundred years later the firm passed under the ownership of three Du Pont cousins, Coleman, Pierre, and Alfred, associated with whom was a young French-Irish stenographer, John Jacob Raskob. During the next four years the cousins created a gunpowder trust, acquiring control of 70 per cent of the business; and when the government sued under the Sherman Act, the Supreme Court found it impossible to dissolve the trust into its constituent units.

During the war the Du Ponts made 40 per cent of all explosives used by the Allies. They built fourteen square miles of factories, increased the capital value of the corporation from $83,000,000 to $308,000,000, and earned net profits of $237,000,000. When the United States entered the war, the Du Ponts refused to reveal their trade secrets, and the government was compelled to ask them to supervise the building of the Old Hickory explosives plant at Nashville, Tennessee. The Du Ponts asked at first for 10 per cent of the construction costs and 15 per cent of the operation returns of the plant, but agreed finally to a contract which gave them a gross profit of about 2 million dollars; they then undertook the task with remarkable efficiency and completed the plant several months ahead of schedule.

At the end of the war the Du Pont corporation had $90,000,000 in its treasury. Turning from the manufacture of explosives to that of chemicals, and creating a large and very efficient staff of research experts, the Du Ponts began to produce numerous coal tar and cellulose products. By 1930 they were making eleven hundred separate articles and owned eighty different factories in thirty different states. A large number of the more spectacular applications of science to industrial processes in the twenties and thirties were the work of the Du Pont laboratories. Coleman and Alfred had retired before the end of the war, and the firm was now controlled by three brothers, Pierre, Irénée, and Lammot. The family dominated the State of Delaware; and genuine political conflicts rarely occurred in that state except when different branches of the family espoused different policies. Normally Republican, the family was persuaded by their business associate, John Jacob Raskob, to support the Democratic candidates in the elections of 1928 and 1932, chiefly because of their opposition to prohibition. Subsequently the Du Ponts returned to Republicanism and were among the most vigorous opponents of the New Deal.

POWER

Another industry which grew rapidly during the twenties was the production of electrical power. Between 1902 and 1929 the kilowatt hours of energy produced increased from 4,768,000,000 to 97,352,-000,000. In terms of horsepower the increase was from 7,500,000,-000 in 1912 to 20,300,000,000 in 1922 and 43,200,000 in 1930. By 1931 the capital invested in the industry totaled about 12 billion dollars. The manufacture of electrical equipment was still dominated by the two corporations which had been founded before the end of the nineteenth century, General Electric and Westinghouse Electric.

The production of power, however, originally handled by numerous small companies, became in the twenties a field for ambitious and unscrupulous financing.

By 1930 more than half the power produced in the United States was controlled by four billion-dollar corporations—Electric Bond and Share, Middle West Utilities, Commonwealth and Southern, and United States Electric Power. A number of extraordinarily complex systems of pyramided holding companies had been constructed, and financiers were dominating large aggregations of capital through relatively small initial investments. The most notorious example of the holding company technique was Middle West Utilities, by means of which the English-born Samuel Insull, formerly an employee of Thomas A. Edison, controlled no less than 150 different public utility corporations.

Power production was a natural monopoly and presented the same problems of public control as had the railroads a generation earlier. Critics of the industry believed that rates were generally too high; that the financiers who controlled it had not learned the lesson taught by the automobile industry; and that, if they lowered their rates, they would stimulate a wider use of electrical equipment and actually earn larger profits, in addition to benefiting society. That this opinion was justified was proved after 1933 when the T. V. A. began to force down the rates of the private power companies operating in the Tennessee Valley, the result being that those companies increased their earnings.

Meanwhile the state governments, following the lead of Wisconsin and New York, attempted to regulate the industry, but with little success. The state public utility commissions were hampered by the fact that much power crossed state lines, and by the difficulty of determining capital values, in terms of which the rate of profit allowed to the companies had to be assessed. The courts, moreover, declared that holding companies were not public utilities and were therefore not subject to regulation. Effective control over the industry could be established only by the Federal government, which took little action until 1933. Meanwhile all the public utility corporations fought government control by means of extensive propaganda campaigns, which were financed not by individual owners but out of corporate profits. The different branches of the industry combined to form state committees to watch their interests in the state legislatures and a National Joint Committee on Utilities to represent them at Washington. It set out to educate the American public as to the benefits of private ownership through the medium of school and college textbooks and by subsidizing journalists, teachers, and public lecturers.

MOTION PICTURES

Another new major industry was the production of motion pictures. The motion picture was a new art form of the greatest importance, both aesthetically and as a vehicle of propaganda. It is discussed from those angles in a later chapter. It was also, however, a branch of big business, and its history exhibited the usual development from competition to combination.

The first attempts to photograph motion by taking a succession of pictures were made in the eighteen-eighties. In 1882, for example, the railroad magnate Leland Stanford adopted this method in order to discover whether a galloping horse lifted all its feet from the ground at the same time. The use of celluloid instead of glass for making such pictures originated with George Eastman and Hannibal Goodman. Finally, in 1889, Thomas A. Edison discovered how to reflect a series of pictures on a screen by using perforated film and a sprocket wheel which ensured regularity in starting and stopping. Similar inventions were being made independently at the same period in Europe.

Edison had already invented the phonograph; and having patented both inventions, he exploited them commercially in penny arcades where people could simultaneously listen to a phonograph and watch a brief moving picture. He regarded both inventions as cheap toys which could never become important. The public, however, quickly became interested in "vitascopes," as the first motion pictures were called; and when, in 1896, the Edison Company exhibited a vitascope at Koster and Biall's Music Hall in New York, it created a sensation. The Edison Company sold projection machines to numerous individuals who had perceived the financial possibilities of the invention, among them being two furriers, Marcus Loew and Adolph Zukor; a New York garment worker, William Fox; and the manager of a clothing store, Carl Laemmle. Since Edison was unable to satisfy the demand for vitascopes, numerous independent producers entered the field, in violation of Edison's patent rights. Vitascopes steadily grew longer; they began to tell stories; and the leading performers in them began to become well-known.

The first film to tell a story was *The Great Train Robbery*, produced by E. S. Porter in 1903. In 1908 David Wark Griffith, the first American who fully grasped the aesthetic potentialities of the motion picture, became a producer. In 1909 began the career of the first motion picture star, Mary Pickford. The motion picture had, moreover, developed beyond the penny arcade and the music hall and had created its own theater, the "nickelodeon," of which there were nearly 10,000 by 1909. During the same period the motion picture was also being developed in Europe, especially in France and Italy, where it was treated from the beginning as a serious art-form and not merely as a popular toy. In 1913 the Italian picture *Quo Vadis* was shown in New York in a regular theater with seats priced at a dollar—an event which marked an epoch in motion picture history.

Meanwhile Edison was fighting to maintain a strangle hold over the new industry by means of his patent rights. In 1909 he combined with nine of his leading competitors to form the Motion Pictures Patents Company, which was to handle production, and the General Film Company, which was to control distribution. All independents were to be totally excluded from the business. There followed a long battle between Edison and the independents, fought partly in the courts and partly by hired strong-arm men. Edison and his associates, however, consistently underestimated the possibilities of the motion picture and the tastes of the public. The independents captured the market by steadily improving the quality of their pictures and by developing such stars as Mary Pickford, Charlie Chaplin, Tom Mix, Broncho Billy, Theda Bara, and John Bunny. By 1914 the Motion Pictures Patents Company, rejected by the public and threatened with prosecution under the Sherman Act, had to accept defeat. One incident of the struggle was the removal of most of the independents to Hollywood, whence they could escape into Mexico in case of pursuit by Edison's lawyers and detectives.

After the defeat of Edison the leading figure in the industry was Adolph Zukor, who joined Jesse Lasky and Samuel Goldfish (later called Goldwyn) in 1916 in forming Famous Players' Lasky, allied with which was the distribution company known as Paramount Pictures Corporation. Zukor aspired to dominate the industry; but he was fought by a number of rival producers. Since the chief desire of the public was to see their favorite stars, the producers began to bid against one another for control of the stars, thus driving up salaries. By 1916 Chaplin and Mary Pickford were probably earning a million dollars a year. The same process brought about a steady improvement in the technique of production, more luxurious theaters, and higher admission prices. In 1921 Paramount was still in the lead, but its supremacy was contested by William Fox, First National, and United Artists. There were half-a-dozen medium-sized production companies, and between thirty and forty small producers on "Poverty Row."

After the World War the motion picture rapidly developed into a major industry. By 1926 there were 20,000 theaters in the United States, with an average attendance of 100,000,000 persons a week. Hollywood, moreover, had defeated its European competitors and captured the market of the entire world. Some 2 billion dollars was invested in the business, and enormous sums were passing through its treasuries. The men who had developed the industry— most of them immigrants from eastern Europe who had started in the clothing trades—had not only become rich; they also controlled an instrument for moulding popular customs and beliefs to which there was no parallel in world history.

This period saw the consolidation of most of the theaters into a few major chains. Zukor attempted to squeeze out his competitors in production by establishing a monopoly of distribution—a project which was checked by the Federal Trade Commission in 1922. In order to fight Zukor the other leading producers began to acquire theaters, while a number of independent exhibitors were combined into a rival chain by Marcus Loew. Loew subsequently joined forces with a group of producers to form Metro-Goldwyn-Mayer, while his chain of theaters passed under the control of William Fox. Another chain of theaters was created by R. K. O., formed in 1928 as an affiliate of the Radio Corporation of America. The result was that the exhibitors lost their independence. Production and exhibition passed under the control of the same individuals; and under the system of block-booking those theaters which remained nominally free were required to show whatever pictures were sent them by the producers—a practice which made it difficult for the smaller producers who did not control theaters to stay in business.

The chief subsequent event in motion picture history was the appearance of the sound or talking picture. The first sound picture, *The Jazz Singer*, was made in 1927 by the four Warner brothers, who had hitherto been on Poverty Row, but who developed into producers of major importance as a result of their initiative. The development of the sound picture was at first impeded by patent difficulties, most of the patents being the property of A. T. and T. By 1929, however, the victory of the talking picture was complete. Another development was the growth of affiliations between Hollywood and Wall Street. Wall Street money began to flow into the industry, and some of the production and distribution companies began to be controlled by bankers. William Fox, for example, lost control of both the production and the distribution companies which bore his name.

In the thirties attendance at motion picture theaters in the United States averaged 85,000,000 a week—a decrease from the high figure of the twenties—and American producers had a world audience estimated at 250,000,000 a week. The industry made between five hundred and seven hundred feature pictures a year, of which there were usually about forty costing more than a million dollars each. Most of the theaters in the United States were combined into four chains, Paramount, Warner Brothers, R. K. O., and Fox-Loew. The leading production corporations were Paramount, M. G. M., Warner Brothers, Twentieth-Century-Fox, R. K. O., United Artists, Universal, and Columbia. These eight companies made 90 per cent of all American pictures.

The motion picture industry was, however, more directly depend-ent on popular favor than any other form of big business, and this made it difficult for any small group of producers to establish a permanent monopoly. The history of the industry showed again and again that the leading production companies were likely to underestimate both the aesthetic tastes of motion picture audiences and their desire for novelty. Smaller producers continued, from time to time, to achieve importance by displaying more courage and a greater respect for their public.

RADIO

Radio had been made possible early in the twentieth century by the inventions of Guglielmo Marconi and Lee De Forest. Commer-cial broadcasting, however, did not begin until November 2, 1920, when Westinghouse Electric began regular broadcasts over KDKA at Pittsburgh, beginning with the returns of the Harding-Cox elec-tion, in order to promote the sale of receiving sets. The sale of advertising became the regular method by which broadcasting was financed in 1923.

The industry then grew rapidly, and by 1938 there were about 30 million receiving sets in use and 700 broadcasting stations. Although most of these were small local stations, the industry was dominated by three large companies with national networks, the National Broadcasting Company, the Columbia Broadcasting Sys-tem, and the Mutual Broadcasting System. There were also twenty-five regional networks. Radio was closely affiliated with the motion pictures, Columbia being partially owned by Paramount, while N. B. C. was under the same control as R. K. O.

The fact that wave lengths had to be allotted to various stations in such a way as to prevent interference made some kind of govern-ment supervision necessary. Wave lengths were at first distributed by the Department of Commerce, which claimed authority under an act of Congress passed in 1912. In 1926 the Department was denied power by a court decision, the result being that by the following year there were 732 different stations and the air was overcrowded. Congress then established the Federal Radio Commission, with power to allot wave lengths, and in 1934 this was replaced by a Federal Communications Commission, which had seven members. The F. C. C. was authorized to give licenses to broadcasting stations which would run for not more than three years; but in practice it limited licenses to six-month periods and used its power to refuse renewal in order to compel stations to devote part of their time to educational programs and to prohibit programs which violated accepted moral standards. The radio was thus considerably less free than the press, and there were occasional complaints of government censorship. On the other hand, the radio was much more nearly impartial on political questions, as a result particularly of a government regulation that rival candidates for political offices must be allowed equal radio facilities. Even the Communist Party, whose policies rarely received fair treatment in the newspapers, was allowed to state its case over the air. Since the political influence of the radio was probably greater than that of the press, this enforcement of impartiality was of great importance for the preservation of democratic processes.

BIBLIOGRAPHY

Annals of the American Academy of Political and Social Science, *Radio* (Jan., 1935)
R. C. Epstein, *The Automobile Industry* (1928)
H. Ford, *My Life and Work* (1922)
Federal Trade Commission, *The Electric Power Industry* (1927)
E. E. Freudenthal, *The Aviation Business* (1940)
J. G. DeR. Hamilton, *Henry Ford* (1927)
B. B. Hampton, *History of the Movies* (1931)
C. O. Hardy, *Recent Growth of the Electric Light and Power Industry* (1929)
*E. C. Kirkland, *History of American Economic Life* (1933)
J. N. Leonard, *The Tragedy of Henry Ford* (1932)
M. L. Ramsay, *Pyramids of Power* (1937)
H. S. Raushenbush and H. W. Laidler, *Power Control* (1928)
L. H. Seltzer, *Financial History of the American Automobile Industry* (1928)
J. K. Winkler, *The Du Pont Dynasty* (1935)

33

LABOR AND AGRICULTURE

THE DECLINE OF TRADE UNIONISM

DURING the twenties the working class enjoyed a higher standard of living than at any previous period. The workers continued, however, to have real grievances. Wages, though higher than formerly, were still too low to provide an adequate standard of living; the average working-class family earned less than $1,500 a year. Insecurity and unemployment was increasing, one out of every twenty workers being required to change his job in each two-year period; and workers who were displaced by machinery after they had passed the age of forty-five often found it impossible to obtain new jobs. Many forms of labor, particularly on the assembly lines of the automobile factories, were becoming more intense and more exhausting. And in certain industries, such as coal mining in Kentucky and West Virginia and textile manufacturing in North Carolina, hours remained abnormally long and wages subnormally low. The employers were still able, through their ownership of the workers' houses and their control over the local governments and police authorities, to exercise a feudal domination.

There was, nevertheless, a marked decline in labor militancy and in the power of the trade unions. Strikes were relatively rare, and many unions adopted a policy of co-operating with the employers by helping to reduce costs and prevent waste. The total number of union members decreased from 5,110,800 in 1920 to 4,330,000 in 1929, only about two-thirds of whom belonged to the A. F. of L. The membership of some of the larger unions decreased with special rapidity. This was particularly true of the United Mine Workers, which was defeated in a series of strikes in 1922 and weakened by the growth of nonunion coal fields in West Virginia and Kentucky.

The A. F. of L. retained control over the skilled crafts; but under the leadership of William Green, who succeeded Gompers in 1924, it became a wholly conservative organization. The chief function of the Federation officials was to settle jurisdictional disputes between different craft unions and to be the official representatives of labor at public meetings. There was, moreover, a marked growth of corruption among some of the unions affiliated to the A. F. of L. Certain union locals, whose leaders devoted themselves primarily to establishing the closed shop and compelling workers to become members in order that they might collect dues from them, became almost indistinguishable from criminal rackets.

The decline of trade unionism was due, in the first place, to the decrease in the importance of skilled labor. In many of the newer highly mechanized industries, such as the automobile industry, almost all labor was only semiskilled, and there was no place for the trained and privileged workers who had always composed the bulk of the A. F. of L. membership. The A. F. of L., however, made little attempt to adapt itself to these new conditions. It continued to represent mainly the skilled workers in the craft unions, and it still set out to benefit its members by establishing labor monopolies, limiting the numbers of the skilled workers by insisting on long apprenticeships and high union initiation fees. It scarcely attempted to organize the unskilled workers, nor did many of its affiliated unions admit Negroes to membership. Yet between 1915 and 1930 more than 1,000,000 Negroes became industrial workers in the North; and, being excluded from the unions, they were willing to work for low wages and could be used as strikebreakers.

In the second place, many employers in the twenties both carried on an elaborate campaign for the Open Shop and also adopted a policy of outbidding the trade unions by instituting various measures of welfare capitalism. They remedied many of the grievances of the workers by adopting safety devices and improving sanitation in the factories, building hospitals and workers' houses, and establishing playgrounds, athletic teams, and orchestras. United States Steel, for example, continued to pay low wages and require long hours, yet between 1915 and 1923 alone it spent 60 million dollars on welfare work. By 1926 nearly 250 corporations, employing nearly 3 million workers, had adopted pension plans. Three hundred corporations were encouraging their employees to become stockholders by selling them stock on credit and at less than the market price. Although less than 1 per cent of all outstanding stock was held by workers, this measure had some influence on working-class psychology. The works' council, or company union, was, moreover, spreading rapidly. By 1926 there were 430 company unions; and although they did not intervene in questions of wages and hours, they enabled the workers to voice their grievances on matters of smaller importance.

Meanwhile employers in the basic industries were still strongly opposed to the formation of independent unions. "Yellow-dog contracts," by which workers pledged themselves not to join unions, were frequently employed. In 1907 a Federal court in West Virginia had enjoined the United Mine Workers from attempting to unionize workers under yellow-dog contracts, and in 1917 this use of the injunction was upheld by the Supreme Court in the case of *Hitchman v. Mitchell*. Throughout the twenties the courts frequently granted injunctions limiting the powers of the unions, particularly with reference to the boycotting of firms employing nonunion labor. It was not until 1932 that Congress made another attempt to restrict this practice. By the Norris–La Guardia Federal Anti-Injunction Act of that year, the Federal courts were forbidden to issue injunctions for the purpose of breaking strikes, destroying unions, or upholding yellow-dog contracts. It was declared that an injunction could be issued only after a hearing in open court and that labor leaders accused of violating an injunction must have a jury trial. In addition to obtaining help from the courts, many corporations continued also to spend considerable sums on labor spies provided by private detective agencies.

COMMUNISM IN THE LABOR MOVEMENT

The I. W. W. never recovered from the repressive measures inflicted upon it during the war period, and by 1924 it was virtually dead. Its leader, William D. Haywood, who had been condemned to prison in 1918, forfeited his bail in order to escape to the Soviet Union, where he died a few years later. The place of the I. W. W., as the principal sponsor of radicalism in the labor movement, was now taken by the Communist Party. The chief Communist trade unionist was William Z. Foster, who joined the party after the defeat of the steel strike of 1919 which he had led.

The Communists provided leadership in several strikes, particularly in the furriers and cloakmakers strikes in New York in 1926, the textile workers strike at Passaic, New Jersey, in the same year, and the textile workers strike at Gastonia, North Carolina, in 1928 and 1929. In these strikes there was considerable use of violence, both by employers and by workers. During the Gastonia strike the local chief of police was killed in a riot; and seven Communist organizers, although there was no reliable evidence directly implicating them, were condemned to prison sentences of from five to twenty years. All of them forfeited the bail put up on their behalf and fled to the Soviet Union. Two of them, Fred Beal and Red Hendricks, subsequently returned to serve their sentences, having decided that they would rather face imprisonment in the United States than live under a Communist dictatorship.

The Communists, however, did not succeed in gaining any real strength in the American labor movement, and the Fur Workers' Union was the only important union which retained Communists among its officials. Their primary purpose was not to win immediate gains for the workers but to overthrow capitalism; and for this reason they were often unwilling to allow strikes to be settled, even on terms advantageous to the workers. They were, moreover, required to obey the instructions of the Communist International, the leaders of which lived in Moscow and had little understanding of American conditions.

After the Passaic and Gastonia strikes they retained little support among the textile workers; and after the cloakmakers strike they lost the positions which they had won in the International Ladies' Garment Workers. This union was subsequently reorganized under the more conservative leadership of David Dubinsky, who brought it quickly to the position of one of the strongest, best managed, and most genuinely progressive unions in the country. The Communists failed also in a long campaign to capture the United Mine Workers. For a number of years they supported a dissident group among the miners, which was led by John Brophy and which attempted to oust John L. Lewis from leadership. There was a prolonged, unscrupulous, and sometimes violent conflict between the two groups, Lewis being denounced by the Communists as an agent of the capitalist class. He succeeded, nevertheless, in retaining leadership of the union.

This phase of Communist activity ended abruptly in 1929, after the Sixth Congress of the Communist International, meeting in Moscow, had ordered the American Communists to abandon their policy of trying to capture established unions and to start organizing new rival unions. As their instrument for carrying out this new program of dual unionism and for splitting the labor movement, the Communists organized in 1929 the so-called Trade Union Unity League. This new policy, however, failed even more completely than did its predecessor. Discontented American workers might be willing temporarily to accept Communist leaders during a strike; but they would not permanently adopt Communist ideals or follow all the deviations of the Communist policies.

AGRICULTURE

If the industrial workers were somewhat better off in the twenties than they had been before the war, the farmers were distinctly worse off. During the war years they had increased the acreage under crops in order to raise food for Europe, and there had been a rapid rise in farm prices, land values, and the quantity of farm mortgages. The end of the war was followed by a catastrophic fall in prices. European countries no longer needed American farm products to the same degree; and there developed a condition of chronic agricultural overproduction, from which the farmers were never able to recover. In 1921 the index of farm prices registered a drop of nearly 44 per cent; and, although prices subsequently rose slowly, the increase was not enough to redress the balance. In terms of the ratio of farm prices to other prices, the farmers were 9.1 per cent better off in 1929 than they had been in 1921; on the other hand, they were 11 per cent worse off than they had been in 1913.

Although the war had intensified the problems of American agriculture, it must not be supposed that it created them. The fundamental causes of the agricultural depression were to be found in the development of the economic system. There was a steady increase in agricultural production. Between 1910 and 1930 the acreage under crops increased from 331,308,000 to 369,136,000, while at the same time output per acre was also increasing. The twenties were a period of especially rapid mechanization in agriculture. Between 1919 and 1932 productivity per acre increased by 16 per cent, and productivity per agricultural worker increased by 25 per cent. Meanwhile the markets for American agricultural products were diminishing. The internal market was limited by the decrease in the rate of population growth (due to immigration restriction and the fall in the birth rate) and by a steady shift in consumption habits away from such agricultural staples as meat and grain and toward fruit and vegetables. The external market grew smaller for a number of reasons, the most important being the development of new agricultural areas in the Argentine and the British Dominions, the policy of encouraging economic self-sufficiency which was adopted by many European governments, and the expansion of American exports of manufactured goods, as a result of which the nations which bought them had less dollar exchange with which to buy agricultural goods.

As a result of these factors, total farm incomes decreased from about 15 billion dollars in 1919 to about 12 billion dollars in 1929. During the same period the total value of all farm properties decreased from 78 billion dollars to 57 billion dollars, while the total value of farm mortgages, which had amounted to 3.8 billion dollars in 1912, had risen by 1930 to 9.2 billion dollars. Whereas in 1912 the farmers were paying 3 per cent of their total gross income as interest on mortgages, by 1930 they were paying 6 per cent. During the same period their real estate taxes also rose from 3 per cent to 6 per cent of gross income. The result was that farm tenancy continued to increase, the proportion of farms operated by tenants reaching 42.4 per cent by 1930. The figures were very much higher in the cotton-growing area in the South; and the southern cotton sharecroppers, 750,000 in number, continued to be the most poverty-stricken group of people in the entire country. Outside the south a majority of the landlords were themselves farmers, not absentee businessmen. Many tenants were relatives or former employees of their landlords, and they had reasonably stable and prosperous lives. There were, however, a large number who were migratory, incompetent, and miserably poor, rarely staying on the same farm for more than two or three years at a time. In 1935, according to a committee of Congress, one-third of all tenant farmers had moved within the previous twelve months.

The result of the increase of farm mortgages and farm tenancy (when the landlord was not himself a farmer) was that a large proportion of the gross income from agriculture did not become purchasing power for the farmers but flowed back immediately to the cities. In a considerable degree urban America was exploiting rural America. In this connection the steady flow of population from the country into the cities was also of significance. Since the population of the urban areas did not fully reproduce itself, young men and women from rural areas, where the birth rate was always higher, found jobs in the cities. The cost of rearing and educating these workers, which may be estimated at $2,000 each, had, however, been carried by the agricultural communities where they were born. O. E. Baker, of the U. S. Department of Agriculture, has calculated that the total wealth which flowed from the farms into the cities as a result of these various factors amounted between 1920 and 1929 to perhaps 25 billion dollars.

Another significant feature of agricultural development was the increase of economic differences among the farmers themselves. The better trained and more vigorous farmers were very much more prosperous than their less fortunate neighbors. By 1929, 11 per cent of all farmers were receiving half of the total farm income, while 49 per cent were receiving only 11 per cent of the income. Half of the farm families each produced less than $1,000 worth of products a year, while there were 750,000 families, two-thirds of them in the South, who produced less than $400 worth a year each.

In a smoothly working economic system, functioning in accordance with the rules of supply and demand, there should be a considerable reduction in the size of the farm population. Several million of the less successful farmers should be stimulated by falling farm prices to seek jobs in industry. Throughout the twenties, however, industrial employment did not expand sufficiently for this to be possible. There was unemployment in the cities as well as poverty on the farms. The actual decrease in the number of males employed in agriculture amounted to less than 900,000 for the entire period from 1910 to 1930, the figures being 10,415,000 for 1910 and 9,554,000 for 1930. The depression period 1930–1935 saw, moreover, an actual increase in the farm population, since unemployed workers turned to subsistence agriculture and the children of farmers were unable to find city jobs. Between 1930 and 1935 the number of farms increased by 523,702, and the total farm population increased by no less than 2,334,000.

Under such conditions the remedies which had been adopted during the Progressive Era—government control of railroad rates, easier credit facilities, and the organization of co-operative grain elevators and co-operatives for the marketing of farm products—were no longer adequate. The farmers themselves hoped for an increase in their foreign markets, but there was little likelihood that such a reversal of economic trends would take place. Their leaders put forward various proposals for Federal government assistance; but the Republican administration rejected the more drastic of them. Meanwhile the depressed condition of agriculture, which limited the internal market for American industry and caused a steady increase in indebtedness, weakened the whole economic system of the United States, and thereby helped to precipitate the crisis of 1929.

BIBLIOGRAPHY

L. Adamic, *Dynamite: The Story of Class Violence in America* (1931)
*O. E. Baker, R. Borsodi, and M. L. Wilson, *Agriculture in Modern Life* (1939)
*J. R. Commons and others, *History of Labor in the United States,* Vols. III and IV (1935)
R. W. Dunn, *Company Unions* (1927)
R. C. Engberg, *Industrial Prosperity and the Farmer* (1927)
W. Z. Foster, *From Bryan to Stalin* (1937)
J. S. Gambs, *The Decline of the I.W.W.* (1932)
B. Gitlow, *I Confess* (1939)
*E. C. Kirkland, *History of American Economic Life* (1933)
G. S. Mitchell, *Textile Unionism and the South* (1931)
E. G. Nourse, *American Agriculture and the European Market* (1924)
J. Oneal, *American Communism* (1927)
B. Ostrolenk, *The Surplus Farmer* (1932)
D. J. Saposs, *Left-Wing Unionism* (1926)
H. Seidman, *Labor Czars: A History of Labor Racketeering* (1938)
E. R. A. Seligman, *Economics of Farm Relief* (1929)

34

FOREIGN TRADE

AND INVESTMENTS

THE UNITED STATES AS A CREDITOR NATION

DURING the World War the United States had changed from a debtor into a creditor nation; and for ten years after the war American capital investments abroad continued to increase. There was also a steady growth in the volume of American export trade, although at the same time the ratio between exports and total production was declining. The American economic system had a surplus of capital and of goods; and until 1929 the policy of both the American government and American industrial leaders was to find outlets for these surpluses in foreign countries. Such a policy, however, created certain problems the importance of which was not fully grasped by American public opinion.

In the first place it is impossible for a nation to continue indefinitely both to invest capital abroad and at the same time to export more goods than she imports. This, however, was what the United States did between 1919 and 1928. Foreign nations that were in debt to American investors could not pay either the principal or the interest on those debts unless America would consent to buy a sufficient quantity of goods from them. Such a policy, however, would be detrimental to American industry and agriculture, which would have to admit foreign competitors into the home market. Foreign lending was thus incompatible with the maintenance of a

high protective tariff, and sooner or later the United States would
have to decide which of them should be abandoned.

In the second place, the growth of American investments in
Europe, South America, and the Far East meant that the United
States had become a world power, vitally interested in the maintenance of peace and prosperity and in the defense of her economic
interests in all parts of the world. The United States, in fact, was
moving into the position which had been occupied by Great Britain
during the nineteenth century. This development, however, involved
an abandonment of the doctrine of isolation from European
entanglements, and American public opinion was by no means prepared to accept the consequences of such a change. Three possible
courses presented themselves. First, the United States could accept
the responsibilities of a world power and intervene in Europe and
the Far East for the purpose of maintaining peace and thereby promoting her trade and protecting her investments. Second, she could
sacrifice her economic connections with other parts of the world
and attempt to reorganize her internal economic system on a basis
of self-sufficiency. Third—as a compromise between these two
extremes—she could concentrate on maintaining peace and extending her economic ties in the western hemisphere. Throughout the
twenties and thirties American public opinion remained undecided
among these three courses; nor was there any general realization of
the responsibilities and sacrifices which each of them would involve.

IMPORTS AND EXPORTS

Down to 1929 there was a steady increase in the volume of
imports. Between 1901 and 1905 the average annual value of
imports had been $972,000,000; between 1926 and 1930 it was
$4,033,000,000. During the latter period 49.4 per cent were raw
materials and 50.6 per cent were manufactured goods; 29.9 per cent
came from Europe, 29.7 per cent from Asia, 24.9 per cent from
Latin America, 11.9 per cent from Canada, 2.3 per cent from Africa,
and 1.3 per cent from Oceania. The most significant trend was the
declining importance of Europe, which had contributed 52.6 per cent
of American imports at the beginning of the century, and the rising

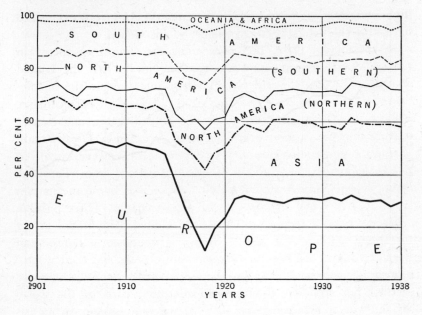

Figure 7. SOURCES OF AMERICAN IMPORTS

importance of the Far East. The United States bought its silk from Japan and its rubber and much of its tin from the British and Dutch East Indies. Although, moreover, a large part of the import trade could be sacrificed without serious losses, it included a number of mineral products not available at home, which were of vital importance to American industry. The steel industry, for example, required forty different commodities, which were imported from fifty different countries.

Between 1901 and 1905 the average annual value of American exports had been $1,454,000,000; between 1926 and 1930 it was $4,777,000,000. The proportion of exports to total production had, however, declined from 12.8 per cent in 1899 to 9.8 per cent in 1929. Between 1926 and 1930, 36.1 per cent of exports were agricultural goods, and 63.9 per cent were mineral products or manufactured goods. Of the exports, 46.8 per cent went to Europe (as

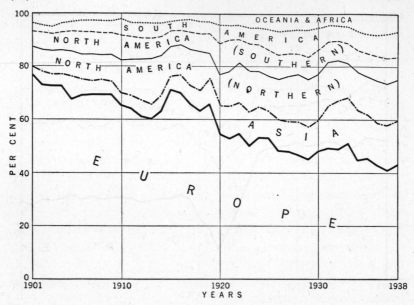

Figure 8. DESTINATION OF AMERICAN EXPORTS

contrasted with 76.7 per cent in 1900), 17.8 per cent to Latin America, 17.4 per cent to Canada, 12.0 per cent to Asia, 3.7 per cent to Oceania, and 2.3 per cent to Africa. In spite of the decreasing importance of exports, from the viewpoint of the economic system as a whole, there were certain branches of production the prosperity of which was mainly dependent on it. In 1929 the United States exported 54.8 per cent of its cotton, 41.2 per cent of its tobacco, and 17.9 per cent of its wheat. The value of the cotton export averaged $765,000,000 a year.

Throughout the twenties American industrialists vigorously pushed their exports in all parts of the world and received assistance from the Federal government, especially from the Department of Commerce under Secretary Hoover. In 1921 a Bureau of Foreign and Domestic Commerce was organized in the Department of Commerce, and commercial attachés were added to the American diplomatic service. William R. Castle, Assistant Secretary of State, told an exporters' convention in 1928 that "Mr. Hoover is your advance agent and Mr. Kellogg is your attorney."

THE EXPORT OF CAPITAL

Meanwhile the Republican administration was also encouraging the growth of American investments abroad, apparently without realizing that this policy would ultimately prove to be incompatible with its tariff policy. A considerable part of the exports of American manufactured goods was, in fact, financed by loans extended by American bankers. American foreign investments consisted partly of the acquisition of mines and factories in foreign countries, and partly of the purchase of foreign securities. Investments of the former kind were motivated, in part, by a desire to burrow under the tariff walls erected by foreign countries. In some instances they were detrimental to American producers. Thus, the American meat-packing corporations acquired factories in the Argentine, which tended to injure American cattle raisers; and American capital helped to rebuild the German merchant marine, which competed with American shipping.

The purchase of foreign securities by American citizens was encouraged by American bankers, who collected commissions on such transactions; and many of the foreign loans floated in the United States, particularly those issued by some of the Latin American countries, were very unsound and were soon in default. By 1938, 66 per cent of all Latin American loans were no longer paying interest. American bankers were so eager to acquire more foreign bonds which they could sell to American investors, at a profit to themselves, that they paid lavish commissions to the relatives of Latin American presidents who were willing to borrow American capital. Thus, the son of the president of Peru received $415,000 from J. & W. Seligman and Company, and the son-in-law of the president of Cuba received $500,000, in addition to a regular salary of $19,000 a year, from the Chase National Bank.[1] Many of the Latin American loans were not spent on productive economic invest-

1. See the Hearings before the Senate Committee on Finance, investigating the sale of foreign bonds in the United States, 1932.

ments, but served to keep dictatorial regimes in power. The ultimate result was that Latin American dictators got the money and the bankers got their commissions; but the American investors who had been induced to buy the bonds in many instances came out with nothing. In 1922 the State Department asked to have advance information about all foreign loans; but it does not appear to have exercised any real supervision over the export of capital.

By 1930 American capital invested abroad (exclusive of the war debts due to the American government) amounted to about $16,-104,000,000. Of this sum $8,238,000,000 represented American holdings of foreign securities, and $7,866,000,000 represented American ownership of properties in foreign countries. Of the latter figure, $1,610,000,000 was invested in transportation, $1,534,000,-000 in factories, $1,185,000,000 in mines, $1,118,000,000 in oil fields, and $874,000,000 in agricultural properties. Since foreigners held about $4,500,000,000 worth of investments in the United States, America's credit balance was about $11,600,000,000.

Nearly $5,000,000,000 was invested in Europe, especially in Germany and Great Britain. German industry after the World War was largely rebuilt with the aid of American capital. Many of the leading American corporations, including General Motors, Ford, General Electric, Standard Oil, and American Telephone and Telegraph, built factories in Europe and established financial alliances with German and British corporations.

Nearly $4,000,000,000 was invested in Canada. By 1930 Americans owned one-third of all the capital in Canadian industry and one-twelfth of the total wealth of the Dominion. There was a greater volume of trade between Canada and the United States than between any other two countries in the world. Fortunately the relations between the two peoples remained amicable. The result was that Canada became an important link between the United States and Great Britain. Whether the final consequence will be the gradual detachment of Canada from the British Empire, or the growth of community of interest between the United States and the rest of the Empire, is a question which provokes speculation.

More than $5,500,000,000 was invested in Latin America. United

States capital had become predominant in Mexico and the Caribbean before 1914; during and after the war United States investments rapidly increased throughout South America, and United States corporations acquired ownership of South American mines, oil fields, and fruit and rubber plantations. Parts of South America, however, particularly the Argentine, which exported chiefly meat and foodstuffs that competed with the products of United States farms, remained within the British orbit. Certain political problems resulted from this development. In the first place, the United States found itself in competition for trade and control of raw materials with Great Britain and with Germany. In the second place, many of the Latin American governments were financially unstable and likely to repudiate their obligations. The peoples of Latin America, moreover, suffered from acutely low standards of living and were beginning to resent the high profits which often accrued to foreign investors and to demand that foreign corporations either pay higher wages or undergo expropriation. This occurred particularly in Mexico. The United States government was, in consequence, under pressure from businessmen with Latin American interests to use force to protect these interests and to intervene in the internal affairs of the Latin American countries.

Investments in Asia and the Pacific totaled about $1,500,000. Of this sum about $300,000,000 was invested in Japan, and $130,000,-000 in China. China had been regarded since 1898 as a suitable field for American investments, but this hope had never materialized. In spite of the Open Door policy, the bulk of the foreign capital in China was contributed by Great Britain and by Japan.

The export of American capital reached its peak in 1928, the figure for that year being $944,000,000. The flow of capital abroad throughout the twenties enabled foreign countries to buy American goods, thus providing markets for American industry. It also contributed to the recovery of Europe from the World War and made it possible for Germany to pay reparations and for the Allies to pay the war debts. Sooner or later, however, the interest payments on the total investment must exceed the amount of new investments; and when this happened, American industry would lose some of its foreign markets, the recovery of Europe would be endangered, and there would be difficulty in maintaining the structure of reparation and war debt payments. This point was reached in 1929. In that year new investments abroad totaled only $306,000,000, whereas the interest payments made to the United States on previous investments amounted to $408,000,000. This was an important contributory cause to the world-wide economic depression which began in the autumn of that year.

During the depression there was no revival of foreign lending, and the existing American investments abroad were drastically cut down, many securities held by Americans being canceled or reduced in value by foreign governments, particularly by the Nazi government in Germany. By 1936 American foreign investments totaled only about $11,500,000,000. Many of the securities included in this figure were, moreover, in permanent default. What had virtually happened in the case of many foreign securities, therefore, was that foreign countries had received free gifts of American goods, while the bills had been paid out of American capital contributed by American investors. American industry during the twenties had been given the stimulus of a kind of public works program conducted for the benefit of Europe and Latin America.

Some critics of the economic system deduced from this experience that the money should have remained at home and been used to increase the purchasing power of the American workers and farmers. Others argued that the export of capital was a beneficial process, which tended to promote world unity and world peace and to improve the standard of living of backward countries. They also held that these foreign loans would not have gone into default if the United States had lent its money more intelligently, had changed its tariff policies in order to make possible an increase in its imports, and had conducted its foreign policy in order to promote world peace and an increase in international trade.

INTERNATIONAL TRADE RIVALRIES

The growth of American foreign trade and investments involved the United States in economic and diplomatic conflicts with other nations. On a number of occasions countries which controlled raw materials needed by American industry adopted plans for restricting production and raising prices. There was, moreover, constant rivalry between the leading powers for control of mineral resources and for export markets.

In the nineteen-twenties the chief competitor of the United States was Great Britain, and it was sometimes suggested that the two nations would eventually go to war with each other. American and British oil companies were constantly in conflict; and while the Americans secured control of the oil fields in Venezuela and Colombia, the British won victories in Persia and Mesopotamia and obtained the more valuable of the Mexican oil fields. The British controlled the world's chief source of rubber, in the East Indies; and in 1922, by the Stevenson Restriction Act, they set out to raise prices. The project failed, however, owing to competition from rubber producers outside the British Empire, and it was abandoned in 1928.

The industrialists of the two nations competed with each other for control of the export markets in South America, and their governments supported them by endeavoring to win popularity. Herbert Hoover (when President-elect) and the Prince of Wales paid good-will visits to the more important Latin American republics. The British, moreover, endeavored to prevent American financiers from winning control over British industries, attempting occasionally to disfranchise American stockholders. This British-American rivalry ended, however, in the nineteen-thirties. The rise of Nazi Germany. which adopted much more aggressive methods of pushing its trade and excluding foreigners from its export markets, caused Great Britain and the United States to draw together.

The United States was alarmed also by the growing power and aggressiveness of Japan, but this hostility was political rather than economic. The United States had much closer economic ties with Japan than with any other country of the Far East. In 1927 Japan supplied 10 per cent of all American imports, silk being the chief item, and bought 5 per cent of all American exports. The relation between the two nations was even more important to the Japanese;

one-third of all Japanese trade, both import and export, was with the United States. In this instance, therefore, there was some discrepancy between the political and the economic interests of the United States.

BIBLIOGRAPHY

L. Denny, *We Fight For Oil* (1928)
———— *America Conquers Britain* (1930)
R. W. Dunn, *American Foreign Investments* (1926)
*L. Hacker, *American Problems of Today* (1938)
F. M. Halsey, *Investments in Latin America* (1925)
*E. C. Kirkland, *History of American Economic Life* (1933)
J. Klein, *Frontiers of Trade* (1929)
C. Lewis, *The American Stake in Foreign Investments* (1938)
J. T. Madden and others, *America's Experience as a Creditor Nation* (1937)
M. A. Marsh, *The Bankers in Bolivia* (1928)
H. Marshall and others, *Canadian-American Industry* (1936)
P. M. Mazur, *America Looks Abroad* (1930)
H. Motherwell, *The Imperial Dollar* (1929)
S. Nearing and J. Freeman, *Dollar Diplomacy* (1925)
J. F. Rippy, *The Capitalists and Colombia* (1931)
F. A. Southard, *American Industry in Europe* (1931)
*B. H. Williams, *Economic Foreign Policy of the United States* (1929)
M. Winkler, *Investments of United States Capital in Latin America* (1928)

35

THE HARDING AND

COOLIDGE ADMINISTRATIONS

HARDING

FROM the election of 1920 until the depression of the thirties conservative Republicanism was in control of the Federal government. There was no revival either of the strong presidential leadership or of the attempts to limit the powers of big business which had characterized the Progressive Era. This return to McKinleyism was in conformity with public opinion and was reflected also in the policies of the Democratic Party, which became almost as conservative as the Republicans. The only effective opposition was provided by a group of Progressive senators, belonging to both parties, who came from Western agricultural states. Since, however, the Progressives frequently held the balance of power between the two parties in the Senate, they were able to exercise an influence out of proportion to their numbers and to prevent some of the wishes of the administration from being carried into effect.

Harding had been nominated for the presidency by the Republican bosses in the belief that he would make an amiable, unassuming, and popular figurehead, who would allow the major decisions of policy to be made in the Senate. This anticipation proved to be correct. Unfortunately Harding's weaknesses of character made him totally unsuited for high office. Personally honest and well-meaning, he was easily victimized by unscrupulous associates. During the

Harding regime an extraordinary collection of corrupt and disreputable adventurers assembled in Washington and were able to use their acquaintance with the President for private profit. Harding's unfitness for the presidency was strikingly illustrated by the quality of his guests at parties in the White House and by the fact that neither he nor his friends obeyed the Prohibition Act which it was his constitutional duty to enforce.

Harding's cabinet contained three outstanding figures. Andrew Mellon, a Pittsburgh multimillionaire with interests in aluminum, banking, and oil, who had previously been unknown to the general public, became Secretary of the Treasury—a position which he retained until 1931; Charles Evans Hughes became Secretary of State; and Herbert Hoover became Secretary of Commerce. These three men determined most of the policies of the administration. Harding's dearest wish, however, had been to give high office to his personal friends. He accordingly appointed his friend, Senator Albert B. Fall, of New Mexico, Secretary of the Interior, with charge over conservation; and his friend, Harry M. Daugherty, Attorney General, with charge over law enforcement. Other appointments, outside the cabinet, were equally unsuitable. Harding's boyhood friend, Daniel R. Crissinger, a small-town lawyer who had once presided for a few months over a bank at Marion, Ohio, became head of the Federal Reserve System. Crissinger was still in office in 1927 when the Federal Reserve System adopted a policy of encouraging cheap money, which had the most disastrous consequences. Colonel Charles R. Forbes, whom Harding had met and liked on a trip to Honolulu, became director of the Veterans' Bureau, greatly to the profit of himself and his friends; and Albert D. Lasker, a Chicago advertising agent, became chairman of the United States Shipping Board, in which capacity he sold, at $30 a ton, as many as possible of the ships which the government had built during the war.

The most important of the spectacular series of scandals which disgraced the Harding administration had to do with oil. Presidents Taft and Wilson had set aside certain oil fields on public land for permanent government ownership, in order that the navy might be assured a supply of oil. Among these oil fields were Naval Oil Reserve Number One, at Elk Hills, California, and Naval Oil Reserve Number Three, at Teapot Dome, Wyoming. These oil fields had been placed under the control of the Secretary of the Navy. In May, 1921, by an executive order signed by Harding and approved by the Secretary of the Navy, Edwin Denby, control was transferred to the Secretary of the Interior, Albert B. Fall. In April, 1922, Fall leased the Teapot Dome field to Harry F. Sinclair; and in December of the same year he leased the Elk Hills field to Edward L. Doheny. These leases were made secretly and without any competitive bidding by rival oil producers. Fall justified them on the plea that the oil was being drained off into diggings on adjoining land. Sinclair and Doheny agreed in return to store a part of the oil in tanks for the use of the navy.

The secrecy with which these transactions had been made aroused criticism among a few Progressive senators, particularly La Follette; and their suspicions increased when they discovered that Secretary Fall had been spending money much more freely than formerly. Senator Walsh of Montana was appointed chairman of a Senate committee of investigation; and after eighteen months of preparation, he began hearings in October, 1923. His activities were at first bitterly denounced by the press and throughout the country as a partisan attempt to smear the administration; but he gradually extracted from a series of very unwilling witnesses evidence of corruption which could not be confuted. Fall had received $260,000 in Liberty bonds from Sinclair, while Doheny had "loaned" him $100,000 without interest or security. Among the discoveries incidentally made during the investigation was that the Liberty bonds given by Sinclair had been part of the profits of the Continental Trading Company, a corporation which had been formed by several oil executives in order to buy oil at $1.50 a barrel and subsequently sell it to the companies which they controlled at $1.75 a barrel. By this device the oil executives had mulcted the stockholders, whose interests they supposedly represented, of more than $8,000,000. Out of the profits of the Continental Trading Company Sinclair had not only bribed Fall but had also made loans to the campaign fund of the Republican Party—a fact which was known to Andrew Mellon and to Will H. Hays, chairman of the Republican National Committee, but which they succeeded in keeping secret until 1928.

Fall resigned from the cabinet in 1923. In 1929 he was convicted of accepting bribes and sentenced to a year in prison and a fine of $100,000. In another trial, however, Sinclair and Doheny were acquitted of bribing Fall, though Sinclair was subsequently sentenced to prison for contempt of the Senate and for hiring detectives to shadow members of the jury appointed to try him. After Walsh had proved that Sinclair and Doheny had obtained the oil fields corruptly, President Coolidge appointed Atlee Pomerene and Owen D. Roberts to serve as government prosecutors, and the oil fields were recaptured by the government through a Supreme Court decision in 1927.

Other scandals occurred in the Department of Justice, headed by Harding's friend, Daugherty. Daugherty antagonized the Progressives by refusing to prosecute businessmen accused of fraud in connection with government contracts during the war, by refusing to enforce the antitrust laws, and—in 1922—by obtaining a sweeping injunction in order to break a railroad strike. In 1924 a Senate committee, with Smith W. Brookhart of Iowa as chairman and Burton K. Wheeler of Montana in charge of the investigation, examined the activities of the department. It was discovered that the enforcement of the Prohibition Act was corrupt, with officials selling liquor permits on a large scale to bootleggers, and that the Alien Property Custodian, Thomas W. Miller, had been defrauding the government by selling properties confiscated from German citizens during the war for much less than their value.

Daugherty retaliated by ordering government detectives to investigate the previous activities of Wheeler and Brookhart, in the hope of discovering something discreditable; and he subsequently declared that the Department of Justice had been the victim of a Communist conspiracy. Daugherty's complicity in the misconduct of his subordinates was never definitely proved, although it was significant that his closest friend, Jess Smith, who had assisted him in administering the department, had committed suicide in 1923. In

1927 Miller was sentenced to eighteen months in prison and a fine of $5,000. Daugherty, tried on the same charge, was acquitted after he had refused to testify and had defended his refusal in a statement which implied that his testimony would have incriminated Harding. Daugherty's enemies, however, thought it more probable that he was using the reputation of the dead President in order to shield himself.

Another Harding official who found his way to the penitentiary was Colonel Forbes, of the Veterans' Bureau. Forbes was guilty of wholesale corruption in the making of contracts for the construction of hospitals and in the sale and purchase of supplies. Out of $1,000,000,000 appropriated for the Bureau in two years, about $200,000,000 was stolen or wasted. In 1923 Forbes resigned, and the legal advisor to the Bureau, Charles F. Cramer, committed suicide. In the following year, after a Senate committee had made an investigation, Forbes was sentenced to two years in prison and a fine of $10,000.

In the summer of 1923 public opinion was still unaware of what had been happening in Washington, and Harding still enjoyed widespread popularity. He appears, nevertheless, to have realized that he had been betrayed by a number of his friends and that he would be lucky if he escaped impeachment. From this fate, however, he was spared. After a visit to Alaska he died suddenly of a blood clot on the brain at San Francisco, on August 2, 1923.

COOLIDGE

Calvin Coolidge, who succeeded to the presidency, saved the reputation of the Republican Party. While there was no spectacular housecleaning, Harding's friends gradually disappeared from office; and there was a marked and salutary change in the tone of White House society. Honest, shrewd, parsimonious, and taciturn, Coolidge carried into the presidency the characteristic traits of the Yankee farmers of his native Vermont. Before coming to Washington he had been Mayor of Northampton, State Senator, Lieutenant Governor, and Governor of Massachusetts, in all of which positions he had displayed considerable political ability, unimpeachable integrity, and a remarkable capacity for winning popular support. He believed in private enterprise, individual initiative, no government interference with business, and strict economy; and he could express these ideals with a forcefulnesss and a clarity which were proofs of his sincerity. Coolidge's doctrines were perhaps a century behind the times and had little relation to the world of huge corporations and stock exchange speculation in which he lived, but they were doctrines which still had great popular appeal. Americans liked to believe the Coolidge philosophy, just as they enjoyed the wry Yankee humor of many of Coolidge's utterances. It was part of the good fortune which accompanied Coolidge's whole career that he left office before the inadequacy of his program to twentieth-century conditions became apparent.

In 1924 the Republican convention nominated Coolidge for reelection to the presidency almost unanimously, Charles G. Dawes receiving the vice presidential nomination. In the Democratic convention, which met at New York, the division between the rural, Protestant, and conservative South and the urban, Catholic, and liberal North developed into open conflict. The differences were now intensified by the growth of the Ku Klux Klan, with its program of preserving Protestant supremacy, and by the question of Prohibition. The two leading candidates were William G. McAdoo and Alfred E. Smith. McAdoo, formerly of Wilson's cabinet, was the candidate of the South. Smith, who had been born of Irish parentage in a New York East Side slum, had entered politics by way of Tammany Hall, and had been elected Governor of New York in 1918 and again in 1922. He was a Catholic, an opponent of Prohibition, and a representative of the urban and immigrant populations of the Northeast. Balloting continued for nine days, neither candidate being willing to give way to the other. Finally both of them agreed to withdraw, and on the 103rd ballot the nomination was given to John W. Davis, a New York corporation lawyer who had been born in West Virginia.

Since both Coolidge and Davis were conservatives, Progressive leaders resolved to nominate a third candidate who would appeal to the farmers and organized labor. In 1922 a Conference for Progressive Political Action, supported chiefly by the railroad brother-hoods, had been formed. In July, 1924, the Conference offered a presidential nomination to La Follette. La Follette chose Senator Wheeler as his running mate, and wrote his own platform, which demanded—in the style of prewar Progressivism—more political de-mocracy and more government control of business. La Follette's can-didacy was endorsed by the American Federation of Labor and also by the Socialist Party.

There was little popular interest in the campaign, and only half the electorate took the trouble to vote. Coolidge carried every north-ern and western state except Wisconsin and won a popular vote of 15,725,000 and an electoral vote of 382. Davis carried only the South and won a popular vote of 8,386,500 and an electoral vote of 136. La Follette, with a popular vote of 4,826,400, had the elec-toral vote of Wisconsin. After the election the La Follette organiza-tion was dissolved, and its leaders returned to their previous party allegiances. La Follette himself died in 1925, and his policies were inherited by his sons, Robert, who succeeded him in the Senate, and Philip, who served as Governor of Wisconsin from 1931 until 1933 and from 1935 until 1939.

THE ELECTION OF 1928

Coolidge's good fortune continued throughout his second term, and there were no setbacks to the prosperity of business and no breaks in the rising trend of stock market prices. There was talk of a third term, but on August 2, 1927, Coolidge curtly declared that he did not "choose to run." The wording of the announcement pro-voked speculation, and some persons suggested that Coolidge hoped for another nomination; but the support of the administration was now given to the candidacy of Herbert Hoover, who had continued to serve as Secretary of Commerce. The chief rival candidates were Vice President Dawes and Frank Lowden, former Governor of Illinois, both of whom, unlike Hoover, favored farm relief legisla-tion which Coolidge had vetoed. In the Republican convention of 1928 Hoover received the nomination on the first ballot. Senator Charles Curtis of Kansas was nominated for the vice presidency.

The Democratic convention gave its nomination to Alfred E. Smith, also on the first ballot, with Senator Joseph T. Robinson of Arkansas as his running mate. Since 1924 Smith had been twice re-elected Governor of New York, had been widely applauded for the efficiency and the liberality of his administration, and had demonstrated remarkable capacity for winning votes. The Southern leaders were now compelled to recognize that he was the only Democrat capable of winning the election. There was still, however, widespread opposition throughout the South to the nomination of a Catholic and a Wet.

On basic economic questions there was little difference between the two candidates. Hoover cited the record of the Republican Party since 1921 and claimed that his election would mean continued prosperity. "We in America today," he declared in his acceptance speech, "are nearer to the final triumph over poverty than ever before in the history of any land. The poorhouse is vanishing from among us. We have not yet reached the goal, but given a chance to go forward with the policies of the last eight years, we shall soon, with the help of God, be in sight of the day when poverty will be banished from this nation. There is no guaranty against poverty equal to a job for every man. That is the primary purpose of the policies we advocate." Smith was somewhat less conservative than Hoover. As Governor of New York he had sponsored social welfare legislation and had opposed private ownership of power sites. He denounced the use of injunctions in labor disputes and promised some kind of farm relief. On the other hand he did not oppose the Republican tariff policies, and his general friendliness to big business was proved by his choice of John J. Raskob, of Du Pont and General Motors, as Chairman of the Democratic National Committee.

The campaign, nevertheless, was one of the most bitter in American history. Hoover, born on a farm in Iowa and educated at Leland Stanford, was the symbol of Anglo-Saxon Protestant supremacy. Smith embodied the aspirations of the immigrant populations of the cities. Social snobbery and religious prejudice played a prominent role in the campaign. Smith was denounced because of his East Side accent and his associations with Tammany Hall; and the fear that his election would put the American government under the control of the Vatican was widely propagated through the areas of rural Protestantism. The candidates were, moreover, in opposition over the issue of Prohibition; while Hoover described Prohibition as "a great social and economic experiment, noble in motive and far-reaching in purpose," Smith, disavowing the Democratic platform, recommended repeal of the Eighteenth Amendment and the return of liquor control to the state governments. In the cities of the Northeast Smith received a popular acclaim probably unprecedented in American history. But five states of the hitherto solid South rejected him; and though he received the largest popular vote ever given to a Democratic candidate, he was defeated in the electoral vote by an unprecedented margin. Hoover won 21,392,000 popular votes and 444 electoral votes. Smith, with a popular vote of 15,016,000, carried only Massachusetts and Rhode Island and six Southern states, with an electoral vote of 87. Norman Thomas, the Socialist candidate, received a popular vote of 267,420, and William Z. Foster, the Communist candidate, received a popular vote of 48,770.

BIBLIOGRAPHY

S. H. Adams, *The Incredible Era* (1939)
C. Coolidge, *Autobiography* (1929)
*C. M. Fuess, *Calvin Coolidge* (1940)
C. O. Johnson, *Borah* (1936)
R. L. Neuberger and S. B. Kahn, *Integrity: The Life of George W. Norris* (1937)
H. F. Pringle, *Alfred E. Smith* (1927)
R. V. Peel and T. C. Donnelly, *The 1928 Campaign* (1931)
A. E. Smith, *Progressive Democracy* (1928)
M. Sullivan, *Our Times,* Vol. VI (1935)
M. R. Werner, *Privileged Characters* (1935)
W. A. White, *A Puritan in Babylon: The Story of Calvin Coolidge* (1938)
——— *Masks in a Pageant* (1928)

36

REPUBLICAN LEGISLATION

FINANCE

THE policies of the Harding, Coolidge, and Hoover administrations were designed, in general, to assist big business, in the belief that if corporations earned large profits and were encouraged to expand their capital equipment, they would pay higher wages and provide greater employment, so that all sections of the nation would benefit. This attitude was especially noticeable in the financial policies of Andrew Mellon, who served as Secretary of the Treasury from 1921 until 1931. Mellon made a considerable reduction in the national debt. His chief desire, however, was to reduce taxes, especially in the higher brackets, in the belief that this was necessary in order to release capital for business expansion.

In the Revenue Act of 1921 the excess profits tax imposed during the war was repealed. The corporation income tax was, however, raised from 10 to 12½ per cent; and, in spite of Mellon's recommendations, Congress refused to reduce the maximum surtax, paid by millionaires, to less than 50 per cent. In 1924 the minimum income tax was reduced from 4 to 2 per cent; the minimum income liable to surtaxes was raised from $6,000 to $10,000; and the maximum surtax was reduced to 40 per cent. Many wartime excise duties were abolished. Congress, however, increased the estate taxes, imposed a new tax on gifts, and ordered publicity for income tax returns. In 1926 Mellon secured the repeal of these three measures; the maximum surtax was reduced to 20 per cent; and the exemption figure for heads of families was raised from $2,500 to $3,500. Finally, in 1929, the minimum income tax was reduced to 0.5 per cent, and the corporation income tax was reduced to 11 per cent. Another conspicuous feature of Mellon's administration of the Treasury Department was the willingness of its officials to allow wealthy men to take advantage of loopholes in the laws in order to reduce their tax payments.

In spite of the drastic tax reductions, the national debt was reduced from $24,298,000,000 in 1920 to $16,185,000,000 in 1930, and there was always a surplus of receipts over expenditures. Another good feature of Republican financial policy was the establishment in 1921 of a Bureau of the Budget, with Charles G. Dawes as its first director, thus making possible a more integrated control of Federal expenditures. Mellon was hailed by his admirers as the greatest Secretary of the Treasury since Alexander Hamilton. Actually, however, his program of surtax reductions probably helped to cause the surplus of capital savings, in excess of the investment needs of the country, which appears to have been an important factor in provoking the overspeculation of 1929 and the depression of the thirties.

THE TARIFF

The return to power of the Republicans meant a repeal of the Underwood Tariff and a restoration of high tariff protection for big business. There was considerably less opposition than formerly to tariff increases, since industries which wanted protection were now developing in the South and the West, and the farmers were becoming afraid of foreign competition in the American market and were therefore willing to allow protection for industry in return for protection for themselves. Few Republican leaders realized that their tariff policy was inconsistent with America's new status as a creditor nation; that, if foreign nations were denied access to American markets, they could pay neither their war debts nor the interest on American private investments; and that, since nations could not buy unless they could also sell, the curtailment of American imports would eventually result in a decline of American exports.

In May, 1921, an Emergency Tariff Act raised the duties on agricultural commodities, wool, sugar, and chemicals. In September of the following year, after prolonged studies by committees of both houses of Congress, the Fordney–McCumber Tariff was passed. This tariff restored many of the rates to the levels of the Payne-Aldrich Tariff, and also imposed prohibitive duties to protect a number of new industries. The average ad valorem duty was 33.22 per cent. The principle on which the tariff was supposedly based was to equalize the manufacturing costs of foreign industry with those of American industry, and a Tariff Commission was appointed to investigate differences in costs. On recommendations from the Commission the President was empowered to change the rates by not more than 50 per cent either upward or downward. Actually, however, the proposals of the Commission resulted in 32 increases and only 5 very unimportant decreases.

During the campaign of 1928 Hoover promised a revision of the tariff, refusing to take warning from the experience of President Taft. The farmers were to be given greater protection; some rates were to be lowered to please the investment banking and foreign trade interests; other rates were to be raised to please the industrialists. Congress was called into special session in the spring of 1929. As a result of attempts by Progressive senators to secure special benefits for the farmers and to transfer to Congress the power to change rates, the new tariff bill, known as the Hawley-Smoot Tariff, was not passed until May, 1930. Big business, whose chief spokesman in Congress was Senator Grundy of Pennsylvania, had dictated most of the changes; and almost all the duties were raised, the average being 40.08 per cent. The bill was not at all what Hoover had wanted, and more than a thousand of the leading economists in the country urged him to veto it, declaring that it would raise prices, protect inefficiency, prevent the payment of international debts, reduce exports, and compel foreign nations to raise their own tariffs against American goods. Hoover, nevertheless, signed the bill on June 17, 1930. His chief reason for doing so was that the bill gave increased powers to the Tariff Commission. The latter would, he hoped, be able gradually to reduce excessive schedules and to make the tariff a non-political question. Within the following year twenty-five other nations retaliated by either raising their own tariffs or threatening to do so; and the results were a general decrease in world trade and an intensification of the rapidly growing world depression.

AGRICULTURE

The problem of the farmers was ably presented by their spokesmen in the Senate, where an agricultural bloc had been organized under the leadership of William S. Kenyon of Iowa. The Republican leaders refused, however, to enact any of their more drastic proposals for solving it.

During the Harding administration Congress passed the Packers and Stockyards Act, prohibiting monopolistic practices by the meatpacking corporations; the Capper-Volstead Co-operative Act, exempting co-operatives for the marketing of farm products from prosecution under the Sherman Act; and the Federal Intermediate Credits Act, creating twelve banks with capital subscribed by the government which were to lend money to co-operatives, with crops stored in warehouses as collateral. These measures, however, which had been part of the Populist program in the eighteen-nineties, did not meet the basic farm problem of overproduction. The farm leaders hoped to solve this problem by securing new foreign markets, and they propounded two methods of attaining this object. Under the McNary-Haugen Bill, the author of which was George N. Peek of the Moline Plow Company, it was proposed that a Federal farm board be created with a revolving fund of $400,000,000 which it was to loan to co-operatives in order to assist them in keeping surpluses out of the home market and thus maintaining high prices. The co-operatives would then market these surpluses abroad for whatever they would fetch, and the difference between what the co-operatives had paid to the farmers and what they had received from these foreign sales was to be met by subsequently requiring the farmers to pay an "equalization fee." The McNary-Haugen Bill passed Congress in 1927 and 1928, but each time it was vetoed by President Coolidge.

The second proposal was the export debenture scheme, under

which export bounties in the form of "debentures" were to be paid to the exporters of the chief agricultural commodities. These debentures could be used to pay import duties, and they would thus be returned to the government. A Federal farm board was to control production by reducing the debenture rates or canceling them if production increased. The export debenture scheme passed the Senate in 1926, 1928, and 1929, but it was always rejected by the House of Representatives.

President Hoover agreed with Coolidge in rejecting schemes which involved government subsidies or agricultural price-fixing; but he recognized that overproduction might occasionally exist, and he believed that the Federal government might legitimately assist the farmers in limiting production by voluntary and co-operative methods. In June, 1929, the special session of Congress passed the Agricultural Marketing Act, which embodied Hoover's recommendations. A Federal Farm Board with eight members was to be established; it was to encourage the organization of co-operatives for marketing farm products; and it was to have a fund of $500,000,000, which it was to loan to the co-operatives. When there had been overproduction the co-operatives would hold surplus crops until the market adjusted itself. Special stabilization corporations might be established for handling particular commodities.

Hoover's assumption was that agricultural overproduction was occasional and not chronic. He believed that, when there was overproduction of one particular crop, the Agricultural Marketing Act would assist farmers to transfer their land to a different crop for which there was greater demand. The Federal Farm Board, however, began functioning during a depression period when the prices of all farm commodities were dropping catastrophically for lack of markets and when the decrease in farm incomes made it impossible for the farmers to reduce production. In 1930 stabilization corporations were established for grain and cotton. The Grain Corporation bought 330 million bushels of wheat in 1930 and 1931, but it could find no purchasers and was finally compelled to stop buying. The price of wheat then dropped, and the storage charges for the wheat held by the corporation soon exceeded its cash value. The history of the Cotton Corporation was similar. It bought 3¼ million bales of cotton; then it stopped buying and the price fell, resulting in a loss to the corporation of 150 million dollars. In the spring of 1932 the Cotton Corporation was urging the growers to plough under one-third of that year's crop.

THE RAILROADS

The restoration of the railroads to private operation was accomplished before Harding took office. McAdoo had proposed that they be operated by the government for five more years in order to test the value of unification. The workers, on the other hand, had put forward a plan, suggested by Glenn E. Plumb, by which the government should purchase the railroads from the stockholders and transfer control to a corporation in which the managers, the workers, and the public should have representation. The general opposition to any form of socialism prevented the adoption of either of these proposals. In February, 1920, Congress passed the Esch-Cummins Transportation Act. The railroads were given back to their owners, but the powers of the Interstate Commerce Commission were considerably enlarged. The Commission, which was to consist henceforth of eleven members chosen from both parties and having seven-year terms, was to fix rates which would yield "a fair return upon the aggregate value of the railway property of the country." A profit of 5½ per cent was indicated as a fair return. By the "recapture clause" railroads earning more than 6 per cent were to transfer half their excess earnings to the Commission, which would lend it to the less prosperous railroads. The Commission was also to plan the consolidation of the railroads into a small number of integrated systems, which would be exempt from antitrust prosecutions, and it was to supervise the issuance of new securities. A Railway Labor Board was created to deal with labor disputes, and the employees of the railroads were guaranteed the right to belong to unions. The Labor Board, however, did not succeed in preventing strikes, several of which occurred as a result of wage cuts in 1921 and 1922; and in 1926 it was replaced by boards of arbitration.

The Interstate Commerce Commission was, in practice, unable to enforce the recapture clause or to bring about consolidation; and its rate-fixing powers were incomplete unless it could also determine the capital value of the railroad properties. But the method by which capital value was to be assessed remained indefinite. The method preferred by the Commission was to take the reproduction cost of the railroads in 1914 and then to make allowance for improvements and depreciation. The railroad corporations, on the other hand, insisted on the rule of reproduction cost new in terms of 1920 price levels, declaring that "it is that property and not the original cost of it, of which the owner may not be deprived without due process of law." In the case of the St. Louis and O'Fallon Railway Company, which was decided by the Supreme Court in 1929, the Commission fixed the capital value at $850,000, while the railway corporation insisted on a figure of $1,350,000. In this case the Supreme Court, following the precedent of *Smyth v. Ames,* decided against the Commission, although it did not lay down any clear-cut rule as to how values were to be calculated.

POWER REGULATION

Problems similar to those of the railroads were presented by the rapidly growing power industry. Power production was a public utility, constituting a natural monopoly. Like the railroad corporations in the seventies and eighties, the power companies were becoming a field for unscrupulous manipulation by financiers; and as with the railroads, so much power crossed state lines and so much of the business was controlled by a few corporations that only the Federal government could establish effective regulation.

In 1920 Congress created a Federal Power Commission, composed of three cabinet members and a secretary. In 1930 the Commission was changed into a body of five full-time members and was given a status similar to that of the Interstate Commerce Commission and the Federal Trade Commission. The chief function of the Commission was to give licences to power corporations who wished to build plants on navigable rivers. The corporations were to pay annual fees, and the Commission was to regulate the rates charged to consumers. Preference was to be given to enterprises owned by states or municipalities. Between 1920 and 1930 the Federal Power Commission granted 449 licences.

The Progressives in Congress, however, recommended Federal regulation of all interstate power corporations, and some of them advocated government ownership. The chief enemy of the power corporations was Senator Norris of Nebraska. Norris believed that the American people could derive almost unlimited benefits from the development of cheap electrical power, and he was convinced that these benefits could never be fully realized as long as the industry was controlled by a few financiers for private profit. He believed that only government ownership could ensure rates low enough for a widespread use of power by farmers and workers. Throughout the twenties Norris conducted, almost single-handed, a long crusade against the power corporations. Norris chose as his test case the question of Muscle Shoals, on the Tennessee River in Alabama. During the war the government had built at Muscle Shoals two nitrate plants for the manufacture of explosives and had begun to construct dams on the Tennessee River to provide power for the plants. The total cost had been $145,000,000. After the war the nitrate plants were no longer used, and the power plants, which had never been completed, were operated by the U. S. Army Corps of Engineers, the power being sold to local corporations. The Republican administration proposed to transfer the whole enterprise, both nitrate plants (which were to be used for fertilizer) and power plants, to private operation on very easy terms.

Norris succeeded in blocking this proposal and recommended instead that the power plants be completed and that a government-owned corporation operate the plants and sell the nitrates and the surplus power. Congress passed a bill embodying Norris's ideas in 1928, but Coolidge pocket-vetoed it. In 1931 Congress passed a similar bill, which was vetoed by Hoover. Hoover declared, in a vehement protest to Congress, that he hesitated "to contemplate the future of our institutions, of our government, and of our country, if the preoccupation of its officials is to be no longer the promotion of justice and equal opportunity but is to be devoted to barter in the market. That is not liberalism; it is degeneration."

SHIPPING

A similar opposition to government ownership was displayed by the Republican Party with respect to shipping. Since, however, the shipping industry was unable to stand on its own feet, it finally became necessary for even the Republicans to accept measures tending toward state socialism.

In 1920 the Republican majority in Congress passed the Merchant Marine Act. The vast fleet of merchant ships which had been constructed during the war was to be sold by the Shipping Board to private operators. Until the sales had been completed the government-owned Merchant Fleet Corporation was to continue to operate certain of the ships and shipping routes. The Shipping Board began by selling ships at from $200 to $250 a ton. In 1921, however, Albert D. Lasker, who became head of the Board by appointment of President Harding, proceeded to sell a large part of the government fleet to private corporations at $30 a ton, which was about one-eighth of what the ships had cost the government. Buyers were allowed to take their pick, and all sales were made in private.

Even the virtual gift of millions of tons of shipping to the operators did not enable them to hold their own against foreign competition, and by 1928 the proportion of American foreign trade carried in American ships had decreased from 42.7 per cent to 32.2 per cent. In that year Congress came to the rescue with another Merchant Marine Act. The government was to loan $250,000,000 to the companies for new construction, and was to pay them an annual subsidy by means of mail-carrying contracts. Meanwhile the Shipping Board continued to sell them ships at very low prices. In spite of these measures it was still necessary to continue the Merchant Fleet Corporation. The Merchant Marine Act of 1928 resulted in some increase in the number of American ships; and by the end of 1930 there were 1,778 ocean-going ships of more than 1,000 tons, with a total tonnage of about 9½ million. Of these,

1,345 were owned by private corporations and 433 by the Merchant Fleet Corporation.

BENEFITS TO VETERANS

During the war the government had made what it considered adequate provision for veterans' relief. Disabled veterans were to have hospital treatment; pensions were to be paid to all totally disabled men and to their dependents at the rate of $30 a month per person; and life insurance was sold by the government on easy terms. At the end of the war a discharge bonus, totaling $256,000,-000, was paid to all veterans. The pension demands of the Grand Army of the Republic had played an important part in American politics after the Civil War; and it was hoped that this experience would not be duplicated in the case of the American Expeditionary Force. This hope, however, was frustrated. The veterans' lobby soon became one of the strongest pressure groups in Washington, and few congressmen were able to resist its demands.

In 1924 veterans suffering disabilities of various kinds which had developed prior to January 1, 1925, were given pensions, and the compensation scales were increased. In 1930 the pension system was again extended to cover disabilities acquired before the beginning of that year. The veterans, moreover, demanded an additional bonus, which would compensate them for the difference between their pay as soldiers and the high wages which had been received during the war by civilian workers. Congress passed a bonus bill, over Coolidge's veto, in 1924. By this bill veterans received twenty-year endowment policies, at the rate of $1.25 for each day they had spent in the army overseas and $1.00 for each day of home service, with compound interest at 4 per cent. Veterans could borrow up to 22½ per cent of the value of these policies. By the end of 1930 about 3½ million persons held policies, and the total value amounted to about 3½ billion dollars. During the depression the veterans began to demand, first, that the percentage which might be borrowed be increased to 50 per cent and, subsequently, that the whole bonus be paid immediately. The first of these proposals was passed, over

Hoover's veto, in 1931; and the second, over Roosevelt's veto, in 1936.

By the end of 1930 the total cost of veterans' relief, including the unpaid bonus certificates, amounted to about 5½ billion dollars; and the annual cost of hospital and other services provided by the Veterans' Bureau was 500 million dollars.

IMMIGRATION RESTRICTION

The most important legislation enacted during the twenties remains to be mentioned. Reversing the policies which had prevailed since the first colonization of the United States three hundred years before, Congress imposed drastic limitations upon immigration. The propaganda carried on against unrestricted immigration since the eighteen-eighties had now begun to permeate public opinion. There was, morever, a widespread fear, especially among the labor organizations, that the postwar poverty of Europe might result in such an extensive migration to America as would seriously lower the American standard of living. The justification for restriction was that excessive immigration would make it impossible for the newcomers to be assimilated into American civilization and the American way of life. The authors of restriction were, however, influenced to some extent by the very narrow and intolerant conception of Americanism which had developed during the war and by the belief that certain racial groups were more desirable than others.

Between 1916 and 1920 immigrants averaged about 300,000 a year. In the year 1920–1921 the number increased to more than 800,000, about two-thirds of whom came from southern and eastern Europe. In 1921 Congress passed the Emergency Quota Act, limiting the number of immigrants of each nationality to 3 per cent of the persons of that nationality resident in the United States in 1910. The act did not apply to persons born in the Old World but resident in the western hemisphere, and it was therefore followed by a very rapid growth of immigration by way of Canada and Mexico. From 1921 to 1925 immigration averaged 650,000 a year.

Finally, in 1924, Congress passed the Immigration Quota Act. Immigration was to be immediately restricted to 2 per cent of the persons of each nationality resident in the United States in 1890. Meanwhile a committee was to determine the racial composition of the American people in 1920. When the committee finished its work, immigration from the Old World was to be limited to 150,000 a year, and it was to be distributed among the various national groups in proportion to the number of persons descended from that national group in the American population of 1920. Persons born in the western hemisphere might enter the United States without quota restrictions; and the children and wives of American citizens, and teachers, students, and ministers of religion were also allowed to enter freely. The purpose of this act was to limit immigration from southern and eastern Europe and to increase the proportion of immigrants from northern and western Europe. In spite of the fact that the quota requirement would have permitted only a negligible immigration from Japan, the admission of Japanese for permanent residence was totally prohibited. This insult to Japan was strongly criticized by Secretary of State Hughes, and it resulted in a most dangerous increase of Japanese hostility. The committee which was studying the racial composition of the American people reported, after several years of work, that it was unable to arrive at any scientifically accurate figures. Congress, however, insisted that it do the best it could, with the result that the national origins quota was finally put into effect on March 22, 1929.

The immigration acts limited entries from Europe but did not restrict immigration from the western hemisphere. Throughout the twenties large numbers of French Canadians and Mexicans took advantage of the fact that American employers could no longer obtain cheap labor from Europe. French Canadians had already entered the United States in considerable numbers in the eighteen-eighties, the new wave of immigration in the twenties brought the total number of entries from French Canada to more than $1\frac{1}{2}$ million. More than a million of these settled in New England, where they became, for the most part, factory workers. During the same period more than a million Mexicans came to the United States, half of them to Texas. Mexican standards of living were very much lower than those in the United States, and Mexican immigrants were paid excessively low wages. Being largely of Indian descent, they were also the victims of color prejudice. The exploitation of Mexican workers by American employers created labor problems, especially in Texas, which occasionally resulted in bitter conflicts.

After 1930 the depression reduced immigration of all kinds drastically. Many persons wishing to come to America were refused visas lest they become public charges, and many aliens either left the United States voluntarily or were deported by the Department of Labor. In 1933 there were only 23,068 immigrants, as contrasted with 80,081 departures. Departures continued to exceed arrivals until 1936, when the growth of persecution in some of the European countries caused immigration to increase.

Most Americans felt that the continuance of unrestricted immigration would tend to weaken American traditions and institutions. Restriction, however, was by no means an unmixed benefit. It meant that the rate of increase of the population was sharply reduced. And since the American economic system, both in industry and in agriculture, had always been keyed to rapid expansion, such a reduction would eventually necessitate considerable economic readjustments. It would, for example, increase the problem of agricultural overproduction. The new American policy had, moreover, most deleterious consequences on Europe. The density of population in some of the European countries was ten times as great as in the United States; and the inability of the European nations to dispose of their surplus population through emigration to the United States was one of the factors which helped to cause the international hostilities of the nineteen-thirties.

The adoption of policies of racial, religious, and political persecution by certain European governments created, moreover, a refugee problem which constituted one of the greatest tragedies of world history in recent times. The most valuable citizens of Germany and Italy found life under Fascism intolerable. Those who secured admission to the United States included such world-famous figures as Thomas Mann and Albert Einstein, who could make a great contribution to American culture and science. But many thousands of others were denied admission under the American immigration laws.

Prior to the enactment of the laws of 1921 and 1924 no such problem could have occurred. Considerable areas of America had been first colonized by refugees, and hospitality to the victims of persecution had been the oldest, and one of the noblest, of American traditions.

BIBLIOGRAPHY

J. D. Black, *Agricultural Reform in the United States* (1930)
J. E. Boyle, *Farm Relief* (1928)
J. S. Davis, *The Farm Export Debenture Plan* (1929)
D. R. Dewey, *Financial History of the United States* (revised edition, 1938)
H. L. Elsbree, *Interstate Transmission of Electric Power* (1931)
C. Eliot, *The Farmer's Campaign for Credit* (1927)
M. Gamio, *Mexican Immigration to the United States* (1930)
R. L. Garis, *Immigration Restriction* (1929)
*L. Hacker, *American Problems of Today* (1938)
J. M. Jones, *Tariff Retaliation* (1934)
J. G. Kerwin, *Federal Water Power Legislation* (1926)
D. P. Locklin, *Railroad Regulation since 1920* (1928)
R. MacVeagh, *The Transportation Act* (1923)
K. Mayo, *Soldiers, What Next?* (1934)
National Industrial Conference Board, *The American Merchant Marine Problem* (1929)
R. L. Neuberger and S. B. Kahn, *Integrity: The Life of George W. Norris* (1937)
H. S. Raushenbush and H. W. Laidler, *Power Control* (1928)
E. E. Schattschneider, *Politics, Pressures and the Tariff* (1935)
E. R. A. Seligman, *Economics of Farm Relief* (1929)
I. L. Sharfman, *The I.C.C.* (1931–37)
D. A. Smith and P. V. Betters, *The United States Shipping Board* (1931)
E. S. Spahr, *History and Theory of Agricultural Credit in the United States* (1932)
E. A. Stokdyk and C. H. West, *The Farm Board* (1930)
F. W. Taussig, *Tariff History of the United States* (revised edition, 1931)
H. D. Wolf, *The Railroad Labor Board* (1927)

37

FOREIGN POLICY, 1921-1933

ISOLATION OR CO-OPERATION?

ALTHOUGH a majority of the Senate had been in favor of entry into the League of Nations, either with or without the reservations, and although many people had voted for Harding in the belief that he was in favor of the League with the reservations, it was the opinion of the twelve or thirteen Senate isolationists which finally prevailed. After the rejection of the treaty in 1920 the question of American entry into the League was not revived, and isolationism became the official American policy. Public opinion accepted the isolationist doctrine that the United States must never again become entangled in the traditional rivalries of the European nations; that she must not pledge herself to support any program for checking war by measures of collective security; and that, if war came, she must keep out of it. This attitude was frequently expressed in a tone of self-righteous complacency which aroused considerable indignation in Europe.

It was, however, the State Department which actually conducted American foreign policy; and successive Secretaries of State, Charles Evans Hughes (1921–1925), Frank B. Kellogg (1925–1929), and Henry L. Stimson (1929–1933), found themselves unable to adopt complete isolationism. State Department officials were necessarily aware of the degree to which the safety and prosperity of the United States were dependent upon the maintenance of peace and tranquillity in other parts of the world. They realized, moreover, that if Europe were again plunged into war, the economic and psychological ties of the United States with European nations would make it difficult for us to preserve neutrality, for which reason it was desirable that we should participate in measures likely to prevent war. But although the State Department favored international co-operation, it was always prevented by the Senate isolationists from asserting effective United States leadership and from making binding pledges of United States support in any program for maintaining peace by collective security. American officials had to content themselves, therefore, either with making futile pacifistic declarations which did not commit the United States to any kind of action or with trying to persuade other nations to take action against aggressors. Thus, during the twenty-year period in which Europe first failed to organize peace and then plunged into a second catastrophic war, the most powerful nation in the world, and the only nation which was capable of viewing European rivalries impartially, refused to undertake any of the responsibilities of leadership.

The isolationists justified their position by pointing to the narrowly selfish policies pursued by all the European nations and to the manner in which the League of Nations was used to maintain Franco-British supremacy. The deficiencies of the League were, however, partly due to the rejection of it by the United States. Lacking any assurance of United States support in the maintenance of peace, none of the European nations felt secure; nor did they have any confidence that the League of Nations could effectively check aggression by economic sanctions if the co-operation of the United States remained doubtful. It was this universal insecurity which made a lasting European peace impossible.

As soon as the United States Senate rejected the Treaty of Versailles, including not only the League of Nations but also the pledge of support against German aggression which had been promised by Wilson during the dispute over the Rhineland, the French government began to build up a system of alliances with the succession states of eastern Europe. In 1923, after Germany had defaulted on the reparations payments, the French army occupied the Ruhr, and thereby precipitated the crisis of inflation which ruined the German middle classes. The attempt of the French to achieve security by such methods aroused bitter resentment in Germany and was to contribute eventually to the rise of the Nazis. The British, on the other hand, favored conciliation with Germany. Great Britain was, however, no longer strong enough to exercise the leadership which had belonged to her during the nineteenth century, nor did she produce men capable of the statesmanship which Europe required. After the World War, except for two brief intervals, she had conservative governments whose primary concern was the defense of their imperial interests and who used the American rejection of the League as a pretext for giving only very lukewarm support to its objectives.

MOVES TOWARD INTERNATIONAL CO-OPERATION

The United States refused at first even to acknowledge the fact that the League existed. The State Department did not answer letters sent to it by the League; and, when the League officials wanted information from the American government, they had to ask the government of the Netherlands to serve as intermediary. The Senate isolationists were deeply suspicious of any American co-operation with the League, even when it concerned merely control of the opium and white slave traffics.

After 1922, however, the fear of contamination began to subside, and the State Department began to send "unofficial observers" to a number of the League conferences. Secretary Hughes, moreover, declared in a speech at New Haven in the autumn of that year that on both economic and humanitarian grounds the United States was interested in European peace, and he offered American help in settling the reparations problem. In the autumn of 1923 the Dawes Commission was appointed with ten members, of whom the chairman and one other were Americans. The recommendations of the Dawes Commission led to a reduction in reparations payments and the stabilization of German finances. Another American, Parker T. Gilbert, was appointed agent-general to supervise the payments. This settlement was followed by the French evacuation of the Ruhr and in 1925 by the Locarno Treaties, which, it was hoped, would put an end to Franco-German hostility and create a lasting peace. In

1928, when Germany again had difficulty in meeting her obligations, Owen D. Young headed another commission which again modified the schedule of reparations payments. The year 1988 was fixed as the date when the payments were to be completed.

Americans, especially Elihu Root, assisted in the establishment of the World Court of International Justice, which was set up by the League in 1921. One of the nine judges of the Court was always an American. In 1923 Harding recommended American adherence to the Court, but without result. In 1926, when Coolidge took up the question, the Senate consented to American adherence, but laid down five reservations and declared that each of the forty-eight nations which had signed the World Court protocol must agree to them. Five nations, all of them small ones, declared that they would accept the reservations, while the other forty-three ignored this ultimatum. In 1929 Elihu Root worked out a formula to which both the forty-eight nations in the World Court and the isolationists in the United States Senate could agree; but the Senate took no action on this proposal until 1935, and then rejected it.

The most conspicuous gesture made by the United States in the cause of world peace was its sponsorship of the Pact of Paris, better known as the Kellogg Pact. For a number of years a Chicago lawyer, Samuel O. Levinson, had been urging that all nations pledge themselves to outlaw war and to settle disputes only by pacific means. In the spring of 1927 the French minister of foreign affairs, Aristide Briand, suggested that France and the United States sign a bilateral pact renouncing any resort to war between each other. Secretary of State Kellogg at first paid no attention; but Senator Borah and President Butler and Professor James T. Shotwell of Columbia University began to arouse public opinion in favor of the proposal and to urge that Briand's suggestion be adopted and enlarged into a multilateral pact of the kind advocated by Levinson. In December, Kellogg began negotiations with the governments of other great powers; and on August 27, 1928, the representatives of fifteen nations signed the Pact of Paris promising never to resort to war. The Pact was subsequently accepted by forty-four other nations. Almost every nation, however, made reservations which deprived the Pact of much of its meaning, and no method was provided for enforcing obedience upon nations which violated it. The United States Senate, for example, declared when it ratified the Pact that it did not curtail the right of the United States to self-defense or the powers which she exercised under the Monroe Doctrine, and that it did not commit her to take any positive action to check aggression. Outside the United States the Pact was generally regarded as a peculiarly futile and meaningless moral gesture. Its only visible consequence was that henceforth when nations resorted to war, they often omitted to make any formal declaration of it.

DISARMAMENT

In promoting disarmament, American diplomacy was somewhat less ineffectual and more realistic. During the war the United States had made plans for enlarging its navy until it would be at least equal to that of Great Britain. After the war, however, both governments were anxious to avoid any expensive and dangerous race for naval supremacy. The United States was, moreover, alarmed by the possibility that the Anglo-Japanese Alliance might be continued; while Canadian opposition to the alliance made Great Britain anxious to find some method of abandoning it which would not offend Japan. It was therefore easy for the governments of the two countries to agree on a conference for the purposes of naval disarmament and the maintenance of peace in the Pacific.

The Washington Conference met on November 12, 1921, the leading delegates being Hughes for the United States, Balfour for Great Britain, and Kato for Japan. With respect to disarmament the conference resulted in a Five-Power Naval Treaty, signed by the United States, Great Britain, Japan, France, and Italy. As soon as the conference opened Hughes took the bull by the horns and made specific proposals, as carefully prepared as they were daring, for naval reductions. Hughes recommended that the various powers scrap a total of sixty-six ships, built or under construction, with a total tonnage of 1,878,043. In the words of the English journalist, Colonel Repington, "Secretary Hughes sank in thirty-four minutes more ships than all the admirals of the world have sunk in a cycle of centuries." By the Five-Power Treaty the United States and Great Britain accepted the principle of naval equality, each power limiting the tonnage of its capital ships to 525,000. Japan was allotted a capital ship tonnage of 272,000; while France and Italy were each to have 175,000 tons. No agreement could be made about smaller ships. The Washington Conference was, however, the only one of the various postwar disarmament conferences which actually brought about any disarming.

Subsequent conferences, at Rome in 1924 and at Geneva in 1927, endeavored to reach agreements about smaller ships, but without success. The failure of the second of these conferences was due partly to the efforts of William B. Shearer, the hired agent of certain American corporations which were engaged in warship construction. In January, 1930, there was another conference in London, which had been preceded by more careful preparations, including a visit of the British Prime Minister, Ramsay MacDonald, to the United States. No settlement could be made which included France and Italy; but the United States, Great Britain, and Japan agreed to build no more battleships until 1936, while the building of smaller ships was to be regulated by a series of ratios. These ratios, however, permitted considerable extra construction by all three powers. By an "escalator clause" the treaty was to be modified if other countries began to build in excess of their relative strength at the time of the treaty. The rapid increase of the German and Italian navies after 1933 soon brought the escalator clause into effect and made the treaty a dead letter. Equally futile was a general Disarmament Conference which met at Geneva in February, 1932, and in which the United States participated. Planned in the hope of limiting land and air armaments, the conference could not overcome the desire of the European nations for more security, and was abandoned after the establishment of the Nazi dictatorship a year later.

WAR DEBTS

Meanwhile the United States was endeavoring to secure payment of the war debts. These debts represented credits extended to the Allied Powers for purchases of goods in the United States during the war and in 1919. At the time when the credits were made little thought had been given to the question of repayment, and a number of congressman had declared, without being rebuked, that the United States should not insist on being repaid. The credits, it was said, represented America's contribution to the common cause and were a recognition of the fact that the losses and expenditures of the Allied Powers had been far greater than those of the United States and that America's military assistance had been negligible for twelve months after her entry into the war.

In 1922, however, Congress decided to demand repayment and appointed the World War Foreign Debt Commission. Few Americans realized that payment of the debts was rendered difficult by the high protective tariff of the United States, and that the attempt to enforce payment without opening American markets to European goods would result in a flow of gold to the United States which might disrupt the monetary systems of Europe. The insistence on payment of the debts made America acutely unpopular in Europe, which began to refer to the United States as "Uncle Shylock."

Between 1923 and 1930 the Debt Commission made agreements with fifteen out of the sixteen nations who had received credits, the only exception being Russia. The total credits had been $10,350,-490,597. Allowing for accrued interest these credits were funded at $11,671,953,489. Payment was to be extended over more than sixty years, and the average rate of interest was 2.1 per cent. Since the interest rate originally provided for had been 5 per cent, this represented a considerable reduction. Total payments, including both principal and interest, would, however, amount to almost twice the original credits. Some nations received much more favorable terms than others. Of the three principal debtors, Great Britain owed $4,600,000,000 and was to pay 3.3 per cent interest; France owed $4,025,000,000 and was to pay 1.6 per cent interest; Italy, now governed by the Fascist dictatorship of Mussolini, owed $2,042,-000,000, but she was asked to pay only 0.4 per cent interest.

Meanwhile the Allies were extracting reparations from Germany; and, although the United States refused to recognize any connection between reparations and war debts, the Allies would not reduce reparation payments as long as the war debt payments continued. In practice all these payments were rendered possible only by large-scale lending to Germany on the part of Allied and American bankers. By 1931 the world depression made a continuance of payments impossible. In the summer of that year the Hoover moratorium suspended payments for twelve months; and in the following year, at the Lausanne Conference, Great Britain and France agreed to remit 90 per cent of their claims to reparations on condition that a "satisfactory settlement" could be made with reference to the war debts. Although the United States Congress refused, in December, 1931, to consider cancellation, Germany, under the rule of Hitler, abandoned all reparation payments in 1933, and the Allies then ceased payment of the debts. France stopped payment in 1932; Great Britain, who had already canceled debts due to her from other nations, which were considerably larger than her own debt to the United States, made a last "token" payment in June, 1933. Of the fifteen debtor nations Finland alone, whose debt totaled $9,000,000, continued payments. These defaults aroused much indignation in America, and in 1934 Congress passed the Johnson Act forbidding any government whose debt to the United States was in default from floating fresh loans.

Throughout the period during which reparation and war debt payments had been made, Germany had borrowed about $6,000,-000,000 from foreign investors, of which about $2,500,000,000 had come from the United States; and she had paid $4,470,000,000 in reparations. The Allies had paid $2,606,000,000 on their war debts. After 1933 the Nazi dictatorship in Germany ceased to pay interest on German foreign debts, and proceeded to repatriate German bonds held by foreigners at a discount rate which in some cases was as high as 70 per cent. By this method she repudiated most of Germany's foreign debt. Thus, the paradoxical result of the attempt to maintain the structure of international debt payments was that, taking into consideration both public and private debts, the payments and receipts of each nation during the postwar period almost balanced each other. Germany seems to have gained more than she paid out; the United States paid out almost as much as she received.

THE FAR EAST

In the Far East Secretaries Hughes, Kellogg, and Stimson continued the policies which had been initiated before the war. They wished to guarantee the Philippines against attack and to preserve the Open Door in China. They continued, therefore, to oppose the imperialist policies pursued by Japan.

At the Washington Conference the Anglo-Japanese Alliance was enlarged into a Four-Power Treaty, signed by the United States, Great Britain, Japan, and France. The four nations agreed to respect one anothers' possessions in the Pacific and to consult with one another in case any of them was endangered by attack from any nation not included in the treaty. By a Nine-Power Treaty, signed by the United States, Great Britain, Japan, France, Italy, Belgium, Holland, Portugal, and China, the Open Door and the territorial integrity of China were reaffirmed. Japan was allowed to retain her economic predominance in Manchuria and in the Shantung peninsular, but she agreed to withdraw her troops from Shantung and also to restore to the Soviet Union territories which she had occupied in eastern Siberia. The treaty did not, however, provide any method for enforcing its provisions; and the result of the disarmament provisions of the conference was that the Japanese fleet could control the Asiatic end of the Pacific. Maintenance of the treaty would depend, therefore, on the good faith of the Japanese.

The Four-Power Treaty was subsequently criticized by certain senators on the ground that it was an entangling alliance. The Republican administration had, however, assured itself of Senate support by including Senators Lodge and Underwood among the delegates to the conference. Harding, moreover, reassured doubters by explaining, in that cloudy verbiage which characterized all his speeches, that although the United States had promised to maintain the status quo in the Pacific, she had not really committed herself to anything.

A Far Eastern power which was not included in the settlement was the Soviet Union. Throughout the twenties the United States refused to recognize the Communist government in Russia. The chief reason was the unwillingness of the Soviet government to undertake

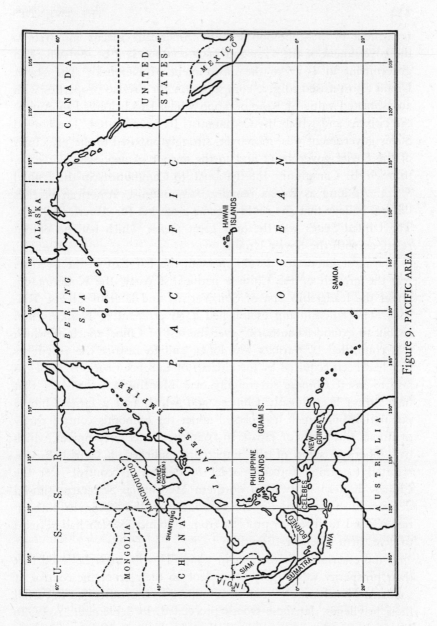

Figure 9. PACIFIC AREA

repayment of $75,000,000 lent by American citizens in 1916 to the government of the Czar and $192,000,000 lent by the American government in 1917 to the government of Kerensky. The Soviet Union also refused to give compensation for private properties with an estimated value of $430,000,000 which had belonged to American citizens and which the Communists had confiscated. The United States government was, moreover, strongly opposed to the principles of the Soviet government and to the encouragement which it gave, through the Communist International, to Communists in the United States. As long as Russia remained Communist, American officials did not believe that she could become a market for American goods. The United States was the only great power which had no official relations with the Soviet Union.

The most important development in the Far East in the twenties was the growth of the Chinese nationalist party, the Kuomintang, under the leadership first of Sun Yat-sen and later of Chiang Kai-shek. The Kuomintang established a government at Nanking and set out to extend its authority over the rest of China, much of which was controlled by various war lords, and to restrict the privileges that had been acquired by the citizens of European nations. It began also to assert Chinese sovereignty over Manchuria, a province that had always been legally Chinese and which had a large Chinese population but which had passed under the economic control partly of Russia and partly of Japan. In 1929 the Soviet government, which had inherited some of the imperialist policies of Czarist Russia, resorted to armed force in order to defend its control over the Chinese Eastern Railway in northern Manchuria. Secretary Stimson denounced this violation of the Kellogg Pact, but the Soviet authorities refused to listen to protests from a country which had refused to give them official recognition.

A more serious crisis began in 1931. The Japanese believed that their prosperity was largely dependent on their economic control of southern Manchuria. When the Chinese government began to curtail their privileges, Japanese troops proceeded, in September, 1931, to undertake military conquest of the province. In February, 1932, they organized Manchuria into a puppet state, under the name of

Manchukuo. They also attacked the Chinese city of Shanghai, hundreds of miles to the south of Manchuria. In January Shanghai was mercilessly bombed by Japanese airplanes. Meanwhile China appealed to the League of Nations and to the government of the United States.

Secretary Stimson was anxious that Japan be checked, not so much because of his interest in the Open Door policy as because be believed that successful violation of the Covenant of the League of Nations, of the Kellogg Pact, and of the Washington treaties would destroy all hope of establishing the rule of law in international affairs, would encourage aggression by other nations, and would lead inexorably to another world war. Although the Senate isolationists had refused to allow any teeth to be put into the Washington treaties or the Kellogg Pact, Stimson felt that if those documents meant anything at all, they meant that the United States should not only obey them herself but should also require other nations to obey them.

Joint action against Japan could, however, be organized only through the League of Nations; and, since the United States was not a member of the League, Stimson was unable to exert much influence on its proceedings or to co-ordinate United States policies successfully with those adopted by the League powers. And while all the smaller nations who belonged to the League wanted action, some of the great powers, particularly Great Britain, were sympathetic to Japan, Sir John Simon, the British Foreign Secretary, had no faith in the ideal of collective security, which he believed would tend to provoke wars rather than to prevent them. The British Foreign Office, moreover, disliked Chinese nationalism, which might endanger British economic interests in the Yangste valley, and was inclined to regard Japan as a useful ally.

In September Stimson embarked upon a course of "parallel action" with the League by urging Japan to cease fighting; in October he authorized the American consul at Geneva to attend meetings of the League Council, and he urged the League to "assert all the pressure and authority within its competence." In November he promised that the United States would do nothing to impede the enforcement of economic sanctions. The League, however, merely urged both Japan and China to abandon military operations, and appointed a commission, headed by Lord Lytton, to study the situation.

In January Stimson went beyond the League by declaring that the United States would not recognize any territorial changes made in violation of treaties—a policy which became known as the Stimson Doctrine. The British government replied by publishing a communique in which it refused to support the Stimson Doctrine, declaring that it had no reason to believe that the Japanese would exclude other nations from the trade of Manchuria and making no mention of the questions of Chinese territorial integrity and protection against aggression. In February Stimson held several telephone conversations with Sir John Simon, asking for joint action under the Nine-Power Treaty, but Simon remained noncommittal. Stimson then wrote an open letter to Senator Borah, in which he pointed out that the United States had accepted the naval limitations of the Washington treaties only because all the other signatories to the treaties had promised to maintain the status quo in the Far East. In March the Assembly of the League of Nations met, and the representatives of the smaller nations joined in denouncing the refusal of the British government to take action. Since the Japanese were now becoming active in the Yangste valley, the British were more willing to oppose them. Japan was induced to evacuate Shanghai, and the League accepted the policy of nonrecognition.

Nothing, however, was done to discipline Japan for her seizure of Manchuria. The British were interested only in the defense of their own interests; and, despite Stimson's promises, the attitude of the United States was uncertain. Many Americans, including President Hoover, were opposed to the adoption of economic sanctions; the United States navy was afraid lest sanctions lead to a Japanese attack on the Philippines; and the isolationists in the Senate were again becoming alarmed and were demanding that the United States remain strictly neutral. No further action was taken by the League until October, when the report of the Lytton Commission was published. The report admitted that the Japanese had had grievances, but it condemned unequivocally their resort to war, and it worked out a solution which might satisfy the legitimate claims of both China and Japan. At the next Assembly of the League Sir John Simon eloquently pointed out all the extenuating circumstances for the Japanese action and declared that the only purpose of the League was conciliation. The League, however, adopted the report; and, when Japan refused to accept it, she was expelled from membership. Japan then continued her program of aggression at the expense of China, moving into Mongolia early in 1933. No further attempt was made to stop her.

It is possible, as critics of Secretary Stimson have argued, that any serious action against Japan would have extended the conflict instead of checking it and would have committed the British and American navies to war in the Far East. It is, however, certain, that Japan's successful defiance of the Covenant of the League of Nations and of the Kellogg Pact showed that the great powers were unwilling to maintain peace by measures of collective security and set an example which was subsequently followed by Italy and Germany. And while the failure of the League to act appears to have been due primarily to the government of Great Britain, it was caused also by the fact that the United States was not a member of the League and by the possibility that the policies advocated by her Secretary of State might be repudiated by her Congress.

LATIN AMERICA

The chief tendency in the relations between the United States and Latin America in the nineteen-twenties was toward the abandonment of the Roosevelt corollary to the Monroe Doctrine, which had justified armed intervention by the United States in order to forestall the danger of European intervention. The policy of intervention had alarmed and alienated all the Latin American nations and had thereby impeded the growth of United States trade and investments. Latin American protests were particularly vehement at the Pan-American Congress at Havana in 1928.

The new attitude of the United States was expressed most clearly in a memorandum by J. Ruben Clark, Undersecretary of State, which was written in 1928 and published in 1930. Clark declared that the sole purpose of the Monroe Doctrine was to protect the American hemisphere from European imperialisms, and that the Roosevelt corollary was not justified by the terms of the doctrine. "So far as Latin America is concerned," said Clark, "the Doctrine is now, and always has been, not an instrument of violence and oppression, but an unbought, freely bestowed and wholly effective guaranty of their freedom, independence, and territorial integrity against the imperialist designs of Europe." This repudiation of the right of intervention was strengthened by a Pan-American Arbitration Conference, which met at Washington in 1929, and at which the United States and the Latin American nations agreed to the compulsory arbitration or conciliation of all disputes with one another.

The United States continued, however, to assert special interests in the Caribbean region, in order to guard the approaches to the Panama Canal. The Roosevelt corollary was replaced by the Isthmian Doctrine, formulated by Secretary Stimson, which meant that the United States must claim certain rights of supervision over the small Caribbean and Central American republics. "The failure therefore of one of these Republics to maintain the responsibilities which go with independence," said Stimson, "may lead directly to a situation imperiling the vital interests of the United States in its seagoing route through the Panama Canal. Out of this situation has followed our national policy—perhaps the most sensitive and generally held policy that we have—which for half a century has caused us to look with apprehension upon even the perfectly legitimate efforts of European nations to protect their rights within this zone."

The retreat from the Roosevelt corollary was a gradual process which did not become immediately effective everywhere. Cuba resumed full self-government in 1922, and the marines left the Dominican Republic in 1924. In Haiti, on the other hand, American rule was in 1922 made stronger; but in 1930 President Hoover promised eventual withdrawal, and the promise was honored in 1934. In both the Dominican Republic and Haiti an American receiver-general continued to exercise financial supervision after the departure of the American officials and marines.

Nicaragua was of special concern to the American government, both because of American financial interests and because of its proximity to the Panama Canal. The marines were withdrawn in 1925, but were sent back, as a result of civil war, in the following year. By 1927 there were 5,000 American troops and marines in the republic, who were apparently enforcing the rule of the conservative president Díaz, whose policies were favorable to American financial interests. This large-scale intervention, which verged on war, had never been sanctioned by Congress, and was vigorously opposed by Democratic and Progressive senators.

In 1927 President Coolidge sent Henry L. Stimson to Nicaragua. Stimson succeeded in persuading almost all the different factions in Nicaragua to agree that an election should be held in 1928 under American supervision. The election resulted in a victory for the liberals, who accordingly took over the government. Similar American-controlled elections were held in 1930 and 1932. One Nicaraguan leader, Augusto Sandino, refused to agree to American supervision; and for some years the American troops were engaged in an attempt to capture or suppress him and his small band of followers. Nicaragua finally resumed complete independence in 1933.

Mexico presented the United States government with more serious problems. The regime which had taken power in Mexico in 1920, after the fall of Carranza, set out to achieve the purposes of the Mexican Revolution. These were: to restore the land to the peasants; to improve the living conditions of the workers; to limit the privileges of foreign capital; to regain Mexican ownership of oil fields and other natural resources; and to reduce the powers of the Catholic Church. Such a program was inevitably distasteful to Americans who had economic interests in Mexico, and was opposed by the Catholic Church in both countries. President Obregón, however, who governed Mexico from 1920 until 1924, proceeded along this revolutionary path very slowly and cautiously; and in 1923, in order to obtain United States recognition, he promised not to interfere with American mineral and subsoil rights which had been acquired before 1917. In the following year, when the Obregón regime was threatened by a rebellion, it was allowed to purchase munitions in the United States.

In 1924, however, Obregón was succeeded by Calles. The latter pursued the program of land distribution with greater vigor, ordered the foreign oil companies to exchange their titles of ownership for fifty-year leases, and, by insisting on government control over the Church, provoked the Catholic priests into open opposition. The result was a conflict with the United States, which threatened to end in war. American oil magnates and American Catholics demanded intervention; and William Randolph Hearst, who owned large estates in northern Mexico, published a series of forged documents purporting to show that four American senators who opposed intervention were in the pay of the Mexican government. The situation became worse when Secretary Kellogg informed the Senate that the Communist International was using Mexico as a base of operations.

In September, 1927, however, Coolidge sent his friend, Dwight Morrow, as ambassador to Mexico. Morrow adopted a somewhat novel approach. Instead of threatening the Mexicans, he set out to make friends with them; and, instead of assuming an attitude of aloof superiority, he endeavored to understand the Mexican point of view. The result was that Morrow, for the time being, was remarkably successful in winning security for American economic interests in Mexico. Two months after his arrival the Mexican Supreme Court declared that the constitution of 1917 was not retroactive and, hence, that subsoil rights acquired by oil companies before that date could not be disturbed. Morrow then proceeded to arrange a settlement between the Mexican government and the Catholic Church, and he brought about an almost complete cessation of the program of land distribution. As a result partly of Morrow's influence and partly of internal political developments, the Mexican government virtually abandoned its revolutionary program, which was not resumed until the accession of Cárdenas to the presidency in 1934 and the subsequent destruction of the political power of Calles.

Morrow was at first hailed as one of the most successful diplomats in American history. Later verdicts were, however, less flattering. He had failed to realize that there was a real need for fundamental changes in the economic and social structure of Mexico and that the demand of the Mexican people for reform would eventually sweep away any obstacles which might be imposed by their rulers. By using his influence to prevent such changes from being made, he had strengthened the feeling of many Mexicans that the United States was concerned primarily with the defense of its own economic interests. Mexican radicals drew the conclusion that the United States might be even more dangerous as a friend than as an enemy.

THE PHILIPPINES

In the Philippines the Republican administration reversed the trend toward independence which had been instituted by the Democrats. Harding sent the Wood-Forbes Commission to the islands; and the commission declared that the Filipinos were misusing the powers which had been entrusted to them. General Leonard Wood was then appointed Governor General, and he set up what was almost a military dictatorship. He controlled every branch of the executive, allowed little power to the legislature, and turned over to private capital the economic enterprises which the Harrison regime had placed under government ownership. The Filipinos began to protest, and in 1926 Coolidge sent a commission headed by Carmi A. Thompson to investigate the situation. The commission recommended more self-government; and steps in this direction were taken in 1927, when Wood died and was succeeded by Henry L. Stimson. In 1929, when Stimson became Secretary of State, he was followed by Dwight F. Davis.

Meanwhile sentiment in favor of Philippine independence was increasing in the United States. The islands were a military liability, and they had brought few economic benefits. In 1930 American capital invested in the Philippines amounted to only $160,000,000; exports from America to the islands amounted in that year to $89,702,173; imports from the islands into America amounted to $113,547,960. Two-thirds of all the trade of the Philippines was with the United States, but to the United States the value of the trade was negligible. The Philippines, moreover, sold more than $50,000,000 worth of sugar each year to the United States. This sugar was admitted duty-free; it was grown mostly by Filipino and

Spanish planters; and it competed with the sugar grown in the United States. Another factor of importance was popular opposition, especially in California, to the admission of Filipino immigrants. The sugar producers and the enemies of colored immigration joined, therefore, with the isolationists and the anti-imperialists in demanding that the United States abandon the islands. This combination of idealism and self-interest caused Congress to pass, over the veto of President Hoover, the Hawes-Cutting Act of January, 1933, by which the islands were to become independent in twelve years. The act was, however, unacceptable to the Filipinos, and a definite settlement was not made until the Tydings-McDuffie Act of 1934.

BIBLIOGRAPHY

*T. A. Bailey, *Diplomatic History of the United States* (1940)
*S. F. Bemis, *Diplomatic History of the United States* (1936)
G. H. Blakeslee, *The Pacific Area* (1929)
R. L. Buell, *The Washington Conference* (1922)
R. M. Cooper, *American Consultation in World Affairs* (1934)
The Council on Foreign Relations, *The United States in World Affairs* (1931–. . .)
*D. F. Fleming, *The United States and World Organization, 1920–33* (1938)
*A. W. Griswold, *The Far Eastern Policy of the United States* (1938)
E. Gruening, *Mexico and its Heritage* (1928)
C. W. Hackett, *The Mexican Revolution and the United States* (1926)
*C. P. Howland (ed.), *Survey of American Foreign Relations* (1928–30)
M. O. Hudson, *The Permanent Court of International Justice* (1925)
C. L. Jones, *The Caribbean since 1900* (1936)
Y. Ichihashi, *The Washington Conference and After* (1938)
D. H. Miller, *The Peace Pact of Paris* (1928)
H. G. Moulton and L. Pasvolsky, *War Debts and World Prosperity* (1932)
W. S. Myers, *Foreign Policies of Herbert Hoover* (1940)
H. Nicholson, *Dwight Morrow* (1935)
H. S. Quigley and G. H. Blakeslee, *The Far East* (1938)
F. L. Schuman, *American Policy towards Russia since 1917* (1928)
——— *International Politics* (1933)
J. T. Shotwell, *War as an Instrument of National Policy* (1929)
F. H. Simonds, *American Foreign Policy in the Post-War Years* (1935)
H. L. Stimson, *American Policy in Nicaragua* (1927)
——— *The Far Eastern Crisis* (1936)

E. Tupper and G. E. McReynolds, *Japan in American Public Opinion* (1928)

B. H. Williams, *The United States and Disarmament* (1931)

W. W. Willoughby, *The Sino-Japanese Crisis and the League of Nations* (1935)

Q. Wright (ed.), *Interpretations of American Foreign Policy* (1930)

38

ASPECTS OF SOCIETY

AN AGE OF MATERIALISM

FROM some points of view the decade of the twenties appears, in retrospect, as a golden age. By contrast with the thirties, it was a period when money was easy to acquire and when men had few doubts or fears about the future. It was also a period of steady cultural advance, in which the literature and art of the United States appeared for the first time to have passed beyond the stage of colonialism or provincialism and to have achieved maturity. Yet the tone of American society in the twenties was in many way very unhealthy, and the American people were left dangerously unprepared to face the catastrophic events of the period which followed. There was probably more materialism, more illiberality, and more cynicism than ever before in American history. Ideals lost their meaning as a result of the World War and Versailles, and for a considerable proportion of the population financial success had become the only objective worth striving for. Much of the spirit of the era might be summarized in the word (coined by W. E. Woodward) "debunk."

The most trusted leaders of America were unanimous in agreeing with President Coolidge that "the business of America is business." Such a sentiment was unexceptionable insofar as business meant the making and distribution of goods. But business also included speculation, advertising, and pressure salesmanship; and these activities, which involved the making of money rather than the making of goods, assumed in the twenties an exaggerated importance.

Speculation had always been a favorite American occupation; but it had never before been pursued so vigorously or by a larger number of people. The hope of getting something for nothing culminated in the stock exchange fever of 1928 and the catastrophe of October, 1929; but throughout the decade there were numerous epidemics of speculative excitement. The most extraordinary of these was perhaps the Florida land boom of 1924 and 1925. Thousands of hopeful individuals from all over the country swarmed into Coral Gables, Miami, and Palm Beach to buy real estate on the installment plan, hoping to sell it again within a few weeks before the next installment was due. Thousands of others bought land without even seeing it. The price of a lot in the business section of Miami rose from $800 to $150,000. The Florida realtors dexterously stimulated the fever, hiring William Jennings Bryan, former champion of agrarian radicalism and Secretary of State of the United States, to make speeches in praise of the Florida climate. The inevitable collapse began in 1926, and was completed by a hurricane which killed four hundred persons along the Florida coast. But many gullible persons who had lost their savings were undaunted by the experience and only too willing to transfer their hopes the following year from Miami to Wall Street.

Meanwhile the salesman and the advertising man seemed to be replacing the engineer as the key figures in the economic system. Confronted by a consumers' market which was apparently too small to absorb all the products of American industry, corporation managers found that their principal problem was not the improvement of production but the capturing of new customers. Qualities which made for successful salesmanship—aggressiveness and lack of scruple —acquired a new value; and the ability to "sell oneself," which had formerly denoted dishonesty, now indicated a desirable accomplishment. The glorification of the advertising man reached its peak in a book, *The Man Nobody Knows,* which was written by the New York advertising agent Bruce Barton. Jesus Christ, declared Mr. Barton, "would be a national advertiser today" and he was "the founder of modern business." The appeal of the salesman and the advertising man was largely to motives of envy and cupidity. Luxuries began to be represented as necessities; and millions of American families were induced to emulate their neighbors by running into debt in order to maintain a higher standard of living than they could afford. In this popularization of luxury the advertising man received valuable assistance from the motion pictures and from the large-selling magazines.

The desire for material satisfactions, which was stimulated by all the new propagandist devices of salesmanship, expressed itself in a general relaxation of traditional ethical standards. Moral taboos, both in speech and in behavior, grew rapidly weaker. In every age, of course, the older generation has viewed with alarm the conduct of the young; and, since there is no statistical evidence, it may be doubted whether there have been any considerable variations in the amount of immorality in different periods. Two generalizations, however, may safely be made about the so-called "jazz age" of the twenties: conversation was freer than for a number of generations, and—largely as a result of the automobile—the traditional double standard was breaking down. Obsession with the problems of sex among persons who considered themselves emancipated ended abruptly in the thirties, when they turned instead to the problems of economic reform or revolution.

A more indubitable symptom of a weakening of moral fiber was the series of waves of popular excitement which were whipped up by the ballyhoo of sensationalist newspapers. Motion picture stars, sports champions, celebrated criminals, and successful gangsters occupied in turn the spotlight of national attention. College football, played by teams of semiprofessionals, became a big business in which a single university could collect a million dollars in admission fees in a single season; 1½ million dollars was paid to see Dempsey beat Carpentier, and ten persons died of excitement while listening to radio reports of the fight between Dempsey and Tunney. The most popular motion picture idols were almost deified; and the death of Rudolph Valentino caused astonishing outbursts of feminine hysteria. Among the different figures who attained the rôle of a national hero, it seemed refreshing to find one, Colonel Lindbergh, who had earned his fame by genuine achievement and who hated the notoriety which he had thereby acquired.

THE INCREASE OF CRIME

Many tendencies which appeared to some people as indicating a growth of materialistic standards of value and a decay of morality might be regarded by others as unimportant or not wholly reprehensible. There was, however, one feature of American life in the twenties which provoked the most justified alarm and which indicated a genuine danger of social disintegration: the extraordinary increase of lawlessness.

Disrespect for the law had always been an American characteristic; and during the twenties it was especially widespread. Encouraged by examples on Wall Street and—during the Harding regime—in Washington, the officials of numerous state and city governments reverted to the ways of the post–Civil War period. Outstanding among the examples of municipal misgovernment were the Democratic regime of Mayor James J. Walker of New York, which combined a corruption reminiscent of the Tammany of Boss Tweed with a polished sophistication appropriate to the richest city in the world, and the Republican regime of Mayor William Hale Thompson of Chicago, who won his election by appealing to the German and Irish vote with a promise to keep "King George's snoot" out of the city.

Law enforcement being frequently in venal hands, organized crime flourished as never before in American history. Thanks to the Eighteenth Amendment, criminal groups were able to take over the very lucrative business of supplying the American people with liquor. They were aided also by corrupt connections with local politicians, by the deficiencies of the American legal system, which enabled shyster lawyers to prevent convictions by means of technicalities, and by the extraordinary tolerance of public opinion, which sometimes treated a clever criminal as a figure of national importance. Another factor in the growth of crime was the American system of states rights; while law-enforcement was local, crime, thanks to the automobile, was organized on a national scale. The jurisdiction of the police stopped at state lines, but murderers and bank robbers often traveled a thousand miles from the scene of their activities.

Bootlegging necessarily involved many criminal activities in addition to the manufacture and sale of liquor. Since the liquor gangs could not claim legal protection against their business competitors, they were compelled to provide for their own defense, using machine guns to guard against the theft of their property by hijackers and to intimidate retailers into buying their liquor. The growth of the liquor gangs, armed with the most modern weapons of warfare and earning revenues equal to those of all but the largest corporations, stimulated crimes of other kinds: particularly the organization of rackets by which retail storekeepers were compelled to pay for "protection," the robbing of banks, and the kidnapping and holding for ransom of members of wealthy families. The crime statistics of the United States in the twenties far exceeded those of any other nation in the world. Homicides averaged 10,800 a year; and the homicide rate was twice that of Italy, sixteen times that of England, and thirty-six times that of Switzerland. Thefts cost the American people a direct sum of 250 million dollars a year, while the indirect costs of crime ran into many billions of dollars. In a single twelve-month period in 1928 and 1929, in only four states, there were 12,000 hold-ups, in which 22 million dollars was stolen. Only 12 per cent of the criminals were caught and only 4 per cent of the money was ever regained. By the year 1935 there were no less than 3 million persons in the United States who had been either convicted or under arrest on criminal charges.

Chicago had the greatest notoriety as a center of criminal activity. In 1920 a young New Yorker, Alphonse Capone, established himself in Chicago as the organizer of a liquor gang. By 1927 his group was earning an annual revenue from the sale of liquor of 60 million dollars, while Capone himself had accumulated a private fortune of 20 million dollars, which enabled him to control the town of Cicero and to own an estate in Florida. Numerous battles were fought between the Capone gang and the rival gang of Dion O'Banion; and when O'Banion was killed he was buried in a casket worth

$10,000 and accompanied by twenty-six truckloads of flowers. By 1929 there had been more than five hundred gang murders in Chicago, many of which had occurred on the public streets and in open daylight, and for which there had been virtually no convictions. In addition to the liquor business the gangs had organized ninety-one rackets which cost the law-abiding citizens of Chicago a total of 136 million dollars a year. Conditions in a number of other cities were probably almost as bad. Nor was it only the immigrant groups in the big cities which produced criminals; gangsters from rural and Anglo-Saxon stock, of the type of Nelson and Dillinger, were quite as vicious as the big-city racketeers.

After 1929 crime decreased. The revenues of the gangs were diminished first by the depression and subsequently by the repeal of prohibition. The Federal government also discovered several legal devices which enabled it to assume responsibility for law enforcement. A number of leading criminals, headed by Capone, were sent to jail on the charge of income tax evasion; while the Dyer Act making it a Federal offence to transport stolen automobiles across state lines could be applied to most of the gangs. The Federal Bureau of Investigation, founded in 1924 and headed by J. Edgar Hoover, became one of the most efficient detective agencies in the world. During the thirties the leading "public enemies" were systematically hunted down and eliminated.

THE GROWTH OF INTOLERANCE

While American society was paying rewards, in an increasing degree, to the qualities of egotism, aggressiveness, and lack of scruple, it was at the same time encouraging timidity and conformity in intellectual questions. The war-time fear of radicalism continued; and persons who doubted the merits of business civilization provoked considerable antagonism.

Certain economic developments, particularly the growth of debt, strengthened the pressure toward conformity. Creditor interests, enjoying economic power, began to claim also rights of intellectual supervision. The ability to borrow depended on a sound credit status; and credit status, as interpreted by small-town bankers, was likely to be assessed not only by strictly economic considerations but also by adherence to the established political and ethical conventions. The intellectual control which was thus acquired by bankers was especially important when it affected the publishers of newspapers. Meanwhile the national habit of speculation was making optimism appear a patriotic duty.

Speculative profits, whether in real estate or on Wall Street, depended on rising values, and rising values were impossible if any public exposure of abuses caused confidence to be impaired. Critics of the economic and social system were thus a menace to its financial stability. The exhortations, frequently expressed in the twenties, that one should "boost" one's native city instead of "knocking" it, and that one should be a "bull upon the United States," were not merely an indication of a homely patriotism; they expressed also a fear lest an injudicious honesty check the rise of monetary values.

The hostility toward anything radical, alien, or "un-American" assumed also more dangerous forms—movements of organized intolerance and repressive legislation. The most formidable of these threats to the ideals upon which America had been built was the Ku Klux Klan. The postwar Klan, which had no connection except its name with the Klan of the Reconstruction Period and which was dedicated to the suppression of Negroes, Catholics, and Jews, had been founded in 1915 by W. J. Simmons. In 1921 the "Imperial Kleagle," Edward Y. Clarke, embarked on an aggressive membership campaign, sending out "kleagles" who sold membership cards for ten dollars apiece and kept for themselves 40 per cent of the proceeds. By 1924 the Klan had a membership of perhaps 4½ million, most of whom were small farmers, storekeepers, and wage earners. It was elaborately organized into "dominions" headed by "Grand Goblins" and "realms" headed by "King Kleagles." From its headquarters at Atlanta, Georgia, it exercised considerable political power throughout the Black Belt in the South, as well as in Texas, Oklahoma, Ohio, Indiana, Oregon, and California. It was responsible for much intimidation and suppression of persons and activities whom it chose to regard as "un-American." Fortunately for American democracy, the Klan had lost most of its influence before the depression of the thirties.

The same fear of anything new or unusual showed itself in numerous restrictions on cultural and intellectual freedom. There was much censorship of books and plays which were regarded as immoral, particularly in Boston where laws originally enacted by Puritans were now being enforced by Catholics. On several occasions American customs officials made their country ridiculous by refusing to allow the importation of European classics which they held might endanger the morals of American citizens. State legislatures displayed considerable faith in their capacity to make men virtuous and God-fearing by law; and in three Southern states, Tennessee, Oklahoma, and Mississippi, the teaching of the Darwinian theory of evolution in the public schools was prohibited. In the Tennessee town of Dayton a high-school teacher, John Thomas Scopes, defied the law; and in the subsequent trial, which occurred in July, 1925, Clarence Darrow appeared for the defence and William Jennings Bryan for the prosecution. Scopes was convicted, although the Supreme Court of the state later released him on a technicality; and the law remained on the statute books. Bryan's cross-examination by Darrow as to his belief in the Garden of Eden and in Jonah and the whale was his last public appearance, since he died a week after the trial.

PROHIBITION

The most striking example of the American faith in moralistic legislation was the thirteen-year attempt to enforce prohibition. In January, 1920, it became illegal by the Volstead Act to sell liquor containing more than 0.5 per cent alcohol, except for medicinal purposes or as sacramental wine. Enforcement was at first entrusted to the Bureau of Internal Revenue in the Treasury Department, and the prosecution of offenders was handled by the Department of Justice.

The number of Federal prohibition agents was only 1,520 in 1920 and 2,836 in 1930; and, since their salaries were generally lower than $2,000 a year, they were under considerable temptation to increase their incomes illicitly, particularly while Harry Daugherty was Attorney General. These men were expected to police the personal habits of the American people and to enforce a law which perhaps a third of the population had no intention of obeying. To what extent the law actually diminished the consumption of alcohol it is impossible to say. In 1930 the director of the Prohibition Bureau calculated that the domestic production of liquor for sale was about 40 per cent of the figure for 1914, but this did not include smuggling from abroad, the diversion of industrial alcohol and of medicinal and sacramental wines, and home brewing. The law was enforced in some rural areas, but there was probably no city of any size which was not adequately supplied with speak-easies and staffed with bootleggers. The most conspicuous results of the Eighteenth Amendment were to encourage disrespect for the law, increase the revenues of criminals, add a spice of adventure to the consumption of liquor, and strengthen the preference of the American people for hard liquor rather than for beer or wine.

For a period the Anti-Saloon League was strong enough to prevent any public admission of the failure of prohibition by politicians. In 1928, however, Alfred E. Smith advocated repeal, and in 1930 a number of candidates for Congress, notably Dwight Morrow in New Jersey, were bold enough to run as Wets and were elected. President Hoover appointed the Wickersham Commission to consider the problem of crime and law enforcement; and, although the commission as a whole was induced to recommend continuance of prohibition, five of its eleven members came out individually for modification and two for repeal. Opposition to prohibition was further strengthened by the depression; rich men, who feared a rise in the income tax, began to advocate the legalization and taxation of liquor as a revenue measure. In the campaign of 1932 the Democratic platform demanded repeal. Congress voted for repeal in February, 1933, and amended the Volstead Act to allow 3.2 per cent beer in March. By December repeal had been ratified by two-thirds of the states. States which wished to continue Dry were to be protected by the Federal government against the importation of liquor from Wet states; but by 1937 only seven states were still

Dry. Of the remainder, fifteen made the sale of liquor a state monopoly, and twenty-six established central licensing bodies with strict rules which would, it was hoped, prevent any return of the evils of the saloon.

CRITICS OF AMERICAN SOCIETY

American society in the twenties did not lack critics. Never before, in fact, had American intellectuals been so nearly unanimous or so bitter in condemning their environment. Unfortunately their attitude was almost wholly destructive; it encouraged escape or cynical acquiescence rather than effort toward constructive change.

Movements for economic reform or revolution had very little support. A few small groups continued to denounce the capitalist system. The Socialist Party, headed after the death of Debs by Norman Thomas, was still functioning, although seriously weakened by the appearance of the Communist Party. The Communists hopefully prophesied revolution in the near future and won some adherents among metropolitan intellectuals, but they were largely occupied by conflicts among the various factions which aspired to party leadership. These controversies were referred to Moscow which —in 1929—awarded control of the party machinery to the group headed by William Z. Foster and Earl Browder, their rivals being expelled from the party and subsequently declared to be fascistic counter-revolutionaries. But the opposition to capitalism was considerably weaker than before the World War. Business prosperity appeared to be firmly established and likely to continue for an indefinite period; and very few individuals, either conservative or radical, were acute enough to predict the debacle of 1929. There was little comprehension of the real weaknesses of the economic system and, consequently, little attempt to prepare a constructive program which might have been applied in the nineteen-thirties. Many of the intellectual leaders of the Progressive Era—such men as Veblen, Brandeis, Dewey, Beard, Steffens—were still active; but there appeared to be no social critics of comparable weight among the younger generation.

Most critics of the American scene now thought primarily in terms not of politics and economics but of aesthetic experience and

of the life of the individual. American society was no longer de·
nounced because it was insufficiently democratic; some of the more
influential figures of the twenties were, in fact (like H. L.
Mencken), disposed to ascribe its deficiencies to too much democ·
racy. The Americans were now denounced as a people who were
blind to aesthetic values and among whom civilized and cultured
living was impossible. The terms of the indictment were compre·
hensive and emphatic. The United States was a country of dollar-
chasing materialism, of standardized mediocrity, of a repressive
puritanism, and of hypocrisy; it did not understand the values of
aesthetic experience or of leisure or of personal freedom. The ablest
and most plausible statement of these opinions was in the writings
of Van Wyck Brooks; but they first achieved notoriety in *Civilization in the United States,* edited by Harold Stearns and published
in 1922, in which thirty different contributors examined thirty dif·
ferent aspects of American life and found almost all of them un·
satisfactory.

Harold Stearns subsequently fled to Paris, where he was joined by
numerous other refugees from prohibition; while other dissidents
from the civilization of the Coolidge era retired to Majorca, Vienna,
Mexico, or the Pacific islands. Meanwhile this attitude of super·
cilious disgust was popularized and vulgarized by H. L. Mencken,
who founded the *American Mercury* in 1924 and who enjoyed con·
siderable influence, particularly among college undergraduates, un·
til 1927, when he made the mistake of ridiculing the campaign to
save Sacco and Vanzetti. Contempt for almost all that America
stood for continued to be the correct attitude for intellectuals until
almost the middle of the thirties, when the rise of Fascism in Eu·
rope, coupled with a new hopefulness in the United States, caused
a rediscovery of national traditions and ideals.

The flight of the intellectuals from America was in many ways
deplorable; but similar viewpoints expressed themselves, on a higher
plane, in a considerable cultural achievement. The decade of the
twenties was probably the most productive period in literature and
art that the United States had known. And although much of its
work was vitiated by a lack of sympathy and a tendency toward

satire, by a desire to "debunk" ideals and expose the falsity of accepted traditions, and by an ivory-tower aloofness and intellectuality, it produced a number of commentaries on American life which seem likely to have a lasting importance.

BIBLIOGRAPHY

F. L. Allen, *Only Yesterday* (1931)
J. T. Adams, *Our Business Civilization* (1929)
E. S. Bates, *This Land of Liberty* (1930)
*Van Wyck Brooks, *Three Essays on America* (1934)
S. G. Cole, *History of Fundamentalism* (1931)
D. L. Colvin, *Prohibition in the United States* (1926)
M. Ernst and A. Lindey, *The Censor Marches On* (1940)
H. Feldman, *Prohibition: Its Economic and Industrial Aspects* (1930)
I. Fisher, *Prohibition at its Worst* (1926)
W. Frank, *The Rediscovery of America* (1929)
W. E. Garrison, *Intolerance* (1934)
N. Hapgood, *Professional Patriots* (1927)
A. G. Hays, *Let Freedom Ring* (1928)
——— *Trial by Prejudice* (1933)
W. Lippmann, *American Inquisitors* (1928)
*R. S. and H. M. Lynd, *Middletown* (1929)
J. M. Mecklin, *The Ku Klux Klan* (1924)
C. Merz, *The Dry Decade* (1931)
H. Stearns (ed.), *Civilization in the United States* (1922)
A. Siegfried, *America Comes of Age* (1927)
*P. W. Slosson, *The Great Crusade and After* (*History of American Life*, Vol. 12, 1931)
F. Tannenbaum, *Crime and the Community* (1938)

The Thirties

PART FIVE

39

THE DEPRESSION

THE STOCK EXCHANGE

THE factor immediately responsible for the economic depression of the thirties was the bull market of 1927, 1928, and 1929. For nearly three years stock prices had continued to rise, with few interruptions, and a considerable proportion of the American people engaged in speculation on a scale hitherto unprecedented. The stock market no longer existed primarily as a means of providing capital for productive enterprise; it had become a place where men expected to make fortunes by gambling on the prices of stocks. Billions of dollars were diverted from investment into speculation; and stock values, pushed upward by competitive buying, ceased to bear any relation to their real capacity for earning dividends.

Orthodox economists attributed this phenomenon to the easy-money policy pursued by the Federal Reserve Board, and particularly to its lowering of the rediscount rate in 1927. Winthrop W. Aldrich, Chairman of the Board of the Chase National Bank, declared in 1938: "The real trouble in 1928 and 1929 was, I believe, . . . an excess of bank credit going into capital uses and speculative uses due to the cheap money policies of the Federal Reserve System during the nineteen-twenties. When a prolonged period of artificially cheap money generates a volume of bank credit which outruns the needs of commerce and industry and runs over on a grand scale into capital and speculative uses, we inevitably lay the foundation for a crisis and depression, because we inevitably create a situation in which debt outruns production."

The Federal Reserve System had lowered its rediscount rate at the request of European bankers, who wished to check the drain of gold from Europe to America; but its failure to abandon the easy-money policy the following year was due chiefly to pressure from the financial community in New York, many of whose leading members were making enormous profits through the rise in stock prices. As a result, it was too late before the Board raised its rediscount rate. For the same reason President Coolidge and Secretary Mellon failed to take any action to discourage speculation. Coolidge, in fact, declared early in 1928 that in his opinion brokers' loans were not too large.

While conservative financiers thus blamed the Federal Reserve System, and by inference the Federal government, other observers attributed the bull market to more fundamental causes. They argued that it was due to an excess of capital savings, which—as a result of the restricted purchasing power of workers and farmers—could find no outlet in productive investment.

The number of persons interested in the stock exchange in 1928 and 1929 probably ran into the millions. The profits to be derived from stock speculation were widely and vigorously publicized by many of the leading bankers, who were themselves engaged in speculation but who omitted to point out that when the inevitable crash occurred it would be the individuals without inside knowledge who would take most of the losses. The National City Company, for example, an affiliate of the National City Bank, combed the whole of the United States for possible buyers of stocks. It divided the country into seventy districts, used contests to stimulate its salesmen to sell more stocks, and made use of eleven thousand miles of private telegraph wires. Many members of the general public were induced to put their savings into Wall Street through the medium of investment trusts, which conducted speculative operations on a large scale.

Between January and September of 1929 investment trusts sold to the public more than 2 billion dollars' worth of their own securities. Many small speculators were, moreover, buying on margin.

Buying on margin meant that the speculator would pay only a small part of the price of his stocks and would borrow the remainder from his broker. The broker, in turn, would borrow from the bank, leaving the speculator's stocks as collateral. This practice greatly increased the instability of the financial system, since a fall in the value of stocks would compel the banks to demand additional collateral or payment of the brokers' loans. This, in turn, would cause the brokers to sell their customers' stocks for whatever they would fetch in order to cover themselves. By September, 1929, loans to brokers totaled more than 8½ billion dollars.

In March, 1929, the Federal Reserve Board put pressure on the banks to limit brokers' loans. This action, which would tend to check speculation and thereby to prevent stock prices from continuing to rise, was bitterly resented by some of the New York bankers; and Charles Mitchell, Chairman of the Board of the National City Bank, promptly declared that his bank would increase its loans to brokers by 25 million dollars. Many industrial corporations were, moreover, pouring their savings into Wall Street, and these reserves of money could not be controlled by the Federal Reserve System. In August the Board raised its rediscount rate from 5 to 6 per cent, thus curtailing the supply of bank credit. This action was, however, too late to prevent the crisis.

By this date there were already indications of a coming depression. Building had fallen off in 1928; production was now beginning to decline in the steel and automobile industries. Stock prices reached their peak in September and then showed a tendency to fall. Since, however, so many persons had bought stocks which they could not afford in the expectation of selling them at a profit, any gradual decline of prices was impossible. As soon as it became obvious that the bull market had ended, there would be a frenzied rush to sell. October 19 was the first bad day; but the real break came on the morning of October 24, when nearly 13 million shares were traded. In the afternoon a group of bankers endeavored to restore confidence by buying stocks at more than their market prices, and it was believed that the situation had been saved. On October 29, however, came another and even more acute crisis; 16½ million shares were traded, and the bankers abandoned all hope of checking the stampede. Stock prices dropped in some cases as much as 80 per cent below their September levels; no buyers at all could be found for many of them; and hundreds of thousands of margin accounts were liquidated.

Subsequently the stock market coasted slowly downward for two and a half years, with occasional brief rises which were not maintained. In September, 1929, the stock market index of *The New York Times* had stood at 311.90; by July, 1932, it had dropped to 34.43.

STATISTICS OF THE DEPRESSION

The break in the stock market meant only a decline in paper values which did not directly affect the productive capacity of American industry and agriculture; the real wealth of the American people was as great in November, 1929, as it had been in September. It was therefore believed by President Hoover and by the majority of the American people that the economic system would quickly adjust itself and that prosperity would continue. Actually, however, what had happened on Wall Street put in motion a chain of events which was to cause the greatest depression in American history. Real wealth had not diminished, but paper wealth had decreased by about 30 billion dollars. In other words, the American people were to that extent poorer in terms of money values in November, 1929, than they had supposed themselves to be in September. The consequence was that they began to limit their purchases of new goods, particularly of the durable goods which had played such an important role in maintaining prosperity throughout the twenties. Moreover, because of both lack of capital and lack of confidence, businessmen began to invest less money than formerly in industrial expansion. The result was that production of capital goods and durable consumption goods declined; workers in these industries were unemployed; and the growth of unemployment caused further contractions of purchasing power, which led in a vicious cycle to still more unemployment. After the stock market crash, the economic system could have righted itself only through a reduction in all other monetary values, including prices and debts, in proportion to the decrease in stock prices. That, however, was impossible.

The country did not feel the full effects of the crash for several years. Economic conditions slowly deteriorated during 1930 and the early months of 1931, but by the summer of that year many people believed that the corner had been turned. What had happened on Wall Street had, however, caused repercussions in Europe, which reacted back upon the United States. The cessation of American loans and the decline of American foreign trade, coupled with the intrinsic weaknesses of the European economic system due to the war, led in the summer of 1931 to the collapse of central Europe—an event which was to bring about the emergence of the Nazi dictatorship. From Austria and Germany the chain of disaster then spread to Great Britain and returned to the United States. According to President Hoover, "there came to us a concatenation of catastrophes from abroad such as we have not experienced in the whole of our economic history." The lowest point of the depression was not reached until July, 1932. Then after a slight recovery in the autumn, the trend turned downward again until March, 1933.

The production of national income decreased from $82,691,-000,000 in 1929 to $40,089,000,000 in 1932, and the total output of goods decreased by 37 per cent. The decrease of production was very much greater in industry than in agriculture. Agricultural production declined by only 6 per cent; industrial production, on the other hand, declined by 48 per cent. The decline in construction was 86 per cent.

The total income of labor decreased between 1929 and 1932 by 40 per cent. The number of unemployed in March, 1933, was variously estimated at between 12 and 15 million. Factory employment fell off by 38 per cent. Although the reductions in hourly wage rates were relatively small and were more than counterbalanced by the fall in prices, a considerable number of the workers still in employment were working on a part-time basis. The real wages of

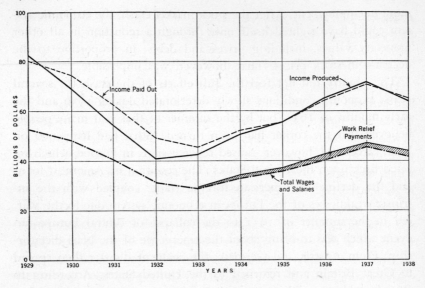

Figure 10. NATIONAL INCOME, WAGES, AND SALARIES DURING THE
DEPRESSION

the average employed wage earner decreased by about 16 per cent. In 1929 industry had paid $10,909,000,000 in wages; in 1932 it paid only $4,608,000,000. Meanwhile the farmers had suffered from a sharp drop in farm prices, which were 61 per cent lower in 1933 than in 1929. Farm incomes in 1929 totaled about $12,791,-000,000; in 1932 they amounted to $5,562,000,000. In March, 1933, the purchasing power of the farmers was exactly half what it had been ten years before.

The total incomes from property decreased between 1929 and 1932 by 31 per cent. In 1929, 269,400 corporations had reported profits, and 186,600 corporations reported deficits; the net profits of all corporate enterprise had totaled $8,740,000,000. In 1932 only 82,600 corporations reported profits, whereas 369,200 corporations reported deficits. The net deficits of all corporate enterprise amounted to $5,640,000,000. The number of bank failures in

1930, 1931, and 1932 was 4,377, involving deposits totaling $2,752,000,000.

REASONS FOR THE SEVERITY OF THE DEPRESSION

For more than a hundred years the American economic system had suffered from periodic depressions, which had always been followed by a return of prosperity. Recovery, moreover, had been due to economic causes and not to any action taken by the American government. For a number of reasons, however, the depression which began in 1929 was exceptionally acute, and recovery was so long delayed that the American people finally insisted that the government intervene.

In the first place, the expansion of the capital and durable goods industries in the twenties had been on a wholly unprecedented scale. By 1929 the supply of factories, machinery, office buildings, automobiles, and other durable goods appears to have been out of all proportion to the effective purchasing power of the nation's consumers. The result was that the revival of these industries was exceptionally slow. Many observers, indeed, doubted whether any revival was possible without government intervention.

In the second place, the price-fixing policies of the big corporations meant that in the capital and durable goods industries prices remained high, while production and employment were drastically reduced. In agriculture and in the more competitive consumption goods industries, on the other hand, prices were reduced while production was maintained. According to Gardiner C. Means, "the whole depression might be described as a general dropping of prices at the flexible end of the price scale and a dropping of production at the rigid end with intermediate effects between." With the exception of the railroads, most of the large corporations continued to make profits, though on a reduced scale, all through the depression. Their policy of maintaining prices, however, tended to delay any real recovery in the capital goods industries, while their drastic reduction of employment prolonged the depression by decreasing consumer purchasing power. Means illustrates his statement by the following figures, showing percentage decreases in prices and production between 1929 and the spring of 1933.

	FALL IN PRICES	FALL IN PRODUCTION
Agricultural implements	6%	80%
Motor vehicles	16	80
Cement	18	65
Iron and steel	20	83
Textile products	45	30
Food products	49	14
Leather	50	20
Agricultural commodities	63	6

Price maintenance was particularly conspicuous in the case of certain mineral products. Throughout the depression nickel remained at 35 cents a pound; sulfur remained at $18 a ton, its leading producer, Texas Gulf, making a 50 per cent profit on every sale; aluminum sold for 24 cents a pound in 1929 and 23 cents in 1932. The effects of price fixing on a consumption goods industry are illustrated in the case of cigarettes. By maintaining prices and taking advantage of decreased costs of production, the seven leading cigarette corporations were able to increase their profits from 85 million dollars in 1929 to 105 million dollars in 1932.

In the third place the depression deprived American industry of many of its foreign markets. In 1929 American exports had a total value of $5,240,995,000; by 1932 the value had decreased to $1,611,016,000. Recovery of these foreign outlets for American surpluses proved to be impossible. Much of the American export trade before 1929 had been financed by American loans; since, however, many of these loans went into default during the depression, American investors were unwilling to continue foreign lending. Other nations, moreover, began to raise tariff barriers, to adopt import quota systems, and to adopt policies of economic nationalism, partly in retaliation for the Smoot-Hawley Tariff and partly in the hope of shielding their own industries from the force of the world depression.

In the fourth place, the severity of the depression was increased by the extraordinarily intricate system of debt obligations. Interest payments which could be handled easily in 1929 were a crushing burden in the deflationary conditions of 1932; and these payments could not be scaled down except through bankruptcies. In the early stages of the depression the share of the national income going to the creditor classes was increased, which meant that the purchasing power of the remainder of the population was proportionately reduced. In 1930 the total amount of interest and dividend payments was actually greater than in 1929. Even in 1932 interest payments (though not dividend payments) were only 3.5 per cent less than in 1929. And when defaults and bankruptcies began, they threatened to spread so widely and to involve so many institutions in a common ruin, that even the government of President Hoover, which professed to believe in laissez-faire principles, was compelled to intervene. Rather than allow economic mechanisms to take their natural course, the government began to give support to the financial structure. Such an intervention moderated the severity of the depression; but by preventing debt obligations from being wiped out, it probably delayed any genuine recovery.

HUMAN EFFECTS OF THE DEPRESSION

Statistics chart the growth of the depression; but they only hint at the extraordinary misery and suffering that it caused—the widespread malnutrition; the deprivation of savings, homes, and properties; and the loss of self-respect on the part of men who found themselves unemployed and dependent on charity.

The total of human misery was slowly growing through 1930, 1931, and 1932. For about a year after the stock market crash, although unemployment was steadily increasing, no unusual measures were taken to meet the crisis. Private charity was considered to be adequate for feeding the unemployed. The autumn of 1930, however, brought the first catastrophic bank failures—the failure in November of the brokerage house of Caldwell and Company in Nashville, Tennessee, which carried down with it 129 banks; and the failure of the Bank of the United States in New York in December. In Arkansas, moreover, the man-made crisis of the depression was coupled with a severe drought which brought many thousands of farmers to the verge of starvation. During the winter of 1930–1931 most of the city governments were giving direct relief, and unemployed persons selling apples at street corners became a familiar sight.

By the summer of 1931 New York, Chicago, Philadelphia, Detroit, and Boston were all close to bankruptcy. Compelled to borrow from large financiers in order to continue paying relief, they were, in return, required to reduce payments to a minimum. Detroit, for example, was able to obtain funds from the automobile corporations only on condition that relief be limited to 7½ cents a day for each individual. Thousands of the unemployed began to build themselves huts out of refuse timber on vacant city lots. These colonies became known ironically as "Hoovervilles." Thousands of others were drifting about the country, walking the roads and taking possession of railroad box cars in such numbers that the railroad detectives were unable to eject them. In Pennsylvania and Kentucky hundreds of thousands of bituminous coal miners went on strike against starvation wages; conditions of virtual civil war prevailed; and the miners and their families lived on payments averaging 4 cents a day per person which were contributed by the Socialist Relief Fund.

By the end of 1931 the resources of private charity and of the city governments were almost exhausted, and most of the state governments had been compelled to appropriate money for relief. The year 1932 brought new financial disasters: the suicide of Ivar Kreuger, the Swedish match king, in March, and the subsequent discovery that the company of Kreuger and Toll, to which American investors had contributed 250 million dollars, was nothing but a gigantic fraud; the break-up of the Insull public utilities empire with its 150 interlocked corporations; and more epidemics of bank failures which threatened by the end of the year to engulf even the strongest institutions in the country. By September, 1932, it was estimated that the total number of unemployed was about 13 million, that 1 million of them were living in Hoovervilles, and that nearly 2 million more, including 200,000 children, had become homeless migrants. Another large body of unemployed had returned to the land and were endeavoring to support themselves by subsistence agriculture. During the depression the number of farmers increased by more than half a million. Moreover, 154 different organizations in twenty-nine states had established barter and scrip systems, under which unemployed persons, having virtually seceded from the established economic system, exchanged the products of their labor with one another without the use of legal money. One such system, in California, had 200,000 members; another, in Minneapolis, included factories, restaurants, and stores.

Probably the most remarkable feature of the depression was the docility with which most of its victims accepted their fate. The depression had been caused by the mechanisms of society and not by the forces of nature; the families who lived on the verge of starvation were surrounded by plenty. Yet throughout the depression the American people displayed an extraordinary respect for law, order, and the established rights of property. Only on three or four occasions was there any organized resort to violence. In July, 1931, the starving farmers of Arkansas seized food from the local storekeepers. Later in the year there were demonstrations of unemployed workers outside the Ford plant at Dearborn, Michigan, which ended in a riot and the killing of four men by the police. In August, 1932, a National Farmers' Holiday Association, headed by Milo Reno, was organized in Iowa, with the purpose of raising prices by preventing farm products from being shipped into the cities. For about a month farmers in Iowa barricaded roads and forcibly held up shipments. Finally, in January, 1933, opposition to mortgage and tax foreclosure sales developed on a large scale throughout the middle western farm belt. Farmers forcibly prevented courts from hearing foreclosure cases or saw to it that the foreclosed land and chattels were sold for trifling sums and subsequently returned to their original owners. This technique, reminiscent of Shays' Rebellion 150 years before, proved to be successful; and state governors finally intervened to prevent further sales. These, along with the Pennsylvania coal strike, appear to have been the only cases of organized resistance to the workings of the economic system. In the larger cities labor conflicts were conspicuous by their absence.

POLITICAL REPERCUSSIONS

In the European countries the depression caused a rapid growth of Communist and Fascist parties; it destroyed democracy in Germany and Austria, and seriously weakened it elsewhere. No such development, however, was visible in the United States. Most Americans remained faithful to the traditional two-party system, and the only considerable shift of sentiment was from the Republicans to the Democrats.

The Socialist Party made gains, but, in spite of the able leadership of Norman Thomas, its voting strength remained smaller than it had been in 1912 and 1920. A growing number of litterateurs became converts to Communism. The Soviet Union at this period was apparently undergoing a rapid economic development; and the much-advertised triumphs of its Five Year Plan seemed to present a startling contrast to the chaotic conditions which prevailed in the United States. But although books in defense of Communism began to appear in considerable numbers, and the probability of a proletarian revolution became a favorite subject of conversation in middleclass intellectual and university circles, particularly in New York, the Communist Party continued to be a small and weak organization with very few working-class supporters. Its membership increased from 7,545 in 1930 to 25,000 in 1934. It organized a number of unemployed demonstrations and hunger marches, but such importance as it seemed to have was due chiefly to the excessive precautions which were taken to check its activities by the police authorities, especially in New York City and in the District of Columbia. A number of fascistic organizations also appeared, especially in the South. The best-known of these was William Dudley Pelley's Silver Shirts. But these groups were apparently as weak as the Communists.

The depression did, however, produce three movements of greater importance. These were at first purely American in their inspiration and ideals, but to many observers they began to present alarming analogies to the Fascist parties of Europe. They were the three movements headed respectively by Senator Huey Long, Dr. Francis E. Townsend, and Father Coughlin.

Huey Long, born in 1893, was elected governor of Louisiana in

1928 and entered the Senate in 1930. He established a totalitarian dictatorship over the State of Louisiana, of a kind unprecedented in the annals of American government; but he used his power not only for the benefit of himself and his friends but also to increase corporation taxes and to give the farmers of Louisiana better schools and an excellent system of roads. During the depression he became a vitriolic enemy of high finance, and he began to build a broad popular organization for the redistribution of property, with the slogans of "Share Our Wealth" and "Every Man A King." With his flamboyant personality, his inordinate ambition, his great ability for politics and mob oratory, and his apparently genuine egalitarian idealism, he combined the characteristics of an old-fashioned Populist leader with those of a Caribbean dictator. He was assassinated in the Louisiana state capitol at Baton Rouge in the summer of 1935; and both his "Share Our Wealth" movement, leadership of which was assumed by Gerald Smith, and his Louisiana political machine disintegrated after his death.

Dr. Townsend, a leader of a very different type, was at the outset of the depression a retired physician living at Long Beach, California. The incident which is said to have stimulated him to become a political crusader was the spectacle of three elderly women searching a garbage can for food. He declared that all persons past the age of sixty ought to receive a pension of $200 a month raised by means of a sales tax. In order to increase purchasing power and stimulate industry, the pensioners were to be required to spend their pensions immediately. The Townsend pension plan was regarded as impracticable by competent economists; but the simplicity of the proposal, coupled with the sincerity and the apostolic zeal of Dr. Townsend himself and the political cleverness of some of his associates, won for it wide popular support. Millions of persons signed petitions in support of the plan; and by organizing themselves as a pressure group and voting for congressmen who were willing to promise them assistance, the Townsendites soon developed into a formidable political force.

Father Coughlin was a Canadian-born Irish Catholic priest, who was attached to the Shrine of the Little Flower at Royal Oak, Michi-

gan. He began to deliver radio addresses on religious subjects in
the twenties, and during the depression he turned to politics. His
highly emotional radio oratory won for him a large audience, including Protestants as well as Catholics. The reforms which he advocated were derived partly from the papal encyclicals and partly
from the traditions of American Populism. He denounced the Wall
Street financiers, demanded government control over banking, and
called for inflation by means of the coinage of silver. During the
Roosevelt administration, however, he gradually abandoned the liberal elements in his program and developed red-baiting and anti-
Semitism with marked Nazi sympathies. The extent of his influence
is difficult to estimate; but it undoubtedly constitutes a dangerous
menace to American democratic traditions.

BIBLIOGRAPHY

F. L. Allen, *Since Yesterday* (1940)
G. Adams, *Workers on Relief* (1939)
L. V. Armstrong, *We Too Are the People* (1938)
*C. A. Beard, *America in Midpassage* (1939)
C. A. Beard (ed.), *America Faces the Future* (1932)
A. M. Bingham, *Insurgent America* (1935)
M. Davis, *The Lost Generation* (1936)
*L. Hacker, *American Problems of Today* (1938)
M. Hallgren, *Seeds of Revolt* (1933)
J. N. Leonard, *Three Years Down* (1939)
*R. S. Lynd, *Middletown in Transition* (1937)
G. C. Means, *Industrial Prices and their Relative Inflexibility* (1935)
J. Rorty, *Where Life is Better* (1936)
G. Seldes, *Years of the Locust* (1933)
R. G. Swing, *Forerunners of American Fascism* (1935)
The Unofficial Observer, *American Messiahs* (1935)
T. J. Woofter and E. Winston, *Seven Lean Years* (1939)

40

THE HOOVER ADMINISTRATION

PRESIDENT HOOVER

HERBERT HOOVER, who became President seven and a half months before the beginning of the depression, took office with a great reputation for administrative efficiency and humanitarian sympathies, which he had earned by his work as supervisor of Belgian relief, as food controller during the war, and as Secretary of Commerce. He left office four years later with a larger body of more bitter opponents than any previous President since Andrew Johnson. This unpopularity may be regarded as Hoover's misfortune rather than his fault; but there is no doubt that he lacked certain of the qualities needed for the position to which he had been elected. Hardworking and widely experienced, with a remarkable grasp of detail and a strong sense of the dignity of the presidential office, he had little ability to work with people, to conciliate opponents, or to win popularity. Having spent most of his early life as a mining engineer in the Far East and in Europe, and having never been elected to any office previous to the presidency, he was tragically lacking in practical experience of American politics. He found it difficult to secure co-operation from Congress—a fact which became obvious immediately after his accession to office, during the debates on the Smoot-Hawley Tariff. Nor could he successfully dramatize his personality and his program in such a way as to obtain popular support. It soon became apparent that opposition was apt to make him irritated and resentful.

Hoover was, moreover, a strong believer in the American system of individualistic capitalism, as it had operated in the nineteen-twenties. He believed that government should assist business and should avoid any measures tending toward socialism or toward bureaucratic control. He was convinced that if unemployed or needy persons acquired the habit of expecting financial assistance from the Federal government, the American system would soon be destroyed. He was therefore sternly opposed to any grants of direct relief by the Federal government. Unemployed persons must be supported by private charity or by the local governments. "The moment responsibilities of any community, particularly in economic and social questions, are shifted from any part of the nation to Washington," he declared on February 12, 1931, "then that community has subjected itself to a remote bureaucracy. . . . It has lost a large part of its voice in the control of its own destiny. . . . Where people divest themselves of local government responsibilities they at once lay the foundations for destruction of their liberties. . . . At once when the government is centralized there arises a limitation upon the liberty of the individual and a restriction of individual opportunity . . . (which) can lead but to the superstate where every man becomes the servant of the State and real liberty is lost." Hoover's faith in "rugged individualism" and in voluntary co-operation was the expression of a clearly integrated philosophy of government; and to persist in such a position during the depression years required considerable courage. But such an attitude, whatever merits it may have had, inevitably caused him to be regarded as callously indifferent to human suffering and unaware of the realities of the crisis.

THE FIRST TWO YEARS

For nearly two years after the Wall Street debacle Hoover appears to have taken the view that the economic system would quickly adjust itself without large-scale government action. The chief thing needed, he felt, was a revival of confidence. In the autumn and winter of 1929–1930 the Federal Reserve System lowered the rediscount rate to 4½ per cent, and made possible a credit expansion of $500,000,000; the Farm Board set up under the Agricultural Marketing Act took action to keep agricultural surpluses off the market; and Hoover increased government expenditure on public works.

The total Federal spendings on public works, which had averaged $275,000,000 a year before the depression, amounted to $410,420,-141 in 1930, $574,874,107 in 1931, and $670,299,000 in 1932. The number of persons employed increased from 180,000 in 1929 to 760,000 in 1932. The most important piece of construction undertaken under this program was the building of a dam at Boulder City on the Colorado River. Hoover also called several conferences of business leaders, at which he urged them not to reduce wages and to undertake capital expansion. Business carried out the Hoover program to the extent of making no serious wage cuts until the autumn of 1931; but it was unable to undertake expansion, nor was anything done to check the growth of unemployment. In 1930 Hoover appointed Colonel Woods to supervise the collection of money for relief; Woods was succeeded in 1931 by Walter S. Gifford, and in 1932 by Fred C. Croxton.

Otherwise Hoover's chief activity during the first two years of the depression was the making of reassuring statements designed to restore business confidence. Unfortunately the causes of the depression were not merely psychological, and the constant reiteration by members of the administration that prosperity was just around the corner soon began to seem ridiculous. Senator Fess, complaining that "every time an administration official gives out an optimistic statement about business conditions the market immediately drops," even suggested that there must be a Wall Street plot to discredit President Hoover by prolonging the depression.

Meanwhile the Arkansas drought provoked the first of many conflicts between the President and Congress on the question of relief. In December, 1930, Hoover asked Congress to vote $45,000,000 to save the animals of the Arkansas farmers, but he insisted that none of the money be used to provide food for human beings, who were to be assisted by such private organizations as the Red Cross. When members of the Senate urged government aid for men as well as for animals, Hoover replied that they were "playing politics at the expense of human misery." Eventually Congress compromised by voting an additional $20,000,000 to feed the farmers, but stipulated that this money was to be a loan and not a gift. In approving of this measure Hoover declared that for the Federal government to give money for relief "would have injured the spiritual responses of the American people." "We are dealing with the intangibles of life and ideals. . . . A voluntary deed is infinitely more precious to our national ideals and spirit than a thousandfold poured from the Treasury."

HOOVER TAKES ACTION

The thesis of the administration was that during the summer of 1931 the American economic system was beginning to recover but that the depression was subsequently prolonged by catastrophes abroad. In May of that year the financial structure of central Europe began to crumble. From this date on Hoover began to act vigorously and quickly.

His first measure, taken on June 20, was to recommend a moratorium on all payments of war debts and reparations. This proposal was designed to save Austria and Germany from financial collapse and to protect the large investments of American and British financiers in those countries. Private debts were to have precedence over government debts. Unfortunately the French government, still hostile to Germany and indignant over a proposed customs union of Germany and Austria, delayed acceptance until July 23, by which time it was too late to prevent financial disaster. Catastrophe spread throughout central Europe, and from it emerged, eighteen months later, the Nazi dictatorship.

In the autumn of 1931 Hoover began to put into effect a program for ending the depression. He proposed to give financial aid to business institutions, particularly banks and railroads; to refinance mortgages on farms and houses in order to check foreclosures; to increase the volume of money in circulation; and to balance the Federal budget by reducing expenditures and increasing taxes. Unfortunately for him the Democrats had made considerable gains in the congressional elections of 1930, and the two parties were now almost equal in both houses. Since a number of the Republicans were western Progressives, the opponents of the administration were in the majority. Democrats and Progressives criticized Hoover's program of pouring in money at the top of the economic system, and they demanded that it be distributed instead among the unemployed workers at the bottom, whose needs were more desperate. Some of Hoover's opponents were not averse to playing politics with the situation in order to improve the chances of the Democratic Party in the 1932 election. There were, therefore, a series of conflicts between President and Congress, and it was a number of months before Hoover's recommendations were put into effect.

In December, 1931, the National Credit Corporation was organized with a capital of $500,000,000, which was subscribed by large banks and designed to aid small banks in danger of failure. In January, 1932, Congress established the Reconstruction Finance Corporation, which was to loan money to banks, railroads, and other institutions. The corporation was to have a capital of $2,000,000,000, subscribed by the Federal government, which was increased by an additional $1,500,000,000 in July. In February was passed the Glass-Steagall Bill, which liberalized the discount requirements of the Federal Reserve System and would make possible an extension of bank credit amounting to $2,500,000,000. Meanwhile the Federal Land Banks had been given $125,000,000 for the refinancing of farm mortgages. In April, in order to offset a decrease in Federal revenue amounting to about $2,000,000,000, taxes were increased to provide an additional revenue of $1,000,000,000; the income tax exemption was reduced to $1,000 for single persons and $2,500 for married persons, and the initial tax was increased to 2 per cent. Congress also authorized Federal economies of about $300,000,000. These figures meant a deficit for 1932 of $2,685,000,000, and a total deficit for the Hoover administration of $3,593,500,762, against which could be set recoverable loans made by the R. F. C. amounting to about $2,500,000,000. In July Congress passed the Federal Home Loan Bank Bill, authorizing the establishment of twelve banks with a total capital of $125,000,000 for the relief of home owners in danger of foreclosure. Congress also authorized the R. F. C. to lend $300,000,000 to the states for relief. Hoover opposed various proposals by Democrats and Progressives to vote up to $2,000,000,000 of Federal money for direct relief or for public works. All these proposals were either defeated in Congress or killed by presidential veto. Hoover described proposals of this kind as "the most gigantic pork barrel ever proposed to the American congress" and as "an unexampled raid on the public treasury."

Meanwhile the veterans of the World War had been demanding immediate payment in full of the bonus which had been voted them in 1924. In February, 1931, Congress had passed over Hoover's veto a bill allowing them to borrow up to 50 per cent of the value of the bonus, but on June 17 it defeated a proposal for immediate payment in full. About 20,000 unemployed veterans, who called themselves the Bonus Expeditionary Force and who were headed by Walter W. Waters, had come to Washington to agitate for payment. After Congress rejected their demand, between 8,000 and 9,000 of them, having no other place to go, stayed in Washington, living in shacks on an empty lot on Pennsylvania Avenue and in Anacostia Park. After insinuating that many of these veterans were criminals or Communists—accusations which were totally untrue— the authorities decided to eject them from the city. This operation was accomplished on July 28. After the police had met with some resistance, during which two of the veterans were killed, the ejection was completed by General Douglas MacArthur, Chief of Staff of the United States army, who called out four troops of cavalry, four companies of infantry, a machine gun squadron, and six tanks. The veterans were expelled by means of drawn sabres, bayonets, and tear-gas bombs; and then their encampment was burned. Probably no incident of the Hoover administration contributed more to make the President unpopular or to reveal his profound misunderstanding of the psychology of the American people.

THE ELECTION OF 1932

For the presidential election of the autumn the Republican Party renominated Hoover and Curtis. The leading contender for the Democratic nomination was Governor Franklin D. Roosevelt of New York, his chief rivals being John Garner, of Texas, Speaker of the House of Representatives since 1931, and Alfred E. Smith. An agreement between the Roosevelt and Garner forces gave Roosevelt the presidential nomination on the fourth ballot, while Garner was subsequently nominated for the vice presidency. The Democratic platform was mainly a conservative document, which promised— among other things—a balanced budget, a 25 per cent reduction in government expenditures, a sound currency, and no government interference with private enterprise. It included also, however, demands for regulation of the stock exchanges, Federal supervision of power companies, enforcement of antitrust laws, and a restoration of international trade by reciprocal tariff agreements. It promised in vague terms that Federal money should be appropriated for relief and public works and that farm surpluses should be controlled.

During the campaign Hoover argued that the chief causes of the depression were world conditions over which the American government had no control and that the measures which he had adopted would now bring about a rapid recovery. A short-lived upswing on the stock market during the summer seemed to give some support to this assertion; and when stock prices turned down again in the fall, it was argued by Republicans that this was due to fears of a Democratic victory.

Since a Democratic victory was almost a foregone conclusion, Roosevelt's chief task during the campaign was to avoid making any damaging mistakes. In his speeches he gave expression to the main principles of what afterwards became the New Deal, but in such vague and general phraseology that it was difficult for his opponents to attack them. Only once, in a speech at San Francisco in which he declared that the epoch of rapid business expansion had ended and that the task now to be undertaken was to solve the problem of underconsumption, did he make any statement which could be denounced as radical. Only once, on the other hand, in a speech at Pittsburgh, in which he denounced Hoover's failure to balance the budget, did he say anything which he afterwards had cause to regret. The result of these cautious tactics was an overwhelming victory. Roosevelt won a popular vote of 22,821,857 and an electoral vote of 472. Hoover, with a popular vote of 15,761,841, carried only the eight states of Maine, New Hampshire, Vermont, Connecticut, Pennsylvania, and Delaware, having an electoral vote of 59. Of the minor candidates Norman Thomas, for the Socialists, had a vote of 884,781; William Z. Foster, for the Communists, had a vote of 102,991.

The election was followed by a deterioration of financial conditions which threatened finally to ruin every bank in the country. Republicans ascribed this development to a fear lest the coming Democratic administration adopt an unsound money policy, as well as to the refusal of the Democratic Congress to adopt Hoover's proposals for banking reform. Democrats pointed out, on the other hand, that there were good reasons for believing that many of the banks genuinely were unsound. Since the start of the depression 18 per cent of the banks in the country had already failed, although most of them had been small institutions in western and southern farming communities. In January, 1933, it became known that total bank resources had decreased from $74,000,000,000 in 1930 to $57,000,000,000 in June, 1932, and that during 1931 and 1932 bank deposits had decreased by $12,000,000,000. In February it was revealed that the Reconstruction Finance Corporation had made large loans to a number of banks. For nearly a year, moreover, the Senate Committee on Banking and Currency had been conducting inquiries into banking practices during the boom and had brought to light a number of astonishing cases of dishonesty and unscrupulousness on the part of leading New York financiers. The public had, therefore, good reasons for distrusting the banks, and began to remove their deposits in such quantities that the state governments were compelled to intervene. On February 14 Michigan decreed a bank holiday, and other states quickly followed this example. By March 4, when the new administration took office, every bank in the entire country was closed.

BIBLIOGRAPHY

R. S. Allen, *Washington Merry-go-round* (1931)
*C. A. Beard, *America in Midpassage* (1939)
W. Irwin, *Herbert Hoover* (1928)

R. Moley, *After Seven Years* (1939)
W. S. Myers, *State Papers of Herbert Hoover* (1934)
W. S. Myers and W. H. Newton, *The Hoover Administration* (1936)
R. V. Peel and T. C. Donnelly, *The 1932 Campaign* (1935)
R. G. Tugwell, *Mr. Hoover's Economic Policy* (1932)
R. L. Wilbur and A. M. Hyde, *The Hoover Policies* (1937)

41

THE NEW DEAL

PERSONNEL OF THE NEW DEAL

FRANKLIN DELANO ROOSEVELT came from an old New York patrician family, distantly related to that of President Theodore Roosevelt. Born in 1882, he had been educated at Groton and Harvard, had been elected to the New York State Senate in 1910, had served as Assistant Secretary of the Navy from 1913 until 1920, and had been Democratic candidate for the vice presidency in 1920. Attacked by infantile paralysis in 1921, he had remained in retirement until 1928, when he had accepted the Democratic nomination for the governorship of New York in order to assist Smith in his campaign for the presidency. Elected governor, and re-elected in 1930, he had advocated public ownership of power sites and had been the first state governor to secure the appropriation of money for relief during the depression. For these reasons he was regarded as a Progressive. Few people, however, expected that as President he would display any unusual talents or adopt any very novel policies.

The Roosevelt administration, nevertheless, was to enact legislation of an importance and a variety that had been equaled by none of its predecessors, and its leader was to inspire both admiration and hatred of an intensity almost without precedent in American history. Any balanced judgment of its achievements and deficiencies must be left to posterity. However, Roosevelt's remarkable political ability, as exhibited in his capacity to win popular approval and to understand and respond to popular sentiment, may be granted without dispute. Likewise, it may be granted that he had a warm sympathy for the underprivileged and a desire to improve their condition; that he displayed courage, persistence, and a willingness to make innovations and to abandon doctrines and practices which he believed to be no longer valuable; and that in his numerous public addresses he showed an awareness of national and international problems which was unusual both for its penetration and for its comprehensiveness. His friends held that these qualities ranked him among the greatest of American presidents. His enemies, on the other hand, declared that he was too eager for personal power, that he made political stability and economic recovery impossible by constant changes in his methods and tactics, and that in the execution of his policies he showed himself a careless and incompetent administrator and a poor judge of men.

There was equal disagreement as to the objectives of the Roosevelt administration. The heir of pre-war Progressivism, Roosevelt himself wished to preserve and strengthen the American system of political democracy and of private capitalistic enterprise. He believed, however, that it was now necessary for the government to intervene in economic processes and to enforce new methods upon capitalistic industry and finance. He became President at the time when the Nazi dictatorship was being established in Germany; and he was convinced that unless capitalist democracy in the United States could reform itself, it would eventually be either overthrown by revolution or replaced by dictatorship. Roosevelt's enemies, however, insisted that he was bringing about the very thing which he wished to avoid: that in attempting to reform the economic system, he was depriving it of its freedom and subjecting it to bureaucratic control; and that in trying to save democracy by government action, he was laying the foundations of dictatorship.

As head of the Democratic Party Roosevelt endeavored to work in co-operation with the Democratic leaders in Congress. Like Theodore Roosevelt and Woodrow Wilson, however, he greatly extended presidential authority; and most of the legislation of the New Deal originated in the executive rather than in the legislative department of the government. Many of the Democrats in Congress, moreover, were unsympathetic to the more radical aspects of the New Deal.

Much of the voting strength of the party came from the South; and, while some of the Southern Democrats were the spokesmen of workers and tenant farmers, there were a number who represented the interests of landlords and industrialists and were likely to rebel against some of Roosevelt's proposals. In the North the Democratic organization consisted partly of corrupt city machines, such as those in New York, Chicago, Boston, Jersey City, and Kansas City, and partly of conservative elements with Wall Street connections. While the city machines continued to support the New Deal for purely partisan reasons, many of the conservative Democrats became its outspoken opponents. The most genuine adherents of the New Deal were, for the most part, outside the Democratic Party organization. They included the trade unions, the bulk of the farm population, many Progressive Republicans who had supported Theodore Roosevelt in 1912 and La Follette in 1924, and a number of young intellectuals, lawyers, and college professors who believed in the need for radical reforms in the economic system. Although, however, the New Dealers comprised a considerable proportion of the voting population, as was proved in the elections of 1934 and 1936, they were inadequately represented in Congress. The machinery of the American political system failed to provide a fair representation of the popular will.

The discordancy between the Democrats and the New Dealers was reflected in Roosevelt's cabinet and among his advisers. Vice President Garner, Secretary of State Hull, Secretary of War Dern, Secretary of the Navy Swanson, Attorney General Cummings, Secretary of Commerce Roper, and Postmaster General Farley were members of the Democratic Party. Farley was the Chairman of the Democratic National Committee and had been one of the chief engineers of Roosevelt's nomination and election; he was regarded as one of the ablest political managers in American history. The other members of this group were believed to have little influence over the program of the New Deal. Cordell Hull, however, gradually asserted himself as one of the strongest figures in the administration and as its most universally respected member. Of the other members of the cabinet Secretary of the Interior Ickes and Secretary of Agriculture Wallace were Progressive Republicans, Secretary of Labor Frances Perkins had formerly been a New York social worker, and Secretary of the Treasury Woodin was a personal friend of the President. Roosevelt, however, gathered round him also a group of personal advisers who became known as the "brain trust." Among the original members of the brain trust were Raymond Moley, R. G. Tugwell, and A. A. Berle, all of whom were professors at Columbia University, and General Hugh S. Johnson. This group had been formed in order to gather material for Roosevelt's speeches during the presidential campaign, and its members continued to supply him with information and advice during the early period of the New Deal. Subsequently Moley and Johnson became opponents of Roosevelt, but their places as advisers to the President were taken by a number of lawyers and social workers who had received administrative appointments in Washington.

PURPOSES OF THE NEW DEAL

In discussing the New Deal one can to some extent distinguish between measures designed to restore economic activity and bring about recovery, measures designed to reform the economic system and prevent future depressions, and measures of long-range planning which pointed to the eventual growth of a new kind of economic order. The recovery measures, which predominated during the early months of the New Deal, had the purpose of checking the process of deflation and bankruptcy by a general raising of prices and wages and by making possible an expansion of credit. These measures may be regarded as a continuation of the Hoover program in a more drastic and comprehensive form. Meanwhile Federal money was appropriated for unemployment relief, and no attempt was made to balance the budget. Some of the New Dealers regarded large-scale Federal spending for relief as in itself a recovery measure, which would stimulate purchasing power. Roosevelt himself, however, does not appear to have accepted this point of view until 1938. If he left the budget unbalanced, it was not from choice but because the resources of the states and municipalities were almost exhausted and there was now no other method of feeding the unemployed.

These recovery measures failed to end the depression, from which the New Dealers drew the conclusion that more radical changes in the functioning of the economic system were required. Business leaders, moreover, had vigorously opposed even the relatively conservative measures of government regulation adopted at the outset of the New Deal. For these reasons Roosevelt was gradually driven to adopt more radical policies, and reform began to prevail over recovery. Among the measures of reform may be included collective bargaining for labor, raising of wages and shortening of hours, insurance against unemployment and old age, and government regulation of the stock exchanges and of public utilities. These measures were adopted in the belief that the primary cause of depression was deficiency of purchasing power on the part of workers and farmers. Government action, it was argued, must establish a fairer balance between the different sections of the community. Roosevelt emphasized the conception of balance in a number of his speeches. "What we seek," he declared on March 5, 1934, "is balance in our economic system—balance between agriculture and industry and balance between the wage earner, the employer and the consumer. We seek also balance that our internal market be kept rich and large, and that our trade with other nations be increased on both sides of the ledger."

Meanwhile the New Deal had also adopted certain measures of long-range planning, of a kind which Progressives had favored for a long time and which probably interested Roosevelt himself more than any other part of his program. These measures included the conservation of natural resources, particularly of the soil, the development of cheap electrical power, and provision for rural communities of the facilities made possible by modern science. In their ultimate effects these measures of the New Deal might prove to be more important than its program of reform, while its program of reform would probably be considered more significant than its program of recovery.

Although many of the changes made by the New Deal were admitted, even by a number of its opponents, to be necessary and permanent, the New Deal failed conspicuously in its primary task—

that of ending unemployment and reviving full economic activity. Opinions differed, however, as to the causes for this failure. While conservatives maintained that the New Deal made recovery impossible by interfering with business and destroying confidence, reformers argued that the New Deal had not gone far enough. Among reformers themselves, moreover, there still prevailed the differences of viewpoint which had characterized the Progressive movement before the war. While one group argued that monopolistic conditions must be accepted and subjected to government control, others continued to favor a trust-busting program which would restore effective competition. Among Roosevelt's advisers the former of these opinions prevailed in 1933, and the latter in 1938.

Although friends of the New Deal occasionally declared that it was the equivalent of a revolution, its enemies maintained that it was a violation of American traditions, that it was destroying democracy and private enterprise, and that it resembled the dictatorships of Germany and Russia. Both of these viewpoints were unjustified. The New Deal was certainly no revolution, since it did not involve any transfer of economic power and privilege from one class to another. On the contrary, one of the most legitimate arguments against it was that many of its measures had the effect of making the government a guarantor of the economic *status quo*. Nor were its interventions in the economic system lacking in precedent in American history. Business had always claimed government assistance in the form of the tariff, gifts of public land and natural resources, and—during the Hoover administration—the Reconstruction Finance Corporation. What was novel in the New Deal was that it gave assistance of a similar kind not merely to business but also to agriculture and labor. And although the New Deal undoubtedly involved a great extension of bureaucratic power, it was following examples set not only by the European dictatorships but also by the democracies. Some New Deal measures, such as unemployment and old-age insurance, had been adopted by almost every European country at least a generation earlier; others had been instituted in Europe since the outset of the depression. There was no New Deal measure to which there did not exist parallels in the European democracies; and there was no democratic nation which had not found it necessary to take similar actions. Many students of social development regarded the extension of bureaucratic power as an alarming tendency; but this tendency was world-wide, and no country, either democratic or dictatorial, had discovered how to avoid it.

Probably the most justifiable criticisms against the New Deal were those made not against its principles but against their execution and administration. For such practical deficiencies, however, the New Dealers themselves were not wholly to blame. Between 1914 and 1933 there had been little progressive legislation; and the New Dealers were compelled to make up for lost time by carrying out within a single administration reforms which should have taken a generation. Many New Deal measures were therefore adopted with inadequate preliminary study and discussion. The nature of the American form of government, moreover, made the enactment of a consistent program singularly difficult. Different pressure groups were able to secure special favors through influence in Congress. The division of responsibility between President and Congress meant that the conservatives in Congress could sometimes block parts of the President's program but were unable to carry out any alternative program of their own. The powers of the Supreme Court meant that measures which were regarded by the administration as essential parts of the recovery program were liable to be declared unconstitutional several years after they had been put into operation. The American Federal government had not been designed as an agency for economic planning, and the attempt to use it for this purpose encountered considerable difficulties.

Another handicap of the New Deal was the lack of a sufficiently large body of trained and nonpartisan civil servants. The young lawyers and college professors who filled many of the newly created administrative positions represented an attempt to remedy this deficiency; but it was frequently declared that their idealism and enthusiasm did not compensate for their lack of practical wisdom and experience. Some of the New Deal agencies were, moreover, partially controlled by Democratic politicians, who were likely to abuse the new government responsibilities for partisan objectives.

SUMMARY OF NEW DEAL LEGISLATION

On March 4, 1933, when Roosevelt took office as President, most of the banks in the nation were closed, the depression was at its worst, and there was a widespread feeling that democratic government must be abandoned and some form of dictatorship established. Never before, in the whole history of the United States, had pessimism been deeper or more nearly universal. Roosevelt responded to the challenge by promising in his inaugural address that he would take immediate action against the depression along a broad front; and on March 9 Congress was called into special session. During the next three months Congress enacted, at the President's request, a series of laws so far-reaching in their implications that in normal times they would have occupied the legislative energies of a generation. The result of Roosevelt's vigorous action was that, for the time being, almost every group in the nation rallied enthusiastically to his support; party and class differences were temporarily forgotten, and men who a few years later became his most bitter opponents acclaimed the President as a great national leader. Whatever may be the verdict of history on the Roosevelt administration, one achievement will always stand to its credit: during its first hundred days it restored the faith of the American people in democracy and in their future.

The principal measures of the special session were the National Industrial Recovery Act, for the reform of industry; the Agricultural Adjustment Act, for the control of farm surpluses and the legalization of certain forms of currency inflation; the Banking Act and the Securities Act, for the regulation of banking and finance; the Unemployment Relief Act creating the Civilian Conservation Corps, the Emergency Relief Act appropriating money for the unemployed, and the establishment (under the National Industrial Recovery Act) of the Public Works Administration, for relief of unemployment; the Farm Relief Act and the Home Owners' Refinancing Act, for assistance to debtors; the creation of the Tennessee Valley Authority, for the development of government-owned power plants; the Economy Act, which slashed government salaries and veterans' pensions by nearly a billion dollars, for the reduction of government expenditure (in accordance with the Democratic platform); and, as a revenue measure, the legalization and taxation of 3.2 per cent beer.

The later New Deal congresses devoted themselves mainly to modifying and making more complete the measures adopted during the special session. In 1934 Congress passed the Securities and Exchange Act, strengthening the Securities Act of 1933; the Cotton Act and the Tobacco Act, strengthening the Agricultural Adjustment Act; the Gold Reserve Act and the Silver Purchase Act, increasing government control over the currency; the Reciprocal Tariff Act, enpowering the administration to make trade agreements with other countries; the National Housing Act; the Federal Communications Act; and the Soil Conservation Act. In 1935 the most important measure was the enactment of social security legislation. Congress also reorganized the system of unemployment relief, creating the Works Progress Administration and the National Youth Administration; passed the Wagner Labor Relations Act; adopted a Revenue Act which was denounced by Republicans as a "soak the rich" measure; and passed a new Banking Act, a Public Utilities Act, and a bill for immediate payment of the bonus to war veterans.

In 1936, after the Supreme Court veto of the Agricultural Adjustment Act, Congress passed the Soil Conservation and Domestic Allotment Act. It also passed a Revenue Act imposing taxes on capital gains and on undistributed corporation profits, a Merchant Marine Act, and the Walsh-Healey Government Contracts Act. During 1937 Congress was chiefly occupied with the conflict over the proposal to reorganize the Supreme Court. It passed, however, the Farm Tenant Act, and established the United States Housing Authority. In 1938 Congress passed the second Agricultural Adjustment Act, the Fair Labor Standards Act (better known as the Wage and Hour Act), and the Food, Drug, and Cosmetic Act. This virtually ended the record of New Deal domestic legislation since the Congress elected in the autumn of 1938 had a conservative majority; public attention, moreover, began to be concentrated on the international crisis.

INDUSTRY AND LABOR

The principal objectives of the industrial and labor legislation of the New Deal were to increase wages and shorten hours, especially in certain sweated industries, and to guarantee to the workers the right to bargain collectively through unions of their own choice. Social legislation of this kind had formerly been left to the state governments. The states, however, were unable to regulate labor conditions effectively since industries were able to move from areas where labor was protected to other areas where low wages and long hours still prevailed. The New Dealers favored labor legislation not only as a step toward a more genuine democracy but also in the belief that reduced hours would bring about greater employment and that higher wages would mean increased purchasing power and, hence, greater production.

The question of wage and hour legislation was, however, complicated by the question of prices. If industrialists were required to pay higher wages, they would compensate themselves by charging higher prices, as a result of which the increase in purchasing power would be canceled. A number of New Deal economists, moreover, believed that the high prices exacted by semimonopolistic industries constituted the basic weakness of the economic system. On the question of prices the New Deal did not adopt a consistent policy. In 1933 its spokesmen declared that a generally higher price level was desirable in order that debt obligations might become less burdensome. In 1938, on the other hand, government economists apparently believed that a number of prices ought to be reduced. They were, however, unable to discover any effective method by which this might be accomplished.

The first attempt by the New Deal to regulate industry was the National Industrial Recovery Act. This was almost the only New Deal measure which represented an attempt at co-operation with big business. It was notable also because it was both the most extravagantly publicized and also the most generally unsuccessful of all the New Deal laws. The principal authors of the N. I. R. A. were certain business leaders who wanted the assistance of the Federal government in checking cut-throat competition and legalizing the price-fixing practices of the trade associations. It was suggested that government co-operation would enable business to plan production and maintain price levels and that this was what was needed to bring about recovery. Proposals to this effect had been made during the Hoover administration by Gerard Swope, president of General Electric, and Henry I. Harriman and were supported by the United States Chamber of Commerce. But they had been rejected by President Hoover as unconstitutional. Of the forty-nine principal speakers at the sessions of the Chamber of Commerce in May, 1933, more than half wanted more government regulation of business. Meanwhile liberal and labor leaders were asking for higher wages, shorter hours, and guarantees of collective bargaining. Also a thirty-hour-week bill had passed the Senate.

The administration decided that these various objectives might be achieved at the same time. Industrialists should be given government support in restricting competition. In return, they should be asked to make concessions to labor. The N. I. R. A. declared that codes of fair competition, regulating wages and hours and checking price-cutting, should be drafted for each industry. Public hearings should be held on the codes, which should be submitted to the President and, when approved, have the force of law. Any action permitted under the act should be exempt from prosecution under the antitrust laws. Section 7A of the act declared that employees might join unions and "bargain collectively through representatives of their own choosing." Some of the New Deal economists disapproved of the N. I. R. A., believing that it would tend to raise prices faster than it raised wages. Roosevelt, in signing the law, declared that if it had this effect, it would prove to be futile. It was, however, loudly hailed by many spokesmen of the administration as the measure which would end the depression.

The National Recovery Administration, which was to enforce the N. I. R. A., was headed by General Hugh S. Johnson, the principal author of the draft legislation of 1917 and subsequently a partner

of George N. Peek in the Moline Plow Company. Johnson was a
singularly forceful personality, with a gift for picturesque language;
and he had the confidence of the big industrialists. The codes of fair
competition were being drafted throughout the summer of 1933. It
was considered desirable to complete them as rapidly as possible,
in order to stimulate recovery; and many of them were adopted with
little study. The trade associations were, in general, allowed to make
their own terms in return for concessions on wages and hours; and,
although an advisory board had been appointed to represent consumers, little attention was paid to the latter. Of 557 basic codes,
441 included price-fixing regulations. Child labor was banned, and
in a number of codes wages were raised and hours were reduced.
These reforms, however, affected mostly the more backward industries, especially in the South. In the more developed industries there
were few improvements, and there was a tendency for minimum
wages to become also maximum wages. Section 7A was vigorously
opposed by certain employers, particularly by Henry Ford and by
Ernest T. Weir of National Steel, while others attempted to counteract it by forming company unions. It gave, however, considerable
stimulus to a number of trade unions, particularly to the United
Mine Workers.

On the whole organized labor appears to have benefited from the
N. R. A. Almost every other group in the community, however,
soon became disillusioned with it. Consumers opposed it because its
policies resulted in a sharp rise in prices, which the condition of the
market did not warrant. Small businessmen disliked it because they
felt that the codes had been drafted to serve the interests of big
business and because they were often unable to pay even the minimum
wages which the codes prescribed. Big industrialists turned against
it because they suspected that once the principle of government
regulation had been admitted it might eventually be used to limit
their powers and because they disliked section 7A.

In 1934 a number of industrial leaders asked that government
regulation be abandoned and that business be allowed to regulate
itself. They were willing to accept wage and hour rules, but they
made no mention of collective bargaining or of price reductions.

The opposition to the N. R. A. was strengthened by the report of the National Recovery Review Board, set up in February, 1934, under the chairmanship of Clarence Darrow, which criticized it because of its encouragement of monopoly. Many price-fixing regulations in the codes proved, moreover, to be unenforceable because of opposition from consumers and from small businessmen. There was widespread indignation when in New Jersey, which had passed a miniature N. R. A. of its own, a small tailor was sent to jail for pressing a pair of pants at less than the code price.

Johnson left the N. R. A. in 1934 and was succeeded first by Donald Richberg and later by S. Clay Williams. Many of the codes were relaxed, and the price-fixing rules began to be abandoned. Some of the New Dealers hoped that the control over business which the government had acquired through the N. R. A. might be maintained and used for somewhat different purposes, in particular for the reduction of monopoly prices. Such ideas ended, however, on May 27, 1935, when the Supreme Court unanimously declared the National Industrial Recovery Act unconstitutional.

According to the government the N. R. A. had brought about a decrease of average hours of labor from 42.6 a week to 36.2 a week and an increase of average wage rates from 42 cents an hour to 52 cents an hour. Its effect on the economic system was impossible to calculate. The establishment of the N. R. A. had been followed by an increase in production, but this increase had not been maintained for more than a few months. On the other hand, the dissolution of the N. R. A. was followed by another and more vigorous increase in production.

After the demise of the N. R. A. the administration was compelled to adopt other methods of achieving the same objectives. In July, 1935, Congress passed the National Labor Relations Act, commonly known as the Wagner Act. Workers were guaranteed the right of collective bargaining through unions of their own choice, and employers were forbidden to discriminate against union members or to support company unions. A National Labor Relations Board, composed of three members and modeled on the Federal Trade Commission, was to supervise enforcement of the act. The

Board was to hold elections, when necessary, in order that workers might choose which union should represent them; and workers whose rights were violated might complain to the Board, which could summon employers for hearings and could issue cease-and-desist orders enforceable by the courts. J. Warren Madden was appointed chairman of the Board.

Many employers expected that the Wagner Act would be declared unconstitutional; and for eighteen months the N. L. R. B. was paralysed by injunction suits. In 1937 and 1938, however, in a series of decisions which marked an epoch in American labor history, the Supreme Court upheld the Wagner Act, declaring that workers had a "fundamental right" to organize and that unions were "essential to give laborers opportunity to deal on an equality with their employer." The N. L. R. B. could then proceed with the duties assigned to it. During its first five years the Board and its subsidiary agencies finished 26,724 cases, of which 48 per cent were settled by agreement, 27 per cent withdrawn by the unions, 17 per cent dismissed, and only 8 per cent ended by decisions of the Board. It also prevented 869 strikes, settled 2,161 strikes which had already been called, and ordered the reinstatement of 21,163 workers who had been dismissed for union activities.

The N. L. R. B., nevertheless, probably provoked more violent controversy than any other New Deal agency. In two respects the Board could exercise considerable discretion in the performance of its duties. In the first place, it was difficult to say what constituted discrimination against union members. Whereas an employer could maintain that he had dismissed or refused employment to a worker on the ground of incompetence or refusal to obey orders, the Board might argue that the real reason was membership in a union. In the second place, when there were two or more competing unions, so that it was necessary to hold an election to determine which of them represented a majority of the workers, the Board could decide whether the bargaining unit should be the craft or the industry. In other words, it had to choose between the claims of craft unionism (represented by the A. F. of L.) and those of industrial unionism (represented by the C. I. O.). Conservatives violently attacked the

N. L. R. B., declaring that in the exercise of its discretionary authority it displayed bias against employers and against the A. F. of L., that it was acting both as prosecutor and as judge, and that many of the young lawyers whom it employed were radical and incompetent. The defenders of the N. L. R. B. pointed out, in reply, that a number of its decisions had been hostile to the C. I. O. They argued that the real objection was not to any bias on the part of the Board but to the principle of collective bargaining.

Another objective of the N. R. A.—the improvement of wages and hours, especially in the more backward industries—was achieved through the Walsh-Healey Public Contracts Act of 1936 and the Fair Labor Standards Act of 1938. The legislative problem was complicated by the influence exercised by Southerners in the Democratic Party. Many of the industries likely to be affected were in the South, and certain Southern spokesmen regarded low wages and long hours as a method by which their section could deprive the North of the economic supremacy which it had enjoyed since the Civil War. Under the Walsh-Healey Act, corporations making contracts with the Federal government must pay the prevailing wages, must give their workers an eight-hour day and a forty-hour week, and must employ nobody under the age of sixteen. The Fair Labor Standards Act fixed minimum wages and maximum hours for all industries engaged in interstate commerce. Minimum wages were to begin at 25 cents an hour and were to rise to 40 cents an hour within seven years; maximum hours were to begin at 44 a week and were to be reduced to 40 a week within two years. Wage committees were to determine minimum wages for different industries, making allowances for differences in costs of production and transportation. Industries in which work had to be completed quickly were exempt from the maximum-hour regulations. An administrator was to enforce the decisions of the committees, employers having the right of appeal to the courts. Employers who violated the regulations were liable to a fine of $10,000 or imprisonment for six months. Shipment of goods made by child labor (except in agriculture) was forbidden. It was calculated that the act meant an increase in wages for 650,000 workers, and a decrease in hours for 2,380,000 workers.

The most important problems presented by the industrial system—those of adjusting prices to purchasing power and of expanding production until unemployment disappeared—remained unsolved. After the invalidation of the N. R. A. there was a rapid growth of production, and the administration made no further attempt to regulate industry. In the autumn of 1937, however, the boom collapsed even more quickly than it had developed, and industry soon found itself back almost where it had been in March, 1933. For several months the administration hesitated, and its spokesmen denounced big business one week and tried to promote business confidence the next. The more influential of the New Deal economists attributed the recession to monopolistic price-raising; Roosevelt finally accepted their point of view, and on April 29, 1938, he sent a message to Congress in which he analysed the American economic system in detail and denounced the growth of monopoly and inequality. In June Congress appointed a Temporary National Economic Committee. This committee conducted an elaborate study of the workings of American corporate enterprise and made a number of very illuminating discoveries. Meanwhile the immediate policy of the administration was apparently to enforce the antitrust laws. Thurman Arnold was appointed to take charge of the antitrust division of the Department of Justice; and he instituted a campaign, directed against both business corporations and trade unions, with the purpose of forcing down prices which were being kept high by monopolistic practices.

AGRICULTURE

The chief objectives of the New Deal agricultural program were to reduce production and thereby to raise prices and increase farm incomes. That American farmers were producing more than the nation could consume was a fact; and in an epoch of economic nationalism it was unlikely that they could find new foreign markets for their surpluses. The Farm Board set up under Hoover's Agricultural Marketing Act had urged the farmers to plant less, and in 1932 it had recommended that the cotton planters plough under one-third of their crop. But the farmers, unlike the big industrial corporations, could not restrict production by voluntary effort; government assistance was essential. The New Deal proposed, by government intervention, to extend to agriculture the power to raise prices by limiting production—the same power that was enjoyed by big business. This policy of subsidizing scarcity was regretted by the New Dealers themselves, but under the circumstances no other policy seemed to be possible.

The personnel of the Department of Agriculture probably typified the spirit of the New Deal more fully than did that of any other branch of the government. Henry A. Wallace of Iowa, the Secretary, was the son of Harding's Secretary of Agriculture and the editor of a farm weekly. He was a scientific student of farm statistics and of genetics, and he had made important improvements in the breeding of corn, hogs, and chickens. He was interested also in religious mysticism and was a friend of the Irish poet, A. E. Associated with Wallace were such men as R. G. Tugwell, Mordecai Ezekiel, Louis H. Bean, Gardiner C. Means, and Jerome Frank.

The basic principles of the New Deal farm program had been first suggested by M. L. Wilson, of the Montana State College of Agriculture, and had been adopted by Roosevelt during the presidential campaign. The Agricultural Adjustment Act passed Congress on May 12, 1933. This act was to apply at first to wheat, cotton, corn, hogs, rice, tobacco, and milk. A contract was to be made with each farmer who chose to adopt the program in accordance with the "historic base" of his farm, in other words with the acreage which he had normally devoted to each crop. The farmer agreed to reduce the acreage by a fixed percentage and to use the surplus land for soil-improving crops or for crops to be consumed only by his family. Farmers who entered the program were, in return, to receive government payments, which would be financed through excise taxes levied on processors. The excise tax was disliked by some of the New Dealers since it would tend to raise consumers' prices, but it was considered desirable to make the plan self-supporting and avoid outright government subsidies. Enforcement of the A. A. A. was entrusted, as far as possible, to local committees of farmers rather than to federal officials, in order to prevent bureaucratic regimentation.

The Agricultural Adjustment Administration was headed first by George N. Peek, author of the McNary-Haugen Bill. Subsequently Wallace decided that Peek was allowing consumers' prices to increase too greatly, and he was replaced by Chester C. Davis, a farmer and farm journalist from Montana. The total area taken out of production by the A. A. A. amounted to 10,400,000 acres in 1933, 35,700,000 acres in 1934, and 30,300,000 acres in 1935. The cash income of farmers rose from $4,606,000,000 in 1932 to $6,805,-000,000 in 1935. Incomes from wheat, cotton, tobacco, corn, and hogs increased by 90 per cent. In terms of the ratio between prices received and prices paid, the farm population was 35 per cent better off in 1935 than in 1932. In 1934 and 1935 a referendum was taken among certain classes of farmers, and 3,707,642 of them, out of a total of 4,288,510, voted for a continuance of the program.

In addition to the A. A. A., the New Deal refinanced numerous farm mortgages through a Farm Credit Administration; it made a series of marketing agreements, fixing prices and rationing sales, with the producers of milk, fruit, and vegetables; and it established a Federal Surplus Commodities Corporation which purchased surplus foodstuffs for distribution among the unemployed. In May, 1939, this corporation adopted a plan by which surplus foodstuffs were distributed through the regular commercial channels, and persons on relief could purchase them by means of food stamps which they received in addition to their relief payments. This device, which increased the business of the retail stores, proved to be very popular, and was quickly adopted in a large number of cities. Congress was, moreover, dissatisfied with the A. A. A. because it restricted only acreage and not actual production. In 1934 and 1935 Congress imposed production quotas on cotton, tobacco, and potatoes, and taxed farmers who produced more than their quotas. These measures were disliked by the New Dealers since they involved too much regimentation of the farmers, and they were passed with the aid of Republican votes.

Criticisms of the A. A. A. were numerous. In the first place, it was attacked on the ground that it set out to create scarcity. In 1933 the program caused the ploughing under of 10,500,000 acres of

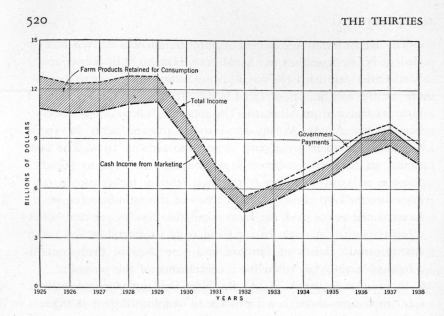

Figure 11. FARM INCOMES IN PROSPERITY AND DEPRESSION

cotton, which had been planted before the act was passed, and the slaughtering of 6,500,000 pigs, which were processed into food for the unemployed. Wallace and the New Dealers replied that the encouragement of scarcity was not an inherent part of the program, and that when the condition of the market warranted it, the government could plan for abundance as easily as for scarcity. In the second place—and this was perhaps the most unfortunate feature of the program—the chief beneficiaries of the A. A. A. were the more prosperous commercial farmers and landowners. Tenant farmers, sharecroppers, and hired laborers derived few benefits from it, and —owing to the restriction of production—were often worse off than before. The A. A. A., in fact, tended to intensify the already serious problem of rural unemployment. In the third place, the A. A. A. resulted in a loss of foreign markets, particularly in the case of cotton. The cotton planters and sharecroppers were, in point of fact, caught in a vicious circle. They could hold their export trade only through low prices, but low prices meant a continuance of their low standard of living. In 1938 and 1939 the government was compelled to begin paying export subsidies to exporters of wheat and cotton. Other criticisms of the A. A. A. were that it caused too sharp an increase in prices and that it deprived farmers of their individual freedom and subjected them to bureaucratic regimentation. Opponents of the A. A. A. were, however, unable to suggest any feasible alternative program. The basic problem of American farming was that there were too many commercial farmers; and, as long as industry was unable to provide jobs for the surplus rural population, the restriction of production, by one method or another, was unavoidable.

On January 6, 1936, the A. A. A. was declared unconstitutional by the Supreme Court. As a substitute measure Congress then passed, on February 29, the Soil Conservation and Domestic Allotment Act. The Federal government was to pay subsidies to the producers of staple crops who would agree to withdraw part of their land from commercial production and use it for soil-conserving crops. This act did not, however, provide any sufficient check on overproduction. The harvests of 1937 and 1938 were the largest since the World War, and prices began to fall sharply.

On February 16, 1938, Congress passed the second A. A. A., an extraordinarily complicated measure by which Wallace hoped to achieve his ideal of an "ever-normal granary." The government was to allot acreage quotas among the producers of staple crops, allowing for the normal domestic and foreign demand and for a surplus which would be stored as a reserve in case of crop failures in future years. Farmers were not compelled to keep to these quotas, but those who did so would receive subsidies, which would be planned with a view to raising farm incomes to the 1909–1914 level. If there was overproduction in spite of the quota system, the government would store surplus crops and make loans to the producers; and, if two-thirds of the producers agreed, the government might restrict sales, by means of marketing quotas, and impose taxes on those who sold above their quotas. The act also established a Federal Crop Insurance Corporation to insure farmers against the uncertainties of the weather. In 1939 nearly 6 million farmers were included in the

A. A. A. program, and about 30 million acres had been taken out of production. The subsidies totaled 482 million dollars in 1938 and 675 million dollars in 1939. As a result of overproduction in 1937, farm prices and farm incomes in 1938 and 1939 did not recover the ground which had been lost.

The two A. A. A.'s benefited the wealthier commercial farmers; but the much more serious problems of the tenant farmers and sharecroppers remained unremedied. The tenant farmers, unlike the more prosperous farmers of the West, were not represented by powerful organizations that could bring pressure on congressmen; and, unlike the landlords of the South, they did not have champions among the leaders of the Democratic Party. The attempts of the New Deal to solve the problem of farm tenancy were, judged as experiments, of considerable interest; but by contrast with the magnitude of the evil, their scope was negligible.

In 1933 a Division of Subsistence Homesteads was established, with a fund of 25 million dollars. In 1935 this was replaced by the Resettlement Administration. These organizations removed destitute farmers from submarginal lands, resettled them in semirural co-operative communities, loaned them money for tools and seeds, and planned for them to combine part-time work in industry with part-time agriculture. By 1936, 124 such communities had been established. The sponsors of these projects, believing strongly in the moral values of rural life, hoped that this combination of industry and agriculture would become a pattern for the social organization of the future. Critics, on the other hand, declared that in view of existing economic conditions such expectations were totally impractical. In 1936, at the President's request, Congress appointed a committee to study farm tenancy; and a majority of the committee arrived at the revolutionary conclusion that the traditional public land policy of the American government should be abandoned. Instead of converting public land into private property, the government should retain legal ownership in order to protect farmers from expropriation through mortgage foreclosures, to prevent speculation, and to check soil erosion.

Congress, however, preferred the traditional individualistic policy and disliked the co-operative ideals of the Resettlement Administration. In 1937 it passed the Farm Tenant Act, creating the Farm Security Administration and appropriating money which tenants could borrow at 3 per cent for the purchase of land. This act enabled tenants to become owners at the rate of only about 5,000 a year, whereas the total number of tenants was nearly 3 million. More successful were the rehabilitation loans, averaging $350 each and numbering about 750,000 in three years, which the Farm Security Administration gave to tenant farmers who could use them profitably. The value of these loans was chiefly due to the fact that they were accompanied by careful advice as to how they could best be spent.

CREDIT, CURRENCY AND FINANCE

The growth of debt was one of the most serious problems of the American economic system, particularly during the depression. By 1932 interest payments on long-term debts amounted to nearly one-fifth of the total national income. According to the rules of laissez-faire economics, this problem should have been allowed to adjust itself through bankruptcies. Such a solution might have had beneficial results in the long run, but its immediate effects would have been so catastrophic that no government could have tolerated it. The Hoover administration had therefore set out to prevent bankruptcies through the Reconstruction Finance Corporation and through aid to owners of homes and farms. It also attempted to increase the amount of money in circulation through the Glass-Steagall Act. The New Deal continued these Hoover policies, and extended them in order to assist a larger number of people. It also endeavored to prevent any repetition of the speculative boom of the twenties by increasing government control over the credit structure and over the stock exchanges.

Under the chairmanship of Jesse Jones the Reconstruction Finance Corporation continued to lend money to banks, trust companies, railroads, and other institutions. By the end of 1937 the R. F. C. had made loans totaling $6,512,518,000, of which $4,452,121,000 had been repaid. For the relief of farmers, whose obligations amounted in 1933 to about $8,500,000,000 in mortgages and to about $3,500,000,000 in short-term debts, Congress in 1933 and 1934 created the Farm Credit Administration. The F. C. A. refinanced farm mortgages, making reductions in both the principal and the rate of interest. By the end of 1937 about half the farm mortgage debt appears to have been held by agencies of the Federal government. The urban mortgage debt, which amounted in 1932 to about $26,000,000,000, was to be refinanced, when necessary, by the Home Owners' Loan Corporation, which was established in 1933. Under the terms of the act, the corporation could give no more loans after 1936 and was to be dissolved in 1951. The H. O. L. C. took over more than a million mortgages with a total value of $3,093,000,000, reduced interest payments by $60,000,000 a year, and arranged for the repayment, within fifteen years, of the principal of the debts which it assumed. Further reorganization of the urban mortgage debt was undertaken by the Federal Housing Authority, set up under the National Housing Act of 1934. The F. H. A. created a mortgage-insurance scheme, designed to encourage borrowing by guaranteeing credit institutions against losses and by reducing interest rates. In four years the F. H. A. underwrote $1,825,000,000 of home mortgages. New loans for improvements and building, on the other hand, amounted to only $775,000,000.

The reorganization of the debt structure by the New Deal benefited both creditors and debtors. Creditors received repayment from the government instead of being required to foreclose on properties whose immediate value was often far smaller than the sums for which they were mortgaged; debtors kept their properties and paid lower rates of interest. The ratio of debt obligations to the national income continued, nevertheless, to be dangerously high; and the H. O. L. C. soon found itself compelled to foreclose on a number of the householders whom it had attempted to rescue. Unless there should be a rapid increase in the income of the debtor classes, it would probably become necessary for the government to undertake a more drastic reduction of debt burdens and a further extension of its creditor functions.

With reference to currency, the New Deal set out to increase the amount of money in circulation, including both cash and bank credit, in the hope that this would lower interest rates, reduce debt burdens, and assist industrial expansion. It also planned to strengthen government control over the currency, in the hope of checking cycles of inflation and deflation and maintaining a stable price level. This program involved a devaluation of the dollar—a step which was vigorously opposed by conservatives on the ground that it would end in uncontrolled inflation. Every other important country in the world, however, had already devalued its currency, and in each case devaluation appeared to have given a stimulus to economic recovery.

The United States formally abandoned the gold standard in April, 1933, and in June, by the Gold Repeal Joint Resolution, it was declared that debts were to be paid in legal tender and not in gold. The dollar then began to fall in relation to foreign currencies, thus stimulating American exports, and prices began to rise. In June the World Economic Conference discussed immediate currency stabilization. Roosevelt believed that stabilization would give an advantage to those countries whose currencies were already devalued more than the United States currency, and he therefore refused to consider such a proposition. Meanwhile a number of western senators, particularly those from the silver-mining states, were demanding outright inflation. Roosevelt counteracted such proposals, which he regarded as dangerous, by having included in the A. A. A. a clause giving him certain discretionary powers of inflation.

In October prices began to fall, and western leaders renewed their demand for inflation. Roosevelt then adopted a gold-purchase plan, proposed by Professor Warren of Cornell, by which the government bought gold at increasing prices, thus making the dollar cheaper. The buying of gold caused the dollar to fall in relation to foreign currencies, but it did not have the effect, expected by its sponsors, of raising prices. In January, 1934, Congress passed the Gold Reserve Act. The government was allowed to fix the dollar at between 50 and 60 per cent of its former value, and by means of an Exchange Stabilization Fund of 2 billion dollars it could manage its value within these limits. The government could, moreover, impound all gold into the treasury, giving gold certificates to its former owners. The purpose of this nationalization of gold was to prevent it from being hoarded or exported by persons who lacked confidence or hoped for speculative profits. One of its results was a large profit for the treasury. Roosevelt then stabilized the dollar at 59.06 per cent of its former value; and, being afraid of inflation, he undertook no further monetary experiments. The treasury continued, however, to buy gold and to bury it at Fort Knox, Kentucky. By 1940 it had about 19 billion dollars' worth of gold, nearly three-quarters of the total world supply. What purposes were served by the accumulation of this hoard were not apparent; and it was suggested that the remainder of the world might eventually be driven to abandon the use of gold, with the result that it would become wholly valueless.

Western senators, faithful to the traditions of Bryan and 1896, demanded that something be done for silver, and in December, 1933, the treasury announced that it would buy all silver mined in the United States for the next four years at 64½ cents an ounce, the current price being 43 cents. In June, 1934, Congress passed the Silver Purchase Act. Silver was to be nationalized in the same manner as gold; the government was to buy silver at its own prices; and 25 per cent of the nation's currency was eventually to be based on silver. By June, 1938, the treasury had bought 1,687,000,000 ounces of silver, more than three-quarters of which came from abroad; and the price had risen to 75 cents an ounce. Some silver certificates were put into circulation, but no serious attempt was made to reach the 25 per cent proportion stipulated by Congress. The program, incidentally, brought considerable benefits to Mexico, which produced large quantities of silver, and caused hardships to China, whose currency was based on silver.

In order to increase government control over bank credit, Congress passed, in August, 1935, the Banking Act. The Federal Reserve Board was henceforth to be known as the Board of Governors of the Federal Reserve System, and all members were to be appointed by the President, with fourteen-year terms. An Open Market Committee, consisting of the Board of Governors and five representatives of the Federal reserve banks, was to control bank credit by buying and selling government securities and by raising and lowering the reserve requirements of the member banks. Roosevelt appointed Marriner S. Eccles of Utah to be Chairman of the Board. By the summer of 1936 the easy-money policy seemed to have overshot the mark; excess reserves were accumulating in the banks, and there seemed to be danger of a speculative boom. The Open Market Committee then began to raise the reserve requirements of the banks, while the treasury sterilized part of its gold reserve by refusing to issue gold certificates for it. A year later the economic system was again entering a depression, so these policies were reversed.

The effects of the New Deal currency and credit policies were difficult to estimate. The purpose of the gold and silver purchase program was to increase the amount of money in circulation in a manner which would not create a threat of uncontrolled inflation. By 1936 the total amount of currency amounted to $6,542,800,000, as contrasted with only $4,746,300,000 in 1929. But the increase in the quantity of money did not in itself bring about recovery, as its supporters had expected; more money in the banks did not necessarily mean more money in circulation. The powers of currency manipulation which had been acquired by the government were, moreover, regarded by many people as dangerous. It was argued, on the other hand, that a wise currency policy could help to stabilize the economic system if it were associated with appropriate measures of other kinds.

Two other New Deal reforms in the field of finance related to banking and to the issuance of securities. Immediately after taking office in March, 1933, the administration set out to restore public confidence in the banks and to reopen as quickly as possible those which appeared to be sound, when necessary with the aid of loans from the R. F. C. By virtue of war powers which had been granted to the Wilson administration and never repealed, it took control of the banking system. Within six weeks nearly 13,000 banks, more than three-quarters of the total number that had survived the depression, were authorized to resume business. In order to prevent panics in the future, Congress passed the Banking Act of June, 1933, by which deposits were to be guaranteed by the Federal Deposit Insurance Corporation. The funds of the corporation were to be contributed partly by the government, partly by the Federal reserve banks, and partly by those commercial banks which accepted the plan. Deposit and investment banking were, moreover, to be separated from each other. During the four years 1934–1937 there were only 194 bank failures, as contrasted with an average of about 500 a year throughout the twenties.

Regulation of the stock exchanges was established by the Securities Act of 1933 and the Securities and Exchange Act of 1934. These acts were fruits of the Senate investigation of 1932 and 1933, which had brought to light the manner in which Wall Street financiers during the boom had unloaded worthless securities upon small investors and had stimulated excessive speculation in order to profit by it. By the act of 1934 a Securities and Exchange Commission (the S. E. C.) was established. All securities were to be registered with the S. E. C., which was to require full and accurate information about them. Various forms of stock manipulation prevalent in the twenties were forbidden; and the Federal Reserve Board was to control the use of credit for brokers' loans and other speculative purposes. Persons buying stocks on margin were required to pay at least 55 per cent of their value. Joseph P. Kennedy, himself a wealthy financier, was the first chairman of the S. E. C., his successors being James M. Landis, William O. Douglas, and Jerome Frank. The S. E. C. proved to be one of the most controversial of the New Deal agencies. Supporters of the New Deal argued that the S. E. C. was disliked by Wall Street because it checked unscrupulous speculation by protecting small investors from fraud. Wall Street, on the other hand, declared that the S. E. C. acted as a deterrent to business expansion by surrounding the issuance of new securities with too much red tape, insisting on too much detailed information, imposing too many delays, and charging too heavy registration fees.

UNEMPLOYMENT RELIEF

When Roosevelt became President there were probably about 15 million persons unemployed, out of a total working population of about 50 million. During the Hoover administration the unemployed had been supported by the state and municipal governments, whose financial resources were now almost exhausted, and by private charity. It was, therefore, necessary for the Federal government to assume direct responsibility. There was a distinct break with previous American custom in the recognition that it was the duty of the Federal government to protect unemployed persons from starvation and that, when men were unable to find jobs, it should be regarded as their misfortune rather than as their fault. The Roosevelt administration wanted, moreover, to provide the unemployed with work and not merely with a dole; work relief might cost more than a dole, but it would prevent demoralization, and it would give the community something in return for its money.

The earliest of the Roosevelt relief agencies was the Civilian Conservation Corps, created in March, 1933, and placed under the control of Robert Fechner. Boys between the ages of eighteen and twenty-five, a large number of whom had never worked before, were drafted into the Corps, and were sent to camps where they worked on reforestation, soil conservation, and other useful projects. Payment amounted to $30 a month, of which $25 was sent to the boys' families. The Corps employed between 300,000 and 500,000 boys at a time for periods averaging nine months each. By 1940 about 2 million boys had served in it. Because of both the utility of its work and the physical and moral value to its members, the C. C. C. probably won more widespread approval than any other New Deal agency.

In the hope of stimulating the capital goods industries, the New Deal adopted a program of building public works. The Public Works Administration was established under the National Industrial Recovery Act, and Secretary of the Interior Ickes was appointed administrator. The P. W. A. was to construct public buildings, bridges, dams, sewage systems, housing developments, and similar projects; and it was to loan money to states and municipalities for similar purposes. In order to stimulate private industry, a large proportion of the money was to be spent on materials. Ickes supervised the spending of P. W. A. funds with what seemed to many people to be excessive care, so that many of the operations were slow in getting under way. Although the P. W. A. projects were generally well-chosen, they apparently did little to stimulate recovery. By 1936 the P. W. A. had spent about 4 billion dollars. Actually, less money was spent on public works under the New Deal than in the twenties. During the twenties states and municipalities had spent an average of 3 billion dollars a year on roads and public buildings and had incurred heavy debts in order to do so. The only novel feature of the New Deal policy was that it was now the Federal government which spent the money and incurred the debts.

The second of the Federal relief agencies was the Federal Emergency Relief Administration, established in May, 1933, and placed in charge of Harry Hopkins. The F. E. R. A. gave funds to local authorities, who were required to contribute part of the costs of relief themselves. Between 1933 and 1935, 71 per cent of all relief costs was paid by the F. E. R. A. In November the Civil Works Administration was created. The purpose of the C. W. A. was to create jobs, controlled by the Federal government, as quickly as possible. In January the C. W. A. was giving employment to 4,250,000 persons. Much of the work, however, was of a makeshift character; the administration was often lax; and the whole program was temporary. The C. W. A. was dissolved in March, and its employees were turned back to the local authorities. The F. E. R. A. had meanwhile been reorganized; its funds were to be used for work projects and not for direct relief; and the Federal government undertook more careful supervision of the wage schedules, the conditions of labor, and the persons eligible for employment. Relief rates were increased, the monthly family allowance averaging $15 in May, 1933, and $35 in July, 1935. In addition to contributing relief funds to the local authorities, the F. E. R. A. also built a number of transient camps, which were giving shelter to 300,000 persons by 1935, bought cattle during the drought of 1934 and used it as food for the unemployed, and spent money for health and education.

The administration had apparently been hoping that the unemployment problem would prove to be temporary and that a quick economic recovery would solve it. By the beginning of 1935, however, it had become apparent that unemployment would have to be regarded as more or less permanent. At that time 5,500,000 persons were receiving relief for themselves and their dependents. The total number of persons living on relief amounted to more than 20½ million, 17 per cent of the entire population, more than 7 million of them being children of under sixteen. This did not include those who were unemployed but receiving no relief and those who were working on other government projects, such as the C. C. C. In January, 1935, Roosevelt proposed that the Federal government assume control of work relief and that direct relief be left to the local governments. In accordance with this proposal Congress established the Works Progress Administration. This was to furnish the unemployed with work of a kind which would not require much expenditure on material, which would be useful, and which—as far as possible—would eventually return money to the government. Wage rates varied from $19 a month in the South to $55 a month in the northern cities, with higher schedules for professional workers. Minimum hours were at first 140 a month. Harry Hopkins was placed in charge of the W. P. A.

The number of persons employed by the W. P. A. varied between 1,400,000 and 3,300,000. It was handicapped by the difficulty of finding projects which would not compete with private business, as well as by the fact that a large majority of its employees were unskilled. Since the program was generally regarded as primarily for relief rather than for work, morale and discipline among the employees were often low. Also, the local administrators of it were not always efficient or nonpartisan. The W. P. A., nevertheless, built or repaired 457,000 miles of streets and roads, constructed 23,000 new schools and other public buildings and improved 65,000 others, and completed numerous other useful projects. It conducted a large number of enterprises in the field of adult education, reducing the national rate of illiteracy among persons above the age of ten from 4.3 per cent to less than 1.0 per cent; and it established a number of projects for professional workers in literature, art, music, and the theater. Particularly notable was the Federal Theater, which was supervised by Hallie Flanagan. In 1937 the Federal Theater gave employment to 12,700 persons, and put on performances which were seen by 22 million persons. Sixty per cent of these performers were in communities where theatrical performances had hitherto been unknown. The work of the Federal Theater was remarkable both for the high quality of its productions and for its remarkable freedom from government censorship. The art projects, most of which consisted of the painting of murals for public buildings, were equally laudable examples of public patronage exercised with a due regard for freedom of aesthetic expression.

Another Federal relief agency was the National Youth Administration, created in June, 1935, and supervised by Aubrey Williams. The N. Y. A. provided part-time work for high school and college students at a maximum rate of $6 a month for the former and $15 a month for the latter. It also established a number of classes for vocational training. The greatest number of persons employed at any one time by the N. Y. A. was 428,818.

The relief rolls decreased throughout 1936 and the early part of 1937. By September, 1937, when the lowest point was reached, 4,400,000 families were living on relief. After this date, however, there was a rapid increase in unemployment and in the number of persons on relief. In 1939 the number of workers unable to find employment in private industry was probably about 11,000,000, although some authorities regarded this figure as a considerable overestimate. In 1938, at Roosevelt's request, Congress increased the appropriations for the W. P. A., and for various forms of public works. In 1939, on the other hand, Congress favored economy; the W. P. A. appropriation was reduced, which meant that a number of its employees were transferred to the local relief agencies; and the Federal Theater and some of the other professional projects were abolished. There was also a reduction in the W. P. A. wage schedules, except in the South.

Down to June, 1940, the Roosevelt administration spent on relief agencies (chiefly the F. E. R. A. and the W. P. A.) a total sum of $16,231,000,000, and on public works (including various housing and power projects not covered by the P. W. A.) a total sum of $7,032,000,000. The smallest appropriations were for the year ending June, 1938, when $1,966,000,000 was spent on relief, and $880,000,000 on public works; the largest appropriations were for the year ending June, 1939, when relief cost $2,741,000,000 and public works cost $1,229,000,000.

The relief agencies of the New Deal, particularly the W. P. A., were vigorously attacked by conservatives. It was argued that the government could not afford to spend such large sums, that those employed by the W. P. A. did little work and were being pampered and demoralized, and that the W. P. A. and the other public works and relief agencies constituted a vast pork barrel designed to secure votes for the Democratic Party. Many Republicans declared that the Federal government should abandon relief and that it should be given back to the local governments—a change which would probably have been followed by large reductions in the scale of payments. It was true that in some states, notably in Pennsylvania, Kentucky, and Tennessee, there was a tendency to use the W. P. A. as an election agency for the benefit of Democratic candidates, although Hopkins and his associates in Washington appear to have been sincerely anxious to maintain its nonpartisan character. In order to prevent this, Congress passed in 1939 the Hatch Act against "pernicious political activity," which forbade employees of the Federal government (with the exception of policy-making officials) from taking part in politics. There was also a growing tendency among persons who were not unemployed to treat W. P. A. workers as a kind of inferior caste, to be viewed with contempt by respectable citizens. Conservatives, however, often refused to recognize the real sufferings caused by unemployment, and the genuine desire of most of those employed by the W. P. A. to find permanent jobs. Men who lived in daily fear of receiving the pink slips indicating dismissal from the W. P. A. were far from being pampered; and, if they were demoralized, it was more from poverty and uncertainty than because they were receiving temporary support from the Federal government.

The real weaknesses of the relief program of the Roosevelt administration were, perhaps, due chiefly to the fact that unemployment was not accepted as a permanent problem. The W. P. A. necessarily had some of the elements of an election agency for the Democratic Party as long as the size of the relief appropriations were determined by the President and Congress, rather than by economic needs, and as long as the right of unemployed persons to receive either work or relief was not generally recognized and established. Although, however, economic developments suggested that large numbers of workers were unlikely ever again to find employment in private industry, the people of the United States were not yet prepared to face the consequences of this unpleasant fact.

SOCIAL SECURITY

The only attempt by the New Deal to provide a permanent unemployment policy was the Social Security Act, which was signed on August 14, 1935. The principle of state insurance for unemployment and old age had already been accepted by all other important nations; and the United States could therefore profit by their experience. The American social security system differed, however, from those of most other nations in that it provided for a smaller scale of payments and made no provision for health insurance.

It was decided that unemployment insurance should be administered by the states, which were to be allowed considerable liberty to experiment with different methods. The money was to be raised by a tax on pay rolls. The Federal government would make no direct contribution, but would hold the reserve funds, which would be drawn on by the states as needed. Previous to 1935 Wisconsin was the only state that had established unemployment insurance. By the summer of 1938, however, all the state governments had adopted satisfactory plans. The amount of the pay-roll tax averaged 2.7 per cent a year. About 27 million persons were covered, agricultural laborers, domestic servants, casual laborers, various categories of salaried employees, and—in many states—employees of small businesses being excluded. In 1938 the largest payment was $15 a week; the average payment was $10.93 a week; and the longest period during which an unemployed person might continue to receive payments was sixteen weeks. Persons who were unemployed for more than this period were expected to apply for regular relief.

Generous old-age pensions were demanded by the followers of Dr. Townsend, and pressure from this group was partly responsible for the passage of the Social Security Act. The act provided both for Federal assistance to state pension plans and also for the establishment of a separate Federal annuity system. The states were to pay half the cost of their pension plans and were to receive the other half from the Federal treasury, but the Federal contribution was not to exceed $15 per person. By the summer of 1938 it was estimated that 22 per cent of the population past the age of sixty-five were receiving pensions. Payments varied between $32.33 a month in California and $4.79 a month in Mississippi, the average being $19.48 a month. The Townsendites continued to agitate for larger pensions; but schemes of this kind, put forward in California and Ohio in the elections of 1939, were defeated. In 1939 the Social Security Act was amended to provide for greater Federal control over state pensions systems in order to prevent their abuse for political purposes.

The Federal annuity system, as drafted in 1935 and amended in 1939, was to be financed by equal contributions from employers and employees, which would amount at first to 1 per cent of wages but which was to be increased later. About 46 million persons were covered by the act, each of whom would have a right to a pension when he reached the age of sixty-five, regardless of need. Payments were to begin in 1940, and would be proportionate to contributions. The maximum payment would be $85 a month. In order to receive this an individual would be required to have worked for forty-three years at a salary of more than $3,000 a year. The act of 1935 also provided for the creation of an enormous reserve fund, which would have amounted to 50 billion dollars by 1970. This feature of the plan was sharply criticized and was virtually abandoned in 1939. The act was also attacked because its scheme of pay-roll taxation diminished purchasing power and had a deflationary effect; this caused the scheme of payments provided for in 1935 to be revised downward in 1939.

Plans for health insurance were not discussed in Congress until 1939. Opposition from the medical profession to "socialized medicine" made any immediate adoption of such a measure unlikely.

RAILROADS, SHIPPING, AND HOUSING

The three major industries of railroads, shipping, and housing were alike in that they required special attention from the Federal government. In each of them there was need for a program of replacement, modernization, and new construction, on a scale large enough to stimulate the capital goods industries and contribute substantially to the ending of the depression. In none of them, however, was private enterprise able to function successfully without government assistance.

The depression reduced at least one-third of the American railroad system to bankruptcy. Owing to the decrease in the volume of freight, the railroads suffered more directly than any other part of the economic system. They were, moreover, suffering from overcapitalization and from the rise of the automobile; and their debts were exceptionally large. Sixty-two per cent of their securities consisted of bonds, the interest on which amounted to about 500 million dollars a year. The railroads borrowed heavily from the Reconstruction Finance Corporation; and in June, 1933, Congress passed the Emergency Railroad Transportation Act, under which Joseph B. Eastman was appointed Federal Coordinator of Transportation. Eastman was, however, able to do little to remedy the situation. Reduction of the railroad debt was what seemed to be required, but the bulk of the debt was held by insurance companies, educational and philanthropic bodies, and other institutions which could not be expected to sacrifice it. Purchase of the railroads by the government was felt to be too costly. Although, therefore, it was generally admitted that the railroads needed to spend large sums on new equipment, no method was devised for making this expenditure possible.

Shipping had received special attention from the government since the World War, but the subsidy programs of 1920 and 1928 failed to enable the industry to compete with that of other nations. Relatively few ships were built after 1918, and by 1933 the bulk of the American merchant fleet was rapidly becoming obsolete. According to liberals this situation was due to mismanagement by the shipping companies, while conservatives attributed it to high labor costs. In 1936 Congress passed a Merchant Marine Act, under which a Maritime Commission was set up. The Commission was given wide powers to plan trade routes and to work out a long-range building program, including both subsidies to private builders and, if necessary, direct building by the government. In 1938 the act was amended to give the Commission power to prescribe wages and working conditions, while a Maritime Labor Board was to arbitrate labor disputes. In the opinion of Joseph P. Kennedy, the first head of the Commission, at least 2.5 billion dollars was required for new shipping. Since private capital seemed unlikely to enter the industry to this extent, the Commission adopted a program of building by the government which would provide fifty new ships a year for ten years. When completed, the ships were to be operated by the private shipping companies.

In the housing industry the great need was for low-cost apartment buildings for working-class families. The needs of the wealthier families had been adequately met before 1929, but private enterprise seemed to be incapable of providing new apartments at rentals which the working class could afford to pay. A large proportion of the urban population continued, therefore, to live in slum tenements. The high cost of housing was due to a number of different factors, among them being heavy real estate taxes, excessive real estate speculation, high cost of material caused by monopolistic price-fixing by business corporations, and high cost of labor caused by monopolistic wage-fixing by the A. F. of L. building unions. From the outset of the New Deal it was frequently suggested that housing was one of the industries which might carry America out of the depression; but the problems involved were so complex that these hopes were not fulfilled.

The F. H. A., which insured construction loans and limited rates of interest, gave some stimulus to the building of houses for middle-income families. By 1940 it had underwritten loans for new houses totaling about 2 billion dollars, and houses were being built at the rate of 460,000 a year, half of which were covered by the F. H. A. The only attempt to solve the problems of low-cost housing in the early stages of the New Deal was through the P. W. A. In three years, however, the Housing Division of the P. W. A. was responsible for the building of only 30,000 family units. In 1937 the United States Housing Authority was established, with Nathan Straus as Administrator. The U. S. H. A. was empowered to loan 800 million dollars to local governments for low-cost housing. Ten per cent of the cost was to be raised locally, and the loans were to be repaid in sixty years, with 3 per cent interest. The U. S. H. A. could also grant annual subsidies of 28 million dollars for the reduction of rents, on condition that costs and rentals be kept below a certain figure and that only families earning less than a certain income be accepted as tenants. By the spring of 1940 the U. S. H. A. had loaned 600 million dollars for 134,000 family units in 179 different projects in 24 states. The average rental to be charged was $14 a month per unit, and only those families were to be admitted whose incomes did not exceed five times the rent. Although, however, the U. S. H. A. had given a considerable stimulus to housing, it seemed likely that the industry could never become really healthy until some method for reducing costs had been discovered. In 1939 and 1940 the Federal government began to take action against the building unions under the antitrust laws; but the more complicated problems presented by local real estate taxes and by the high cost of material remained unsolved.

POWER

The power industry also was the object of special attention on the part of the New Deal. During the twenties a large part of the industry had been controlled by unscrupulous financiers, who had created public utility empires, controlled by means of holding companies, with inflated capital values upon which dividends had to be earned.

They had also conducted elaborate propaganda campaigns against government control. During the depression some of these enterprises, particularly the Insull system, had gone into bankruptcy, in spite of a relatively low fall in their earnings. The industry had consequently acquired a particularly bad reputation among the American public. Roosevelt had for a long time been an enthusiast of cheap power and an enemy of financial manipulation of the industry, and during his campaign for the presidency he formed an alliance with Senator Norris and gave his support to Norris's long campaign against the power corporations. Roosevelt was a strong believer in the traditional values of rural life; and one of his most cherished ideals was that of a rural society whose members should enjoy economic security and all the advantages of modern technology. In the achievement of this ideal cheap electrical power would play an essential part.

In 1935 Congress passed the Public Utility Act. The Federal Power Commission was given extended powers and was to regulate all companies which transmitted power across state lines. The S. E. C. was to supervise the acquisition of new properties by utility companies, and "as soon as practicable after January 1, 1938," it was to limit the operations of the holding companies so that each of them would control only "a single integrated public utility system." This "death sentence" for holding companies was bitterly opposed by the power corporations, who tried to influence Congress against it by sending thousands of telegrams of protest. It was, however, upheld by the Supreme Court in 1938, and a number of the corporations then agreed to accept it.

Meanwhile the P. W. A. gave funds to municipalities for building publicly owned power plants, and the Rural Electrification Administration, headed by Morris L. Cooke, began to build generating plants and power lines in rural areas. By September, 1939, the R. E. A. had built 135,000 miles of line, supplying 300,000 homes, and had made plans for 240,000 more miles which would supply an additional 700,000 homes. The most spectacular efforts of the New Deal to provide cheaper power consisted, however, in the construction of a number of large hydroelectric plants. Among these were Boulder Dam on the Colorado River in the Southwest, which had been initiated by the Hoover administration, Grand Coulee Dam and Bonneville Dam on the Columbia River in the Northwest, and Fort Peck Dam on the Missouri River. These gigantic engineering projects of the democratic government of the United States were far larger than any of the more loudly publicized building achievements of the European Communist and Fascist dictatorships.

Meanwhile a project had been undertaken on the Tennessee River which involved not only the building of dams but also the forcing down of the electrical rates charged by the power corporations as well as an elaborate scheme of economic and social rehabilitation. Senator Norris's proposal that the government complete and operate the power plant at Muscle Shoals was accepted by Roosevelt and enlarged into a program of social planning which aroused more enthusiasm among Progressives than did any other part of the New Deal. The Tennessee Valley Authority was created by Congress in May, 1933. The T. V. A. was to complete the dams at Muscle Shoals and to build other dams along the Tennessee River. It was also to build transmission lines for rural districts, to generate and sell power, giving preference to public bodies, and to fix the resale rates of the power, thus creating a "yardstick" by which the rates charged by private corporations might be measured. It was also to improve navigation, to carry out flood control operations, to undertake reforestation, to manufacture and sell cheap fertilizer, and to promote the economic and social welfare of the communities living in the area watered by the Tennessee River. This area included parts of seven states and covered about 40,000 square miles with a population of 2 million. It had previously been one of the most backward and poverty-stricken regions in the United States. The original members of the Tennessee Valley Authority were A. E. Morgan, an engineer and flood control expert who had previously been president of Antioch College; David Lilienthal, a lawyer who had reorganized the public utility commission of the State of Wisconsin; and Harcourt Morgan, president of the University of Tennessee and an agricultural scientist.

The T. V. A. proceeded rapidly with the construction of a series of dams and completed seven by 1940. It also began to reduce rates and campaigned to extend the use of electrical appliances, thus enormously increasing the consumption of power. By 1940 the inhabitants of the Tennessee Valley were using 1,179 kilowat hours of energy per person per year, as contrasted with a national average of 850, and were paying 2.14 cents per kilowatt hour, as contrasted with a national average of 4.21. The growth of the T. V. A. was bitterly opposed by the utility companies. Most of the companies operating in the Tennessee Valley were a part of the Commonwealth and Southern system, which was headed after 1933 by Wendell L. Willkie. Willkie declared that the T. V. A. yardstick was unfair since the T. V. A. did not make sufficient allowance, in fixing rates, for the fact that it obtained its capital interest-free from the government and was exempt from taxation. A champion of private enterprise and an enemy of socialism, Willkie maintained that the threat of government competition prevented private capital from entering the power industry and thus impeded economic recovery.

The controversy with the utility companies caused disputes among the three members of the T. V. A.; and in 1938 A. E. Morgan, who had supported some of the claims of the companies, was dismissed by Roosevelt and replaced by James P. Pope, former United States Senator from Idaho. It was decided finally that the T. V. A. should purchase all private utility plants in the region which it served and—in order not to discourage construction by private corporations in other parts of the country—that the price should be a generous one. In 1939 Commonwealth and Southern sold its Tennessee Valley properties to the T. V. A. for $78,600,000, of which $45,000,000 was paid by the T. V. A. itself and the remainder by the local governments. The long fight conducted by the private companies had, however, apparently prevented any extension of the T. V. A. idea to other parts of the country. In 1937 Roosevelt had proposed the creation of seven other public bodies similar to the T. V. A. for other regions of the United States, but Congress failed to take any action on this recommendation.

CONSERVATION

Closely allied to Roosevelt's desire to promote the widespread use of cheap power was his belief in the duty of the Federal government to conserve the soil and other natural resources. Earlier administrations, particularly that of Theodore Roosevelt, had campaigned for conservation, but it was not until 1933 that the Federal government undertook a really comprehensive campaign to check soil erosion and promote reforestation. In view of the enormous importance of this problem to future generations, the conservation program of the New Deal may ultimately be regarded as one of its most valuable achievements.

In the nineteen-thirties public opinion was at last becoming aware of the irreparable damage already done to the land of the United States. Throughout the nineteenth century the cutting of timber, careless farming, and the destruction of grass lands by overgrazing and by putting them under the plough had destroyed much of the soil available for agriculture. The warnings against soil erosion which had repeatedly been delivered by the great Virginians of the eighteenth century had been forgotten. By the nineteen-thirties one-sixth of all American agricultural land had been totally ruined, and an additional one-third had been seriously damaged. The meaning of these facts was brought home to the American people by a series of floods and dust storms. Catastrophic floods, due to the disappearance of forests and topsoil, occurred on the Ohio, Mississippi, and Connecticut Rivers. In the great dust storm of 1934, 300 million tons of topsoil from Kansas, Oklahoma, and Texas were blown out into the Atlantic. The storms of this and subsequent years reduced large areas of western agricultural lands virtually to desert and left their inhabitants destitute. The subsequent migration of thousands of the victims of the Dust Bowl from Kansas and Oklahoma into California and their exploitation by the fruit-growing corporations of that state were the theme of one of the most widely read novels of the decade, John Steinbeck's *The Grapes of Wrath*.

The conservation program of the New Deal interlocked with its recovery program, and a number of measures which were open to justifiable criticisms from the viewpoint of recovery appeared much more commendable when they were regarded in terms of conservation. This was notably true of the A. A. A. The latter was condemned by many critics of the New Deal because it paid farmers to produce less, but it was also a soil conservation project on a very wide scale. Farmers were required to devote the land withdrawn from production to sorghums, legumes, grasses, and other soil-conserving crops. The purpose of the A. A. A. was to preserve, for the use of future generations, the land not immediately needed. Similarly much of the money spent on work relief was invested in conservation projects. The Civilian Conservation Corps constructed dams for checking soil erosion, built firebreaks and lookout towers for checking forest fires, campaigned against tree-destroying diseases and animals, and carried out reforestation measures. Much of the money spent by the F. E. R. A., the C. W. A., and the W. P. A. was also devoted to conservation. These agencies worked on the prevention of soil erosion and undertook large scale engineering projects for the control of floods. Another New Deal agency which combined conservation with other purposes was the T. V. A.

Government responsibility for soil conservation had first been recognized by Congress in 1929. In that year Congress had authorized the establishment of ten experimental stations for the study of soil erosion. In September, 1933, a Soil Erosion Service was created. In April, 1934, by the Soil Conservation Act, this was changed into a Soil Conservation Service and made a bureau of the Department of Agriculture. It was headed by Hugh Bennett, who had been studying the subject for thirty years. The Soil Conservation Service employed 13,000 permanent officials and made use of C. C. C. labor. By establishing experimental erosion projects to demonstrate the value of conservation, the officials of the Service set out to persuade farmers to accept their co-operation in building terraces on sloping lands and in adopting other devices for checking wind and water erosion. Meanwhile the New Deal speeded up the purchase of forest reserves by the government and urged the private timber companies to adopt a policy of cutting no timber in excess of the annual growth. The Resettlement Administration purchased submarginal farm land for reforestation; and, by the Taylor Grazing Act of 1934, the grazing of cattle on public land was restricted. In 1934, in order to check dust storms, the government began to plant trees along a "Shelter Belt" one hundred miles broad, east of the Dust Bowl, from Canada to Texas, thereby conserving moisture and breaking the force of the wind. By 1940, 100 million trees had been planted.

One other New Deal measure which may be considered under the heading of conservation was the Indian Reorganization Act of 1934. The previous Indian policy of the government had been to integrate the Indians into white civilization and to break up the Indian common lands into private properties. This policy had been conspicuously unsuccessful, since the Indians refused to accept amalgamation, and the creation of private property in land had meant, in practice, the transfer of Indian land to white ownership at the rate of 2 million acres a year over a forty-five year period. By 1934 the Indians retained only 47 million acres, of which half was desert or semidesert and the remainder was grass land that had been largely ruined by excess grazing. A program of rehabilitation in order to save the Indians from starvation was therefore necessary. John Collier, who became Commissioner of Indian Affairs under the New Deal, believed that there were values in the traditional communal life of the Indians which deserved to be rescued and that the Indians should be encouraged to remain Indian instead of being forcibly transformed into bad imitations of white men. By the Indian Reorganization Act the land which still belonged to the Indians was to remain as communal tribal property. The Indians were, moreover, given credits and additional land, and were to receive assistance in the checking of overgrazing.

THE FEDERAL BUDGET

The feature of the New Deal which provoked most vigorous and widespread criticism was its failure to balance the budget. Businessmen and conservative economists believed that the continuance of deficit financing would result in steadily increasing taxes and might end in uncontrolled inflation. They further believed that the government was absorbing capital which would otherwise have financed business expansion, that these funds were being used wastefully and unproductively, and that a balanced budget was essential in order to create business confidence and thereby make possible an economic recovery.

Roosevelt himself appears originally to have favored a balanced budget; during his campaign for the presidency he had criticized Hoover for his failure to prevent deficits; and one of the earliest measures of the Roosevelt administration was the Economy Act of March 20, 1933, which reduced government salaries and veterans' benefits. The promise to balance the budget was, however, incompatible with other promises of the Democratic platform—with its support of adequate relief for the unemployed, reduction of agricultural production, and Federal expenditures for public works. In March, 1933, moreover, any sudden contraction of government expenses would have diminished purchasing power and have had a deflationary effect that might have done more harm than good to the economic system.

Roosevelt, therefore, accepted an unbalanced budget as inevitable; the Federal government spent large sums on public works and unemployment relief; and, with the expansion of government services under the New Deal, its normal expenditures also began to rise. Roosevelt still regarded a balanced budget as desirable in the abstract, but he continued to postpone any serious attempt to achieve it. And although the Republican leaders denounced the New Deal financial policies, few of them were willing to commit themselves as to where, specifically, economies should be made. Congressmen had always found that they were more likely to be re-elected if they voted for the spending of money; and many Republican senators and representatives who denounced New Deal extravagance were, when confronted by concrete issues, willing to appropriate even larger sums than was the administration. This was conspicuously the case with the veterans' bonus, which Congress voted over Roosevelt's veto in 1935, and with subsidies for the farmers.

Meanwhile some of the New Deal economists were putting forward a new point of view. They argued that large-scale government spending was essential during periods of depression in order to maintain purchasing power and compensate for the lack of spending by private capital. Eventually the growth of the national income would enable the budget to be balanced by increasing government revenues. The budget should be planned over long periods, with deficits in times of depression and surpluses in times of prosperity. It was suggested also that much of the government debt should be considered as an investment; insofar as government borrowings were used to finance public works, conservation, and improvements of health and education, they served, directly or indirectly, to increase the national wealth. When a private business corporation borrowed capital in order to enlarge its plant and equipment, it was regarded as a sign of prosperity; government borrowing, it was suggested, should be judged in the same manner.

The New Dealers argued, furthermore, that much of the alarm provoked by the growth of the national debt reflected an inability to distinguish between a public debt and a private debt. A private debt was a burden upon the debtor; but a public debt was a debt owed by the nation to itself. Payment of a public debt meant merely the transference of wealth from one group of citizens to another; it did not diminish the wealth of the nation as a whole. The only question to be asked about an increase in the public debt was whether the government was making the best possible use of the capital and labor which it was putting into motion. Would the capital have been employed more advantageously if it had been left in private hands?

During the depression there was a decrease in government revenue, particularly in the income tax. A larger proportion of the revenue than formerly was represented by indirect taxes, which were paid by the whole population, not merely by those persons in the upper income brackets. The most important of the indirect taxes were those levied on liquor and tobacco, which accounted for nearly a quarter of all government revenues under the New Deal. During the ten years 1931–1940 total revenues were $41,033,000,000; income tax payments amounted to $15,789,000,000, more than half of which was supplied by the corporation income tax, while internal indirect taxes brought in $16,035,000,000.

Government expenditure increased during the Hoover adminis tration as a result of public works and the R. F. C. In 1933 normal government expenses were temporarily reduced, but they quickly began to rise as a result of the growth of the civil service, which contained 568,345 members in 1932 and 813,302 in 1937. Abnormal expenditure reached its peak in 1936 and 1937 as a result of pay ment of the veterans' bonus. During the fiscal year 1937–1938, after a business recovery, relief spendings were reduced and the budget was almost balanced; during a part of the year, in fact, the govern ment was taking in more money than it paid out. This was followed by a sharp business recession, and in the spring of 1938 the govern ment embarked on another large-scale spending program. Roosevelt had apparently accepted the viewpoint of those New Deal economists who believed that an unbalanced budget was necessary in a depres sion period. In 1939 the conservatives in Congress insisted on a reduction of government spending, and the demand for a balanced budget began to win considerable support. In the spring of 1940, however, the United States was compelled to adopt a large-scale armament program, which made a continuance of treasury deficits for some years to come almost inevitable.

In the spring of 1940 the gross national debt amounted to $44,458,000,000, having increased by $21,929,000,000 since the beginning of the New Deal. In 1919, at the conclusion of the World War, the debt had amounted to $25,482,000,000. Since, however, there was nearly $2,250,000,000 in the Treasury, and another $2,000,000,000 in the Stabilization Fund, the net debt amounted to about $40,250,000,000. The administration calculated, moreover, that it had spent $16,431,000,000 on public works and other dur able improvements and on recoverable loans, and that of this sum $3,234,000,000 would eventually be paid back to the Treasury. Government borrowings had come almost wholly from the banks, and the interest rate had been abnormally low. Until 1940 interest payments on the national debt amounted to a smaller figure than in 1919.

Government receipts and expenditures from June 30, 1930, until June 30, 1940, were as follows:

FISCAL YEAR ENDING JUNE	RECEIPTS	ORDINARY EXPENDI- TURES	ARMAMENTS, VETERANS, A.A.A., SOCIAL SECURITY, INTEREST ON DEBT, ETC.	PUBLIC WORKS, RELIEF	TOTAL EXPENDI- TURES	DEBT
			(IN MILLIONS OF DOLLARS)			
1931	3190	647	2340	684	3671	16,801
1932	2006	756	2407	1372	4535	19,487
1933	2080	584	2267	1013	3864	22,539
1934	3116	458	2193	3360	6011	27,053
1935	3800	562	2895	3553	7010	28,701
1936	4116	675	4634	3357	8666	33,778
1937	5294	689	3974	3779	8442	36,425
1938	6242	712	3934	2980	7626	37,165
1939	5520	799	4452	4241	9492	41,732
1940	5669	865	4882	3458	8995	44,458

The New Deal made few permanent alterations in the tax system. In 1933 and 1934 the only changes were the imposition of liquor taxes and a tightening of the income tax regulations in order to block loopholes. In 1935, however, Roosevelt asked Congress for higher taxes on large incomes and inheritances and on big corporations. The purposes of this proposal appear to have been social and political rather than financial; Roosevelt hoped to check the growth of big business, and he seems to have wished to steal the thunder of Huey Long, whose "Share our Wealth" movement was reaching dangerous proportions. In the Revenue Act of 1935 Congress imposed higher taxes on gifts and estates; it raised income taxes on incomes above $50,000, the maximum being 75 per cent on incomes above $5,000,000; it raised the corporation income tax, the maximum being 15 per cent; and it imposed an excess profits duty, with a maximum of 12 per cent on profits exceeding 15 per cent.

The Revenue Act of 1936 provoked even more controversy. Its chief features were a tax of from 7 to 27 per cent on undistributed corporation profits, and a heavy tax on profits realized through the transfer of capital assets. In the opinion of the New Dealers the failure of corporations to distribute their profits was often a device by which wealthy stockholders evaded income tax payments; such undistributed profits, moreover, were often spent uneconomically on unwise expansion. Business, on the other hand, vigorously opposed these two new taxes. They declared that corporations accumulated surpluses for use in depression periods, that taxing these surpluses would weaken business, and that the tax on capital gains would discourage new investments. In 1938 Congress made drastic reductions in both these taxes, and Roosevelt expressed his disapproval by allowing the Revenue Act to become law without his signature. In 1939 the undistributed profits tax was abolished; while the corporation income tax was raised to a maximum of 18 per cent. Another feature of the 1939 Revenue Act was that for the first time Federal taxes were imposed on the employees of state and municipal governments—a measure which had been made possible by a recent Supreme Court decision.

BIBLIOGRAPHY

J. Alsop and R. Kintner, *Men Around the President* (1939)
C. Aronovici, *Housing the Masses* (1939)
L. P. Ayres, *Economics of Recovery* (1934)
*C. A. Beard, *America in Midpassage* (1939)
H. H. Bennett, *Soil Conservation* (1939)
A. A. Berle and others, *America's Recovery Program* (1934)
J. C. Bonbright, *Public Utilities and the National Power Policies* (1940)
*Brookings Institution, *The Recovery Problem in the United States* (1936)
D. V. Brown and others, *Economics of the Recovery Program* (1934)
J. C. Brown, *Public Relief 1929–39* (1940)
*A. R. Burns, *The Decline of Competition* (1936)
E. M. Burns, *Towards Social Security* (1936)
P. Campbell, *Consumer Representation in the New Deal* (1940)
J. P. Clark, *The Rise of a New Federalism* (1938)
C. L. Dearing, *The A.B.C. of the N.R.A.* (1934)
P. H. Douglas, *Social Security in the United States* (1936)
*Editors of *The Economist, The New Deal* (1937)
A. Epstein, *Insecurity* (revised edition, 1938)
J. T. Flynn, *Country Squire in the White House* (1940)
J. Franklin, *1940* (1940)

G. B. Galloway, *Industrial Planning under the Codes* (1935)
A. F. Gustavson and others, *Conservation in the United States* (1939)
L. Hacker, *Short History of the New Deal* (1934)
*——— *American Problems of Today* (1938)
M. A. Hallgren, *The Gay Reformer* (1935)
*A. H. Hansen, *Full Recovery or Stagnation* (1938)
S. High, *Roosevelt—and then?* (1937)
C. L. Hodge, *The Tennessee Valley Authority* (1938)
G. C. Johnson, *The Treasury and Monetary Policy, 1933–38* (1939)
M. D. Bane and F. Steegmuller, *America on Relief* (1938)
*E. K. Lindley, *Halfway with Roosevelt* (1936)
D. and E. K. Lindley, *A New Deal for Youth* (1938)
L. S. Lyon and others, *The National Recovery Administration* (1935)
W. MacDonald, *The Menace of Recovery* (1934)
R. Moley, *After Seven Years* (1939)
New Republic, Supplement on *The New Deal in Review* (May 20,
    1940)
E. G. Nourse and others, *Three Years of the A.A.A.* (1937)
W. F. Ogburn and others, *Social Change and the New Deal* (1934)
J. D. Paris, *Monetary Policies of the United States, 1932–38* (1938)
C. F. Roos, *N.R.A. Economic Planning* (1937)
F. D. Roosevelt, *Public Papers and Addresses* (1938)
J. Rosenfarb, *The National Labor Policy* (1940)
I. M. Rubinow, *The Quest for Security* (1934)
*E. Stein and others, *Labor Problems in America* (1940)
M. Stevenson and R. E. Spear, *The Social Security Program* (1936)
M. S. Stewart, *Social Security* (1937)
B. Stolberg and W. J. Vinton, *Economic Consequences of the New Deal*
    (1935)
N. W. Straus and T. Wegg, *Housing Comes of Age* (1938)
G. Swope, *The Swope Plan* (1931)
The Unofficial Observer, *The New Dealers* (1934)
H. A. Wallace, *New Frontiers* (1934)
——— *America Must Choose* (1934)
S. C. Wallace, *The New Deal in Action* (1934)
G. S. Watkins and P. A. Dodd, *Labor Problems* (1940)

42

POLITICS AND

THE SUPREME COURT

OPPOSITION TO THE NEW DEAL

AT THE beginning of the New Deal there was little open opposition to the administration among any section of the population. All classes had been alarmed by the spread of the depression and by its culmination in the closing of the banks, and all classes were willing to accept almost any program which Roosevelt might recommend. Many conservative Democrats disapproved of much of the New Deal, but few of them ventured to oppose it publicly; and many Republicans in Congress voted for a number of New Deal measures.

In 1934 and 1935, on the other hand, as the Progressive tendencies of the New Deal became more apparent, public opinion began to crystallize. The New Deal ran counter to the traditional party divisions; and, while the bulk of the farming and wage-earning groups, both Democratic and Republican, supported the administration, the majority of the business classes opposed it. As in 1800, in 1828, and in 1896 American opinion was becoming divided along class lines. The business classes were by no means unanimous. While the representatives of the capital goods industries were against the New Deal, a number of spokesmen of the consumption goods industries and of retail trade, the prosperity of which depended directly on mass purchasing power, supported Roosevelt. Other businessmen favored the New Deal because they disliked the isolationist tendencies of Republican foreign policy and because they approved of New Deal efforts to increase international trade and promote international peace. Or they favored the New Deal because they believed that drastic reforms in the American economic system were the only alternative to collapse and revolution.

A large proportion of the wealthier families in America, however, became most bitter antagonists of the whole New Deal program. They declared that Roosevelt was making himself a dictator, that he was destroying the American form of government by making Congress into a rubber stamp, and that he had Communistic leanings. They denounced the growth of bureaucracy, the failure to balance the budget, the squandering of public money on unemployment relief, the encouragement given to organized labor, the raising of wages and shortening of hours, and the regulation of the stock exchanges; and they insisted that any economic recovery was impossible as long as a group of impractical theorists in Washington were allowed to destroy business confidence and to shackle business expansion with unnecessary regulations. The intensity with which many wealthy families hated Roosevelt was probably unparalleled in American history. The weakness of the opposition to the New Deal was, however, that it was almost wholly negative. Whatever justification there may have been for specific criticisms of the New Deal, many of its opponents gave the impression that they wanted to return to the days of Harding and Coolidge, or to those of McKinley and Mark Hanna, that they were incapable of recognizing that the American system could not survive unless it were reformed, and that they had learned nothing by the depression.

That the New Deal had the support of a majority of the population was proved in the election of 1934, when the Democrats made further gains in both the Senate and the House. Opposition to the New Deal was, however, strongly entrenched in the Supreme Court. The members of the Court, with the dates of their appointment, were as follows: four were conservatives—Van Devanter (1911), McReynolds (1914), Sutherland (1922), and Butler (1922); three were liberals—Brandeis (1916), Stone (1925), and Cardozo (1932); two occupied the middle of the road—Chief Justice Hughes

(1930), and Roberts (1930). Throughout the depression the Court had maintained a conservative trend, and had frowned upon attempts by state legislatures to regulate economic conditions. In 1934, on the other hand, it showed liberal tendencies; in particular, in a five to four decision in the Nebbia case, in which the majority decision was written by Justice Roberts, it upheld a New York State law fixing the minimum price of milk.

The year 1935 brought a return to conservatism. The Court voided several minor New Deal measures, and on May 27, in the Schechter Case, it declared the N. R. A. unconstitutional by a unanimous vote. The reasons for the decision were, first, that Congress had unconstitutionally transferred legislative power to the executive, and, second, that the scope of the N. R. A. had been unconstitutionally extended beyond the sphere of interstate commerce. January, 1936, brought a veto of the other main pillar of the New Deal recovery program, the A. A. A. By six to three, the majority opinion being written by Justice Roberts, the Court declared that the A. A. A. was an unconstitutional interference with the rights of the states and that Congress had made an unconstitutional use of its power to levy taxes. The decision was notable because of an eloquent dissenting opinion by Justice Stone, in which he warned his colleagues against the assumption that the courts were "the only agency of government that must be assumed to have capacity to govern." Later in the year several other New Deal measures were invalidated, making a total of eight decisions against it and only two in its favor. In June a New York State minimum wage law for women was declared unconstitutional by five to four—a decision which appeared to conflict with the ruling in the Nebbia Case. The voiding of this state wage law, coupled with the earlier voiding of the N. R. A., meant that, according to the Court, no government body in the country had authority to regulate wages. In the opinion of the Court the constitution of the United States still enforced the rules of laissez-faire economics.

Roosevelt expressed bitterness over the decisions of the Court, declaring that the justices had interpreted the constitution according to the practices of "horse and buggy days" and pointing out that they defined interstate commerce very broadly when it was a question of issuing injunctions against strikers and very strictly when Congress attempted to raise wages and reduce hours. He did not, however, commit himself as to what policy he proposed to adopt.

THE ELECTION OF 1936

For the 1936 election the Republicans nominated Alfred M. Landon, governor of Kansas, for the presidency, and Frank Knox, proprietor of the Chicago *Daily News,* for the vice presidency. Both men had formerly been followers of Theodore Roosevelt, and were regarded as liberals. Their platform did not promise any repudiation of the New Deal, though it demanded changes in detail. The unemployed, for example, were still to receive relief from the Federal government, but it should be administered by the states; the farmers were still to be given Federal subsidies, but they were to be assisted in finding foreign markets for their surpluses; the antitrust laws were to be enforced; labor was to be guaranteed the right of collective bargaining; and—according to Landon—the constitution should, if necessary, be amended to allow regulation of wages and hours.

The Democrats renominated Roosevelt without opposition, adopted a platform praising the achievements of the New Deal, and declared that if the Court continued to prohibit Federal regulation of economic conditions, they would seek a "clarifying amendment." This clause in the Democratic platform was so phrased in order to imply that the barrier to Federal regulation was not the constitution itself but the manner in which the Court had interpreted it.

The campaign was very bitter, but few concrete issues were presented to the electorate. Roosevelt ran on his record and promised the country more of the same kind of thing, but he made no definite commitments. Landon was no match for Roosevelt as an orator; and during the campaign his liberalism grew less evident and the influence of his more conservative supporters grew more marked. The most vigorous opponents of Roosevelt were a group of wealthy businessmen, headed by the Du Pont family, who had recently organized the so-called Liberty League to fight the New Deal; a number of conservative Democrats from Northern states, including two former presidential candidates, Alfred E. Smith and John W. Davis; and the newspaper proprietor William Randolph Hearst, who had now totally abandoned his semisocialism of a generation earlier. These men declared that the college professors whom Roosevelt had called to Washington and the labor leaders who supported him were Communists. At least two-thirds of the press was against the New Deal, and many of the newspapers which supported it were lukewarm. On the other hand, Roosevelt had the support of most of the trade unions, whose leaders had formed Labor's Nonpartisan League in order to campaign for his re-election, and particularly of the United Mine Workers, who gave him a campaign contribution of $469,870. He could rely on most of the farm organizations and on the unemployed; and, for the first time, the Democrats received the votes of most of the Northern Negro population—a change of party allegiance which had considerable importance.

The election resulted in the most sweeping political victory for more than a century. Roosevelt, with a popular vote of 27,476,000 had an electoral vote of 523. Landon, with a popular vote of 16,680,000, carried only Maine and Vermont, which gave him 8 electoral votes. Of the minor candidates, William Lemke, who had been nominated by the followers of Father Coughlin, Dr. Townsend, and the late Huey Long, received 882,000 votes; Norman Thomas, the Socialist candidate, received 194,000 votes; Earl Browder, the Communist candidate, received 80,000 votes.

ROOSEVELT AND THE SUPREME COURT

After his second inauguration Roosevelt startled the country by proposing, on February 5, 1937, a reorganization of the Federal judiciary. Declaring that many judges were too old to perform their duties efficiently, Roosevelt recommended that whenever a judge passed the age of seventy without retiring, the president should have the power to appoint an additional judge to assist him. Under this plan the membership of the Supreme Court might, if necessary, be increased to fifteen. Roosevelt appears to have made this proposal without consulting the Democratic leaders in Congress, and against the wishes of most of his usual advisers.

The Court plan was Roosevelt's first serious political mistake.

Many persons who disapproved of the Court's conservative decisions would have preferred some other method of dealing with the problem—a constitutional amendment, for example, or a restriction of the Court's power of review. Many liberals believed that Roosevelt's proposal would seriously impair the dignity and independence of the judiciary. The arguments with which Roosevelt supported his plan were very disingenuous; and, by failing to publish his proposal until after the election, he had shown a disregard for the democratic process. Strong opposition developed in the country and in Congress, its leader being Senator Wheeler, who was himself a Democrat and a Progressive. Meanwhile the Court proceeded to take the wind out of its opponents' sails by spectacularly reversing itself. In March, by another five to four decision, the Court upheld a minimum wage law enacted by the State of Washington. Thus, as a result of a change of mind on the part of Justice Roberts, the constitution no longer prohibited wage-fixing. In April the Court adopted a broader definition of interstate commerce than in the Schechter Case, and accepted the Wagner Labor Relations Act; and in May, abandoning the narrow interpretation of the taxing power which had caused it to invalidate the A. A. A., it accepted the Social Security Act. The result was that the chief arguments in favor of the Court plan had been removed. In August, after the sudden death of Senator Robinson, who had legislative charge of the plan, Roosevelt accepted defeat. Congress passed the Judicial Procedure Act, limiting certain minor abuses of judicial power, and abandoned the proposal to enlarge the Supreme Court.

In his ultimate objective Roosevelt, nevertheless, proved to be victorious. In June Justice Van Devanter resigned and was succeeded by Hugo Black, Senator from Alabama. A controversy was provoked by the subsequent discovery that Black had once been a member of the Ku Klux Klan; but the new justice soon showed himself a vigorous champion of civil liberties, while the able dissenting opinions in which he maintained that the Fourteenth Amendment should not apply to corporations were of remarkable interest. In 1938 Justices Sutherland and Cardozo were succeeded by Stanley Reed, former Solicitor General, and Felix Frankfurter, of the

Harvard Law School; in 1939 Justice Brandeis was succeeded by William O. Douglas, of the S. E. C., and in 1940 Justice Butler was succeeded by Frank Murphy, former governor of Michigan and Attorney General.

Thus, for the first time since before the Civil War, the Supreme Court had a liberal majority. The dissenting opinions which had been delivered in earlier years by Holmes, Brandeis, Stone, and Cardozo now became the official interpretations of the constitution. The Court allowed much more latitude than formerly to the legislative power; it showed a new concern for the rights and needs of labor, particularly in the series of decisions in which it upheld the Wagner Act; and in a number of cases it defended, more fully and vigorously than had been its custom, the civil liberties guaranteed by the first article of the Bill of Rights. This revolution on the Supreme Court was probably as important a development in American constitutional history as had been its swing toward conservatism in the eighteen-eighties and nineties.

THE ELECTIONS OF 1938

Roosevelt did not quickly regain the prestige which he had lost during the Court fight. A large part of his own party was now in open revolt against his leadership; and his difficulties were increased by the sudden economic recession, which began in August, 1937, and continued until the following summer. In the spring of 1938 Congress accepted Roosevelt's new spending program, and it passed several New Deal laws, notably the second A. A. A., the Fair Labor Standards Act, and the Food, Drug, and Cosmetic Act, which revised the act of 1906 by giving the Department of Agriculture stronger power to prohibit the sale of adulterated foods and harmful drugs. On the other hand, Congress refused to grant Roosevelt authority, which he had requested in January, 1937, to reorganize the executive branch of the government. It had been agreed by most students of the problem for many years that such a reorganization was needed and that only the President could do it efficiently. But the fears, provoked during the Court fight, that Roosevelt was aiming at dictatorship, caused Congress to reject this proposal. It was, however, passed in a modified form in 1939, as a result of which a number of changes were made. The most important was the assembling of most of the New Deal bureaus into three major agencies: the Federal Security Agency, the Federal Works Agency, and the Federal Loan Agency. The first administrators of these three agencies were Paul V. McNutt, John Carmody, and Jesse Jones.

In the elections of 1938 the New Dealers attempted to transform the Democratic Party into a consistently Progressive organization by preventing five conservative senators and one congressman from securing renomination as Democratic candidates. This party "purge" was unsuccessful except in the case of the congressman, Representative O'Connor of New York; and the elections resulted not only in the strengthening of conservative influences in the Democratic Party but also in Republican victories. The Republicans elected governors in Pennsylvania, Michigan, Minnesota, Wisconsin, and Oregon, all of which had previously been governed by Democrats or Progressives; and they won eighty seats in the House of Representatives and eight in the Senate. In co-operation with a group of sixty conservative southern Democrats, the Republicans in the House were able to prevent any extension of the New Deal. In 1939 Congress showed a marked inclination to amend a number of New Deal laws, particularly the Wagner Act; and it cut the relief and public works appropriations recommended by the President. This victory for economy was, however, counteracted by an increase in the benefits to be paid to the farmers. In spite of Republican denunciations of government extravagance, Congress was still, by preference, a spending agency; and the total appropriations which it voted were actually larger than those which Roosevelt had requested.

FARMER-LABOR PARTIES

Third-party movements continued during the thirties to be numerically as weak as they had been in the nineteenth century. As a result of events in Europe, however, they won considerably more attention.

Immediately to the left of the Democratic Party were various labor and farmer-labor organizations which aimed at the gradual transformation of capitalism into some form of democratic socialism but which, on immediate issues, generally supported the New Deal.

The oldest of these was the Minnesota Farmer-Labor Party. This party had been formed in 1918 and had elected a United States Senator in 1922. From 1932 until 1938, under the leadership first of Floyd B. Olson and later of Elmer Benson, it controlled the state government. In 1936 it supported Roosevelt in return for the withdrawal of the state ticket of the Democratic Party. In Wisconsin, the traditional stronghold of agrarian liberalism, a Progressive Party was organized in 1934 and was successful in electing several congressmen. The La Follette family continued to be powerful; Robert La Follette represented the state in the Senate, first as a Republican and afterward as an Independent, while his brother Philip served as governor for three terms. In 1938 Philip La Follette launched a national Progressive Party but won very little support. The only result was that in the election of the autumn he was defeated for re-election to the governorship by a conservative Republican. Similar progressive and farmer-labor organizations won some strength in other Middle Western and Far Western states, especially in Washington and California. In California in 1934 Upton Sinclair, the socialist novelist, captured the Democratic nomination for governorship and was defeated by the Republican candidate by a narrow margin. In 1938, when the Democrats won control of that state, their candidates had Communist support and were considerably to the left of the New Deal.

In the East the most significant third party movement was in New York. In 1933 New York City conducted one of its periodic political housecleanings. Tammany Hall, which had controlled the city since 1917, was discredited by revelations of corruption made by a legislative investigation with Samuel Seabury as counsel. Fiorello H. LaGuardia, officially a Republican but actually a Progressive, was elected mayor. Mayor LaGuardia gave the city a New Deal administration whose energy, efficiency, and liberality won wide applause. His strongest support came from the trade unions of the city, who organized in 1936 the American Labor Party, the leadership of which came chiefly from the clothing unions. In 1936 nearly

250,000 persons voted for Roosevelt on the Labor Party ticket; and in 1937, when LaGuardia was re-elected mayor as candidate both of the Republicans and of the Labor Party, the Labor Party vote reached nearly 500,000. The Labor Party was not strong enough to elect candidates of its own to important offices, but it was in a position to hold the balance of power in New York State between the two major parties.

There was considerable talk of a national farmer-labor party; but as long as the Democratic Party adopted New Deal candidates and supported Progressive policies, such a development was unlikely. The importance of these various third-party movements was that, if the Democratic Party lost their support, it might be defeated by the Republicans. The independent Progressive vote was probably strong enough to enforce Progressive policies upon the Democrats.

The Socialist Party, meanwhile, had fallen upon evil days. Attacking the New Deal as not sufficiently radical, it lost all its right-wing supporters, who turned to Roosevelt and to the American Labor Party. In the election of 1936 its vote was smaller than in any presidential election since 1900.

COMMUNISM AND FASCISM

Numerically, the Communists remained even weaker than the Socialists, the party membership in 1939 being about 75,000; but their influence was considerably broader. They developed a technique for penetrating non-Communist organizations, which they often succeeded in controlling as a result partly of their secretiveness and partly of the energy and enthusiasm with which they undertook onerous and dangerous duties.

In the early stages of the New Deal the Communists denounced Roosevelt as a Fascist, declaring that in political essence and direction his program was identical with that of Hitler. In 1935, however, the Communist International instructed its various subsidiary parties throughout the world to join other progressive organizations in a Popular Front and to demand that the aggressive policies of the Fascist states be checked by a program of collective security. The chief reason for this change of policy appears to have been the fear of the Soviet government that it would be attacked by Nazi Germany. The Communist Party of the United States thereupon abandoned its program of dual unionism, dissolved the Trade Union Unity League, and set about winning influence in the established labor unions by "boring from within." It formed numerous "transmission belt" organizations for middle-class liberals, most of whom were quite unaware that these organizations were under Communist control. And it began to support Roosevelt, approving particularly of his desire that the United States help the European democracies to check Nazi Germany. In 1936, although the Communist Party ran Earl Browder as its own candidate, many Communists voted for Roosevelt in order to defeat Landon, who was being depicted by the party as a Fascist. The Communist cause was advocated by numerous writers, artists, and intellectuals, and the allegation was made that it had a number of supporters in government agencies and among trade union officials.

The extent of Communist influence was probably much exaggerated by both the friends and the enemies of the party. The chief importance of the activities of the party was that it played into the hands of conservatives by enabling the latter to denounce as communistic many liberal movements that were temporarily receiving Communist support. In two directions, however, the Party had indisputable success: it controlled the Workers' Alliance, an organization formed to represent the interests of the unemployed; and it had great influence in a number of youth organizations, particularly in the American Student Union and in the American Youth Congress.

In the summer of 1939, when Stalin signed a pact with Hitler, Communist policy immediately reversed itself. The Communists declared that the war in Europe was not between democracy and dictatorship but between rival imperialisms, the governments of Great Britain and France being even more guilty than that of Germany. They began to denounce Roosevelt as a war-monger and to support isolationism. Most of the intellectuals who had formerly supported the party quickly abandoned it; but the Communists were able, to some extent, to capitalize upon American antiwar sentiment, particularly among young men of military age.

Of the two forms of totalitarianism, most Americans regarded Communism as constituting the more dangerous internal menace to democracy. Fascistic sentiment had, however, a rapid growth after 1933 and was probably stronger than Communism. The German-American Bund was the only body which was openly affiliated with European Fascism; but by 1940 there were several hundreds of small organizations which imitated the Nazis in preaching anti-Semitism, exaggerating the Communist menace, and advocating dictatorship. Of the three demagogic movements which had appeared during the depression and which had combined to support the candidacy of Lemke in 1936, two—those headed by Father Coughlin and by Gerald Smith—became definitely fascistic. Father Coughlin advocated policies which grew increasingly similar to those adopted in Germany, and he continued to have considerable popular influence both through his radio speeches and through his magazine *Social Justice*. Opposition to the growing strength of the labor movement, as represented by the C. I. O., sometimes assumed fascistic forms, especially in the South, where the Ku Klux Klan began to revive.

The growth of these un-American activities, both on the left and on the right, caused considerable alarm and threatened to cause a restriction of civil liberties. Many conservatives, who were disturbed by the spread of propaganda sponsored by the dictatorship states, began to demand that the United States herself adopt dictatorial policies in self-defense. In 1938 a congressional committee headed by Martin Dies began to investigate un-American activities. The Dies Committee discovered much significant information; but some of its members were notably lacking in regard for civil liberties and appeared anxious to pin the Communist label indiscriminately on all liberals and Progressives. In the spring of 1940 the fear of un-American movements was increased by the success of Fifth Column agencies in helping Nazi Germany to conquer Norway and Holland. It became obvious that some kind of check on similar agencies in the United States was necessary; and there was considerable danger that all aliens, however innocent, and all radicals, however free from foreign affiliations, might be the victims of popular hysteria. Whether the United States could take adequate measures against un-American groups working in the interests of foreign governments, and at the same time preserve unimpaired her traditional liberties, began to seem dubious.

BIBLIOGRAPHY

D. Alfange, *The Supreme Court and the National Will* (1937)
*C. A. Beard, *America in Midpassage* (1939)
I. Brant, *Storm over the Constitution* (1936)
G. Britt, *The Fifth Column* (1940)
E. Browder, *The People's Front* (1938)
R. K. Carr, *Democracy and the Supreme Court* (1936)
E. S. Corwin, *Court over Constitution* (1938)
I. Feinstein, *The Court Disposes* (1937)
O. K. Fraenkel, *The Supreme Court and Civil Liberties* (1937)
D. Pearson and R. S. Allen, *The Nine Old Men* (1936)
M. J. Pusey, *The Supreme Court Crisis* (1937)

43

TRADE UNIONISM

UNDER THE NEW DEAL

THE UNIONS AND THE N. R. A.

ONE of the most important results of the New Deal was the stimulus which it gave to labor organization.

During the depression the trade unions had declined both in numbers and in importance. The official membership of the A. F of L. decreased from 2,769,700 in 1929 to 2,317,500 in 1933, and the real decrease in dues-paying members was considerably larger. The membership of unions outside the A. F. of L. amounted in 1933 to 655,500. The growth of unemployment reduced the financial resources of the unions and made successful strikes almost impossible. William Green and the other A. F. of L. leaders were, moreover, conservatives who were incapable of making the militant demands for reform which the situation required. Many of them had voted for Herbert Hoover in 1928, and they were fully as helpless and bewildered when confronted by the depression as were the leaders of organized capital.

The coming of the New Deal brought an immediate and decisive change. The administration was known to be friendly to organized labor; and the inclusion of Section 7A in the National Industrial Recovery Act meant that workers now had a legal right to join unions of their own choosing. The economic recovery meant, moreover, that labor was in a strong position to win concessions, and in its struggle to do so it was stimulated by all the bitterness which had accumulated during the years of wage cuts and dismissals. While employers hastily tried to protect themselves from Section 7A by forming company unions, ten of thousands of workers who had hitherto been wholly unorganized began to flock into the A. F. of L., declaring that the government wished them to join unions and that it was their patriotic duty to obey the N. R. A. During 1934, 1,466,695 workers participated in strikes—a figure which had been exceeded only in 1916, 1917, and 1919. Particularly notable were the ten-day San Francisco general strike of July, which was precipitated by the grievances of the longshoremen and marine workers, and the textile workers strike of September.

There were three unions in particular which were able to take advantage of this situation in order to make large permanent additions to their membership—the United Mine Workers under the leadership of John L. Lewis, the International Ladies Garment Workers under David Dubinsky, and the Amalgamated Clothing Workers under Sidney Hillman. The growth of the United Mine Workers was especially rapid. In 1932 its membership had not exceeded 150,000 and may have been as low as 50,000; by 1935 it had increased to 500,000, and had established itself in areas where the yellow-dog contract had prevailed hitherto and where union organizers had been excluded by terroristic methods. John L. Lewis had formerly been regarded as one of the most conservative of union leaders; he had fought a long battle to prevent progressive and radical leaders from capturing the union, and had been accused by his opponents of retaining control by fraud and intimidation. In 1928 he had been a supporter of Herbert Hoover. After 1933, however, Lewis joined forces with his former enemies in the United Mine Workers, who were headed by John Brophy, and displayed great energy, aggressiveness, and political skill in rebuilding the union.

Meanwhile other A. F. of L. leaders failed to capitalize on the new pro-union sentiment of American workers. While the workers were militant and enthusiastic, the old-fashioned labor leaders were slow-moving, conservative, and wedded to a policy of collaboration with the employers. Faithful to the traditions of the A. F. of L., they endeavored to distribute the new union members among the different craft unions; and workers who wanted vigorous action to consolidate their right to collective bargaining found that the chief activity of the union officials was the settlement of jurisdictional boundaries and disputes. The inapplicability of craft union methods to the new situation was particularly marked in the steel, automobile, and rubber industries. It became apparent that such industries could most effectively be organized by the methods of industrial unionism, already used in the United Mine Workers, under which all the workers in an industry, whatever specialized task they might perform, belonged to the same organization.

THE C. I. O.

At the A. F. of L. convention of 1934, which met at San Francisco, the advocates of industrial unionism secured passage of a compromise resolution admitting the need for industrial unions in certain industries. The leaders of the craft unions disliked this program, which would tend to diminish their own jurisdictions; and the A. F. of L. took no action to implement it. In the 1935 convention, meeting at Atlantic City, the industrial unionists demanded action and were defeated by a vote of 10,933 to 18,024. The industrial unionists then decided to ignore the A. F. of L., and on November 9, 1935, their leaders formed the Committee for Industrial Organization. Lewis was elected chairman and John Brophy director. The C. I. O. began its career with nearly 1,000,000 members, a large majority of whom belonged to the United Mine Workers, the International Ladies Garment Workers, and the Amalgamated Clothing Workers. In August, 1936, the A. F. of L. suspended the C. I. O. unions, and the split became definitive. In November, 1938, the C. I. O. was reorganized on a permanent basis. It changed its name to the Congress of Industrial Organizations and adopted a constitution. Lewis was elected president, Sidney Hillman and Philip Murray vice presidents, and James Carey of the Electrical, Radio, and Machine Workers secretary.

The most spectacular successes of the C. I. O. were in steel and automobiles—two industries in which trade unionism had hitherto been negligible. In the steel industry the labor movement had suffered three crushing defeats, in 1892, in 1902, and in 1919. In 1933 only 4,800 steel workers were unionized, and the A. F. of L. Amalgamated Association of Iron, Steel, and Tin Workers had been dormant for more than a decade. In June, 1936, the C. I. O. formed the Steel Workers Organizing Committee, headed by Philip Murray of the United Mine Workers. The S. W. O. C. rapidly gathered members, and was assisted by the sympathetic attitude of Governor Earle of Pennsylvania. On March 1, 1937, Myron C. Taylor, Chairman of the Board of United States Steel Corporation, which had traditionally been regarded as the chief stronghold of antiunionism in the country, agreed to establish collective bargaining with the S. W. O. C. The workers gained a forty-hour week and a ten per cent increase in wages. By the end of the year a large number of other steel corporations had accepted collective bargaining, and the membership of the S. W. O. C. had risen to more than 400,000.

A group of powerful corporations in Pennsylvania, Ohio, and Illinois, generally known as Little Steel, refused, however, to abandon their traditional hostility to unions. In May and June the S. W. O. C. called strikes against Republic Steel, Youngstown Sheet and Tube, Inland Steel, and Bethlehem Steel. The chief spokesmen of the employers were Tom Girdler of Republic and Eugene Grace of Bethlehem. Girdler's vituperative denunciations of the Roosevelt administration and of the C. I. O. and his adherence to the ideals of the era of President McKinley made him, for a period, a figure of national prominence. Some 90,000 steel workers went on strike; but the employers made extensive use of propaganda and of strikebreakers and were aided by the local police authorities. In July the S. W. O. C. had to accept defeat. The most important episode of the strike was the Memorial Day massacre in South Chicago. A group of strikers who were engaged in peaceful picketing outside a plant belonging to Republic Steel were attacked by the police. Ten of the workers were killed, seven of them being shot in the back, fifty were wounded by gunfire, and twenty-five were injured by clubbing. Of the policemen, who declared that they had acted in self-defence, three were slightly injured. The defeat of the S. W. O. C. by Little Steel was not, however, permanent, since the National Labor Relations Board, in a decision upheld by the Supreme Court, subsequently ordered Republic Steel to reinstate several thousand of the strikers and to accept collective bargaining with the S. W. O. C.

Workers in the automobile industry began to join unions in 1933 and soon became disillusioned with the leaders given them by the A. F. of L. In April, 1936, a convention of the United Automobile Workers repudiated A. F. of L. control and elected Homer Martin, a former clergyman, as their president. Soon afterward they joined the C. I. O. In December there began a series of strikes in the plants of General Motors, which eventually included 140,000 workers. These strikes were notable for the extended use of a new technique, the "sit-down," which had been first adopted by the rubber workers at Akron, Ohio, in January. Governor Frank Murphy of Michigan refused to use force to expel the strikers from the plants and endeavored to bring about a settlement by arbitration. On February 11 General Motors agreed to bargain with the union, although without accepting the closed shop; and the subsequent negotiations brought about an increase in wages. In March, 1937, the U. A. W. called a sit-down strike in the Chrysler plant; and a month later Chrysler agreed to a settlement similar to that made by General Motors. The Ford Motor Company continued to be an uncompromising enemy of unionism; but by the end of 1937 the U. A. W. had made contracts with every other important automobile corporation and claimed a membership of 400,000. Subsequently the union was split by factional quarrels, provoked chiefly by the personality and tactics of Homer Martin. In 1939 Martin was expelled from leadership, and replaced by R. J. Thomas. Martin and his followers formed a small rival union, which was admitted into the A. F. of L.

The C. I. O. also established unions in a number of other industries. Among the more important were the Textile Workers; the Electrical, Radio, and Machine Workers; the Rubber Workers; the Transport Workers; the Oil Workers; the Shoe Workers; and a number of different sailors' and longshoremen's organizations. Through its Cannery, Agricultural, Packing and Allied Workers it endeavored to extend unionism to agriculture; and it included also several unions of white-collar and professional workers, the most successful of which was the American Newspaper Guild, which had been started at Cleveland, Ohio, in the summer of 1933 and had joined the C. I. O. in 1937. At the time of the 1938 convention the C. I. O. included 42 national unions and organizing committees. It claimed an enrollment of 3,787,877, although the actual number of dues-paying members was probably considerably smaller.

THE C. I. O. *VERSUS* THE A. F. OF L.

Meanwhile the A. F. of L. had also been making large gains. It profited by the growth of union sentiment among the American working class; and it was assisted by a number of employers who hastened to sign contracts with A. F. of L. unions in order to protect themselves from the militant C. I. O. By 1940 each organization was claiming a membership of about 4,000,000. The conflict between them had become exceedingly bitter; and efforts on the part of President Roosevelt and members of his cabinet to bring about a reunion of the labor movement were unsuccessful. It was difficult to arrange a satisfactory compromise between the claims of craft unionism and those of industrial unionism. Both organizations, moreover, had internal weaknesses.

In 1939 and 1940 officials of certain union locals affiliated to the A. F. of L. were indicted as criminals and racketeers; and the A. F. of L. leaders were denounced for having allowed such men to occupy responsible positions. The C. I. O., on the other hand, was open to attack because the Communist Party, which had decided to support it in 1937, had captured control of some of the C. I. O. unions. There was considerable discontent within the C. I. O. because of this growth of Communist influence and also because of the increasingly erratic policies and egotistical attitudes of John L. Lewis. One powerful organization, the International Ladies Garment Workers, left the C. I. O. in 1938 and returned two years later to the A. F. of L. In 1940 some students of the labor movement believed that the C. I. O'., in spite of its claims to increased membership, was beginning to disintegrate.

Meanwhile the conflict between the two organizations was weakening the labor movement. By accusing the New Deal and the Labor Relations Board of being sympathetic to the C. I. O., and by opposing New Deal candidates who had C. I. O. support in the elections of 1938, the A. F. of L. strengthened the forces of conservatism. Struggles between A. F. of L. and C. I. O. unions, moreover, resulted in strikes, picketing, and other labor disturbances, which tended to discredit the whole union movement with the general public.

OPPOSITION TO UNIONISM

In spite of the growth of collective bargaining, many employers continued to fight unionism by the traditional methods. A Senate Committee on Civil Liberties, headed by La Follette, discovered that almost every big corporation in the country employed professional detective agencies to break up labor organizations. Between January, 1934, and July, 1936, General Motors alone spent nearly a million dollars on espionage; 304 Pinkerton detectives had joined unions as spies and *agents provocateurs;* and 100 of these had become union officials, one of them becoming the national vice-president of a union, and fourteen others being elected presidents of union locals. The Ford Motor Company created an organization known as the Ford Service Men, whose function was to spy on labor organizations and to intimidate them by physical attacks on union leaders. According to a report published in December, 1937, by the National Labor Relations Board, the Ford Service Men had "been vested with the responsibility of maintaining surveillance over Ford employees, not only during their work but even when they are outside the plant, and of crushing at its inception, by force if necessary, any signs of union activity. . . . The River Rouge plant has taken on many aspects of a community in which martial law has been declared and in which a huge military organization . . . has been superimposed upon the regular civil authorities." Employers also carried on extensive propaganda campaigns in order to create the impression that all labor leaders were self-interested agitators with communistic tendencies. When a strike occurred, they frequently obtained help from the local police in order to crush picketing, and they created and financed organizations of vigilantes and "citizens' committees."

The technique of strikebreaking was explained by James H. Rand, of Remington Rand Corporation, in a bulletin published by the National Association of Manufacturers. This technique was known as the "Mohawk Valley Formula" and was applied in a strike at the Remington Rand plant at Ilion, New York. The employer, said Mr. Rand, should represent the labor leaders as agitators and declare that they represented only a minority of the workers. He should create a Citizens' Committee to defend law and order, and he should win the support of storekeepers and other middle-class citizens, pointing out that they lost money through the strike. He should threaten that if the strike were not defeated, the plant might close down permanently and thus ruin the town. He should organize a "back to work" movement to demoralize the strikers, and he should call on the police to protect those workers who returned to work.

That workers had a right to bargain collectively through unions of their own choosing had been stated by Congress in the Wagner Act and had been subsequently affirmed by the Supreme Court. The Roosevelt administration, through its Labor Relations Board, had considerable success in making this right a reality. Organized labor under the New Deal had, in consequence, made its greatest advances in American history; and by 1940 about one-quarter of the American working class had been unionized. But whether labor would hold the ground which it had won was uncertain. Some of the new unions used their powers irresponsibly, calling strikes unnecessarily and abusing the sit-down technique (which was finally declared illegal by the Supreme Court in 1939, in the Fansteel Metallurgical Corporation Case). After the Republican victories in the elections of 1938 a number of states passed laws limiting the right to strike and restricting picketing and other forms of labor struggle. In the spring of 1940 the national need for a rapid increase in the construction of armaments provided an additional argument for limiting the powers of unions. Labor leaders would have to display considerable powers of statesmanship if the unions were to retain all the rights which they had received under the New Deal.

BIBLIOGRAPHY

R. R. Brooks, *When Labor Organizes* (1937)
——— *Unions of their own Choosing* (1939)
——— *As Steel Goes* (1940)
H. Harris, *Labor's Civil War* (1940)
E. Levinson, *Labor on the March* (1938)
J. Rosenfarb, *The National Labor Policy* (1940)
*E. Stein and others, *Labor Problems in America* (1940)
B. Stolberg, *The Story of the C.I.O.* (1938)
J. Walsh, *The C.I.O.* (1937)
K. White, *Labor and Democracy in the United States* (1939)

44

THE NEW DEAL AND

THE ECONOMIC SYSTEM

THE effects of the New Deal on the economic system remained a subject of violent controversy. Throughout 1933 and 1934 business conditions fluctuated. In the spring of 1935 there began a steady improvement, which continued until August, 1937. The national income produced, which had amounted to $82,691,000,000 in 1929 and $40,089,000,000 in 1932, reached $71,853,000,000 in 1937. The number of wage earners in employment increased from 25,973,000 in 1933 to 32,546,000 in 1937, 2,317,000 less than in 1929. Corporate business, which had reported a deficit of about $5,640,000,000 in 1932, made in 1937 a net profit of about $4,000,000,000, while payments of dividends for 1937 stood at 90 per cent of the 1929 figure. Industrial production was 77 per cent greater than in 1932, though it was still 7½ per cent less than it had been in 1929. There were, however, relatively few new investments; about 7,500,000 persons were unemployed; and nearly 4,500,000 families were still living on relief. The recovery was not maintained, and from September, 1937, until June, 1938, there was a sharp recession, during which unemployment increased by about 4,000,000. The autumn of 1938 brought an improvement which, however, was not fully maintained through 1939.

The working class—that part of it, at least, that was fortunate enough to retain employment in private industry—made definite gains under the New Deal. The average weekly wage for factory workers rose from $17.57 in 1933 to $25.14 in 1937. Prices remained somewhat lower than before the depression, so that by 1937 the real earnings of the average employed worker were nearly 10 per cent greater than they had been in 1929. Hours of labor in manufacturing decreased from an average of 37.9 a week in 1933 to 34.5 in 1934, chiefly as a result of the N. R. A.; after the invalidation of the N. R. A. they rose to 38.6 in 1937, but remained considerably lower than before the depression. These figures seemed to support the claim of business leaders that recovery was impeded by high labor costs. Defenders of the New Deal pointed out, however, that there had been a considerable increase in the productivity of labor, chiefly as a result of new mechanical devices; fewer hours of labor were needed to produce the same quantity of goods. In 1939 industrial production was 12 per cent less than in 1929, but the total wages paid to factory workers were 17 per cent less.

Between 1932 and 1937 farm prices rose by 86 per cent, and the cash income of farmers increased from $4,606,000,000 to $8,988,000,000. Their real income in 1937, in terms of price levels, was about the same as in 1929. This was a result partly of the A. A. A. and partly of the droughts of 1934 and 1936. After 1937 farm prices and incomes decreased as a result of overproduction after the voiding of the first A. A. A. In 1939 farm prices were 23 per cent lower than in 1937, and the cash income of farmers was $8,518,000,000. Some progress had been made in reducing farm indebtedness. The total mortgage debt decreased from $9,214,-278,000 in 1930 to $7,082,000,000 in 1937. In spite of a number of foreclosures, the number of owner-farmers increased from 3,568,-394 in 1930 to 3,899,091 in 1935, and the percentage whose farms were mortgaged decreased from 42.3 per cent to 39.6 per cent. The growth of the ratio of tenancy was, at least, temporarily checked; while owner-farmers increased by 9.3 per cent, the number of tenant-farmers increased from 2,664,365 to 2,865,155—a rise of only 7.5 per cent. But the problems presented by the tenant-farmers and sharecroppers had been scarcely touched.

The most conspicuous feature of economic development in the thirties was, however, the lack of business expansion and the consequent stagnation of the capital goods industries. New issues of stocks and bonds for productive investment, which had averaged about $5,000,000,000 a year throughout the twenties, amounted to only $1,225,000,000 in 1937, $872,000,000 in 1938, and $371,-000,000 in 1939. The function of borrowing capital and putting it back into circulation by investment, which had been performed by private business before 1929, was now being performed by the Federal government. The American people still had many needs which could not be satisfied by means of the existing industrial equipment; in the fields of power production, housing, shipping, and railroad facilities, for example, there was room for great expansion. But private capital did not enter these fields in sufficient quantities.

The growth of mechanization, moreover, was increasing the maladjustments of the economic system. Industry needed a decreasing number of workers to produce the same amount of wealth and to pay the same quantity of dividends. Production in the thirties was always lower than it had been in 1929; but even a return to the 1929 level of production would not have meant a return to the 1929 level of employment (except insofar as the growth of productivity was compensated by the decrease in hours of labor). It would, moreover, have left unemployed the millions of new workers who had been added to the adult population since that date.

A significant example of the decrease in the labor needs of industry was afforded by the record of American Telephone and Telegraph. Between 1929 and 1935 this corporation reduced the number of its employees from 454,000 to 269,000, thereby cutting its wage bill by 139 million dollars. This reduction was chiefly due to an increased use of the dial system and to an increase in the work required of each operator from 134.6 units an hour to 173 units an hour. Use of the telephone by the general public decreased during the depression but rose after 1933, and by 1937 it had exceeded 1929 levels. During the same period the corporation continued to pay $9 dividends on its stock; and, owing to an expansion in its capital equipment, total dividend payments rose from 116 million dollars in 1929 to 168 million dollars in 1935. The gross revenues of the corporation decreased, but not to the same degree as the decrease in its wage bill. A. T. and T. was a well-managed corporation, and in improving its equipment and putting the interests of its stockholders above all other considerations the managers of the corporation were only doing their duty.

In a healthy economic system the corporation's decreased need for labor would have been regarded as a sign of economic progress; in an expanding capitalism its dismissed workers would have found other jobs where they were more needed, and the increase in its dividends would have provided additional capital for new investments. In a period of economic contraction, however, such policies had a different effect. By performing honestly their functions as custodians of the stockholders' money, the managers of A. T. and T. were extending unemployment, diminishing mass purchasing power, and increasing that proportion of the total national income which went to the rentier class. Nor were the policies of A. T. and T. unique; they were, to a greater or less degree, the policies generally pursued by American corporate business.

Under such conditions the future of American capitalism appeared to be somewhat gloomy. Large-scale unemployment seemed likely to become a permanent problem; and—a consideration of grave significance—the problem would be particularly acute for young men leaving colleges and high schools. During the thirties a large proportion of the nation's youth had been unable to find jobs, and it did not appear that the normal processes of American capitalism were likely to remedy this situation. In certain of the European countries a similar situation had been a considerable factor in the rise of Fascism. Hitler's storm troopers had been, for the most part, young men who had found themselves barred from employment and from economic opportunities.

Enemies of the New Deal declared that recovery had really begun in the summer of 1932, that the New Deal had impeded rather than assisted it, and that the lack of new investments and the recession of 1937–1938 were caused by New Deal legislation which interfered with business, gave too many privileges to labor, and destroyed confidence. The New Dealers, on the other hand, argued that the continuance of the depression was due chiefly to the high prices charged by the big corporations and to the lack of sufficient purchasing power among the mass of the people. They maintained that the government was responsible for such recovery as had occurred and that the remedy for the nation's economic maladjustments was not to decrease the economic activities of the government but to extend them and make them more effective. The actual economic consequences of the various New Deal experiments cannot be calculated with any accuracy. The only fact which seems to be indisputable is that recovery was dependent upon large-scale government spending, and that when—as in 1937—the government began to economize there was an immediate slump. Few people, however, would maintain that heavy government borrowings and spendings could become a permanent policy.

The year 1940 saw these problems postponed. Large-scale armaments and possible war would lead to an industrial boom and to the absorption of many of the unemployed into munitions and aviation factories or into the armed forces of the United States. The search for a remedy to America's economic problems could therefore be delayed until the end of the international conflict.

BIBLIOGRAPHY

The same as for Chapter 41.

45

FOREIGN POLICY, 1933-1940

ISOLATION OR INTERVENTION?

PRESIDENT ROOSEVELT and his advisers were as actively interested in the maintenance of peace abroad as they were in the restoration of prosperity at home. Roosevelt's belief in the need for a vigorous foreign policy was not, however, reciprocated by Congress or by American public opinion; and the New Deal administration was therefore compelled to adopt a much more passive attitude toward world problems than its leaders would have liked.

The international order established by the Treaty of Versailles had begun to break up in 1931 when Japan seized Manchukuo and the League of Nations failed to give protection to China. In 1933 the Nazis set up a dictatorship in Germany and began to build armaments in order to avenge the defeat of their country in the World War and ultimately to achieve world domination. International peace and security were henceforth threatened by three aggressive and militaristic powers—Germany, Italy, and Japan—who were contemptuous of treaty obligations and of the rights of weaker nations. In response to this challenge the governments of the two leading European democracies, Great Britain and France, both of whom possessed large colonial empires which were coveted by the aggressor powers, failed to maintain their initial superiority in armaments, refused until too late to rally the small nations in an effective program of collective security, and for a long time tolerated aggression as long as it was not directed against their own possessions. The weakness of the democracies was due partly to pacifistic sentiment, similar to that which prevailed in the United States, partly to concentration on internal reforms, and partly—it would appear—to sympathy for Fascism among the wealthier and more conservative classes.

Opinion in the United States was sharply divided between isolationism and interventionism. The isolationists included the industrialists and farmers whose markets were at home, and those liberals who believed chiefly in avoidance of war. The interventionists included the economic groups, such as the cotton planters of the South and the bankers and exporters of New York, who were interested in foreign trade, and those liberals who believed that Fascism was a menace to democracy everywhere. There was an isolationist wing and an interventionist wing in each of the two major parties.

The principal arguments of the isolationists were as follows. First, since, as the Treaty of Versailles had proved, the United States could not end the perpetual cycle of wars and rivalries in Europe, it would be foolish for her to become entangled in them for a second time. Second, American intervention in Europe meant, in practice, American support for British and French imperialism, which differed from German and Italian imperialism only in being satiated and hence passive but which was not intrinsically nobler. Third, the chief responsibility of Americans was to build democracy and preserve freedom at home, saving the rest of the world by their example rather than by meddling in Europe, and democracy and freedom would be destroyed if America became involved in war. And fourth, the correct American foreign policy was to maintain the Monroe Doctrine and to exclude European influences from any part of the western hemisphere, north or south. The weakness of the isolationist argument was that it overlooked the dangers to American security and democracy which would be presented by a Nazi victory over Great Britain and France. The United States navy was not strong enough to control both the Atlantic and the Pacific at the same time; and since the Washington Conference, by a tacit agreement with Great Britain, the American navy had been concentrated in the Pacific, while the British policed the Atlantic. Destruction of the British fleet might be followed by a combined Japanese-Nazi attack on the western hemisphere; and the United States would then be compelled, in self-defense, to become a militaristic power. The major, but unconscious, premise of the isolationists was that British sea power would never be crushed by Nazi Germany.

The interventionists' arguments were as follows. First, Great Britain and France were the first line of defense of the American hemisphere against Fascism and the United States should therefore support them. Second, Fascism was necessarily hostile to all democracy everywhere and, if it were triumphant in Europe, it would immediately proceed—partly by open attack and partly by subsidizing American fascistic movements—to undermine democracy in the United States. Third, since the United States could not divorce herself, either politically, economically, or ideologically, from the remainder of the world, she should, in her own interests, act in order to promote international peace, security, the rule of law, and adherence to treaty obligations. The weakness of the interventionist position was that, prior to 1939, the two European powers with whom the interventionists proposed to co-operate—Great Britain and France—displayed no particular wish to check Fascist aggression and had little regard for the security of small nations or the enforcement of treaties. The result was, as we have already seen, that American isolationists and British conservatives continued to play into each others' hands. While the isolationists pointed to the misdeeds of the British as an argument against American intervention, the British declared that they could not adopt a policy of collective security as long as America remained isolated.

The preferences of the Roosevelt administration were definitely for intervention. Roosevelt's personal attitude underwent some variations; but his general belief was that Fascist aggression represented a danger which Americans could not safely overlook and that the United States, as the strongest and richest country in the world, had international responsibilities and obligations to fulfill. The viewpoint of Secretary of State Cordell Hull was even more strongly internationalist. Hull believed that the United States should use her influence on behalf of international law and the fulfillment of treaties. His strongest conviction was that trade barriers and economic nationalism were the chief cause both of economic depression and of war, and that the United States could most usefully promote world peace and prosperity by lowering tariffs and increasing world trade. In the pursuit of these objectives Hull showed a sincerity and a persistence which won the admiration even of those who disagreed with him.

Prior to 1940, however, American public opinion did not allow Roosevelt and Hull to take any very vigorous action in support of their policies. The arguments of the isolationists were strengthened by the general distaste of the American people for foreign adventures and entanglements and by their conviction that they could, if they chose, remain aloof from the next European war. Roosevelt and Hull were, therefore, unable to do much more than make speeches denouncing aggressors. American foreign policy consisted of little except a series of moral gestures, which probably caused the peoples of the democracies to put too great a trust in American assistance in the event of war. Since these gestures were not implemented by actions, they had no visible effect in checking the Fascist nations.

THE TRADE TREATIES

At the outset of his administration Roosevelt appeared to be in favor of a program of economic nationalism. Any attempt to restore world trade would be incompatible with the price-raising and cheap-money policies of the New Deal. The Hoover administration had previously agreed to American participation in an international economic conference, which met at London in June, 1933; and Cordell Hull led the American delegation. But when the conference began to discuss currency stabilization, Roosevelt sent a message denouncing such a project as contrary to American interests. The message virtually ended the conference, though it is doubtful if it would have accomplished anything of value even without Roosevelt's intervention. Roosevelt's action was loudly applauded by the isolationists and deplored by the interventionists. Three years later, however, the United States joined Great Britain and France in the stabilization of their respective currencies.

Cordell Hull refused to accept defeat; and he subsequently succeeded in winning Roosevelt's support for his ideals and in checking those individuals in the administration who opposed them. In June, 1934, Congress passed the Trade Agreements Act. The power to make tariff agreements was delegated to the executive for three years. In 1937 the act was renewed for another three years. Tariffs might be lowered as much as 50 per cent, although no changes might be made in the free list. Under this plan tariff schedules were worked out by government committees, which heard any complaints that might be made by business interests and then made recommendations to the Secretary of State. Tariff making was thus removed from Congress, which—on account of the influence of pressure groups and the practice of log-rolling—had always found it easier to raise schedules than to lower them, and was entrusted to experts.

By 1940 Hull had made treaties with twenty different countries, covering 55 per cent of America's export trade and 15 per cent of its import trade. The precise effect of the treaties was difficult to estimate. American exports to treaty countries increased by 61 per cent, while exports to nontreaty countries increased by only 37 per cent. On the other hand, imports from treaty countries rose by 35 per cent, and imports from nontreaty countries rose by 37 per cent. The most important effects of the treaties were probably psychological rather than economic; they removed much of the resentment which had been caused by the Smoot-Hawley Tariff and promoted friendly relations, especially with the Latin American countries. The trend toward economic nationalism throughout the world was, however, too strong for one country to stop it, and foreign trade in the thirties remained much smaller than in the twenties. In 1937, the year of greatest activity, American exports had a value of $3,349,000,000, as contrasted with $5,241,000,000 in 1929, and imports had a value of $3,084,000,000, as contrasted with $4,399,000,000 in 1929. There were, moreover, few new foreign investments by Americans, and after 1935 capital tended to flow into the United States from abroad. European investors felt that the United States was the safest place for their money. By 1938 America's credit balance on investments was only $3,800,000,000.

LATIN AMERICA

Probably the most successful achievement of the Roosevelt-Hull foreign policy was to bring about more friendly relations with Latin America. All groups in the United States were united in regarding this as desirable, whatever opinion they might hold with reference to the problems of Europe.

The Hoover administration had disclaimed any right on the part of the United States to intervene in the internal affairs of the Latin American countries. This attitude was reiterated by Roosevelt in what he termed his "Good Neighbor" policy. In a speech delivered on December 28, 1933, Roosevelt declared that "the definite policy of the United States from now on is one opposed to armed intervention. The maintenance of constitutional government in other nations is not a sacred obligation devolving upon the United States. The maintenance of law and the orderly processes of government in this hemisphere is the concern of each individual nation within its own borders first of all. It is only if and when the failure of orderly processes of government affects the other nations of the continent that it becomes their concern; and the point to stress is that in such event it becomes the joint concern of a whole continent in which we are all neighbors." In other words, the defense of the Monroe Doctrine was no longer to be the responsibility of the United States alone; the Doctrine was to become the joint policy of all the nations of the hemisphere, all of whom were to be regarded as equals in a common opposition to European encroachments.

In accordance with this policy American marines were withdrawn from Haiti in 1934; and in the same year the Platt Amendment, under which the United States enjoyed the right to intervene in Cuba, was repealed. In August, 1933, there had been a revolution in Cuba, due chiefly to bad economic conditions caused by a fall in the price of sugar and by the necessity to pay interest on the loans which had been made by American bankers. President Machado was overthrown and was succeeded first by Grau San Martin and subsequently by a regime in which the dominant influence was exercised by an army leader, Fulgencio Batista. United States pressure was regarded as responsible for the rapid fall of Grau San Martin, who was somewhat radical, and for the consolidation of the more conservative Batista regime. On the other hand, the United States used its influence to persuade Batista to conform to democratic processes and to make social reforms; and Cuban economic conditions were improved by a trade treaty which reduced the American duty on sugar. Latin America was, moreover, favorably impressed by the fact that no American troops or marines were landed in Cuba during the revolution.

The Good Neighbor policy encountered its greatest difficulties in Mexico. The Mexican revolutionary movement, which had been checked since 1929, resumed its progress in 1934, when Lazaro Cárdenas was elected president. Cárdenas distributed land on a large scale to the peasants and reduced the estates of the big landowners, among whom were some Americans. He also supported the trade unions in their demand for a higher standard of living. In March, 1938, the foreign oil companies, both American and British, were expropriated after they had declared themselves unable to obey a government order to pay higher wages. While the Mexican government insisted that the companies deserved expropriation because they had refused to obey Mexican law, the oil interests replied that the wage increases would have ruined them and that the dispute about wages was merely an excuse, and not a reason, for the expropriation.

The Mexican government stated that it was willing to pay the companies for their properties but that such payment should cover only what the companies had invested in equipment; the companies, on the other hand, claimed payment also for the oil, valuing their properties at 400 million dollars. The companies, moreover, prevented Mexico from marketing its oil in Great Britain and the United States; and the Mexican government, although strongly opposed to Fascism, was then compelled to make contracts for the sale of oil with Germany, Italy, and Japan. Secretary Hull supported the claims of the companies to full compensation but did not condemn the expropriation itself. And in spite of considerable pressure from the oil interests and from American newspapers, he made no attempt to coerce the Mexican government. In 1940 the Sinclair Oil Company came to terms with Mexico and was paid the first installment of its compensation; and the prospects seemed good for an amicable ending of the controversy.

Roosevelt and Hull made their principal attempts to promote unity in the western hemisphere by means of a series of conferences. Regular Pan-American conferences were held at Montevideo in 1933 and at Lima in 1938; and a special conference to discuss methods of preserving peace was held at Buenos Aires in 1936. Roosevelt visited the Buenos Aires conference in person and declared that any non-American state seeking "to commit acts of aggression against us will find a Hemisphere wholly prepared to consult together for our mutual safety and our mutual good." The attempts of the United States at the Buenos Aires and Lima conferences to create a kind of American League of Nations, in which each state would have definite obligations to maintain collective security, were unsuccessful. At the Lima conference, however, a pact was signed for mutual consultation in case of danger; and in September, 1939, after the outbreak of the European war, a conference was held at Panama, at which plans were devised for keeping the war out of the western hemisphere.

The traditional hostility of Latin America to the United States, and its traditional suspicion of Yankee imperialism, by no means disappeared. The German and Italian governments engaged in vigorous campaigns to increase their trade with Latin America and to win sympathy and support. They were aided by the presence of considerable German and Italian populations in Brazil, the Argentine, and elsewhere, and by the Fascist sympathies of many of the wealthier Latin Americans. In its official utterances the United States government found it wise to maintain the fiction that the western hemisphere was wholly dedicated to democracy, but in reality most of the Latin American governments were dictatorships. The Nazi government pushed its exports to Latin America by underselling its competitors and by using barter methods which compelled countries which sold to Germany to take German goods in exchange. Between 1933 and 1939 German trade with Latin America increased rapidly, chiefly at the expense of Great Britain.

The Roosevelt-Hull policies had, however, considerable success in counteracting this Fascist penetration. In 1939 the United States government began to promote trade not only through the trade treaties but also through a government-owned Export-Import Bank, which made loans to Brazil and other Latin American countries. Between 1933 and 1938 the share of the United States in the import trade of Latin America increased from 29.2 per cent to 35.8 per cent. In 1937 Latin America bought 34.3 per cent of its imports from the United States, in contrast to 15.3 per cent from Germany, and sold 31.3 per cent of its exports to the United States, in contrast to 8.7 per cent to Germany. The modesty and friendliness of Cordell Hull had, moreover, made a most favorable impression upon Latin American diplomats. A German victory in Europe would be followed by a vigorous German campaign to win political and economic control of South America. But in 1940 the United States was certainly better liked by the Latin Americans than at any previous period.

THE FAR EAST

In the Far East Japan continued her career of conquest in China, and talk of an eventual war between Japan and the United States grew more frequent. The most important American interest in the Far East was in the Dutch and British East Indies, whence the United States imported most of its rubber and its tin; and Japanese imperialists were now beginning to claim these islands as within the Japanese sphere of influence.

It was possibly on account of the aggressive policies of Japan that the Roosevelt administration decided to initiate diplomatic relations with Soviet Russia. This step was taken also in the hope of stimulating trade between the two countries. Maxim Litvinoff, Soviet Commissar for Foreign Affairs, came to Washington in November, 1933; and notes were exchanged in which the Soviet government pledged itself not to spread propaganda in the United States. No settlement was made about the debts which had been incurred by previous Russian governments and repudiated by the Bolsheviks, or about the claims to compensation of Americans who had owned properties in Russia which the Bolsheviks had confiscated.

The Philippines continued to be the Achilles' heel of the American defense system, but arrangements were made for eventual American withdrawal. After the Filipinos had refused to accept the Hawes-Cutting Act, Congress passed, in March, 1934, the Tydings-McDuffie Act. During a transitional period the Philippines were to have a native chief executive, but the United States was to retain certain rights and obligations in the islands; duties were gradually to be imposed on imports from the Philippines into the United States; and the Philippines were to become completely independent in 1946. Under this arrangement Manuel Quezón was elected as the first President of the Philippines. Subsequently many of the Filipinos, alarmed by the power of Japan and by the prospect of exclusion from American markets, began to reconsider their desire for independence. Many Americans, on the other hand, realizing the difficulty of defending the Philippines in case of Japanese attack, felt that the United States should withdraw even sooner than 1946.

With reference to the Japanese seizure of Manchukuo, Roosevelt and Hull continued Stimson's nonrecognition policy. On the other hand, they stopped sending protests to Japan, and they endeavored to induce Great Britain, whose economic interests in China were far larger than those of the United States, to adopt a more vigorous policy. On July 7, 1937, after five years of relative peace, war again broke out between China and Japan. The Japanese undertook the conquest of large areas of central China, and the loss of life, among both soldiers and the Chinese civilian population, was enormous. Japan apparently proposed both to dominate the whole of China, thereby destroying whatever remained of the Open Door, and to deprive the western nations of their economic privileges in the Far East. The American government took "parallel" action with Great Britain and with the League of Nations in protesting to Japan. Mere protests, however, were futile, and none of the western powers was able to take action. In November, 1937, representatives of nineteen nations, including the United States, met at Brussels to discuss the Far Eastern situation; but the conference adjourned without accomplishing anything. American citizens in China, of whom there were about 10,000, were urged by the State Department to leave, and warships were sent to protect them. On December 12 one of these warships, the gunboat *Panay,* and three American oil tankers, were sunk by Japanese airplanes. The Japanese, however, quickly apologized and paid reparation. Under the neutrality legislation of 1937 the President was required to prohibit the export of munitions to countries which were at war. Roosevelt did not, however, apply the law to the war in China, on the excuse that the war had never been officially declared; his reason appears to have been that an embargo on munitions would hurt China more than it would hurt Japan. As the war proceeded, American sympathies for China grew stronger, and American protests to the Japanese government against its economic policies and its methods of waging war grew stronger. But apart from the abrogation by the United States government in 1939 of the trade treaty of 1911 with Japan, no action was taken. American exporters continued to ship to Japan large quantities of scrap iron and other materials for the making of munitions.

EUROPE

At the outset of his administration Roosevelt made it plain that he was alarmed at the growth of aggressive policies and anxious that the United States should use her influence on behalf of peace. In May, 1933, he sent a message to the government of every nation in the world, in which he denounced aggression. This appears to have been intended chiefly as a warning to Hitler.

Meanwhile the disarmament conference which had been convened in 1932 was still meeting; and Norman Davis, who represented the United States, promised that if a substantial degree of disarmament were achieved, then the United States would pledge herself to do nothing which might interfere with the imposition of sanctions by the League of Nations to restrain an aggressor nation. Owing to the establishment of the Nazi dictatorship, however, it was now too late for any kind of disarmament. In 1935 a naval conference met at London, as had been provided for in the naval treaty of 1930. Japan demanded naval equality with the United States, which the United States could not accept; and although in March, 1936, the United States, Great Britain, and France signed another naval treaty with one another, the conference could do nothing to prevent a new armaments race.

The isolationists were now becoming alarmed by the threat of another world war; and, whereas Roosevelt believed that the United States should endeavor to prevent war, the primary concern of the isolationists was to ensure that when war came, the United States should stay out of it. In 1934 a Senate committee under Gerald P. Nye of North Dakota investigated the munitions industry, and paid special attention to its activities prior to April, 1917. Finding that bankers and munitions manufacturers had made large profits by supplying the Allies and that they had been generally in favor of American participation, the Nye Committee concluded that this economic tie between the United States and the Allies had been one of the chief causes for the American entry into the war. It followed that if the United States were to remain neutral in the next war, she should immediately adopt legislation which would prevent economic involvement.

The desire for neutrality was strengthened by a number of books and articles denouncing the international bankers and the "merchants of death" and by novels and moving pictures which depicted the horrors of war and conveyed the impression that all wars were evil and that a country could avoid war by merely choosing not to fight. Pacifistic sentiment grew rapidly, especially among the younger generation and in the colleges.

One measure tending to prevent economic involvement had already been taken in 1934, when Congress passed the Johnson Act prohibiting the governments which were in default on their war debts from floating fresh loans in the United States. In August, 1935, Congress passed the first of a series of Neutrality Acts. When a war started, the President was to prohibit the export of munitions to belligerent countries, and he might also withhold protection from

American citizens who traveled on ships belonging to the belligerents. This act was disliked by the administration, which would have preferred a measure allowing it to discriminate against an aggressor nation.

In October war started between Italy and Ethiopia, and Roosevelt declared the Neutrality Act in force. Meanwhile the League of Nations, for the first and last time, was attempting to maintain peace by the adoption of economic sanctions. The British conservative government appears to have originally been willing to allow Italy to conquer Ethiopia; but in the summer of 1935 British public opinion became aroused; and, in deference to the popular demand for action, the British government took the lead in condemning Italy. The sanctions voted by the League were, however, mild, and did not cover any commodities which Italy bought from the United States. In particular, they did not include oil, the most vital of all the materials needed for modern warfare. Roosevelt and Hull gave a clear invitation to the League of Nations to adopt more rigorous sanctions by declaring, in their Neutrality Proclamation, that the United States government would give no protection to American citizens who traded with Italy. In other words, if the League powers chose to blockade Italy, the United States would not interfere. The State Department tried by moral pressure to prevent Americans from selling to Italy oil and other raw materials needed for war. Since these materials were not covered by the League sanctions, American exporters saw no reason why they should obey this moral embargo; and Italian purchases of oil and metals from the United States increased by between 200 and 300 per cent. It soon appeared that the British government was not in earnest in its support of sanctions.

In November there was a general election in Great Britain, and the government, appealing for support on the basis of its foreign policy, was returned to power. This was followed, in December, by the announcement of the Hoare-Laval Pact, which revealed that the British and French were willing to allow Italy to absorb a large part of Ethiopia. In the following spring, after Italy had completed her conquest, the sanctions were abandoned. The British declared that they would have asked the League to adopt more effective sanctions if they had been assured of American co-operation. Most Americans, on the other hand, believed that the British government had never been genuinely desirous of the defeat of Italy.

In February, 1936, the Neutrality Act was amended in order to prohibit the granting of loans and credits to belligerents. In July civil war began in Spain. The Spanish democratic government, which was composed of a Popular Front coalition of liberals, Socialists, and Communists, was attacked by conservative elements, under the leadership of General Franco, who planned to establish a dictatorship with the assistance of the Italian and German governments. The British and French governments then adopted a "nonintervention" program, which was supposed to prevent either of the two factions from receiving foreign assistance. Actually, however, "nonintervention" helped the rebels, who continued to receive troops and munitions from Italy and Germany, while the government could obtain only some very meager assistance from the Soviet Union.

In January, 1937, at the request of the administration, which wished to co-operate in the "nonintervention" program, Congress extended its neutrality legislation to cover civil as well as international war. Shipments of munitions to Spain were then embargoed. This measure was vigorously condemned by liberals, who pointed out that the Spanish government, both by international law and by a treaty signed in 1902, had a legal right to buy munitions from the United States. They also held that, by participating in the Anglo-French "nonintervention" policy, the United States was, in practice, helping Fascism. Isolationists argued that this was a fresh proof of the duplicity of the British and of the dangers of Anglo-American co-operation.

The next Neutrality Act was passed in May, 1937. Upon the outbreak of a war, the President was to prohibit the sale of munitions to belligerents, the sale of securities in the United States by belligerents, and travel by Americans on belligerent-owned ships. The President might also, at his discretion, enforce "cash-and-carry" rules, by which belligerents purchasing other commodities from the United States would be required to pay cash for them and to transport them in their own ships. This act was a compromise, which pleased neither interventionists nor isolationists. The administration wanted more power to use American influence to restrain aggression. The isolationists, on the other hand, distrusted Roosevelt and felt that more stringent measures were needed to keep America neutral. One such proposal was for an amendment to the constitution, sponsored by Representative Ludlow, which would require a popular referendum before the United States could declare war. In 1938 the House of Representatives defeated the Ludlow Amendment by only a narrow margin, the vote being 209 to 188.

Meanwhile international conditions were steadily degenerating, and a second world war seemed to be rapidly approaching. On October 5, 1937, in a speech at Chicago, Roosevelt declared that 90 per cent of the peoples of the world wanted peace and that only 10 per cent were war-mongers, and he called for concerted action by the peace-loving powers to quarantine the aggressors. The immediate occasion for this declaration was the outbreak of the war in China. The general reaction to the President's speech was hostile; and, when it became obvious that the American people were unwilling to support Roosevelt in taking action to prevent aggression, the European democracies ignored Roosevelt's proposal. After the failure of the Chicago speech, Roosevelt drew the conclusion that, since any hope of maintaining security by collective action must be abandoned, the United States must arm in self-defense. In January, 1938, he asked Congress to pass a billion dollar naval expansion program, and later in the year he recommended an enlargement of the air force to 6,000 planes. There was considerable opposition to these proposals, most of the opponents being—somewhat paradoxically— isolationists who had refused to support collective security; and Congress did not pass the naval expansion bill until April.

In August, 1938, in a speech at Kingston, Ontario, Roosevelt declared that the obligations of the United States under the Monroe Doctrine included the defense of Canada against foreign aggression. In September, during the Czechoslovakian crisis, Roosevelt sent notes to Germany and Italy, urging a settlement by negotiation. The crisis ended with the Munich conference, at which Great Britain and France agreed to German annexation of a large part of Czechoslovakia. In November came violent anti-Semitic persecutions in Germany. Roosevelt protested to the Nazi government and recalled the American ambassador. In January, 1939, it became known that Roosevelt had approved of the sale of American-built airplanes to Great Britain and France. When the isolationists denounced this action, Roosevelt held a secret conference with a number of congressmen, at which he apparently explained that Great Britain and France were America's first line of defense. When, however, the press announced that Roosevelt had said that the American frontier was in France, such widespread hostility was aroused that Roosevelt denied having made such a statement. In March, Germany annexed what was left of Czechoslovakia, and in April Italy annexed Albania. Roosevelt once again sent messages to the German and Italian governments denouncing aggression.

It cannot be said that American diplomacy was of any avail in postponing the advent of war. The sympathies of a large proportion of the American people were against Fascism; but as long as they were unwilling to take any action against aggressors, the European dictators knew that they could safely ignore Roosevelt's messages and speeches. Nor were relations between the people of the United States and those of the European democracies particularly friendly. While the British and French felt that the United States ought to promise them assistance in case of war, the Americans deplored the Anglo-French policy of surrender which had culminated at Munich. If—in the words of the title of a book by an American author— many Englishmen expected every American to do his duty, many Americans would have been willing to defend the independence of Czechoslovakia to the last drop of English and French blood.

In April the British and French governments, abandoning the policy of surrender, promised to defend Poland against Nazi attack. Roosevelt and Hull believed that war was imminent, and they asked Congress to alter the neutrality legislation in order to make possible greater American assistance to the Allies, hoping that such a measure would serve as a warning to Germany. The isolationist leaders in the Senate declared, however, that war was improbable; and Congress refused to change the neutrality laws.

On August 23 the Nazis concluded a pact with the Soviet Union, thus safeguarding their eastern front. On August 24 Roosevelt cabled more appeals for peace. On September 1 the German army invaded Poland, and on September 3 Great Britain and France declared war. On September 21 Roosevelt called Congress into special session, and asked it to make the amendments in the neutrality laws which it had been unwilling to make in the spring. Congress debated the question for six weeks, but finally agreed to repeal the embargo on munitions, thus making it possible for the Allies to purchase airplanes and guns in the United States. They were to be sold under cash-and-carry rules, the Allies paying for them immediately and transporting them in their own ships. As an additional safeguard against American involvement, no American ships were to be allowed to enter the European combat zone. This new Neutrality Act was signed on November 4.

The Nazis completed their conquest of Poland in seventeen days, after which there was a lull in the war until the following spring. Most Americans hoped that Germany would be defeated; but, since the Allies did not appear to be in any need of immediate assistance, scarcely anybody in the United States advocated American participation. The British, moreover, had once again declared a blockade of Germany; and as in the previous war, the British blockade regulations caused some irritation in the United States. Meanwhile American exporters were shipping considerable quantities of metal to Italy and the Soviet Union, some of which was probably resold to Germany.

The American feeling of security abruptly ended in the spring of 1940. In April the Nazis suddenly seized Denmark and Norway; and in May the German army, violating neutral rights even more brutally than in 1914, smashed through Holland and Belgium and inflicted a crushing defeat upon the Allied armies in Flanders. A complete Nazi victory within a few months appeared to be not impossible. The change in American sentiment was immediate and cataclysmic. The American people suddenly became aware that their own interests were much more deeply involved in the European conflict than they had realized and that, if Germany seized the

British fleet, the United States would be confronted by the gravest perils in the whole of its history. Although relatively few persons demanded any immediate entry into the war, only a small minority of the population continued to advocate the kind of isolationism that had prevailed since the repudiation of the League of Nations. On May 16 Roosevelt appeared before Congress to recommend expansion of the American aviation industry to the point where it could construct 50,000 war planes a year. With scarcely a dissenting voice, billions of dollars was voted for the army, the navy, and the air force; and the United States set about the task of arming herself with as much speed as possible. Whatever achievements or catastrophes the future might hold, the events of May, 1940, certainly marked a decisive turning point in both the internal and the external history of the American people.

BIBLIOGRAPHY

American Academy of Political and Social Science, *Democracy and the Americas* (July, 1939)
*T. A. Bailey, *Diplomatic History of the United States* (1940)
C. Beals, *The Coming Struggle for Latin America* (1938)
*C. A. Beard, *America in Midpassage* (1939)
E. Borchard and W. P. Lage, *Neutrality for the United States* (1937)
*R. L. Buell, *Isolated America* (1940)
K. Carr, *South American Primer* (1939)
The Council on Foreign Relations, *The United States in World Affairs* (1931–..)
S. P. Duggan, *The Two Americas* (1934)
*A. W. Griswold, *The Far Eastern Policy of the United States* (1938)
S. G. Inman, *Latin America* (1937)
H. J. Tasca, *The Reciprocal Trade Policy of the United States* (1938)

46

LITERATURE AND

THE ARTS

GENERAL CHARACTERISTICS

THE history of literature and the arts in the United States since 1900 is one of steadily increasing achievement. There has been a remarkable growth in both the quantity and the quality of American contributions to all the various arts and an equally significant improvement in the standards of popular taste. It can plausibly be argued that more good work in literature, painting, and music has been produced in the United States since 1900 than in the whole of the preceding three hundred years. There have been, perhaps, no single figures equal in importance to Emerson or Melville or Whitman, nor has the United States produced individual masters comparable to those of contemporary Europe—to Proust and Mann in the novel, to Picasso and Matisse in painting, and to Sibelius and Stravinsky in music; but there have been a very large number of men and women capable of distinguished work on all levels but the highest. Today the United States can no longer be regarded—aesthetically—as a colony of Europe; since 1900 its artistic achievements have had an importance equal to those of the leading European countries.

Since the time of Emerson, critics have frequently urged American intellectuals to break away from European influences and to develop an indigenous American culture. It has been suggested that the United States was in need of an artistic Declaration of Independence. Some of the features of American aesthetic development in the twentieth century have been inspired by this recommendation. American writers and painters have set out to depict the American environment more realistically than did their predecessors; they have abandoned European forms and conventions which did not seem to be adapted to American material; and they have repudiated the traditional belief in the artistic superiority of Europe. It would, however, be an error to attach too much importance to nationalistic influences in the arts. The arts, like the sciences, have always been international; and the writers and artists of different nations have always borrowed from one another freely. Throughout the twentieth century there has been a constant and fruitful interchange between the United States and Europe. New techniques and new ideas, first conceived on one continent, have often been adopted and developed in the other. Many American artists have settled in Europe, and many European artists have transplanted themselves to America. America and Europe have been confronted by similar social and economic problems, and artists on both sides of the Atlantic have been dealing with the material presented by the same kind of industrial civilization.

The artistic interchange between the United States and Europe has been paralleled by a similar interchange among the different regions of the United States. Since the end of the nineteenth century, New York has been the cultural capital of the country, and it has often seemed to attract too large a proportion of the nation's intellectuals and to exercise too widespread an influence over the nation's artistic development. Groups of writers and artists have, however, established themselves in other cities, particularly in Boston, Chicago, San Francisco, New Orleans, and Santa Fe, or have set out to record the distinctive physical and cultural characteristics of the regions from which they have sprung. In the twentieth century good novels have been written, and good pictures have been painted, in every part of the United States; and the steady growth of cultural activities has by no means been confined to the great metropolitan areas.

The arts in America have been enriched also through the interplay of racial differences. In the nineteenth century most of the leading American intellectuals were of English stock, but since 1900 the children of the immigrants and the descendants of the slaves have played an increasingly important part in American cultural development. American writers, painters, and musicians have been German, Irish, Jewish, Italian, Negro, Slavic, Scandinavian, Spanish, and Portuguese as well as Anglo-Saxon.

Perhaps the two dominating tendencies in American aesthetic development since 1900 have been realism and intellectualism. The realists have set out to tell the whole truth about modern American society, with special emphasis on those dark features of it which appeared to contradict the optimistic beliefs cherished by conservatives. They have often accepted a materialistic and deterministic philosophy of life and have usually been sympathetic to some form of political and economic radicalism. Meanwhile, writers and artists with more intellectual inclinations have endeavored to record complex experiences with the greatest possible subtlety and precision, and in so doing they have frequently produced works of such obscurity that their audiences have been very limited.

Both of these tendencies have been vigorously denounced by the academic conservatives, who have remained faithful to the traditions established in the nineteenth century. The realists have been condemned for their pessimism and their unrestricted frankness, while the work of the intellectualists has been dismissed as unintelligible and nonsensical. Throughout the past four decades there has been continual controversy between the conservatives and the exponents of the different forms of modernism. The conservatives appear, however, to have been fighting a losing battle; and the modernists have been steadily increasing their influence not only among writers and artists but also among the general public.

Meanwhile, the development of the arts has been profoundly affected by the growth of machine technology. During the nineteenth century the aesthetic effects of industrialism appeared to be wholly bad. The new industrial cities were of an unparalleled ugliness and sordidness; and the traditions of craftsmanship in the construction of buildings, furniture, and utensils disappeared. In such a society the arts were no longer a vital part of life and were in danger of becoming merely amusements for a small leisure class. What was useful ceased to be artistic, and what was artistic had no apparent utility. During the twentieth century, however, it has become apparent that the machine is not incompatible with beauty. Architects and designers have gradually begun to produce new styles which are both suited to the requirements of machine technology and also aesthetically attractive. Poets, painters, and composers have accepted the sights and sounds of the machine age as appropriate material for aesthetic treatment. During the twenties and thirties, moreover, industrialists discovered that the public is more willing to buy their commodities if they are good looking as well as useful; they have given increasing attention to the appearance of the articles which they manufacture, and have stressed this fact in their advertising. Machine civilization, it appears, may eventually create an environment as well adapted to humane living as was that of the agrarian civilizations of earlier periods.

The machine has also made possible a much broader appreciation of the fine arts. Improvements in the printing of books and the reproduction of pictures, the propagation of good music by the phonograph and the radio, and the development of such new art-forms as the motion picture have greatly enlarged the audiences to which artists can appeal. It has frequently been argued that this popularization and commercialization of art has caused tastes to be vulgarized rather than elevated; and there is much evidence, particularly in the early history of the motion picture, to support this belief. But in the main, artists can view the future with optimism. In the thirties there was a marked improvement in the quality of the books and motion pictures which won popular acclaim; while the growth of musical appreciation, as measured by the time given to good music over the radio, was very rapid. One can plausibly maintain that the future development of the United States will be characterized both by high artistic achievement and by a high level of appreciation among the general public.

CRITICAL TRENDS

The origins of the more important aesthetic tendencies of the twentieth century can be traced back to the last two decades of the nineteenth century. The earliest of the literary realists were Stephen Crane and Frank Norris, who began publication in the eighteen-nineties, and Theodore Dreiser, whose *Sister Carrie* appeared in 1900. The same decade saw a similar trend toward realism in painting, in the work of Robert Henri, John Sloan, and their associates in the so-called Philadelphia Group. Meanwhile, Henry James was developing the novel into an instrument for communicating the most subtle and complex experiences; and, although his audience was restricted, he was to exercise a profound influence upon the more intellectual writers of the twentieth century. Another significant artistic movement of the eighties and nineties was the attempt to create new architectural forms which would be appropriate to the methods of machine construction. The most important of the architectural pioneers was probably Louis Sullivan.

The first decade of the twentieth century, on the other hand, was a period of relative stagnation. During the Progressive Era intellectual leaders were interested primarily in political questions, and little work of permanent importance was done in any of the arts. The most prominent writers of the period dealt with political and economic questions in a journalistic spirit, while in painting and architecture the new movements made little headway.

Until the World War the spokesmen of academic conservatism and of a narrowly moralistic reticence dominated literary opinion in the universities and in journalism, and most of the leading contemporary writers and artists of the European countries were denounced by them as unhealthy and un-American. Conservative viewpoints were similarly dominant in the fields of painting, music, and architecture. This type of criticism was represented in literature by such men as Henry Van Dyke and Hamilton Wright Mabie and by a younger and more vigorous writer, who changed after the war into a champion of the literary radicals, Stuart P. Sherman. A more healthy influence was exercised by the critic William Cary Brownell and the philosopher George Santayana, both of whom had a deep understanding of the meaning of culture and an appreciation of what was best in the civilization of Europe. But these two men had little direct influence upon the development of the arts in America. More immediately useful functions were performed by James Gibbons Huneker, who was a mediocre critic but who popularized in America the ideas of many important contemporary European writers.

A decisive turning point in the history of the arts in America occurred during the years 1912–1915. These four years saw the first appearance of a large number of new poets and novelists, notably Robert Frost, Edgar Lee Masters, Vachel Lindsay, Carl Sandburg, Edna St. Vincent Millay, Amy Lowell, and Sherwood Anderson. In 1912 the magazine *Poetry,* edited by Harriet Monroe, began publication; and in 1914 appeared the first *Imagist Anthology.* These two events marked the beginning of what has often been called a Renascence of Poetry. In the other arts the same period was notable for the Armory Exhibition of modern painting in 1913, which introduced to America the leading European modernists; the foundation in 1915 of both the Washington Square Players and the Provincetown Players, which were to vitalize the American theater; and the completion in the same year of D. W. Griffith's *The Birth of a Nation,* the first motion picture to exhibit the aesthetic potentialities of this new art form.

This artistic activity was accompanied by the advent of a number of young critics, particularly Randolph Bourne and Van Wyck Brooks, whose work appeared in such magazines as *The Seven Arts, The Liberator,* and *The Masses.* These men sympathized with the political aspirations of the Progressive Era; and, while they were severe in indicting the deficiencies of American society and traditions, they accepted American democratic ideals and were not unduly pessimistic about the future. In their opinion the American people had too little esteem for aesthetic and intellectual activities; were governed by standards of value that were largely utilitarian, materialistic, and narrowly puritanical; and were apt to consider the arts as merely superficial adornments and not as a vital element in daily life. Bourne died in 1918; but Brooks, who became the most influential spokesman of the group, continued his critical activities into the twenties and won even wider acclaim in the thirties by his history of the literature of nineteenth-century New England. An important younger writer with similar ideas, who specialized in the criticism of painting and architecture, was Lewis Mumford.

American participation in the World War, with intolerance and hysteria at home and the defeat of Wilsonian idealism abroad, was followed by disillusionment and cynicism. The movements which had been initiated before the war continued to develop; and the ten years from the Peace of Versailles to the Wall Street debacle were the most fruitful period in artistic activity that the United States had known. But it was a period in which the leading writers and artists either set out to expose and condemn American civilization in a spirit of pessimism or else adopted an ivory-tower aloofness from society and declared that the function of the artist was to give pleasure only to himself and his friends. The tone of disillusionment was reflected in almost all the important writings of the period. It was apparent at one extreme in the best-selling realistic novels of Sinclair Lewis, who published *Main Street* in 1920 and *Babbitt* in 1922; it found expression in a totally different manner in the highly intellectual poetry of T. S. Eliot, who lived in England but exercised great influence over American writers and whose *Waste Land* appeared in 1922.

Meanwhile, Americans were learning many new techniques and ideas from Europe. Such European innovators as Proust and Joyce in the novel and Picasso in painting were studied in America; and new currents of thought, particularly those represented by Freud and the Vienna school of psychoanalysis, by Marx and Russian Communism, and by the revival of the Thomist philosophy of the Catholic Church, began to have considerable influence among American intellectuals. An influential movement of native origin was the Humanism of Irving Babbitt and Paul Elmer More. This was to a large extent a continuation of the academic and moralistic conservatism of earlier generations, but Babbitt and More far excelled such men as Van Dyke and Mabie in breadth of learning and power of logic. Another new development was the reformulation of the agrarian ideals of the South by a group of southern writers headed by John Crowe Ransom and Allen Tate. This group, whose members wrote some of the best poetry and ablest criticism of the period, were opposed to industrialism and the pretensions of modern science and were sympathetic to traditional religion.

These different intellectual and aesthetic trends found expression in a large number of so-called "little magazines," which were usually published with the aid of subsidies from patrons and which performed a most valuable function in printing the work of younger writers. Leadership along the "little magazines" was exercised from 1920 until 1928 by *The Dial*, from 1930 until 1934 by *The Hound and Horn* and *The Symposium*, and subsequently by *The Southern Review* and *The Kenyon Review*. Other important "little magazines" were *The Little Review, Broom, The Fugitive, Secession, transition, The Gyroscope,* and *Pagany*. Almost every important American writer of the younger generation began his career by appearing in these magazines.

The depression, which coincided with the apparent success of the first Five Year Plan in Russia, was followed by a general swing to the left. Marxism never won many adherents among American workers, but for a period it captured almost an entire generation of American intellectuals. A few writers had been Communists before 1929, notably Michael Gold and Joseph Freeman, and *The New Masses* had criticized literature and art from a Communist viewpoint. In the early thirties most of the younger poets, novelists, painters, and musicians adopted the slogan of "proletarian" art; they declared that art was an instrument of class warfare and that the correct functions of the artist in modern society were to express the viewpoint of the workers and to arouse their revolutionary fervor. The proletarian works of art which were produced in accordance with this formula do not appear to have exercised any influence among the working class, which had little leisure or inclination for artistic appreciation; but they helped to spread Communistic ideas among the middle classes and in the universities. The chief spokesman of orthodox Communism in the arts was Granville Hicks, who served as literary editor of *The New Masses*; while similar ideas were propagated in *The Modern Monthly* by V. F. Calverton, who preached Marxism but was opposed to the policies of the Communist Party. Considerable greater subtlety and aesthetic understanding were displayed by two left-wing critics who wrote chiefly for *The New Republic,* Edmund Wilson and Kenneth Burke. With the exception of Van Wyck Brooks, Wilson was probably the ablest literary critic who had appeared in the United States in the twentieth century.

Literary Communism reached its zenith in the middle of the thirties. Subsequently many intellectuals became disillusioned by the policies adopted by the Russian government and by the American Communist Party and were dubious of the validity of the Marxist philosophy. The growth of Fascism in Europe, moreover, stimulated a new understanding of the value of the American democratic tradition. Many of the ablest European scholars and writers sought refuge in the United States and adopted American citizenship; and most of them were better able to appreciate the unique virtues and potentialities of the American way of life than were native intellectuals, who had never experienced tyranny. The culture of Europe appeared to be close to destruction; and it became apparent that it would be the function of the United States to preserve individual freedom, democratic institutions, and the aesthetic and intellectual standards of western civilization through the dark days which seemed to be imminent. The belief that the United States had a special mission to perform, which had animated the founders of the republic and had been stated again by Lincoln and Woodrow Wilson, but which had almost disappeared in the twenties, was now being recovered. The latter years of the thirties were a period of much bewilderment and gloom, and they were less fruitful in aesthetic creation than the twenties. But the strongest trend was toward a reinterpretation of the permanently vital elements in American history and tradition and a new appreciation of the vigor and richness of American democracy.

POETRY

The only important writer of poetry whose career spanned the entire period from the eighteen-nineties to the nineteen-thirties was

Edwin Arlington Robinson, a native of a Maine seaport. Robinson's best works, delineations of characters, were noted for intellectual depth and for clarity and precision in the expression of emotion. His writings were pervaded by an ironic bitterness which was typical of much of the culture of twentieth-century urban New England. Another New England poet was Robert Frost, who published his first book in 1913. Frost, who wrote with a classic simplicity, displayed in his poetry the integrity and the reticence of a Yankee farmer. These two men, who were little influenced by the experiments of the modernists, have usually been regarded as the leading twentieth-century American poets. Of the younger writers who continued to use the traditional conventions and techniques, the most widely read and probably the best was Edna St. Vincent Millay, also a New Englander.

Most of the poets who appeared after 1912 abandoned the verse forms and the conventions of nineteenth-century poetry and experimented with various kinds of free verse, derived partly from Whitman and partly from the Symbolist poets of nineteenth-century France. Much of their work was characterized by a bold use of startling metaphors and images, in a manner often resembling that of the latter Elizabethans. They attempted also to extend the subject matter of poetry so that it included the phenomena of industrial civilization. For these reasons their work frequently seemed to conservative readers to be obscure or unpoetic and provoked considerable antagonism. Their most useful champion was Amy Lowell, of Boston. Miss Lowell, whose own "imagist" poetry was mediocre but who was a very formidable personality, conducted an elaborate campaign to win recognition for the new poetry.

The poets of the period following 1912 can be roughly divided into the realists and the intellectualists. The most prominent of the realists were three Middle Westerners: Vachel Lindsay, who expressed the beliefs of American evangelical Protestantism; Carl Sandburg, who celebrated the industrial civilization of Chicago; and Edgar Lee Masters, whose *Spoon River Anthology* delineated the life of a Middle Western small town. A later writer, who resembled the realists in style, though not in his subject matter, was Robinson

Jeffers, of California. Jeffers' narratives of crime and incest reflected a most pessimistic attitude toward the future of the human race.

The intellectualist trend was responsible for work of greater value and vitality. Its most prominent representatives were two Americans who had settled in Europe before the war, Ezra Pound and T. S. Eliot. Pound was a leader in evolving new techniques of writing verse, but the matter of his poetry was less important than its manner. His most ambitious work, the *Cantos,* was a confused melange of history and anecdote, notable chiefly for the virtuosity of its crafts-manship. T. S. Eliot, on the other hand, who derived much of his verse technique from Pound, used it to express a repudiation of twentieth century civilization and an acceptance of religious tradition which influenced numerous disciples. He was often regarded as the leading figure in postwar Anglo-American literature. Other American poets whose work displayed a similar intellectual sophistication were Wallace Stevens, of Hartford, Connecticut, and several members of the southern agrarian group, especially John Crowe Ransom and Allen Tate. Writers whose work was less complex but equally baffling to conservatives were E. E. Cummings, of Cambridge, Massachusetts, whose impulse was mainly lyrical; William Carlos Williams, of Rutherford, New Jersey, who was primarily an observer of the American scene; and Hart Crane, of Cleveland, Ohio, an ambitious writer of great rhetorical power, who endeavored in his *Bridge* to convey a unified vision of the civilization of America. Some of these writers, especially Eliot and Tate, were important also as critics, while other criticism that was equally subtle and rigorous was written by Yvor Winters and by R. P. Blackmur. The best criticism of the twenties and thirties appeared in the *Hound and Horn* and in *The Southern Review.*

The growth of the ideal of proletarian art influenced most of the writers of verse who appeared after 1930; but, although significant "proletarian" work was done by—among others—Horace Gregory, Edwin Rolfe, and Muriel Rukeyser, the decade of the thirties was less productive in good poetry than had been the twenties. In 1940 the most generally acclaimed American poet was probably Archibald MacLeish. MacLeish was a disciple of Pound and Eliot and a writer of less originality; but he was able to reconcile their technical innovations with a more popular appeal, while he showed also a healthy awareness of the central problems which confronted contemporary American civilization. His appointment by President Roosevelt to be Librarian of Congress gave him added influence as a spokesman of the arts in the life of the nation.

THE NOVEL

The novelists of twentieth-century America were so numerous, and their audience was so large, that the writing of fiction might almost be regarded as a branch of big business. But, although the bulk of what was written was intended merely for entertainment and was quickly forgotten, there was a notable increase in both the quantity and the quality of novels of artistic value. It is impossible, in any brief discussion, to convey the extraordinary richness and variety of American fiction during the past quarter of a century.

The modern American novel has been dominated by the trend toward sociological realism, of which the leading representative before the World War was Theodore Dreiser. Dreiser's work had little subtlety and was marred by a very clumsy prose style; but his delineation of contemporary American life had a massive strength and honesty, and his insistence on his right to tell the truth as he saw it, in defiance of accepted conventions, removed many obstacles from the path of his successors. Of the other twentieth-century novelists who were prominent before the war, only two—Edith Wharton and Booth Tarkington—still continue to have considerable audiences. Mrs. Wharton, a disciple of Henry James and a very accomplished artist, wrote studies of New York wealthy society, some of which were masterpieces but which had little influence on later writers. Booth Tarkington had great technical skill but he used it to defend all the favorite prejudices and narrownesses of American middle-class society. Good work was done also by Robert Herrick, by Jack London, and—in the short story—by O. Henry; but little of it now seems likely to survive.

After 1912 new novelists of importance appeared in steadily increasing numbers, most of them being primarily concerned with the realistic depiction of different aspects of the American scene. In the early twenties the most prominent figures, in addition to Dreiser, were Sinclair Lewis, Sherwood Anderson, Willa Cather, and James Branch Cabell. Lewis' bent was primarily toward satire, and his strength lay in his gift for accurate observation. His first serious novels, *Main Street* and *Babbitt,* were generally considered to be denunciations of American middle-class society, although Lewis himself, as was shown in his later books, had considerably more sympathy with the average American businessman than had most other writers of the period. He was awarded the Nobel Prize, the first American to be so honored, in 1930. Anderson's leanings were mystical rather than sociological; most of his novels dealt with middle-class Americans who were dissatisfied with their environment and were seeking a new and more emotionally satisfying way of life. Willa Cather was more purely an artist than any other novelist of the period; and some of her studies of pioneer life, particularly *My Antonia,* which described Czech immigrants in Nebraska, were of classic perfection. Meanwhile Cabell, repudiating the realism of almost all his contemporaries, constructed an elaborate mythical country which he called Poictesme; he wrote a cycle of romances, the main theme of which was that only poetic illusions could make human life worth living. Some critics regarded Cabell as a great artist; others were infuriated by his withdrawal from the problems of contemporary life.

Of the novelists who first became prominent in the latter twenties, the most widely discussed were John Dos Passos, Ernest Hemingway, William Faulkner, and Thomas Wolfe. Dos Passos first attracted attention with a disillusioned war novel, *Three Soldiers,* and then went on to equally bitter descriptions of American society as a whole. His *U. S. A.* was an ambitious panoramic survey of life in the United States from 1900 to 1929, written from a radical point of view. Hemingway, a very careful artist, specialized in studies of simple human beings confronted by the elemental experiences of sex, danger, and death; he was probably more successful as a writer of short stories than as a novelist. Faulkner dealt always with crime, suicide, degeneracy, and insanity in his native state of Mississippi.

He won praise chiefly as a stylist, but the significance of his stories was always obscure, and in his later books his verbal tricks and his obsession with meaningless acts of violence were exaggerated to the point of absurdity. Wolfe told the story of his own life in four long volumes, which had a most enthusiastic reception from some critics, who liked their vividness and vitality, but repelled others because of their lack of form and discipline and of any coherent point of view.

The realistic trend (except in the case of Sinclair Lewis) was closely affiliated with political radicalism; and most of the younger realists who appeared after 1930 accepted Marxist doctrine and—for a few years—were inclined to support Communism. None of the proletarian novelists could be ranked in importance with the figures already mentioned, and the numerous studies of working-class life and of class warfare which were written during the thirties usually had little artistic value. Good work from a proletarian point of view was, however, written by James T. Farrell, who described Catholic Irish middle-class society in Chicago; Erskine Caldwell, who wrote chiefly (in a spirit that was more fantastic than realistic) about Georgia sharecroppers; Grace Lumpkin, who dealt with labor conflicts in North Carolina textile mills; John Steinbeck, whose *The Grapes of Wrath* was a best seller; and several Negro writers who were concerned with the problems of their own race, particularly Richard Wright. A Marxist novelist of an older generation was Waldo Frank, who viewed Marxism as a religion rather than as a science. Frank, who shared many of the ideas of Brooks and Mumford, was also important as a critic.

Many of the novelists of the twenties and thirties who concentrated on describing the life of a particular section of the country can most conveniently be classified as regionalists. Some of the best writing of the period was done by the Southern agrarians, particularly in the Civil War novels of Caroline Gordon, Allen Tate's *The Fathers,* and Robert Penn Warren's *Night Rider.* Other important southern novelists were Ellen Glasgow, of Virginia, a writer of an earlier generation whose first book appeared before the end of the nineteenth century, and Elizabeth Madox Roberts, of Kentucky. The best of the western regionalists were Ruth Suckow, of Iowa; Glenway Westcott, of Wisconsin; Vardis Fisher, of Utah; and H. L. Davis, of Oregon. Much of this regionalist writing belonged to the classic tradition and was free from the pessimism and the materialism of the realists. Similar qualities, though on a lower artistic level, were displayed in some of the novels of American history, particularly those of Kenneth Roberts and Esther Forbes, which began to appear in increasing numbers during the thirties.

Apart from the main stream were those writers who valued style above observation and for whom manner was more important than content. Critics with a preference for delicate artistry over breadth and vigor liked the novels of Elinor Wylie, Thornton Wilder, and Robert Nathan. During the twenties there were a number of writers who specialized in sophistication, including particularly F. Scott Fitzgerald, Carl Van Vechten, and Ben Hecht; but much of their work was meretricious and was soon forgotten. In general, Paris rather than any part of the United States was the headquarters of the devotees of style; and their high priestess was Gertrude Stein, whose own writings (with the exception of her *Autobiography of Alice B. Toklas*) were unintelligible to most readers but who exercised a considerable personal influence. The concentration on stylistic perfection by writers who also had something to say resulted occasionally in work which, though small in quantity, was of the highest quality. For some critics this high quality was exemplified in *Nightwood* of Djuna Barnes and, for a larger number, in the short stories of Katherine Anne Porter.

Many of the writers who have been mentioned achieved only limited audiences, but a number of them became figures of national prominence. Throughout the twentieth century there was a marked improvement in popular taste, as reflected in the quality of the works which became best sellers; and the audiences for work of genuine value grew steadily larger. The four big selling novels of the thirties were *Anthony Adverse* by Hervey Allen, *The Good Earth* by Pearl Buck (who received a Nobel Prize in 1938), *Gone With the Wind* by Margaret Mitchell, and *The Grapes of Wrath* by John Steinbeck. None of these, perhaps, will take rank as a

classic; but at least three of them were the products of honest crafts-
manship and will not quickly be forgotten.

PAINTING

The American achievement in painting has been on a high level
since the Colonial period, and its healthiest and most vigorous
tendency has always been toward the realistic depiction of the
American environment. In the latter decades of the nineteenth
century, however, although much good work of this kind was being
done, its merits were not recognized by established critical opinion.
The two most prominent American artists of the period were J. M.
Whistler and J. S. Sargent, both of whom lived mainly in Europe;
but in the opinion of modern critics their work was surpassed by
that of three men whose genius was not perceived until after their
deaths: Thomas Eakins, a scientific realist; Albert Pinkham Ryder,
a mystic and romantic; and Winslow Homer, an illustrator whose
best work was done in water colors. Accepted standards of taste at
this period were dominated by the academic conservatism represented by the National Academy of Design (founded in 1825),
whose preferences were for the romanticism of early nineteenth-
century Europe. In opposition to the Academy was the Society of
American Artists, founded by a group of disciples of the French
Impressionists, the ablest of whom were John Twachtman, J. Alden
Weir, Maurice Prendergast, and Childe Hassam. But Impressionism
was now ceasing to seem radical, and the two organizations were
combined in 1906.

Meanwhile wealthy men were becoming interested in collecting
pictures, numerous public and private galleries were being established, and large sums of money were being paid to dealers. Most of
it went, however, to the purchase of old masters and very little to
the support of contemporary artists. The United States might perhaps pride herself on the growth of her art collections; but the
presence of Italian primitives in art galleries probably did very little
to stimulate the growth of a living American art.

Since 1900 much American painting has continued to be academic,
some of which, such as the work of Harry Watrous, has been on a

high level. But the two most vital tendencies in painting, as in literature, have been realism and intellectualism. Modern realism, which was derived partly from Eakins and Homer, originated at Philadelphia in the eighteen-nineties with a group headed by Robert Henri and John Sloan. Included also were George Luks, George Bellows, George Overbury Hart, Jerome Myers, William Glackens, and Everett Shinn. Described by conservatives as the "ash-can school," these men were primarily illustrators, sympathetic to political radicalism, who liked to depict urban working-class life. They joined two of the ablest of the older men, the romanticist Arthur B. Davies and the Impressionist Maurice Prendergast, in a series of annual exhibitions which gradually made their work known. In 1917 they founded the Society of Independent Artists.

Henri and Sloan exercised great influence on American painters of a later generation; and their methods have been continued by Reginald Marsh and Peggy Bacon, and—less obviously and with greater individual variation—by such men as Glenn Coleman, Rockwell Kent, Boardman Robinson, Edward Hopper, Eugene Speicher, Leon Kroll, and Guy Pené Du Bois. Another development of the realist tradition has been the growth of regionalism, as exhibited by Thomas Benton of Missouri, Grant Wood of Iowa, and also Charles Burchfield and John Steuart Curry.

The intellectualist trend in painting has been represented by such movements as cubism, expressionism, abstractionism, and surrealism, which have in common with one another the abandonment of verisimilitude. The members of these schools propose to create forms with aesthetic significance, and in order to do so they claim the liberty to distort the subjects which they depict or to produce abstractions which have no direct relation to visual realities. This tendency, which originated in Europe, first reached the United States through the influence of the photographer Alfred Stieglitz, who began in 1908 to display the work of European modernists in his New York gallery, and through the International Exhibition at the Armory of the Sixty-ninth Regiment in New York in 1913. Among the American painters whose work has belonged mainly to one or another of the intellectualist schools have been Max Weber, John Marin,

Stuart Davis, Bernard Karfiol, Preston Dickinson, Charles Sheeler, and Peter Blume.

American painting received the greatest stimulus in its history during the Roosevelt administration, when the Federal government assumed the role of art patron. The Federal Art Project of the W. P. A. gave employment to 5,300 painters, most of whom were commissioned to paint murals for public buildings. It also conducted a number of art schools, organized experimental art galleries in different parts of the country, and collected material on the early history of the arts in America. An especially significant aspect of the Art Project was that painters were encouraged to stay at home, instead of gravitating to New York or some other metropolitan area, and to choose subjects from the history or daily life of their own locality. The result of this public patronage and decentralization of art was not only to make possible much good work but also to create a wide popular interest in contemporary American painting.

MUSIC

The development of serious music in the United States has been slower than that of any of the other arts, and there have been few, if any, American composers of the first rank. Probably the most significant feature of American musical history in the twentieth century has been the increase not so much of original contributions as of popular appreciation.

American interest in good music received its greatest stimulus from the German immigrants who came to the United States after 1848. They were active in the organization of musical performances and ultimately in the establishment of permanent symphony orchestras in the leading cities. In the latter years of the nineteenth century the most useful figure in American music was Theodore Thomas, who conducted orchestras in Chicago and New York. The steady growth of appreciation had resulted, by the nineteen-twenties, in the establishment of half a dozen or more first-class symphony orchestras, of opera companies in New York and Chicago, and of three good schools of music, the Juillard in New York, the Curtis in Philadelphia, and the Eastman in Rochester. The greatest growth of popular appreciation came, however, as a result of the radio. Early in the thirties a few radio stations, very cautiously and with considerable hesitation, began to broadcast symphony concerts. They quickly discovered that there was a large audience for classical music. The time given to good music by the leading stations steadily increased, while the growth of interest is indicated by the fact that whereas in 1929 the total number of symphony orchestras in the United States was 73, it had increased by 1940 (according to John Erskine) to no less than 270.

Prior to 1900 the United States had produced only one reputable composer of serious music, Edward McDowell (1861–1908), who is remembered chiefly for his piano sonatas. Since that date, and more especially since the World War, a large number of Americans have made significant contributions to music, among the more important being Deems Taylor, Howard Hanson, Ernest Schelling, Roy Harris, Aaron Copland, Roger Sessions, Charles Ives, Henry Cowell, Carl Ruggles, Louis Gruenberg, J. Alden Carpenter, Wallingford Riegger, Virgil Thomson, Edgar Varese, Harl McDonald, Bernard Wagenaar, Vladimir Dukelsky, William Grant Still, William Schuman, and George Antheil. A number of persons born in Europe but resident in America, such as Charles Martin Loeffler and Ernest Bloch, have also been considered American composers. Some of those in the former group, such as Deems Taylor and Howard Hanson, can be classified as traditionalists; but music of greater vitality has been written by the modernists, the most prominent of whom are Aaron Copland and Roy Harris. In the securing of recognition for American music, particularly that of the modernists, important work has been done by the League of Composers, founded in 1923.

For the average citizen modern music means popular music; and any history of American music should include some reference to the American supremacy in the field of popular songs and dance tunes, as evidenced at the beginning of the twentieth century by Victor Herbert and after the World War by such figures as George Gershwin, Vincent Youmans, Jerome Kern, Cole Porter, Richard Rodgers, and Irving Berlin, who have had audiences as international as has Hollywood. The distinctive American contribution to popular music was, however, the tendency known at different times as ragtime, blues, jazz, and swing, which appears to have originated in Negro cabarets in Memphis and New Orleans. The best work in this genre was done by Negro composers, such as W. C. Handy (who published *Memphis Blues* in 1912), and by Negro orchestra leaders, such as Louis Armstrong and Duke Ellington, although it was softened, sentimentalized, and given a wider popularity by white conductors, particularly by Paul Whiteman. What relation jazz and swing have to genuine music is a subject of controversy; but there is no denying the force and vitality of the best examples of it, and a number of serious composers did not disdain to learn from it.

ARCHITECTURE

During the nineteenth century there was little attempt to apply aesthetic standards to a large majority of the buildings that were erected. The growth of cities and the construction of factories, railroad stations, and urban tenements were governed by purely financial considerations. Art was applied only to churches, which were usually Gothic, to government buildings, which were usually Classical, and to the houses of the rich, which were often designed in the style of Renaissance chateaux. In other words, art was divorced from daily life and was considered appropriate only to give dignity to religion and government or as an amenity for those individuals who could afford to pay for it. Under such conditions it was inevitable that architecture should have no real vitality and should consist principally of antiquarian reconstructions of styles developed in earlier societies.

A new and more vigorous architecture began to develop when architects began to plan buildings with a view to utility as well as appearance. The greatest American architect of the post–Civil War period was Henry Hobson Richardson (1838–1886). Although Richardson is remembered chiefly for the strength and dignity of his Romanesque churches, his chief significance in architectural history is that he exhibited the same qualities in the designing of office buildings and railroad stations, paying attention both to the needs which they were intended to serve and to aesthetic values. Richardson's methods were developed further by Louis Sullivan (1856–

1924) of Chicago. Meanwhile the engineers who constructed bridges and factories were beginning to discover that the pursuit of technical efficiency often resulted in art. A striking example of the aesthetic potentialities of engineering was provided by the Brooklyn Bridge in New York, which was built by John A. and Washington R. Roebling and was completed in 1883.

The basic ideas of modernist architecture were first expressed by Louis Sullivan, who declared that "form follows function." The architect should consider first the purposes of the building which he is designing and the material out of which it is to be constructed; he should express the purposes and the material honestly, instead of trying to conceal or disguise them; and the form and decoration of the building should develop out of its function and should be in harmony with it. During the period when this point of view was being formulated, methods of construction were being revolutionized by the substitution of metal for masonry. Henceforth, most large buildings consisted primarily of steel skeletons—a technical development which made the skyscraper possible.

The work of Sullivan and of his associates, Daniel Burnham and John W. Root, ought to have resulted in the growth of a new architectural style appropriate to the new method of construction. In 1893, however, the progress of modernist architecture was abruptly checked by the Columbian Exposition at Chicago. Many of the buildings at the Exposition were designed in the Classical Greek and Roman styles; and the spectacle which they presented aroused such enthusiasm that classicism dominated American architecture for the next generation. Under the leadership of the New York firm of McKim, Mead, and White, public buildings, office buildings, libraries, and railroad stations were made to resemble Roman temples or Roman baths, with little regard to their purposes and methods of construction; and the metal skeletons of the skyscrapers were hidden behind irrelevant façades and decorations. Alongside these classical reminiscences there were also imitations both of Gothic, many of which were contributed by the firm of Cram, Goodhue, and Ferguson, and of Renaissance. American architecture continued to be an academic and eclectic combination of different styles of the past, none of which had any real relation to contemporary needs.

The most important American architect of the early twentieth century was Sullivan's pupil, Frank Lloyd Wright, of Wisconsin, who is best known for his "prairie houses." Wright's work is characterized by direct expression of methods of construction, fresh use of new building materials, consideration of the environment in which the building is to be erected, and preference for horizontal rather than for vertical lines. Wright had little direct influence in the United States, but he received wide recognition in Europe. European architects, while they rejected the insincerity of the more pretentious American buildings of the early twentieth century, were also strongly attracted by the aesthetic qualities of the more modern American factories, power plants, grain elevators, and other buildings which had been erected by engineers for purely useful ends. These American influences helped to produce the so-called "International Style," which was based on Sullivan's formula that "form follows function" and which was developed chiefly in Holland, Sweden, and Germany.

In the twenties and thirties there was a considerable improvement in American architectural standards, as Classical and Gothic reminiscences began to give way before the International Style. After 1920 not all government buildings had to look like Greek temples, and not all public libraries were built to resemble Roman baths. The style of the newer skyscrapers became more appropriate to their purposes and methods of construction—a development which was hastened by the zoning regulations established in New York and elsewhere in 1917 and later; and wealthy men who commissioned country homes no longer expected them to be duplicates of French chateaux. The growth of architectural honesty—considerable as it was—was, however, not universal. A number of buildings were still being erected, especially on the campuses of universities, which were painstaking reproductions of thirteenth-century Gothic. And although some of the newer state capitols, notably that designed by Bertram Goodhue for Nebraska, were approved by the modernists, many new government buildings in the District of Columbia continued to recall the Parthenon.

For most people modernist architecture meant chiefly the skyscraper; but there were very few skyscrapers that could be considered aesthetically satisfying. The economic and social forces that produced them were in many ways reprehensible. The skyscraper resulted from the rise in real estate values, which made it desirable to make the greatest possible use of every inch of ground. This had the effect of increasing the congestion of urban areas. In the words of Louis Sullivan, it was "the eloquent peroration of most bald, most sinister, most forbidding conditions." The healthiest tendencies in modern American architecture were exemplified not in the skylines of the cities but in those suburban and country houses that reflected the influence of Frank Lloyd Wright, in some of the power plants and other industrial buildings of the age of electricity, and in some of the public buildings erected in various parts of the country by the P. W. A. during the period of the New Deal.

THE THEATER

Prior to 1915 the drama was not considered in America as a serious art form. The leading playwrights, such as Clyde Fitch and Augustus Thomas, were interested merely in producing competent entertainment; and, except in the work of William Vaughn Moody, who died in 1910 before he was able fully to realize his talents, there had been no attempt to use the stage as a vehicle for genuinely creative work. Acting and production were on a high level; but performances of Shakespeare were the only contact of the theater with literature.

Meanwhile, the European drama had been reinvigorated and used for the expression of philosophical and political ideas by such writers as Ibsen, Strindberg, and Shaw. Since work of this kind did not reach the American commercial theater, groups of amateurs began to organize "little theaters" for the production of good plays. The most important of the little theater organizations were the Washington Square Players, which later became the Theatre Guild, and the Provincetown Players, both of which were founded in 1915. The existence of these groups encouraged serious American writers to turn to the writing of plays. Good plays found steadily increasing audiences; and eventually plays of genuine literary value began to be produced in the Broadway commercial theater. During the twenties and thirties the New York theater was often considered to be superior to that of any European city. And although the number of theatrical performances outside the metropolitan areas has decreased as a result of the growth of the motion picture, a healthy interest in the stage has been maintained in other parts of the country by a number of little theaters and drama festivals.

The best-known American dramatist of this period was Eugene O'Neill, who was discovered by the Provincetown Players. Beginning as a realist, O'Neill gradually evolved into a mystic concerned primarily with spiritual salvation. He was always dissatisfied with the limitations imposed by traditional stage technique, and he experimented constantly with new methods of expression. His recognition in Europe as one of the leading dramatists of modern times led to the award of a Nobel Prize in 1936. Many critics, however, preferred his early studies of elemental working-class characters to the more pretentious explorations into complex emotions which filled his later work.

Of the other dramatists who became prominent during the twenties, the most important were Maxwell Anderson, who preferred tragic themes and attempted in his later work to re-establish the poetic drama; George Kelly and Sidney Howard, who were primarily realists; S. N. Behrman, Robert Sherwood, and Philip Barry, who excelled in different forms of sophisticated comedy; and George S. Kaufman, a writer exhibiting the best qualities of the commercial theater, who wrote comedies with a broader and more colloquial humor. There were also some interesting attempts, notably by Elmer Rice and John Howard Lawson, to abandon realistic methods of presentation and to introduce the technique of German expressionism.

The early thirties saw an effort to create a proletarian drama; and several organizations, particularly the Group Theatre, were founded in order to produce plays with a radical point of view. The Group

Theatre produced one writer of great promise, Clifford Odets, who dealt with the middle-class Jewish life of New York in a style that was partly realistic and partly poetic. But probably the most interesting example of "social significance" on the stage was provided not by any of the radical intellectuals but by a trade union, the International Ladies Garment Workers, which produced a musical entertainment, *Pins and Needles,* that had a long run in a Broadway theater.

Another important development that should be mentioned in connection with the theater is the growth of the American dance. At the beginning of the twentieth century the United States produced, in Isidora Duncan, one of the greatest dancers of modern times. Miss Duncan was notable not only for her own work but also because she introduced a greater sincerity and naturalness into ballet technique throughout the world. During the twenties and thirties there was a rapid growth of interest in stage dancing in the United States, and a number of dancers, such as Martha Graham and Ruth St. Denis, became widely known. It was suggested by critics that the international leadership in the field of the ballet, which had belonged to Russia before the Bolshevik Revolution, was now being assumed by the United States.

THE MOTION PICTURE

Sociologically, although not aesthetically, the motion picture is incomparably the most important art form of the twentieth century, and its potentialities both for aesthetic expression and for the guidance of popular taste and opinion are immense. There have been, however, many obstacles to the full realization of these potentialities. The production and displaying of motion pictures is a business, which is pursued for profit and for which large outlays of capital are necessary. Most motion pictures are designed to appeal to large audiences, including children as well as adults, and must therefore be comprehensible to persons of a low level of mentality. Motion picture producers, moreover, have to refrain from offending the political, religious, or moral convictions of any considerable section of the public; and they are, therefore, compelled to treat controversial questions with great caution. The available subject matter is further limited by the international scope of the motion picture market. Producers have to respect not only the accepted beliefs of Americans but also the nationalistic attitudes of European and Latin American peoples, and they must refrain from giving offense to foreign governments.

It is, therefore, inevitable that most motion pictures should deal with the time-worn themes of love, adventure, and financial success, and should offer their audiences merely an escape from reality and not any enrichment of their understanding of it. The average motion picture, particularly during the twenties, has been aesthetically and intellectually contemptible; and many people have concluded that Hollywood is synonymous with vulgarity and stupidity and that the invention of the motion picture was an unmitigated disaster. There have been, nevertheless, a certain number of pictures of genuine merit, and during the thirties they appeared to be increasing in number. In view of all the impediments to the aesthetic development of the motion picture, it is perhaps surprising that good pictures are not even more infrequent.

The general public go to the movies chiefly to see their favorite stars perform their familiar roles of romantic hero and glamorous heroine. For the average movie-goer Hollywood has meant such personalities as Douglas Fairbanks, Rudolph Valentino, Clark Gable, Greta Garbo, Marlene Dietrich, and Joan Crawford. From the aesthetic point of view, however, the most important individual is not the star but the director; and the aesthetic development of the motion picture is dependent primarily upon the appearance of gifted directors and upon the degree to which they are able to express their own ideas freely, instead of being controlled by producers interested primarily in commercial considerations.

The first notable director was D. W. Griffith, whose career began in 1908. Griffith was the first person to grasp the fundamental elements of motion picture technique and to realize how it differed from the technique of the stage. He understood that a motion picture should be built up not from scenes but from shots. Instead of filming continuous scenes from a single angle, he made the camera mobile, switched quickly from one scene to another in order to build up suspense, introduced the close-up, and included shots of the details of scenery or background which had a symbolic value. He also promoted a more realistic style of acting than had previously been customary, used plots with more intellectual content, and lengthened the film from four to twelve or more reels. His chief weakness was that his attitude to political and social questions was apt to be sentimental and naïve. Many critics believe, nevertheless, that his two greatest pictures, *The Birth of a Nation* (1915) and *Intolerance* (1916), have never been surpassed. Griffith created no important pictures after 1922, and abandoned direction altogether in 1931.

Of the directors who were contemporary with Griffith, the most important were Thomas Ince, who excelled as a story-teller; Maurice Tourneur, who developed the pictorial possibilities of the film; and Mack Sennett, who specialized in slap-stick comedy. Much more widely known were the early stars, Douglas Fairbanks, Mary Pickford, Theda Bara, and Charlie Chaplin. Chaplin, whose career began in 1913, was originally a slap-stick comedian; but in the twenties he began to direct films as well as to act in them and to develop the slap-stick technique into a vehicle for genuinely aesthetic commentary on modern civilization. Remaining independent of Hollywood commercialism and preserving his artistic integrity, he created pictures which won both world-wide popularity and enthusiastic praise from serious critics.

During the twenties the American motion picture suffered from an artistic retrogression. There was no advance upon the work of Griffith, and commercialism was dominant. Hollywood began to produce pictures dealing chiefly with sexual license and material luxury, in which it was implied that wealth and pleasure were what made human life worth while. Enormous sums were spent on the creation of lavish scenery and backgrounds. This tendency reached its climax in *Ben-Hur* (1926), the costliest picture ever made and artistically one of the worst. The typical director of this period was Cecil B. De Mille, an accomplished technician not hampered by any artistic ideals, who began to create sophisticated sex dramas in 1919.

By 1922 demands for censorship were beginning to arise. In order to prevent this, Hollywood established its own board of censors in the form of the Motion Picture Producers and Distributors Association, of which Will H. Hays, Postmaster General in the Harding cabinet, became president. The Hays office prohibited any open display of sexuality and insisted upon moral endings; but it did not create any fundamental change in the ethical standards of Hollywood. In its anxiety not to offend public opinion in any part of the world, it discouraged any honest treatment of political and religious controversies.

The greatest director who appeared in the twenties was probably Erich Von Stroheim who created pictures (notably *Greed*, 1923) which had a harsh realism reminiscent of Zola and Dreiser. Von Stroheim was too scrupulous an artist to satisfy the producers who employed him, and he left Hollywood in 1925. Other notable directors were Ernst Lubitsch, a master of sophisticated comedy who was still creating pictures in 1940, Rex Ingram (*The Four Horsemen of the Apocalypse*, 1921), James Cruze (*The Covered Wagon*, 1923), and F. W. Murnau (*Sunrise*, 1927). Artistic leadership, however, belonged to the Europeans—to the Germans from 1921 to 1926, to the Russians from 1926 to 1929, and to the French in the early thirties. Nothing produced in Hollywood during the same period equaled the work of such European masters as Eisenstein and Pudovkin in Russia, and René Clair and Jean Renoir in France.

During the thirties there was a marked improvement in the standards of Hollywood. Although the large majority of its pictures were still purely commercial products, it created perhaps half a dozen a year which were of genuine artistic merit. Good directors began to achieve greater freedom; the technique of camera work and of acting advanced; and, although most producers were still shy of controversial material, some of them ventured occasionally to handle subjects of political and social significance. Hollywood gradually became aware that there had been a depression; and when it dealt with contemporary subjects, it did not always—as in the twenties— glorify American capitalism. The most remarkable example of this change of viewpoint, apart from the work of Charlie Chaplin, was

John Ford's *The Grapes of Wrath* (1939), a frank study of poverty and exploitation. From this point of view the European crisis, which deprived American producers of some of their foreign markets, was a positive blessing. Hollywood was no longer careful not to produce anything that might annoy Mussolini or Hitler, and it was henceforth able to produce pictures that exhibited the benefits of democracy and denounced Fascism.

Among the outstanding directors of the thirties were John Ford (*The Informer*, 1935; *The Grapes of Wrath*, 1939), Frank Capra (*It Happened One Night*, 1934; *Mr. Deeds Goes to Town*, 1936), William Wyler (*Jezebel*, 1938; *Wuthering Heights*, 1939), William Wellman (*The Public Enemy*, 1931), William Dieterle (*Zola*, 1937), Lewis Milestone (*All Quiet On the Western Front*, 1930; *The Front Page*, 1931), Mervyn Le Roy (*Little Caesar*, 1930; *I Am a Fugitive*, 1932), King Vidor (*The Citadel*, 1938) and Rouben Mamoulian (*Dr. Jekyll and Mr. Hyde*, 1931; *Love Me Tonight*, 1932). It was sometimes suggested, however, that the American motion picture was at its best in pure fantasy. Chaplin excluded, the most widely acclaimed figure in Hollywood was Walt Disney, who began to create animated cartoons in 1920, invented Mickey Mouse in 1928, and made his first long picture, *Snow White*, in 1938. Another form of fantasy was the humorous extravaganza evolved by the Marx brothers, who were appearing in pictures throughout the thirties.

Some of the best work in the field of the motion picture was done outside Hollywood by the makers of documentary films, most of whom were private individuals relatively free from the restrictions of commercialism. The founder of the documentary film was Robert Flaherty, who created *Nanook of the North* in 1922. Important work in this genre was done subsequently by Pare Lorentz, who made two pictures for the U. S. Department of Agriculture, *The River* and *The Plough that Broke the Plains*, by Joris Ivens and by Paul Strand.

BIBLIOGRAPHY

M. Bardeche and R. Brasillach, *History of Motion Pictures* (1938)
*H. Cahill and A. H. Barr (eds.), *Art in America* (1935)

O. Cargill, *American Literature: A Period Anthology* (1933)
S. Cheney, *New World Architecture* (1930)
H. Cowell (ed.), *American Composers and American Music* (1933)
M. Cowley (ed.), *After the Genteel Tradition* (1937)
G. H. Edgell, *American Architecture of Today* (1928)
G. Hicks, *The Great Tradition* (1935)
H. R. Hitchcock, *Modern Architecture* (1929)
J. T. Howard, *Our American Music* (1931)
*L. Jacobs, *The Rise of the American Film* (1939)
H. L. Kaufman, *From Jehovah to Jazz* (1937)
F. P. Keppel and R. L. Duffus, *The Arts in American Life* (1933)
S. F. Kimball, *American Architecture* (1928)
*J. W. Krutch, *American Drama since 1918* (1939)
S. La Follette, *Art in America* (1929)
J. J. Martin, *America Dancing* (1936)
L. Mumford, *Sticks and Stones* (1924)
———— *The Brown Decades* (1931)
A. H. Quinn, *History of American Drama* (1923)
L. Reis, *Composers in America* (1938)
P. Rosenfeld, *An Hour with American Music* (1929)
P. Rotha, *The Film Till Now* (1930)
———— *Documentary Film* (1936)
W. Sargeant, *Jazz Hot and Hybrid* (1939)
L. H. Sullivan, *Autobiography of an Idea* (1924)
T. E. Tallmadge, *Story of Architecture in America* (1936)
W. F. Taylor, *History of American Letters* (1936)
*C. Van Doren, *The American Novel* (Revised edition, 1940)
*C. and M. Van Doren, *British and American Literature since 1890* (Revised edition, 1939)
F. L. Wright, *Modern Architecture* (1931)
———— *Autobiography* (1932)
M. D. Zabel (ed.), *Literary Opinion in America* (1937)

47

AMERICA FACES

THE FUTURE

IN THE first chapter of this book it was suggested that twentieth-century America is confronted by five main problems, and that the continued growth of American civilization depends on their solution. These are the problems of economic insecurity, economic inequality, the waste of natural resources, international rivalries and wars, and the clash of values and traditions among different sections of the American people.

During the first four decades of the twentieth century the leaders of American opinion were occupied largely in exploring these different problems and in propounding possible methods of solving them. Successive governments, both Federal and local, put into effect a number of the remedies that had been recommended. Yet in spite of all the constructive labors of intellectuals and statesmen, and in spite of the immense changes in political practice and viewpoint between the America of McKinley and the America of Franklin Roosevelt, it cannot be said at the end of this period that any of these problems have become less urgent or that the American people can face the future with equanimity. Reform has been extensive and sometimes rapid, but meanwhile the underlying maladjustments have become more widespread and more dangerous.

In the hope of preventing insecurity, limiting inequality, and checking waste, the Federal government extended its authority over industry and agriculture and assumed responsibility for providing relief for the unemployed. The economic system has continued, nevertheless, to operate at less than its full capacity, and millions of men have been unable to find work in private industry. Meanwhile the growth of bureaucratic power has appeared to many people to present a threat to individual liberty.

In the pursuit of security against aggression by foreign powers, the American people have oscillated between isolation and international co-operation. But they have been unable to adopt either of these attitudes with sufficient consistency; nor is there any certainty that either of them, even though adopted wholeheartedly and put into practice wisely, will protect America from war. The peace of the American hemisphere, as of Europe and Asia, is perpetually menaced by international antagonisms inherited from the past and by the aggressive policies of European and Asiatic dictatorships.

The growth of national unity has been furthered by the limitation of immigration and by the inculcation of American ideals through the public schools and in the press. The beginning of the fifth decade of the century finds the overwhelming majority of the American people loyal to the traditions (insofar as they understand them) of freedom and democracy. Yet there remain acute social and economic divisions and deep-rooted racial and religious prejudices which threaten, in any time of crisis, to cause dangerous conflicts.

Meanwhile the urgency of these problems has been increased by events in Europe and Asia. Other powers, confronted by economic maladjustments and class conflicts similar to those which exist in the United States, have come under the rule of aggressive dictatorships. These dictatorships aspire to dominate the world, and they encourage internal conflicts in the democratic nations in order to weaken them and make them ripe for conquest. The American people appear to be faced with perhaps the greatest challenge in their history—a challenge which necessitates not only the building of armaments and the adoption of a more vigorous foreign policy but also the removal of every element of inner weakness of which the dictatorships can take advantage. The problem of defense is both external and internal, and what is at stake is the preservation of the American tradition.

Americans, however, are in no danger of failing to recognize the gravity of the crisis. Since 1933 there has been a growing awareness of the double threat presented by aggression abroad and insecurity and division at home. Fortunately able to take warning by the catastrophes which have overwhelmed the nations of Europe, the American people have acquired a more vivid understanding of the values of their tradition and of the forces which threaten it. The discussion of political and sociological issues in recent years has resembled, in keenness, lucidity, and awareness of fundamentals, the debates over the constitution in the seventeen-eighties and over slavery and states' rights in the eighteen-fifties. For, although nearly all groups in the United States are agreed as to the importance of individual liberty and democratic government, there is considerable disagreement as to how these ideals should be given practical application. There is controversy over the internal reconstruction of the American system, over the external policies which America should adopt, and over the philosophical implications of democracy.

Few persons in America advocate a return to the kind of *laissez faire* which prevailed in the era of President McKinley. Few people, on the other hand, favor complete government ownership and operation of the economic system. Between these two extremes, nevertheless, there is room for wide differences of opinion. Conservatives argue that the preservation of liberty and continued cultural and economic progress require a system of free capitalistic enterprise. The activities of the government must necessarily be greater than in the nineteenth century; but the primary object should be to maintain private enterprise and to enable it to function more smoothly and more equitably. The ablest and most convincing statement of this attitude is in the writings of Walter Lippmann. In opposition to this position, numerous liberal and radical intellectuals argue in favor of increased government intervention in economic affairs, with the hope of achieving either some form of "democratic collectivism" or a mixed system in which some branches of the economic system would be publicly owned, while others would still be operated for private profit. Examples of this point of view are to be found in the writings of such men as Max Lerner, Jerome

Frank, Alfred Bingham, John Chamberlain, Eduard Heimann, Stuart Chase, George Counts, George Soule, and David Cushman Coyle. Meanwhile, a third school of thought, of which the chief spokesman is Herbert Agar, regard both capitalistic ownership and government ownership as destructive of individual liberties. Their program is to encourage small-scale private property and consumers' co-operatives.

Scarcely anyone in America advocates a policy of imperialist expansion. Scarcely anyone, on the other hand, argues that Americans should remain wholly indifferent to what happens outside their own country. It is believed almost universally that the United States has special responsibilities for the preservation of world civilization and that, as Washington, Lincoln, and Wilson declared during earlier times of crisis, it is her mission to protect the institutions of freedom. Men disagree, however, as to whether this task can best be fulfilled through intervention or through example. Should the United States adopt a policy of military opposition to the Fascist powers and undertake the function of leadership in the creation of a new world order? Or should she set out instead to create a finer form of democracy within her own borders and to make herself an impregnable stronghold of peace, freedom, and constructive civilization? The political dangers of tolerating the growth of Fascism have been set forth by such writers as Dorothy Thompson, Raymond Leslie Buell, and Hamilton Fish Armstrong, while the moral issues involved have been the theme of eloquent appeals for action by Lewis Mumford, Waldo Frank, and Archibald MacLeish. The isolationist position, on the other hand, has been ably defended by Charles A. Beard, John Chamberlain, and Stuart Chase.

Of more fundamental importance, but more intangible and less easy to define, are the philosophical and moral implications of the American tradition. Much American thinking of the twentieth century has been permeated by the philosophies of pragmatism and instrumentalism, which emphasize the need for perpetual experiment and exploration and oppose the belief in absolute and unchanging moral standards and intellectual formulas. In the opinion of the instrumentalists, doctrines of moral and intellectual abso-

lutism lead to authoritarian methods in government and to the
forcible suppression of ideas which are deemed to be heretical.
This point of view has been expressed in numerous writings by
John Dewey, the dean of American philosophers, whose career has
spanned more than half a century; and it is supported by the numerous younger philosophers and sociologists who have been influenced
by him.

Opponents of the instrumentalist position are equally vigorous in
upholding democratic ideals; but they argue that democracy depends
on the common acceptance by all citizens of certain moral and intellectual truths, that its preservation requires a capacity for individual discipline and surrender, and that only faith in certain
enduring values provides a sufficient stimulus for self-sacrifice. It
is not moral absolutism but the relativism of the instrumentalists,
they maintain, which will end in dictatorship since it implies that
the end justifies the means and will thereby encourage disrespect
for individual rights and liberties. The instrumentalist attitude has
always been attacked on these grounds by traditionalists of different
kinds, particularly by the adherents of the Catholic philosophy of
Thomism, by the Humanists of the school of Babbitt and More,
and by the southern agrarians. During the thirties, as the need for
a faith strong enough to resist Fascism became more apparent, asser-
tions of moral absolutism became more frequent. The need for beliefs, whether revealed by religion or grasped by intuition, has been
emphasized by conservatives like Walter Lippmann and by liberals
like Lewis Mumford and Waldo Frank. Controversy between the
exponents of the two points of view is especially vehement in the
field of education. American educational theory for a long time has
been dominated by the instrumentalists; and their methods have now
been challenged by such men as President Hutchins of Chicago,
who believe both in indoctrination of truths established by tradition
and in a more rigorous mental discipline.

There is much truth in the contentions of each party; and, important though the controversy is, the two groups are perhaps not
so far apart from each other as appears on the surface. Progress, as
the instrumentalists correctly contend, is impossible without experi-

ment and exploration. Constant testing of accepted theories by examining their results in practice, refusal to be bound by inherited dogmas which are no longer relevant to actual conditions, willingness to try out new methods and new hypotheses—the preservation of these characteristics, on which the American people have always rightly prided themselves, is indispensable for the continued growth of civilization. On the other hand, it is also necessary that men maintain a sense of civic responsibility and discipline, that they be willing to sacrifice themselves for the common good, and that they refuse to condone any form of injustice or dishonesty. The preservation of all civilization, and more particularly of civilization in a democracy, depends on the sensitivity, the strength, and the enlightenment of the consciences of individual men and women. Certain moral ideals are inherent in the American tradition—the ideals, particularly, of human freedom and human equality—and the belief in these ideals will remain vital only so long as they are recognized as absolutes.

Both some of the habits recommended by the instrumentalists and some of the beliefs affirmed by the traditionalists are necessary for an enduring civilization. The greatness of America has consisted, in the last resort, in the character of her citizens, in their allegiance to ultimate values, and, particularly, in their willingness to make experiments. As long as these two qualities are unimpaired, there is no valid cause to fear the future or to suppose that any problems, however difficult, will prove to be ultimately insoluble. To what extent the moral fiber of the American people may have been weakened by the cynicism of the twenties and by the economic failures of the thirties is a question that sometimes provokes gloomy speculation, but the manner in which America has begun to brace herself to meet the challenge of Fascist aggression does not suggest that she has genuinely lost any of the qualities which made her great.

BIBLIOGRAPHY

H. Agar, *Land of the Free* (1935)
H. Agar and A. Tate (eds.), *Who Owns America?* (1936)
H. F. Armstrong, *"We or They"; two worlds in conflict* (1936)
*C. A. Beard, *The Open Door at Home* (1934)

*C. A. Beard, *A Foreign Policy for America* (1940)

A. Bingham, *Man's Estate* (1939)

R. Borsodi, *Prosperity or Security* (1938)

*R. L. Buell, *Isolated America* (1940)

*J. Chamberlain, *The American Stakes* (1940)

G. S. Counts, *The Prospects of American Democracy* (1938)

D. C. Coyle, *Roads to a New America* (1938)

S. Chase, *The New Western Front* (1939)

────── *Idle Money, Idle Men* (1940)

L. Dennis, *The Coming American Fascism* (1936)

A. W. Dulles and H. F. Armstrong, *Can We Be Neutral?* (1936)

M. Ezekiel, *$2500 a Year* (1936)

────── *Jobs for All* (1939)

*J. Frank, *Save America First* (1938)

W. Frank, *Chart for Rough Water* (1940)

L. Hartley, *Is America Afraid?* (1937)

────── *Our Maginot Line* (1939)

Q. Howe, *England Expects Every American To Do His Duty* (1937)

E. Heimann, *Communism, Fascism or Democracy* (1938)

H. W. Laidler, *A Program for Modern America* (1936)

*M. Lerner, *It Is Later Than You Think* (1938)

────── *Ideas are Weapons* (1939)

*W. Lippmann, *The Good Society* (1937)

L. Mumford, *Men Must Act* (1939)

*────── *Faith for Living* (1940)

G. Soule, *The Coming American Revolution* (1934)

N. Thomas, *The Choice Before Us* (1934)

Twelve Southerners, *I'll Take My Stand* (1930)

E. J. Young, *Powerful America* (1936)

48

THE SECOND WORLD WAR

THE ELECTION OF 1940

AFTER the German victories in the spring of 1940 the people of the
United States realized that they must now concentrate their energies
on the tasks of national defense; and a substantial majority of them
believed that they should also give support to the nations which were
fighting aggression in Europe and Asia. The first steps toward creating effective armed forces and sending aid to Great Britain were
taken during the summer; but full adoption of these policies had
to be postponed until after the presidential election in November.

The result of the Republican Convention, which met at Philadelphia
in June, was an encouraging proof of the vitality of American democratic processes. The three leading contenders for the presidential
nomination had been District Attorney Dewey of New York, Senator
Taft of Ohio, and Senator Vandenberg of Michigan. All these men
were inclined toward isolationism; and none of them had shown any
understanding of the revolutionary forces which had destroyed democracy in Europe and had carried mankind into the greatest conflict
in history.

Fortunately these were not the only available candidates. The rank
and file of the Republican Party were demanding a more inspiring leader, and had found one in Wendell Willkie, a former Democrat who had been a corporation lawyer and the president of a power
company and had never held any political office. In spite of his Wall
Street associations Willkie was a man of genuinely liberal convictions, who was opposed to Roosevelt not because he failed to appreciate
the need for reform but because he believed that the New Deal had

been applied inefficiently and extravagantly and with too much bureaucratic regimentation; and in spite of his German descent and Indiana background he was an outspoken advocate of aid to Great Britain. He was, moreover, refreshingly free from the timidity and insincerity which characterized so many of the nation's professional politicians. It became obvious early in the convention that whatever the Republican party bosses might want, the people wanted Willkie; and the result of this popular pressure was that he received the nomination on the sixth ballot.

Meanwhile it had become apparent that the Democratic Party was going to challenge tradition by nominating President Roosevelt for a third term. Roosevelt himself, as he afterwards explained, had originally planned to retire, but had changed his mind and decided to accept renomination on account of the unprecedented world crisis. He made no public pronouncement of his intentions; but his silence prevented any alternative candidate from gathering support. A number of the Democratic leaders disliked this violation of the no-third-term tradition, but they were unwilling to disrupt the party by openly opposing its leader; and when the Democratic Convention met, Roosevelt was renominated on the first ballot. At Roosevelt's insistence, and contrary to the wishes of a number of the delegates, Henry A. Wallace was nominated for the vice-presidency.

The campaign showed that the American people did not regard the third-term question as a matter of vital importance. The essential issue was whether Roosevelt or Willkie would provide more effective leadership in the task of defending the American way of life. The two candidates were substantially in agreement in their appraisal of the international crisis; and they differed only in details in their approach to domestic policies. And although Willkie was able to point to a number of weaknesses in Roosevelt's administration of the New Deal and—less plausibly—in his handling of foreign affairs, a majority of the electorate decided that they did not wish to entrust their destinies to a new and untried chief executive. Some voters felt that Willkie had shown a dangerous propensity for rash and reckless utterances, while others were alarmed by the quality of some of his supporters. The reactionaries who wished to return to the Coolidge era and the isolationists who hated Great Britain or sympathized with Naziism were all trying to defeat Roosevelt; and in spite of Willkie's liberalism they would inevitably have regarded his election as a victory for themselves. As in the campaign of 1936, many Americans decided to vote for Roosevelt because of the enemies whom he had made.

The result was the reelection of the president by a reduced majority. The Middle Western farm vote reverted to its traditional Republicanism, but the Democratic Party retained its hold over the cities and—in spite of the support given to Willkie by John L. Lewis—over organized labor. With a popular vote of twenty-seven million, Roosevelt carried thirty-eight states having an electoral vote of 449. Willkie, receiving a popular vote of twenty-two million, nearly six million more than any previous Republican candidate, won ten New England and Mid-Western states with an electoral vote of 82.

THE ROAD TO WAR

While the United States had been engaged in political campaigning, the nations across the Atlantic had been passing through one of the most terrible and momentous summers in their entire history. The German offensive in the West, which had begun on May 10, swept across Holland and Belgium, broke through the French lines near Sedan, and within four weeks had virtually destroyed the French army, which military experts only a month before had believed to be the best in the world. On June 10 Mussolini, convinced that German victory was now certain and eager for a share in the plunder, entered the war; and on June 17 a new French government, headed by the semi-Fascist Marshal Pétain, ended democracy in France and sued for an armistice. After one of the shortest and most brilliant military campaigns on record, Hitler had become master of most of western Europe.

To many observers, both in Europe and in the United States, it seemed certain that the Nazis would now complete their victory by subduing Great Britain. The British army had been rescued from capitulation by the evacuation at Dunkirk, but it had abandoned the whole of its equipment; Great Britain had barely begun to organize her energies for war; and until May she had been governed by men who had shown a tragic inability to understand the enemy whom they were facing. But the British people now displayed a courage and a capacity in meeting the crisis which showed that free institutions had not lost their virtue and which earned the admiration of all democratic nations throughout the world. They had already found a leader equal to the occasion in Winston Churchill, gifted both in knowledge of war and in command of eloquence; and after Dunkirk they prepared to deal with the threatened invasion. Hitler never ventured to send troops across the Channel; he attempted first to secure mastery of the skies and to knock out Great Britain from the air. And in a series of battles over British cities in August and September the Royal Air Force won a decisive victory over the German Luftwaffe. German plane losses were rarely less than twenty per cent, and sometimes exceeded twice that proportion; on one day alone, September 15, the Luftwaffe lost more than two hundred out of a raiding force of less than five hundred. In October Hitler abandoned daylight raiding, and had to postpone indefinitely his invasion plans. The Battle of Britain—one of the most important battles of all time— had been won; and the ultimate victory of the democracies had become possible.

Meanwhile in the Far East Japan was preparing to take advantage of the European war in order to satisfy her imperialist ambitions. The Japanese war lords had been engaged in war with China for three years; but although their armies had occupied a large part of that country, they had never been able to end the resistance of the Chinese people under the leadership of Chiang Kai-Shek. The German victories now opened easier and more profitable areas for conquest. For a generation or more, Japanese militarists had been looking forward to the conquest of the French, Dutch, British, and American possessions in the Far East, with their vast resources in rubber, oil, tin, and other raw materials; and the prospect of a German victory in Europe was too good an opportunity to be overlooked. The European powers could no longer defend their Asiatic possessions; and the United States, it was hoped, could be intimidated by a show of force. In September, 1940, an alliance between Germany, Italy, and

Japan was signed at Berlin. The Nazis and the Japanese war lords agreed to support each other in their plans for a "new order" in Europe and Asia respectively, and promised to come to each other's assistance if either of them were attacked by any power at present neutral—a threat which could refer only to the United States. It appeared that Japan had signed the treaty in order to obtain German sanction for the absorption of French Indo-China. Japanese troops had already begun to occupy bases in that region, and were not opposed by the officials of the German-controlled government of Marshal Pétain.

The United States was thus in danger of finding herself confronted by aggressive militaristic powers across both oceans. Hitler had failed to conquer Great Britain by direct attack, but he might starve her into submission by submarine warfare; and the British, as their Prime Minister admitted, could not hope to defeat him without American assistance. Japan could occupy the East Indies whenever she felt that the time was ripe; and only the armed forces of the United States could prevent her from acquiring permanent control of the whole of the western Pacific. The crisis precipitated one of the most important debates in American history. Should the United States take action to prevent hostile powers from controlling the European and African coasts of the Atlantic and the Asiatic coast of the Pacific? Or should she assume that she could do business with a victorious Germany and Japan and could successfully defend herself if either or both of these powers should choose to attack her?

Of the numerous organizations which endeavored to mobilize public opinion, the most influential were the interventionist Committee to Defend America by Aiding the Allies and the isolationist America First Committee. The Committee to Defend America, headed by William Allen White, was supported from the outset by a majority of the most respected leaders of American opinion; and as the war proceeded a large number of former pacifists and isolationists began to reconsider their opinions. The United States, they declared, could not hope to preserve her free institutions and her traditional ideals if all Europe and Asia passed under the rule of aggressive and cynical military dictatorships; and it was improbable that she could defend the western hemisphere from German and Japanese attack if she had no allies in other parts of the world. British seapower had always been America's first line of defense; and if the British Empire were overthrown, not even the United States, in spite of her vast resources, could hope to outbuild the Nazis in a race for naval and air superiority. Both the ideals and the security of America required that adequate aid should be given to the British and the Chinese. These arguments were supported by a growing majority of the American people, particularly in the Northeast and in the South.

The isolationists, on the other hand, were handicapped in their appeals to public opinion by the quality of their supporters. They included a number of sincere and patriotic citizens, who genuinely believed that the United States had no interest in the preservation of British seapower and that neither Germany nor Japan would ever venture to attack her; but they included also men whose motives were much more dubious. Nazi sympathizers who believed that democracy had failed and that fascism represented the "wave of the future," business men who wanted to end the New Deal and preferred Hitler to Roosevelt, Irish-Americans whose hatred of Great Britain outweighed their loyalty to the United States, antisemitic agitators who propagated the Nazi doctrines of racial hatred, office-seekers who believed that the American electorate wanted primarily to stay out of war and would be pleased by assurances that they were not in danger, and politicians who had based their careers on the theory that all wars were provoked by bankers and munitions manufacturers and were now unwilling to admit that they had been wrong—men of this kind supported the America First Committee and preached isolationist doctrines in Congress and in the newspapers. They made it increasingly obvious that a victory for isolationism would mean a victory for all the most sinister forces in American public life.

Supported by a majority of the electorate, the Roosevelt administration began slowly to give help to the British and the Chinese. When Italy entered the war, Roosevelt vigorously denounced the Italian dictator in a speech at Charlottesville, Virginia, in which he declared that the American government would "extend to the opponents of force the material resources of this nation." Surplus guns and planes were released by the War Department for sale to Great Britain; and in September an agreement was concluded with the British government by which the United States leased a number of bases situated on British territory in Newfoundland, the West Indies, and Guiana, which were necessary for the security of the western hemisphere. The British, in return, received fifty over-age destroyers, which they particularly needed for defense against the submarine campaign. When France capitulated, American influence was exerted to prevent the French navy and North African colonies from falling into German hands; and although the Pétain government refused to send the navy to American ports for safekeeping, it was encouraged by American pressure to offer some resistance to the Germans. In the Far East the American government answered the Japanese-Nazi alliance by giving loans to China, embargoing sales of scrap to Japan, and ordering American citizens in Japanese-controlled territory to return home. The United States began to cooperate with the Chinese, the British, and the Dutch in defense of their common interests; and it was made obvious to Japan that the democratic powers would not submit to intimidation. Meanwhile progress was made in unifying the nations of the western hemisphere against Nazi penetration. The United States began to buy up the surplus commodities of the Latin-American nations in order to compensate them for the loss of their European markets and to outbid the German offer of profitable contracts to be fulfilled at the end of the war. And at the Havana Conference of July it was agreed that the American nations should exercise a collective trusteeship over any European possessions, such as the French West Indies, which might be in danger of transference to Nazi control.

Through the summer the chances of continued British resistance seemed uncertain; and since the American economic system was not yet geared for war production, it was difficult to decide whether the United States should gamble on British strength by sending all her available resources abroad or concentrate on building her own defenses. By the end of the year, however, it had become evident that Great Britain was capable of defending herself. The November elections, moreover, showed that public opinion in the United States would support a bolder program. American policy now assumed a more definite shape. Roosevelt declared in a radio address on December 29 that the

United States was determined that "the Axis powers are not going to win this war"; there could be no negotiated peace; and nothing but a democratic victory could ensure the kind of world in which nations could live in security. Roosevelt had pledged himself during the presidential campaign that the United States would not herself enter the war unless she were attacked; but she would give the democracies sufficient material aid to enable them to defeat the aggressor powers. "We must be the great arsenal of democracy," said the president; "there will be no 'bottlenecks' in our determination to aid Great Britain."

In addition to shipping war material to Great Britain, the United States also endeavored to check Hitlerism in other directions. Admiral Leahy was sent as American minister to the Vichy government of Marshal Pétain, with the task of encouraging the Vichy officials to resist their Nazi overlords; and political and economic relations were fostered with the Soviet Union. In spite of the Nazi-Soviet pact of August, 1939, American diplomats believed that a rupture between the two nations was likely, and that American friendship might encourage Stalin to resist Hitler's demands. As early as January, 1941, the State Department was able to warn the Soviet Union to expect a Nazi attack in June. Meanwhile, in the Far East, American policy was to remain firm but passive; the United States would not surrender to Japanese demands, but at the same time she would not provoke Japan into aggressive action. The defeat of Hitler was to have priority in the American program. In spite of the American sympathy for China, Japan continued to receive shipments of American oil, since it was believed in Washington that if oil were embargoed, the result would be a Japanese attack on the East Indies.

Hitherto, in accordance with the Neutrality Act of 1939, the British had been required to pay in cash for all American war materials and to transport them in their own ships. It was now becoming obvious that Great Britain would need more direct help. Her cash reserves were almost exhausted, and although she still had large foreign investments, she could not liquidate them quickly and without heavy sacrifices. The German submarines, moreover, were inflicting severe losses upon British shipping; and it was absurd for the United States to export war material which would go only to the bottom of the Atlantic.

In December Roosevelt proposed a method for dealing with the first of these problems. Credits to Great Britain were prohibited by both the Johnson Act and the Neutrality Act. The history of the war loans made during the First World War, moreover, did not encourage a repetition of such a policy. Roosevelt suggested instead that goods should be lent to Great Britain, who would make repayment after the war not in money but in kind. This "lend-lease" program, embodied in an act of Congress which was passed in March, 1941, was subsequently broadened into an instrument both for winning the war and for implementing American policies of post-war reconstruction. Goods might be shipped to any country "whose defense the President deems vital to the defense of the United States"; and the return to the United States might be "payment or repayment in kind or property, or any other direct or indirect benefit." In a series of agreements with nations which received lend-lease aid, it was stipulated that they should promote freer international trade after the war.

The problem of ensuring that American goods actually reached the British could be solved only by sending American merchant ships into the combat zone and by giving them adequate defenses against submarines. The first of these measures was prohibited by the Neutrality Act, while the second would mean that America would become a belligerent. In April Roosevelt declared that the Red Sea and Indian Ocean were not a combat zone, thus allowing American ships to supply the British army in Egypt; and the air force was instructed to patrol the Atlantic as far as Iceland in order to warn British merchant ships of the locality of submarines. American troops occupied Greenland in the same month, and Iceland in July. In September the American destroyer *Greer* was attacked by a submarine while proceeding to Iceland; and Roosevelt announced that henceforth the American navy would defend the freedom of the seas by attacking any German submarines which were encountered. In the following month another destroyer, the *Reuben James,* was sunk, and a third, the *Kearny,* was damaged. The United States was now becoming engaged in an undeclared naval war in the Atlantic.

The growing partnership of the United States and the British Commonwealth became more intimate in August, when Roosevelt and

Churchill met and conferred with each other for several days on a battleship near the coast of Maine. The two statesmen discussed the progress of the war, and set forth their ideas of post-war reconstruction in an eight-point program which became known as the Atlantic Charter. In his message to Congress in January Roosevelt had already formulated four freedoms which, he believed, should be guaranteed everywhere: freedom of religion, freedom of speech, freedom from want, and freedom from fear. The Atlantic Charter declared that the peace settlement should be based on the following principles: no nation should seek territorial aggrandizement; no territorial changes should be made except by the wish of the population concerned; all nations should be allowed to choose their own form of government; all nations should have equal access to markets and to raw materials; nations should collaborate with each other in the raising of standards of living; there should be security against war; the seas should be free to all in time of peace; and the aggressor nations should be deprived of their weapons, and efforts should be made to lighten the burden of armaments for all nations. The eight points of this Atlantic Charter were reminiscent of the fourteen points of President Wilson, but the differences were perhaps more significant than the similarities. Unlike the Fourteen Points, the Atlantic Charter was not merely an American program; it was formulated jointly by the Americans and the British. It confined itself to general statements of policy, and did not attempt to forecast specific territorial changes. It laid considerable emphasis on economic cooperation. And it did not propose that the victorious nations should themselves disarm, or that they should commit themselves to freedom of the seas in wartime. The American government, it appeared, had taken warning from some of the errors which had been made in 1918 and 1919.

By this date the European war had spread eastward, and another group of unoffending neutrals had become the victims of Nazi imperialism. The winter of 1940–41 had been relatively quiet, except for the night raids of the Luftwaffe over British cities and the continuous pressure of the submarine campaign. The British had made use of the lull in Nazi activity to complete their liquidation of Mussolini's East African empire and to destroy Italian armies in Libya. The spring and summer saw more demonstrations of Nazi blitzkrieg tactics. Hungary, Rumania and Bulgaria had been absorbed into the Nazi "New Order" during the autumn and winter without resistance; but the Jugo-Slavs and the Greeks were less compliant. Hitler's drive into the Balkans began on April 6, and within less than three weeks the Jugo-Slav and Greek armies had been crushed, and the Nazis were on the Aegean. The seizure of Crete, accomplished by troops transported entirely by air and in spite of British control of the sea, followed in May; and it seemed inevitable that the next move would be the conquest of the entire Middle East. German troops, taking over Libya from the Italians, had already driven the British back into Egypt.

Hitler, however, had other plans. The Soviet government had shown a disconcerting unwillingness to accept Nazi dictation, and had viewed the Nazi conquest of the Balkans with obvious displeasure. Hitler apparently felt that it was unsafe for him to engage in an all-out struggle with Great Britain as long as he had a potentially hostile army in his rear; and having based his whole career on the thesis that communism meant disorder and degeneracy, he was incapable of a realistic appraisal of Soviet military power. On June 22 the German army began its invasion of the Soviet Union, hoping to crush the Soviet armies in a single campaign; and during the next five months it occupied half a million square miles of Russian territory. The Soviet armies, nevertheless, were able to conduct an orderly retreat; and by the end of November the German advance was definitely halted, and the Russians were able in some sections to take the offensive. For the second time Hitler had failed to achieve his objective. The Nazis may have hoped that their attack on the Soviet Union would create divisions among the democracies; but the British and American governments, in spite of their hostility to communism, believed in cooperation with any power opposed to Germany. Lend-lease aid was given to the Soviets; and the vigorous resistance made by the Russian army and people won the sincere admiration of the people of the United States.

The conflict in Europe had the front place in the minds of most Americans; and by the autumn of 1941 the United States had come as close to belligerency as it was possible to go without ceasing to be officially at peace. Nevertheless, as many students of foreign affairs had always predicted, it was the course of events in the Far East which finally precipitated the American people into open war. The Japanese military caste were steadily increasing their control over the Japanese government and people—a process which culminated in October, 1941, when General Tojo became prime minister. Probably they did not wholly trust the Nazis; but they realized that it was only by openly allying themselves with Germany against the democracies that they could hope to achieve their ambition for a "Greater East Asia." In July they completed their occupation of French Indo-China—a move which caused the American government to restrict sales of oil to Japan and to freeze Japanese assets in the United States—and began to make preparations for seizing the East Indies. Meanwhile the Japanese government had initiated negotiations with the United States; and between March and December, 1941, the Japanese ambassador in Washington, Admiral Nomura, held no less than sixty meetings with Cordell Hull. Whether the Japanese had any genuine belief in the possibility of coming to terms, or whether they were merely trying to distract American attention until their military plans had been completed, it was difficult to say. Certainly they made no offers which the United States could regard as suitable bases for a real settlement. They declared that they would be willing to leave Indo-China and the East Indies alone if the United States, in return, would accept Japanese political and economic control of China, would cease giving any support to the Chinese, and would refrain from any embargoes or restrictions upon Japanese trade.

Cordell Hull, in reply, reiterated the traditional Far Eastern policy of the United States: maintenance of the status quo, full political independence for China, and the Open Door in economic relations. In November Admiral Nomura was joined by another Japanese diplomat, Saburu Kurusu. The American government was willing to prolong the negotiations, since allied preparations for the defense of the East Indies were far from complete; but it was not deceived as to Japanese intentions, and sent warnings to American military and naval commanders that war was imminent. The majority of the American people, on the other hand, their attention fixed upon the European war, did not appreciate the gravity of the situation; underestimating the military and economic power of Japan, they never suspected that the

Japanese would have the audacity to launch an attack upon the United States. It was therefore with complete surprise that they learnt, on the afternoon of December 7, that while negotiations in Washington were still continuing and no declaration of war had been made, the Japanese air force had made a surprise attack upon the American Pacific fleet at Pearl Harbor. The United States, like so many other nations in Europe, Asia and Africa during the previous decade, had become the victim of aggression.

On the following day Congress declared that a state of war existed with Japan; and three days later Germany and Italy, removing any doubts as to the common purposes of the aggressor nations, declared war upon the United States. Meanwhile Great Britain had declared war on Japan. The European and Asiatic conflicts were now merged into a single global war.

THE HOME FRONT

The immense task of preparing the United States for total war began in the summer of 1940. The three major necessities of the war program were to build a large army and navy, to transfer industry to war production, and to establish controls over the economic system which would assure an equitable distribution of the available commodities and prevent inflation. For these three purposes it was necessary for the government to assume far-reaching powers over the lives and activities of all the people of America. This necessity was generally recognized; and in spite of much distrust of the New Deal among Republicans, it was agreed that the government must have the requisite authority.

The United States adopted peacetime conscription for the first time in her history by the Selective Training and Service Act of September, 1940. All men between the ages of 20 and 36 were required to register, and were subsequently classified by local draft boards into four groups according to their relative availability for service. Those who were not given deferment on account of occupation, support of dependents, or physical disability were to be called for military training, the order being determined, as in 1917, by lottery. They were to be released at the end of a year's service, and the total number of drafted men at any one time was not to exceed 900,000. This measure, it was hoped, would provide a body of trained soldiers who could be called back for duty if the United States entered the war.

After Pearl Harbor, service was no longer limited to one year; and by a new draft law, passed on December 19, all men between the ages of 18 and 65 were to register, and all those between the ages of 20 and 45 were made liable to service. In the autumn of 1942 it was decided that men past the age of 38 should be deferred, and that a larger number of younger men were required; and on November 12 the age of liability to service was lowered to 18. By October, 1942, there were 4,250,000 men in the army and 1,300,000 in the navy. Government plans called for an expansion of the army to 8,200,000 and of the navy to 2,600,000 by the end of 1943. It was apparent that if these totals were to be reached, it would be necessary for many men with dependents to be called into service. Before the end of 1942, draft boards were beginning to call up married men without children; and in February, 1943, it was announced that men of draft age who had dependent children would become liable to service if they were not working in an essential occupation. In the spring of 1942 Congress had authorized payments to the dependents of drafted men; but the scales were low, and the problem of providing for the children of men who might be drafted had not yet been adequately dealt with.

The calling of men for military service and the movement of workers into those war industries which paid high wages resulted in a shortage of labor in many occupations which were equally important to the prosecution of the war, particularly in agriculture. To some extent the scarcity could be met by the employment of women, who began to become factory workers in much larger numbers than ever before. By the end of 1942 there were 12,500,000 men and 4,000,000 women engaged in war industries. It became apparent, however, that the government would find it necessary to assume much greater powers over the disposition of labor and that it might be necessary to conscript men and women for work in industry and agriculture. In December, 1942, Paul V. McNutt was appointed to control all questions of manpower as head of a War Manpower Commission. It was likely that he would eventually be authorized to use compulsion to meet the needs of factories and farms in addition to those of the armed forces.

The process of shifting industry to war production began in the summer of 1940, with the appointment of an Advisory Commission of seven members, which was to supervise the armament program. There was, however, a lack of centralized and responsible authority, and the various members of the Commission lacked adequate powers. As in the First World War, it was gradually recognized that efficient production could best be obtained by giving full authority to a single individual. A move in this direction was taken in December, when the Office of Production Management was established with William S. Knudsen, formerly president of General Motors, as Director, and Sidney Hillman, formerly president of the Amalgamated Clothing Workers, as Assistant Director. This dual control, under which authority was divided between an industrialist and a trade-union leader, impeded efficiency; and the O. P. M. still lacked adequate authority. Finally, in January, 1942, the O. P. M. was replaced by the War Production Board, and Donald Nelson, formerly of Sears Roebuck, was placed at the head of it with full responsibility.

In spite of many unnecessary delays and much waste and inefficiency, American industry responded to the challenge presented by the national crisis even more remarkably than in the First World War. The building of new factories and the transfer of labor and equipment to war production necessarily required much time, although many observers believed that it might have been accomplished more quickly. But once the new war industries were ready, they began to produce war materials in quantities which justified the most optimistic prophecies and with which the Axis powers would not hope to compete. The total sums spent by the United States government on war purposes amounted to six billion dollars for the fiscal year 1940–41 and to twenty-five billion for the year 1941–42; the estimated total for 1942–43 was seventy-four billion, while the budget for 1943–44 called for the staggering total of one hundred billion—a sum larger than the total income of all the American people in any year of peace. In 1942 the nation produced 746 merchant ships with a total tonnage of over eight million, and 48,000 planes. It was expected that these figures would be more than doubled in 1943.

Undoubtedly the most complicated of the problems which confronted the government was that of preventing a price inflation which would vastly increase the cost of the war and cause acute sufferings and dislocations among the civilian population. The quantity of goods and services available for civilian use was being drastically reduced, while at the same time the payments of wages and salaries were being raised through government purchases of war materials to the highest totals in American experience. Between 1939 and 1942 wages and salaries increased from forty-four billion to seventy-five billion, and farm incomes from nine billion to fifteen billion. In 1942 individual incomes amounted to a total of 114 billion, of which 82 billion was spent on goods and services. In 1943 there would be no reduction in individual incomes, but the quantity of goods and services available for consumers was expected to decrease by about thirty billion. If inflation was to be avoided, this excess of purchasing power over goods must be recaptured by the government through loans and taxes, and wage and price levels must be stabilized. Adequate controls over the economic system were rendered difficult by the influence of different pressure groups, each of which was afraid of incurring more than its due share of the necessary sacrifices. To reconcile the divergent interests of business, agriculture, and labor in order to apportion equitably the costs of the war seemed to be an almost impossible task.

Taxes on all income brackets were steadily increased, and the total number of persons liable to income tax was enlarged from less than four million in 1939 to nearly thirty million in 1943. Government revenues amounted to 7,607 million dollars in 1940–41, and to 12,799 million in 1941–42, and were estimated at 24,552 million in 1942–43. In 1942–43 between one-quarter and one-third of the total government expenditures were being met out of taxes. It was estimated that by the summer of 1944 the national debt would reach the astronomical total of 210 billion dollars. These figures meant that, in spite of greatly increased tax collections and in spite also of considerable purchases of bonds by the general public, there was still a large surplus of purchasing power. Even higher taxes were therefore to be expected in 1943 and 1944.

The task of preventing price increases was entrusted to the Office of Price Administration, established in April, 1941, and headed by Leon Henderson. The O. P. A. at first lacked adequate powers, and by April, 1942, the cost of living was fifteen per cent higher than in September, 1939, while the increases in most wholesale prices had been considerably larger. Congress passed a price control act in February, 1942, authorizing the O. P. A. to fix price ceilings; but pressure from the farmers caused it to include a clause authorizing an increase of farm prices to 110 per cent of parity and giving the Secretary of Agriculture the right to veto price ceilings on agricultural products. Meanwhile critics of the administration were denouncing its willingness to allow wage increases to labor. A National War Labor Board had been established in January, 1942, under the chairmanship of William H. Davis, in order to supervise wages and prevent labor disputes. The policy of the N. W. L. B., announced in connection with a grant of a fifteen per cent wage increase to the workers in Little Steel, was to allow raises which would compensate for the higher cost of living.

By the spring of 1942 there seemed to be real danger of a disastrous inflation. In April Roosevelt sent a message to Congress laying down a five-point anti-inflation program; and in September he asked for full authority over prices and wages, declaring that if Congress failed to act he would assume the necessary power himself. The result was the enactment, on October 2, of the Stabilization of the Cost of Living Act. Salaries, wages, and prices were, in general, to be frozen at the levels which they had reached by September 15; proposals to allow general further increases in farm prices were defeated, although it was stated that such prices should allow for increased costs of farm labor. On the day after the passage of the Act Supreme Court Justice James F. Byrnes was appointed head of the Office of Economic Stabilization.

Meanwhile certain acute shortages in articles for civilian consumption had developed, and the O. P. A. had begun to put into effect a gradual program of rationing. Sugar, gasoline, and coffee were rationed before the end of 1942, and it appeared that many other articles of food and clothing would be similarly limited during 1943. There was an alarming amount of grumbling against the O. P. A., but it was difficult to decide how much of it indicated an inability among some sections of the population to realize that winning the war required real sacrifices and how much of it was due to blunders and lack of political tact among O. P. A. officials. Leon Henderson, against whom most of the complaints were directed, resigned in December, 1942, and was succeeded by Prentiss Brown, formerly senator from Michigan.

One of the most satisfying features of the war at home was that civil liberties were much more generally respected than in 1917 and 1918. Enemy agents were taken into custody by the F. B. I., and subversive literature was removed from circulation; but the general public showed little of that intolerance toward alleged pro-Germans which had disfigured the American record in the First World War, and critics of the war program continued to express their opinions with great freedom. The government undertook to publicize its aims and activities, both at home and in foreign countries, for which purpose the Office of Facts and Figures, headed by Archibald MacLeish, was established in February, 1942. In May the O. F. F. was expanded into the Office of War Information, and Elmer Davis, a former newspaperman and radio commentator, was given general charge of government publicity. For the most part these agencies restricted themselves to the function of giving out information, and there was little attempt to stir up popular excitement. The chief danger on the home front, in fact, was not fanaticism but apathy. The conduct of the men in the armed forces and merchant marine proved that American civilization had not weakened in any degree the capacity for heroism in facing danger; but many observers were dubious as to whether the civilian population would be prepared to surrender the comforts of a high standard of living with equal patriotism.

THE FIRST YEAR

Entry into the war as a belligerent made the United States a member of a world-wide combination of nations engaged in defending themselves against aggression. On January 1, 1942, a pact was signed by the representatives of twenty-six governments, in which they accepted the

Atlantic Charter, pledged themselves not to make peace until the enemy had been defeated, and—at Roosevelt's suggestion—assumed the title of the United Nations. Immediate steps were taken to coordinate the activities of the United States with those of her allies. Prime Minister Churchill of Great Britain visited the United States at the end of December for discussions with Roosevelt; and joint boards were afterwards established in Washington for common planning of war operations and of the production and allocation of munitions, shipping and raw materials. Roosevelt and Churchill held subsequent conferences at Washington in June and at Casablanca in North Africa in January, 1943; and the military and production chiefs of the United States and Great Britain made frequent crossings of the Atlantic to consult with each other. But although there was much greater coordination among the allied powers than had been achieved during the First World War, there could be no real unity of command in a war which covered so vast an area and included so many diverse peoples. Great Britain and the United States were able to establish a close partnership, in which the policy was adopted of appointing single commanders, sometimes British and sometimes American, with full powers in different theatres of war; but their collaboration with the Soviet Union and with China was much more distant, and was not free from mutual suspicions and recriminations.

The Japanese attack on Pearl Harbor brought into the common struggle not only the resources of the United States but also those of a large part of Latin America. The sagacious and patient labor which Cordell Hull and Sumner Welles had given to the Good Neighbor policy now met with a most gratifying response. A conference of the American nations was held at Rio de Janeiro in January; and the sentiments of most of the participants were voiced by Ezequiel Padilla, Mexican Secretary of State, who declared that: "The attack by Japan was not on the United States but on America. In the Philippines that small force of men are dying not for the United States but for America. . . . We are going to defend America." As a result of the opposition of Argentina, the conference could go no further than to "recommend" that all the American nations should break diplomatic relations with the Axis; but all except Argentina, Chile, and Ecuador followed the recommendation immediately, and Chile and Ecuador did so within a year. Between

December, 1941, and August, 1942, eleven of the twenty Latin-American countries, including Mexico and Brazil, entered the war as belligerents. By January, 1943, only Argentina remained entirely neutral; and even in that country the sentiment of public opinion, if not of the government, seemed to be strongly in favor of the United Nations. The western hemisphere was thus more nearly united than ever before; and much of the suspicion and hostility which Latin America had formerly felt for the United States had disappeared.

The American war program was to take the offensive first against Germany, if possible in 1943, and not to undertake large-scale operations against Japan until after Germany had been defeated. During most of 1942 neither the United States nor her allies could expect to be strong enough for offensive action anywhere, and the initiative would necessarily remain with the Axis. This was particularly true in the Pacific. The forces which the Americans, the British, and the Dutch could immediately muster for the defense of the East Indies were very weak; and the Japanese enjoyed initially an overwhelming superiority. Japanese military and naval operations, moreover, had been planned with great skill and care. During the winter and spring of 1942, therefore, the American people were to taste defeat.

The results of the raid on Pearl Harbor were not made public for a year. A total of 105 Japanese planes had participated, of which 48 had been shot down; and they had destroyed 247 American planes and had hit 18 warships, including every one of the 8 battleships of the Pacific fleet. Although only one of these battleships was considered to be a total loss, 4 others had been damaged so severely that they could not be put back into service for many months. The Japanese had thus inflicted upon the United States one of the worst naval disasters suffered by any power in modern times, and had made it impossible for the American fleet to interfere with their invasion of the East Indies. Their success was apparently due to over-confidence and lack of cooperation among the American naval and military commanders at Pearl Harbor; in spite of warnings from Washington, they had regarded a surprise attack as impossible and had failed to take precautions against it. Four days after Pearl Harbor the naval superiority of the Japanese was increased by the sinking of two British capital ships by Japanese planes off the coast of Malaya.

On the same day as the attack on Pearl Harbor Japanese planes, by means of another successful surprise attack, crippled the American air force in the Philippines. Guam was captured on December 12, and Wake, after a gallant resistance, on December 23. Meanwhile Japanese invasion forces, putting into effect plans which had been carefully prepared many months before, proceeded to the conquest of the allied possessions in the western Pacific. Armies operating from Indo-China invaded the British colony of Malaya and forced its defenders back to the island fortress of Singapore, which had long been regarded as the key to the defense of the whole East Indian archipelago. Allied hopes for a long siege were disappointed, and the fortress, along with 70,000 British troops, fell into Japanese hands on February 15. Thailand had already been occupied without resistance, and another Japanese army had advanced into Burma, planning to cut the road by which supplies from the western powers were shipped to China. By the end of April all Burma had been occupied, and Japanese planes were bombing Indian cities, apparently in preparation for an invasion. Japanese troops had landed in the Philippines on December 22, and early in January the American and Filipino defending army, led by General MacArthur, had been forced to abandon most of the territory of the islands and to take up defensive positions on the rocky peninsula of Bataan. The prolonged and heroic defense first of Bataan and afterwards of the island of Corregidor, which was not finally captured until May 6, provided the only note of encouragement among the events of this gloomy winter. Especially gratifying was the cooperation of the Filipino government and people with the Americans, which was in marked contrast with the apathy displayed by the inhabitants of the British and Dutch colonies. The United States was now earning her reward for forty years of good government and encouragement of democratic aspirations.

Elsewhere the United Nations were unable even to delay the Japanese assault. Borneo, Celebes, and New Britain were occupied during January. Allied warships succeeded in smashing a convoy of Japanese troop transports in the Macassar Straits at the end of January, and another off Bali three weeks later; but the Japanese were prepared for heavy losses, and continued to enjoy an overwhelming superiority in manpower and equipment. Macassar and Sumatra were taken during February; and Java, the richest and most densely populated of all the East Indian islands, could now be attacked from three sides. The Dutch and American warships in the region were virtually annihilated in the battle of the Java Sea on February 27; and by March 10 all resistance in Java had ended. Meanwhile another Japanese army had landed on the northern coast of New Guinea; and Australia seemed to be in danger of invasion.

By the end of the first five months of war Japan had almost completed her conquest of the East Indies. Whether the United Nations would succeed in retaining any strongholds in the western Pacific seemed more than doubtful. The beginning of May, however, marked the turn of the tide, at all events for the year 1942. The United Nations were able to hold India and Australia, the two essential bases for future offensives against the Japanese positions in the islands. India was primarily a British responsibility, although the inability of British officials to secure cooperation in the defense of the country from the Indian nationalist leaders caused much concern in Washington and among the American people. The British General Wavell was appointed to command the allied forces in that country.

Australia, on the other hand, although a British dominion, turned to Washington rather than to London for assistance. American troops were sent to Australia; and in March General MacArthur, who had earned both the applause of military experts and the admiration of public opinion by his skilful defense of Bataan, was ordered to leave the Philippines to assume the command. Early in May a Japanese armada appeared in the Coral Sea, off the northeast coast of Australia; but in a five-day battle (May 3–8) American planes, operating from carriers, put them to flight, winning the first definite American victory of the war. Thwarted in their plans for an attack on Australia, the Japanese then turned eastwards for a direct assault upon American bases. They occupied several of the Aleutian islands, and sent a strong naval force across the Pacific with the apparent intention of attacking the center of the American defense system at Hawaii. Between June 3 and June 6 this force was defeated in the battle of Midway. Once again the American victory was won by planes, operating on this occasion from land bases rather than from carriers, and the two opposing fleets never even sighted each other. Meanwhile the Japanese land forces, ignoring India for the time being, were again launching an offensive in China; and in July the Chinese, in spite of their lack of equipment, put to shame the European armies who had failed so decisively in Malaya, Burma, and Java by winning a considerable victory.

In Europe it was generally believed that the campaigns of 1942 would be of crucial importance. As in the First World War it would be at least a year before American troops could reach Europe in any large numbers; and during that year Hitler would probably employ all his available resources in an effort to achieve victory before the United States could prevent it. German successes were therefore to be expected, and the question was whether they would be decisive.

During the winter the Soviet forces had succeeded in pushing back the invaders, although they had failed to capture any important strongholds. In the spring the German armies, resuming the initiative, ended Russian resistance in the Crimea; and at the end of June they launched a general offensive across the plains of southern Russia, hoping to drive through to the Caspian and to cut off the Soviet armies from the oil of the Caucasus. The German advance continued through the summer, and by September it had almost reached the Volga. Here, at the city of Stalingrad, Soviet forces made a final stand, knowing that the fate of Russia depended on the outcome. For two months the Germans assaulted the city, but the Soviet defenses held; and the German losses were so heavy that by the third week in November they were beginning to lose the initiative. This was probably the real turning point in the war. If the battle of Britain, two years earlier, meant that Hitler had failed to win the war, the defense of Stalingrad marked the point when he began to lose it.

The titanic struggle on the Russian front, in which larger armies and greater material resources were employed than in any previous war in history, dwarfed all other military operations. It was hoped that the British and Americans would be able to relieve the strain on the Russians by invading the continent of Europe and thereby initiating a second front; but during 1942 they lacked men, supplies, and—particularly—ships for such an enterprise; and an experimental raid on the French port of Dieppe in August suggested that the German defenses had great strength. In spite of Soviet appeals for help, therefore, they had to content themselves with the shipping of supplies to Russia and with attempts to cripple German production by bombing raids. The British raids of the spring and summer were far heavier than the biggest efforts of the Luftwaffe in the battle of Britain; and considerable areas of German industrial cities were destroyed. The military results were controversial. Some authorities maintained that Germany could be defeated by air raids alone, at considerably less expense than by an invasion of the continent; but whether this was true or not, it was certain that the United Nations had not yet built air armadas large enough to make the experiment.

Africa was the only theatre of war where the British and Americans met the Germans in land fighting; and although the forces engaged were small, the strategic importance of the area was considerable. In June the German army in Libya, commanded by Marshal Rommel, inflicted a crushing defeat on the British and drove into Egypt almost as far as Alexandria. But supplies from the United States, arriving at the opportune moment, saved the British from disaster; and by October they were strong enough to take the offensive. The battle of El Alamein, concluded on November 4, was the first occasion in the war when any German army was decisively defeated. The remnants of Rommel's army were then driven back through Libya and Tripoli and proved to be too weak for further resistance.

El Alamein was followed by the first important American action in the European theatre of war. The convoying of American troops to the British Isles had started in January, and by the summer a considerable army, commanded by General Eisenhower, had been formed; but they had not yet been engaged in battle. On November 7 an American Expeditionary Force landed in the French colonies of Morocco and Algeria. This project was one of the fruits of the long and much criticized maintenance of American diplomatic relations with the Vichy government; two of the objectives of American diplomacy had been to prevent the Nazis from taking over North Africa and to establish friendly relations with the French officials in that region. The operations were carefully planned and beautifully coordinated; and all French resistance had ceased at the end of five days. The Vichy officials in the area, under the leadership first of Admiral Darlan and afterwards of General Giraud, then agreed to support the United Nations. It was hoped that this move would be followed by the expulsion of the Germans from all North Africa. Unfortunately German troops, ferried across from Italy, reached Tunisia ahead of the allies, and were able to establish strong positions there. They were subsequently joined by the defeated army of Marshal Rommel. Although it seemed certain that the Germans would eventually be expelled, it became increasingly apparent that prolonged and costly fighting might be necessary, and that the allies could not hope for any immediate invasion of the continent from North Africa. Meanwhile the reluctance of the French officials to adopt democratic policies and the hatred which French liberals felt toward men who had served the Vichy government caused a number of disheartening disputes.

The difficulties of the United Nations in Africa were, however, overshadowed by the successes of the Russians. Hitler's failure to capture Stalingrad made possible a Soviet winter offensive, which was launched in the third week of November. During December and January the Russians encircled and destroyed considerable sections of the German army, regained most of the territory which had been lost during the summer, and threatened to drive through into the plains of the Ukraine and to cut off even larger bodies of German troops from their sources of supply. These victories were the first convincing proof that military superiority had passed to the United Nations. How long the offensive of the Russians could continue, and how soon the British and Americans would be able to join them in an invasion of the continent, could not be predicted. Germany might yet show an unexpected capacity for defending herself. Allied operations would, moreover, be severely hampered by the submarine campaign, which was increasing in intensity; it was announced in January that submarines were being built twice as fast as they were sunk, and that from five to seven hundred of them would be in action by the spring. Yet in the winter of 1943 one thing seemed certain: that sooner or later Germany would be compelled to accept defeat.

By the autumn of 1942 the United Nations had not only wrested the initiative from the Germans; they had also begun to undertake more limited offensive operations against Japan. It was essential that the sea route from the United States to Australia should be kept open, and for this reason American forces early in August landed at Guadalcanal in the Solomon Islands, which had previously been held by the Japanese. Persistent attempts by Japanese land, air, and sea forces to regain Guadalcanal were unsuccessful; in particular, a major naval engagement was fought on November 13, 14, and 15, in which the Japanese fleet was repulsed with even heavier losses than in the battles of Midway and the Coral Sea. Meanwhile General MacArthur was undertaking a painful and difficult offensive against Japanese forces in the jungles of New Guinea; and General Wavell was opening a campaign for the reconquest of Burma. These were all operations of minor importance; but they engaged the attention of the Japanese, and they were essential preliminaries to that general Pacific offensive which would be undertaken whenever the United Nations could spare enough troops and resources from the European war fronts. Prior to such an attack American forces in the Pacific set themselves the task of weakening Japan by a process of attrition, sinking ships and destroying planes faster than the Japanese could replace them. In this endeavor they appeared to be successful, Japanese losses of merchant ships from American submarine attacks being particularly heavy.

AFTER THE WAR

By the beginning of 1943 it could be considered certain that the United Nations would eventually win the war. But whether they would also win the peace remained to be seen.

The war aims of the United States government had been stated in the Atlantic Charter, which had been formally accepted by all the United Nations, and had been subsequently elaborated in speeches by Vice-President Wallace and by Under-Secretary of State Sumner Welles.

The United States government looked forward to a world in which men would have security against war, in which prosperity would be assured through freer international trade, in which the imperialist control of subject races would be ended, and in which governments would be based on the free consent of the governed. These propositions were not utopian visions plainly impossible of fulfillment; they were sober necessities which were essential to the preservation of civilization and the prevention of the catastrophe of war. They were in harmony with the ideals which had always animated the republic of the United States and with the hopes of the oppressed nations of Europe and Asia. What remained to be seen was whether the people of the United States, after the war had been concluded, would have sufficient wisdom to conduct their foreign policy in accordance with these objectives.

After the First World War the United States had attempted to withdraw from Europe, disclaiming all responsibility for defending the victory which her armed forces and her industries had helped to win; and she had subsequently adopted tariff and war debt policies which showed a total ignorance of the economic interdependence of all nations. The fruits of this evasion of responsibility, and of the similar errors which had been committed by other nations, had been a decade of disaster, followed by a global war, in which the nations of the world had paid the penalty of their errors through lower standards of living and through the killing of their young men in battle. As the economic crisis of the thirties and the war of the forties have shown, the world had become a unity; and whatever happened in any part of it might affect, for good or ill, the lives of all people everywhere. No nation, and particularly not the richest and most powerful of all nations, could hope to escape her obligation to defend the peace of the world and to promote its common welfare.

Would the United States after the war be willing to continue collaborating with her allies in order to preserve and extend the fruits of victory? Or would war-weariness and suspicion, ignorance of political and economic realities, and unwillingness to make sacrifices, cause her to break her connections with the British Commonwealth, with the Soviet Union, and with China, and to adopt a policy either of complacent and short-sighted isolationism or of imperialist aggrandizement? As the tide of battle began to turn and the day of victory grew nearer, this was the all-important question which began to occupy the minds of men of good will not only in the United States herself but throughout the world.

APPENDIX

STATISTICAL TABLES

Except where otherwise stated, all figures are from the *Statistical Abstract of the United States,* published annually by the U. S. Department of Commerce.

1. Population by States.
2. Immigration by Country of Origin.
3. Population by Racial Origin.
4. Manufactures.
5. Earnings in Manufacturing Industries, 1921–1938.
6. Earnings of All Wage-earners, 1890–1926.
7. Distribution of Income in Manufacturing, 1919–1938.
8. Estimated Long-term Debt.
9. Agriculture.
10 and 11. Exports.
12 and 13. Imports.
14. Government Finance.
15. Cabinet Ministers.
16. Vote in Presidential Elections.

1. POPULATION BY STATES

	1900	1910	1920	1930	1940
CONTINENTAL U. S.	75,994,575	91,972,266	105,710,620	122,775,046	131,409,881
NEW ENGLAND	5,592,017	6,552,681	7,400,909	8,166,341	8,426,556
Maine	694,466	742,371	768,014	797,423	845,139
New Hampshire	411,588	430,572	443,083	465,293	489,716
Vermont	343,641	355,956	352,428	359,611	357,598
Massachusetts	2,805,346	3,366,416	3,852,356	4,249,614	4,312,332
Rhode Island	428,556	542,610	604,397	687,497	711,669
Connecticut	908,420	1,114,756	1,380,631	1,606,903	1,710,112
MIDDLE ATLANTIC	15,454,678	19,315,892	22,261,144	26,260,750	27,419,893
New York	7,268,894	9,113,614	10,385,227	12,588,066	13,379,622
New Jersey	1,883,669	2,537,167	3,155,900	4,041,334	4,148,562
Pennsylvania	6,302,115	7,665,111	8,720,017	9,631,350	9,891,709
EAST NORTH CENTRAL	15,985,581	18,250,621	21,475,543	25,297,185	26,550,823
Ohio	4,157,545	4,767,121	5,759,394	6,646,697	6,889,623
Indiana	2,516,462	2,700,876	2,930,390	3,238,503	3,416,152
Illinois	4,821,550	5,638,591	6,485,280	7,630,654	7,874,155
Michigan	2,420,982	2,810,173	2,668,412	4,842,325	5,245,012
Wisconsin	2,069,042	2,333,860	2,632,067	2,939,006	3,125,881
WEST NORTH CENTRAL	10,347,423	11,637,921	12,544,249	13,296,915	13,490,492
Minnesota	1,751,394	2,075,708	2,387,125	2,563,953	2,785,896
Iowa	2,231,853	2,224,771	2,404,021	2,470,939	2,535,430
Missouri	3,106,665	3,293,335	3,404,055	3,629,367	3,775,737
North Dakota	319,146	577,056	646,872	680,845	639,690
South Dakota	401,570	583,888	636,547	692,849	641,134
Nebraska	1,066,300	1,192,214	1,296,372	1,377,963	1,313,468
Kansas	1,470,495	1,690,949	1,769,257	1,880,999	1,799,137

SOUTH ATLANTIC	10,443,480	12,194,895	13,990,272	15,793,589	17,771,099
Delaware	184,735	202,322	223,003	238,380	264,003
Maryland	1,188,044	1,295,346	1,449,661	1,631,526	1,811,546
District of Col.	278,718	331,069	437,571	486,869	663,153
Virginia	1,854,184	2,061,612	2,309,187	2,421,851	2,664,847
West Virginia	958,800	1,221,119	1,463,701	1,729,205	1,900,217
North Carolina	1,893,810	2,206,287	2,559,123	3,170,276	3,563,174
South Carolina	1,340,316	1,515,400	1,683,724	1,738,765	1,905,815
Georgia	2,216,331	2,609,121	2,895,832	2,908,506	3,119,953
Florida	528,542	752,619	968,470	1,468,211	1,877,791
EAST SOUTH CENTRAL	7,547,757	8,499,901	8,893,307	9,887,214	10,762,967
Kentucky	2,147,174	2,289,905	2,416,630	2,614,589	2,839,927
Tennessee	2,020,616	2,184,789	2,337,885	2,616,556	2,910,992
Alabama	1,828,697	2,138,093	2,348,174	2,646,248	2,830,285
Mississippi	1,551,270	1,797,114	1,790,618	2,009,821	2,181,763
WEST SOUTH CENTRAL	6,532,290	8,784,534	10,242,224	12,176,830	13,052,218
Arkansas	1,311,564	1,574,449	1,752,204	1,854,482	1,948,268
Louisiana	1,381,625	1,656,388	1,798,509	2,101,593	2,355,821
Oklahoma	790,391	1,657,155	2,028,283	2,396,040	2,329,808
Texas	3,048,710	3,896,542	4,663,228	5,824,715	6,418,321
MOUNTAIN	1,674,657	2,633,517	3,336,101	3,701,789	4,128,042
Montana	243,329	376,953	548,889	537,606	554,136
Idaho	161,772	325,794	431,866	445,032	523,440
Wyoming	92,531	145,965	194,402	225,565	246,763
Colorado	539,700	799,024	939,629	1,035,791	1,118,820
New Mexico	195,310	327,301	360,350	423,317	528,687
Arizona	122,931	204,554	334,162	435,573	497,789
Utah	276,749	373,351	449,396	507,847	548,393
Nevada	42,335	81,875	77,407	91,058	110,014
PACIFIC	2,416,692	4,192,304	5,566,871	8,194,433	9,682,781
Washington	518,103	1,141,990	1,356,621	1,563,396	1,721,376
Oregon	413,536	672,765	783,389	953,786	1,087,717
California	1,485,053	2,377,549	3,426,861	5,677,251	6,873,688

2. IMMIGRATION BY COUNTRY OF ORIGIN

COUNTRY	1841–50	1851–60	1861–70	1871–80	1881–90	1891–1900	1901–10	1911–20	1921–30
GRAND TOTAL	1,713,251	2,598,214	2,314,824	2,812,191	5,246,613	3,687,564	8,795,386	5,735,811	4,107,209
TOTAL EUROPE	1,597,501	2,452,660	2,065,270	2,272,262	4,737,046	3,558,978	8,136,016	4,376,564	2,477,853
Austria }			7,800	72,969	353,719	592,707	2,145,266	453,649	32,868
Hungary }								442,693	30,680
Belgium	5,074	4,738	6,734	7,221	20,177	18,167	41,635	33,746	15,846
Bulgaria						160	39,280	22,533	2,945
Czechoslovakia								3,426	102,194
Denmark	539	3,749	17,094	31,771	88,132	50,231	65,285	41,983	32,430
Finland								756	16,691
France	77,262	76,358	35,986	72,206	50,464	30,770	73,379	61,897	49,610
Germany	434,626	951,667	787,468	718,182	1,452,970	505,152	341,498	143,945	412,202
Greece	16	31	72	210	2,308	15,979	167,519	184,201	51,084
Italy	1,870	9,231	11,725	55,759	307,309	651,893	2,045,877	1,109,524	455,315
Netherlands	8,251	10,789	9,102	16,541	53,701	26,758	48,262	43,718	26,948
Norway			71,631	95,323	176,586	95,015	190,505	66,395	68,531
Sweden	13,903	20,931	37,667	115,922	391,776	226,266	249,534	95,074	97,249
Poland	105	1,164	2,027	12,970	51,806	96,720	69,149	4,813	227,734
Portugal	550	1,055	2,658	14,082	16,928	27,508	53,008	89,732	29,994
Rumania				11	6,348	12,750		13,311	67,646
Soviet Union (Russia)	551	457	2,512	39,284	213,282	505,290	1,597,306	921,201	61,742
Spain	2,209	9,298	6,697	5,266	4,419	8,731	27,935	68,611	28,958
Switzerland	4,644	25,011	23,286	28,293	81,988	31,179	34,922	23,091	29,676
Turkey in Europe	59	83	129	337	1,562	3,626	79,976	54,677	14,659

UNITED KINGDOM	1,047,763	1,338,093	1,042,674	984,914	1,462,839	659,954	865,015	487,589	550,804
England	32,092	247,125	222,277	437,706	644,680	216,726	388,017	249,944	157,420
Ireland	780,719	914,119	435,778	436,871	655,482	388,416	339,065	146,181	220,591
Scotland	3,712	38,331	38,769	87,564	149,869	44,188	120,469	78,357	159,781
Wales	1,261	6,319	4,313	6,631	12,640	10,557	17,464	13,107	13,012
NOT SPECIFIED	229,979	132,199	341,537	16,142	168	67			
YUGOSLAVIA								1,888	49,064
OTHER EUROPE	79	5	8	1,001	682	122	655	8,111	22,983
TOTAL ASIA	82	41,455	64,630	123,823	68,380	71,236	243,567	192,559	97,400
China	35	41,397	64,301	123,201	61,711	14,799	20,605	21,278	29,907
Japan	47	58	186	149	2,270	25,942	129,797	83,837	33,462
Turkey in Asia	47	58	2	67	2,220	26,799	77,393	39,389	19,165
Other Asia			141	406	2,179	3,696	15,772	8,055	14,866
TOTAL AMERICA	62,469	74,720	166,607	404,044	426,967	38,972	361,888	1,143,671	1,516,716
Canada and Newfoundland	41,723	59,309	153,878	383,640	393,304	3,311	179,226	742,185	924,515
Mexico	3,271	3,078	2,191	5,162	1,913	971	49,642	219,004	459,287
Central America	368	449	95	157	404	549	8,192	17,159	15,769
South America	3,579	1,224	1,397	1,128	2,304	1,075	17,280	41,899	42,215
West Indies	13,528	10,660	9,046	13,957	29,042	33,066	107,548	123,424	74,899
Other America									31
AFRICA	55	210	312	358	857	350	7,368	8,443	6,286
AUSTRALIA, TASMANIA AND NEW ZEALAND			36	9,886	7,017	2,740	11,975	12,348	8,299
PACIFIC ISLANDS				1,028	5,557	1,225	1,049	1,079	427
ALL OTHER COUNTRIES	53,144	29,169	17,967	790	789	14,663	33,523	1,147	228

3. POPULATION BY RACIAL ORIGIN

	TOTAL	WHITE OF NATIVE PARENTAGE	WHITE OF FOREIGN OR MIXED PARENTAGE	WHITE FOREIGN BORN	NEGRO
1900	75,994,575	40,949,362	15,646,017	10,213,817	8,833,994
1910	91,972,266	49,488,573	18,897,837	13,345,543	9,827,763
1920	105,710,620	58,421,957	22,686,204	13,712,784	10,463,131
1930	122,775,046	70,136,714	25,361,186	13,366,407	11,897,143

4. MANUFACTURES

YEAR	NUMBER OF ESTABLISH-MENTS	VALUE OF PRODUCTS IN THOUSANDS OF DOLLARS	WAGE EARNERS	WAGES IN THOUSANDS OF DOLLARS
1899	205,237	11,103,726	4,509,684	1,895,414
1904	213,935	14,345,545	5,189,895	2,444,221
1909	265,509	20,067,674	6,273,293	3,210,277
1914*	269,223	23,443,659	6,613,991	3,787,767
1914*	173,656	23,065,565	6,478,713	3,783,259
1919	210,426	60,053,895	8,431,157	9,673,134
1921	192,275	41,748,686	6,484,447	7,467,690
1923	192,293	58,288,281	8,202,779	10,166,713
1925	184,108	60,925,575	7,879,508	9,994,341
1927	187,801	60,471,716	7,857,015	10,118,713
1929	206,811	68,178,340	8,380,536	10,909,815
1931	171,450	39,829,888	6,136,144	6,688,541
1933	139,325	30,557,328	5,787,611	4,940,146
1935	167,916	44,993,699	7,203,794	7,311,329
1937	166,794	60,712,872	8,569,231	10,112,883

* These and subsequent figures exclude establishments with products worth less than $5,000.

5. EARNINGS IN MANUFACTURING INDUSTRIES, 1921–38

(1923–25 AVERAGE 100)
(in thousands of dollars)

YEAR	PRODUC-TIVITY*	AVERAGE WEEKLY EARNINGS	COST OF LIVING	ADJUSTED WEEKLY EARNINGS
1921	88.3	92.2	103.6	89.0
1922	97.8	89.5	97.2	92.1
1923	93.7	99.1	99.0	100.1
1924	100.6	99.6	99.2	100.4
1925	105.7	101.3	101.8	99.5
1926	107.5	102.5	102.6	99.9
1927	110.2	102.9	100.6	102.3
1928	120.3	103.8	99.5	104.3
1929	121.6	104.2	99.5	104.7
1930	125.0	96.8	97.0	99.8
1931	131.6	86.8	88.6	98.0
1932	129.3	70.4	79.8	88.2
1933	134.4	68.3	75.8	90.1
1934	135.0	75.3	78.6	95.8
1935	141.8	81.2	80.7	100.6
1936	147.3	87.5	81.6	107.2
1937	143.2	96.4	84.3	114.4
1938	143.8	89.3	83.0	107.6

* Figures for productivity are taken from S. Bell, *Productivity, Wages, and National Income,* published by the Brookings Institution.

6. EARNINGS OF ALL WAGE-EARNERS, 1890–1926

From P. H. Douglas, *Real Wages in the United States,* Houghton Mifflin Company, 1928.

YEAR	AVERAGE ANNUAL WAGE IN DOLLARS	RELATIVE WAGE	COST OF LIVING (1914 = 100)	REAL WAGE
1890	486	71	75	96
1891	487	71	73	98
1892	495	73	73	99
1893	480	70	72	98
1894	448	66	70	94
1895	468	69	70	98
1896	462	68	72	95
1897	462	68	72	94
1898	468	69	72	95
1899	480	70	74	96
1900	490	72	76	94
1901	508	74	78	96
1902	519	76	80	95
1903	543	80	84	95
1904	540	79	83	96
1905	554	81	83	98
1906	569	83	86	97
1907	595	87	91	96
1908	563	83	87	95
1909	594	87	87	100
1910	630	92	92	100
1911	629	92	95	97
1912	646	95	96	99
1913	675	99	99	100
1914	682	100	100	100
1915	687	101	98	103
1916	765	112	107	105
1917	887	130	129	101
1918	1115	163	157	104
1919	1272	187	178	105
1920	1489	218	206	106
1921	1349	198	177	112
1922	1305	191	165	116
1923	1393	204	168	121
1924	1402	206	169	122
1925	1434	210	173	122
1926	1473	216	174	124

7. DISTRIBUTION OF INCOME IN MANUFACTURING, 1919–1938
(From S. Bell, *Productivity, Wages, and National Income*, published by the Brookings Institution)

YEAR	TOTAL INCOME*	WAGES*	PER CENT	SALARIES*	PER CENT	EARNINGS ON CAPITAL*	PER CENT
1919	17,317	9,673	55.9	2,776	16.0	4,868	28.1
1920	18,477	11,568	62.6	3,118	16.9	3,791	20.5
1921	10,544	7,468	70.8	2,446	23.2	630	6.0
1922	14,308	8,017	56.0	2,491	17.4	3,800	26.6
1923	17,838	10,166	57.0	2,884	16.2	4,788	26.8
1924	16,344	9,482	58.0	2,923	17.9	3,939	24.1
1925	17,967	9,995	55.6	3,015	16.8	4,957	27.6
1926	18,623	10,302	55.3	3,218	17.3	5,103	27.4
1927	17,968	10,119	56.3	3,359	18.7	4,490	25.0
1928	19,269	10,229	53.1	3,534	18.3	5,506	28.6
1929	20,874	10,909	52.3	3,802	18.2	6,163	29.5
1930	15,265	8,828	57.8	3,654	24.0	2,783	18.2
1931	10,208	6,689	65.5	3,023	29.6	496	4.9
1932	6,077	4,608	75.8	2,280	37.5	—811	—13.3
1933	8,076	4,940	61.2	2,069	25.6	1,067	13.2
1934	10,750	6,369	59.3	2,411	22.4	1,970	18.3
1935	12,806	7,311	57.1	2,536	19.8	2,959	23.1
1936	15,265	8,466	55.4	2,776	18.2	4,023	26.4
1937	17,174	10,113	58.9	3,081	17.9	3,980	23.2
1938	12,685	7,690	60.6	2,814	22.2	2,181	17.2

* In millions of dollars.

8. ESTIMATED LONG-TERM DEBT
(in millions of dollars)

YEAR	TOTAL PRIVATE DEBT	RAIL-WAY	PUBLIC UTILITIES	INDUS-TRIAL	FARM MORT-GAGE	URBAN REAL ESTATE	FEDERAL GOVERN-MENT	LOCAL GOVERN-MENT
1912	31,324	10,720	5,272	4,500	3,832	7,000	965	4,284
1922	51,186	11,898	8,438	6,750	8,900	15,200	22,483	9,893
1934	74,300	13,413	13,597	8,800	7,645	30,845	27,944	18,823
1937	70,335	13,109	13,874	7,762	7,082	28,508	36,715	19,152

9. AGRICULTURE

YEAR	NUMBER OF FARMS	ALL LANDS IN FARMS (1000 ACRES)	OWNERS NUMBER	OWNERS PER-CENTAGE	MORTGAGES ON FARMS OPERATED BY OWNERS NUMBER	MORTGAGES ON FARMS OPERATED BY OWNERS PER-CENTAGE	TENANTS NUMBER	TENANTS PER-CENTAGE
1850	1,449,073	293,561						
1900	5,737,372	838,592	3,653,323	63.7			2,024,964	35.3
1910	6,361,502	878,798	3,948,722	62.1	1,006,511	30.0	2,354,676	37.0
1920	6,448,343	955,884	3,925,090	60.9	1,193,047	35.4	2,454,804	38.1
1930	6,288,648	986,771	3,568,394	56.7	1,231,668	42.3	2,664,365	42.4
1935	6,812,350	1,054,515	3,899,091	57.2	1,270,107	39.6	2,865,155	42.1

10. EXPORTS

Percentage of Total

YEAR	NORTH AMERICA NORTH-ERN	NORTH AMERICA SOUTH-ERN	SOUTH AMERICA	EUROPE	ASIA	OCEANIA	AFRICA
1901	7.3	6.0	3.0	76.4	3.6	2.1	1.7
1902	8.1	6.7	2.8	73.0	5.0	2.1	2.4
1903	8.9	6.3	2.9	72.5	4.4	2.4	2.7
1904	9.2	6.9	3.5	72.4	4.4	1.9	1.7
1905	9.4	7.7	3.7	67.2	8.9	1.8	1.2
1906	9.2	8.5	4.3	68.8	6.4	1.7	1.1
1907	9.9	8.7	4.4	69.0	5.4	1.7	.9
1908	9.2	8.3	4.5	69.0	6.1	1.9	1.1
1909	10.1	8.5	4.6	69.0	5.0	1.8	1.0
1910	12.6	9.5	5.3	65.1	4.5	2.0	1.1
1911	13.4	8.9	5.3	63.8	5.1	2.3	1.2
1912	15.1	8.3	6.0	60.9	6.4	2.2	1.1
1913	17.0	8.0	5.9	60.0	5.7	2.2	1.2
1914	14.8	7.5	5.3	62.9	6.0	2.4	1.2
1915	11.1	6.2	3.6	71.2	5.0	1.9	1.0
1915 (6 mo.)	11.0	6.5	4.5	69.7	5.1	2.1	1.1
1916	11.2	5.7	4.0	69.6	7.1	1.5	1.0
1917	13.5	6.8	5.0	65.2	7.5	1.2	.8
1918	14.6	6.9	4.9	62.8	8.1	1.8	1.0
1919	9.5	6.9	5.6	65.5	9.7	1.6	1.2
1920	12.0	11.5	7.6	54.3	10.6	2.1	2.0
1921	13.4	11.8	6.1	52.7	11.9	2.5	1.6
1922	15.2	8.7	5.9	54.4	11.7	2.7	1.5
1923	15.8	10.2	6.5	50.2	12.3	3.5	1.5
1924	13.8	9.9	6.8	53.3	11.2	3.4	1.5
1925	13.4	9.8	8.2	53.0	9.9	3.9	1.8
1926	15.5	8.9	9.2	48.0	11.8	4.4	2.1
1927	17.3	8.4	9.0	47.5	11.6	4.0	2.2
1928	18.1	7.7	9.4	46.3	12.7	3.5	2.3
1929	18.3	8.3	10.3	44.7	12.2	3.6	2.5
1930	17.5	9.1	8.8	47.9	11.6	2.8	2.4
1931	16.7	7.7	6.5	49.0	15.9	1.7	2.5
1932	15.3	7.4	6.0	48.7	18.1	2.3	2.2
1933	12.8	7.5	6.8	50.7	17.4	2.1	2.6
1934	14.4	8.3	7.6	44.5	18.8	2.7	3.6
1935	14.4	8.8	7.6	45.1	16.6	3.2	4.2
1936	15.9	9.2	8.3	42.5	16.2	3.2	4.6
1937	15.5	9.6	9.5	40.6	17.3	3.0	4.5
1938	15.4	8.5	9.7	42.8	16.7	3.0	3.8

11. EXPORTS

YEAR	TOTAL IN THOUSANDS OF DOLLARS	PERCENTAGE OF CRUDE MATERIALS	PERCENTAGE OF CRUDE FOOD-STUFFS	MANUF. FOOD-STUFFS	PERCENTAGE OF SEMI-MANU-FACTURES	FINISHED MANU-FACTURES
1901	1,487,765	28.17	16.83	23.09	10.16	21.76
1902	1,381,719	28.60	13.63	24.26	9.75	23.75
1903	1,420,142	29.85	13.31	23.22	10.10	23.52
1904	1,460,827	32.54	9.46	21.52	12.19	24.30
1905	1,518,562	32.08	7.92	18.97	14.07	26.96
1906	1,743,865	29.53	10.32	20.22	13.17	26.76
1907	1,880,851	32.40	9.03	18.65	14.00	25.93
1908	1,860,775	30.70	10.30	18.10	14.23	26.68
1909	1,663,011	32.27	8.28	18.47	14.11	26.87
1910	1,744,985	33.57	6.42	15.16	15.66	29.19
1911	2,049,320	35.79	5.13	14.01	15.35	29.72
1912	2,204,322	33.69	4.60	14.69	16.04	30.98
1913	2,465,884	30.48	7.49	13.23	16.83	31.97
1914	2,364,579	34.33	5.90	12.59	16.06	31.11
1915	2,768,589	21.77	18.66	16.74	13.10	29.73
1915 (6 mo.)	1,852,863	16.66	8.67	16.08	14.72	43.87
1916	5,482,641	15.04	7.76	11.95	16.82	48.43
1917	6,233,513	13.50	8.28	13.08	21.39	43.77
1918	6,149,088	16.07	9.05	23.25	17.41	34.22
1919	7,920,426	20.94	8.75	25.32	11.90	33.08
1920	8,228,016	23.30	11.36	13.82	11.86	39.66
1921	4,485,031	22.46	15.38	15.66	9.38	37.12
1922	3,831,777	26.25	12.18	15.62	11.63	34.32
1923	4,167,493	29.54	6.29	14.26	13.78	36.12
1924	4,490,984	29.63	8.73	12.75	13.57	35.32
1925	4,909,848	29.51	6.60	11.90	13.73	38.26
1926	4,808,660	26.77	7.11	10.67	13.91	41.54
1927	4,865,375	25.07	8.85	9.74	14.70	41.64
1928	5,128,356	25.71	5.86	9.26	14.24	44.93
1929	5,240,995	22.15	5.23	9.40	14.13	49.09
1930	3,843,181	21.93	4.72	9.59	13.56	50.20
1931	2,424,289	34.83	5.34	10.38	13.35	47.10
1932	1,611,016	32.60	5.67	9.65	12.48	39.60
1933	1,674,994	35.85	2.94	9.38	14.39	37.44
1934	2,132,800	31.08	2.81	7.98	16.28	41.85
1935	2,282,874	30.45	2.62	7.01	15.60	44.33
1936	2,455,978	27.62	2.40	5.94	16.32	47.71
1937	3,349,167	21.88	3.17	5.39	20.56	29.00
1938	3,094,440	19.44	8.14	6.02	16.58	49.82

12. IMPORTS

Percentage of Total Imports

YEAR	NORTH AMERICA		SOUTH AMERICA	EUROPE	ASIA	OCEANIA	AFRICA
	NORTH- ERN	SOUTH- ERN					
1901	5.2	12.4	13.4	52.2	14.8	.8	1.1
1902	5.4	11.3	13.3	52.6	15.1	.8	1.5
1903	5.4	13.1	10.5	53.4	15.5	.9	1.2
1904	5.3	14.7	12.15	50.3	15.7	.8	1.0
1905	5.7	14.6	13.5	48.4	15.6	1.1	1.0
1906	5.7	13.5	11.4	51.6	15.7	1.0	1.0
1907	5.2	13.2	11.2	52.1	15.6	1.3	1.5
1908	6.4	13.6	10.5	50.9	16.0	1.2	1.4
1909	6.1	13.2	12.5	49.9	15.8	1.3	1.2
1910	6.2	13.5	12.6	51.8	13.5	1.3	1.1
1911	6.7	13.3	12.0	50.3	15.1	.8	1.8
1912	6.7	13.5	13.0	49.6	15.0	.8	1.4
1913	6.7	13.2	12.0	49.2	16.4	.9	1.5
1914	8.6	14.0	11.8	47.3	16.1	1.3	1.0
1915	9.6	18.6	15.6	36.7	16.2	1.7	1.5
1915 (6 mos.)	11.8	15.4	18.2	29.8	21.0	2.0	1.8
1916	10.0	17.5	17.9	26.5	23.0	2.5	2.6
1917	14.2	15.3	20.3	18.7	27.8	1.2	2.5
1918	15.1	17.1	20.2	10.5	31.0	3.4	2.8
1919	12.8	16.8	17.6	19.2	28.4	2.3	2.9
1920	11.6	19.9	14.4	23.3	26.5	1.5	2.8
1921	13.5	16.6	11.8	30.5	24.6	1.4	1.6
1922	11.8	14.6	11.5	31.8	26.6	1.6	2.1
1923	11.0	15.4	12.3	30.5	26.9	1.6	2.3
1924	11.1	16.4	12.9	30.4	25.8	1.4	2.0
1925	10.9	12.3	12.3	29.3	31.2	1.8	2.2
1926	11.0	11.9	12.8	28.8	31.8	1.5	2.2
1927	11.6	12.0	12.4	30.2	30.3	1.3	2.2
1928	12.2	11.3	13.9	30.5	28.6	1.3	2.2
1929	11.7	10.6	14.5	30.3	29.1	1.3	2.5
1930	13.5	11.3	14.2	29.8	27.9	1.1	2.2
1931	13.3	11.5	14.7	30.6	27.4	.9	1.6
1932	13.7	11.9	15.2	29.5	27.4	.6	1.8
1933	13.2	8.8	14.0	31.9	29.3	.9	1.9
1934	14.4	9.7	13.8	29.6	29.6	.9	2.0
1935	14.3	9.8	13.7	29.2	29.5	1.3	2.0
1936	15.7	9.8	12.0	29.6	29.2	1.5	2.1
1937	13.2	9.2	13.7	27.3	31.4	2.2	3.0
1938	13.6	11.4	13.4	28.9	29.0	.8	2.8

13. IMPORTS

YEAR	TOTAL THOUSAND DOLLARS	CRUDE MATERIALS	PERCENTAGE OF CRUDE FOOD-STUFFS	MANUF. FOOD-STUFFS	SEMI-MANU-FACTURES	FINISHED MANU-FACTURES
1901	823,172	30.88	13.43	15.25	15.49	24.96
1902	903,321	34.16	13.31	10.56	16.34	25.62
1903	1,025,719	32.80	11.62	11.37	19.08	25.13
1904	991,087	33.05	13.34	11.93	16.17	25.51
1905	1,117,513	35.42	13.08	13.01	15.91	22.88
1906	1,226,562	34.55	10.95	11.44	17.96	25.10
1907	1,434,421	34.00	10.44	11.06	19.11	25.39
1908	1,194,321	31.31	12.19	12.31	16.43	27.77
1909	1,311,920	35.13	12.51	12.63	16.94	22.80
1910	1,556,947	37.11	9.30	11.66	18.31	23.62
1911	1,527,226	34.36	11.87	11.26	18.84	23.67
1912	1,653,265	34.66	13.93	11.86	17.77	21.78
1913	1,813,008	35.82	11.68	10.72	19.27	22.51
1914	1,893,926	34.31	13.09	12.02	16.86	23.72
1915	1,674,170	35.33	13.38	17.07	14.17	20.04
1915 (6 mos.)	912,787	41.46	14.29	12.43	15.75	16.08
1916	2,391,635	43.04	10.88	14.16	17.47	14.45
1917	2,952,468	43.56	13.07	11.90	18.18	13.28
1918	3,031,213	40.70	11.41	13.12	21.43	13.45
1919	3,904,365	43.57	13.97	14.23	15.60	12.64
1920	5,278,481	33.79	10.94	23.46	15.20	16.61
1921	2,509,148	34.23	11.96	14.68	14.41	24.71
1922	3,112,747	37.91	10.59	12.44	17.76	21.30
1923	3,792,066	37.10	9.58	13.98	19.00	20.34
1924	3,609,963	34.86	11.77	14.45	18.17	20.76
1925	4,226,589	41.36	11.71	10.24	17.87	18.83
1926	4,430,888	40.47	12.18	9.42	18.15	19.78
1927	4,184,742	38.25	12.06	10.77	17.92	21.00
1928	4,091,444	35.85	13.44	9.91	18.65	22.15
1929	4,399,361	35.43	12.24	9.63	20.12	22.58
1930	3,060,908	32.74	13.07	9.59	19.87	24.73
1931	2,090,635	30.72	14.58	10.63	17.80	26.27
1932	1,322,774	27.09	17.61	13.15	16.40	25.75
1933	1,449,559	28.85	14.61	14.17	20.14	22.23
1934	1,655,055	28.16	15.54	16.11	18.78	21.41
1935	2,047,485	28.57	15.81	15.64	20.09	19.89
1936	2,422,592	30.24	14.38	15.93	20.22	19.22
1937	3,083,668	32.26	13.73	14.62	21.07	18.31
1938	1,960,428	29.57	13.34	15.93	19.75	21.42

14. GOVERNMENT FINANCE
(in thousands of dollars)

YEAR	TOTAL RECEIPTS	TOTAL EXPENDITURES	GROSS DEBT
1901	587,685	524,617	1,221,572
1902	562,478	485,234	1,218,031
1903	561,881	517,006	1,159,406
1904	541,087	583,660	1,136,259
1905	544,275	567,279	1,132,357
1906	594,984	570,202	1,142,523
1907	665,860	579,129	1,147,178
1908	601,862	569,196	1,177,690
1909	604,320	693,744	1,148,315
1910	675,512	693,617	1,146,940
1911	701,833	691,202	1,153,985
1912	692,609	689,881	1,193,839
1913	724,111	724,512	1,193,048
1914	734,673	735,081	1,188,235
1915	697,911	760,587	1,191,264
1916	782,535	734,056	1,225,146
1917	1,124,325	1,977,682	2,975,619
1918	3,664,583	12,697,837	12,243,629
1919	5,152,257	18,522,895	25,482,034
1920	6,694,565	6,482,090	24,297,918
1921	5,624,933	5,538,209	23,976,251
1922	4,109,104	3,795,303	22,964,079
1923	4,007,135	3,697,478	22,349,688
1924	4,012,045	3,506,678	21,251,120
1925	3,780,149	3,529,643	20,516,272
1926	3,962,756	3,584,988	19,643,183
1927	4,129,394	3,493,585	18,510,174
1928	4,042,348	3,643,520	17,604,291
1929	4,033,240	3,848,463	16,931,198
1930	4,177,942	3,994,152	16,185,308
1931	3,189,639	4,091,598	16,801,485
1932	2,005,725	4,947,777	19,487,010
1933	2,079,697	4,325,150	22,538,672
1934	3,115,554	6,370,947	27,053,086
1935	3,800,467	7,583,434	28,701,167
1936	4,115,957	9,068,886	33,545,385
1937	5,293,840	8,546,380	36,427,091
1938	6,241,661	7,691,287	37,167,487
1939	5,667,824	9,268,338	40,445,417

15 PRESIDENTS AND CABINET MEMBERS, 1901–1940

Year	President	Vice-Pres.	Sec. of State	Sec. of Treas.	Sec. of War
1901	T. Roosevelt		John Hay	Lyman Gage	Elihu Root
1902				Leslie Shaw	
1903					
1904					Wm. H. Taft
1905		Chas. Fairbanks	Elihu Root		
1906					
1907				G. B. Cortelyou	
1908					Luke Wright
1909	Wm. H. Taft	Jas. Sherman	Robt. Bacon	F. MacVeagh	J. Dickinson
1910			P. C. Knox		
1911					H. L. Stimson
1912					
1913	W. Wilson	Thos. Marshall	Wm. Bryan	W. G. McAdoo	L. M. Garrison
1914					
1915			Robt. Lansing		
1916					N. D. Baker
1917					
1918				Carter Glass	
1919					
1920			Bainbridge Colby	D. F. Houston	
1921	W. G. Harding	C. Coolidge	C. E. Hughes	Andrew Mellon	John Weeks
1922					
1923	C. Coolidge				
1924					
1925		C. G. Dawes	Frank Kellogg		Dwight Davis
1926					
1927					
1928					
1929	H. C. Hoover	Chas. Curtis	Henry L. Stimson		James W. Good
1930					Pat. J. Hurley
1931					
1932					
1933	F. D. Roosevelt	J. N. Garner	Cordell Hull	Wm. H. Woodin	Geo. H. Dern
1934				H. Morgenthau Jr.	
1935					
1936					H. A. Woodring
1937					
1938					
1939					
1940					H. L. Stimson

PRESIDENTS AND CABINET MEMBERS, 1901-1940 (*Continued*)

	Sec. of Navy	Sec. of Inter.	Postmaster General	Attorney General	Sec. of Commerce	Sec. of Labor
1901	John Long	E. A. Hitchcock	Chas. Smith	P. C. Knox		
1902	Wm. Moody		Henry Payne			
1903						
1904	Paul Morton		Robt. Wynne	W. H. Moody		
1905	C. J. Bonaparte		G. B. Cortelyou			
1906						
1907	V. Metcalf	J. R. Garfield	G. vonL. Meyer	C. J. Bonaparte		
1908	T. H. Newberry					
1909	G. vonL. Meyer	R. A. Ballinger	F. H. Hitchcock	G. W. Wickersham		
1910						
1911						
1912		W. L. Fisher				
1913	Joseph. Daniels	F. K. Lane	A. S. Burleson	J. C. McReynolds	Wm. Redfield	Wm. Wilson
1914				Thomas Gregory		
1915						
1916						
1917						
1918						
1919				A. M. Palmer	Joshua Alexander	
1920		J. B. Payne				
1921	Edwin Denby	Albert Fall	Will H. Hays	H. M. Daugherty	H. C. Hoover	J. J. Davis
1922			Hubert Work			
1923		Hubert Work	Harry S. New			
1924	C. D. Wilbur			Harlan F. Stone		
1925				J. G. Sargent		
1926						
1927		R. O. West				
1928					W. F. Whiting	
1929	Chas. F. Adams	R. L. Wilbur	W. F. Brown	Wm. D. Mitchell	R. P. Lamont	
1930						Wm. N. Doak
1931						
1932					R. D. Chapin	
1933	C. A. Swanson	H. L. Ickes	Jas. A. Farley	H. S. Cummings	D. C. Roper	Frances Perkins
1934						
1935						
1936						
1937						
1938					H. L. Hopkins	
1939	C. Edison			Frank Murphy		
1940	Frank Knox		F. C. Walker	R. A. Jackson	Jesse Jones	

16. VOTE IN PRESIDENTIAL ELECTIONS

YEAR	REPUBLICAN		DEMOCRAT		MISCELLANEOUS		SOCIALIST AND SOCIALIST LABOR	COMMUNIST
	POPULAR	ELECTORAL	POPULAR	ELECTORAL		ELECTORAL		
1900	7,219,530	292	6,358,071	155	50,232[1]		127,519	
1904	7,628,834	336	5,084,491	140	114,753[1]		436,184	
1908	7,679,006	321	6,409,106	162	28,131[1]		434,645	
1912	3,483,922	8	6,286,214	435	4,126,020[2]		926,090	
1916	8,538,221	254	9,129,606	277		88	598,516	
1920	16,152,200	404	9,147,353	127			950,974	
1924	15,725,003	382	8,385,586	136	4,826,471[2]	13	27,650	36,386
1928	21,392,190	444	15,016,443	87			289,023	48,770
1932	15,761,841	59	22,821,857	472			918,057	102,991
1936	16,679,583	8	27,476,673	523	882,479[3]		200,522	80,159
1940								

1 Populist.   2 Progressive.   3 Union.

INDEX

Accidents (industrial), 69
Adams, Henry, 205
Adams, Samuel Hopkins, 211
Adamson Act, 262
Addams, Jane, 217, 301, 321
Adkins v. Children's Hospital, 224
Advertising, 376
Agar, Herbert, 629
Agricultural Adjustment Act, 509, 510, 518–22, 543, 553
Agricultural Marketing Act, 434–5, 494
Aguinaldo, E., 147, 151
Air Mail Act (1925), 392; (1934), 393
Alabama Midland Case, 123
Alaska, 56, 153, 286
Albert, Dr. H., 300
Aldrich, N. W., 114, 231, 242, 243, 258
Aldrich, T. B., 203
Aldrich, S. W., 479
Aldrich-Payne Tariff, 243–4
Aldrich-Vreeland Act, 258
Algeciras Conference, 286
Algonquin, Sinking of, 320
Alien Property Custodian, 334, 424
Allen, Hervey, 610
Allgeyer v. Louisiana, 134
Altgeld, J. P., 72
Amalgamated Clothing Workers, 78, 565
Amalgamated Copper Company, 55
Amendments to Constitution, 14th, 33, 133–8; 16th, 243; 17th, 223, 243; 18th, 224–6, 471–4; 19th, 226–8
America First Committee, 637, 638
American Birth Control League, 227
American Can Company, 375
American Defense Society, 316
American Federation of Labor, 73–9, 179, 262, 335, 336, 402–4, 427, 564–6, 569–70
American Labor Party, 559
American Legion, 316
American Newspaper Guild, 569
American Petroleum Institute, 378
American Protective Association, 160, 178
American Protective League, 338
American Railway Union, 76, 140
American Rights Committee, 316

American Smelting and Refining Company, 56
American Student Union, 561
American Sugar Refining Company, 59, 242
American Telephone and Telegraph Company, 58, 59, 371 372, 390, 399, 416, 575
American Tobacco Company, 59, 232
American Truth Society, 301
American Youth Congress, 561
Anaconda Copper Company, 55, 56
Ancona, Sinking of, 312
Anderson, Maxwell, 619
Anderson, Sherwood, 608
Anderson, W. H., 225
Angell, J. B., 183
Antheil, George, 614
Anthony, S. B., 227
Anti-Saloon League, 225
Apperson brothers, 388
Arabic, Sinking of, 312
Archbold, J. D., 50, 51, 235
Argentina, 415, 417, 585, 651, 652
Armstrong, H. F., 629
Armstrong, Louis, 615
Armstrong Committee, 221
Arnold, Thurman, 517
Association for Protection of American Rights in Mexico, 282
Atchison, Topeka and Santa Fe, 46
Atlantic Charter, 642, 651
Austria, 158, 163, 292–3, 319, 347, 352, 353, 483, 416
Automobile industry, 388–91, 568
Aviation industry, 330, 391–3

Babbitt, Irving, 602
Bacon, Peggy, 612
Baer, G. F., 234
Baker, N. D., 218, 325–6, 334, 342
Baker, O. E., 408
Baker, R. S., 210
Balfour, A. J., 448
Ballinger, R. A., 245
Baltimore and Ohio, 45, 46, 48
Bank of the United States, 487

Banking Act (1933), 509, 528; (1935), 510, 526
Baptist Church, 169, 174, 225
Bara, Theda, 397
Barnard, F. A. P., 183
Barnes, Djuna, 610
Barry, Philip, 619
Barton, Bruce, 465
Baruch, B. M., 329
Batista, F., 584
Beal, Fred, 405
Bean, L. H., 518
Beard, Charles A., 213, 473, 629
Beecher, H. W., 175, 177, 189
Behrman, S. N., 619
Belgium, 293, 319, 452, 594, 635
Bell, A. Graham, 58
Bellamy, Edward, 198
Bellows, George, 612
Belmont, August, 253
Bennett, Hugh, 90, 543
Benson, Elmer, 559
Benton, Thomas, 612
Berger, Victor, 198, 335
Berle, A. A., 372, 374, 505
Berlin, Irving, 614
Bery, Carl, 388
Bethlehem Steel, 53, 567
Beveridge, A. J., 243, 251, 268
Billings, W. K., 317
Bingham, Alfred, 380, 629
Birth Rate, 195-6
Black, Hugo L., 586
Blackmur, R. P., 606
Blaine, J. G., 145
Blair, J. M., 383
Bland-Allison Act, 121
Bliss, T. H., 349
Bloch, Ernest, 614
Blume, Peter, 613
Bok, Edward, 189
Bonus (veterans'), 439, 498, 510
Bonus Expeditionary Force, 498
Borah, W. E., 80, 354, 364, 447, 456
Bourne, Randolph, 601
Bowles family, 185
Boy-Ed, Captain, 301
Brandeis, L. D., 78, 141, 202, 214, 221, 377, 473, 552, 557
Brazil, 585, 586, 652
Bristow, Senator, 243
"Broncho Billy," 397
Brookhart, S. W., 424
Brooks, Phillips, 177
Brooks, Van Wyck, 474, 601
Brophy, John, 406, 565, 566
Browder, Earl, 473, 555, 561

Brown, Prentiss, 650
Brown, W. F., 392
Brownell, W. C., 600
Brussels Conference, 588
Bryan, W. J., 121-2, 148, 233, 240, 252, 256, 273, 286, 299, 301, 304, 310, 312, 465, 471
Bryant, W. C., 185
Bryce, James, 300
Buck, Pearl, 610
Bucks' Stove and Range Company Case, 77, 140
Buell, R. L., 629
Buenos Aires Conference, 585
Buick Company, 390
Bulgaria, 293, 347, 643
Bullard, R. L., 344
Bunau-Varilla, P., 270-3
Bunny, John, 397
Bunting v. Oregon, 138
Burchfield, Charles, 612
Bureau of the Budget, 431
Bureau of Foreign and Domestic Commerce, 414
Bureau of Immigration, 161
Burke, Kenneth, 604
Burleson, A. S., 338
Burnham, Daniel, 616
Butler, E. R., 218
Butler, N. M., 365, 447
Butler, P., 552, 557
Byrnes, J. F., 649

Cabell, J. B., 608
Cadillac, 389
Caldwell, Erskine, 609
Caldwell and Company, 487
Calles, P. E., 460
Calverton, V. F., 604
Cameron, Simon, 109
Canada, 64, 158, 246, 286, 304, 416, 440, 441
Cannery, Agricultural, Packing and Allied Workers, 569
Cannon, J. G., 113, 231, 236, 242, 245
Capone, "Scarface," 468
Capper-Volstead Act, 433
Capra, Frank, 624
Cardenas, L., 460, 584
Cardozo, Benjamin, 141, 552, 556
Carey, James, 566
Carmody, John, 558
Carnegie, Andrew, 29, 38, 52, 53, 79
Carpenter, J. A., 614
Carranza, Venustiano, 280-2
Carver, G. W., 171